PORT

THE ROUG

CW00363965

PORTUGAL ROUGH GUIDE CREDITS

Text Editors: Mark Ellingham, Jules Brown and Richard Trillo
Portuguese editors: Luís Miguel da Costa, Jorge Bochechas & Fernanda Valente
Proofreading: Celia Woolfrey and Rob Jones
Production: Susanne Hillen
Typesetting: Gail Jammy

Series Editor: Mark Ellingham

Acknowledgments

A thousand thanks to Jules Brown, Rob Jones, Greg Ward and Jonathan Buckley in London, and to Luís, Fernanda, and Jorge in Portugal for all their editing, past and present, and to Paul Blaney, Paul Sutcliffe and Kevin Rose, Matthew Hancock and Amanda Tomlin, Judith Clifton and Christian Kerslake, and John W. Smith, for their fabulously detailed updates and fresh research.

We're also greatly indebted to the following for their help on the ground: Felipa Pedrosa, Maria Ernestina Pires de Silva, Zé-Carlos and Maria-José Menezes, Zé-Manuel and Joana Pedrosa, Maria dos Prazeres, Iréna and Dr. Francisco, Jean and John Martin, Zé-Victor, Santos, Zita and *Pensão Estoril*, Charlie Millar, David Evans and Julia Rochester.

And we'd like to say a big thankyou to the many **readers of the previous edition** of the guide who took time to annotate our errors, omissions and lapses of taste; the roll of honour appears on p.378 – apologies to anyone whose name we missed or whose signatures we couldn't quite decipher

This fifth edition published in June 1992 by Rough Guides, 149 Kennington Lane, London SE11 4EZ.
Previous editions published by Harrap Columbus.
Distributed by Penguin Books, 27 Wrights Lane, London W8 5TZ.
Typeset in Linotron Univers and Century Old Style to an original design by Andrew Oliver.
Printed in the United Kingdom by Cox & Wyman, Reading.

Illustrations in Part One and Part Three by Ed Briant; Basics illustration by Andrew Harris;
Contexts illustration by Helen Manning.

British Library Cataloguing in Publication Data:
A catalogue record for this book is available from the British Library.

ISBN : 1-85828-022-2

PORTUGAL

THE ROUGH GUIDE

written and researched by

MARK ELLINGHAM, JOHN FISHER, GRAHAM KENYON and ALICE MARTIN

With additional accounts by
Luís Miguel da Costa, Fernanda Valente, Jorge Bochechas,
Manuel Dominguez, Matthew Hancock, Amanda Tomlin,
Jules Brown, Paul Blaney, Paul Sutcliffe and Kevin Rose.

THE ROUGH GUIDES

CONTENTS

Introduction vi

INTRODUCTION

Portugal is an astonishingly beautiful country. Especially if you've come from the arid plains of central Spain, the rivers, forests and lush valleys are so total a contrast that it's hard, at first, to take in. Suddenly the landscape is infinitely softer and greener, with flowers and trees everywhere. Life also seems easier-paced and the people more courteous; the Portuguese themselves talk of their nation as a land of *brandos costumes* – gentle ways.

For so small a country, Portugal has tremendous variety both in landscape and in its ways of life and traditions. Along the coast around Lisbon, and on the now well-developed Algarve in the south, there are highly sophisticated resorts, while Lisbon itself, in its idiosyncratic, rather old-fashioned way, has enough diversions to please most city devotees. But in its rural areas – the southern Alentejo, the mountainous Beiras, or northern Trás-os-Montes – this is still a conspicuously underdeveloped country, the "Third World of Europe" as its inhabitants put it. Tourism and EC membership is changing many areas, but for anyone wanting to get off the beaten track, there are limitless opportunities to experience smaller towns and countryside areas that still seem rooted in the past century.

In terms of population, and of customs, differences between the **north and south** are particularly striking. Above a roughly sketched line, more or less corresponding with the course of the river Tagus, the people are of predominantly Celtic and Germanic stock. It was here, at Guimarães, that the "Lusitanian" nation was born, in the wake of the Christian reconquest from the North African Moors. South of the Tagus, where the Moorish, and Roman, civilisations were most established, people tend to be darker-skinned (*moreno*) and maintain perhaps more of a "Mediterranean" lifestyle (though the Portuguese coastline is, in fact, entirely Atlantic). **Agriculture** reflects this divide as well, with oranges, figs, and cork in the south, corn and potatoes in the north – where the methods of farming date back to pre-Christian days, amid a mass of tiny plots divided and subdivided over the generations.

More recent events are woven into the pattern. The 1974 **revolution**, which brought to an end 48 years of dictatorship, came from the south – an area of vast estates, rich landowners and a dependent workforce – while the conservative backlash of the 1980s came from the north, with its powerful religious authorities and individual smallholders wary of change. Two-thirds of the support for the PCP, the largest Communist party outside the region of the old East European "Bloc" (and by now quite possibly the largest), derives from the Alentejo. More profoundly even than the revolution, **emigration** has altered people's attitudes and the appearance of the countryside. After Lisbon, the largest Portuguese community is in Paris, and there are migrant workers spread throughout France and Germany. Returning, these emigrants have brought in modern ideas and challenged many traditional rural values. New ideas and cultural life have arrived, too, through Portugal's own recent immigrants from the old African colonies of Cape Verde, Mozambique and Angola.

The greatest of all Portuguese influences, however, is **the sea**. The Atlantic seems to dominate the land not only physically, producing the consistently temperate climate, but mentally and historically. The Portuguese are very conscious of themselves as a seafaring race; mariners like Vasco da Gama led the way in the discovery of Africa and the New World, and until less than twenty years ago Portugal remained a colonial power, albeit one in deep crisis. Such links long ago brought African and South American strands into the country's culture: in the distinctive music of *fado*, blues-like songs heard in Lisbon and Coimbra, for example, or the Moorish-influenced *Manuelino*, Baroque "Discovery" architecture that provides the country's most distinctive monuments.

This "glorious" history has also led to the peculiar national characteristic of *saudade*: a slightly resigned, nostalgic air, and a feeling that the past will always overshadow the possibilities of the future. The years of isolation under the dictator Salazar, which yielded to democracy after the 1974 revolution, reinforced such feelings, as the ruling elite spurned "contamination" by the rest of Europe. Only in the last decade or so, with Portugal's entry into the European Community, have things really begun to change. A belated industrial revolution is finally underway, and the Portuguese are becoming increasingly geared toward Lisbon and the cities. For those who remain in the countryside, however, life remains traditional – disarmingly so to outsiders – and social mores seem fixed in the past. Women still wear black if their husbands are absent, as many are, working in France, or Germany, or at sea.

Where to go and when

Since Portugal is so compact, it's easy to take in something of each of its elements – northern river valleys, southern coast, and mountains – even on a brief visit. Distances are small and easily covered, whether you rent a car or make your own way by public transport.

Scenically, the most interesting parts of the country are in the north: the **Minho**, green, damp, and often startling in its rural customs; the sensational gorge and valley of the **Douro**, followed along its course by the railroad, off which a couple of antiquated branch lines veer into remote **Trás-os-Montes**; and the wild, mountainous *serras* of **Beira Alta**. For contemporary interest, spend at least some time in both **Lisbon** and **Porto**, the only two cities of real size. And if it's monuments you're after, the whole centre of the country – above all **Coimbra**, **Évora** and the **Estremadura** region – retains a faded grandeur dating from the Age of the Discoveries in the sixteenth century and from the later gold and diamond wealth of Brazil.

The **coast** is virtually continuous beach – some five hundred miles of it – and only on the **Algarve** (and there, only the western half) and in a few pockets around Lisbon and Porto has there been really large-scale tourist development. Elsewhere, while a number of beach areas have seen casual development on a relatively small scale, resorts remain low-key and thoroughly Portuguese, with great stretches of deserted sands between them. Perhaps the loveliest are along the northern **Costa Verde**, around Viana do Castelo, or, for isolation, the wild beaches of **southern Alentejo**. It must be added, however, that the Portuguese coast *is* the Atlantic and can often be windswept and exposed. If you like your swimming warm, the only area where the water approaches Mediterranean temperatures is the **eastern Algarve**, where a series of sandbank islands, the still unexploited *ilhas*, protect the shore.

Swimming aside, **when you go** seems to matter little. The entire country is warm from **April to October**, if slightly erratically so in the rainy north, while the Algarve is amazingly mild throughout the year – it hardly has a winter and January can be delightful when the almond blossoms are out. The **Serra da Estrêla**, in contrast, does – with snow for skiers and plenty of chilly winds. Throughout the year, escaping the crowds, outside the Algarve and Lisbon, is little problem. Especially on the Algarve, booking accommodation is essential in high season; elsewhere, however, you should find rooms without great difficulty throughout the year.

AVERAGE DAYTIME TEMPERATURES (F)						
	JAN	MARCH	MAY	JULY	SEPT	NOV
LISBON	53	57	63	70	70	59
PORTO (Costa Verde)	49	53	59	67	65	53
COIMBRA (Costa da Prata)	50	56	60	67	67	56
FARO (Algarve)	54	57	65	75	72	60

PART ONE

THE
BASICS

GETTING THERE: FROM BRITAIN AND IRELAND

You need at least two full days to travel overland from Britain to Portugal, so for most visitors flying is the most viable option. There are scheduled flights year-round to Lisbon, Porto and Faro (in the Algarve) from London and from five regional British airports – Birmingham, Edinburgh, Glasgow, Manchester and Newcastle (some flights via London). Numerous package companies also sell charter flights from a variety of British regional airports – most of them to Faro. Alternatively, if time isn't the most important factor, you can approach Portugal overland from Spain, to which there are many more and often cheaper charter deals.

Road or rail alternatives are worth considering if you plan to visit Portugal as part of an extended trip through Europe. There is no direct ferry from Britain to Portugal but drivers can knock off much of the journey by taking the ferry from Plymouth to Santander in northern Spain.

Irish travellers will generally need to travel via Britain. *TAP*, the Portuguese national airline, have connecting flights from Dublin to Manchester, and have an arrangement with *British Airways* for add-on flights from Belfast.

CHARTER FLIGHTS FROM BRITAIN

Most of the cheaper flights to Portugal are **charter** deals, sold either with a package holiday or, through 'consolidators', as a flight-only option. They have fixed and unchangeable outward and return dates, and a maximum stay of one month.

Travel agents throughout Britain sell **charter flights** to Portugal (see box overpage) and even the high street chains frequently promote 'flight-only' deals, or heavily discount all-inclusive holidays, when their parent companies have chartered too many airline seats. The greatest variety of flights, however, tends to be from the **London** airports to Faro; Lisbon and Porto are less on the package trail. Flying from **elsewhere in Britain**, you'll often find flights have a connection or stop in London or Manchester.

Obviously the more flexible you can be on dates the better your chances of a rock-bottom deal; if you're prepared to take a 'leaving tomorrow at 2am from Luton Airport' flight, you can often pick up a real bargain. It's well worth an hour on the phone asking for a range of offers.

Student/youth charters are also sporadically available to Lisbon – though more frequently and cheaper to Madrid (which has easy train connections to Lisbon) or Málaga (for trains to the Algarve). The main operators are *USIT/Campus Travel* (see box overpage).

SCHEDULED FLIGHTS FROM BRITAIN

The advantages of **scheduled flights** are that they can be pre-booked well in advance and remain valid for three months – sometimes longer. As with charters, discount deals are available from many high street travel **agents**, as well as from a number of specialist flight and student/youth agencies (see overpage). And, again, you will usually do well to phone around a number of outlets to compare prices.

TAP (Air Portugal) fly from London (Heathrow) to Lisbon, Porto and Faro, and from Manchester to Lisbon, with connections to Porto and Faro. **British Airways** also fly to Lisbon and Porto from London (Heathrow).

TAP and *BA* actually work in conjunction with each other, so you can book a flight to Portugal from any airline in Britain, with a low-cost add-on fare for the routing through London or Manchester. There are a bewildering variety of fare structures, ranging from around £99 to £400 return, depending on class, ticket status and season. For a summer flight reckon on £120–160 return from London; a little more from elsewhere in Britain.

SPECIALIST HOLIDAY AGENTS

Virtually every UK holiday company operates in Portugal – though many are limited to the Algarve. Those listed below are the smaller companies, whose holidays tend to be oriented towards individuals; many of them rent villas, and a few offer manor house and *pousada* (see p.21) rooms; all should be able to arrange flights and car rental. The Portuguese Tourist Office publishes a list of 155 tour operators.

Abreu, 109 Westbourne Grove, London W2, (☎071/229 9905/6/7). Portuguese-run agency – always worth a call for flights or coaches.

Allegro Holidays, 15a Church St, Reigate, Surrey (☎0737/221 323). Minho, Lisbon area and Algarve.

Beach Villas, 8 Market Passage, Cambridge (☎0223/311 113). Costa Verde, Sintra and Algarve.

Caravela Tours, 38/44 Gillingham St, London (☎071/630 9223). Charter wing of Air Portugal. Offers stays in manor houses in the north, plus *pousadas* throughout the country.

Destination Portugal, 37 Corn St, Witney, Oxon (☎0993/773 269). A most unusual agent, who claims to accommodate literally any Portuguese needs, from a flight-only deal, plus a cheap pension booking, to car rental, villas and manor house lets. Highly recommended.

Explore Worldwide, 1 Frederick St, Aldershot (☎0252/344 161). Hiking specialist that offers small group tours in the Douro and Gerês.

Portugalicia, 110 Ladbroke Grove, London W10 (☎071/221 0333). Another agency run by (and mainly for) Portuguese in London.

Portugal Travel, 84 York St, London W1 (☎071/723 7774). Full range of flights and holidays.

Portuguese Options, 26 Tottenham St, London (☎071/436 3246). Tailor-made holidays.

Portuguese Travel Centre, 13 Beauchamp Place, London SW3 (☎071/581 3104). Good value flights, car rental, hotels and villas.

Something Special, 10 Bull Plain, Hertford, Herts (☎0992/552 231). Algarve villas.

Sunvil Holidays, Upper Square, Old Isleworth, Middx (☎081/568 4499). Tailor-made itineraries to suit most budgets.

Travel Club of Upminster, Station Rd, Upminster, Essex ☎07082/25000). Long established villa operator.

Travelscene, 11/15 St Ann's Rd, Harrow, Middx (☎081/427 4445). Weekend breaks.

Unicorn Holidays, 34–35 Cam Centre, Wilbury Way, Hitchin, Herts (☎0462/422 223). *Pousadas*, manor houses and fly-drive.

FLIGHT AGENTS

Below are a slection of **recommended agents** for finding a **flight-only deal**. Other sources worth checking include the classified travel sections of newspapers like *The Independent* and *The Guardian* (Saturday editions), *The Sunday Times* or – in London – *Time Out* and *The Evening Standard*. High street travel agents are also worth a look for reductions on package holidays and charter flights.

Campus Travel, 52 Grosvenor Gardens, London SW1W 0AG (☎071/730 8111). Student/youth specialists.
Other branches at: 39 Queen's Rd, Bristol; 5 Emmanuel St, Cambridge; 5 Nicholson Sq, Edinburgh; 13 High St, Oxford.

South Coast Student Travel, 61 Ditchling Rd, Brighton BN1 4SD (☎0273/570226). A good agent with plenty to offer non-students as well.

Springways Travel, 71 Oxford St, London W1 (☎071/734 0393). Reliable discount flight agent.

STA Travel, 74 Old Brompton Rd, London W7 (☎071/937 9962, autoqueue). Reliable independent agent, with good value flights (including student/youth discounts) and a small range of complete holidays. 20 offices in the UK include: 117 Euston Rd, London; 25 Queen's Rd, Bristol; 38 Sidney St, Cambridge; 75 Deansgate, Manchester; and 36 George St, Oxford.

AIRLINES

TAP, 19 Regent St, London SW1 (☎071/839 1031); or Room 25, level 7, Manchester International Airport (☎061/499 2161).

British Airways, 156 Regent St, London W1 (☎081/897 4000).

PACKAGE HOLIDAYS

If you're considering a brief trip, or want things easy, you may prefer to take one of the numerous **package deals** available. Like flights, these concentrate on the Algarve, but there's a fair range of other possibilities if you shop around.

In addition to standard beach-and-villa or beach-and-hotel holidays, there are companies who rent rooms in manor houses and *pousadas* (the state-run chain, which, like Spanish para-dores tend to be monuments in themselves); others who run economic weekend breaks to Lisbon; and a range of sporting (mainly tennis and golf) holidays. The box opposite contains some

recommendations; for full lists, contact the Portuguese Tourist Office (See p.17 for addresses).

FLIGHTS FROM IRELAND

Comments on the previous page on charters and scheduled flights apply equally to Ireland as a starting point. Costs, however, are generally higher. Reckon on £140–180 for a return flight in summer. The cheaper flights, including most of the youth/student offers, are often via London or Manchester, with a tag-on fare from Ireland for the connection. As ever, it's worth spending the time to shop around.

FLIGHT AGENTS IN IRELAND

USIT. Student and youth specialist.
O'Connell Bridge, 19/21 Aston Quay, Dublin 2 (☎01/778 117).
10–11 Market Parade, Cork (☎021/270 900).
31a Queen St, Belfast (☎0232/242 562).

Joe Walsh Tours, 8–11 Baggot St, Dublin (☎01/789 555). General budget fares agent.
Thomas Cook, 118 Grafton St, Dublin (☎01/771 721). Mainstream package holiday and flight agent, with occasional discount offers.

AIRLINES

Aer Lingus, 42 Grafton St, Dublin (☎01/370 011); 46 Castle St, Belfast (☎0232/245 151).
TAP, 54 Dawson St, Dublin (☎01/798 844).

British Airways, 60 Dawson St, Dublin (☎01/610 666); 9 Fountain Centre, College St, Belfast (☎0232/245 151)

BY TRAIN FROM BRITAIN

From London to Lisbon takes a minimum of 40 hours by train, setting out from Victoria Station at around 9am, changing trains in Paris (and trans-fering stations, from Nord to Austerlitz) around 6–8pm, and again at the Spanish border (at Hendaye/Irún or Cerbère/Port Bou) around dawn. It's a good way to travel if you want to stop off in France and/or Spain on the way, though – unless you qualify for under-26 or over-65 discounts – you are likely to pay more than if you just bought a flight.

There are two **main routes into Portugal**: from Paris, via Irún, San Sebastián, Vilar Formoso, Guarda, and Pampilhosa, to Porto, Coimbra, and Lisbon; and from Madrid, via Cáceres to Marvão-Beirã, Abrantes, and Entroncamento (where the line splits to Lisbon, or to Coimbra and Porto). For other crossings, see our train network map, and the travel details at the end of each chapter.

TICKETS AND PASSES

The current fare for a **standard rail ticket** from **London to Lisbon** is £220 return (sea-crossing included). If you're under-26, this comes down to £190 as a *BIJ* ticket (valid for two months; avail-able from *Eurotrain* or *Wasteels*, see box over-page). Stops are allowed anywhere along the way on a pre-specified route.

Neither of these tickets is a very good deal when compared to an **InterRail pass**. If you're under-26, this costs £180 for a month and gives unlimited travel on all European (and Moroccan) railways, and fifty percent discounts in Britain, on the English Channel ferries, and on ferries from Spain to the Balearic Islands or Morocco. For other ages, there's an **InterRail "26-plus" pass** at £260 for a month, £180 for fifteen days; note, however, that this doesn't include travel in Spain, nor discounts on ferries or travel within Britain.

Both passes have an elegibility requirement of six months' residence in Europe, though travel agents aren't always too particular about this.

TRAIN AND BUS INFORMATION

Eurotrain, 52 Grosvenor Gardens, London SW1 (☎071/730 3402).

British Rail European Travel Centre, Victoria Station, London SW1 (☎071/834 2345).

Wasteels, 121 Wilton Rd, London SW1 (☎071/834 7066).

Eurolines, 121 Wilton Rd, London SW1 (☎071/730 0202).

EurRail, the official rail pass for North American residents, is nowhere near as good a deal, unless you're planning to virtually live on European trains for the month or two of its validity. Under-26 **EurRail youth passes** cost US$470 for a month and US$640 for two months. If you're over-26 has to buy a **first class pass**, at US$680 for one month, US$920 for two months, or US$1150 for three months. Various **Flexipass** deals are alos available, offering 14days travel in a month, etc. For further details, call *STA Travel* in North America (see overpage).

Lastly, European-resident senior citizens holding a Senior Citizen Railcard can purchase a Rail Europe Senior Card for just £7.50. This allows 50 percent discounts on rail fares throughout Europe, plus 30 percent off most ferry crossings. Details and tickets from British Rail.

BY BUS FROM BRITAIN

The cheapest, open-to-all, year-round, fixed price means of getting to Portugal is **by bus**. If you can tolerate the long journey (40–45hr depending on destination) it's a dependable method.

Eurolines, the foreign travel wing of *National Express*, operates weekly services from London to Lisbon, Coimbra, Porto, Viseu, Guarda, Vilar Formoso, Faro, and Lagos. The current fare to Lisbon is £110 return (£62 return for children aged four to twelve); there are no student discounts. Tickets are available in Britain from any *National Express* or *Eurolines* agent (in effect most travel agents), or from Victoria Coach Station.

Buses leave Victoria Coach Station on Saturdays. You have to change in Paris from the London terminus at Place Stalingrad to the southbound one at Porte de Charenton – there should be a transfer bus, but it's an easy enough journey on the metro (Line 4: *Direction Creteil*).

Alternatively, if you make your way to **Paris**, there are buses six days a week (not Monday) to Lisbon, and fairly regular services to most other towns in Portugal. Coming back, providing you've made bookings in advance, you can join these buses at any stage. In Paris, tickets are sold at the Porte de Charenton terminus, and by a Portuguese agent at 75 Boulevard Poniatowski, Paris (☎43 07 44 58). **Return** bookings can be made in Portugal at *Intercentro* in Lisbon (Avda. Casal da Ribeiro 18), *Internorte* in Porto (Praça da Galiza 96), and elsewhere at larger travel agencies and coach stations.

Tiring though these journeys are, they're comfortable enough, and broken by frequent rest and meal stops. As long as you take plenty to eat, drink, and read, as well as a certain amount of French and Spanish currency to use along the way, you should emerge relatively unscathed.

DRIVING FROM BRITAIN

There's been talk for a while of a direct ferry service starting up from England to Viana do Castelo, which at present is a cargo route. For the present, the only way of substantially cutting down on the driving time to Portugal is to take the ferry from **Plymouth to Santander** in northern Spain. This is an expensive route – and it still leaves a long day's driving before you reach Portugal itself.

Driving through France, your route obviously depends on what you want to see along the way. Quickest is to take the **coast road** via Nantes and Bordeaux, entering Spain at Irún. This can be followed from the standard channel ports or, further to the west, off the **ferries** from Portsmouth–Cherbourg (4hr 30min; *P&O*), Poole–Cherbourg (4hr; *Brittany Ferries*),Weymouth–Cherbourg (4hr; March–Oct only; *Sealink*), Portsmouth–Caen (5hr 45min; *Brittany Ferries*), Portsmouth–St Malo (9hr; *Brittany Ferries*) or Plymouth–Roscoff (6hr; *Brittany Ferries*).

Ferry costs vary enormously and depend on the size of car, number of passengers and, especially, the season – from October to March there are very good deals on all the longer crossings. Full details can be obtained from travel agents or from **Sealink** (☎01/828 4142), **P&O** (☎01/734 4431) and **Brittany Ferries** (☎0752/21321).

THE SANTANDER FERRY

The journey from **Plymouth to Santander** takes 24 hours and the boat runs twice weekly for most of the year (once a week in January, and with a three-week gap around Christmas) carrying cars and passengers. Seat prices for a one-way trip range from around £70 according to the season, cars from £80–150. Details and tickets, again, from most agents or direct from **Brittany Ferries**, Plymouth (☎0752/21321).

MOTORAIL THROUGH FRANCE

Easy too, but very expensive, is the **Motorail Service** from Boulogne–Biarritz – details from Victoria Station (☎01/834 2345). There are also *Motorail* services across Spain. If you've flown from the US or Canada to Madrid, it's an easy matter to get to Lisbon, and if you have time and no need to rush to the city, there are a number of worthwhile stops along the way.

HITCHING FROM BRITAIN

If you're **hitching** the best plan is to get as far south into France as you can afford by some other means. Hitching out of the channel ports is a nightmare, as is Paris and the 100km or so around the capital. Try taking the coach (see Eurolines, opposite) as far as Tours or the train to Chartres. From there it's not too far to Irún, and once in Spain local buses and trains are cheap fallbacks if necessary.

For anyone planning to spend some time in Paris en route, one possible alternative is to join *Allostop*, the French hitch-hiking association. For the princely sum of 35F they will enrol you for a single journey and put you in touch with a driver going your way (to whom you contribute petrol costs). The Paris *Allostop* office is at 84 Passage Brady (☎42 46 00 66: open Mon–Fri 9am–1pm and 2–6pm).

GETTING THERE VIA SPAIN

Flying to **Madrid** or **Málaga** may well work out cheaper than to Portugal. From either, connections west are routine and there are rewarding stops en route.

MADRID CONNECTIONS

Coming from Madrid, it's easiest to make your way west by rail. The most direct trains leave from **Madrid's** Estacion Atocha, reaching **Lisbon** (Estação Santa Apolonia) six to ten hours later. The fastest route is **via Badajoz**, the "gateway to Portugal" and a close neighbour of the star-shaped fortress town of Elvas (see the *Alentejo* chapter), the first stop the train makes in Portugal. Other stops along this line, such as the lofty towns of Portalegre and Abrantes (described in the *Alentejo* and *Estremadura and Ribatejo* chapters respectively) make this the recommended route through the country. Departures from Madrid are at 7.40am, 2.25pm, or 6pm.

OTHER RAIL CROSSINGS

Another attractive route from Madrid goes **through Valencia de Alcantara**, reaching Lisbon in nine to ten hours. Trains depart at 10.10am and 10.55pm, stopping only at the border – a point to keep in mind when you're deciding on provisions for the trip.

Alternatively, if you're working your way around Spain first, you can cross from Old Castile at **Fuentes de Onoro** (1.22am, 3.48am, or 4.31am: 1hr to Guarda, 6hr to Lisbon) or, at more sociable hours, from **Vigo** in Galicia (7.10am, 1.50pm, or 8.25pm; 3hr to Porto, 9hr to Lisbon).

MALAGA CONNECTIONS

From **Málaga** you are well placed to head for the **Algarve** – Portugal's prime coastal strip. If you have the time, you could take in a loop through the great Andalucian cities of Granada, Córdoba and Sevilla – the latter caught up in the throes of the World Expo Fair throughout 1992. The Málaga–Granada and Granada–Córdoba journeys are quicker and easier by bus than train. From Córdoba, you're back on a main train line to Sevilla and thence, through Huelva, to the Portuguese border at Ayamonte–Vila Real de Santo Antonio. Once across the border at Vila Real (a couple of minutes' ferry ride across the Guadiana estuary), you can join the Algarve train line, towards Tavira and Lagos.

GETTING THERE FROM NORTH AMERICA

Flying to Portugal directly from North America is more feasible than it used to be. *TAP* (the Portuguese national airline) has a range of flights, and deals and routes have opened up in general as it dawns on both the travel industry and consumers that Portugal is one of the few countries where the dollar is still worth something.

However, unless time is your only consideration, you can, on the whole, get better-priced tickets to Spain, making your own way on to Portugal by train or bus. Similarly, you may want to consider flying first to London and then picking up one of the cheap British charters on to Portugal. For Canadians, in particular, this can make a large saving on travel budgets.

DIRECT FROM THE US

Most scheduled and charter flights to Portugal go from **New York, Boston, Miami, or Los Angeles**, and if you want to travel direct you will in general do best to buy an add-on to one of these "gateway" cities. There's more choice if you're prepared to fly to Madrid, or to London.

The cheapest tickets are available through discount outlets advertised in the Sunday newspaper travel sections. The Sunday travel section of the *New York Times* is the best single source of information. It is a good idea to research these **well in advance**, though with some fares you cannot actually purchase tickets until the month before you plan to travel – nerve-wracking, but

these tour operators often have good fares. If you can **reserve ahead** (sometimes without commitment), do so. At peak times, flights are often full to capacity.

TAP, the Portuguese national airline, and *TWA* are the main scheduled operators to Lisbon and the ones most often used by the handful of block-buyers and discounters. **Student/youth agencies** frequently offer better fares to Madrid than to Lisbon.

FROM THE EAST COAST

In the summer, charters on the **New York–Lisbon** route are likely to be the cheapest option. A good first phone call is to *Access International*, 250 W. 57th St, Suite 511, New York, NY 10107 (☎212/ 465 0707). From **Washington, DC** a few charters are available for slightly higher prices.

As for scheduled flights, as we go to press *TAP* (☎800/221 7370, ☎212/944 2100) offers APEX return fares to Lisbon from around $700–1000, from **New York** or **Boston**. Fares depend on season and day of departure (Fri, Sat, Sun are more expensive.

Iberia (☎800/772 4643) fly **New York–Madrid**; APEX fares are $602–652 low season, $680–730 mid, and $934–984 high season. You can book until 14 days before departure.

Out of **Miami**, *Iberia* has relatively expensive 7–90-day APEX fares in the $857 (low season midweek) to $1050 (high season weekend) range.

Among the **independent travel/student/youth discount** chains, best fares with *STA* to Lisbon are from $550 mid season to $630 high. *CIEE* has competitive offers on the *New York–Madrid* route.

One-way fares are always considerably more than half the price of the APEX or discount fare.

FROM THE WEST COAST

It's possible to find high season **charter fares** from $440 one way, $840 return to **Lisbon** out of **San Francisco or Los Angeles**.

Among the most consistent outlets offering deals at these prices are *Airkit*, 1125 W. 6th St, Los Angeles, CA 90017 (☎213/957 9304) and *Access International* (☎800/TAKE-OFF, or ☎212/ 465 0707). Flights are via New York, must be reserved at least a month in advance, and tend to fill up early.

AGENTS AND TOUR OPERATORS IN NORTH AMERICA

Access International, 101 W 31st St, Suite 104, New York, NY 10001 (☎800/TAKE-OFF). *Good East Coast and central US deals to Europe.*

Airkit, 1125 W 6th St, Los Angeles, CA 90017 (☎213/957-9304). *West Coast flight consolidator with seats to Europe from San Francisco and LA.*

American Express, World Financial Center, New York, NY 10285 (☎212/640-2000 or 800/800-8891). *Packages, city breaks, etc, all over Europe.*

Contiki Holidays, 1432 Katela Ave, Anaheim, CA 92805 (☎714/937-0611 or 800/626-0611). *Coach tours for under-35s through Europe.*

Cosmos/Global Gateway, 92-25 Queens Blvd, Rego Park, NY 11374 (☎800/221-0090). *The leading US budget tour operators to Europe. Bookable through travel agents only.*

Council Travel, 205 E 42nd St, New York, NY 10017 (☎212/661-1450); 312 Sutter St, Suite 407, San Francisco, CA 94108 (☎415/421-3473); 14515 Ventura Blvd, Suite 250, Sherman Oaks, CA 91403 (☎818/905-5777); 1138 13th St, Boulder, CO 80302 (☎818/905-5777); 1210 Potomac St NW, Washington, DC 20007(☎202/337-6464); 1153 N Dearborn St, Chicago, IL 60610 (☎312/951-0585); 729 Boylston St, Suite 201, Boston, MA 02116 (☎617/266-1926); 1501 University Ave SE, Room 300, Minneapolis, MN 55414 (☎612/379-2323); 2000 Guadalupe St, Suite 6, Austin, TX 78705 (☎512/472-4931); 1314 Northeast 43rd St, Suite 210, Seattle, WA 98105 (☎206/632-2448). *Nationwide US student travel organisation.*

Discount Club of America, 61-33 Woodhaven Blvd, Rego Park, NY 11374 (☎718/335-9612). *East Coast discount travel club.*

Discount Travel International, Ives Bldg, 114 Forrest Ave, Suite 205, Narbeth, PA 19072 (☎215/668-2182 or 800/221-8139). *East Coast deals.*

Encore Short Notice, 4501 Forbes Blvd, Lanham, MD 20706 (☎301/459-8020 or 800/638-0830). *East Coast travel club.*

Europe Through the Back Door Tours, 109 Fourth Ave N, C-2009, Edmonds, WA 98020 (☎206/771-0833). *Excellent travel club which publishes a regular newsletter packed full of travel tales and advice, sells its own guides and travel accessories, Eurail passes, and runs good-value bus tours taking in the biggest European cities. Worth joining for the newsletter alone.*

Europe Train Tours, 198 Boston Post Rd, Mamaroneck, NY 105431 (☎814/698-9426 or 800/551-2085). *Rail specialist.*

Interworld, 3400 Coral Way, Miami, FL 33145 (☎305/443-4929). *Southeastern US consolidator.*

Jet Vacations, 1775 Broadway, New York, NY 10019 (☎212/247-0999 or 800/JET-0999). *European package specialist.*

Moment's Notice, 425 Madison Ave, New York, NY 10017 (☎212/486-0503). *Last-minute deals.*

Nouvelles Frontières, 12 E 33rd St, New York, NY 10016 (☎212/779-0600); 800 bd de Maisonneuve Est, Montréal, PQ H2L 4L8 (☎514/288-9942). *French discount travel firm. Other branches in LA, San Francisco and Quebec City.*

STA Travel, ☎800-777-0112 (nationwide); 48 E 11th St, Suite 805, New York, NY 10003 (tele-sales ☎212/986 9470); 7202 Melrose Ave, Los Angeles, CA 90046 (tele-sales ☎213/937 5781); 82 Shattuck Sq, Berkeley, CA 94704 (☎510/841 1037); 166 Geary St, Suite 702, San Francisco, CA 94108 (☎415/391 8407); 273 Newbury St, Boston, MA 02116; (☎617/266-6014). *Worldwide specialist in independent travel.*

Stand Buys, 311 W Superior St, Chicago, IL 60610 (☎800/331-0257). *Midwestern travel club.*

Travel Cuts, Head Office: 187 College St, Toronto, ON M5T 1P7 (☎416/979-2406). *Others include:* MacEwan Hall Student Centre, University of Calgary, Calgary, AL T2N 1N4 (☎403/282-7687); 12304 Jasper Av, Edmonton, AL T5N 3K5 (☎403/488 8487); 6139 South St, Halifax, NS B3H 4J2 (☎902/494-7027); 1613 rue St Denis, Montréal, PQ H2X 3K3; (☎514/843-8511); 1 Stewart St, Ottawa, ON K1N 6H7 (☎613/238 8222); 100–2383 CH St Foy, St Foy, G1V 1T1 (☎418/654 0224); Place Riel Campus Centre, University of Saskatchewan, Saskatoon S7N 0W0 (☎306/975-3722); 501–602 W Hastings, Vancouver V6B 1P2 (☎604/681 9136); University Centre, University of Manitoba, Winnipeg R3T 2N2 (☎204/269-9530). *Canadian student travel organisation.*

Travelers Advantage, 49 Music Sq, Nashville, TN 37203 (☎800/548-1116). *Reliable travel club.*

Travac, 1177 N Warson Rd, St Louis, MO 63132 (☎800/872-8800). *Good central US consolidator.*

Travel Avenue, 130 S Jefferson, Chicago, IL 60606 (☎312/876-1116 or 800/333-3335). *Discount travel agent.*

Unitravel, 1177 N Warson Rd, St Louis, MO 63132 (☎800/325-2222). *Another consolidator.*

Worldwide Discount Travel Club, 1674 Meridian Ave, Miami Beach, FL 33139 (☎305/534-2082). *Florida-based travel club.*

AIRLINES IN THE US AND CANADA

Air Canada, 26th Floor, Place Air Canada, 500 Dorchester Blvd W, Montréal, PQ H2Z 1X5 (☎514/879 7000).

Air France, 888 Seventh Ave, New York, NY 10106 (☎212/830-4000 or 800/237-2747); 875 N Michigan Ave, Chicago, IL 60611 (☎312/440-7922); 2000 rue Mansfield, Montréal, PQ H3A 3A3 (☎514/284-2825); 151 Bloor St W, Suite 600, Toronto, ON M5S 1S4 (☎416/922-5024).

American Airlines, PO Box 619616, Dallas/Fort Worth International Airport, Dallas, TX 75261 (☎817/267-1151 or 800/433-7300).

British Airways, 530 Fifth Ave, New York, NY 10017 (☎800/2479297); 1001 bd de Maisonneuve Ouest, Montréal, PQ H3A 3C8 (☎800/668-1059); 112 Kent St, Ottawa, ON K1P 5P2 (☎613/236-0881); 1 Dundas St West, Toronto, ON M5G 2B2 (☎416/250-0880).

Canadian Airlines, 2500 Four Bentall Center, 1055 Dunsmuir St, Box 49370, Vancouver, BC V7X 1R9 (☎604/270 5211)

Continental Airlines, 2929 Allen Parkway, Houston, TX 77019 (☎713/821-2100 or 800/231-0856).

Delta Airlines, Hartsfield Atlanta International Airport, Atlanta, GA 30320 (☎404/765-5000).

Icelandair, 360 W 31st St, New York, NY 10001 (☎212/967-8888 or 800/223-5500).

KLM, 565 Taxter Rd, Elmsford, NY 10523 (☎212/759-3600 or 800/777-5553); 225 N Michigan Ave,

Chicago, IL 60601 (☎212/861-9292); 1255 Green Ave, West Mount, Montréal PQ H3Z 2A4 (☎514/933-1314 or 800/361-5073).

Northwest Airlines, Minneapolis/St Paul International Airport, St Paul, MN 55111 (☎612/726-1234 or 800/225-2525).

Sabena, 720 Fifth Ave, New York, NY 100022 (☎800/955-2000); 5959 W. Century Blvd, Los Angeles, CA 90045 (☎213/642-7735); 1001 bd de Maisonneuve Ouest, Montréal, PQ H3A 3C8 (☎514/845-0215).

Swissair, 608 Fifth Ave, New York, NY 10020 (☎718/995-8400 or 800/221-7370); 2 Bloor St W, Suite 502, Toronto, ON M5S 2V1 (☎416/960-4270).

TAP Air Portugal, 399 Market St, Newark, NJ 07105 (☎201/344-4490 or 800/221-7370); 1010 Sherbrooke St West, Montreal, PQ H3A 2R7 (☎514/849-4217).

TWA, 100 South Bedford Rd, Mount Kisco, NY 10549 (☎212/290-2141 or 800/892-4141).

United Airlines, PO Box 66100, Chicago, IL 60666 (☎708/952-4000 or 800/241-6522).

US Air, Crystal Park Four, 2345 Crystal Drive, Arlington, VA 22227 (☎703/418-7000 or 800/622-1015).

UTA, 323 Geary St, Suite 401, San Francisco, CA 94102 (☎415/397 84 00)

Virgin Atlantic Airways, 96 Horton St, New York, NY 10014 (☎212/206-6612 or 800/862-8621).

If a less than direct arrival appeals to you, return fares in the $850–970 range, from San Francisco or LA to **Madrid**, are constantly advertised in the Sunday travel sections of the *Los Angeles Times* and the *San Francisco Examiner/Chronicle*. One-ways on this route cost from about $450 to $480, depending on the agent and season.

Among the **scheduled airlines' own fares**, *Iberia* (☎800/772 4642) offers nonstop service between **Los Angeles** and **Madrid** two to four days of the week. seven–180-day APEX fares are from $950 low season to $1250 high season (with around a $50 supplement for weekend travel) – prices that are made more appealing by the inclusion of a connecting flight to Los Angeles from anywhere on the West Coast and

the offer of a free Spanish domestic flight to Málaga, Las Palmas, Tenerife, or Santiago (the latter most useful for travel in northern Portugal). *Pan Am's* rates out of **San Francisco, Los Angeles, or Seattle to Madrid** are almost identical to *Iberia*'s, although they connect via through New York and can't offer deals on onward flights within Spain.

Most of the **independent travel chains** can't do much better than the scheduled airlines' own fares in their offerings to Lisbon. APEX fares from $860 mid season to $960 high season from **LA** and **San Francisco** to **Lisbon** on *TWA* (open to anyone) is about the lowest *STA* or *CIEE* has to offer, with **Madrid** return fares, from any Pacific city through New York, for a hundred or so dollars cheaper depending on season.

CENTRAL US

A few **charter fares** ($421 one way, $808 return) are advertised from **Chicago to Lisbon** but from most places in the central US it's probably best to get yourself a cheap flight to New York first. There are no direct scheduled flights from the central US to Lisbon.

Pan Am has APEX tickets from **Dallas to Madrid** (price structure virtually identical to Pacific Coast fares) and from **Chicago to Madrid** ($656 low season, $864 mid, $1030 high, with $50 weekend surcharge and 180-day maximum stay), but again all these flights connect via New York.

Iberia offers direct nonstop flights out of Chicago to Madrid which are marginally cheaper and have the added advantage of including a connection to Santiago, just north of the Portuguese frontier.

DIRECT FROM CANADA

TAP fly direct twice a week from Toronto via Montréal to Lisbon, and you might want to call them and see if they have any current deals. **Toronto–Lisbon**, CDN$924 low season, CDN$1065 mid, CDN$1161 high season are the fares as we go to press for 7–120-day APEX seats, with CDN$60 weekend supplement. *Air Canada's*

Lisbon and Madrid service has been suspended indefinitely.

Student/youth flights can be arranged to **Madrid** through *Travel CUTS* (known as *Voyage CUTS* in Québec); fares from **Toronto** or **Montréal** start at CDN$789 low season, CDN$909 mid, CDN$1019 high, with one ways at CDN$459 low and CDN$579 mid and high season. All these go via London, which is much cheaper. Except in summer, you may find an onward ticket in London for less than the difference.

West of the Canadian Rockies you're probably better off flying **Vancouver–London** (from CDN$399 one way, CDN$749–899 return), and then continuing on to Lisbon, or alternatively getting a flight from Seattle to Madrid.

TRANSITING VIA BRITAIN

As flights to London are often the cheapest way to get overseas, a lot of people start their European travels in England. *Virgin Atlantic* offers inexpensive fares from Newark, and charters are available to London from most major US and Canadian cities. Especially if you're under 26, you may pay no more in total transport cost, and you will have a good deal more flexibility than those travellers who cross the Atlantic directly to Portugal.

GETTING THERE FROM AUSTRALASIA

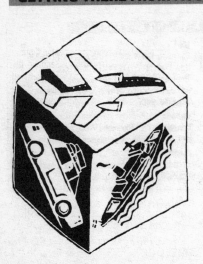

There are no direct flights to Portugal from Australia or New Zealand. As usual with European destinations, it is almost always cheapest to transit via London, picking up flights or rail tickets on from there.

You're unlikely to find any special deals from Australia or New Zealand that offer connections to Portugal; it makes more sense to fly another European route and then make your own arrangements.

STA Travel, who have offices throughout Australia and New Zealand, are usually a good bet for discount (and youth/student) flights to London, and they can arrange connections on to Portugal if you want.

Their head office addresses are:

Australia
STA, 1a Lee St, Sydney 2000 (☎212/1255).

New Zealand
STA, 10 O'Connel St, Auckland (☎399/191).

VISAS AND RED TAPE

Citizens of European Community states and Australia need only a valid passport for entry to Portugal, and can stay on an ordinary stamp for up to three months; American and Canadian nationals can stay up to sixty days. Only New Zealanders must, for some reason, obtain a visa, allowing a three month stay.

EXTENDED STAYS

For **longer stays** you can either get a special visa before you leave – from a Portuguese Consulate – or apply for an extension once you're in the country.

These are issued by the nearest District Police headquarters or the Foreigner's Registration Service, (Avenida Antonio Augusto de Aguilar 18, Lisbon (☎01/554 047) which has branch offices – *Serviço de Estrangeiros* – in most major tourist centres. You should apply at least a week before your time runs out and be prepared to prove that you can support yourself without working (for example by keeping your bank exchange forms every time you change money).

One well-used way around the bureaucracy is simply to leave the country for a couple of days and get a new two-month stay stamped in your passport when you return.

Visas or extended stay visas are also available through any **Portuguese Consulate** abroad. See the box below for addresses.

PASSPORT STAMPS

It's worth pointing out that although you may not get a **stamp in your passport**, especially if you arrive by a land border, it's important to have one if you plan to do any driving while in the country, as the various police and traffic controllers like to check foreigners' passports and may not be impressed by a blank one.

PORTUGUESE CONSULATES AND EMBASSIES

Britain
Consulate: 83 Brompton Road, London SW3 (☎071/581 8722).

Ireland
Embassy: Knock Sinna House, Fox Rock, Dublin 18 (☎01/893 569).

Netherlands
Willenskade 18, 3016 TL, Rotterdam (☎010/411 1540).

Sweden
Embassy: Fredrikshovagadam 5/3, PO Box 27004, Stockholm (☎8/662 6028).

USA
Consulate General: 630 Fifth Avenue, Suite 655, New York, NY 10111 (☎212/765 2980).
There are other branches in Boston, Providence, and San Francisco, as well as the Embassy in Washington DC.

Canada
Consulate: 1221 Richmond West, #701, Toronto (☎416/360 0663). The embassy is in Ontario.

Australia
Embassy: 6 Campion Street, 1st floor, Deakting Act 2600, Canberra (☎852 084).

COSTS, MONEY AND BANKS

Portuguese costs of living have been edging up since entry into the EC in 1986 but as a tourist, you're unlikely to feel the pinch. Accommodation, transport, food and drink are all way cheaper than in northern Europe – or North America – and a fair bit less than in Spain. Except in the most upmarket resorts of the Algarve, you can get by with little hardship on a budget of less than £15 ($25) a day. On £30 (US$50) a day you'll be living pretty well.

SOME BASIC COSTS

Costs for a double room in the cheaper pensions work out about £8–12 (US$14–20), rising to around £16–25 (US$26–44) in a two- or three-star hotel, £25–50 (US$44–90) in four-star places like most of the state-run *pousadas*. **Campsites** are an absolute bargain at around £2 ($3.50) a night per person, tent included, in all but the fanciest coastal sites.

Portuguese **food** is usually excellent and though prices vary you should always be able to get a substantial basic meal for around £5 (US$8.50), while breakfast of a bun and large cup of coffee will be little over £1 (US$2). **Drink** too is more than reasonable – a bottle of house wine rarely costs more than £2 (US$3.50), a glass of the local brew in a bar around 30p (US 50c).

Even **transport** is hardly going to break the bank. Distances are small and fares (especially on trains) low. From Porto to Lisbon, or Lisbon to the Algarve, for example, costs just £7 (US $12).

To some extent all these **prices depend on where and when you go** – the cities and developed tourist areas are invariably more expensive than elsewhere, and costs in the Algarve, in particular, are noticeably higher. As always, too, if you're travelling alone you'll spend considerably more than you would in a group of two or more people, sharing rooms and meals.

An **International Student Identity Card (ISIC)** is well worth having if you're eligible – it'll get you free or reduced admission to many museums and sights as well as occasional other discounts. The cards are available through *STA* and *USIT* in Britain and Ireland, *CIEE* in the US and *Travel CUTS* in Canada (see "Getting There" for addresses). Also of some use, giving similar discounts, is a **Federation of International Youth Travel Organisations (FIYTO)** youth card. This and available to anyone under 26, from the same outlets.

CURRENCY AND EXCHANGE

The Portuguese currency unit is the **escudo ($)**, which is divided into 100 **centavos**. It is written with the $ sign in the middle: thus 100$50 is 100 escudos and fifty centavos. For the last few years, exchange rates have hovered around 250$00 to the pound sterling, 150$00 to the American dollar.

You can buy **escudos** in advance at most European, US and Canadian banks but are supposed to take in no more than 5000$00 (around $40). In any case, rates tend to be better from banks in Portugal.

CARRYING/CHANGING MONEY
Travellers' cheques – sold at most British banks (even if you don't have an account), or from offices of *Thomas Cook* – are probably the safest and easiest way to carry money. They are accepted by all Portuguese banks and by exchange bureaux (*cambios*) at airports and major railway stations. **Eurocheques** are also widely accepted, and the cards work in many cash dispenser machines.

Visa, *Amex*, and *Mastercard* are the most useful **credit cards** in Portugal, though many smaller places and even some upmarket hotels have no facilities to take payment with them.

Additionally, many places will take either Access/Mastercard and Visa or Amex and Diners but don't rely on them. In the banks of large towns, however, there are increasing numbers of "Multibanco" ATMs for *Visa* and *Mastercard/Access* **cash advances** (don't forget your PIN number). They charge interest on the withdrawal from day one, plus a currency conversion fee, as do the banks which give cash advances on the cards over the counter. Among banks offering this service are *Banco Fonsecas & Burnay* and *Banco Pinto & Sottomayor*.

In Lisbon you may also find a branch of your **British or American bank** (*Lloyds, Barclays, Chase Manhattan, Citibank* and *Manufacturers Hanover* are all represented), at which you can obtain cash advances. *Lloyds* are represented also in Porto and Faro.

All banks charge fairly hefty **commissions** on transactions – up to 1000$00 for each exchange

– so it is worth changing a reasonable amount of money at a time. There are much lower commissions (200–300$00) on foreign currency exchanges at *caixas* – savings banks or building societies – some of which may also change cheques.

You'll find a **bank** and/or *caixa* in all but the smallest towns. Standard **opening hours** are Monday to Friday 8.30am to 3pm. In Lisbon and in some of the Algarve resorts they may also open in the evening to change money, and some banks are now installing **automatic exchange machines** for various currencies and denominations. These are useful and charge a set two percent commission instead of the high counter rates.

When travelling in rural areas, don't get stranded without **small notes and change**. A 5000$00 note (less than £20/US$35) can be hard to change at a small village market.

HEALTH AND INSURANCE

No inoculations are required for Portugal, though, as throughout southern Europe, it's a sensible precaution to have a typhoid shot and an up-to-date polio booster. A Hepatitis jab is also worth considering, as there have been outbreaks in the past year along parts of the coastline around Porto. Whatever you might hear from hypochondriacs, water is drinkable from the tap anywhere in the country, and from some freshwater sources, too. Be wary, however, of pools and streams in the south of the country.

Otherwise, Portugal poses few health problems. **Mosquitoes** can be an intolerable menace at certain times of year and in certain localities, but there seems to be no predictability about this, though the north is often cited as being particularly bad. December and January are usually mosquito-free. Mosquito-repellent lotion and coils are widely sold in towns and resorts.

PHARMACIES AND DOCTORS

For minor health complaints you go to a **farmácia** (drugstore), which you'll find in almost any village; in larger towns there's usually one where English is spoken. Pharmacists are highly trained and can dispense many drugs that would be available only with a prescription in the US or Canada.

Tampons are available at *farmácias* (ask for them by brand name), as are most forms of contraception, including (on prescription) the Pill. **Condoms** – *preservativos* – are rarely on display, but always available. Ask, and the pharmacist will set out an array on the counter, in the best formal Portuguese manner.

In the case of serious illness, you can get the address of an **English-speaking doctor** from a British or American Consular Office or, with luck, from the local police or tourist office. There's a **British hospital** in Lisbon at Rua Saraiva de

Carvalho 49 (☎01/602 020). In an **emergency** dial ☎115 (free) for the National Ambulance Service.

TRAVEL INSURANCE

As an **EC** country, Portugal has free reciprocal health agreements with other member states. To take advantage you'll need form E111, available from main post offices. Reassuring as the EC health agreements may sound, however, some form of **travel insurance** is still worthwhile – and essential for **North Americans and Australasians**, who must pay for any medical treatment in Portugal.

In many parts of Portugal public health care lags behind much of northern Europe and you may well prefer to get private treatment. With insurance you have to pay on the spot, but will be able to claim back the cost – along with any drugs prescribed by pharmacies. Be sure to keep all receipts. Travel insurance provides cover for your **baggage, money and tickets**, too, should they be stolen, though to reclaim from your insurance company you must register any theft with the police within 24 hours.

EUROPEAN COVER

In Britain and Ireland, travel insurance schemes (from around £20 a month) are sold by almost every travel agent and bank; *ISIS* policies, available from most student/youth travel agents, and useable by anyone, are good value. Also well worth considering is the special student/youth policy issued by *Campus Travel* (see p.4).

Be aware, too, of the cover offered by various **credit card companies** for holidays bought on their account; *VISA* and *American Express* offer some medical and theft coverage against items and travel arrangements paid for with them.

NORTH AMERICAN COVER

North Americans should check on existing cover (including bank and charge card benefits) before buying special travel insurance. For example, **Canadians** are usually covered for medical expenses by their provincial health plans. Holders of **ISIC** student identity cards are entitled to accident coverage and sixty days of hospital in-patient benefits for the period during which the card is valid. **University students** will ofen find that their student health coverage extends for one term beyond the date of last enrolment.

Company plans may take care of most contingencies, and **homeowners' or renters'** insurance may cover overseas theft or loss of documents, money, and valuables.

If, after exhausting the above possibilities, you feel you still need additional **travel insurance**, your travel agent can usually recommend a policy. Most offerings are quite comprehensive, anticipating everything from charter companies going bankrupt to delayed or lost baggage, as well as sundry illnesses and accidents. **Premiums** vary widely, from the very reasonable ones offered through student/youth agencies (often available to everyone; talk to *STA*) to ones so expensive that the cost for anything more than two months' coverage would likely equal the cost of the worst possible combination of disasters. Be aware, though, that very few insurers will be able to arrange on-the-spot payments in the event of a major expense or loss; you will usually be reimbursed only after going home.

An important thing to keep in mind, too, is that none of the currently available American policies **insure against theft** of anything while overseas. US and Canadian insurance policies apply only to items **lost** from, or **damaged** in, the custody of an identifiable, responsible third party, ie. hotel porter, airline, luggage consignment, etc. If you are travelling for some length of time in Europe, and you are stopping en route in Britain, it is worth considering taking out a **British travel insurance policy** which will normally include cover for theft and is reassuring if you have an expensive camera, camping equipment, or other precious items.

TRAVEL WITH A DISABILITY

Portugal is only slowly coming to terms with the needs of travellers with **disabilities** and you should not expect much in the way of wheelchair access or special facilities. That said, the Portuguese themselves always seem ready to help and people will go out of their way to make your visit as straightforward as possible.

Portuguese tourist offices abroad can rarely offer any more than the contact addresses listed below, but your first port of call in any town in Portugal should be the local **Turismo**. They will invariably find you a suitable hotel and, in smaller towns, may personally organise your needs.

For North Americans, the choice of **airline to choose** to get to Portugal (or Europe), is an important consideration. On the basis of an informal survey, *Virgin* and *Air Canada* came out tops in terms of disability awareness (and seating arrangements) and might be worth contacting first for any information they can provide.

Lastly, try to get hold of a copy of *Nothing Ventured: Disabled People Travel the World* (Harrap-Columbus, UK), published in North America as *Out and About* (Prentice Hall).

USEFUL CONTACTS
● The **National Rehabilitation Secretariat** (Secretariado Nacional de Reabilitação), Avenida.

Conde de Valbom 63, 1000 Lisbon (☎01/761 081) provides guides to transport facilities and Lisbon access, but in Portuguese only.

● The **Institute for the Promotion of Tourism** (*IPT*), Rua Alexandre Herculano 51, 1200 Lisbon (☎01/681 174) publishes a list of hotels that are "without barriers or with few obstacles to wheelchair users".

● **ARAC**, Rua Dr António Candido 9, 1097 Lisbon (☎01/563 836) is able to provide **hire cars** with hand controls, though you are advised to write or call first to confirm.

INFORMATION AND MAPS

This guide includes maps of all Portugal's major towns and other places where you'll need them. You can pick up a wide range of pamphlets, and some additional maps, for free from the *Portuguese National Tourist Organisation* (see box on facing page). Though some of their descriptions are best taken with a grain of salt, it is well worth visiting one of their offices (or writing) for information before you leave home.

In Portugal itself you'll find a tourist office, or *turismo*, in almost every town of any size. Most are detailed in the guide and the vast majority are exceptionally helpful and friendly. Aside from the help they can give you in finding a room (some will make bookings, others simply supply lists), they often have useful local maps and

leaflets that you won't find in the national offices. Local tourist office hours are generally Monday to Saturday 9am to 6pm (sometimes later).

MAPS

The National Tourist Organisation can provide you with a reasonable map of the country. However, if you're doing any real exploration, or driving, it's worth investing in a good **road map** of the country. There are three good candidates, published by *Michelin* (#437); *Plaza y Janés* (Spain); and the *Automóvel Clube de Portugal* (which also publishes an excellent regional map of the Algarve). All are widely available in Portugal. If you're planning on spending more than a day or two in **Lisbon**, the German *Falk Plan* of the city is unequalled.

More detailed **topographic** maps for walkers can be obtained from the army in Lisbon at the *Serviços Cartográficos do Exército* (Avenida Dr. Alfredo Bensaúde, Olivais Norte). They're not available anywhere else in Portugal except in Porto (*Porto Editora*, Rua da Fábrica), and there you need Portuguese assistance (see *Porto* chapter). In Britain, *Stanfords*, 12 Long Acre, Covent Garden, London WC2 (☎071/836 1321) hold stocks of some of the more popular tourist areas, like Geres National Park.

Many of these topographic maps are disastrously out of date – none have been revised since Portugal began its motorway programme – but they're the best you'll get.

GETTING AROUND

Distances are small in Portugal and you can get almost everywhere easily and efficiently by either train or bus. Trains are often marginally cheaper, and some lines highly scenic, but it's almost always quicker to go by bus – especially on shorter or less obvious routes. Approximate times and frequencies of most journeys are printed in the "Travel Details" at the end of each chapter and local peculiarities are also pointed out in the text.

Car hire is also worth considering, if time is limited and you want to cover a lot of ground, though you may find you need nerves of steel to drive on Portuguese roads.

TRAINS

CP, the Portuguese railway company, operates all trains. About ninety percent are designated *Regional*, stop at most stations en route, and have first- and second-class cars. For these there are standard charges and if you're travelling on InterRail or EurRail your pass will be valid. The next range up, *Intercidades*, are twice as fast and twice as expensive, and you should reserve your seat if using them. The fastest, most luxurious, and priciest services are the *Rápidos* (known as "Alfa"), which speed between Lisbon and Porto – sometimes they have only first-class seats. Both these latter classes involve supplements for rail pass holders.

Always turn up at the station with time to spare; long queues often form at the ticket desk – and on certain trains, even with a rail card, you'll need to queue up for seat bookings too. If you end up on the train without buying a ticket first, beware: you could end up paying a huge supplement to the ticket controller, or be kicked off the train by the guard at the next stop.

CP sells its own **Bilhete Turístico rail passes** (valid for first class travel on all trains except the Lisbon–Madrid *Talgo*) for around £45 (US$75) a week, £65 (US$110) for two weeks, and £90 (US$150) for three weeks. **Over-65s** can get half-price travel if they buy a **Cartão Dourado** (for next to nothing), valid on most trains except suburban ones during rush hour.

Complete **train timetables**, and timetables for individual lines, are sporadically available from information desks at main stations. If they don't have copies they'll often photocopy the sections you need.

PORTUGAL: TRAINS

To Tuy & Vigo
Valença
Caminha
Viana do Castelo
Braga
Barcelos
Guimarães
Póvoa de Varzim
Vila Real
Amarante
Lousado
Porto
Espinho
Régua
Tua
Pocinho
Sernada
Vouzela
Vilar Formoso
Viseu
To Salamanca & Paris
Nelas
Aveiro
Cantanhede
Sta. Comba Dão
Guarda
Pampilhosa
Figueira da Foz
Coimbra
Covilhã
Lousã
Fundão
Pombal
Castelo Branco
Leiria
SPAIN
Tomar
Caldas da Rainha
Abrantes
Marvão
Torres Vedras
Entroncamento
To Madrid
Santarém
Setil
Portalegre
Sintra
To Sevilla
Estremoz
Elvas
Cascais
LISBON
Vendas Novas
Badajoz
Vila Viçosa
Évora
Setúbal
Casa Branca
Alcácer do Sal
Moura
Ermidas-Sado
Beja
Sines
Funcheira

Bragança
Mirandela
Vila Real

Atlantic Ocean

1. Tâmega Line
2. Corgo Line
3. Tua Line
4. Douro Line
5. Vouga Line
6. Norte Line
7. Minho Line
8. Póvoa Line
9. Beira-Alta Line
10. Beira-Baixa Line
11. Leste Line
12. Portalegre Line
13. Oeste Line
14. Sul Line
15. Sado Line
16. Algarve Line

0   100 km

Lagos
Silves
Tunes
Tavira
Portimão
Faro
Vila Real de Sto. António
To Huelva & Sevilla

- - - - **Lines replaced with CP buses**

Sadly, several of the old narrow-gauge **mountain railways** of the north have been phased out, with the Tâmega, Corgo and Tua lines terminating, respectively, at Amarante, Vila Real and Mirandela. Several other minor lines have been closed, too, though some have at least been replaced by buses operated by *CP*. Regular train tickets and passes are valid on these bus lines.

Lastly, two **points to beware.** First, railway stations can be some miles from the town or village they serve – Portalegre station and town are 12km distant, for example – and there's no guarantee of connecting transport. Second, forget about using trains on **Friday and Sunday evenings** unless you enjoy playing sardines with the army – all on the move for weekend furlough.

BUSES

Buses can often be more flexible than trains and fares are usually competitive. There are express buses and standard multiple-stop buses serving most longer routes, most of which were operated until recently by the state-owned **Rodoviaria Nacional** (*RN*). This is currently in the throes of regional division and privatisation but a national network of expresses (*Rede Expressos*) has been maintained and there are many other private companies operating in competition.

The local tourist office will usually have all the timetables and will tell you where the various buses leave from, if there is no central bus station. Addresses are also detailed in the text of the guide, along with basic information on routes. As usual, buses are considerably less frequent at weekends – when they may be non-existent on some rural routes.

DRIVING AND CAR RENTAL

Driving gives obvious benefits in the freedom to visit out-of-the-way places, and with car hire rates among the lowest in Europe it's an option worth thinking about – even for just a part of your travels. Petrol (*super*), however, is relatively expensive: about 25 percent more than in Britain, and nearly twice the US equivalent.

Before you set out, bear in mind that Portugal also has one of the highest **accident** rates in Europe and some very tortuous highways, most notoriously the Lisbon–Cascais coast road and the main route south from Lisbon/Setúbal to Faro and the Algarve. The Lisbon-Porto route, once the most dangerous in the country, has improved since completion of the motorway. However, on the whole it is safer to stick to the smaller roads which have potholes but less traffic. Portuguese driving can be crazy – no one seems to recognise the same set of rules and you'll find people driving at you at night on full beam, or coasting down the middle of the road and never observing a right-of-way. August is especially lethal, with Portuguese emigrant workers returning home in fast cars to show off to relatives.

If you **break down** you can get assistance from the *Automóvel Clube de Portugal* which has reciprocal arrangements with the *AA/AAA* and most other automobile clubs. In the north, phone their Porto service at ☎02/29271 or ☎02/29272; in the south, phone Lisbon ☎01/775 475 or ☎01/775 402. Both operate 24 hours a day.

CAR RENTAL

Car rental companies can be found in all the major towns and at the airports in Lisbon, Porto, and Faro. Local firms usually charge less than the big three – *Hertz, Avis*, and *Europcar* – and we've listed addresses for some of them in the Lisbon and Porto chapters; tourist offices can give details of others.

Rates are reasonable, at around £100–120 (US$170–200) a week for the cheapest category car with unlimited mileage, though prices get inflated on the Algarve in high season – times when it's best to **arrange rental in Britain** before setting out. Several of the package holiday companies detailed on p.4 will arrange car hire in conjunction with flights. A particularly good specialist for car hire throughout Europe is *Holiday Autos*, 12 Bruton St, Berkeley Square, Mayfair W1X 7AJ (☎071/491 1111).

When picking up your car, check such important details as brakes and, if you're renting locally, **insurance coverage**. As you might have gathered, collision insurance is a good idea and unless you pay a separate supplement the initial several thousand escudos' worth of damage may be on your head. If you make any repairs along the way, keep the receipts – you may be able to get some money back from the company.

HITCHING

Hitching is variable. It can take hours to get out of Lisbon or Porto because there's nowhere good to stand – and quite often competition from Portuguese national servicemen. But most other towns are very small, their centres within easy reach of the main highways, and present no problems. The Portuguese are a kind, strikingly generous people and the main difficulty – in a predominantly rural, village-oriented country – is that they tend not to be driving very far. If you have time this won't bother you.

BIKES, MOPEDS AND MOTORBIKES

Bicycles are a great way of seeing the country, though everywhere north of Lisbon is hilly and you'll find pedalling hard work in mountainous Beira Alta or across the burned plains of southern Alentejo. Bikes can be hired in Lisbon from *TIP Tours*, Avenida. Costa Pinto 91A (☎01/286 5150). It's inexpensive to transport them on trains (about 200$00), but the procedure can require some patience – you should arrive at the baggage office a good hour and a half before your train, and be prepared to pester someone into opening up the office. On long-distance international trains allow three days for the bike to arrive.

Although it's a hassle taking your own **bike by plane**, it really is worth it to have a decent set-up with gears and brakes you can trust. Take sufficient **spares**, as you're not likely to find what you need except in large cities. In Portugal, cycle-touring is uncommon, though you will come across the odd road race or team practice.

If all that legwork is not to your taste, you can hire **mopeds** and low-powered (80cc) **motorbikes** in many tourist areas, especially on the Algarve. Go easy, wear a helmet, and check all the cables before setting off.

ACCOMMODATION

In almost any Portuguese town you can find a pension offering a double room for under 2500$00 (£10/US$17). Unlike in Spain, you'll rarely find anything much cheaper than this – but then you're unlikely to have to pay much more either, except in Algarve resorts in high season, or in Lisbon. If you have the money to move upmarket, you're often spoilt for choice, with some wonderful manor houses in the north and a network of state-run *pousadas* (similar to the Spanish paradores) scattered about the country.

Even in mid-season you shouldn't have much problem finding a bed in most of the Portuguese regions. However, over the last couple of summers, due in large part to the collapse of tourism in Yugoslavia, the Algarve has been a very different matter, with all rooms booked up for days ahead, overflowing campsites, and casual arrivals reduced to sleeping out in the parks.

YOUTH HOSTELS

There are fifteen **youth hostels** (*Pousadas de Juventude*) in Portugal, all open year-round. The price for a dormitory bed is around 750$00 (£3/US$5) a night, a little extra if you need to hire sheets and blankets.

Most have a curfew (usually 11pm or midnight) and all demand a valid *IYHA* card – available in Portugal from the *Associação Portuguesa de Pousadas de Juventude*, currently in a temporary base at Avenida Duque de Ávila 133, Lisbon (Mon–Fri 1–8pm, Sat 9.30am–12.30pm), if you haven't obtained one from your home-based *IYHA* before leaving.

All of the hostels are detailed in the guide. Among the best are those at Lindoso (in the Gerês National Park), Penhas de Saúde (in the Serra de Estrêla – skiing country), Sagres (on the site of "Henry the Navigator's Fortress"), São Martinho do Porto, Areia Branca, Oeiras (on the seafront near Lisbon), Coimbra, Alcoutim (north-east Algarve), Portalegre (in a monastery) and Leiria (perhaps the best of the lot).

ROOMS AND PENSIONS

After hostels, the next rung up in the accommodation scale consists of **rooms** (*quartos* or *dormidas*) let out in private houses. Most common in the seaside resorts, these are sometimes advertised, sometimes just hawked at the bus and train stations. Unless everything else in town is full – a fact hawkers will be well aware of – their rates should be a little below that of a pension, say 1500–2000$00 (£6–8/US$10–14). On the Algarve, in high season, you can expect to pay up to twice as much. Elsewhere, however, if demand for accommodation isn't tight, you might try some haggling over prices, especially if you're prepared to commit yourself to a longish stay.

The main budget travel standbys are **pensions** – *pensões* (*pensão* in the singular) – which are officially graded from one to three stars (often, it seems, in quite random fashion). Most serve meals, often in a bargain-priced, all-

ROOM PRICE SCALES

All the establishments listed in this book have been price-graded according to the following scale. Costs may have risen slightly overall, but the relative comparisons should remain valid. The **prices quoted** are for the **cheapest available double room** in high season.

Effectively this means that rooms in all ① and most ② range hotels will be without private bath, though there's usually a washbasin in the room. In the ③ category and above you will probably be getting private facilities. Remember, though, that many of the cheap places will also have more expensive rooms including en suite facilities.

① 2000–2500$00 (£8–10/US$14–17)   ④ 5000–8000$00 (£20–32/US$34–60)

② 2500–3500$00 (£10–14/US$17–24)   ⑤ 8000–12,000$00 (£32–44/US$60–80)

③ 3500–5000$00 (£14–20/US$24–34)   ⑥ 12,000$00 and upwards (£44/US$80 upwards)

Note that in our accommodation listings, price codes are not given for **youth hostels** (whose standard rates are given below), nor for **private rooms** – which generally hover just below the ① mark. .

inclusive package, but they rarely insist that you take them. Pensions that don't serve meals are sometimes called *residencials*. In price and all other respects they are virtually identical.

Similar to *pensões*, and generally at the cheaper end of the scale, are *hospedarias* or *casas de hóspedes* – boarding houses, similar to the Spanish *fondas* and *casas de huespedes*. They can be characterful places, though you don't see very many of them around these days.

Pension **prices** for a double room range from 2000–7000$00 (£8–28/US$14–50), depending on their location, season and facilities. Wherever you arrive, ask to see the room before you take it. If you want a cheaper one – and especially if you're travelling alone, in which case you'll frequently be asked to pay more or less the full price of a double for your single occupancy – one can usually be found. *"Tem um quarto mais barato?"* ("do you have a cheaper room?") is the relevant phrase.

HOTELS AND *POUSADAS*

A **one-star hotel** usually costs about the same price as a three-star *pensão* – say 5000–6000$00 (£20–24/US$35–44). Again, however, quirks abound in the official municipal grading/pricing systems and establishments classified as one-star hotels don't show any notable differences to pensions. Indeed, it's not uncommon to find a two- or three-star *pensão* offering much better quality rooms than a one-star hotel.

Prices for **two- and three-star hotels**, though, see a notable shift upscale, with doubles around 9000–20,000$00 (£36–80/US$65–140).

There's a further and more dramatic shift in rates as you move into **four-star** hotel league, which charge anything from 15,000$–30,000$00 (£60–120/US$105–210) a double. Five-star hotels can charge what they like, starting at around 40,000$00 (£160/US$280), though the very fanciest can reach almost double that.

The four-star hotel category includes **pousadas**, often converted from old monasteries or castles or located in dramatic countryside settings. The most interesting are those at Évora, Estremoz, and Óbidos; if you can't afford to stay in them, have a drink and look around. *Estalagems* and *albergarias* are other designations of hotels in the same range.

MANOR HOUSES AND VILLAS

An attractive alternative in the three- to four-star hotel price range is the accommodation marketed as *Manor and Country Houses of Portugal*: in effect upmarket B & B, offered by owners of "houses of distinction", ranging from great homes to more modest farmhouses. There are various schemes in operation around the country, most widely in Minho and around Sintra, where they are marketed as *Turihab* (*Turismo de Habiação*). Local tourist offices usually have information and leaflets, or, if you want to book up in advance, several of the specialist holiday operators detailed on p.4 can make arrangements for you.

Note that British holiday operators are also the best sources if you want to rent a **villa** for your stay in Portugal. Unless travelling well out of season, you are unlikely to be able to rent a villa on the spot. Prices for villas, especially in the north, or for the Algarve out of season, can be very reasonable.

Portugal has over a hundred authorized **campsites**, most of them small, low-key and attractively located – and all of them remarkably cheap. Charges are per person and per tent, with showers and parking extra; even so, it's rare that you'll end up paying more than 500$00 (£2/US$3.50) a person, and some work out even less. The most useful are again detailed in the text but you can get a fairly complete map list from any Portuguese tourist office, or a detailed booklet called *Roteiro Campista* (with prices, exact locations, facilities,

etc) from Portuguese bookshops or large newsstands.

Camping outside official grounds is legal – but with certain restrictions. You're not allowed to camp "in urban zones, in zones of protection for water sources, or less than 1km from camping parks, beaches, or other places frequented by the public". What this means in practice is that you can't camp on tourist beaches, but with a little sensitivity you can pitch a tent for a short period almost anywhere in the countryside.

The **Algarve** is again an exception, however. This is the only region where freelance camping is banned and where campsite thefts are a regular occurrence. Over most of the rest of the country the locals are extremely honest and you can leave equipment without worrying.

EATING AND DRINKING

Portuguese food is excellent, cheap, and served in quantity. Virtually all cafés, whatever their appearance, will serve you a basic meal, or at least a snack, for around 1250$00 (£5/US$8), while for 1500–3000$00 (£6–12/US$10–20) you have the run of most of the country's restaurants; even on the luxury level, only a handful of Portuguese restaurants will cause a credit card crisis. Do beware, however, of eating anything you haven't explicitly asked for and expecting it to be free, or included: it won't be.

CAFÉS AND SNACK FOOD

In addition to their food, all **cafés** serve alcohol – and they're much cheaper places to drink than bars, which tend to have slightly cosmopolitan pretensions and prices. If they cook in a big way you'll probably see blackboard lists of dishes or maybe just a sign reading *Comidas* (meals) or *Sandes* (sandwiches).

Often you'll find a whole range of dishes served at a café but the classic Portuguese **snacks and basic fare include** *prego na pão* (steak sandwich) which is usually served with a fried egg (*prego no prato*), *bitoque* (steak, fries, fried egg), *rissóis* (deep-fried meat patties, often wonderful), *pasteis de bacalhau* (cod fishcakes).

In the north you may also find *lanches* (pieces of sweetish bread stuffed with ham) and *pasteis de carne* or *pastels de chaves* (puff pastries stuffed with sausage meat).

Among **sandwiches** (*sandes*) on offer, the most common fillings include *queijo* (cheese), *fiambre* (ham), *presunto* (smoked ham) and *chouriço* (smoked sausage). *Sandes mista* are usually a combination of ham and cheese.

Sometimes, too, you'll see food displayed on café counters, particularly **shellfish** – if you see anything that looks appealing, just ask for *uma dose* (a portion). *Uma coisa destas* (one of those) can also be a useful phrase.

A LIST OF FOODS AND DISHES

Basics

Pão	Bread	*Queijo*	Cheese
Arroz	Rice	*Salada*	Salad
Manteiga	Butter	*Ovos*	Eggs
Legumes	Vegetables	mexidos	scrambled
Batatas fritas	Chips	estrelados	fried
Acepipes	Hors d'oeuvres	*Pequeno almoço*	Breakfast
Sal	Salt	*Almoço*	Lunch
Pimenta	Pepper	*Jantar*	Dinner

Soups

Açorda (de Marisco)	Bread soup (with shellfish)	*Sopa à alentejana*	Garlic/bread soup with poached egg on top
Caldo verde	Cabbage/potato broth		
Canja de galinha	Chicken soup with rice and boiled egg yolks	*Sopa de grão*	Chickpea soup
		Sopa de legumes	Vegetable soup
Gaspacho	Chilled vegetable soup (only served in the south)	*Sopa de marisco*	Shellfish soup
		Sopa de peixe	Fish soup

Fish (*peixe*) and shellfish (*mariscos*)

Ameijoas	Clams	*Espadarte*	A large kind of swordfish
Arroz de marisco	Seafood paella		
Atum	Tuna	*Gambas*	Shrimp
Bacalhau	Dried salted cod, the standard Portuguese fish: 365 ways of cooking include *com batatas e grão* (with boiled potatoes and chickpeas), *à Brás* (with egg and chips), *na brasa* (roasted on coals), *à Gomes de Sá* (sliced, with boiled eggs and potatoes), and *à minhota* (with chips)	*Garoupa*	(Like) bream
		Lampreia	Lamprey (similar to eel)
		Lagosta	Lobster
		Linguado	Sole
		Lulas or *Chocos*	Squid
		Mexilhões	Mussels
		Peixe espada	Scabbardfish
		Pescada	Hake
		Polvo	Octopus
Caldeirada	Fish stew	*Robalo*	Sea bass
Camarões	Shrimp	*Salmão*	Salmon
Carapaus	Mackerel	*Salmonetes*	Mullet
Cataplana	Pressure-cooked clams with bacon, sausage, and peppers; an Algarve speciality	*Sarda*	Mackerel
		Sardinhas	Sardines
		Truta	Trout

Meat (*carne*), poultry (*aves*) and game (*caça*)

Almondegas	Meatballs	*Coelho*	Rabbit
Bife á Portuguesa	Steak in mustard sauce, usually topped with a fried egg; a cheap standard	*Codorrniz*	Quail
		Costeleta	Chop
		Cozido à Portuguesa	Boiled casserole of chicken, lamb, pork, beef, sausages, offal, beans, etc. Served with rice and vegetables.
Borrego	Lamb		
Cabrito	Kid		
Carne de porco	Pork (*lombo*, loin; *à alentejana*, with clams)		
Carneiro	Mutton	*Dobrada*	Tripe (*tripas à moda do Porto*, tripe curry with beans and vegetables)
Chanfana, Ensopado, Sarapatel	Lamb and/or goat stews		

Meat and Poultry (continued)

Fígado	Liver	*Perú*	Turkey
Frango	Chicken	*Salsicha*	Sausage
Iscas	Pork liver	*Vitela*	Veal
Leitão	Suckling pig		

Terms

Assado/no speto	Roasted/spit-roasted	*Grelhado*	Broiled
Cozido	Boiled/stewed	*Molho*	Sauce
Frito	Fried	*No forno*	Baked

Vegetables and Fruits

Alface	Lettuce	*Laranja*	Orange
Alho	Garlic	*Limão*	Lemon
Ameixas	Plums	*Maçã*	Apple
Arroz	Rice	*Melão*	Melon
Batatas	Potatoes	*Morangos*	Strawberries
Cerejas	Cherries	*Pimenta*	Pepper
Favas	Broad beans	*Salada*	Salad
Feijão	Beans	*Uvas*	Grapes
Figos	Figs		

Cheeses

The best of the cheeses is the *Queijo da Serra* (from the Serra da Estrêla). *Cabreiro* or *Queijo de cabra* is a goat's cheese like Greek *feta*. Also worth trying are the soft cheeses of *Tomar* and *Azeitão*.

Restaurant variations

Restaurants – *restaurantes* – can appear in a number of other guises. These include:

***Tasca*.** Small, neighbourhood "taverna" style restaurant, often good for "home" cooking.

***Casa de pasto*.** Similar to the Spanish *casa de comidas*, this is a workers' dining room or diner, often found in the poorer or more industrial parts of town. They usually have a set three-course menu.

***Cervejaria*.** Literally a "beer house", common In larger towns. *Cervejarias* are more informal than restaurants, with friends dropping in at all hours for a beer and a snack. Most serve complete meals, too.

***Marisqueiria*.** Specialising in seafood, this stands midway between *cervejarias* and *restaurantes* on the formal scale. In larger cities *marisquerias* can be very upmarket.

MARKETS

Markets – often held in indoor covered sites – are always good hunting grounds for snacks. At many of them you'll find stands serving complete meals, or at least some local delicacy. In the north, especially, the most delicious standby is a chunk of *broa* (corn/rye bread) with local cheese and *marmelada* (thick quince spread).

RESTAURANT MEALS

Even if your money's fairly tight, you won't need to depend exclusively on snacks and market picnics. **Restaurants** are rarely too expensive. In addition, servings tend to be huge – especially in the north – so you can often have a substantial meal by ordering a *meia dose* (half portion), or *uma dose* between two. This is normal practice; you don't need to be a child.

It is often worth checking out the *ementa turística*, too. This is by no means necessarily a "tourist menu" as such, but more like the French *menu du jour*. It can be good value, particularly in pensions that serve meals, or in the cheaper workers' diners. Smarter restaurants, however, sometimes resent the law that compels them to offer the *ementa turistica*, responding with stingy portions or, where there's any deviation from the set fare, declaring the whole menu *à lista* (*á la carte*) and consequently twice as expensive.

Otherwise, the one thing to watch for when eating out in Portugal – especially if you've grown happily complacent in Spain on a regular intake of free *tapas* – is the plate of **starters** usually placed before you when you take a table and before you order. These can be quite elaborate, or consist of little more than rolls, butter, and cheese, but what you eat is counted and you will be charged for every bite.

DISHES AND SPECIALITIES

Regional differences and specialities aren't as great as in Spain but it's always worth taking stock of the *prato do dia* (plate of the day) and, if you're on the coast, going for **fish and seafood**. Crabs, king prawns, crayfish and huge barnacles are all fabulous, while fish on offer always include superb mullet and sardines, and an infinite range of dishes created from *bacalhau* – dried cod. On the Algarve, you shouldn't miss the amazing *cataplana* – seafood and hams pressure-cooked.

Meat dishes are less special – except for steaks and pork, above all the ubiquitous *porco à alentejana* (pork cooked with clams), and smoked hams (*presunta*). Don't be fooled by Porto's exotic-looking **tripas** (tripe) dishes: the beans and spice can taste good but the heart of the dish is still recognisably chopped stomach-lining.

Soups, everywhere, are extraordinarily cheap, and the thick vegetable *caldo verde*, kale cooked with pieces of ham and blood sausage, can be almost a meal in itself; it's served mainly in the north. *Canja de galinha* (chicken broth) is available nationwide and again very filling.

If you've had enough rich food, any restaurant will fix a **salada mista** (a mixed salad), which usually has tomatoes, onions, and olives as a base, and you can ask for it to be served *sem óleo* (without oil). Incidentally, the lack of **salt** in Portuguese cooking – and on tables – can take some getting used to. Portuguese compensate by the consumption of large quantities of salted codfish (*bacalhau*).

PASTRIES AND SWEETS

Lastly a word about **pastries** – *bolos* or *pasteis*. These are usually at their best in *casas de chá* (tea-rooms), though you'll also find them in cafés and in *pastelarias* (pastry shops), which themselves often serve the whole range of drinks.

Pastries are serious business and enthusiasts won't be disappointed. Among the best are the Sintra cheesecakes (*queijadas de Sintra*), *palha de ovos* (egg pastries) from Abrantes, *bolo de anjo* (angel food cake), *pastéis de nata* (delicious little custard tarts), and the full range of marzipan cakes from the Algarve. The incredibly sweet egg-based *doces de ovos* – most infamously from Aveiro – are completely over-the-top.

Unfortunately, few of these delicacies are available in restaurants as **desserts**. Instead, you'll almost always be offered the ubiquitous *Ola* ice cream price list, *pudim flan* (crème caramel) or *arroz doce* (rice pudding).

WINES, SPIRITS AND BEER

Portuguese **wines** (*tinto* for red, *branco* white, and *rosé*) are dramatically inexpensive and of an amazing overall good quality. Even the standard *vinho da casa* that you get in the humblest of cafés is generally a very pleasant bevy.

TABLE WINES

Among table wines the best reds are from the **Dão** region, a roughly triangular area between Coimbra, Viseu, and Guarda around the Rio Dão. Tasting a little like burgundy, and produced mainly by local cooperatives, they're available throughout the country.

The light, slightly sparkling **vinhos verdes** – "green wines", in age not colour – are again produced in quantity, this time in the Minho. They're drunk early and don't mature or improve with age, but are great with meals, especially shellfish. There are red and rosé *vinhos verdes*, though the whites are the most successful.

Portugal also produces an interesting range of sparkling, champagne-method, wines, known as **espumantes naturais**. The best of these come from the Bairrada region, northwest of Coimbra. They are designated *bruto* (extra dry), *seco* (fairly dry), *meio seco* (quite sweet) or *doce* (very sweet).

Rosé wines are known abroad mainly through the spectacularly successful export of *Mateus Rosé*. This is too sweet and aerated for most tastes, but other rosés – the best is *Tavel* – are definitely worth sampling.

Among other smaller regions offering interesting wines are **Colares** (near Sintra), **Bucelas** in the Estremadura (crisp, dry whites), **Valpaças** from Trás-os-Montes, **Reguengos** from Alentejo and **Lagoa** from the Algarve.

PORT AND MADEIRA

The fortified **port** (*vinho do Porto*) and **madeira** (*vinho da Madeira*) wines are Portugal's best known wine exports – and you should certainly sample both.

Ports are produced in the valley of the Douro and are stored in huge wine lodges at Vila Nova de Gaia, a riverside suburb of Porto (you can visit them for tours and free tasting). Alternatively, for reasonable prices you can try any of 300 types and vintages of port at the *Instituto do Vinho do Porto* (Port Wine Institute) bars in Lisbon and Porto. But even if your quest for port isn't serious enough to do either, be sure to try the dry white aperitif ports, still little known outside the country.

Madeira, from Portugal's Atlantic island province, has been exported to Britain since Shakespeare's time – it was Falstaff's favourite tipple, known then as sack. Widely available, it comes in three main varieties: *Sercial* (a dry aperitif), *Verdelho* (a sweeter aperitif) and *Bual* or *Malmsey* (sweet, heavy dessert wines). Each improves with age and special vintages are greatly prized and priced.

SPIRITS (*LICOR*)

The typical Portuguese measure of *licor* is equivalent to at least two shots in Britain or North America, making drunkenness all too easy. Low prices, too, are an encouragement, so long as you stick to local (*nacional*) products.

The national **brandy** is arguably outflanked by its Spanish rivals – which are sold almost everywhere, and very cheaply – but the native spirit is available in two varieties (*Macieira* and *Constantino*), each with loyal followings. It's frighteningly cheap at around 700$00 a bottle. Portuguese **gin** is weaker than international brands but again ridiculously cheap.

Local **firewaters** – generically known as *aguardente* – are more impressive in their own right. They include *Bagaço* (the fieriest), *Figo* (made from figs, with which it shares similar qualities when drunk to excess), *Ginginha* (made from cherries), and the very wonderful *Licor Beirão* (a kind of cognac with herbs). *Aguardente velha* (old) and *velhissima* (very old) are smoother versions of the basic hooch.

Lastly, in Lisbon, some bars serve *caipirinhas* – wonderful Brazilian-style cocktails of light rum, lime, and crushed ice.

BEER

The most common Portuguese **beer** (*cerveja*) is *Sagres* but there are a fair number of local varieties – if you're curious, they can all be tasted at the Silves Beer Festival held in the town's castle for a week every June. If you don't get the chance, note that probably the best Portuguese beer is the blue-labelled *Super Bock*, which is rivalled only by *Sagres Europa*. For something unusual (and not recommended on a hot afternoon) try the green-labelled *Sagres Preta*, which is a dark beer, resembling British brown ale.

When **drinking draft beer** order *uma imperial* if you want a regular glass; *uma caneca* will get you a half litre.

And when **buying bottles**, don't forget to take your empties back: they can represent as much as a third of the price!

Coffee (*café*) comes either black, small, and expresso-strong (*uma bica* or simply *um café*), small and with milk (*um garoto* or *um pingo* in some parts of the north), or large and with milk but often disgustingly weak (*um galão*). For white coffee that tastes of coffee and not diluted warm milk, ask for "*um café duplo com um pouco de leite*".

Tea (*chá*) is usually plain; *com leite* is with milk, *com limão* with lemon, but *um chá de limão* is hot water with a lemon rind. *Chá* is a big drink in Portugal (which originally exported tea-drinking to England) and you'll find wonderfully elegant *casas de chá* dotted around the country.

All standard **soft drinks** are available. *Tri Naranjus* is a good local range of fruit drinks (excellent *limão*, lemon), and the fizzy *Sumol*, is extremely fruity and appetising. Fresh orange juice is *sumo de laranja*. Lastly, **mineral water** (*água mineral*) is available almost anywhere in the country, either still (*sem gás*) or carbonated (*com gás*).

COMMUNICATIONS: POST, PHONES AND THE MEDIA

Portuguese postal services are reasonably efficient. Letters or cards take under a week to arrive at destinations in Europe, and a week to ten days to North America.

POSTAL SERVICES

Post offices (*correios*) are normally open Monday to Friday 9am–6pm, larger ones sometimes on Saturday mornings too. The main Lisbon and Porto branches operate a limited 24-hour service.

Stamps (*selos*) are sold at post offices (queue for the counter marked *selos*) and anywhere that has the sign of the red horse on a white circle over a green background and the legend *Correio de Portugal – Selos*.

To receive mail **posta restante**, look for a counter marked *encomendas*. You can have mail sent to you at any post office in the country. Letters should be marked clearly, and your name, ideally, should be written in capitals and underlined. To collect, you need to take along your passport. If you are expecting mail, ask the postal clerk to check for letters under your first name and any other initials (including Ms, etc) as well as under your surname – filing can be erratic.

PHONES

International calls can be made direct from almost any telephone booth in the country, but in most of them, you'll need a a good stock of coins and a great deal of patience with the international lines (always blocked or cutting you off

mid-speech). In busy tourist areas, especially the Algarve and Lisbon, there's a limited number of **credifones** which you can use with the 500$00 and 1200$00 phonecards available from post offices; they don't always work.

Public phones in bars and cafés are usually indicated by the sign of the red horse on a white circle over a green background and the legend *Correio de Portugal – Telefone*, and these should charge the regular, post office price.

The best bet, otherwise, is still to go to the old-fashioned post offices. Except in Lisbon and Porto, most are closed in the evening, which can be inconvenient, but there is no cheap-rate period anyway for international calls, which are pricey by European or North American standards.

To phone Europe dial 00, then 44 for the UK; then dial the city/local code (minus its preceding 1 in the US or 0 in Europe); and finally the number; for **North America**, dial 097 for the international exchange, then the country code (1 for the US and Canada)

Reverse charge (collect) calls can be made from any booth, dialing 099 for a European connection and 098 for the rest of the world.

NEWSPAPERS AND RADIO

The *International Herald Tribune*, and most British **newspapers**, can be bought in the major cities and resorts. The two most established Portuguese dailies are the Lisbon-based *Diário de Notícias* and the *Jornal de Notícias* from Porto. They have their uses for *listings information*, even if you've very sketchy knowledge of the language. A new and popular daily is now outselling them both, however: the stylish and youthful *Público*, which has good foreign news and regional inserts. Another informative read – on the entertainment front – is the weekly paper *SE7E* (*sete* means "7"), and, for a view of the country's culture, *JL* (*Jornal de Letras*).

English-language magazines include the old and staid *Anglo-Portuguese News*, the *Algarve News*, and *Algarve Magazine*. The first two can be useful for finding work, but none are especially informative. Imported **British and various continental European newspapers** (all a day old) are widely available in Lisbon, Porto and the Algarve.

On the **radio** front, you can pick up the **BBC World Service**, with hourly news on 648 KHz Medium wave and 15.07 MHz Short wave, and **BBC Radio 4** after dark on 198kHz long wave. **Voice of America** is sporadically audible on 6040 on the 49m short wave band. **Portuguese radio** also puts out an English-language programme for tourists at 8.30am or 10am (between 558 and 720 KHz/87.9 and 95.7FM depending on where you are).

OPENING HOURS AND HOLIDAYS

Like Spain, Portugal has held onto the institution of the *siesta*. Most stores and businesses, plus smaller museums and post offices, close for a good lunchtime break – usually from around 12.30 to 2.30 or 3pm.

Banks are a rare exception, staying open 8.30am to 3pm, Monday to Friday. **Shops** generally open around 9am, and after re-opening keep going until 7pm; except in the larger cities, they tend to close for the weekend at Saturday lunchtime.

Museums, churches, and monuments open from around 10am to 6pm; the larger ones stay open through lunchtime. Almost all museums and monuments, however, are closed on Mondays.

PUBLIC HOLIDAYS

The main public holidays, when almost everything is closed (and transport service reduced), are: Jan 1; April 25 (commemorating the 1974 revolution); Good Friday; May 1; Corpus Christi (usually early June); June 10 (*Dia de Camões e das Comunidades* – Camões day: the community part was added after the Revolution); August 15 (Feast of the Assumption); October 5 (Republic, Day, dating back to 1910); November 1 (All Saints Day); December 1 (independence from Spain in 1640); December 8 (Immaculate Conception); and December 25. There are, too, local holidays: for example June 13 in Lisbon and June 24 Porto.

FESTIVALS, BULLFIGHTS, FOOTBALL AND SPORTS

Rural and traditional, Portugal maintains a remarkable number of folk customs which find their expression in local carnivals (*festas*) and traditional pilgrimages (*romarias*). Some of these have developed into wild celebrations lasting days or even weeks and have become tourist events in themselves; others have barely strayed from their roots.

Every region is different, but in the **north** especially there are dozens of village festivals, everyone taking the day off to celebrate the local saint's day or the harvest, and performing ancient songs and dances in traditional dress for no one's benefit but their own. The festival list is potentially endless, and only the major highlights are detailed in the box opposite. For more **details** on what's going on around you, check with the local tourist office or buy the monthly *Borda d'Água*, an information leaflet detailing saints' days, star signs, gardening tips, and, most importantly, all the country's annual fairs. It is often the obscure and unexpected event which turns out to be the most fun.

Among major, national celebrations, **Easter Week** and **St. John's Eve** (June 23/24) stand out. Both are celebrated throughout the country

MAJOR POPULAR FESTIVALS

Among the biggest and best known of the other **popular festivals** are:

The **Queima das Fitas**, celebrating the end of the academic year in Coimbra (mid-May).

Santarém's Fair (last Sunday in May for two weeks).

The **Festival of São Gonçalo in Amarante** (1st weekend in June).

Lisbon's Popular Saints, especially Saint Anthony (throughout June).

The **Festa do Colete Encarnado** in Vila Franca de Xira, with Pamplona-style running of bulls through the streets (first week in July and again at the *Festas Bravas*, first week in October).

Vila Viçosa's **horse fair** (mid-August).

The **Festa da Nossa Senhora da Agonia** in Viana do Castelo (third weekend in August)

Lamego's celebrations around the **Romaria de Nossa Senhora dos Remédios** (last week in August to mid-September). On a more strictly religious note are the great **pilgrimages to Fátima**, May 13 and October 13 and, to a lesser extent, on the thirteenth of every month in between.

Look out too for the great **feiras**, especially at Barcelos. Originally they were markets, but as often as not nowadays you'll find a combination of agricultural show, folk festival, amusement park, and, admittedly, tourist bazaar.

with religious processions. The former is most magnificent in Braga, where it is full of ceremonial pomp, while the latter tends to be a more joyous affair. In Porto, where St. John's Eve is the highlight of a week of celebration, everyone dances through the streets all night, hitting each other over the head with leeks.

BULL FIGHTS

The Portuguese **bullfight** is neither as commonplace nor as famous as its Spanish counterpart and as a spectacle it's marginally preferable. In Portugal the bull isn't killed, but instead wrestled to the ground in a genuinely elegant, colourful, and skilled display. After the fight, however, the bull is usually injured and it is always slaughtered later in any case. If you choose to go – and we would urge visitors not to support the events put on simply for tourist benefit on the Algarve – these are the basics.

A *tourada* opens with the bull, its horns padded, facing a mounted *toureiro* in elaborate eighteenth-century costume. His job is to provoke and exhaust the bull and to plant the dart-like *farpas* (or *bandarilhas*) in its back while avoiding the charge – a demonstration of incredible riding prowess. Once the beast is tired the *moços-de-forcado* or simply *forcados* move in, an eight-man team who try finally to immobilise it. It appears a totally suicidal task – they line up behind each other across the ring from the bull and persuade it to charge them, the front man leaping between the horns while the rest grab hold and try to subdue it.

The great Portuguese bullfight centre is **Ribatejo**, where the animals are bred. If you want to see a fight, best to witness it here, amid the local *aficionados*, or as part of the festivals in Vila Franca de Xira and Santarém, or at the Campo Pequeno in **Lisbon**. The season lasts from around April through October.

FOOTBALL

Football (soccer) is the Portuguese national sport, with a long and often glorious tradition of international and club teams. The leading clubs, inevitably, hail from Lisbon (*Benfica* and *Sporting*) and Porto (*FC Porto*). Just about every Portuguese supports one of these three teams, paying scant attention to the lesser, local teams. Of these, F.C. *Guimarães* are the most consistent challengers to the big league boys.

If you want to see a league match, the season runs from September through to May. Tickets are inexpensive, and matches given due prominence in the press. You may also be lucky enough to catch one of the big three teams, or even the national side, in European action. The spectacle of a packed capacity football stadium somewhat puts bullfights in the shade.

PARTICIPATORY SPORTS

Participatory sports on offer in Portugal include windsurfing, golf and tennis – all of which are promoted mainly on the Algarve.

Windsurfing boards are available for rent on most of the Algarve beaches and at the more popular northern and Lisbon coast resorts. The biggest windsurfing destination is **Guincho**, north of Lisbon (see p.84), though the winds and currents here require a high level of expertise.

Tennis courts are a common feature of most of the larger Algarve hotels – their attraction being that you can play year-round. If you want to improve your game, the best intensive coaching is under the instruction of ex-Wimbledon pro Roger Taylor at the **Vale do Lobo** resort complex. Arguably the country's best **golf**

course, designed by Frank Penninck, is just up the road from here at **Vilamoura**, and several others are within reach.

Anyone interested in **fishing** should head to the trout streams of the Minho and other northern regions. Licenses can be obtained from local town halls.

For further information – and addresses of operators promoting sporting holidays – contact the Portuguese National Tourist Office for a copy of their *Sportugal* brochure.

MUSIC, CINEMA AND TV

Portugal's rich musical traditions – and current performers – are covered in some depth in the *Contexts* section of this guide. Suffice to say here that there is much on offer, and much that should be experienced – from the strange laments of *fado* to the African bands from the former Portuguese colonies of Cabo Verde, Guinea-Bissau, São Tomé e Principe, Angola, and Mozambique. The best source for information on these is the weekly paper *SE7E*.

The **rock music** scene is almost exclusively based in Lisbon. To catch the more interesting bands, particularly the African ones, keep your eyes open for bills advertising festivals, and check listings in *SE7E* for Lisbon, Porto, and (in summer) Vila Real de Santo António.

Jazz is active in a small way, too, and there's an excellent international **jazz festival** run by the Gulbenkian Foundation (Fundação Gulbenkian) during the summer, with Cascais hosting a much smaller one around the same time. Vilar de Mouros, near Caminha, sporadically hosts an August jazz and rock week, too.

More **classical** tastes are catered to by the summer **Estoril festival** and events in Lisbon and elsewhere sponsored by the Fundação Gulbenkian. Tourist offices have full schedules.

CINEMA AND TELEVISION

Going to the cinema in Portugal is extremely cheap, and **films** are often shown with the original (usually English) soundtrack with Portuguese subtitles. Listings can be found in the local newspaper or on sandwich boards, invariably placed somewhere in the central square of every small town. Screenings are cheap, with reduced price matinées and all Monday shows.

Portuguese **television**, too, imports many American and British shows – nearly always subtitled rather than dubbed. Increasingly, too, European **satellite TV** stations are spawning their dishes around the country; sports channels are popular in bars. You also get televised bullfights and, above all, *telenovelas* – soaps. Often from Brazil, these are compelling viewing even if you don't understand a word.

TROUBLE AND HARASSMENT

Portugal is a remarkably crime-free country, though there's the usual petty theft in larger tourist resorts and Lisbon is developing a reputation for pickpockets on public transport. Hired cars, too, are always prey to thieves – leave them looking as empty as possible – and campsites in the Algarve are less reliable than elsewhere.

For your own part, violations of **drug laws** (possession of dope is a criminal offense) carry heavy sentences; and you'd be foolish to try to bring any in. **Nude bathing**, still rare and theoretically an arrestable offense, could bring a fine and away from the Algarve even going topless may provoke a warning. Portuguese **police**, though, don't generally go looking for trouble.

SEXUAL HARASSMENT

The ruralism and small-town life of Portugal make it one of the most relaxed of Latin countries for **women travellers**. Which is not to say that the Portuguese **machismo** is any less ingrained than in Spain or Italy: simply that it gets rather less of an outlet.

The main problems come with the **cities**. Walking past sidewalk cafés can be like stepping on a bed of snakes, as men stare and "hiss" their approval in customary fashion. They don't really expect you to notice, perhaps (and may only be doing it to acknowledge they've noticed you to each other…) and after a while it does blend into the background. But it's not something you ever really get used to – or would want to get used to.

Irritation aside, however, Portugal is rarely a dangerous place, and only the following few areas need to be particularly avoided: parts of **Lisbon** (particularly the Cais do Sodré and parts of the Bairro Alto by night), streets immediately around **train stations** in the larger towns (traditionally the red light districts), and **parts of the Algarve**, where aggressive males congregate on the pick-up.

On the whole it's a **rural country**, intensely traditional and formal to the point of prudishness. People may initially wonder why you're travelling on your own – especially inland and in the mountains, where Portuguese women never travel unaccompanied – but once they have accepted that you are a crazy foreigner you're likely to be welcomed, adopted, and offered food and lodging in their homes.

As far as transport goes, **hitching** is extremely easy and safe so long as there are two or more of you. With a man in your party the rides usually take longer to come by, but if you're strolling the streets together you'll find that the sound effects disappear. If you're on your own, get around at night by **taxi** – very cheap anyway. By day public transport is good and quite safe. **Buses** have a cozier feel than trains, and you should avoid the latter on Friday afternoon and evening and late Sunday night when the whole army seems to be going on (or returning from) weekend furlough.

THE WOMEN'S MOVEMENT

There are relatively few women's organisations in Portugal. The best contact points are the *IDM* centre and the feminist bookshop *Editora das Mulheres*, both in Lisbon (see that chapter for addresses). Also of interest is the *Comissão da Condição Feminina* (Avenida da República 32-2° esq, Lisbon), which researches and maintains a watching brief on all aspects of women's lives in Portugal; members organise conferences and meetings, are very active in areas of social and legal reform, and are linked with feminists throughout the country.

WORK

Portugal has employment problems of its own, and without a special skill you're unlikely to have much luck finding any kind of long-term work. One realistic option though is teaching English. For this a TEFL diploma is a distinct advantage, though not absolutely essential. Work is best arranged before you leave as this prevents work permit hassles. But if you're already in Portugal you could just apply to individual schools or advertise your services privately. Au-pair work is also possible; once in Portugal try advertising in the *Anglo-Portuguese News*, Avenida de São Pedro 14D, Monte Estoril.

WORKING ON THE ALGARVE

As far as temporary jobs go, the only opportunities are in **tourist-related work** on the Algarve; foreigners are not normally employed on the harvests and wages are low. The Algarve, however, does offer a range of ways of getting money, all of them dependent to some extent on your self-confidence and/or lack of scruples.

Most obvious of the tourist-related jobs is **bar work**. This is not easy to find – you'll stand the best chance in one of the many British-owned places – and even when you do, it often brings in barely enough money to live on, after very long hours. Better, at least in terms of time involved, is to try your hand walking the streets at night **giving out disco invitations** to holiday makers. This work is available in Albufeira, Lagos, Praia da Oura, etc. It's paid solely on commission but it does leave you free during the day – and much of the night – to seek your own entertainment.

Which leads nicely into the biggest scam in the country – perhaps in Europe – of **selling time shares**. Here possibilities exist for making really big bucks, though not everyone, of course, strikes it rich. The work again involves walking the streets in the major resorts and in Quarteira, Vilamoura, and Monte Gordo, this time inviting British tourist couples to view time-share resorts and villas. It is extremely tiring, soul-destroying, and, at its most successful, pretty disreputable work, but earnings are on a commission basis and this can add up to a fair living if you're the type who enjoys selling your grandmother. Just ask the people who are already doing the job on the street what to do. They'll tell you how to find work and how depressing it is.

One last outlet is to head for the huge new **yacht marina** at **Vilamoura**. Only half-built, it already holds around a thousand craft, slowly being surrounded by trendy bars, boutiques, and cafés. You could try some of these, but it's even better to approach the yachties themselves. Almost all boat owners have hundreds of little tasks that need doing and, given the opportunity, will pay a few thousand escudos to anyone presenting themselves as a handyman/woman. Mostly it's **painting** or **scrubbing down** decks – hardly skilled labor – but if you can convince someone you know what you're doing the quality of work you'll be given may improve.

Between late September and early November, however, there's the chance of **crewing** to the Canaries or the Caribbean; for this sort of angle try *Wellies Bar* as well as word of mouth. For the more menial odd-jobs you just need persistence and a thick skin: spend a couple of days asking around and something should turn up.

If you do decide to stay on in the Algarve to work, you can **extend** your sixty days unofficially by crossing the border at Vila Real de Santo António (the easiest way). The official way, if reliable long-term employment beckons, is to go to one of the *Serviço de Estrangeiros* offices in Portimão, Albufeira, or Faro.

DIRECTORY

ADDRESSES Most addresses in Portugal consist of a street name and number followed by a storey number, eg, Rua de Afonso Henriques 34-3°. This means you need to go up to the third floor of no. 34, but remember: in Europe, the ground floor is not counted as the first floor as it is in the US, so you will be going up four stories. An "esq" or "E" (standing for *esquerda*) after a floor number means you should go to the left; "dir" or "D" (for *direita*) indicates the apartment or office you're looking for is on the right. In a town of any size, the *Rossio* is always the main, central square.

AIRPORT TAX None.

BAGGAGE You can often leave it at a station for a very small sum while you look for rooms. On the whole the Portuguese are highly trustworthy, and even shopkeepers and café owners will keep an eye on your belongings for you.

BEACHES Beware of the heavy undertow on many of Portugal's western Atlantic beaches and don't swim if you see a red or yellow flag. The sea is warmest on the eastern Algarve – the beaches past Faro.

BRING...an **alarm clock** for early morning departures, **ear plugs** if you're a light sleeper, a **glue stick** for gumless stamps if you'll be writing postcards, a **torch**, a pocket **Portuguese dictionary**, and **mosquito repellant** (preferably wrist and ankle bands).

CHILDREN Portugal is very children-friendly and families should find it as easy a place to roam as any other country (or, realistically, at least no harder). Cheap hotels and *pensões* will only rarely charge extra for children in their parents' room, and in restaurants small portions and extra plates are absolutely the norm for all who require them. Lastly, museums and most sights don't usually charge for small children.

CONSULATES AND EMBASSIES See listings for Lisbon and Porto.

DRESS Churches often require "modest dress" – which basicaly just means you shouldn't wear shorts or very flimsy tops.

DUTY-FREE GOODS If you're in the market for duty-frees, try to check out prices when you arrive at the airport. Apart from standard *licor* brands, there are no great savings to be made. For national specialities – including wine, port, and brandy – you're better off buying from local groceries and *licor* stores.

EMERGENCIES Phone ☎115 for ambulance service (no coin required).

FILM is not cheap by Portuguese standards and the price seems shocking compared with food, drink, and other national products. It's best to buy stock at home.

GAY LIFE The gay scene isn't especially prominent, or at least commercialised, though there's a fair sprinkling of clubs, and a gay beach, in Lisbon (see that chapter) and one or two places to meet in Porto and the Algarve. Attitudes in the capital are fairly tolerant; elsewhere a gay consciousness has yet to make much impact. There is no explicit law against homosexuality.

LAUNDRY There are few self-service launderettes, but loads of *lavandarias*, where you can get your clothes washed, mended, and ironed (overnight) at a fairly low cost.

MUSEUMS Entry fees are mostly standardised at 200$00 and are usually free on Sundays.

NATIONAL PARKS The head office in Lisbon (Rua Ferreira Lapa 29-1°) has details on Portugal's parks and reserves, but generally neither head nor district offices have much time for foreign visitors, concentrating on awakening a spirit of wildlife conservation and protection in their compatriots.

PUBLIC BATHROOMS "Ladies" often charge and are clean, "Gentlemen" may look more aesthetic (lots of ironwork) and are free, but usually pretty unattractive inside. A sign that says *Retretes* will head you in the right direction, then it's *homens* for men and *senhoras* for women; the doors will generally have the usual block figure wearing a skirt or trousers.

SWIMMING POOLS Every sizeable town has a swimming pool, usually outdoors, but you'll find that they are often closed from about September to May.

TIME Portugal keeps Greenwich Mean Time – one hour behind Spain (and Britain), five hours ahead of Eastern Standard Time and eight hours ahead of Pacific Standard Time. Daylight Savings Time goes into effect on the last Sunday in March (spring ahead) and ends on the last Sunday in September (fall back).

TIPPING Hotels and restaurants include a service charge but porters and maids expect something. Don't tip cab drivers.

I am very happy here, because I loves oranges, and talks bad Latin to the Monks, who understand it as it is like their own. And I goes into society (with my pocket pistols) and I swims in the Tagus all across at once, and I rides on an ass or a mule and swears Portuguese, and I have got a diarrhoea, and bites from the mosquitoes. But what of that? Comfort must not be expected by folks that go a-pleasuring.

— Byron in Portugal, July 1809.

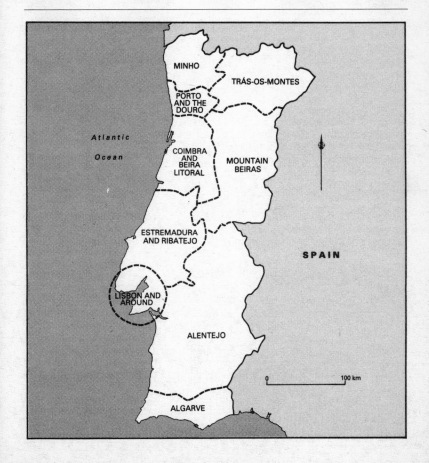

CHAPTER ONE

LISBON AND AROUND

There are few cityscapes as startling and eccentric as that of **Lisbon**. Built on a switchback of hills above the broad **Tejo** (Tagus) estuary, its quarters are linked by an amazing network of trams – pre-war models cranking up outrageous gradients – funiculars and *elevadors*. Down at the river, you are lured across towards the sea by a vast, Rio-like statue of Christ, arms outstretched, by one of the grandest of all suspension bridges, and by a mini-fleet of ferries. As a visitor, it's hard not to feel an element of the funfair about the place: a sense heightened by the castle poised above the Alfama district's medieval, whitewashed streets, by the Manueline fantasy architecture of Belém, the mosaic wave-patterns of the central Rossio square, or the Art Nouveau shops and cafés.

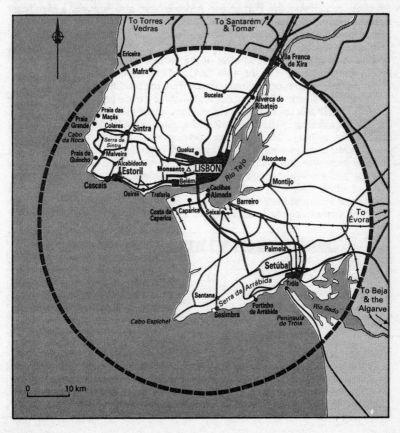

For Americans, San Francisco is an obvious counterpart: a city that has parallels in both its physical make-up and its fault-line position: Lisbon's Great Earthquake, in 1755, levelled most of the old lower town. The two cities stand a further comparison in their tangibly easygoing characters. Lisbon is immediately likable, gentler than any port or capital should expect to be, a city almost provincial in feel and defiantly human in pace and scale. For much of the present century, Lisbon, as the rest of the country, stood apart from the European mainstream. The isolation ended abruptly with the 1974 revolution, and still more so with integration into the European Community a decade later, but the city's identity is strong, and strikingly resistant to any creeping homogenisation of culture. Madrid, for instance, seems as foreign to Lisbon as London or Paris.

None of which is to suggest that the city is static. Over the present century, Lisbon's population has doubled to nearly a million, a tenth of all Portuguese, and following on from the revolution the capital absorbed a vast influx of **refugees** – *retornados* – from Portugal's former African colonies of Angola, Cabo Verde, São Tomé e Principe, Guinea Bissau and Mozambique. The *retornados* imposed a heavy burden on an already strained economy, especially on housing, but their overall integration is one of the chief triumphs of modern Portugal. Like the city's Brazilian contingent, the Portuguese Africans have also brought a significant **cultural** buoyancy. Alongside the traditional *fado* clubs of its Bairro Alto quarter, Lisbon now has superb Latin and African bands, and a panoply of international restaurants and bars. The city has a real sense of involvement in **politics**, too, despite the current, moribund state of the parties. Everywhere you go, graffiti artists seem to have got to the walls first, and in working-class parts of the city, like Alcântara, some superb murals remain from the revolutionary years.

Art and monuments of a more conventional nature are perhaps thinner on the ground, largely as a result of the 1755 earthquake. But there is one building from Portugal's golden age – the **Jerónimos Monastery** at Belém – that is the equal of any in the country. More modern developments include the **Gulbenkian Foundation** museum complex, with its superb collections of ancient and modern art, and some adventurous contemporary architecture, such as Tómas Taveira's amazing post-modernist shopping centre at **Amoreiras**.

All of which makes for a city that demands at least a few days of anyone's Portuguese itinerary. Better still, make the capital a base for a week or two's holiday, with day escapes and excursions in the area. The sea is close by, half an hour's journey taking you to the beach suburb of **Cascais**, or to the miles of dunes along the **Costa da Caparica**. Slightly further afield lie the lush wooded heights and royal palaces of **Sintra**, Byron's "glorious Eden". And if you become interested in Portuguese architecture, there are the rococo delights of the **Palácio de Queluz** and its gardens en route, or the extraordinary monastery of **Mafra** – a good first step into Estremadura (the region immediately to the north, covered in the following chapter).

LISBON (LISBOA)

Physically, **LISBON** is an eighteenth-century city: elegant, open to the sea and carefully planned. The description does not cover its modern expanse, of course – there are suburbs here as poor and inadequate as any in Europe – but is accurate within the old central boundaries of a triangle of hills. This "lower city", the **Baixa**, was the product of a single phase of building, carried out in less than a decade by the dictatorial minister, the Marquês de Pombal, in the wake of the **Great Earthquake** of 1755.

The Earthquake, history and monuments

The **Great Earthquake** – which was felt as far away as Scotland and Jamaica – struck Lisbon at 9.30am on November 1, All Saints' Day, when most of the city's population was at mass. Within the space of ten minutes there had been three major tremors and fires, spread by the candles of a hundred church altars, were raging throughout the capital. A vast tidal wave swept the seafront, where refugees sought shelter: in all, 40,000 of a 270,000 population died. The destruction of the city shocked the continent, with Voltaire, who wrote an account of it in his novel *Candide*, leading an intense debate with Rousseau on the operation of providence. For Portugal, and for the capital, it was a disaster that in retrospect seems to seal an age. Eighteenth-century Lisbon was arguably the most active port in Europe.

Lisbon had been a central and prosperous city since **Roman**, perhaps even Phoenician, times. In the Middle Ages, as **Moorish** *Lishbuna*, it thrived on its wide links with the Arab world and on the rich territories of the south, Alentejo and Algarve. Its reconquest by the Christians, in 1147, was an early and dubious triumph of the Crusades, its one positive aspect the appearance of a first true Portuguese monarch in **Afonso Henriques**. It was not until 1255, however, that the city took over from Coimbra as capital.

Over the following centuries, Lisbon was twice at the forefront of European development and trade, on a scale that is hard to envisage today. The first phase came with the great Portuguese **discoveries** of the **late fifteenth and sixteenth centuries**, such as Vasco da Gama's opening of the sea route to India. The second was in the opening decades of the **eighteenth century**, when a colonised Brazil was found to yield both gold and diamonds.

It is these that are the great ages of Portuguese patronage. The sixteenth century is dominated by the figure of **Dom Manuel I**, under whom the flamboyant national style known as Manueline developed. Lisbon takes its principal monuments, the tower and monastery at Belém, from this era. The eighteenth century, more extravagant but with less brilliant effect, produced **Dom João V**, best known as the obsessive builder of Mafra, which he created in response to Philip II's El Escorial in Spain.

DEVELOPMENT AND DESTRUCTION

In recent years Lisbon has experienced some of the most radical **redevelopment** since the Marquês de Pombal rebuilt the shattered capital after the 1755 earthquake. This is mainly the result of Portugal's economic stability – and extensive grants – since joining the European Community in 1986, guided by prime minister Cavaco Silva. As a result of cheap labour costs, foreign investment has been pouring into the capital, and with it the need for a rapid building programme. This investment has pulled Portugal off the bottom rung of the EC prosperity ladder above Greece, but at a price: much of the old Lisbon has shrunk – including huge swathes of the lovely Parque Eduardo VII, the summit of which is to receive a Hilton hotel; many of Lisbon's beautiful old **mansions** are being demolished to make way for towering office buildings; and it's likely that even most of the **trams** will eventually disappear to make way for faster roads.

Ironically it is **beyond Pombal's statue at Rotunda** that the worst of the damage is being done. Avenida da República's beauty has all but gone. The green gauze goes up across the graceful pre-1920s façades, and the labourers set to, dismantling the buildings with hammers and picks, piece by piece – a dangerous process for both workers and passers-by, who are often showered with lumps of masonry escaping the protective nets. The concrete piles that take the place of the old houses (supposedly more earthquake-proof than their predecessors, if building regulations are being adhered to) are erected with similar disregard for pedestrians: iron girders and stacks of bricks swing perilously over pavements from rickety cranes.

Much of the blame for the scandalous demolition of the grand mansions can be laid at the door of an inconsistent planning department. The city's highly bureaucratic **planning regulations**, which could be used to safeguard old buildings, are rumoured to be easily bypassed with some financial persuasion. At the same time, **pre-revolution rent laws** have contributed to appalling living conditions in Lisbon's older tenements, some of which are literally falling apart and have no chance of being repaired. Only the property developers are prepared to take on such slums – if they're in prime sites.

The cause of this state of affairs is simple. In Lisbon, once tenants move into accommodation, **rents** are fixed for life. This means that pre-revolution tenants are still paying miniscule rents while rents on new accommodation spiral to northern European levels. Landlords of old buildings find themselves with unremovable tenants, and receive such a small income for their property that they can't afford renovations. Nor can they sell, as no one will buy property with tenants already installed; and the slum-bound tenants themselves can't afford to move out to new properties. Enter the **developers**: the impasse has brought about a tidal wave of destruction.

But not all of old Lisbon is lost and at least the **city centre** will retain its elegance. Changes in the rent laws are in the pipeline, while EC funding is helping a renovation scheme in Lisbon's protected areas, including the **Alfama** quarter, Lisbon's oldest. Residents are temporarily rehoused while crumbling buildings are refaced and hot water and reliable electricity are put in. The **Bairro Alto** is next in line – so long as funds hold out.

Parts of the **Baixa** and the wealthy **Lapa** areas are already preserved, while European Community protection orders have also been slapped on some of Lisbon's old buildings, such as the **mansion on Avenida Fontes Pereira de Melo**. The streets of the **Chiado**, burned out in the 1988 fire, are the subject of an ambitious redevelopment plan to restore their original design.

Survivals and the city structure

Eighteenth-century prints show a pre-quake Lisbon of tremendous opulence and mystique, its skyline characterised by towers, palaces and convents. There are glimpses of this still – the **Belém** suburb survived the destruction, as did the old Moorish hillside of **Alfama** – but these are isolated neighbourhoods and monuments. It is instead **Pombal's** perfect, Neoclassical grid that covers the centre. Given orders, following the earthquake, to "Bury the dead, feed the living and close the ports", the king's minister followed his success in restoring order to the city in its rebuilding.

The **Baixa**, still the heart of the modern city, adheres to his strict ideals of simplicity and economy. Individual streets were assigned to each craft and trade and the whole was shaped by public buildings and squares. Only the **Rossio**, the main square since medieval times, remained in its original place, slightly off-centre in the symmetrical design.

Orientation and arrival

It could hardly be easier to get your bearings in the **Baixa**. At one end, opening onto the Rio Tejo, is the broad, arcaded **Praça do Comércio** (popularly known as the **Terreiro do Paço**), with its ferry stations for crossing the river, tram terminus for Belém, and grand triumphal arch. At the other – linked by almost any street you care to take – stands the **Rossio**, more like three squares than one, merging with the **Praça da Figueira** and **Praça dos Restauradores**.

These squares, filled with cafés, occasional buskers, lost-looking tourists and streetwise dealers, form the hub of Lisbon's daily activity. At night the focus shifts to the **Bairro Alto**, high above and to the left of the Baixa, and best reached by funicular (*Elevador da Glória*) or the great street *elevador* (*Santa Justa*) built for the city by Gustave Eiffel. East of the Baixa, the **Castelo de São Jorge**, a brooding landmark, holds a still taller hill, with the **Alfama** district – the oldest, most fascinating part of the city – sprawled below.

Points of arrival

The place to head for on arrival is the **Rossio**. Most of the city's pensions are within walking distance of the square, and in the adjoining Praça dos Restauradores the **Turismo** will provide you with accommodation lists and a good, semi-three-dimensional **map** of the city – useful in that it outlines Belém and other places of interest outside the area of our own plan. The best map for a longer stay in the city is the Falk, ingeniously folded and with a good index.

BY TRAIN

■ **Long-distance trains** – from Coimbra, Porto and the north (and from Badajoz, Madrid and France) – use the **Santa Apolónia station**. This is about fifteen minutes' walk from the Praça do Comércio, or a short ride on buses #9 or #46 to the Rossio. At the station there's a small information office (understaffed and not very reliable) and an 8am-to-8pm money exchange. A useful bus from here is #90, which runs past the Fluvial station (see below), Rossio, Saldanha and the airport (7am–9pm), but costs 190$00.

■ **Local trains** – from Sintra or anywhere else in Estremadura – emerge right at the heart of the city in the **Rossio Station**, a mock-Manueline complex with the trains an improbable escalator-ride above the street-level entrances. It is complete with shops, bank exchange counters and left luggage cabins. At weekends, currently, works on the line mean that trains bypass Rossio, involving a metro ride or taxi to Entrecampos station, 3km to the north.

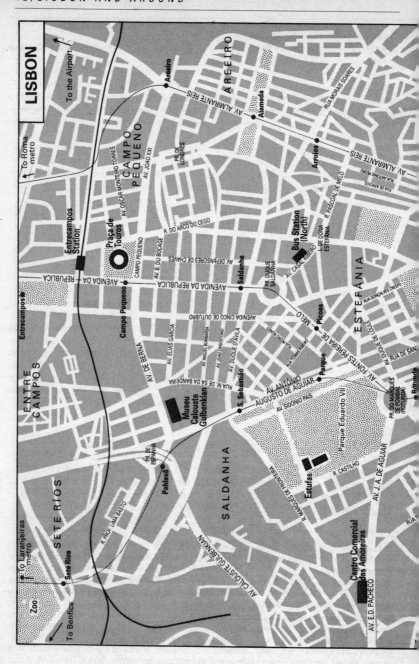

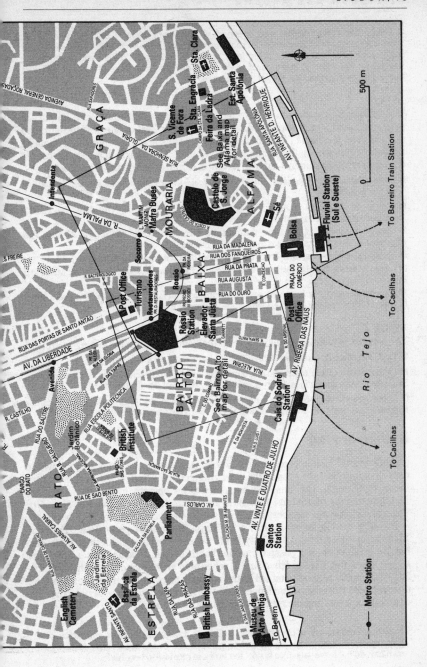

■ **Trains from the Algarve and south.** A slightly more involved but also more scenic approach. The railway lines from the south terminate at the suburb of **Barreiro**, on the far bank of the river, where you catch a ferry (included in the price of the train ticket) to the **Fluvial** (or *Sul e Sueste*) station next to the Praça do Comércio. Buses #1, #2, #9, #32, #39, #44 and #45 run up from the Fluvial to the Rossio.

BY BUS

The various **bus companies** have terminals scattered about the city, but all are positioned near a metro station. Leaving Lisbon, it's best to check at the Turismo on times and terminals. You can usually buy tickets if you turn up half an hour in advance – though for the summer expresses to the Algarve it's best to reserve (through any travel agent) a day in advance. Companies and terminals include:

■ **Avda. Casal Ribeiro** (metro *Saldanha*): *Rodoviária da Estremadura* services to destinations north of Lisbon.

■ **Praça de Espanha** (metro *Palhavã*) and **Avda. Cinco de Outubro 75** (metro *Saldanha*): *Rodoviária da Lisboa* have departures south from both terminals.

■ **Campo Pequeno**: *AVIC* serve the northwest coast; *SOLEXPRESSO* the Alentejo and Algarve. Also long-distance buses to the rest of Europe.

■ **Campo das Cebolas**, near Praça do Comércio: destinations in the Minho.

■ **Largo Martim Moniz**, northeast of the Rossio: *Empresa Mafrense* services for Mafra and Ericeira (hourly).

■ **Algarve departures**: in season several companies run fast, excellent-value express buses between Lisbon and the Algarve. Contact the Turismo for details.

BY AIR

The **airport** is just twenty minutes from the centre. Options for getting in are:

■ **Taxi.** A routine ride, costing 1000–15000$00, depending on traffic.

■ **Linha Verde (#90) express bus.** From the terminal to Rossio, Praça do Comércio and Santa Apolónia train stations. Every 15min from 7.30am to 1.30am; 200$00.

■ **Local buses #44/45.** These leave from the other side of the car parking, to Praça dos Restauradores and Cais do Sodré station. Every 10–15min from 6am to 1am; 50$00.

Getting around

Getting around Lisbon presents few problems. Most places of interest are within easy walking distance – and transport connections are detailed in the text for those that aren't. The bus and tram networks operate from around 6am to midnight and the metro until 1am. Both are free to children – as are the *elevadors*. Taxis are among the cheapest in Europe and a useful complement at all hours.

If you're staying for more than a few days, the **tourist pass** (*Passe Turístico*; 1550$00 for seven days, 1100$00 for four) might be worth considering; it is available, on production of a passport, at the booth by the *Elevador Santa Justa*. For longer stays, there is the *Passe Social*, renewable each calendar month (currently 2670$00); it can also be obtained at the *elevador* or at any metro station (look for the *venta de passes* sign); you'll need a photograph. Both of these passes cover the city's buses, trams and the metro – though not local trains.

Note that although one of the safer cities in Europe, Lisbon has its share of **pickpockets**. Take special care on buses and the metro, and around the main squares. If you have your own **car**, do not leave valuables inside: the break-in rate is also very high.

Trams, funiculars and buses

At the slightest excuse you should ride one of the city's **trams** (*eléctricos*). Ascending some of the steepest gradients of any city in the world, many are worth taking for the pleasure of the ride alone. Highlights include:

■ **#28** The best ride in the city: from São Vicente to the Estrêla gardens, passing through Rua da Conceição in Baixa. In summer, an original open-window tram plies this route.

■ **#12** São Tomé in the Alfama to the Largo Martim Moniz, near Praça da Figueira.

■ **#15/#17** Two tram lines from Praça do Comércio to Belém; #17 doesn't run on Sundays.

■ **Elevador da Gloria** A funicular to the Bairro Alto from the Praça dos Restauradores.

■ **Elevador da Bica** Another funicular, linking Rua do Loreto/Rua Luz Soriano in Bairro Alto to Rua de São Paulo near the Cais do Sodré station.

■ **Elevador Santa Justa** This time a lift, rather than a funicular, transporting you from Rua do Ouro, on the west side of the Baixa, up to a walkway by the Carmo church. See p.58.

Most of the trams and funiculars run every ten to fifteen minutes throughout the day, from around 6.30am to midnight: look up for tram-stop (*paragem*) signs, suspended from the cable. **Buses** (*carris*) run just about everywhere in the Lisbon area and can prove valuable for getting to and from the rather far-flung bus stations, as well as more outlying attractions.

Tickets for trams, funiculars and buses are best bought in *módulos* – blocks of twenty tickets; they cost 560$00 and can be obtained at the Elevador Santa Justa booth and other terminals. You need one of these tickets for an elevador trip and, two (or sometimes three) for most tram and bus journeys, depending on the zones you pass through along the way. Individual tickets (50$00) can also be bought, on board, from the driver.

The Metro

The *Metropolitano* covers a few useful routes – to the Gulbenkian museum, for example – though as a visitor to the city you're unlikely to make extensive use of it. The most central stations are at Praça dos Restauradores and Rossio. **Tickets** are 50$00 a journey; or 400$00 for a ten-ticket *módulo* – sold at all stations.

Trains

There is a local line **west along the coast** through Belém, to Estoril and Cascais, departing from the Cais do Sodré station. Tickets to Estoril/Cascais are 130$00.

Ferries

Ferries cross the Tejo at various points and can be a pleasure in their own right.

■ **Praça do Comércio** (*Sul e Sueste*) to Cacilhas, Barreiro and Montijo. Worth doing for the terrific views of Lisbon alone. 75$00 one way.

■ **Cais do Sodré** to Cacilhas/Almada. Again, fine views. 75$00 one way.

■ **Belém** to Trafaria (buses to Caparica). 200$00 one way.

Taxis

Lisbon's taxis are inexpensive, so long as your destination is within the city limits. All taxis have meters, which are generally switched on, and tips are not expected. A green light means the cab is occupied.

The only problem is persuading a taxi to stop. They can be found quite easily by day – there are ranks in the Rossio, at the near end of Avenida da Liberdade and at Cais do Sodré. At night, going home from a bar or restaurant, it's usually best to phone *Rádio Taxis* (☎01/82 50 61 – or 62/63/64/65/66/67/68/69).

Accommodation

The **listings** that follow are a selection of the better value pension and hotel rooms in the city. They cover all price ranges – from rock bottom to a couple of luxury choices – but most fall into the low- to mid-range budgets, with double rooms between 2500$00 and 5000$00. Our categorisation system is explained in the box below.

If you have money for the more expensive categories of **hotels** (5000$00 and up for a double room), it can save a lot of walking to use the **booking service** at the Praça dos Restauradores **Turismo**. The service operates during normal office hours (Mon–Sat 9am–8pm, Sun 10am–6pm); there is no commission charge. A similar service is available at the **airport hotel desk**, facing you as you pass through customs on arrival – and they're prepared to reserve pension as well as hotel rooms.

Looking around on your own, especially for the cheaper options, pick from one of the **pensions** (*pensão* singular, *pensões* plural) below. These are not exhaustive listings – the city has scores of small, cheap pensions, often grouped one on top of the other in tall tenement buildings – but they do cover all the main concentrations in the central parts of the city. When doing the rounds, be warned that the pensions tend to occupy upper stories (leaving one person with all your bags is a good idea if you're in company) and that those within the same building are generally independent of each other, so try all of them for space. Don't be put off unduly by some fairly unsalubrious staircases. And beware that rooms facing onto the street in Lisbon can be pretty noisy.

ADDRESSES

Addresses – written as 53-3°, etc – specify the street number followed by the storey number.

ROOM PRICE SCALES

The symbols used in our hotel listings denote the following price ranges.

① 2000–2500$00   ③ 3500–5000$00   ⑤ 8000–12,000$00

② 2500–3500$00   ④ 5000–8000$00   ⑥ 12,000$00 and upwards

For a fuller explanation, see p.21.

EASTER AND MIDSUMMER SHORTAGES . . . AND 30-MINUTE ROOMS

At **Easter**, and even more so in **midsummer**, room availability is often stretched to the limit, many single rooms "converted" to doubles, and even rock-bottom prices may start as high as 3000$00. At this time you should be prepared to take anything vacant and look around next day, if need be, for somewhere better, or possibly cheaper.

Fortunately, during most of the year you should have little difficulty in finding a room, and for maybe a third less than midsummer prices within a few minutes' walk of the Rossio: a double, say, for around 2500$00. Anything much cheaper is usually in the **"thirty-minute room"** business, as the Portuguese put it, but most are safe enough. Remember, too, you can always try to knock the price down at quieter times of year, especially if you can summon a few good-natured phrases in Portuguese, or if you are looking for a group room.

| PHONE PREFIXES |

All numbers in the Greater Lisbon area are prefixed ☎01, if you are dialling from elsewhere in the country. From Britain numbers should be prefixed ☎010-351-1.

Around Rossio, Praça da Figueira and in the Baixa Grid

This is the most obvious, central and accessible accommodation area, with dozens of possibilities around the Rossio station, in Praça da Figueira, and in the grid of streets in the Baixa, or lower town.

NEAR ROSSIO STATION/PRAÇA DA FIGUEIRA

Residencial Estrêla do Carmo, Calçada do Carmo 25-2° (☎346 71 09). A bit cramped. ①.

Pensão Estação Central, Calçada do Carmo 17-2° (☎342 33 08). Cleanish, but small and musty rooms. ②.

Pensão Muralha, Rua 1° de Dezembro 3-3° (☎342 24 59). Rather shabby but clean, with showers in rooms. ②.

Pensão Arco da Bandeira, Rua dos Sapateiros 226-4° (☎342 34 78). Superior *pensão* with comfortable rooms. Highly recommended. ③.

Pensão Rossio, Rua dos Sapateiros 173-2° (☎342 72 04). Nice rooms, right on the Rossio, with helpful management. ③.

Pensão Ibérica, Praça da Figueira 10-2° (☎346 18 46). Central location and lots of rooms but noisy and a bit ramshackle. ②.

Pensão Beira Minho, Praça da Figueira 6-2°esq (☎86 74 12). Tiny place, entered through a flower shop. ②.

Pensão Coimbra e Madrid, Praça da Figueira 3-3° (342 17 60). Fairly upmarket pension, next to the *Pastelaria Suíça*, with superb views of the Rossio and Praça da Figueira. ③.

Pensão Lafonense, Rua das Portas de Santo Antão 36-2° (☎346 71 22). A very welcoming pension, just off the Rossio, just behind the national Theatre. ③.

IN THE BAIXA GRID

Pensão Santiago, Rua dos Douradores 222-3° (☎87 43 53). Reasonably clean, but rates tend to depend on what sex you are. Not a first choice. ①.

Pensão Angoche, Rua dos Douradores 121-4° (☎87 07 11). Small, quiet, clean and friendly. Recommended. ①.

Pensão "A Andorinha", Rua dos Correeiros 183-3° (☎346 08 80). Cheap and very tacky last resort. ①.

Pensão Galicia, Rua do Cruxifixio (☎328 430). Very much better – clean rooms and a fine location. ①.

Pensão Prata. Rua da Prata 71-3° (346 89 08). Showers in rooms, clean and friendly. ②.

Pensão Norte, Rua dos Douradores 159 (☎87 89 41). A five-floor warren; cold showers. ②.

Pensão Marinho, Rua dos Correeiros 205-2° (☎36 09 40). Unprepossessing exterior but reasonable enough inside. ②.

Pensão Moderna, Rua dos Correeiros 205-4° (☎346 08 18). Above the *Marinho*, big clean rooms, crammed with elderly furniture. Atmospheric and recommended. ③.

Residencial Primavera, Rua dos Correeiros 161-2° (☎32 59 83). Quiet and friendly, but not uplifting. ③.

Hotel Duas Nações, Rua da Vitória 41 (☎346 20 82). Classy, pleasantly faded, nineteenth-century hotel. ④ – ⑤.

Albergaria Residencial Insulana, Rua da Assunção 52 (☎32 76 25). The most opulent in the Baixa: fine rooms and breakfasts. ⑤.

Chiado area

The upmarket shopping area of Chiado lies just to the west of the Baixa, below the Bairro Alto (see Bairro Alto plan on p.57).

Residencial Nova Silva, Rua Vítor Cordon 11-2º (☎342 43 71). A very comfortable hotel. Small rooms but good beds, kind staff and wonderful views out across the river. ③.

Hotel Borges, Rua Garrett 108–110 (☎346 19 51). Nice position above the *Brasileira* café in Chiado's main street, though the rooms are very ordinary and the hotel rather musty. ⑤.

Bairro Alto

Bairro Alto is a lively, atmospheric part of the city to stay in – if you can find space in one of its few *pensões*. To get up to the heart of the quarter, either take a taxi or the funicular tram from beyond the Turismo in Praça dos Restauradores.

Pensão Duque, Calçada do Duque 53, near São Roque church (☎346 34 44). Just outside the nightclub zone, atmospheric and very reasonably priced. ②.

Pensão Globo, Rua do Teixeira 37 (☎346 22 79). Just behind the famous "Port Wine Institute" and across the road from the Jardim São Pedro de Alcântara (good view across the city) and the *Elevador da Glória*. Shared shower and toilet at the top. Rooms are clean, management fine and the location, in a quiet Bairro Alto street, superb. ②.

Casa de Hóspedes Atalaia, Rua da Atalaia 150-1º (☎346 44 59). At the lower, river end of the Bairro Alto quarter, near Cais do Sodré station.Tolerable at the price, but standards vary and you can find yourself uncomfortably remote from the shared bathrooms. Very active nocturnal life – mostly human rather than insect. ②.

Residencial Cabinda, Rua do Alecrim 20-2º (☎32 24 62). Private bath and phone, but relatively low price reflects dingy rooms. Lively after-dark street life. ②.

Pensão Londres, Rua Dom Pedro V 53 (☎346 22 03). Another nice location: take the Calçada da Gloria funicular from beside the Rossio station and turn right. Pleasant rooms. ②.

Residencial Camões, Travessa do Poço da Cidade 38-1/2/3º (☎346 40 48). Right in the heart of Bairro Alto, for which you pay quite dearly (and more with a private bath). But this is a friendly place, with clean, light rooms. ③.

Residencial Bragança, Rua do Alecrim 12 (☎342 70 61 or 342 11 14). Very large and a bit basic for the price – though the rooms are clean and come with private bath and phone. ③.

Residencial Santa Catarina, Rua Dr Luis de Almeida e Albuquerque 6 (☎346 61 06). Nicely located in a small street just off the Calçada do Combro. Very good value for its range, with exceptional staff. ④.

Lapa

This area, just back from the seafront, west of Bairro Alto, houses most of the foreign embassies and also boasts the city's most characterful upmarket hotel:

Residencial York House, Rua das Janelas Verdes (☎396 25 44); tram #19. Despite the *residencial* classification, this is a four-star hotel installed in a sixteenth-century convent, packed with antiques and its best rooms grouped around a beautiful interior courtyard. The **York House Annexe**, at no. 47 (☎66 24 35), is a pleasant townhouse but not really so special – better to book ahead for the real thing. From 24,000$00. ⑥.

Around the Castle – and Graça

Oddly enough, there are no pensions in the Alfama district, but there are a few attractive places on the periphery – climbing up toward the castle – and a particularly nice, more expensive place in Graça, a little to the north.

Pensão São João da Praça, Rua São João da Praça (☎86 25 91). Reasonably good value choice in a normally quiet area above Alfama. ②.

Pensão Ninho das Águias, Costa do Castelo 74 (☎86 70 00). Rather surly, and unremarkable rooms, but beautifully sited in its own garden on the street looping around the castle. ③.

Albergaria Senhora do Monte, Calçada do Monte 39 (☎86 60 02). Beautiful location with lovely views of the castle and Graça convent from the south-facing rooms. ⑤.

Around Avenida da Liberdade

Among cheaper pensions, the most likely to have space at busy times of year are a group on either side of the **Avenida da Liberdade** and on adjoining streets such as **Rua da Glória** and **Rua Portas de Santo Antão**. All places below are to some extent recommended, which is not something you can say without qualification for Rua da Glória pensions – many of which double up as brothels.

Pensão Dona Maria II, Rua Portas de Santo Antão 9-3° (☎37 11 28). Large airy rooms (with sink) and nice views over Rossio. Good value. ①.

Pensão Modelo, Rua Portas de Santo Antão 12-1° (☎342 70 41). Clean, modern and a bit soulless. ①.

Pensão Monumental, Rua da Glória 21 (☎346 98 07). A mixed bag of rooms in a rambling old pension; hot water is a bit erratic. ③.

Pensão Iris, Rua da Glória 2a-1° (☎32 31 57). A mostly residential guest house, with a homely feel behind the ill-lit entrance. ②.

Pensao Pemba, Avda. da Liberdade 11-3° (☎32 50 10). Decent value rooms, most with private showers. ②.

Pensão Flor da Baixa, Rua Portas de Santo Antão 81-2° (☎32 31 53). Entered through an electrical supply shop. Competently run with pleasant rooms. ②.

Residencial Florescente, Rua Portas de Santo Antão 99 (☎32 66 09 or 32 50 62). Despite the uniformed staff at reception, this is one of the street's best value establishments. Location, however, leaves much to be desired, with a strip-club opposite. ②.

Hotel Lis, Avda. da Liberdade 180 (☎56 34 34). Old-fashioned, nineteenth-century hotel with big rooms and a touch of class. ④.

Around Avenida Almirante Reis

The **Avenida Almirante Reis** and the streets to its west, between Anjos and Arroios metro stops, are fruitful hunting grounds for reasonably priced *pensões*, convenient for the metro and many of Lisbon's central attractions.

Residencial Portugália, Avda. Almirante Reis 112-1° (☎82 36 53). Not too awful considering its price – but not one to choose if you can afford a bit more. ①.

Pensão Fernandina, Rua António Pedro 52-1° (☎53 63 79), just off Praça do Chile near Arroios metro. Clean, but contains rather alarming faded Sixties furnishings. ②.

Residencial Coragem, Rua António Pedro 40-1° (☎57 43 86). Clean, roomy lodgings, all with private bathrooms. Fairly good value. ③.

Pensão Lar do Areeiro, Praça Dr. Francisco de Sá Carneiro 4 (☎89 31 50). Very respectable and well-run pension. ④.

Residencial Luena, Rua Pascoal de Melo 9 (☎54 55 43). Neat, welcoming rooms with private bathrooms; good management. ④.

Residencial Paradouro, Avda. Almirante Reis 106-6° (☎82 23 44). Not overpriced for its high standard. ④.

Around Praça Marquês de Pombal and Saldanha

A number of good places are located some way out from the immediate city centre in the prosperous streets to the **east of the Parque Eduardo VII**. This is an especially promising area for more upmarket choices.

Pensão Embaixatriz, Rua Pedro Nunes 45-2° (☎53 10 29). Outstandingly cheap (even less for a room with a shower instead of a bath) and, while old, clean and respectable. ①.

Residencial Ideal, Avda. João Crisóstomo 16-1° (☎56 12 13). Spotless, spacious rooms with en suite showers and friendly management. ②.

Residencial Bela Veneza, Rua Tomás Ribeiro 40-2°esq (☎54 30 03). A bit shabby but a popular budget choice. All rooms with private bathrooms. ③.

Pensão Pátria, Avda. Duque d'Ávila 42-6° (☎53 06 20). Highly convenient for the main bus station if you're leaving town; less obviously recommendable if you're staying, though the rooms are quite large, clean and cheerful. ④.

Residencial Canada, Avda. Defensores de Chaves 35-1° (☎352 14 41). Excellent value for money, with private bathrooms (and satellite TV. . .) in all the rooms. Kept immaculate by a bevy of charming ladies. Recommended. ④.

Residencial Estrêla do Saldanha, Avda. da República 17-1° (☎54 64 29). Small place, with private bathrooms, but there are better bargains. ④.

Residencial Avenida Alameda, Avda. Sidónio Pais 4 (☎53 21 86). Very pleasant hotel in a top location. ④.

Hotel Fenix, Praça Marquês de Pombal 8 (☎53 51 21). 4-star hotel with all the comforts. Highly recommended if your budget stretches to 18,000$00. ⑥.

Youth Hostels

Lisbon's main youth hostel is currently closed for rebuilding: phone before setting out to check if it has reopened. If it hasn't, your only hostel choice is 20km west along the coast towards Cascais, at Oeiras.

Pousada de Juventude de Lisboa, Rua Andrade Corvo 46 (☎57 33 45). This is – or was – the main city hostel. It's not a bad location, near Parque Eduardo VII, if it re-emerges on the same spot. To get there, take the metro to *Picoas*, then walk a block to the south.

Pousada de Juventude de Catalazete, Forte do Catalazete, Oeiras (☎443 06 38). An attractive small hostel, overlooking the beach at Oeiras, between Belém and Cascais. To reach it, take any train from Cais do Sodré and follow signs from Oeiras station under the coast road (*Estrada Marginal*) and through the park – around 1km. It's small, so phone before setting out. Reception is closed from 2pm to 6pm.

Campsites

The choice comes down to the major municipal campsite, northwest of the centre in the rambling woods of the Parque Florestal de Monsanto, a little campsite at Oeiras (see hostels, above), or making your base across the river from the city at one of the beach campsites along the Costa da Caparica – for more on which, see p.80. Given Monsanto's nighttime reputation – parts are distinctly seedy, with prostitutes taking clients into the woods – Caparica is probably the best option.

Parque Municipal de Turismo e Campismo. The main city campsite is 6km west of the city centre, an inconvenient location for anyone without transportt, though the site itself is pleasant enough, with a swimming pool and shops. In addition to warnings above, be fore-warned that stretches of Monsanto are given over to a semi-permanent community of African refugees and squatters living in ramshackle tents and caravans. The entrance is on the *Estrada da Circunvalação* on the park's west side. If you're using public transport, take a train from Cais do Sodré to Algés, then bus #50 to the campsite; or take bus #14 from Praça da Figueira. To return to the city (Praça da Figueira) take the #43.

Costa da Caparica. An alternative to Monsanto is to camp at one of the beaches along the Costa da Caparica. There are several small and lively campsites here, 30–50min away by bus (signed Caparica) from the Praca de Espanha terminal, or by a ferry from Cais do Sodré to Cacilhas and then local bus on from there.

Oeiras. There's a small campsite here, open summer only. Unfortunately, the river nearby can stink in the heat . . . you have been warned!

The City Quarters

Lisbon's interest lies as much in the everyday aspects of the city as in any specific sights. The cafés, markets, trams, ferries across the Tejo: all these are sufficient stimulation for random wanderings. The most rewarding areas, as you'd expect, are the oldest: the upper and lower towns of **Baixa** and **Bairro Alto**, and the winding lanes and anarchic stairways of **Alfama**. However, other outlying areas of the city provide strong attractions in their museums – above all the **Gulbenkian** and **Antiga Arte** – gardens and palaces. And no stay in Lisbon should neglect the waterfront suburb of **Belém**, to the west, dominated by one of the country's grandest monuments, the **Jerónimos monastery**.

Around the Baixa

The lower town – **the Baixa** – is very much the heart of the capital, housing many of the country's administrative departments, banks and business offices. Yet it is also a speedy introduction to the contradictions of the city. Although it appears on first impressions an imposing quarter – Europe's first great example of neoclassical design and urban planning – it's not long before you realise that the uniform streets, even in the chic shopping districts, are not quite all they seem. For all Lisbon's cosmopolitan air, this is the nearest a Western European capital gets to the Third World. Begging, lottery-ticket selling and shoe-shining are all growth industries, with highly accomplished exponents.

Chiado and the Rossio

Architecturally, and as points toward which to gravitate, the most interesting places in the Baixa are the squares – the **Rossio** and **Praça do Comércio** – and, on the periphery, the lanes leading east to the **Sé** (Cathedral) and west up **toward Bairro Alto**. This latter area, known as **Chiado** – the *nom de plume* of the poet António Ribeiro – suffered much damage from a fire that swept across the Baixa in August 1988, destroying the *Grandella* department store and many old shops in Rua do Cruxifixo. Chiado, however, remains the city's most affluent quarter, focused on the fashionable shops and – fortunately spared from the fire – the beautiful old café-tearooms of the **Rua Garrett**.

Of these **cafés**, *A Brasileira*, at Rua Garrett 120, is the most famous, having been frequented by generations of Lisbon's literary and intellectual leaders – the very readable Eça de Queiroz and Portugal's greatest twentieth-century poet, Fernando Pessoa, among them. It's not an especially expensive place to sit, at least for coffee, although if you're seriously into pastry shops (and Lisbon has a wide range) the best eats are at the *Pastelaria Suíça*, on the Rossio.

For more formal culture, the **Museu de Arte Contemporânea** (Tues–Sun 10am–12.30pm & 2–5pm), at no. 6 on nearby Rua Serpa Pinto 6, might tempt a visit, though don't take the name too seriously. The paintings here, in the main portraits, are all at least three generations old. For real contemporary Portuguese art you need to check the Gulbenkian's collection (see p.61).

Moving down to the **Rossio**, the focus again shifts back to cafés – most with summer terraces. The square itself is modest in appearance, but very much a focus for the city. Its single concession to grandeur is the **Teatro Nacional**, built along the north side in the 1840s. Here, prior to the earthquake, stood the

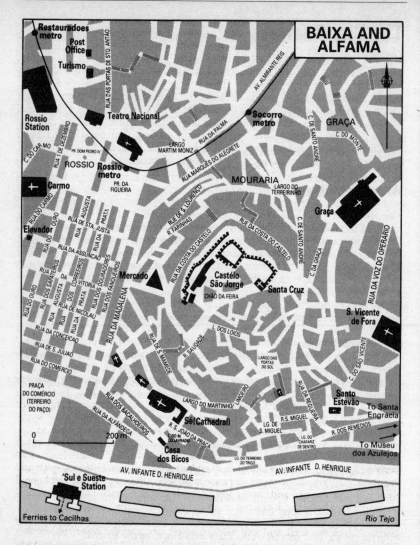

Inquisitional Palace; bullfights, public hangings and *autos-da-fé* (ritual burnings of heretics) used to take place in the square. The nineteenth-century statue atop the central column is of Dom Pedro IV (after whom the square is officially named), though curiously it's a bargain adaptation: cast originally as Maximilian of Mexico, it just happened to be in Lisbon en route from France when news came through of his assassination.

The church beyond the square, **São Domingos**, was where the Inquisition actually read out its sentences; though blackened and gutted by a fire in the 1950s, the building is still in religious use.

Praça do Comércio

At the waterfront end of the Baixa, the **Praça do Comércio** was intended as the climax to Pombal's design, at its centre an exuberant bronze of Dom José, monarch during the earthquake and the capital's rebuilding. Seen from the river – the Fluvial terminus, where ferries across to Barreiro and Cacilhas dock, is just off the square – the design is graceful and impressive, with the streets of the Baixa extending into the distance beyond. Close up, however, it seems less substantial and less glamourous, having been requisitioned as a car park for government employees working in its classical buildings. Today, a walk down here invariably provokes a rash of offers to sell you dope: acceptance is unwise in the extreme and the hashish often adulterated. Lisbon town planners are working on projects to bring the square back into the hub of city life, by pedestrianising the area and opening more cafés, but the only sign of life is still the dimly lit, old-world café of *Martinho da Arcada*, one of the poet Pessoa's haunts. Sadly this has recently been converted into a swanky restaurant and the main room is no longer accessible to casual coffee takers.

Like the Rossio, the Praça do Comércio has a popular name – **Terreiro do Paço**, after the old royal palace which stood here and whose steps still lead up from the Tejo – and has played an important part in the country's history. In 1908, alongside the Central Post Office, King Carlos I and his eldest son were shot and killed, opening the way to the declaration of the Republic two years later.

Streets and markets

A major appeal of the **Baixa** is the survival of tradition. Many of the streets in the grid maintain their crafts and businesses as Pombal devised: Rua da Prata (Silversmiths' St), Rua dos Sapateiros (Cobblers' St), Rua do Ouro (Goldsmiths' St), Rua do Comércio (Commercial St). And they are, along with the mosaic side-walked squares, a visual delight, with tiled Art Deco adverts still surviving.

The **markets** around Baixa are particularly wonderful. A good case in point is the huge **fish market** which takes place, daily except Sundays, from dawn behind the **Cais do Sodré** station, where you can still see *varinas*, fishwives from Alfama who were joined a few years ago by groups from Cabo Verde, bargaining for and carting off great baskets of wares on their heads.

Take a look inside the **Ribeira market**, too, the domed building on the right of Caís do Sodré. Even if you're not tempted by the arrays of food – least of all perhaps by the gruesome slabs of flesh and innards – the fruit, flower, spice and vegetable displays on the upper story are impressive. Rua do Arsenal, just behind the market, is packed with stalls selling fresh fish and dried cod and grocers stocked with everything, including unbelievably cheap wines and spirits.

Just as diverting, and perhaps more desirable after a long recreational night in Bairro Alto, is the **fruit and vegetable market** down by the waterfront further west, toward Belém. Four in the morning is the perfect time to share a glass of hot *cacão* with the traders in the **market bar**.

The Cathedral area

A couple of blocks east of the Praça do Comércio is the church of **Conceição Velha**, severely damaged by the earthquake but retaining its flamboyant Manueline doorway, an early example of this style and hinting at the brilliance that emerged at Belém. It once formed part of the Misericórdia (almshouse) – you'll find one of these impressive structures in almost every Portuguese town or city. Nearby, at Campo das Cebolas, stands the curious **Casa dos Bicos**, set with diamond-shaped stones and again offering an image of the richness of pre-1755 Lisbon; the building is not routinely open, though it sees fairly regular use for cultural exhibitions.

The Sé

The **Cathedral** – or **Sé** (daily 8.30am–6pm) – stands very stolidly above the Baixa grid. Founded in 1150 to commemorate the city's reconquest from the Moors, it has a suitably fortress-like appearance, similar to that of Coimbra, and in fact occupies the site of the principal mosque of Moorish *Lishbuna*. Like so many of the country's cathedrals, it is Romanesque – and extraordinarily restrained in both size and decoration. The great rose window and twin towers form a simple and effective facade, but inside there's nothing very exciting: the building was once splendidly embellished by Dom João V, but his Rococo whims were swept away by the earthquake and subsequent restorers. All that remains is a group of Gothic tombs behind the high altar and the decaying thirteenth-century cloisters.

For admission to these you must buy a ticket (9am–1pm & 2–6pm; 100$00), which also covers the cloisters and Baroque *Sacristia* with its small museum of treasures – including the relics of Saint Vincent, brought to Lisbon in 1173 by Afonso Henriques in a boat piloted by ravens (see "Sagres", in the *Algarve* chapter). For centuries the descendants of these birds were shown to visitors but the last specimen, despite great care from the sacristan, died in 1978. Nevertheless, ravens are still one of the city's symbols.

The Castle

From the Sé, the Rua das Cruzes da Sé leads directly into the heart of the **Alfama**. Rua do Limoeiro winds upward toward the **Castelo**, past sparse ruins of a Roman theatre, the well-positioned **Miradouro de Santa Luzia**, and the *Espírito Santo Foundation*, home of the **Museum of Decorative Arts** (*Museu das Artes Decorativas Portuguesas*). The latter is a seventeenth-century mansion, stuffed with period furnishings and with a handful of truely beautiful pieces. However it's closed at present for restoration: no hardship, as the guided tours (compulsory – and in Portuguese only) used to point out *everything* – "traditional Portuguese, Indian, Brazilian", etc – making for something of an endurance test for any but the most committed tourists.

The **conquest of Lisbon from the Moors** – and the siege of the Castelo de São Jorge – are depicted in *azulejos* on the walls of **Santa Luzia**. An important victory, leading to Muslim surrender at Sintra and throughout the surrounding district, this was not, however, the most Christian or glorious of Portuguese exploits. A full account survives, written by one Osbern of Bawdsley, an English priest and crusader, and its details, despite the author's judgemental tone, direct one's sympathies to the enemy.

The attack, in the summer of 1147, came through the opportunism and skillful management of Afonso Henriques, already established as "King" at Porto, who persuaded a large force of French and British Crusaders to delay their progress to Jerusalem for more immediate goals. The Crusaders – scarcely more than pirates – came to terms and in June the siege began. Osbern records the Archbishop of Braga's demand for the Moors to return to "the land whence you came" and, more revealingly, the weary and contemptuous response of the Muslim spokesman: "How many times have you come hither with pilgrims and barbarians to drive us hence? It is not want of possessions but only ambition of the mind that drives you on". For seventeen weeks the castle and inner city stood firm but in October its walls were breached and the citizens – including a Christian community coexisting with the Muslims – were forced to surrender.

The pilgrims and barbarians, flaunting the diplomacy and guarantees of Afonso Henriques, stormed into the city, cut the throat of the local bishop, and sacked, pillaged and murdered Christian and Muslim alike. In 1190 a later band of English Crusaders stopped at Lisbon and, no doubt confused by the continuing presence of Moors, sacked the city a second time.

Castelo de São Jorge

A triumphant statue of Afonso Henriques – who alone emerges from the account with honour – stands at the entrance to the **Castelo** (daily 9am to sunset; free). Beyond stretch gardens and terraces, walkways and pools, within the old Moorish walls.

At first the Portuguese kings had taken up residence within the castle – in the Alcáçova, the Muslim palace – but by the time of Manuel I this had been superseded by the new royal palace on Terreiro do Paço. Of the Alcáçova only a much-restored shell remains, in which a small, rather insignificant museum (Roman and Islamic tombstones) has been installed. But the castle as a whole is an enjoyable place to spend a couple of hours, wandering amid the ramparts and towers to look down upon the city. Crammed within the castle's outer walls is the tiny medieval quarter of **Santa Cruz**, once very much a village in itself.

To the north sprawls the old **Mouraria** quarter, to which the Moors were relegated on their loss of the town. This, despite a few grand old houses, is largely in decay, at present being substantially redeveloped and the focus of an active prostitution trade (especially along Rua do Benformoso).

Alfama

The oldest part of Lisbon, stumbling from the walls of the castle down to the Tejo, **Alfama** was buttressed against significant damage in the 1755 earthquake by the steep, rocky mass on which it's built. Although none of its houses dates from before the Christian conquest, many are of Moorish design and the kasbah-like layout is much as Osbern described it, with "steep defiles instead of ordinary streets . . . and buildings so closely packed together that, except in the merchants' quarter, hardly a street could be found more than eight foot wide".

In Arab-occupied times Alfama was the grandest part of the city but with subsequent earthquakes – Lisbon averages one every 200 years – the new Christian nobility moved out, leaving it to the fishing community so evident today. Today, it is undergoing some commercialisation, with its cobbled lanes and "character", but although the antique shops and restaurants may be moving in, they are far from taking over. The quarter retains a largely traditional life of its own; you can eat at local prices in the cafés; the flea market engulfs the periphery of the area twice a week; and this is very much the place to be during the June "Popular Saints" festivals (above all on June 12), when makeshift *tavernas* appear at every corner.

The steep defiles, alleys and passageways are known as *becos* and *travessas* rather than *ruas*, and it would be impossible (as well as futile) to try and follow any set route. At some point in your wanderings around the quarter, though, head for the **Rua de São Miguel** – off which are some of the most interesting *becos* – and for the (lower) parallel **Rua de São Pedro**, the main market street leading to the lively **Largo do Chafariz de Dentro**. The most promising areas for café-restaurants are Rua da Regueira, above the Largo do Chafariz and Rua de Santo Estevão.

The Flea Market

The **Feira da Ladra**, Lisbon's rambling and ragged **flea market**, fills the **Campo de Santa Clara**, at the edge of Alfama, on Tuesday mornings and all day Saturday. Though it's certainly not the world's greatest – "you will find stalls with shabby ready-made clothes" advises the cautious Turismo pamphlet – it does turn up some interesting things: oddities from the former African colonies, old prints of the country, and army-surplus gear. Out-and-out junk – students flogging broken alarm clocks and old postcards – is spread on the ground above Santa Engrácia, and half-genuine antiques at the top end of the *feira*. (Tram #28 runs from Rua da Conceição in the Baixa to São Vicente, and bus #12 runs between Santa Apolónia station and the Praça Marquês de Pombal.)

Santa Engrácia and São Vicente de Fora

While at the flea market, take a look inside **Santa Engrácia**, the loftiest and most tortuously built church in the city. Begun in 1682 and once a synonym for unfinished work, its vast dome was finally completed in 1966. If you ask nicely, you may be allowed to take the elevator to the dome – looking down on the empty church and out over the flea market, port and city.

More interesting, architecturally, is nearby **São Vicente de Fora**, whose name – "of the outside" – is a reminder of the extent of the sixteenth-century city. It is also where Afonso Henriques pitched camp during his siege and conquest of Lisbon. Built during the years of Spanish rule by Philip II's Italian architect, Felipe Terzi, its severe geometric facade was an important Renaissance innovation. Through the **cloisters**, decorated with *azulejos* (tiled scenes), you can visit the old monastic refectory, since 1855 the **pantheon of the Bragança dynasty** (daily 10am–5pm; 150$00). Here, in more or less complete (though unexciting) sequence, are the bodies of all Portuguese kings from João IV, who restored the monarchy, to Manuel II, who lost it and died in exile in England in 1932. Among them is Catherine of Bragança, the widow of Charles II and (as the local guide points out) "the one who took the habit of the fifth o'clock tea to that country".

Two museums: weapons and azulejos

A couple of blocks south of Santa Engrácia, opposite the dockside **Santa Apolónia station**, is the city's military museum, the **Museu de Artilharia** (Tues–Sat 10am–4pm, Sun 11am–5pm; 150$00). This is very traditional in lay-out – old weapons in old cases – and lacks much appeal.

Rather more of interest beckons in the form of the **Museu dos Azulejos** (Tues–Sun 10am–5pm; 200$00) at Rua Madre de Deus 4, a little under a kilometre to the east (tram #3 or #16) from the station. It is installed in the church and cloisters of Madre de Deus, whose own eighteenth-century tiled scenes of the life of Saint Anthony are among the best in the city. The highlight, however, is Portugal's longest *azulejo* – a wonderfully detailed 120-foot Panorama of Lisbon, completed around 1738.

Bairro Alto

Bairro Alto, the upper town, is the natural place to wind up at night – in the *fado* houses, bars, excellent restaurants, or even the refined and somewhat dauntingly named *Port Wine Institute* (see "The Facts"). By day, the quarter's narrow seventeenth-century streets have a very different character, with children playing, the old sitting in doorways, and nightlife venues seemingly as much concealed as closed. It is well worth a morning or afternoon's exploration, with two of the city's most interesting churches – **Carmo** and **São Roque** – on the fringes, and a couple of approaches to the quarter that are a treat in themselves.

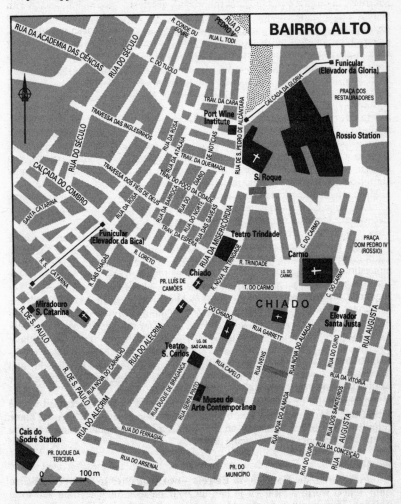

The Elevador, funiculars and Carmo church

Raul Mésnier's *Elevador Santa Justa*, just off the top end of Rua do Ouro on Rua de Santa Justa, is the most startling approach to the quarter. One of the city's most extraordinary and eccentric structures, it whisks you up through metal latticework, depositing you on a platform above the Baixa.

Alternatives, and hardly more conventional feats of engineering, are the two **funicular-like trams**. One, the *Elevador da Glória*, links the quarter directly with the Praça dos Restauradores, taking off just behind the tourist office on the left; the other, *Elevador da Bica*, climbs up to Rua do Loreto (west of the Praça de Camões) from Rua de São Paulo/Rua da Moeda, northwest of Cais do Sodré. Both funiculars and the *elevador* currently cost 30$00 one way (children free).

The ruined Gothic arches of the **Convento do Carmo** hang almost directly above the exit of Mésnier's *elevador*. Once the largest church in the city, this was half-destroyed by the earthquake but is perhaps even more beautiful as a result. In the nineteenth century its shell was adapted as a chemical factory. These days it houses a small "archaeological museum" (10am–6pm; closed Sun; 250$00) with a very miscellaneous collection of medieval tombs and *azulejos* – barely a museum in fact but no less atmospheric for that. At night, in summer, free classical concerts are often held here.

São Roque

The church of **São Roque**, over toward the Chiado in the Largo Trindade Coelho, looks from the outside like the plainest in the city, its bleak Renaissance facade (by Filipo Terzi, architect of São Vicente) having been further simplified by the earthquake. Nor does it seem impressive when you walk inside. But hang around in the gloom and the sacristan will come and escort you around, turning on lights to a succession of side chapels, each lavishly crafted with *azulejos* (some emulating reliefs), multicoloured marble, or Baroque painted ceilings.

The climax – to which you're proudly directed – is the **Capela de São João Baptista**, last on the left. This chapel, for its size, is estimated to be the most expensive ever constructed and was certainly one of the most bizarre commissions of its age. It was ordered from Rome in 1742 by Dom João V to honor his patron saint and, more dubiously, to requite the pope, whom he had persuaded to confer a patriarchate upon Lisbon. Designed by the papal architect, Vanvitelli, and using the most costly materials available (including ivory, agate, porphyry and lapis lazuli), it was actually erected at the Vatican for the pope to celebrate mass before being dismantled and shipped to Lisbon. The cost – then – was about £250,000 sterling, which is perhaps its chief curiosity. But there are other eccentricities. Take a close look at the four "oil paintings" of John the Baptist's life and you'll find that they are in fact mosaics, intricately worked over what must have been years rather than months.

The site of the Crusader camp during the Siege of Lisbon is occupied by the **Igreja dos Mártires**, in the nearby Rua Garrett (see Chiado, p.51). As its name suggests, the church was built on the site of a burial ground, created for the English contingent of the besieging army.

Estrêla

A fourth church, the **Basílica da Estrêla** – two kilometres to the west of Bairro Alto, is also worth a visit – it is half an hour on foot (or take tram #28 from Chiado). The church is memorable not so much for the building itself – a vast monument to late-eighteenth-century Neoclassicism – as for the view across the city from its dome, and for the **public gardens** below. Lisbon takes its gardens seriously, even the small patches amid squares and avenues, and these are among the most enjoyable, a quiet refuge often graced with an afternoon brass band. It has a pool of giant carp, too, and a café.

Through the park and on the Rua de São Jorge is the gate to the post-Crusader **English Cemetery** (ring loudly for entry) where among the cypresses lies Henry Fielding, author of *Tom Jones*, whose imminent demise may have influenced his verdict on Lisbon as "the nastiest city in the world".

Parque Eduardo VII, Amoreiras and the Aqueduto

North of the Praça dos Restauradores are the city's principal gardens – the **Parque Eduardo VII**. The easiest approach is by metro (to *Rotunda*), though you could walk up (energetically) in about twenty minutes along the Avenida da Liberdade or take any bus going to the Rotunda.

The park's big attractions are the **Estufas**, huge and wonderful glasshouses, filled with tropical plants, flamingo pools and endless varieties of palms and cacti. They're near the top end of the park, open 9am to 6/5pm (erratically closed at lunchtime; 60$00 admission).

There are some excellent cafés close by, in which to while away an hour or two of the evening. At the Estufa Fria itself, rock and classical concerts and an antiques fair are occasionally held.

Useful **bus links** from the park are: #31, #41 and #46, which run north a few blocks at the bottom end of the Rotunda to the Gulbenkian museum (10min walk; see below); #27 and #49, from the same stop, which run west to Belém; and #51 which runs to Belém from the top of the park near the Estufa Fria.

Amoreiras

In the daytime, a **free bus** ferries shoppers from the Rotunda to Lisbon's new Post-Modernist shopping centre, **Amoreiras** (Avenida Duarte Pacheco), visible on the city skyline from almost any approach. The complex, designed by **Tomás Taveira**, is Portugal's most adventurous – and most entertaining – modern building: a wild Lego fantasy of pink and blue, sheltering ten çinemas, 60 restaurants, 370 shops and a hotel. Most of the shops stay open until 11pm, seven days a week.

The Aqueduto

Buses #11 (from Rossio; last bus back at 8pm) and #23 go past Amoreiras and then on past the **Aqueduto das Águas Livres**, just behind. So too does the bus from Praça de Espanha to Caparica – affording enough of a view for most people.

The aqueduct was opened in 1748, bringing reliable drinking water to the city for the first time. However, it gained a more notorious reputation through one Diogo Alves, a eigheteenth-century serial murderer who threw his victims off the arches – a 200–foot drop. To visit the structure, check first at the Turismo that it's open; you can reach the entrance by walking to the left from the top of Parque Eduardo VII along Rua Marquês de Fronteira, Rua Carlos Mascarenhas and Calçada da Quintinha, up to Travessa da Quintinha. Once inside and up, you can walk across the aqueduct to the Parque Monsanto and return back via the Alcântara valley – a very scenic walk. En route, don't miss the former **Mãe d'Água cistern** at Rua das Amoreiras, close to Largo do Rato.

The Gulbenkian museums

The **Fundação Calouste Gulbenkian** is *the* great cultural centre of Portugal – and it is a wonder that it's not better known internationally. It is housed in a superb complex, set in its own park, and the museum's collections seem to take in virtually every great phase of Eastern and Western art – from Ancient Egyptian scarabs to Art Nouveau jewellery, Islamic textiles to French Impressionists. In a new, separate building, across the park, a **Centro de Arte Moderna** has also just been opened – its excitingly displayed works, exclusively Portuguese, touch on most styles of twentieth-century art. The complex is located just north of the Parque Eduardo VII, with its main entrance at Avenida de Berna 45; to reach it, take bus #31, #41 or #46 from the Rossio, or the metro to São Sebastião.

Astonishingly, all the main museum exhibits were acquired by just one man, the Armenian oil magnate **Calouste Gulbenkian** (1869–1955), whose legendary art-market coups included buying works from the Leningrad Hermitage after the Russian Revolution. In a scarcely less astute deal made during the last war, Gulbenkian literally auctioned himself and his collections to the European nations: Portugal bid security, an aristocratic palace home (a Marquês was asked to move out), and tax exemption to acquire one of the most important cultural patrons of the century.

Today the **Gulbenkian Foundation** runs an orchestra, three concert halls and two galleries for temporary exhibitions in the capital alone. It also finances work in all spheres of Portuguese cultural life – there are Gulbenkian museums and libraries in the smallest towns – and makes charitable grants to a vast range of projects. The admissions desk of the museum has a schedule of current activities.

Anyone travelling with kids may be equally impressed to know that the Gulbenkian maintains a **Centro Artístico Infantil** in its gardens (entrance just off Rua Marquês de Sá de Bandeira), well-stocked with toys and offering free, ninety-minute **childcare sessions** for 4–12-year-olds between 9am and 5pm.

The Main Museum

Oct–May Tues–Sun 10am–5pm; June–Sept Tues, Thurs, Fri & Sun 10am–5pm, Wed & Sat 2–7.30pm; 200$00; free on Sun.

The **Museu Gulbenkian** is the foundation's public showplace. It is divided into two complete and distinct halves – the first devoted to Egyptian, Greco-Roman, Islamic and Oriental arts, the second to European art – and ideally you'll want to take them in on separate visits. The collections aren't immense in numbers but each contains pieces of such individual interest and beauty that you need frequent unwinding sessions – well provided for by the basement **café-bar** and gardens. Expert explanatory notes in English are usually available in every section; if you want to work out what to see in advance, ask for a complete set at the entrance.

It seems arbitrary to hint at highlights, but they must include the entire contents of the **Egyptian room**, which covers almost every period of importance from the Old Kingdom (2700 BC) to the Roman period. Particularly striking are a carved ivory spoon from the time of Amenophis III and an extraordinarily lifelike *Head of a Priest* from the penultimate, Ptolomaic period. **Mesopotamia** produced the earliest forms of writing and two cylinder seals, one from before 2500 BC, are on display here, along with architectural sculpture from the Assyrian civilisation.

Fine statues, silver and glass from the **Romans** and intricate gold jewellery from ancient **Greece** come soon after, followed by remarkable illuminated manuscripts and ceramics from **Armenia**, porcelain from **China**, and beautiful **Japanese** prints and lacquer-work. Islamic arts are magnificently represented by ornamented texts, opulently woven carpets, glassware (such as the fourteenth-century mosque lamps from **Syria**), and precious bindings from **Persia** and **India** (mostly fifteenth-century).

In the **European section** don't miss a group of French medieval **ivory diptychs** (particularly six scenes depicting the *Life of the Virgin*) and a thirteenth-century copy of Saint John's prophetic *Apocalypse*, produced in Kent and touched up in Italy under Pope Clement IX.

In the **painting** section you'll find work from all the major schools: from fifteenth-century Flanders, there's a pair of panels by **Van der Weyden**; from the same period in Italy comes **Ghirlandaio**'s *Portrait of a Young Woman*; from the seventeenth century, there are two exceptional portraits – **Rubens**' of his second wife, *Helena Fourment*, and **Rembrandt**'s *Figure of an Old Man* – plus works by van Dyck, Frans Hals and Ruisdael; **Fragonard** is the best represented of the eighteenth-century artists, whose company includes Gainsborough, Sir Thomas Lawrence and Francesco Guardi; and finally Corot, Manet, Monet and Renoir supply a good showing from nineteenth- to twentieth-century France.

Sculpture is poorly represented on the whole, though a French sixteenth-century religious statue of *Mary Magdalene*, a fifteenth-century medallion of *Faith* by Luca della Robbia, a 1780 marble *Diana* by Jean-Antoine Houdon, and a couple of Rodins stand out. Otherwise **ceramics** from Spain and Italy; **furniture** from Louis XV to Louis XVI; eighteenth-century works from **French goldsmiths;** fifteenth-century **medals** (especially by Pisanello); tapestries and textiles; and, above all, an Art Nouveau collection with its 169 pieces of fantasy jewellery by **René Lalique** are the best of the tail-end of this great collection.

The Modern Art Centre

Same hours as main museum; 200$00; free on Sun.

To reach the **Centro de Arte Moderna**, cross the gardens with their specially commissioned sculptures. This museum keeps the same hours as the main section (charging a further 200$00) and is also highly recommended.

Big names on the twentieth-century Portuguese scene include Almada Negreiros, the founder of *modernismo* (his portrait of Fernando Pessoa in the *Museu da Cidade* is particularly well known), Amadeu de Sousa Cardoso and Guilherme Santa-Rita (both of Futurist inclinations), Vieira da Silva (a crisscross of lines) and Paula Rego (who paints creepy kids).

North of the Gulbenkian: the Zoo and some outlying palaces and museums

Few visitors explore anything of Lisbon north of Saldanha, unless for a trip to the **Sporting** or **Benfica football stadiums** or the **Campo Pequeno** bullring. Out past the Cidade Universitária, though, are a couple of diverting museums, devoted to the city's **history** and to **costume**. They are both on the route of the #1 and #7 buses, which start, respectively, from the Rossio and Praça da Figueira.

Over to the northwest of the Gulbenkian, further peripheral attractions are provided by the city's **Zoo** and by the nearby **Fronteira Palace**. Buses #31, #41 and #46 (or the metro, to *Sete Rios*) link the Rotunda with the Jardim Zoológico.

The City Museum

The **Museu da Cidade** (Tues–Sun 10am–1pm & 2–6pm; 200$00) was installed quite recently in the eighteenth-century **Palácio Pimenta**, at the top left corner of the Campo Grande. Its principal interest lies in a new and imaginative collection of prints, paintings and models of pre-1755 Lisbon. Pessoa enthusiasts might also want to make the homage for Almada Negreiros' famous portrait of the poet.

The Costume Museum

Another recent creation, the **Museu do Traje** (Tues–Sun 10am–1pm & 2.30–5pm; 300$00) occupies another eighteenth-century palace, the Palácio do Monteiro-Mor, some 2km further north of the city museum. The museum's extensive collections are drawn upon for temporary thematic exhibitions – excellent if costume is your subject. For more casual visitors, the surrounding park is at least as big an attraction – one of the lushest areas of the city, open daily until 5pm and with a good restaurant and café. A small **Museu de Teatro**, of truly specialist interest, is also sited in the grounds.

The Zoo

The **Jardim Zoológico** (daily 9am–7pm; 390$00) is one of the least inspiring of European zoos, exhibiting particularly unhappy captives in utterly miserable conditions. As an establishment with supposed educational, scientific, and conservation objectives it's disgraceful. On the other hand it's really as much a rambling garden as anything else and in this, and in its peculiarly Portuguese eruptions of kitsch (an extraordinary dogs' cemetery), makes for an enjoyable afternoon's ramble, if you're able to ignore the context.

Fronteira Palace

Palace enthusiasts might like to visit the **Palácio dos Marquêses da Fronteira** (Tues–Sat: tours from 11am, 1000$00; 300$00 for the gardens only), which is five minutes' walk from the zoo. After passing the bland housing development on the Rua de São Domingos and crossing the little-used railway line, the fantastic gardens of this small, pink country house feel like an oasis. Have a look at the tiled conversation piece that the Marquês built for messing around in boats. The allegorical panels on the lower level, taken from Camões' tale of the *Doze da Inglaterra*, mark an historic moment in the history of *azulejos* when, in the mid-seventeenth century, the Portuguese dropped the formal Moorish methods of design (as in the upper level) and turned to painting straight onto tiles.

Museu de Arte Antiga

The **Museu de Arte Antigua** (Tues–Sun 10am–1pm & 2–5pm; 200$00), Portugal's national gallery, is the one Lisbon museum that stands comparison with the Gulbenkian collections. It doesn't have the same eclecticism, of course, nor the international highlights, but the core of the museum – fifteenth- and sixteenth-century Portuguese works by such artists as Nuno Gonçalves – is excellent and well displayed in a beautiful converted palace of the period. It is sited at Rua das Janelas Verdes 95 in the wealthy suburb of Lapa, two kilometres west of the Praça do Comércio. To get there, take tram #19 from the Praça do Comércio (10min), bus #40 from Rua do Comércio, or bus #27 or #49 from Belém.

Gonçalves and the Portuguese School

Gonçalves and his fellow painters of the so-called "Portuguese school" span that indeterminate and exciting period when Gothic art was giving way to the Renaissance. Their works, exclusively religious in concept, are particularly interesting in their emphasis on portraiture – transforming any theme, even a martyrdom, into a vivid observation of local contemporary life. Stylistically, the most significant influences upon them were those of the Flemish, "Northern Renaissance" painters: Jan van Eyck, who came to Portugal in 1428, Memling and Mabuse (both well represented here), and Roger van der Weyden.

The acknowledged masterpiece, however, is Gonçalves' *Panéis de São Vicente* (Saint Vincent Altarpiece), a brilliantly marshalled canvas depicting the saint, Lisbon's patron, receiving homage from all ranks of its citizens. On the two lefthand panels are Cistercian monks, fishermen and pilots; on the opposite side the Duke of Bragança and his family, a helmeted Moorish knight, a Jew (with book), a beggar, and a priest holding Saint Vincent's own relics (a piece of his skull, still possessed by the cathedral). In the epic central panels the mustachioed Henry the Navigator, his nephew Afonso V (in green), and the youthful (future) Dom João II pay tribute to the saint. Among the frieze of portraits behind them, that on the far left is reputed to be Gonçalves himself; the other central panel shows the Archbishop of Lisbon.

Later painters and foreign works

Later Portuguese painters – from the sixteenth to the eighteenth century – are displayed too, along with good collections of **ceramics** (showing the influence of Indian and Oriental designs from new trading links).

But after Gonçalves and his contemporaries (notably Gregório Lopes and Frei Carlos), the most interesting works are by **Flemish and German** painters (Cranach, Bosch – a fabulous *Temptation of St. Anthony* – and Dürer), and miscellaneous gems by Raphael, Zurbarán, and, rather oddly, Rodin.

Belém and Ajuda

Even before the Great Earthquake, Belém's great **Monastery of Jerónimos** was Lisbon's finest monument: since then, it has stood quite without comparison. It stands in a pleasant waterfront suburb, close by a small group of museums, plus a palace at nearby Ajuda, and with some fine cafés and restaurants if you want to make a day of it. Don't make that day **Monday**, when the monastery is closed.

The suburb is easily reached by tram – #15 and #17 run from the Praça do Comércio, taking about twenty minutes – or any slow train from Cais do Sodré.

The Monastery of Jerónimos

It was from Belém in 1497 that **Vasco da Gama** set sail for India, and here too that he was welcomed home by Dom Manuel "the Fortunate" (*O Venturoso*). Da Gama brought with him a small cargo of pepper, enough to pay for his voyage sixty times over. The **Mosteiro dos Jerónimos** (Tues–Sun 10am–6.30/5pm) stands as a testament to his triumphant discovery of a sea route to the Orient, which amounted to the declaration of a "golden age". It was built in honour of a vow Dom Manuel made to the Virgin in return for a successful voyage, on the site of the old *Ermida do Restelo* or *Capela de São Jerónimo*, a hermitage founded by Henry the Navigator, where Vasco da Gama and his companions had spent their last night ashore in prayer. Its funding also was a levy on the fruits of his discovery – a five percent tax on all spices other than pepper, cinnamon and cloves, whose import had become the sole preserve of the Crown.

The church and cloister

Begun in 1502 and substantially complete when its funding was withdrawn by João III in 1551, the **monastery** is the most ambitious and successful achievement of Manueline architecture. It is less flamboyantly exotic than either Tomar or Batalha – the great culminations of the style in Estremadura – but, despite a succession of master-builders, it has more daring and confidence in its overall design. This is largely the achievement of two outstanding figures, **Diogo de Boitaca**, perhaps the originator of the Manueline style with his Church of Jesus at Setúbal, and **João de Castilho**, a Spaniard who took over construction from around 1517.

It was Castilho who designed the **main entrance** to the **church**, a complex, shrine-like hierarchy of figures centered around Henry the Navigator (on a pedestal above the arch). In its intricate and almost flat ornamentation, it shows the influence of the then-current Spanish style, Plateresque (literally, the art of the silversmith). Yet it also has distinctive Manueline features – the use of rounded forms, the naturalistic motifs in the bands around the windows – and these seem to create both its harmony and individuality. They are also unmistakably outward-looking, evoking the new forms discovered in the east, a characteristic that makes each Manueline building so new and interesting – and so much a product of its particular and expansionary age.

This is immediately and spectacularly true of **the church** itself, whose breathtaking sense of space alone would place it among the great triumphs of European Gothic. Here, though, Manueline developments add two extraordinary fresh dimensions. There are tensions, deliberately created and carefully restrained, between the grand spatial design and the areas of intensely detailed ornamentation. And, still more striking, there's a naturalism in the forms of this ornamentation that seems to extend into the actual structure of the church. Once you've made the analogy, it's difficult to see the six central columns as anything other than palm trunks, growing both into and from the branches of the delicate rib-vaulting.

Another peculiarity of Manueline buildings is the way in which they can adapt, enliven, or encompass any number of different styles. Here, the basic structure is thoroughly Gothic, though Castilho's ornamentation on the columns is much more Renaissance in spirit. So too is the semicircular apse (around the altar), added in 1572, beyond which is the entrance to the remarkable **double cloister**.

Vaulted throughout and fantastically embellished, the **cloister** (400$00) is one of the most original and beautiful pieces of architecture in the country. Again it holds in balance Gothic forms and Renaissance ornamentation and again is exuberant in its innovations – such as the rounded corner canopies and delicate twisting divisions within each of the arches. These lend a wavelike, rhythmic motion to the whole structure, a conceit extended by the typically Manueline motifs drawn from ropes, anchors and the sea. In this – as in all aspects – it would be hard to imagine an art more directly reflecting the achievements and preoccupations of an age.

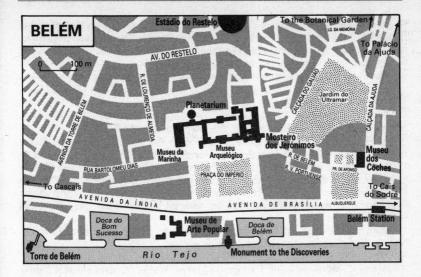

The monastery's museums

In the wings of the monastery are two **museums**. The enormous **Museu da Marinha** (Tues–Sun 10am–5pm; 300$00, free Wed), in the west wing, is more interesting than most of its kind, packed not only with models of ships, naval uniforms, and a surprising display of artefacts from Portugal's oriental trade and colonies, but also with real vessels – among them fishing boats and some sumptuous state barges – a couple of seaplanes and even some fire engines.

In contrast, the **Museu de Arqueologia** (same hours; 250$00), in the east wing, seems sparse and, apart from some fine Roman mosaics unearthed in the Algarve, thoroughly unexceptional. A third museum, **Museu Agrícola do Ultramar** – tropical agriculture – is close to the eastern corner of the monastery and the Jardim Colonial, and speaks for itself.

Around Belém

The Rio Tejo at Belém has receded with the centuries, for when the Monastery of Jerónimos was built it stood almost on the beach, within sight of caravels moored ready for expeditions to India and Brazil, and of the **Torre de Belém**, guarding the entrance to the port.

Torre de Belém

The **Torre de Belém** (10am–1pm & 2.30–6.30/5pm; 400$00), still washed on three sides by the sea, is just a couple of hundred metres down from the monastery. Whimsical, multi-turreted and with a real hat-in-the-air exuberance, it was built over the last five years of Dom Manuel's reign (1515–20). As such, it is the one completely Manueline building in Portugal, the rest having been adaptations of earlier structures or completed in later years.

Its architect, Francisco de Arruda, had previously worked on Portuguese fortifications in Morocco, and a Moorish influence is very strong in the delicately arched windows and balconies. Prominent also in the decoration are two great symbols of the age: Manuel's personal badge of an armillary sphere (representing the globe), and the cross of the military Order of Christ, once the Templars, who took a major role in all Portuguese conquests.

The tower's interior is unremarkable except for a "whispering gallery"; it was used into the nineteenth century as a prison, notoriously by Dom Miguel (1828–34), who kept political enemies in the waterlogged dungeons.

More museums, the Monument to the Discoveries and Ajuda

Close by are a number of museums. The best – if it has reopened after reconstruction work – is the **Museu de Arte Popular** (Tues–Sun 10am–12.30pm & 2–5pm; 200$00), a province-by-province display of Portugal's still very diverse folk arts, housed in a shed-like building on the waterfront. Also well worth a look is the **Museu de Etnologia** (Tues–Sun 10am–12.30pm & 2–5pm), north of the monastery on Avenida Ilha da Madeira, with its displays from the old African colonies.

Almost adjacent to the Popular Arts museum is the **Monument to the Discoveries**, an angular slab of concrete erected in 1960 to commemorate the 500th anniversary of the death of Henry the Navigator. Henry appears on the prow with Camôes and other Portuguese heroes. Within the monument is a small exhibition space, with interesting and changing exhibits on the city's history. For 225$00 you can climb right up to the top for some fine views of the Tejo and Belém tower.

At the corner of Belém's other main square – Praça Afonso de Albuquerque, a few minutes' walk from the monastery along Rua de Belém – there's the **Museu dos Coches** (Tues-Sun 10am–1pm & 2.30–6.30/5.30pm; 400$00; Sun free), oddly the most visited tourist attraction in Lisbon. It consists of an interminable line of royal coaches – Baroque, heavily gilded and sometimes beautifully painted.

Jump on tram #18, on the Calçada da Ajuda behind the coach museum, and you'll be pulled slowly uphill to the **Palacio da Ajuda** (half-hour tours 10am–5pm, closed Wed; 250$00). The palace was built by those crashingly tasteless nineteenth-century royals, Dona Maria II and Dom Ferdinand, and like their Pena Palace folly at Sintra is all over-the-top aristocratic clutter. The banqueting hall, however, is quite a sight; likewise the lift, decked out with mahogany and mirrors.

Football, ferries and cakes

Belém's **football club**, Belenenses, is a bit of joke in Portugal, forever swapping managers, trying to buy players way out of its price range and currently languishing in the second division. Still, a Saturday afternoon at the ground is an enjoyable and far more relaxing experience than the high energy of a visit to Benfica or Sporting, and you always have a very fine view of the Tejo if the action palls.

If you feel like escaping to a **beach** you can get a **ferry** across the Tejo from Belém to TRAFARIA – only three kilometres by bus from Costa da Caparica (see below); boats run on the hour and half hour (daily 6.30am–12.30am) from a terminus right by the electric railway station. Alternatively, trains from here continue to Cascais (see below), with a connection at Oeiras.

Finally, before leaving Belém, it's worth taking a tour of the **coffeeshops**, especially the *Antiga Confeitaria de Belém*, in Rua de Belém, by the tram stop, which bills itself as the "única fábrica de pasteis de Belém" – delicious flaky tartlet specialities filled with custard-like cream.

The Facts

The best sources for all **things going on in the city** is the weekly entertainments paper *Se7e* – a typographical pun, *sete* meaning seven in Portuguese; it is published on Tuesdays and available from most newsstands. The listings sections at the back are fairly comprehensive and easily decipherable; if you're unsure of the details, ask the Turismo staff for help or suggestions on transport.

Restaurants

Lisbon has some of the best-value **restaurants** of any European city – in fact by picking a place at random, outside the city centre, it's hard to go far wrong. **Lunchtime** choices include workers' cafés around Alfama, fish restaurants across the Tejo at Cacilhas, or down the coast at Cascais, or a multitude of set meals on offer to office employees in the Baixa. **By night** the obvious place to be is Bairro Alto, which hosts the city's most adventurous restaurants, and, to a lesser extent, Alfama. Note that many are closed on Sundays, and beware, too, that on Saturday nights in midsummer restaurants get booked up for the evening – phone, or pass by in the day, to reserve a table.

Bairro Alto

Bairro Alto is crammed with small, inexpensive restaurants – interspersed with a few that are unashamed tourist rip-offs: avoid menus in English and uniformed doormen and you should strike lucky. Selections below only scratch at the surface of the possibilities; prices quoted are per person with wine.

A Quinta, Passarela do Elevador de Santa Justa – the exit passageway of the Elevador (☎346 55 88). Good value food and unrivalled views over the Baixa. 1500$00.

Bizarro, Rua da Atalaia 133 (☎347 18 99). Fine and substantial meals for around 1500$00.

O Barriga, Travessa da Queimada 31. Another of the best deals in the quarter. 1500$00.

Casa Faz Frio, Rua Dom Pedro V 96 (☎346 18 60). A beautiful, very traditional restaurant, best at lunchtime; huge portions. 2000$00.

Mamma Rosa, near the top of the Elevador da Gloria, just off Rua São Pedro de Alcântara (closed Sun). Cramped, popular pizza place with famously cheeky waiters. 2000$00.

Cervejaria da Trindade, Rua Nova da Trindade 20 (☎342 3506). Huge, vaulted hall with some of the city's loveliest azulejos on the walls. It's a place to go late at night – it stays open till 2am (last orders at 1.30am) – for beer and seafood. Around 2000–3000$00.

O Bichano, Rua da Atalaia 78 (☎37 25 46). Imaginative menu, including a very special *Bacalhau à Braz*. Go early or book - it's always crowded. 2500$00.

Casa de Pasto Flores, Praça das Flores 40, a little to the northwest of the heart of Bairro Alto (☎395 23 95). Classic Portuguese dishes. 2500$00.

Brasuca, Rua João Pereira da Rosa 7 (☎342 85 42). A lively restaurant with great Brazilian food (and *caipirinhas*) as well as Portuguese standards. Around 2500$00.

Fidalgo, Rua da Barroca 27 (☎342 29 00; closed Sun). A fashionable hangout for arts and media types, who are rewarded by delicious seafood creations. 3000$00.

Cato Baton, Travessa Fiéis de Deus 28 (☎362 63 72). One of the most stylish interiors in Bairro Alto provides a backdrop for pleasant, French-inspired cooking. 3000$00.

O Mais Possivel, Rua do Norte. Highly rated French-Portuguese menu. 3500$00.

Pap'Açorda, Rua da Atalaia 57–59 (☎346 48 11; closed Sun & Mon). Upmarket but excellent. An *açorda* is a bread and shellfish stew, eaten here from clay bowls. 3500$00.

See the bar map on p.71 for detailed coverage of Bairro Alto's maze of streets.

ROCK-BOTTOM BUDGET EATING

For **rock-bottom** eating, there are stalls and picnic food in the **mercado** behind **Cais do Sodré** station. Also worth checking out in summer is the **Jardim do São Pedro** terrace, near the top of the *Elevador da Glória* in Bairro Alto: there is often a band playing here, and when anything's going on, a dozen or so foodstalls – if you're happy to eat standing up you can do so for next to nothing. Another reliable option is a **self-service** restaurant, the *Veranda*, over the Rossio train station.

Sadly, the absurdly cheap student *cantinas*, formerly a budget standby, now require local student passes – ISIC cards won't do.

Campo de Ourique and Lapa

Campo Ourique is a bit out of the way, northwest of Bairro Alto; **Lapa** is the next neighbourhood west of Bairro Alto along the seafront. They have two of the best Indian restaurants in the city, both run by (English-speaking) immigrants from the former Portuguese colony of Goa.

Velha Goa, Rua Tomás da Anunciação, Campo de Ourique (☎60 04 46; closed all day Mon & Sat lunchtime). Slightly pricey but very fine cooking. 3000$00.

Restaurante Zuari, Rua São Jaão da Mata 41, Lapa (☎67 71 49). Again great food, though as a newly established place, prices are a lot lower. 1500$00.

Alfama

Across the city centre, **Alfama** is surprisingly uncommercialised. Restaurants here, with only a handful of exceptions, are more often workers' cafés, good for soups and grilled sardines: **Rua da Regueira**, above the Largo do Chafariz de Dentro, has an especially promising concentration.

Túnel de Alfama, Rua dos Remedios. Cheap and very substantial. Lunchtime only. 1250$00.

Rio Coura, Rua do Limoeiro – just uphill from the Sé. Good value: a full meal and half a bottle of house for 1400$00.

Wong, Calçada da Mouraria 8, near the Mouraria market. Decent Chinese food. 1500$00.

Mestré André, Calçadinha de Santo Estevão 4–6 (☎87 14 87). A fine neighbourhood tavern, with superb pork dishes and good *churrasco* (grills). 2000$00.

Baixa

In the **Baixa** you need to be selective – particularly on **Rua das Portas de Santo Antão**, where several of the famed seafood restaurants have geared their standards and prices very firmly to tourists. **Rua dos Douradores**, toward the right-hand side of the grid, is more rewarding, and Rua dos Correeiros has a number of places where you can buy perfectly good food in rather unexciting surroundings.

Rei dos Frangos/Bom Jardim, Travessa de Bom Jardim 7–11 (the alleyway connecting Restauradores with Rua das Portas de Santo Antão). Always packed with students, this is *the* place for chicken – half ones for about 600$00 – and wonderful *Gelado Bom Jardim*.

Solmar, Rua das Portas de Santo Antão 108 (☎346 00 10). A vast showpiece restaurant, but deserving of its reputation, with very slick service and fine seafood. 4000$00.

O Coradinho, Rua de Santa Marta 4a (the northern extension of Rua das Portas de Santo Antão). Very friendly and excellent value with a full *Ementa Turística* for around 1000$00.

Bar-Restaurante Unidos do Minho, Rua dos Correeiros 215. Northern-style cooking and good value set menus.

Martinho da Arcada, Praça do Comércio/Rua da Prata. Old-established restaurant on the corner of the square, with a loyal lunchtime following of office workers.

O Cantinho do Aziz, 3–5 Rua de São Lourenço 3–5 (☎87 64 72; closed Sun). A little hard to find, up a couple of flights of stairs just to the east of Rossio, but well worth the search. Owned and run by a congenial Mozambican family, it offers a selection of African and Indian food (try the curried goat) for around 600–800$00 per dish.

Adega Triunfo, Rua dos Bacalhoeiros 127 (closed Sun). A great, small fish restaurant, highly recommended. 1500–3000$00.

Hua Ta Li, Rua dos Bacalhoeiros. Almost next to the *Triunfo*, this is one of the city's best value Chinese (Macão-nese, in fact) restaurants. 2000$00.

Estefânia

It's worth making the trip out here for an excellent, traditional eatery.

Cervejaria Portugália, Avda. Almirante Reis 117 (get off at Arroios metro and walk back; open until 1.30am). Top quality *mariscos*; always very busy but large enough to cope. 2500$00.

Belém

At Belém, there are several excellent places on and around the Rua Vieira Portuense, parallel to the main Rua de Belém; most have terraces in summer.

Dionísios, Rua de Belém 124 (☎64 06 32). Dependable Greek restaurant. 2000$00.

O Alexandre, Rua Vieira Portuense 84 (☎363 44 54). Tiny fish restaurant with pavement terrace and views of the monastery. 2000$00.

Associação Regional de Vela do Centro and **Clube Naval de Lisboa**. Two sailing clubs, next door to each other on the Doca de Belém, which have restaurants open to non-members above their boathouses. Feast on seafood at tables overlooking the river and Monument to the Discoveries. 3500$00.

VEGETARIAN RESTAURANTS

There's an increasing number of specifically **vegetarian options** – around twenty restaurants that now tag themselves "macrobiotic". The following listings are arranged geographically, roughly from the Rossio northwards.

Restaurante do Sol, Calçada do Duque 25 (Mon–Fri 9am–10pm, Sat 9am–3pm; closed Sun). Former workers' co-op restaurant. Fantastic fruit juices and good, if unexciting, meals for around 600$00, or just ask for "um prato".

Celeiro, Rua 1 de Dezembro 65. Conveniently just off the Rossio. Health food supermarket with basement restaurant like a school canteen – and like a school canteen the best things get eaten early (open noon–3pm).

O Terraço do Finisterra, Rua do Salitre 117, Metro Avenida (12–2.30pm & 7–9.30pm; closed Sun). Located in the Buddhist Centre, this stripped pine restaurant has superb, unusual veggie food (try the chocolate and chestnut cheescake). Set lunch at 750$00.

Centro Macrobiótico Vegetariano, Rua Mouzinho da Silveira 25, Metro Rotunda (open noon–8pm; turn left up Rua Braancamp from the metro, then left again). The food is much more digestible than the name; in the summer, tables are set outside in a small courtyard.

Espiral, Praça Ilha do Faial 14a, off the Largo de Dona Estefânia, Metro Saldanha (open daily 12–2pm & 6.30–9.30pm). This, Lisbon's "centre for alternatives", has a pleasant and inexpensive macrobiotic restaurant (plus vegetarian, Chinese and fish dishes) with adjacent bookshop and noticeboard detailing information on the city's alternative/green/ therapy scene. Often has live music at the weekend.

Super-Chefe, Avda. Duque de Ávila 22, Metro Saldanha (noon–midnight). Not a veggie restaurant as such – the menu includes burgers – but features crêpes, pizzas, wonderful cheeses and salads at competitive prices.

Instituto Kushi, Avda. Barbosa du Bocage 88, off Avda. da República, Metro Campo Pequeno. Cheap, wholesome food in a friendly place behind a macrobiotic shop.

Bars, clubs and discos

Although there are enjoyable **bars and clubs** scattered all over the city, the densest concentration is to be found in **Bairro Alto**, whose streets shelter around fifty or so bars and clubs, in addition to its dozens of fado houses (see "Music", following) and restaurants. In Bairro Alto, too, are located a handful of discos – and, on the periphery, over towards Rato, much of the city's gay scene. Brasher, more mainstream **discos** cluster further to the west in the quarters of **Santos** and the more outlying **Alcântara**.

Generally, where there's an admission charge to a club or disco, you can expect to pay around 1500$00, which usually includes a drink or two; if you're handed a ticket on entry, keep hold of it and present it when you buy your first round. Friday and Saturday nights tend to be overcrowded and expensive. Places featuring **live music** are covered in the next section (p.74).

Bairro Alto

The **Bairro Alto** streets are a maze – hence the **map** opposite. On this are keyed the pick of (current) places. Wandering through the quarter, though, you're bound to come upon other places that catch your eye: omission in our listings is not a negative sign, as bars and clubs change hands and names and decor every other week. Indeed, several clubs never seem to adopt any name at all, revealing their presence simply by a streetlight and a slot in the door for the frontperson to inspect customers. Don't be intimidated by this rather posey custom: just knock and walk in – and straight out, if you don't like the look of the place.

It is worth being aware that the Bairro Alto is also something of a sex centre – though most people are there just to eat, drink, or listen to music. Beyond the usual whistles, it's not too hustley or threatening for women.

Unless otherwise stated, most of the clubbier bars in Bairro Alto open around 10pm and close around 2am. Fridays and Saturdays are always packed out; on Sundays places tend to close and sleep it off.

KEYED ON THE MAP

[1] O Solar do Vinho do Porto (Port Wine Institute Bar), Rua de São Pedro de Alcântara 45 (Mon–Sat 10am–10pm). A good, if odd, place to precede more serious drinking, or round off an early meal. The *Solar* offers the chance to sample over 300 types and vintages of port, from 100$00 a glass up – although the waiters have a nasty habit of saying the cheaper ports are finished, it's worth at least one trip.

[2] Harry's Bar, Rua de São Pedro de Alcântara 57 (open all night; ring bell for admission). Handy last stop if you're stuck waiting for the first morning tram or train. A tiny little front-room bar, with waiter service, bar snacks and an eclectic clientele – often including a late-night contingent from the nearby gay discos.

[3] Baltigo, Rua do Teixeira 1 (closed Mon). Typical, intimate Bairro Alto style bar, with marble tables and abstract art.

[4] O Tacão Grande, Travessa da Cara. Quiet, low-lit bar.

[5] Coco Giro, Travessa da Boa-Hora. A no-nonsense, regular bar – friendly and informal, with benches and cheap beer from the tap.

[6] Gráficos, Travessa da Água de Flor 40. Fashionable, techno-style bar with loud music.

[7] Boris, Rua do Diário de Notícias (closed Wed). Clientele are mainly black leather youth who regard The Cult as the ultimate art form.

[8] Mascote do Bairro, Rua do Diário de Notícias. Cheap, relaxed bar with a good selection on the jukebox.

[9] Sem Nome, Rua do Diário de Notícias. Currently one of the city's in bars.

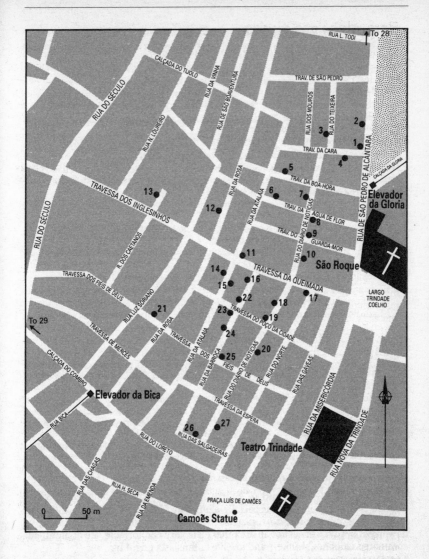

[10] La Folie, Rua da Atalaia 122 (Mon-Sat 10pm–3.30am). Very bright, loud disco-bar.

[11] Frágil, Rua da Atalaia 126 (Mon–Sat 10.30pm–3.30am; free). This is one of the few clubs in the country that maintains a door policy of admitting only its own kind: it's very trendy, partly gay, and can be oppressively pretentious. Pricey drinks, too.

[12] Keops, Rua da Rosa. Small nightspot with Egyptian decor and modern music. Distinctly fashionable but also rather pleasant.

[13] Club Bairro Alto, Travessa das Inglesinhas 50. Relaxed and spacious, with a greater diversity of music than many other Bairro Alto clubs.

[14] Beij'Arte Bar, Rua da Atalaia. Low-key salsa music, paisley decor, bohemian feel.

[15] Thermas d'Atalaia, Rua da Atalaia. Sweaty bar with a very dark interior, a decent range of cocktails and R & B dance music.

[16] Sudoeste, Rua da Barroca 135 (10pm–4am; closed Tues; free entry – ring for admission). Small club, and fun, with current rap and dance tracks.

[17] Tertúlia, Rua do Diário de Notícias 60 (7pm–2am; closed Sun). A place, as its name means, to meet up and talk with circles of friends. Jazz, occasionally live on the piano.

[18] Ártis, Rua do Diário de Notícias 95 (10pm–2am; closed Mon). Jazz decor and music, and a fine range of snacks and dishes.

[19] Páginas Tantas, Rua do Diário de Notícias. Cocktail bar; expensive but good.

[20] Maybe, Rua do Diário de Notícias. Very 1980s decor and style.

[21] Pub Grogs, Travessa dos Fiéis de Deus 82 (10pm–4am; closed Sun). A thoroughly unpretentious tavern – stone walls, wooden benches and regular-priced beers.

[22] Os Três Pastorinhos, Rua da Barroca 111 (nightly 10pm–2am). A good-time place, when it's full: music treads the line between dance and listenability, with lashings of soul and reggae; decor is a rather neat pinball-theme.

[23] Cena de Copos, Rua da Barroca. Not a club to frequent unless you're under-25 and bursting with energy. If you are, this is the place.

[24] 99 da Barroca, Rua da Barroca (nightly 10pm–2am). A pleasant, if a bit over-plush, wine bar with mid-priced drinks and cocktails.

[25] Sensão da Balila, Rua da Barroca. Beautiful people, minimalist design, top prices.

[26] Unnamed bar, Rua das Salgadeiras. A very modish disco-bar – knock for admission. Those that are admitted get to dance to one of the best sound systems in the city.

[27] Estudio Três, Rua do Diário de Notícias. A great little bar: stylish and not expensive.

JUST OFF THE MAP AND OVER TOWARDS ESTRELA

[↦ 28) Pavilhão Chinês, Rua Dom Pedro V 89 (Mon–Fri 2pm–2am, Sat 6pm–2am, Sun 9pm–2am). A wonderfully decorated bar, completely lined with mirrored cabinets of ludicrous and bizarre tableaux of artefacts from around the world. Drinks are moderately expensive, featuring a long list of speciality cocktails.

[↦ 29) Incógnito, Rua dos Poiais de São Bento 37 (10.30pm–3.30am; closed Mon & Tues). Appropriately named – the only indication is a pair of large metallic doors. Once within, you'll find downstairs a low-lit, plush, dance floor with interesting music. Opposite the club is a good, cheap bar/restaurant.

Bar Latino Americano, Rua Buenos Aires 31a, Estrela (Mon–Sat, until 2am). Latin music, as you'd expect from the name. A nice place to round off an evening.

DOWN TOWARDS CAIS DO SODRÉ

Down **towards the river end of Bairro Alto**, the rougher side of town around Cais do Sodré station – and especially along Rua Nova do Carvalho – there are more than a dozen *boites*, most playing music, and ranging from atmospheric to downright seedy. This is not an area that feels very comfortable late at night, but committed clubbers, drinkers and low-life enthusiasts might try:

Jamaica, Rua Nova do Carvalho 6 (nightly 9pm–3.30am). Disco with predominantly reggae/hard rock sounds.

Tokio, Rua Nova do Carvalho 12 (9pm–3.30am; closed Sun). Younger scene and more modern sounds.

Shangri-la, Rua Nova do Carvalho 49/51 (9pm–3.30am; closed Sun). Less crowded than *Jamaica* or *Tokyo* and deserves a mention for its nostalgic 1980s sounds – The Smiths, The Cure, Lloyd Cole . . .

Wagon-Lits, on the seafront in front of Cais do Sodré. This station bar is a real drinkers' dive at night, invariably full of offbeat characters.

GAY/LESBIAN BARS, CLUBS AND DISCOS

While the Lisbon **gay scene** doesn't yet have the high profile common to some other European capitals, there's quite a lively scene around the borders of the Bairro Alto and the Rato quarter to its northwest. All listings below are in this area.

Memorial, Rua Gustavo de Matos Sequeira 42a (10pm–4am). The best scene the city has – and as rewarding for lesbians as gay men. 1000$00 entry covers a couple of beers.

Trumps, Rua da Imprensa Nacional 104b (11pm–4am; closed Mon). The biggest gay disco in Lisbon with a reasonably relaxed door policy. Mostly soul, rap and house. Packed with a broad mix of people from Thursday to Saturday, a bit cruisy midweek.

Tatoo, Rua de São Marçal 15. Favourite bar with cloney types, but more sophisticated and lively at weekends.

Bar 108, Rua de São Marçal 33. More upbeat than *Tatoo*, with a younger and less self-conscious crowd.

Xeque-Mate, Rua de São Marçal 170 (nightly 10pm–2am). Exclusive and obnoxiously cruisy bar and disco, though a bit more cosmopolitan in the summer.

Finalmente, Rua Cecílio de Sousa (between *Trumps* and *Xeque-Mate*). Very busy, with first-class disco but lashings of kitsch. Weekend drag shows feature skimpily dressed young *senhoritas* camping it up to high-tech sounds.

Bric-a-Bar, Rua Cecílio de Sousa 84 (open nightly). Disco.

See also **Harry's Bar** – no. 2 on the Bairro Alto map-listed recommendations.

Santos

Santos – the area northwest of Cais do Sodré – is a very trendy location at present. The key street is Escadinhas da Praia: coming from Santos station, turn left down the main road, Avenida 24 de Julho, and it's the second on the right.

Kremlin, Escadinhas da Praia 5 (nightly 11pm–5am). Currently the city's most fashionable nightspot, this is packed with flash young Lisbonites raving to hip-hop, acid and house. Tough door rules, 5000$00 entrance, and don't bother showing before 1am.

Plateau, Escadinhas da Praia 3 (nightly 11pm–7am). Gentler admission policy here, with more of a rock orientation – and the all-around beaming of MTV as you bop.

O Xafarix, Avda. Dom Carlos I 69/Largo Vitorino Damásio (nightly 10pm–4am). Disco with occasional live music.

Baixa

Wandering around the main **Baixa grid** toward midnight you would imagine that the city had closed up and gone to bed; a single exception is the bar *Bora-Bora* at Rua da Madalena 201. One area worth mentioning is further north, though, on and around **Rua das Portas de Santo Antão**, which runs parallel to the Avenida da Liberdade on the Rossio side, and starts just off Restauradores. The street is packed with cheap, no-nonsense local bars.

Alfama

In **Alfama** most of the action is to be found in the *fado* clubs, detailed with all other live music places in the next section (p.66). Notable bars include:

Chapitô, Costa do Castelo 1/7 (open all day). Multi-media centre, incorporating an open-air bar with a marvellous river view, recording studios, circus tent, exhibition areas, a small theatre, a restaurant, and surreal decoration in the downstairs bar interior. It is youthful, highly fashion-conscious and there's no charge for admission.

Cerca Moura, Largo das Portas do Sol. One of a cluster of bars on the largo, with a nice view of the Tejo and a large esplanade.

Sua Excelência O Marquês, Largo Marquês do Lavradio, behind the Sé. Very trendy bar.

Estefânia and Campo Pequeno

Two disco recommendations for the areas west and north of the Rotunda:

Bamboo, Rua Gonçalves Crespo, Estefânia. African sounds most nights.

Spring-Fellow, Avda. Óscar Monteiro Torres, close to the Praça dos Touros in the north of the city. A fairly welcoming disco – less pretentious than it sounds from the corrupted name.

Alcântara

Traditionally, the city's top discos are in the far-flung area of **Alcântara**, way west of Bairro Alto; to reach them you'll need to take a taxi.

Fonte dos Passarinhos, Calvário (Alcântara's main square). Good cheap place for pre-club food and drink.

Banana-Power, Rua Cascais 51–53 (daily 11pm–4am). A club owned and designed by Tomás Taveira, architect of the post-modernist Amoreiras complex (see p.59). The clientele is dauntingly well-heeled and the prices outrageous, but design enthusiasts will at least want to take a look at the bar and restaurant (☎63 18 15).

Alcântara Mar, Rua Cozinha Económica (Tues–Sat 11pm–6am). Big, glitzy disco, full of business types. Close by is the **Alcântara Café**, Rua Maria Luísa Holstein 15, a bar-restaurant that is currently among the city's trendiest, in decor, clientele – and prices.

Alcântara Terra, Centro Comercial Lusíadas, Rua Lusíadas 5 (daily 11pm–5am). Mostly rap and soul here for a distinctly younger crowd.

Live music

Tourist brochures tend to suggest that Lisbon entertainment begins and ends with **fado**, the city's most traditional music, akin to the French *chansons*, which is offered in thirty or so nightclubs in the Bairro Alto and elsewhere.

There's no reason – except perhaps ever-rising admission prices – not to sample some *fado*, but don't miss out on other possibilities. Portuguese **jazz** can be good, **rock** an occasional surprise, and if you check out *Se7e*, *Sabado* and the posters around the Praça dos Restauradores there's a good chance of catching **African music** from the former colonies of Cabo Verde, Guinea Bissau, Angola and Mozambique, or **Brazilian** artists on tour.

Fado

Fado is thought to have originated, via the Congo, in the Alfama. It is often described as a kind of working-class blues – although musically it would perhaps be more accurate to class it as a kind of light operetta, sung to a vaguely flamenco accompaniment. Alongside Coimbra (which has its own distinct tradition), Lisbon is still the best place to hear it, either at a *Casa de Fado* or in an *Adega Típica*. There's no real distinction between these places: all are small, all serve food (though you don't always have to eat), and all open around 9 to 10pm, get going toward midnight, and stay open until maybe 3 or 4am.

Their drawbacks are inflated minimum charges – rarely, these days, below 2500$00 – and, in the more touristic places, extreme tackiness. Uniformed bouncers are fast becoming the norm, as are warm-up singers crooning Beatles songs and photographers snapping your table. Beware.

BAIRRO ALTO
Adega do Ribatejo, Rua Diário de Noticicias 23. Enjoyable both for the food and fado, this remains a genuine *adega*, popular with locals. The singers include a couple of professionals, plus the doorman, the manager and – best of all – the cooks.

Mil e Cem, Travessa da Espera 38. Good atmosphere and one of the cheaper minimum charges in the city.

Viela, Rua das Taipas 14. Another pleasant and not too touristy fado restaurant.

A Severa, Rua das Gáveas 55, **Adega Machado**, Rua do Norte 91, and **Painel do Fado**, Rua de São Pedro de Alcântara 65. The big three with the big names – and prices.

ALFAMA
Parreirinha d'Alfama, Beco do Espírito Santo 1, just off Largo do Chafariz de Dentro, Alfama. Reasonable music and food at fairly moderate prices.

SANTOS/ESTRÊLA
Fado Menor, Rua das Praças 18. 1000$00 cover charge and good music.

Patio das Cantigas, Rua de São Caetano 27.

ALCÂNTARA
A Cesária, Rua Gilberto Rola 20. Reckoned to be the real McCoy.

Timpanas, Rua Gilberto Rola 16. Likewise recommended.

African music
The best place to hear **African music** – if you're there at the right time – is a summer festival, when the city's bands are sometimes promoted alongside international West African acts. But there are regular gigs through the year and several more or less stable clubs:

Ritz Clube, Rua da Glória 55 (one block west of the Avda. da Liberdade; nightly 10.30pm–3.30am). Lisbon's largest African club occupies the premises of an old brothel-cum-music hall. It's a great place, with a resident Cabo Verdean band, plus the occasional larger-name concert. 1000$00 admission covers your first drink.

Cave Adão, Rua das Taipas 8 – a couple of blocks further west of Rua da Gloria (nightly 10pm–5am). Mix of disco and live bands. Food and drink. 1000$00 admission and drink.

Monte Cara, Rua do Sol ao Rato, off Largo do Rato, northwest of Bairro Alto. Lively and relaxed atmosphere, dancing until 6.30am. Live music sporadically – mainly Cabo Verdean bands – otherwise a disco. A restaurant on the ground floor serves Cabo Verdean food.

Bom Tom, Rua São João da Praça, Alfama. Features occasional Angolan bands.

Brazilian music
Three venues with regular live sounds:

Chafarica, Calçada de São Vicente 81, Alfama. Brazilian bar with live music till late most nights; the decor was recently, alas, given a rather clinical revamp.

Pê Sujo ("Dirty Foot"), Largo de São Martinho 6/7, Alfama (Tues–Sun; free). Five minutes' walk from the Sé in Alfama; ring to gain admission. Drinks feature *caipirinhas*, the lethal Brazilian concoction of rum, lime, sugar and ice, which regularly results in massive audience participation in table-banging samba sessions. Last set about 12.30am.

Johnny Guitar, Calçada do Marquês de Abrantes 72, Santos. Regular live music.

Look out, too, for visiting **Brazilian singers** – the wonderful Milton Nascimento, Maria Bethânia, Gilberto Gil, Ney Matogrosso and Chico Buarque de Holanda are some examples – who, like mainstream American or British bands on tour, tend to play **stadium gigs** (see below).

Rock Venues

Rock music is a chancier business, though there are a handful of established, interesting bands – among them Sétima Legião, Madredeus, GNR, Rádio Macau, Xutos e Pontapés, Rui Veloso and Heróis do Mar. Venues are highly erratic, so check *Se7e* for possibilities.

Anos Sessenta, Largo do Terreirinho 21, Alfama. This small club is one of the few regular rock venues. It's located a few minutes' walk from Largo Martim Moniz near the castle.

The main **stadium venues** for concerts are:

Coliseu dos Recreios, Rua das Portas de Santo Antão.

Pavilhão do Restelo, in Restelo. Belongs to the *Belenenses*, Belém's football team.

Pavilhão de Cascais, out in Cascais.

Jazz and folk

Hot Clube de Portugal, Praça da Alegria, off Avda. da Liberdade (Thurs–Sat 10pm–2am; 600$00 cover and pricier drinks). The city's only regular jazz venue – a tiny basement club which hosts local and visiting artists. In addition to jazz bands, the *Clube* (and other places – see *Se7e*) sometimes hosts **folk** singers, products of the new "political music" that emerged with the 1974 revolution. Names to watch out for include Sérgio Godinho, Vitorino, Fausto and the band Trovante.

Classical music, theatre and dance

Most major **cultural events**, including just about every classical music concert in the city, are sponsored by the **Gulbenkian Foundation**. If you're interested, it's worth picking up a schedule of events from them as soon as you arrive – or checking possibilities with the tourist office. Tickets range from 500$00 to 3000$00.

Free classical concerts are held at the Carmo and São Roque churches in Bairro Alto (every Saturday night at the latter), the Sé (Cathedral) and the Basílica da Estrêla.

There are performances of Portuguese and foreign **plays** at the Teatro Nacional de Dona Maria II (in the Rossio) and an **opera** season (Sept–June) at the Teatro Nacional de São Carlos on Rua Serpa Pinto.

Other entertainments

Music aside, there's a fair amount of other entertainment, including daytime pursuits, in Lisbon: over seventy **cinemas**, two above-average **football** teams, summer season **bullfights**, and a host of cultural and traditional festivals with which your visit might coincide.

Cinemas

Cinema is an unsung glory of a stay in Lisbon. The city and its environs have some seventy-five **cinemas**, virtually all of them showing **original language films** with Portuguese subtitles. You'll find, on any one night, a selection of American, British, French and African movies. Ticket prices are low (350–400$00; on Mondays 250–3000$00) and some of the theatres are beautiful in themselves – Art Nouveau and Art Deco palaces, often with original period bars. Among the most interesting are:

Eden Cinema, Avda. da Liberdade. The city's most beautiful Art Deco cinema: a wonderful sweep of lines, and superb heroic movie friezes, by the architect Cassiano Branco.

Quarteto, Rua das Flores, Bairro Alto. An art cinema with four screens.

Instituto da Cinemateca Portuguesa, Rua Barata Salgueiro 39, near Rotunda metro. The capital's national film theatre, this has shows at 6.30pm and 9.30pm every day, ranging from contemporary Portuguese films to anything from Truffaut to Valentino.

Amoreiras, Avda. Duarte Pacheco. Taveira's post-modern shopping centre features no fewer than ten screens; all, unfortunately, are modest-sized, but this is a good place to catch first-run mainstream movies.

At the corner of Restauradores, near the post office, is a kiosk with **tickets and programme details** for all the city's cinemas and theatres.

Football

Benfica – Lisbon's most famous football team – have a glorious past (the great Eusébio played for the team in the 1960s) and are at present on top form, after a few years in the shadow of F.C. Porto. No visit to the city is complete without taking in a game at their huge, beautiful **Estádio da Luz**. Tickets are cheap by European standards: you can buy them in advance from the *ABEP* kiosk in Praça dos Restauradores at a small commission, or at kiosks (not the turnstiles) at the ground on the night; bring a cushion for the bench seats. The best way to get to matches is on the metro – the Benfica stop is right outside the stadium.

Sporting Club de Portugal, Benfica's traditional rivals, play at the *Estádio José Alvalade* – bus #1 or #36; ticket arrangements are similar to those described above. For somewhat less illustrious action, a trip out to watch First Division **F.C. Estoril** or Second Division **Belenenses** of Belém (see p.66) can also be fun.

Details of matches – most of the regular league fixtures take place on Sunday afternoons (Sunday evening for a few big events) – are printed in all daily papers.

Bullfights

Bullfights take place most Thursdays and Sundays in summer at the principal **Campo Pequeno** bullring (metro Campo Pequeno), at Montijo across the Tejo, and less frequently at **Cascais**.

Other festivals and events

Lisbon's main **popular festivals** are in June, with fireworks, rides and partying to celebrate the **Santos Populares** – Saint Anthony (June 13), Saint John (June 24), and Saint Peter (June 29). Celebrations of each begin on the previous evening, with much partying on the streets; Saint Anthony's is the largest, taking over just about every square in Alfama.

On the cultural front, there is a big annual **International Jazz Festival** at the Gulbenkian in the summer and various events in **Cascais**, mostly held in the Parque Palmela. And through July and August the **Estoril Festival** takes place, with sometimes adventurous performances by internationally known orchestras, musicians and dance groups.

Again at **Estoril**, and a lot better than it sounds, is the state-run **Handicrafts Fair**. Crafts of all kinds are displayed from every region of the country along Avenida Amaral: if you buy anything, bargain at length – *Lisboetas* expect it. The fair runs through July and August, from around 5pm until midnight, with food-stalls included in the attractions.

From May to September there's also a permanent fairground, the **Feira Popular**, opposite the Entrecampos metro station. Cheap eats, cheap rides and a thoroughly Portuguese night out (until 1am, when the metro closes down too).

Shops and markets

The more interesting shopping areas are detailed in the preceding "City Quarters" sections preceding: the post-modernist shopping complex at **Amoreiras** (p.59); the elegant downtown **Chiado** district (p.51); the **flea market** (p.56); and **Ribeira** wholesale and **Cais do Sodré** fish markets (p.53).

Below are a few more selective shopping recommendations for particular goods, plus a handful of additional or specialist markets.

Antiques and crafts

Rua de São Bento, Bairro Alto. Cheapish antique/junk shops are concentrated along this street – none stand out above the others, but they make good browsing.

Fábrica Santana, Rua do Alecrim, 100m down from the Chiado/Largo do Carmo. If you're interested in Portuguese tiles – **azulejos** – check out this factory-shop, which sells copies of traditional designs.

Fábrica Viúva Lamego, Largo do Intendente (metro Intendente). Another azulejo factory shop.

Filartesanato, Feira Internacional de Lisboa, on the waterfront, west of the Ponte 25 de Abril bridge (Tues–Sat 2.30–8pm). General Portuguese regional crafts emporium.

Books, newspapers and maps

Livraria Bertrand, Rua Garrett 75, Chiado. Good general bookshop with novels in English, plus a range of British magazines.

Livraria Britanica, Rua São Marçal, opposite the Jardim Botânico, Rato. Exclusively English-language bookshop – pricey but well stocked.

Livraria Portugal, Elevador de Santa Justa. Excellent Portuguese bookshop which features – among other fine books – *Rough Guides* (known as *Real Guides* in North America).

Valentim de Carvalho, in the Rossio. A record and video shop downstairs with a bookshop, good for browsing, above.

International Press Centre, by the Turismo, on the west side of Praça dos Restauradores. The best place for English-language **newspapers**. Try also the news stands around Rossio.

Serviços Cartográficos do Exército, Avda. Dr. Alfredo Bensaúde, Olivais Norte (Mon–Fri 9–11.30am & 1–4.30pm, bus #25 from Praça do Comércio to *Laboratório Química Militar*. The army's map office is the place to go for ordnance survey maps for hiking. If at all possible, take a Portuguese friend along to facilitate the operation.

Records/CDs

Contraverso, Travessa da Queimada, Bairro Alto; **Valentim de Carvalho** in the Rossio. The city's best record shops, both with a wide range of local and international labels.

Markets

Numismatists' market (Sun am). Old coins and notes from Portugal and its former colonies, underneath the arches on the west side of Praça do Comercio.

31 Janeiro market (Mon–Sat). A food and fancies market opposite the Sheraton hotel on Avda. Fontes Pereira de Melo; metro Picoas or Saldanha.

Praça do Chile (turn right off Avda. Almirante Reis, Metro Arroios). An interesting and friendly general market in a large circular building.

Praça de Espanha clothes market (daily). Handy for supplies and easy to visit while you're waiting for a bus to Caparica.

Rotunda do Aeroporto (daily). The main rag-trade market, with complete wardrobes of clothing for a few thousand escudos. Take an airport bus to get there.

LATE NIGHT SHOPPING

The **Amoreiras** shops stay open till 11pm, Monday to Saturday, with nearby cinemas and restaurants to go on to afterwards. To get there, take bus #11 from Rossio or #23 from Rotunda (after 9.30pm catch any bus to Rotunda, then take a taxi or walk).

For general goods, try the late night **supermarket** just off the Rossio in Rua Jardim do Regedor (Mon–Fri 8am–12pm; Sat 9am–12pm; Sun 9am–11pm).

Directory

Airline Offices Most are along Avda. da Liberdade – including *British Airways* at 36-2° (☎346 09 31), *Air France* at 224A and *Air Maroc* at 225A. *TAP* (☎80 41 21) and *KLM* are in the Praça Marquês de Pombal, at the end of the Avda. de Liberdade.

Airport Information ☎72 11 01. Airport bus services are detailed under "Points of Arrival".

American Express is operated by *STAR Travel*: main office at Avda. Sidónio Pais 4A; a smaller one at Praça dos Restauradores 14 will phone to see if you have mail.

Banks Most main branches are in the Baixa and surrounding streets and standard banking hours are Mon–Fri 8.30–3pm. *Banco Borges & Irmão* (Avda. da Liberdade 9A) is one of the most efficient. There's an 8.30am-8.30pm **currency exchange** at Santa Apolónia station.

Car Rental *Avis*, *Budget* and *Europcar* all have desks at the airport, though there are far often lower prices at smaller agencies like *Dollar Budget* or the local *AutoCerro*. *Avis* is at Praça dos Restauradores 47, *InterHire* at Avda. da Liberdade 12. Turismo has full lists.

Embassies include: **Britain**, Rua São Domingos à Lapa 37 (☎396 11 91); **Ireland**, Rua da Imprensa à Estrêla 1-4° (☎396 15 69); **Australia**, Avda. da Liberdade 244-4° (☎52 33 50); **Netherlands**, Rua do Sacramento à Lapa 4-1° (☎396 1163); **Sweden**, Rua Miguel Lupi 12-2° (☎60 60 97); **USA**, Avda. das Forças Armadas (☎72 66 00); **Canada**, Avda. da Liberdade 144-3° (☎347 48 92).

Emergencies ☎115 is the general number. Red Cross point: Praça do Comércio. Fire: ☎342 22 22. Police: ☎36 61 41.

Hospitals British Hospital, Rua Saraiva de Carvalho 49 (☎60 20 20; night emergency ☎60 37 85; daily clinics 10am–1pm and 6–8pm).

Laundry *Lava Neve*, at Rua de Alegría 37 in Bairro Alto, is excellent, or try the one at Rua Saraiva de Carvalho 171 a little west of Rato (bus #9 from Rossio).

Lost Property See "Theft".

Lost or Stolen Credit Cards American Express and Visa (☎54 56 50).

Phones For international calls, it's easiest to use the telephone office at the corner of the Rossio (no. 65; 8am–11pm; personal cabins). You can also, in theory, make international calls from any phone booth – but the lines are often blocked. Phonecards, available in denominations of 500$00 and up from any post office, make calls from cabins a lot easier.

Police If you need help, or have something stolen, go to the office on Rua Capelo, west of the Baixa near the Teatro São Carlos.

Post Offices Main post office is on the Praça do Comércio (Mon–Fri 9am–7pm), **Posta Restante** section has a separate entrance at Rua do Arsenal 27 (closes at 2pm). Posta Restante letters sometimes delivered to post office in Praça dos Restauradores. At both ask them to check for letters under your surname and first name – and all other initials if possible. **Airmail** and **Express Mail** (the fastest service) leaves from special box in Restauradores post office (open until 11pm).

Student Information *Centro Nacional de Informação Juvenil*, Avda. da Liberdade 194, open 9.30am–7pm; offers practical advice and a library.

Swimming Pools The easiest to reach is *Piscina do Areeiro* (Avda. de Roma, metro Areeiro or Roma); 9am–1pm & 3–7.30pm. *Piscina dos Olivais* is further afield but preferable – bus #31 from the Rossio (45min) or #10 from Areeiro (20min).

Theft Go directly to the 24-hr Tourism Police, Rua Capelo 13, Chiado (☎36 61 41) and report any incident within 24 hours in order to make a claim on travel insurance – in most cases travellers' cheques can be replaced at the bank or agent recommended by the company. See also "Lost/Stolen Credit Cards", above. If you're lucky, property left on the metro will turn up at the **lost property office** at the top of the Elevador de Santa Justa, to the left as you walk out to the Largo do Carmo. Anything left on a bus or anywhere else may have been handed in to the police lost property office at Rua dos Anjos 56a – but allow a couple of days for it to get there.

Tourist Information Phone the Turismo in Praça dos Restauradores on ☎36 33 14.

Trains See "Points of Arrival" for details of station termini for different destinations. Full timetables are available at the Rossio information office. Information ☎87 60 25.

Travel Agencies Can be found along Avda. da Liberdade. Specialists include: *Wasteels*, near Santa Apolónia station, for train tickets; *Tagus Juvenil*, Praça de Londres 9B (☎88 49 57), for youth deals; *Turicoop*, Rua Pascoal de Melo 15 (☎53 18 04); *Intercentro*, Avda. Casal Ribeiro 18B (☎57 17 45), the main international bus agents; *Abreu*, Avda. da Liberdade 160 (☎37 13 41), well-established charter agents.

Women's Movement The best contact points are the *Editora das Mulheres* bookshop, right in the centre of the Baixa at Rua da Conceição 17, and *IDM* (*Informação e Documentação das Mulheres*) at Rua Filipe da Mata 115A (about 500m north of the Gulbenkian; metro Palhavã or bus #31 from the Rossio or Praça de Espanha). *IDM* is a women's centre incorporating a small library and the sole women-only café in Lisbon. Run by a collective, they are very eager to welcome foreign travellers and publicise the centre's activities. English spoken.

AROUND LISBON

Transport around the capital is reliable, and basing yourself in Lisbon you could take in a fair part of Estremadura (Chapter Two) and Alentejo (Chapter Eight) on daytrips. Covered in this chapter are just the attractions within a 50-kilometre or so radius of the capital. Some of these, such as the palaces of **Queluz**, or even **Mafra**, are best seen on a daytrip, but the beautiful town of **Sintra**, the most popular excursion from Lisbon, demands a longer look, revealing a different side if you can stay overnight. However you decide to see them, keep in mind that most of the Sintra palaces are closed on Mondays, and Queluz and Mafra on Tuesdays.

For **beach** escapes from the city, Lisbon has five possibilities within easy reach: at **Carcavelos**, **Estoril** and **Cascais**, along the coast from Belém; at **Guincho**, to the north; and along the **Costa da Caparica**, a 30-kilometre expanse of dunes just south of the capital across the Tejo. If you want to **stay by the sea** (and obviously it's as easy to commute into Lisbon as out from it), there are reasonably priced pensions both along the surburban Estoril coast – at Oeiras, Carcavelos, Parede, Estoril and Cascais – and at Caparica. For **camping**, Guincho has one good campsite and Caparica a whole string. As you might imagine, all beaches in the Lisbon area get very crowded at weekends and throughout August.

Costa da Caparica

It takes something over an hour (outside of rush hours) to reach **Costa da Caparica** from the capital, and it's here that most locals come if they want to swim or laze around on the sand. There are foreign tourists, too, but they're in a minority: this is a thoroughly Portuguese resort, lively, crammed with restaurants and beach cafés and fun. It is also – as far as sea and sand go – more or less limitless. A mini-railway runs along 8km or so of dunes (in season only) and if you're into solitude you need only take this to the end of the line and walk. En route to Caparica, and perhaps more fun if you have kids to entertain, is a **"Wave Park"**, the **Parque Onda**. For 800$00 admission, you can career down all manner of slides into huge pools.

Access: ferries and the Christo-Rei

The most enjoyable approach to Caparica is to take a **ferry from the Fluvial station** (by Praça do Comércio) to **Cacilhas** and then pick up the connecting bus which leaves right in front of the dock where the boats come in. The ferries run every ten minutes, the last returning at 9.35pm (9.10pm at weekends); the crossing takes ten minutes. If you miss the last one you can still get back to the capital by taking a boat to the **Cais do Sodré** terminus; this runs throughout the night.

Alternatively, and (outside traffic rush hours) more speedily, you can take a **bus** from the centre of town direct to Caparica over the swaying **Ponte 25 de Abril**. Buses leave from the main Praça de Espanha terminus (metro Palhavã) and from Areeiro and Campo Pequeno every twenty to thirty minutes.

Either of these routes will give wonderful views of the city and take you past the **Christo-Rei** – a relatively modest version of Rio's Christ-statue landmark. The statue itself is worth a halt: a lift shuttles you up the plinth, via a tacky religious souvenir shop, to a highly dramatic viewing platform. On a good day, Lisbon stretches like a map below you and you can catch the glistening roof of the Pena Palace at Sintra in the distance. If you're travelling by bus, #18 will deposit you at the base, and you can pick up another one on to Caparica. Driving, cross the bridge and turn left off the *autoestrada*, following signs for Almada and *Christo-Rei*.

Caparica

At **CAPARICA** all buses stop in a dusty depot close to the beginning of the sands. If you walk along the beach to the left you come to the main square, where there's a **tourist office**, market, cinema and banks.

There aren't very many hotels in Caparica. If you strike lucky, a particularly attractive place to stay is the *Hotel-Restaurante Pátio Alentejano*, Rua Professor Salazar de Sousa 17 (☎01/290 00 44; ②), just off the beach at the west end of town. Alternatively, the tourist office can book private rooms, and there is a string of campsites. Moving north to south along the beach, these are: *Orbitur* (☎01/ 290 06 61); *Clube de Campismo de Lisboa* (☎01/290 01 00); *Lugar ao Sol* (☎01/290 15 92); *Praia da Saúde* (☎01/290 22 72); *Costa Nova* (☎01/290 30 21); and *Praia da Mata* (☎01/290 26 20). All are pricier than average and crowded in summer.

A recommended **restaurant**, among dozens of fish and seafood places along the main street, Rua dos Pescadores, is the *Casa dos Churros* at no. 13.

The beaches

Caparica's **beaches**, which take in coves and lagoons as they spread southward, speak for themselves. It's useful to know, though, that each of the twenty **mini-train stops**, based around one or two beach-tavernas, has a very particular scene or feel. Earlier stops tend to be family oriented, often with a campsite and pool nearby. Later ones are on the whole younger and more trendy, with nudity (though officially illegal) more or less obligatory. One or more stops are predominantly gay – most recently stop no. 17 was the most fashionable.

West to Estoril and Cascais

Quirks of the Tejo currents have spared Caparica from the pollution of Lisbon and its shipping. The **Estoril coast**, however, has suffered badly, and many locals regard the sea, as far as Cascais, as too much of a health hazard for swimming. Nonetheless, the coast retains its attractions, with a lively summer culture of seafront bars and promenade life. **Cascais**, in particular, makes a pleasant alternative base to a stay in Lisbon, and is well placed for trips to Sintra or the wild Guincho beach.

Access to each of the towns and resorts could hardly be easier. The *Linha de Cascais* **electric train** leaves every twenty minutes from Cais do Sodré station, stopping at Belém and the Greater Lisbon suburbs en route to Cascais. Beware, though, that some trains terminate in Oeiras, while others stop only at Alcântara, Oeiras and stations beyond. By road, the **N6** is the main highway, passing through most of the centres along the seafront, often as the *Avenida Marginal*.

Oeiras to Estoril

The first suburb of any size after Belém is **OEIRAS**, where the Tejo officially turns into the sea. The beach here is nothing special and, unless you're staying at the youth hostel, the only reason for a stop would be to see the **Palácio do Marquês de Pombal**, erstwhile home of the rebuilder of Lisbon. The house is today an adult education centre, and the park is not technically open to visitors. However, if there's nothing special going on, the guard should be able to show you the **gardens**, or at least let you peer over the walls at its massive grotto.

Accommodation at Oeiras is limited to the **youth hostel** (☎01/443 06 38), well sited, overlooking the sea, and a tiny **campsite** (☎01/243 03 30), unfortunately positioned too close to the river – which stinks in summer. There is a small and helpful **Turismo**, across from the fire station on Rua Álvaro António dos Santos. For meals, try the inexpensive *Adega* **wine cellar** on Rua Marquês de Pombal, or the **restaurants** *Vai Vem*, on the same street, and *Bombeiros Voluntários de Oeiras* (☎01/443 00 69), over the fire station; at the latter you rub shoulders with firemen recuperating between emergencies.

Carcavelos

Next stop along the coast is **CARCAVELOS**, popular for its kilometre of beach and plethora of beachfront bars and cafés. The water here, though far from clean, doesn't appear to do lasting damage and it's a busy surfing area. Other possible motivations for a visit are the huge **Thursday market**, which sprawls between the train station and town centre, and a superb and inexpensive Mozambiquan restaurant, *O Palheiro*, on Rua Santarém (☎01/247 0142). *The Pub*, right by the station in an old railway carriage, is the one late-night haunt, open till 2am.

Parede

PAREDE, like Carcavelos, boasts a clutch of culinary highlights, though a rather less impressive beach. If you stop off, don't under any circumstances miss the superb *Lua de Mel* pastellaria – 50m up from the station on the Avenida da República – nor *Eduardo's Café*, right by the station (open until 2am), which draws gastronomes from Lisbon for its seafood (ordered by the gram – so you can sample everything). Other enjoyable feasts are to be had at the nearby *Churrasqueira Brito*, a typical Portuguese *frango* joint, *Limo Verde*, a massive and exuberant *cervejaria* (beer house), and *O Junco*, an unexpectedly marvellous Chinese restaurant; all of these are along the Avenida da República.

São Pedro and São Jorge
Beyond Parede, the beaches improve rapidly, and you reach the beginning of an esplanade which stretches virtually uninterrupted to Cascais. **SÃO PEDRO**, the first stop, has a superb beach, just down from the station, and **SÃO JOÃO** is flanked by two lovely stretches of sand. The whole seafront here is pretty animated in the summer months, swarming with young surfers and Portuguese holiday-makers, with its own bar culture, cafés and restaurants.

Estoril
The major resort along this coast, **ESTORIL** gained a post-war reputation as a haunt of exiled royalty and the idle rich: pretensions towards being a "Portuguese Riviera" that it continues to maintain, with grandiose expatriate villas and luxury hotels. It is little surprise then, that the town's touristic life revolves around a **casino** and **golf course**. The former requires a passport and some semblance of formal attire to get in (open 3pm–3am); minimum bet is 1000$00. If you want to play at the eighteen-hole McKenzie Ross-designed golf course, contact **Estoril Golf Club** on the Avenida da República (☎01/268 01 76).

Estoril's less exclusive plus points include a good number of **bars and clubs** – *Gaiety Bar* (Avenida Fausto Figueiredo) and *Bauhaus* (Avenida Sabóia) are the most dynamic – and a minor First Division football team, **FC Estoril**, whose stadium at the top end of Rua Afonso Henriques, makes a diverting Saturday visit. Following the seafront is pleasant, too, with Cascais under an hour's walk.

If you want to stay in town, there's a very helpful **Turismo** (☎01/268 01 13), right opposite the station across the Avenida Marginal, who can give advice on **private rooms**. Hotels proper are very upmarket and there are just four **pensions**, which themselves are not especially good value:

Pensão Costa, Rua de Olivença 2-1° (☎01/268 16 99). ②.
Pensão Chique do Estoril, Avda. Marginal 60 (☎01/268 03 93). ②.
Pensão Maryluz, Rua Maestro Lacerda 13 (☎01/268 27 40). ③.
Pensão Casa Londres, Avda. Fausto Figueiredo 7 (☎01/268 15 41). ③.

Cascais

At the end of the railway line, with three fair beaches along its esplanade, **CASCAIS** is now a major resort. But it's not too large or difficult to get around and has a much younger, less exclusive feel than Estoril, even retaining a few elements of its previous existence as a fishing village. There's a lively **Wednesday market**, as well as Sunday evening **bullfights** that take place not just for the tourists.

Accommodation
Through the summer, accommodation is at a premium in Cascais, and pensions in any case are sparse. The best plan is to contact the excellent **Turismo** (Rua Visconde da Luz, ☎01/268 0113) on arrival, where the staff will usually phone around on your behalf until you're sorted out. There are quite a few private rooms.

Worth trying among the **pensions** are:

Pensão Avenida, Rua da Palmeira 14-1° (☎01/286 44 17). Basic but tolerable. ①.

Pensão Le Biarritz, Avda. do Ultramar (☎01/28 22 16). ②.

Pensão Costa, Avda. do Ultramar (☎01/28 22 16). ②.

Pensão Casa Lena, Avda. do Ultramar 389 (☎01/286 87 43). ③.

Pensão Residencial Italia, Rua do Poço Novo 1 (☎01/28 01 51). ③.

Pensão Residencial Palma, Avda. Valbom 15 (☎01/28 02 57). Highly recommended. ③.

Pensão Dom Carlos, Rua Latina Coelho 8(☎01/286 51 54). Very attractive pension in a sixteenth-century mansion. ③.

Around town

You'll find the main concentration of bars and nightlife – and consequently most of what makes Cascais tick as a tourist town – on the pedestrian thoroughfare behind the tourist office and the beaches. For a wander away from the crowds, take a right and head into the old, and surprisingly pretty, **west side of town**. One shop is worth noting, too: the *Livraria Galileu*, at Avenida Valbom 24a, which has stacks of new and secondhand books in all languages and a basement full of desirable obscurities. Also worth a look is the afternoon **fish market**, which takes place, around 5pm, on a promontory between the Ribeira and Rainha beaches.

On the outskirts of town, to the west, is the pleasant **Parque Marechal Carmona**, with its mansion of the counts of Guimarães, preserved complete with its nineteenth-century fittings as a house-museum. A little further on – 1.5km walk from the town – is the postcard-image of the **Boca do Inferno** – Mouth of Hell – where waves crash against caves in the cliff face. It's always packed with tourists – likewise the very tacky market on the roadside – and unimpressive except in stormy weather. En route, however, taking the coast road past the military-occupied fort, there's a little **beach** with a nice **grill-café** on a terrace above.

Restaurants and bars

Porta Romana, Rua Afonso Sanches 41 (Mon–Sat 12.30–3pm & 7.30–11pm). Pizza takeaway opposite the police station.

Joshua's, Rua Visconde da Luz 19. Slightly pricey, Middle Eastern-style eatery; open late.

Dom Pedro I, Praça 5 de Outubro (closed Sun). Decent Chinese restaurant.

A Tasca, Rua Afonso Sanches. Pleasant tavern, good for fish dishes.

Van Gogo, Travessa da Alfarrobeira 9. Music bar open till 3.30am.

Coconuts, in the *Hotel Nau*, Rua Dra. Iracy Doyle – near the municipal park. Summer disco.

Praia do Guincho

PRAIA DO GUINCHO (6km direct from Cascais on the inland route; hourly buses) looks out over unpolluted ocean: a great sweeping field of beach with body-crashing Atlantic rollers. It's a superb place to surf or windsurf – World Championships have been held here – but also a dangerous one. The undertow is notoriously strong and people are drowned every year: take care.

The beach is hardly developed, fronted by just a couple of **hotels** – the deluxe-class *Hotel de Guincho* and slightly more moderate *Estalagem O Muchaxo* (☎01/285 02 21; ⑥) – and a **campsite** (☎01/285 10 14). For meals, *O Muchaxo* is acclaimed as the best seafood **restaurant** in the Lisbon area; *O Camponês* at nearby MALVEIRA DA SERRA, toward Colares, is good, too, and rather cheaper.

Sintra

Summer residence of the kings of Portugal, and of the Moorish lords of Lisbon before them, **SINTRA**'s verdant charms have long been celebrated. British travellers of the eighteenth to nineteenth century found a new Arcadia in its cool, wooded heights, recording with satisfaction the old Spanish proverb: "To see the world and leave out Sintra is to go blind about".

Byron stayed here in 1809 and began *Childe Harold*, his great mock-epic travel poem, in which the "horrid crags" of "Cintra's glorious Eden" form a first location. Writing home, in a letter to his mother, he proclaimed the village:

> *perhaps in every aspect the most delightful in Europe; it contains beauties of every description natural and artificial. Palaces and gardens rising in the midst of rocks, cataracts and precipices; convents on stupendous heights, a distant view of the sea and the Tagus . . . it unites in itself all the wildness of the Western Highlands with the verdure of the South of France.*

That the young Byron had seen neither of these is irrelevant: his description of Sintra's romantic appeal is exact – and still telling two centuries later. Move mountains and give yourself the best part of two full days.

Orientation

Sintra loops around a series of green and wooded ravines, a confusing place in which to get your **bearings**, and consists of three distinct and separate villages: **Estefânia** (around the railway station), **Sintra-Vila** (the main town), and, two kilometres to the east, **São Pedro de Sintra**. It's ten to fifteen minutes' walk between the station and Sintra-Vila, passing en route the fantastical **Câmara Municipal** (town hall), and around twenty minutes from Sintra-Vila to São Pedro.

The centre of Sintra-Vila is gathered about the extraordinary **Palácio Nacional**, distinguished by a vast pair of conical chimneys. This is the most obvious landmark, dominating the central square; just downhill is a **Turismo**, which can help with accommodation (see p.89) and provide a useful free map of the town.

The Palácio Nacional

The **Palácio Nacional** (or **Paço Real**; 10am–5pm; closed Wed; 200$00) was probably already in existence under the Moors. It takes its present form, however, from the rebuilding and enlargements of Dom João I (1385–1433) and his fortunate successor, Dom Manuel, heir to Vasco da Gama's inspired explorations. Its style, as you might expect, is an amalgam of Gothic – with impressive roofline battlements – and the latter king's Manueline additions, with their characteristically extravagant twisted and animate forms. Inside, the Gothic–Manueline modes are tempered by a good deal of Moorish influence, adapted over the centuries by a succession of royal summer occupants. The last royal to live here, in the 1880s, was Maria Pia, grandmother of the country's last reigning monarch – Manuel II, "The Unfortunate".

Today the Paço is run as a museum, with guided **tours** every twenty minutes. The tours are fairly informal – best to go early or late in the day to avoid the crowds – and allow you a leisurely stroll through the various rooms and patios. You're taken first to the **kitchens**, their roofs tapering into the giant chimneys, and then to the upper floor. First stop here is a gallery above the palace Chapel,

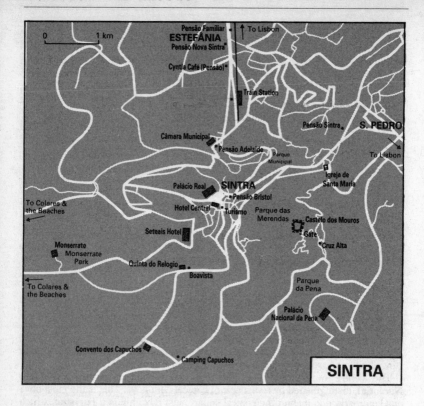

SINTRA

built perhaps on the old mosque. In a room alongside, the deranged Afonso VI was confined for six years by his brother Pedro II; he eventually died here in 1683, listening to mass through a grid, Pedro having seized "his throne, his liberty and his queen". Beyond the gallery, a succession of state rooms climaxes in the Manueline **Sala das Armas**, its domed and coffered ceiling emblazoned with the arms of 72 noble families – originally 74 until the Távoras and Aveiros were erased for their eighteenth-century intrigues against the Crown.

Highlights on the lower floor include the Manueline **Sala dos Cisnes**, so-called for the swans on its ceiling, and the **Sala das Pegas**. This last takes its name from the flock of magpies (*pegas*) painted on the frieze and ceiling, holding in their beaks the legend *por bem* (in honour) – reputedly the response of João I, caught by his Queen Philippa (of Lancaster) in the act of kissing a lady-in-waiting. He had the room decorated with as many magpies as there were women at court in order to satirise and put a stop to their gossip.

The Castle and Pena Palace

From nearby the church of **Santa Maria**, towards São Pedro, a stone pathway leads up to the ruined ramparts of a **Moorish Castle** (Tues–Sun 9am–sunset, free; also accessible from the top – close by Pena Palace – by road).

The Castle

Taken with the aid of Scandinavian crusaders by Afonso Henriques, the **Castelo dos Mouros** spans two rocky pinnacles, with the remains of a mosque spread midway between the fortifications. Views are extraordinary: south beyond Lisbon's bridge to the Serra de Arrábida, west to Cascais and Cabo da Roca (the westernmost point of Europe), and north to Peniche and the Berlenga islands.

Pena Park and Palace

The upper gate of the castle gives onto the road up to Pena, opposite the lower entrance to **Pena Park** (daily 10am–6pm), a stretch of rambling woodland, with a scattering of lakes and follies, ideal for a picnic. At the top of the park, about twenty minutes' walk, rears the fabulous Palácio da Pena.

The **Palácio da Pena** (Tues–Sun 10am–5pm; 400$00) is a wild fantasy of domes, towers, ramparts and walkways, approached through mock-Manueline gateways and a drawbridge that does not draw. A compelling riot of kitsch, it was built in the 1840s to the specifications of Ferdinand of Saxe-Coburg-Gotha, husband of Queen Maria II, and it bears comparison with the mock-medieval castles of Ludwig of Bavaria. The architect, the German Baron Eschwege, has immortalised himself in the guise of a warrior-knight on a huge statue that guards the palace from a neighbouring crag. Inside, Pena is no less bizarre, preserved exactly as it was left by the royal family on their flight from Portugal in 1910. The result is fascinating: rooms of concrete decorated to look like wood, turbaned Moors nonchalantly holding electric chandeliers – it's all here. Of an original convent, founded to celebrate the first sight of Vasco da Gama's returning fleet, a chapel and genuine Manueline cloister have been retained.

Above Pena, past the statue of Eschwege, a marked footpath climbs to the **Cruz Alta**, highest point of the Serra de Sintra. Another footpath (unmarked) winds down to the left from Pena, coming out near Seteais (see below).

Seteais, Monserrate and the Cork Convent

After the castle and Pena, a visit to the palace of **Seteais** and luxuriant gardens of **Monserrate** are the other obvious goals of a Sintra walk; enthusiastic hikers might want to make a circuit of these, via the **Capuchos** "Cork Convent".

Seteais

Seteais ("Seven Sighs") stands just to the right of the Colares road, fifteen-minutes' walk from the centre of town. It is one of the most elegant palaces in

Portugal, completed in the last years of the eighteenth century and entered through a majestically stagey neoclassical arch. It is maintained today as an intensely luxurious **hotel** – offering some of the most expensive accommodation in the country; with more modest money to blow, make for the bar and terrace – downstairs to the left, past a distinctly unwelcoming reception.

Beyond Seteais, the road leads past a series of beautiful private *quintas* (manors or estates) until you come upon Monserrate – about forty minutes' walk.

Monserrate

With its Victorian folly-like mansion and vast botanical park of exotic trees and subtropical shrubs and plants, **Monserrate** is one of the most romantic sights in Portugal. It would be easy to spend the whole day wandering around the paths laid out through the woods – and the charm of the place is immeasurably enhanced by the fact that it's only partially maintained.

The name most associated with Monserrate is that of **William Beckford**, author of the Gothic novel *Vathek* and the wealthiest untitled Englishman of his age. He hired the *quinta* here from 1793 to 1799, having been forced to flee Britain through homosexual scandal – buggery then being a hanging offence. Setting about improving this "beautiful Claude-like place", he landscaped a water-fall and even imported a flock of sheep from his estate at Fonthill. In this Xanadu-like dreamland, he whiled away his days in summer pavilions, entertaining with "bevys of delicate warblers and musicians" posted around the grounds.

Half a century later, a second immensely rich Englishman, **Sir Francis Cook**, bought the estate. His fantasies were scarcely less ambitious, involving the construction of a great Victorian house inspired by the Brighton Pavilion. Cook also spared no expense in developing the grounds, importing the head gardener from Kew to lay out succulents and water plants, tropical ferns and palms, and just about every conifer known. Fernando II, who was building the Pena Palace at the time, was suitably impressed, conferring a viscountcy on Cook for his efforts.

The **gardens** are open daily except on public holidays – officially from 9am to 5pm, though the gates aren't always locked. Cook's **house** is closed but you can still admire the exterior, with its mix of Moorish and Italian decoration (the dome is modelled on Brunelleschi's *Duomo* in Florence) and peer into a splendid series of empty salons.

The Convento dos Capuchos

One of the best long walks in the Sintra area is to the **Convento dos Capuchos** (9am–6pm; closed Tues), an extraordinary hermitage with tiny, dwarflike cells cut from the rock and lined in cork – hence its popular name of "Cork Convent". Philip II, King of Spain and Portugal, pronounced it the poorest convent of his kingdom, and Byron, visiting a cave where one monk had spent thirty-six years in seclusion, mocked in *Childe Harold*:

> Deep in yon cave Honorius long did dwell,
> In hope to merit Heaven by making earth a Hell.

Coming upon the place after a walk through the woods, however, it's hard not to be moved by the simplicity and seclusion of the place.

To reach the convent, the most straightforward approach is by the ridge road from Pena (9km), but there is also an indistinct path through the woods from Monserrate, starting above the fountain opposite the entrance to the gardens.

Sintra practicalities

Sintra's a popular resort and it's worth booking ahead, or turning up early in the day, if you intend to stay. There's a fair range of accommodation: a youth hostel, half a dozen pensions and hotels, a network of private rooms, and, considerably more upmarket, Turihab bed and breakfast in several local *quintas*, or **manor-houses**. Rooms and *quinta* accommodation is best arranged through the efficient and helpful **Turismo** (☎01/293 11 57), just off the central square.

The nearest **campsites** are well out of town: at the **Capuchos convent** (☎01/86 23 50) – a ten-kilometre haul, with no bus – and, more convenient, on the beach at PRAIA GRANDE (see overpage).

Accommodation

Pousada de Juventude, Santa Eugénia (☎01/923 32 11). An attractive hostel located in the hills above São Pedro. It's a 5-km walk from the centre, less with a local bus to São Pedro.

Casa de Hospedes Adelaide, Rua Guilherme Gomes Fernandes 11 (☎01/923 08 73). Welcoming and inexpensive pension, midway between the train station and Sintra Vila. ③.

Pensão Nova Sintra, Largo Afonso d'Albuquerque 25 (☎01/923 02 20). Decent rooms and a handy situation, on the square by the train station. ③.

Residencial Sintra, Travessa dos Alvares, São Pedro (☎01/923 07 38). Big, rambling old pension out at São Pedro. ③.

Quinta da Padernas, Rua da Paderna (☎01/923 50 35). B & B in a lovely old house, just north of Sintra-Vila. ④

Estalagem da Raposa, Rua Alfredo Costa 3 (☎01/923 04 65). An old townhouse run as an inn since the last war; spotless, nicely furnished rooms. ④

Hotel Central, Praça da República 35 (☎01/923 09 63). Characterful and comfortable nine-teenth-century hotel, opposite the Palácio Nacional. ⑤.

Villa das Rosas, Rua António Cunha 4 (☎01/923 42 16). Rural villa on the edge of town, north of the train station. ⑤.

Quinta da Capela, Estrada de Monserrate (☎061/929 01 70). Beautiful sixteenth-century manorhouse on the road to Monserrate, furnished with antiques and equipped with a sauna and springwater pool. Doubles from 14–17,000$00; closed mid-Nov to March 1. ⑥.

Restaurants and bars

There are some fine restaurants scattered about the quarters of Sintra, with the best concentration at São Pedro, well worth the twenty-minute walk from the centre. Local specialities include *queijadas da Sintra* – sweet cheese pastry-cakes.

Tasca do Manel, opposite the Câmara Municipal, Sintra Vila. No nonsense bar with hearty plates of the day and barrelled wine; closes at 10pm.

Casa da Avo, Escadinhas da Audiencia, Sintra Vila. Slightly soulless but the house wine is cheap enough to drown such thoughts – and it's hard to fault dishes like the *caldeirada* (fish stew).

Restaurante Tulhas, Rua Gil Vicente 4, behind the Turismo, Sintra Vila. Imaginative cook-ing in a fine building, converted from old grain silos. Moderate prices.

Bar Loco, by the train station. An old railway dining car converted into a bar-restaurant with good value (if limited) food menu, and an African band playing reggae covers most nights.

Adega do Saloio, Travessa Chão de Meninos, São Pedro. A superb grillhouse, popular enough to have spread to buildings on both sides of the road.

Toca do Javali, Rua 1º Dezembro 18, São Pedro. Outdoor tables in summer and superb cooking at any time of year. Prices are modest for the quality – don't stint!

Solar de São Pedro, Praça Dom Fernando II 12, São Pedro. French-Portuguese dishes served in an azulejo-covered vault.

Fairs and festivals

At São Pedro, on the second and last Sunday of each month, there's a country **fair**, with food, crafts and antiques/junk. In its wake, the village has become something of an antiques centre, with numerous stores year round. The village is also host to a full-blown **festa** over the feast of Saint Peter (June 28–29).

In July, Sintra holds a **music festival**, with classical performances in a number of the town's palaces, and also at Queluz (see opposite).

West of Sintra: Colares, the beaches and Cabo da Roca

About six kilometres west of Monserrate is **COLARES**, a hill village famed for a long-established wine, with much-prized vintages. It has a couple of mid-range **hotels** (*Residencial Conde*, ☎01/929 16 52; and *Hotel Miramonte*, ☎929 12 30; both ④) and a fine **restaurant**, *A Bistro* (closed Mon), in an old apothecary shop.

Praia das Maçãs, Azenhas do Mar and Praia Grande

Continuing west from Colares, the road winds around through the hills to the beach-resort of **PRAIA DAS MAÇÃS** (bus #441 from Sintra train station, or in summer, trams from Colares). This has two pensions (the *Oceano*, ☎01/929 23 99; and *Real*, ☎01/929 20 02; both ④), a scattering of restaurants, and a **bike rental shop** – *Velo-Cidade*, in the Casa da Ancôra, which has Shimano-equipped mountain bikes – superb transport for the area.

Nearby **AZENHAS DO MAR** and **PRAIA GRANDE** (again on the bus #441 route) are in similar mould; Praia Grande has a large **campsite** (☎01/929 05 81).

Cabo da Roca

Fourteen kilometres southwest of Colares, **CABO DA ROCA** can be reached by taking a bus to CRUZ DA AZOIA and walking the remaining 3km from there. It's an enjoyable trip, though the cape comprises little more than a lighthouse and a couple of stalls. At one of these, you can buy a certificate recording that you've visited the "Most Westerly Point in Europe" – which indeed you have.

Mafra

Moving on from Lisbon or Sintra, **MAFRA** makes an interesting approach to Estremadura. It is distinguished – and utterly dominated – by just one building: the vast **Palace-Convent** built in emulation of Madrid's Escorial by João V, the wealthiest and most extravagant of all Portuguese monarchs. It is open from 10am to 1pm and 2.30–5pm daily, except Tuesday; arrive at least an hour before closing times to be sure of getting on a guided **tour** (which lasts for one hour).

The palace-convent

Begun in 1717 to honour a vow made on the birth of a royal heir, **Mafra Convent** was initially intended for just thirteen Franciscan friars. But as wealth poured in from the gold and diamonds of Brazil, João and his German court architect, Frederico Ludovice, amplified their plans to build a massive basilica, two royal wings and monastic quarters for 300 monks and 150 novices. The result, completed in thirteen years at a cost, crippling to the state, of over £4m (US$7m), is quite extraordinary and – on its own bizarre terms – extremely impressive.

In style the building is a mix of Baroque and Italianate neoclassicism, but it is the sheer magnitude and logistics that stand out. In the last stages of construction over 45,000 labourers were employed, while throughout the years of building there was a daily average of nearly 15,000; there are 5200 doorways, 2500 windows and two immense belltowers each containing over 50 bells. An apocryphal story records the astonishment of the Flemish bellmakers at the size of this order: on their querying it, and asking for payment in advance, Dom João retorted by doubling their price and his original requirement.

Parts of the convent are used by the military but an ingenious cadre of guides marches you around a sizeable enough portion. The **royal apartments** are a mix of the tedious and the shocking: the latter most obviously in the **Sala dos Troféus**, with its furniture (even chandeliers) constructed of antlers and upholstered in deerskin. Beyond are the **monastic quarters**, including cells, a pharmacy and a curious infirmary with beds positioned so the ailing monks could see mass performed. The highlight, however, is the magnificent Rococo **library** – brilliantly lit and rivalling Coimbra's in grandeur. Byron, shown the 35,000 volumes by one of the monks, was asked if "the English had any books in their country?"

The **basilica** itself, which can be seen outside the tour, is no less imposing, with the multicoloured marble designs of its floor mirrored in the ceiling decoration.

Practicalities

The **town** of Mafra is dull – and with frequent buses heading on to the lively resort of Ericeira (12km; see Estremadura chapter) there seems no point in lingering. Alternatively, you can see it as a daytrip from Sintra: there's a 10.30am bus from Sintra station and another back at 1.30pm. If you need to stay, the owner of the *Restaurante Primavera* (facing the palace across the main road) lets out clean and comfortable **rooms**; the restaurant here is good, too.

Queluz

The **palace** of QUELUZ (9am–1pm & 2–5pm; tours daily except Tues) is just twenty minutes by train from Lisbon's Rossio station (or thirty minutes on the way back from Sintra); it stands about 800 metres downhill from the station of QUELUZ-BELAS; ask there for the way to the palácio.

The building is as perfect a counterpoint to Mafra as you could imagine: an elegant, restrained structure regarded as the country's finest example of Rococo architecture. Its low, pink-washed wings enclose a series of rambling and beautiful eighteenth-century formal gardens, which, although preserved as a museum, don't quite feel like one – retaining instead a strong sense of its past royal owners. The palace is in fact still pressed into service for accommodating state guests and dignitaries, and hosts classical concerts in the summer months.

The palace was built by Dom Pedro III, husband and regent to his niece, Queen Maria I, who lived here throughout her 39-year reign (1777–1816), quite mad for the last 27, following the death of her eldest son, José. William Beckford (see Sintra) visited when the Queen's wits were dwindling, and ran races in the gardens with the Princess of Brazil's ladies-in-waiting; at other times firework displays were held above the ornamental canal and bullfights in the courtyards. It's all easy to imagine today. Visits can be enhanced, to, by a meal – or at least tea – in the original kitchen, the **Cozinha Velha**.

South of the Tejo: Setúbal and Its Coast

As late as the nineteenth century, the southern bank of the Tejo estuary was an underpopulated area used as a quarantine station for foreign visitors; the village of TRAFARIA here was so lawless that the police only visited when accompanied by members of the army. The huge **Ponte 25 de Abril** suspension bridge, inaugurated as the "Salazar Bridge" in 1966 and renamed after the 1974 revolution, finally ended what remained of this separation between "town and country". Since then, Lisbon has spilled over the river in a string of tatty industrial suburbs that spread east of the bridge, while to the west the Costa da Caparica has become a major holiday resort.

Setúbal

Some fifty kilometres from Lisbon, **SETÚBAL** is Portugal's third port and a major industrial centre. Once described by Hans Christian Andersen as a "terrestrial paradise", most of its visual charm is long gone but it's a friendly, enjoyable place – far more indulgent of tourists than Lisbon. If you're heading south and have time to break up the journey, it's worth stopping at least for a look at the remarkable **Igreja de Jesus**, designed by Diogo de Boitaca and possibly the first of all Manueline buildings. On a more prolonged visit, you can take in several maritime museums and some excellent **beaches** nearby.

Sights

The **Igreja de Jesus** is essentially late Gothic, with a huge, flamboyant doorway, but Boitaca transformed its interior design by introducing fantastically twisted pillars to support the vault. The rough granite surfaces of the pillars contrast with the delicacy of the blue-and-white *azulejos* around the high altar, which were added in the seventeenth century. The church stands on the Praça Miguel Bombarda along the main Avenida 5 de Outubro, about 400m from the train station or the town centre. Next door to the church, housed in the old monastic quarters, is a small but very fine **municipal museum** (Tues–Sun 10am–12.30pm & 2–5pm) with a superb collection of fifteenth- to sixteenth-century Portuguese art as well as sections dedicated to fifteenth- to eighteenth-century jewellery and to local archaeology. You might also climb up to the **Castelo São Felipe**, to the west of the town. This is now a *pousada*, but drinks are affordable and there are fine views over the mouth of the Sado estuary and the Troia peninsula.

A half-hour walk along the coast road, west out of Setúbal, takes you to ALBARQUEL, where a magnificently located **café-restaurant** sits on an outcrop of rock above the sea (reasonable café, expensive and highly renowned restaurant). For more on the continuation of this road, see the "Parque Natural da Arrábida" overpage.

Practicalities

Considering Setúbal's size, **accommodation** is in short supply. However, the **Turismo** (just off Avenida 5 de Outubro; 9am–5pm) runs a helpful accommodation service for **rooms** in private homes. Among **pensions** worth trying are:
Residencial Bom Fim, Praça Bocage (☎065/298 12). Inexpensive and central. ①.
Residencial Alentejana, Avda. Luisa Todi 124 (☎065/213 98). ②.
Residencial Bocage, Rua de São Cristovão 14 (☎065/215 98). ③.

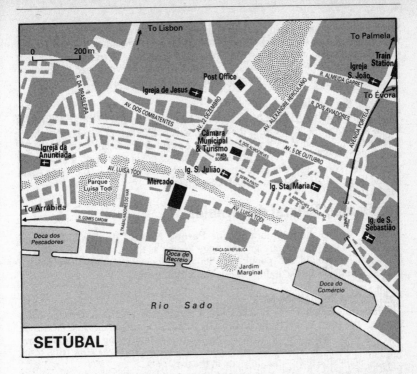

SETÚBAL

The town also has an extremely attractive **pousada**, the *São Filipe* (☎065/523 844; doubles around 20,000$00 – ⑤), which occupies the castle, high above the river, and a muncipal **campsite** (☎065/224 75).

Superb value fish and seafood **restaurants** abound in the dock area and around the western end of Avenida Luisa Todi; *O Capote*, in a small square just off the avenue is one of the best. If you're self-catering, you can buy your own fish from the market opposite the fountain of Luisa Todi. Further supplies are available from the *Pingo Doce* supermarket. In midsummer, you'll find the market area considerably expanded with clothes and touristy bric-a-brac.

Evening diversions in Setúbal are reasonably promising. You could start drinking at the *Cactus* on Praça Bocage and finish at *Torib's* which stays open till about 3am. Between bars you might visit one of the two pool halls or the music club *Absurdia* (usually no entrance charge), or the **Teatro Luisa Todi**, which stages shows at weekends and often runs art-house movies during the week. Alternatively, try the *Seagull* disco, a ten-minute drive along the coast road (2000$00 entrance, including three beers), or the less pretentious *Leo Taurus*, five minutes' drive along the N10 Lisbon (country) road, where entrance is often free.

Tróia

Setúbal's traditional **beaches**, reached by frequent ferry (long queues for cars in summer) from the town, are on the **Península de Tróia**, a large sand spit hemming in the Sado estuary. The peninsula was settled by the Phoenicians and subsequently by the Romans, whose town of *Cetobriga* appears to have been overwhelmed by a tidal wave in the fifth century. There are some desultory remains, including tanks for salting fish, opposite the marina on the landward shore. Once a wilderness of sand and wildflowers, Tróia must once have been magnificent, but it's now a heavily developed concrete resort. To avoid the worst, and the crowds, be prepared to walk for twenty minutes or so south along the beach.

Palmela: the castle-pousada

The small town of **PALMELA**, a couple of kilometres to the north of Setúbal, is worth a visit for the views from the **castle**, which, like that of Setúbal, has been restored and extended as a **pousada**, the *Castelo de Palmela* (☎01/235 12 26; doubles 20,000$00 – ⑥). A fine place to stay, the castle is also worth a trip for the views, which on a clear day encompass Lisbon, Setúbal, the Sado and Tróia – and for the beautiful, *azulejo*-lined chapel of São Filipe.

The Parque Natural da Arrábida

Between Setúbal and Sesimbra lies the **Parque Natural da Arrábida**, whose main feature is the 500-metre granite ridge known as the Serra da Arrábida, visible for miles around and popular for its wild mountain scenery. The twisted pillars of Setúbal's Igreja de Jesus were hewn from here.

Approaches through the park

The **bus** from Setúbal to Sesimbra takes the main road well back from the coast through the town of **VILA FRESCA DE AZEITÃO**, where the José Maria da Fonseca **wine vaults** can be visited. The free tour is interesting and a good introduction to the local *Setúbal Moscatel*. There is a **campsite**, *Picheleiros* (☎065/208 13 22) just outside town – the only site in the park area.

If you have transport, a better route – not covered by buses – is the twisting **coast road N10-4**, which isn't served by public transport. Nestling in the cliffs down this road is the sixteenth-century **Convento da Arrábida**, whose crumbling white buildings with their stunning ocean views are the home of a silent Franciscan order. Nearby is the tiny harbour village of **PORTINHO DA ARRÁBIDA**, which has a couple of excellent, clean beaches, wonderful out of season and always quieter than Tróia. There are **prehistoric cave** sites nearby and a fantastic **restaurant** by the water's edge. Next along is **GALAPOS**, arguably the best beach along this whole coast.

Sesimbra

Although in the throes of rapid development as a resort, with apartment buildings mushrooming on the outskirts, the centre of the little fishing town of **SESIMBRA**, with its steep narrow streets, manages to retain a peaceful and unhurried atmosphere. Indeed, most mornings it's impossible to walk around without tripping over fish baskets, nets being mended and lines being untangled. If there's a drawback to the place, it's the rather tiny strip of beach, located between the town and fishing port.

Sesimbra is well connected by **bus** with Lisbon (Praça de Espanha terminal), Cacilhas and Setúbal. Coming from Lisbon in summer, it's quicker to take the ferry across to Cacilhas and pick up a bus there, as the main bridge road is often jammed solid with traffic.

Around the town

A **Moorish castle** dominates the town from its vantage point, a stiff half-hour climb above. Within the fortress are a church and various ruins, while a circuit of battlements gives amazing panoramas over the surrounding countryside and coastline. Back in the town, the **municipal museum** in the Palácio do Bispo, features archaeological and historical finds from the area. The best of the churches, the Manueline **Igreja da Mai**, is on nearby Rua João de Deus.

The most attractive corner of town is undoubtedly the original fishing port, **Porto de Abrigo**, with its brightly painted boats, daily fish auctions, and stalls selling a superb variety of temptingly well-priced shellfish. It's a pleasant walk from the centre, along the Avenida dos Naufragos – follow the signs towards the **Forte do Cavalo**, where the local anglers try their hand at sea fishing.

Rooms, food and nightlife

Sesimbra is largely a day-trip resort for Lisbon residents, though the wealthier ones have bought up second homes here for the summer. **Accommodation** is sparse at any time of year, with just a handful of pensions and pricey hotels. Your best bet is to try for private rooms through the **Turismo** (9am–6pm; closed 12.30–2pm in winter), on the seafront at Avenida dos Náufragos 17 (☎01/223 3304). There's also a well-located **campsite** at *Forte do Cavalo* (☎01/223 39 05), just past the fishing port.

The more modest pension/hotel possibilities are:

Residencial Chic, Travessa Xavier da Silva 2–6 (☎01/223 31 10). Dead central and with more than adequate rooms. ③.

Pensão Náutico, off Rua Deneral Humberto Delgado. Another comfortable place, up the hill and a little more secluded. ③.

Hotel Espadarte, Avda. 25 de Abril (☎01/223 31 89). Decent, fairly upmarket hotel. ④.

Among the dozens of excellent **fish and seafood restaurants**, try *Sesimbrense*, on the corner of Largo do Município and Rua Jorge Nunes, or for a splurge, *Restaurante Algamar* at 26 Adenida dos Naufragos. Cheaper places, with less of a range of shellfish but consistently good fish, are *O Pescador* and *Tasca do Marítimo* on the square above the Turismo. Finally, two **nightclubs** have a bit of a summer reputation: *Clip*, on Rua P.F. Marques, and *Belle Epoch*, off the Largo do Calvario; both stay open till 4am.

West of Sesimbra: Cabo Espichel and Aldeia do Meco

Six buses a day make the eleven-kilometre journey west from Sesimbra to the **Cabo Espichel**, a desolate end-of-the-world plateau where the road winds up at a wide church square. This is enclosed on three sides by ramshackle eighteenth-century pilgrimage lodgings, which are now hardly used. Beyond, wild and wind-swept cliffs drop almost vertically several hundred feet into the Atlantic.

A few kilometres to the north and up the coast from here is the village of **ALDEIA DO MECO** with four buses a day from Sesimbra, providing easy access to the southern beaches of the **Costa da Caparica** (see p.81 for the northern section). Again these are prone to overcrowding in July and August, but they can be almost deserted and extremely warm and pleasant in, say, May or October. Several villages have **rooms** for rent and there is a growing number of official **campsites** – a particularly good one at FETAIS (☎01/223 29 78), between Aldeia and Praia do Penedo. The best strip of beach is by the lagoon at LAGOA DE ALBUFEIRA: it is extremely clean and excellent for windsurfing.

travel details

Local Trains

FROM ROSSIO STATION

Sintra Line Every 16min to Queluz (20min) and Sintra (50min). Last train back from Sintra departs 1.47am.

Oeste Line 13 daily to Torres Vedras (70–90min), Caldas da Rainha (2hr–2hr 30min) and Óbidos (2hr 30min); 6 to Leiria (3hr–3hr 30min); 4 to Figueira da Foz (3hr 45min). For most of the trains you have to change at Cacém on the Sintra line.

FROM CAIS DO SODRÉ STATION

Cascais Line Every 20min to Estoril (28min) and Cascais (32min). Every other train stops at Belém (7min).

Trains to the South and the Algarve

FROM TERREIRO DO PAÇO (FLUVIAL STATION: VIA BARREIRO, 30min)

Algarve Line 2 daily to Alcácer do Sal (2hr), Albufeira (5hr), Faro (5hr), Tavira (6hr) and Vila Real de Santo António (7hr), plus 2 fast trains daily to Albufeira and Faro. On all trains, change at Tunes for Lagos and Faro for Tavira/Vila Real.

Alentejo Line 3 daily via Casa Branca (2hr) to Évora (3hr) and Beja (3hr 30min). *CP* bus connections at Évora to Estremoz, Vila Viçosa and Reguengos de Monsaraz. Also on this lines is a **night train to the Algarve**, via Beja.

Setúbal Line Hourly to Palmela (75min) and Setúbal (90min).

Other Long-Distance Trains

FROM SANTA APOLÓNIA STATION

Norte Line 10 daily to Coimbra (2hr 30min), Aveiro (3hr) and Porto (3–4hr); some are faster, more expensive express services. Change at Alfarelos (2hr 10min) for Figueira da Foz (15 daily; 20min). *CP* bus connections from Sernada do Vouga to Viseu.

Leste Line 4 daily to Abrantes (2hr 30min), Portalegre (4hr 30min), Elvas (5hr 30min) and Badajoz, Spain (6hr).

Beira-Baixa Line 6 daily to Abrantes (2hr 30min), Castelo Branco (3hr 30min–4hr 30min) and Covilhã (4hr 30min–6hr), with 3 continuing to Guarda (7hr 15min).

Beira-Alta Line 5 daily to Coimbra (2hr 30min) and Guarda (5hr 45min–7hr).

Galiza (Galicia) Line 3 daily to Porto (4hr); connections thence to Valença and into Spain.

International Trains

FROM SANTA APOLÓNIA STATION

Madrid 1 day and 1 night train to Madrid–Chamartin (day 8hr 15min; night 10hr 30min). Both via Entroncamento (1hr), Abrantes (1hr 30min) and Marvão (3hr).

Paris 1 daily (2.35pm) express to Paris–Austerlitz (26hr) via Coimbra B (2hr 30min) and Guarda (6hr 30min).

Buses

For details of bus termini see p.44.

Mafra/Ericeira (10 daily; 90–110min); Torres Vedra (12 daily; 2hr 30min); Sesimbra (hourly; 2hr–1hr 30min); Peniche (8 in 3hr, 2 in 100min); Nazaré (3 daily; 4hr); Tomar (3 daily; 2hr 30min); Évora (6 daily; 3hr 30min).

Daily *Beiras Express* to Leiria (2hr 30min), Coimbra (3hr 30min), Viseu (5hr), Guarda (7hr) and Vilar Formoso (8hr).

Also **express buses** to the **Algarve** (Lagos, Faro, Albufeira, etc) in around 4hr; year-round service, very frequent in summer; details from travel agents or from the tourist offices.

Hitching

Heading **south** (to the Algarve or Madrid), try by the Praça de Espanha bus station or buy a ferry–train ticket to Setúbal, then walk 3km east along N10 to the A2 junction. For the **north**, take the bus to the airport and stand by the A1 (Coimbra/Porto) approach road – or even further back by the tollgate at the beginning of A1.

Flights

Porto Hourly flights on *LAR* and *Portugalia*.

Faro Daily flights on *LAR* and *Portugalia*.

Bragança, **Covilhã**, **Vila Real**, **Viseu** Flights two or more times weekly on *LAR* and *Portugalia*.

Portimão (summer only) and **Chaves** weekly flights on *LAR*.

Also *LAR* and *TAP* flights to **Madeira** and the **Azores**.

CHAPTER TWO

ESTREMADURA AND RIBATEJO

The **Estremadura** and **Ribatejo** regions have played a crucial role in each phase of the nation's history – and the monuments are there to prove it. Encompassing a comparatively small area, they boast an extraordinary concentration of vivid architecture and engaging towns. **Alcobaça, Batalha**, and **Tomar** – the most exciting buildings in Portugal – all lie within a ninety-minute bus ride of one another. But even without them the two regions' attractions are compelling and immensely varied: ferries sail from Peniche to the utopian **Berlenga Island**; **Óbidos** is a completely walled medieval village; spectacular underground caverns can be visited at **Mira d'Aire**, and tremendous castles at **Porto de Mós, Leiria** (itself an elegant town), and on **Almourol**, an islet in the middle of the Tejo.

The Estremaduran coast – the lower half of the **Costa de Prata** – provides an excellent complement to all this, and if you're exclusively after sun and sand it's no mean alternative to the Algarve. **Nazaré** and **Ericeira** are justifiably the most popular resorts but there are scores of less developed beaches. If you want more isolation, try the area around **São Martinho do Porto**, or the coastline west of **Leiria**, backed most of the way by the medieval pine forest of **Pinhal de Leiria**.

Virtually all of these highlights fall within the boundaries of Estremadura, which, with its fertile rolling hills, is second in beauty only to Minho. The flat, bull-breeding lands of **Ribatejo** (literally "banks-of-the-Tejo") fade into the dull expanses of northwestern Alentejo and there's no great reason to cross the river unless you're pushing on to Évora or can catch up with one of the region's lively traditional **festivals**. The wildest and most famous of these are the *Festas do Colete Encarnado* of **Vila Franca de Xira**, with Pamplona-style bull-running through the streets; for details of this and others see p.123.

Ericeira and Torres Vedras

October 5, 1910 marked the end of Portuguese monarchy. Dom Manuel II – "The Unfortunate" – was woken in his palace at Mafra by reports that an angry Republican mob was advancing from Lisbon. Terrified, he fled to the harbour at **ERICEIRA** and sailed into the welcoming arms of the British at Gibraltar, to live out the rest of his days in a villa at Twickenham. Baedeker's guidebook, published the same year, described Ericeira as "a fishing village with excellent sea bathing" and recent development has done little to change the town's original character. There are one or two large hotels and a few nightclubs, and the place is doubtless on the way to resort status – but it hasn't quite happened, yet.

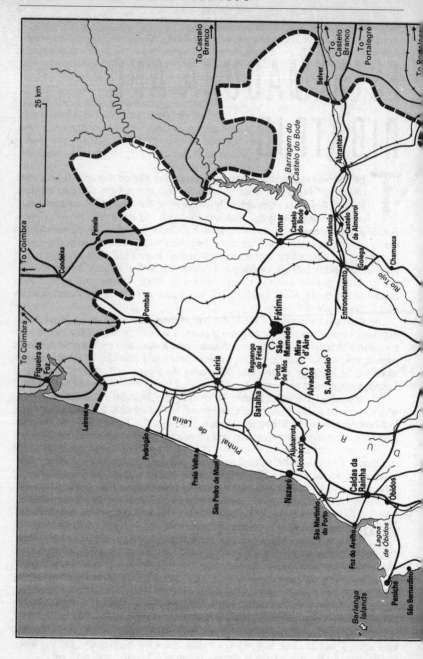

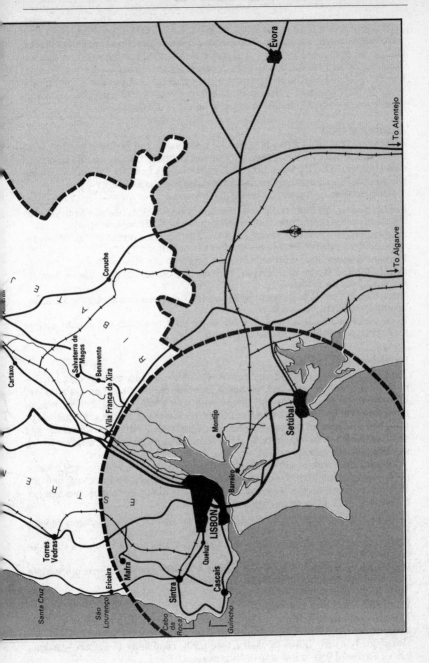

At the centre of town is the Praça da República, a small square busy with side-walk cafés, wonderful pastry shops, and a cinema that shows mainly subtitled Hollywood films. Activity, bars, and restaurants are all concentrated on Rua Dr. Eduardo Burnay, which leads from a corner of the Praça to the town's main **beach**. A second beach, prettier, much less crowded, and popular with surfers – Praia do São Sebastião – lies about 25 minutes' walk north, past the next headland. There's a small, primitive **campsite** here, but not much else.

Accommodation

Accommodation in Ericeira is generally good value and pleasant, though most hotels and pensions are not open all year round (those that are should be a good deal cheaper). The **Turismo** on Rua Mendes Leal is typically helpful for **private rooms** (there are numerous *quartos* above bars and restaurants).

For **pensions or hotels**, try one of the following:

Pensão Severa, Rua Fonte do Cabo 64. Neat and modern, with its fake pine furnishings, on one of four parallel streets between the main Praça and the old fishing quarter. ②.

Pensão Gomes, Travessa J. Mola, just off Praça da República (☎061/636 19). Oldish, but clean and fresh with friendly, if somewhat eccentric, staff. ③.

Pensão Fortunato, Rua Dr. Eduardo Burnay 7 (☎061/628 29). Pleasant. ③.

Pensão Virmus, Rua Prudêncio Franco Trindade 25-1° (☎061/638 30). Clean, modern and airy with a lively bar to boot. ③.

Hotel Vilazul, Calçada da Balcia 10 (☎061/636 69). Good value considering the breakfasts, balconies, and private bathrooms. ④.

Hotel Pedro o Pescador, Rua Dr. Eduardo Burnay 2 (☎061/625 04). A quiet, elegant family place, with an English seaside hotel feel. ④.

Restaurants and nightlife

The lively *pastelarias* around the Praça da República are recommended for lunch – or tea-time indulgences – and the *Snack Bar Bela Sombra*, right on Praia do Sul, has a good range of dishes and prices, with very good seafood. For something more leisurely try *Restaurante Severa* (beneath the *pensão* of the same name), or the *Toca do Caboz* on the same street. The *Restaurante Patio dos Marialvas*, just south of the Praça da República, is also good value, with an *ementa turistica* which includes *arroz de marisco*.

Ericeira after dark is surprisingly animated, popular even with young *Lisboetas* up for a night out from the capital. *Barzinho*, in Ribamar up the coast, and *Big Surprise*, in Seixal on the Mafra road, are a couple of popular out-of-town venues. In Ericeira itself, a few recommended joints:

Disco-Bar Pirata, attached to the *Hotel Turismo* at the top of Praia do Sul. Biggest in town, slightly pricey and exclusive but always a hectic buzz.

Ferro Velho, Rua Dr. Eduardo Burnay (10.30pm–4am). Less trendy, cheaper, a shade too cramped, but fun.

Bar Neptuno, Travessa J. Mola. A real good-time bar with a two-for-the-price-of-one happy hour, frequent live music, and intriguing upstairs rooms.

Onwards – and São Lourenço

The bus north from Ericeira passes a fine series of untouched **beaches**, the best being at SÃO LOURENÇO, a peaceful hamlet with a sandy campsite. There are also virtually hourly buses to **Mafra** (see p.90), continuing to Lisbon – making Ericeira a useful first or last stop in Estremadura.

Torres Vedras: battles and beaches

TORRES VEDRAS, 27km north and inland of Ericeira, is well known in European history: it took its name from the Duke of Wellington's famous defence (*Linhas de Torres*) in the **Peninsular War** against Napoleonic France.

The **Linhas de Torres** consisted of a chain of 150 hilltop fortresses, stretching some 40km from the sea directly west of Torres Vedras to Alhandra, where the Tejo widens out into a huge lake. Astonishingly, they were built in a matter of months and without any apparent reaction from the French. Here in 1810 Wellington and his forces retired, comfortably supplied by sea and completely unassailable; the French, frustrated by impossibly long lines of communication and by British scorching of the land north of the Lines, eventually had to retreat back to Spain in utter despair. Thus from a last line of defence, Wellington completely reversed the progress of the campaign – storming after the disconsolate enemy to effect a series of swift and devastating victories.

The town

In view of this historical glory, modern Torres Vedras is somewhat disappointing. There are a few ruins of the old **fortresses** and a couple of imposing sixteenth-century churches, but all this is swamped by a dull sprawl of recent buildings. Booklets and old maps can be read at the **Turismo** (in the central Praça da República) and directly facing it is the **Museu Municipal** (Tues–Sun 10am–noon & 2–6pm) with a room devoted to the Peninsular War. Unless you get hooked on the local wine, there's not much else to delay your progress.

If you need somewhere to stay, consult the Turismo, which displays a list of **pensions** in its window. In general, however, you'd probably be better off taking one of the many buses on to Peniche, Óbidos, or the popular local resort of Praia de Santa Cruz. The **bus station** is just uphill from the **train station**.

Praia de Santa Cruz and other beaches

Most people at **PRAIA DE SANTA CRUZ** are locals from Torres Vedras, and this gives the place a friendly, easygoing feel, as well as some excellent places to eat. The beach itself is long and wide and there's a **campsite** just five minutes' walk from the sea. By the bus station is the *Pensão Miramar*, one of a number of modest-priced **pensions**.

Quieter resorts – uncrowded outside public holidays or summer weekends – are to be found to the north of here and are easily reached on buses heading to Peniche. **AREIA BRANCA** ("White Sand"), 21km from Torres Vedras, is one of the best, with a **campsite** and very congenial, beachside **youth hostel** (☎061/ 421 27); nearby LOURINHÃ has restaurants and a bank. **CONSOLAÇÃO**, just south of Peniche, also has a good beach and small **campsite**.

Peniche and Berlenga Island

PENICHE, impressively enclosed by ramparts and one of Portugal's most active fishing ports, is the embarkation point for the Ilha Berlenga. As late as the twelfth century the town was itself an island but the area has silted up and is now joined to the mainland by a narrow isthmus with gently sloping beaches on either side and a campsite between them. It's an attractive place for a brief stay, of interest in its own right (above all for the fortress which dominates the south side of town), and with a great market on the *campo*, held on the last Thursday of the month.

The Fortaleza and beaches

The sixteenth-century **Fortaleza** of Peniche was one of the dictator Salazar's most notorious jails. Greatly expanded in the 1950s and 1960s to accommodate the growing crowds of political prisoners, it later served as a temporary refugee camp for *retornados* from the colonies. Today it's a **museum** (Tues–Sun 3–7pm), with the familiar mix of local archaeology, natural history, and craft displays, among which you can still see the old cells (on the top floor), the solitary-confinement pens (*segredos*), and the visitors' grille (*parlatório*): an eerie reminder of Portugal's fascist past.

Just outside the city walls, off the fine **north beach** of the peninsula, there's a **traditional boatyard**. It's fascinating to watch the shipwrights here manoeuvring huge timbers into position to form the skeletal framework of a new fishing vessel. If you've got more time to spare there's a beautiful ninety-minute walk beyond the fortress – out to the tip of **Cabo Carvoeiro**, the rugged, rock-pillared and light-house-tipped peninsula beyond Peniche.

Another rewarding walk, a few kilometres to the north of Peniche, is to **Baleal**, an islet-village, joined to the mainland by a narrow strip of fine sand.

Accommodation and restaurants

Most visitors to Peniche end up staying in **private rooms**. If you aren't offered one on arrival, make your way down to the **Turismo** (☎062/79571), in the gardens by the ramparts, or look out for *quartos* or *dormidas* signs in the windows, especially on Rua Marechal. The earlier you arrive, the more reassuring the choice.

Best of the **pensions** is the comfortable and modern *Pensão Flita*, near the bus station at Largo do Francisco Freire 12 (☎062/72 91 90; ②). Second choices are *Residencial Cristal*, Rua 1 de Decembro (☎062/727 24; ②), and the *Pensão Aviz*, near the Turismo on Largo Jacob Pereira (☎062/721 53; ①).

If you plan on **camping**, try to arrive early in the day and, if the municipal campsite is full, get yourself on the waiting list – vacancies are established at 1.30pm (be there on the dot). The site is a fair walk, or a taxi ride, north of town, near the Baleal beach (see above).

There is a fine array of **restaurants** along the Avenida do Mar – most of them good value, serving huge portions. Just round the corner from the *Pensão Félita*, on the way out of the town centre, is a wonderful **bakery/snack bar** for breakfast or picnic makings, usually full of fishwives in knitted triangular capes and socks, swinging plastic bags of fish as they sip *bicas* and exchange news.

Berlenga Island

The **ILHA BERLENGA**, ten kilometres offshore and just visible from the cape, is a dreamlike place – rather like a Scottish isle transported to warmer climes. Just one square mile in extent, it is the largest island of a tiny archipelago, with a jagged coastline of grottoes, miniature fjords, and extraordinary rock formations. In summer the sea is calm, crystal clear, and perfect for snorkelling and diving – rare in the Atlantic.

The only people permitted to live here are a couple of dozen fishermen, as the whole island has been declared a **National Bird Reserve**, the home of thousands upon thousands of seagulls and eiders (as in down), perched in every conceivable cranny and clearly plotting to leave their mark on every possible victim. Makeshift paths are marked out with stones, and guardians watch out for visitors straying out of bounds and disturbing the birds.

Human (and also rat) life revolves around the main **landing dock** with its colour-washed fishing boats and small sandy **beach**. It can get crowded and noisy down here at the height of the season – it takes very few people to make the place seem packed – though the only actual buildings here are a cluster of huts, a small **bar-restaurant**, a rather basic shop, and a lighthouse.

A short walk beyond the lighthouse, on an islet joined by the narrowest of causeways, is the seventeenth-century **Forte de São João Baptista**. Formerly a youth hostel, and then a *pensão*, the fort is currently in the throes of restoration as a **pousada**. Until this opens, there are no rooms available on the island. However, there is a free **campsite**, which clings to a strictly limited site on the rocky slopes above the harbour. If you want to stay here, you must obtain a **permit** from the Turismo in Peniche. In summer, there are often more applicants than permits, so you may have to wait a day or two. If you're organised, you can write to the tourist office (Turismo, Rua Alexandre Herculano, Peniche) and book in advance.

Rowing boats can be hired at the jetty to explore the intricacies of the coastline, though you may prefer to go in something with a motor if there's any motion on the sea (you can get a guided trip for a few hundred escudos). Don't miss the **Furado Grand**e, a fantastic tunnel 75 metres long which culminates in the aptly named **Cova do Sonho** (Dream Cove) with its precipitous cliffs.

Ferries and permits

The **ferry** from Peniche to Berlenga takes one hour – longer if the sea is rough. The service operates from June 1 to September 20; currently, there are twice daily ferries during July and August (9am & 11am; return at 4pm & 6pm) and once daily in June and September (10am; return at 5pm). In July and August you may have to get up at 6am to secure a boat ticket for the same day. Tickets cost 300$00 one way, 500$00 return.

If the weather is difficult, times will change and boats may be cancelled. In any case, be sure to go without breakfast – it's a rough ride, as evinced by a grim collection of buckets under the seats!

Óbidos

ÓBIDOS, "The Wedding City", was the traditional bridal gift of the kings of Portugal to their queens. The custom was begun in 1282 by Dom Dinis and Dona Isabel, and the town can hardly have changed in appearance since then. It is very small and completely enclosed by lofty medieval walls: streets are cobbled, houses whitewashed with bright blue and yellow borders, and at all points steep staircases wind up to the ramparts, where you can gaze across a ludicrously fable-like countryside of windmills and vineyards.

It's touristy, of course, but perhaps less than you might expect. You can walk right around the town along its perimeter **walls** – a narrow and at times hair-raising walkway with no handrails, and from this vantage point the town still seems to have a private life of its own. If you stay the night, the feeling is reinforced, as the town slowly empties to regain its charm.

Around town

The most striking building in town is Dom Dinis's massively-towered **Castelo**, which has been converted to a very splendid *parador*. It's worth a visit for a meal or drink, even if you couldn't contemplate staying there.

Below the castle, the principal focus of the streets is the parish church, the **Igreja de Santa Maria**, in the central Praça – chosen for the wedding of the ten-year-old child king, Afonso V, and his eight-year-old cousin, Isabel, in 1444. It dates mainly from the Renaissance, though the interior is lined with seventeenth-century blue *azulejos* in a homely manner typical of Portuguese churches. On the left-hand wall is an elaborate tomb designed by Nicolas Chanterene, an influential French sculptor active in Portugal in the first half of the sixteenth century.

The *retábulo* in a side chapel opposite this tomb was painted by **Josefa de Óbidos**, one of the finest of all Portuguese painters – and one of the few women artists afforded any reputation by art historians. Born at Seville in 1634, Josefa spent most of her life in a convent at Óbidos. She began her career as an etcher and miniaturist and this remarkable handling of detail is carried through into her later full-scale religious works. Another of her paintings, a portrait, can be seen in the adjacent **museum** (daily 10am–1pm & 2–5pm).

Óbidos also, a little suprisingly, boasts a modern **sculpture museum**, located in a building opposite the Turismo. This is worth a look both for the creations and for the views from the top floor. On Saturday mornings, the town hosts an excellent morning **market** – still predominantly a local affair. If you're on the lookout for things to buy, the old people's **handicrafts centre**, on the main street, Rua Direita, has a good variety of nicely made items.

Practicalities

Orientation is little problem in Óbidos. **Buses** stop outside the **Porta da Vila**, the principal town gate in the fortifications. From here **Rua Direita** leads straight through the town to the **Turismo** (☎062/952 34). The **train station** is a short walk downhill from the gate.

Accommodation is on the expensive side, unless you get one of a handful of private rooms, advertised in upstairs windows in a few of the houses and sometimes touted to new arrivals at the bus or train stations.

Pensions and hotels include:

Casa de Hóspedes Madeira, Rua Direita (☎062/952 12). The cheapest in town and nicely positoned within the walls. ①.

Residencial Martim de Freitas, Estrada Nacional 8 – on the road to the station (☎062/95 91 85; ②). Very pleasant: huge rooms with four-poster beds. ②.

Albergaria Raina Santa Isabel, Rua Direita (☎062/95 93 23). The best moderate-priced rooms, with balconies looking onto the main street. ④.

Albergaria Josefa d'Óbidos, Rua Dr. João de Ornelas (☎062/95 95 33). Reasonably central position, just outside the walls, but a bit dull. ④.

Estalagem do Convento, Rua Dr. João de Ornelas (☎062/95 92 14). An old convent, rather tackily converted. ⑤.

Pousada do Castelo (☎062/95 91 05). One of the country's finest *paradors* – around 20,000$00 for a double room. ⑥.

Good value **places to eat** include the *Café 1 de Dezembro*, next to the church of São Pedro, and *Bar Império Romano*, down a steep flight of steps by the Santa Cruz church. The *Estalagem do Convento* has a pricier but excellent restaurant.

In the second week of October, the town hosts a long-established **festival of early music**, with free evening performances in many of the churches.

Caldas: a Royal Spa

Five kilometres north of Óbidos, **CALDAS DA RAINHA** ("Queen's Spa") was put firmly on the map by Dona Leonor. Passing by in her carriage, she was so impressed by the strong sulphuric waters that she founded a hospital here, initiating four centuries of noble and royal patronage.

That was in 1484 but the town was to reach the peak of its popularity in the nineteenth century when, all over Europe, spas became as much social as medical institutions. The English Gothic novelist, William Beckford, stopping off on his journey to Batalha and Alcobaça (recorded in *Travels in Spain and Portugal*, one of the best nineteenth-century travel books), found it a lively if depressing place – "every tenth or twelfth person a rheumatic or palsied invalid, with his limbs all atwist, and his mouth all awry, being conveyed to the baths in a chair".

Disappointingly little remains of all the royal wealth poured into the spa, though it is still a pleasant stop on your way to Nazaré or Alcobaça. From the central **Praça da República**, which hosts a fruit market every morning, the **royal spa hospital**, still very much in use, is a short walk downhill. If the idea appeals, you can bathe in a series of warm, sulphurous swimming pools for a nominal entrance fee. Protruding from the back of the spa is the striking Manueline belfry of **Nossa Senhora do Pópulo**, the hospital church. There's a Virgin and Child by Josefa de Óbidos (see opposite) in the sacristy.

At the back of the adjoining park is the **Museu de José Malhoa** (Tues–Sun 10am–5pm), devoted to sculpture, paintings, and ceramics from the turn of the century, when local artist Rafael Bordalo Pinheiro made Caldas something of an arts-and-crafts centre. His own *piece de resistance*, on display here, is a series of lifesized ceramic figures representing the Passion.

Practicalities

It's a short walk from either **bus** or **train station** to the **Praça da República**, where you'll find a **Turismo** (☎062/345 11). Due to the spa, there's a fair amount of **accommodation**, most of it reasonably priced. Two of the most convenient pensions are to be found in Rua Almirante Cândido dos Reis, just off the Praça da Republica: the *Pensão Portugal* at no. 22 (☎062/342 80; ②) and *Residencial Europeia* at no. 64 (☎062/347 81; ③). There's also an *Orbitur* **campsite**, centrally located in the Parque Rainha Dona Leonor.

For **food**, it's hard to beat the spit-roasts and grills at the *Churrasqueria Zé do Barrete* (closed Sun), midway down Rua Almirante Cândido dos Reis on the Travessa da Cova da Onça, though the *Pensão Portugal* has pretty substantial meals, too. Ironically, given the intentions of spa visitors, the town's speciality is *cavacas*, meringues piled high and dripping with sugar. Caldas also remains famed for its traditional **ceramics**, which include peculiar phallus-shaped objects: don't miss the July **Feira Nacional da Cerâmica**.

North along the coast to Nazaré

Heading **north from Caldas**, towards **Nazaré**, buses and trains loop inland, touching the coast only at **São Martinho do Porto**. If you have your own transport, bear off left at Caldas on the N360, which takes you past the **Lagoa de Óbidos**, and then out along the coast on a beautiful clifftop route – a much better option than the busy N8. At **FOZ DO ARELHO**, the first resort you come to, there's a fine beach, fronted by a **campsite** and a couple of decent **pensions**: the *Penedo Furado* (☎062/97 96 10; ④) and *Foz Praia* (☎062/97 94 13; ④).

São Martinho do Porto

SÃO MARTINHO DO PORTO is the main resort between Peniche and Nazaré, and was until recently – like the rest of this stretch – hardly developed. Things have been changing fast over the past few years, however, and this is now one of the more exploited Estremaduran resorts. In midseason, or at weekends, it's probably not worth the struggle to find a room – or even a place in the campsite.

The reason for São Martinho's tourist success is down to its **beach**: a vast sweep of sand which curls around a landlocked bay to form a natural swimming pool. This shelter makes it one of the warmest places to swim on the west coast, with the sands sloping down into calm, shallow, solar-heated water. If you want something more bracing – or less crowded – there's also a a good northern beach, around the bay.

The best bets for budget **accommodation** are the *Residencial Carvalhos* (☎062/981 12; ②) and *Pensão Americano* (062/981 70; ③) or **private rooms** (bookable through the Turismo, if you're not offered one on arrival); other hotels in the resort are quite expensive. There's also a **campsite** by the railway lines and a new **youth hostel** (☎062/999 52) at Mont São Martinho, just out of town on the Alcobaça road. Another youth hostel, the *Pousada de Juventude de São Martinho* (☎062/995 06), is located at the village of Alfererão, 6km inland.

Nazaré

After years of advertising itself as the most "picturesque" seaside village in Portugal, **NAZARÉ** has finally more or less destroyed itself in the process. In summer, the crowds are way too much for the place to cope with, and the enduring characteristics are not so much "gentle traditions", as trinket stalls and high prices. It's a pity, as local traditions happily coexisted with the tourists for some time, women weaving barefoot through the town bearing immense trays of fish on their heads, and the fishermen sitting unperturbed on the beach, mending their nets beside brilliantly painted sardine boats. Nowadays, however, the boats have all but disappeared to a new harbour, fifteen minutes' walk from the village, where cranes have replaced the oxen once used to haul in the boats. In the old village, meanwhile, the traditional dress worn by women drying sardines on the beach looks increasingly quaint and phony.

On public transport, it's simplest to arrive at Nazaré by bus. There are regular connections with most towns in the region, and the bus station is centrally located on the Avenida Vieira Guimarães, parallel to the main drag, Avenida da República. The nearest **train station** is at VALADO, six kilometres inland, though a local bus (from the town's main square) shuttles arrivals into Nazaré.

The village and beaches

Nazaré was originally based on a rock face, 110 metres above the present sprawl of towering holiday apartment buildings – the legacy, by most accounts, of pirate raids which continued well into the nineteeth century. Legend tells of a twelfth-century knight, Dom Fuas Roupinho, who, while out hunting, was led up the cliff by a deer. The deer dived off into the void and Dom Fuas was saved from following by the timely vision of **Nossa Senhora da Nazaré**, in whose name the church was subsequently built.

You can reach this church, and the surrounding **Sítio** district, on a **funicular**, which rumbles up almost continuously from 7.30am to midnight. There is an enjoyable *miradouro* up top, though the shrine itself is unimpressive, despite an icon carved by Saint Joseph and painted by Saint Luke (a handy partnership active throughout Europe). The church does, however, host a well-attended **Romaria** (Sept 8–10) with processions, folk dancing, and bullfights. The Sítio bullring also stages Saturday night *touradas* in summer.

The problem with Nazaré's **beaches** – grand tent-studded sweeps of clean sand, stretching out to the north beyond the headland of Sítio, and south across the narrow Alcoa estuary – is that swimming is dangerous. The Atlantic can be fierce along the Estremaduran coast, so, for safety's sake, stick to the patrolled main beach where the bathers are packed in as tightly as the sardine boats. Alternatively, tramp southwards towards the village of GRALHA, where you'll find a number of small coves and one sheltered beach isolated enough to be a popular spot for nude bathing.

Accommodation
Pensions in Nazaré are heavily booked throughout the summer but **rooms** are plentiful: you'll be accosted at the bus station by their owners. If you have problems finding a place, consult one of the two **turismos**: in the main square in town or down on the seafront.

The more promising **pension possibilities** include:

Casa Durão, Rua do Elevador. The cheapest and tiniest rooms in town. ①.

Pensão Leonardo, Praça Dr. Manuel de Arriaga (☎062/512 59). All the basic necessities and it's right in the centre, above a decent restaurant. ③.

Pensão Europa, Praça Dr. Manuel de Arriaga (☎062/515 36). Much the same as the neighbouring *Leonardo*, and also over a restaurant. Very friendly. ③.

Residencial Cubata, Avda. da República 6 (☎062/517 06). Tacky-looking but respectable enough. ③.

Residencial Beira-Mar, Avda. da República 40 (☎062/514 58). Right on the beachfront and very pleasant, as it should be, at the price; large breezy rooms and private bathrooms. ④.

Restaurants
The main concentration of **restaurants** is around the main Praça Dr. Manuel de Arriaga and Avenida da República. Good choices include:

Adega Oceano, Avda. da República 51. Well-priced and welcoming.

Tasquinha, Rua Adrião Batalha. Another fine place, just off the Avda. da República.

Aquário, Largo das Caldeiras 13. One of the best (and cheapest) for a seafood blow-out.

Casa Bizarro, Rua António Carvalho Laranjo. Follow the sign from the beachfront near the *Residencial Beira-Mar*. Just off the main drag but all the better for that in terms of price and atmosphere. Again, great value seafood and house wine.

Other practicalities
There is no bank in Nazaré but **currency** can be exchanged at the *Viagens Maré* travel office, next to the *Hotel Maré* on Praça Dr. Manuel de Arriaga, and there are **post offices** in the town, and in summer, by the beach.

Alcobaça

From the twelfth to the nineteenth centuries, the Cistercian **Monastery of ALCOBAÇA** was among the greatest in the Christian world. Owning vast tracts of farmland, orchards, and vineyards, it was immensely rich and held jurisdiction over a dozen towns and three seaports. Its church and cloister are the purest and the most inspired creation of all Portuguese Gothic architecture – and, alongside Belém and Batalha, are today the most impressive monuments in the country. In addition, the abbey is the burial place of those romantic figures of Portuguese history, Dom Pedro and Dona Inês de Castro.

The Abbey

The Monastery (daily 8.30am–5.30pm; 300$00), although empty since its dissolution in 1834, still seems to assert power, magnificence, and opulence. And it takes little imagination to people it again with the monks, said once to have numbered 999. Mass was once celebrated here without interruption, but it was the residents' legendarily extravagant and aristocratic lifestyles that formed the common ingredients of the awed anecdotes of eighteenth-century travellers.

Even William Beckford, no stranger to high living, found their decadence unsettling, growing weary of "perpetual gormandising . . . the fumes of banquets and incense . . . the fat waddling monks and sleek friars with wanton eyes, twanging away on the Jew's harp". Another contemporary observer, Richard Twiss, for his part found "the bottle went as briskly about as ever I saw it do in Scotland" – a tribute indeed. For all the "high romps" and luxuriance, though, it has to be added that the monks enjoyed a reputation for hospitality, generosity, and charity, while the surrounding countryside is to this day one of the most productive areas in Portugal, thanks to their agricultural expertise.

Founded by Dom Afonso Henriques in 1147 to celebrate the liberation of Santarém from the Moors, Alcobaça is a truly vast complex. What is not obvious when you go in, because the abbey is so huge, is that only half of it is open to the public – the other part, the south wing, being a state-run **mental hospital** which can be overviewed from the first floor monks' dormitory. It's in a state of apparent neglect, shabby with corrugated iron fences and chickens scratching in the dust.

The Abbey Church

The main **Abbey Church**, modelled on the famous Cistercian abbey of Citeaux in France, is the largest in Portugal. External impressions are disappointing, as the Gothic facade has been superseded by unexceptional baroque additions of the seventeenth and eighteenth centuries. Inside, however, all later adornments have been swept away, restoring the narrow soaring aisles to their original vertical simplicity. The only exception to this Gothic purity is the frothy Manueline doorway to the sacristy, hidden directly behind the high altar, and, as at Tomar and Batalha, encrusted with intricate, swirling motifs of coral and seaweed.

THE TOMBS OF PEDRO AND INÊS

The abbey's most precious treasures are the fourteenth-century **tombs of Dom Pedro and Dona Inês de Castro**, each occupying one of the transepts and sculpted with phenomenal wealth of detail. Animals, heraldic emblems, musicians, and biblical scenes are all portrayed in an architectural setting of miniature windows, canopies, domes, and towers; most graphic of all is a dragon-shaped hell's mouth at Inês' feet, consuming the damned. The tombs are inscribed with the motto "Até ao Fim do Mundo" (Until the End of the World) and in accordance with Dom Pedro's orders have been placed foot to foot so that on the Day of Judgement the pair may rise and immediately feast their eyes on one another.

Pedro's earthly love for Inês de Castro, the great theme of epic Portuguese poetry, was cruelly stifled by high politics. Inês, as the daughter of a Galician nobleman, was a potential source of Spanish influence over the Portuguese throne and Pedro's father, Afonso IV, forbade their marriage. The ceremony took place nevertheless – secretly at Bragança in remote Trás-os-Montes – and eventually Afonso was persuaded to sanction his daughter-in-law's murder. When Pedro succeeded to the throne in 1357 he brought the murderers to justice, personally ripping out their hearts and gorging his love-crazed blood appetite upon them. More poignantly he also exhumed and crowned the corpse of his lover, forcing the entire royal circle to acknowledge her as queen by kissing her decomposing hand (see Coimbra for more on this story's locales).

The Kitchen

From one highlight to another. Beckford – Romantic dilettante that he was – stood bewildered by the charms of these tombs when "in came the Grand Priors hand in hand, all three together. 'To the *kitchen*', said they in unison, 'to the kitchen and that immediately'". They led him past the fourteenth-century Chapter House to a cavernous room in the corner of the cloisters.

This route you can follow. Alcobaça's feasting has already been mentioned but this **kitchen** – with its cellars and gargantuan conical chimney, supported by eight trunklike iron columns – sets it in real perspective. A stream tapped from the River Alcôa still runs straight through the room: it was used not merely for cooking and washing but also to provide a constant supply of fresh fish, which plopped out into a stone basin! At the centre of the room, on the vast wooden tables, Beckford continued to marvel at

> *pastry in vast abundance which a numerous tribe of lay brothers and their atten-*
> *dants were rolling out and puffing up into a hundred different shapes, singing all*
> *the while as blithely as larks in a corn field. "There", said the Lord Abbot, "we shall*
> *not starve. God's bounties are great, it is fit we should enjoy them".*

And enjoy them they did, with a majestic feast of "rarities and delicacies, potted lampreys, strange Brazilian messes, edible birds' nests and sharks' fins dressed after the mode of Macau by a Chinese lay brother"! As a practical test for obesity the monks had to file through a narrow door on their way to the **Refectory**; those who failed were forced to fast until they could squeeze through.

The Cloisters

The **Cloisters of Silence**, notable for their traceried stone windows, were built in the reign of Dom Dinis, the "poet-king" who established an enduring literary and artistic tradition at the abbey. An upper storey of twisted columns and Manueline arches was added in the sixteenth century, along with, in its standard position opposite the refectory, a beautiful hexagonal lavatory.

The **Sala dos Reis** (Kings' Room), off the cloister, displays statues of virtually every King of Portugal down to Dom José, who died in 1777. Blue eighteenth-century *azulejos* depict the siege of Santarém, Dom Afonso's vow, and the founding of the monastery. Also on show here is a piece of war booty which must have warmed the souls of the brothers – the huge metal cauldron in which soup was heated up for the Spanish army before the battle of Aljubarrota in 1385·(for more of which, see "Batalha", below).

The rest of the abbey, including four cloisters, seven dormitories, and endless corridors, is closed to the public. Parts of it are currently occupied by a mental asylum – sad glimpses of which can be caught from some of the windows in the visitable parts. For the best overall view of the abbey, make your way to the ruined hilltop **castle**, about five minutes' walk away.

Practicalities

Though Alcobaça is not a hive of activity, it's not a bad place to stay. A useful first call is the **Turismo** (☎062/423 77) on the central Praça 25 de Abril, opposite the abbey. They can supply maps of the town and advise on accommodation and transport. The bus station is five minutes' walk from the centre of town, across the bridge; coming into town, bear left and head towards the abbey towers. There are reasonably frequent connections to Nazaré and Leiria.

Accommodation

There is a scattering of inexpensive **pensions and hotels**:

Quartos Alcôa, Rua Araujo Guimarães 30 (☎062/427 27)– on the Praça da República. These are usually the town's cheapest – and most central – rooms. ①.

Pensão Mosteiro, Rua Frei Estevão Martins 5 (☎062/421 83). Friendly if a bit basic. ①.

Pensão Corações Unidos, Rua Frei António Brandão 39, just off the main square (☎062/421 42). The best cheap choice: big rooms and decent meals, too. ①.

Hotel Santa Maria, Rua Dr. Francisco Zagalo, off the main square (☎062/432 95). Pleasant hotel with views of the abbey from some rooms. ②.

There's also a well-sited **campsite**, two minutes' walk from the bus station (turn left along Avenida Manuel da Silva Carolino).

Food

The *Restaurante Trindade*, on Praça Afonso Henriques, near the abbey, or *Cervejaria Roma*, opposite the abbey, should go some way toward satisfying your appetite after the Beckford passages quoted above; both are good value. The Pensão Corações Unidos also has a fair restaurant.

Leiria and the Pinhal do Rei

A royal castle hangs almost vertically above the graceful town of **LEIRIA**, a place of cobbled streets, attractive gardens, and fine old squares. If you are travelling around on public transport, you will proabably want to make it your base for a couple of nights, as the three big sites of northern Estremadura – Alcobaça, Batalha, and Fátima – are all easy day excursions by bus, as are the caves of Mira d'Aire. The town itself lacks much in the way of culture or nightlife, but it has enough restaurants and bars to keep the evenings occupied.

Arriving by **bus**, you'll be dropped at a modern terminal, beside the gardens flanking the central **Praca de Goa**; a **Turismo** (☎044/327 48), just across the square, dispenses maps. The **train station** is 4km out of town – a cheap taxi ride.

The castle and town

Leiria **Castle** (daily 9am–7pm; 39$00!) was one of the most important strongholds in Moorish Portugal, reconquered by Afonso Henriques as he fought his way south in 1135. The actual building you see today dates mostly from the fourteenth and eighteenth centuries. Within its walls stands a royal palace, with a magnificent balcony high above the Rio Lis, and the church of Nossa Senhora da Penha, erected by João I in about 1400 and now reduced to an eerie, roofless shell. If you have small children with you, beware: there are several precipitous, unguarded points among the buildings and staircases.

At the heart of the old town is the **Praça Rodrigues Lobo**, surrounded by beautiful arcaded buildings and dominated by a splendidly pompous statue of the eponymous seventeenth-century local poet. It's a promising area, too, for bars and restaurants, as well as for rooms (see below).

Rooms and food

For accommodation, make your way to the Praça Rodrigues Lobo and look around the restaurants (several of which offer rooms) and **pensions** here and on the narrow side streets: try Rua Mestre de Aviz and Rua Miguel Bombarda. Other cheap rooms are to be found in Largo Paio Guterres and Largo Cónego Maia, both near the sixteenth-century cathedral.

The cheaper pensions and hotels include:

Residencial Casa de Santo António, Rua Machado dos Santos 10a (☎044/221 50). Cheapest in town – a bit basic. ①.

Pensão Alcoa, Rua Rodrigues Cordeiro 24–1º (☎044/326 90). Large rooms and great views over the town. ③.

Pensão Leirense, Rua Afonso de Albuquerque 6 (☎044/320 61). Pleasant old rooms, near the Misericórdia church. ④.

Pensão Ramalhete, Rua Dr. Correia Mateus 30–2º (☎044/268 21). Rambling old nineteenth-century inn, close by the Turismo. ③.

Hotel San Luís, Largo Alexandre Herculano 10 (☎044/346 42). Good location and cheap for its class. ④.

There's also a very well-appointed **youth hostel** – one of the most enjoyable in the country – at Largo Cândido dos Reis 7 (☎044/318 68).

As for **restaurants**, a couple of very inexpensive places can be found if you head off down the Rua Dr. Correia Mateus (opposite the Turismo) and past Largo de Santana (try second on the right); seafood is good at *Jardim* (by the Turismo), and real Portuguese cuisine – slightly more expensive, but worth every penny – can be found at *Tromba Rija*, Rua Professores Portelas (☎044/32072), out of town on the Marrazes road; go under EN1 and take a left after the *Casa da Palmeira*.

The Pine Forest and Beaches

Some of the most idyllic spots on this stretch of coast are in the **Pinhal do Rei** (or *Pinhal de Leiria*), a vast 700-year-old pine forest stretching from São Pedro de Muel to Pedrógão.

The coastline of Estremadura has changed drastically over the last few centuries – Peniche was once an island, Nazaré was under the water until the seventeenth century, and in Roman times the sea splashed against the walls of Óbidos. Although there were trees here before, the Royal Pine Forest was planned by Dom Dinis, a king renowned for his agrarian reforms, to protect fertile arable land from the menacing inward march of sand dunes; it has since grown into an area of great natural beauty, with sunlight filtering through endless miles of trees and the air perfumed with the scent of resin.

Official **campsites** are located at the resorts of VIEIRA DE LEIRIA – on the Lis estuary and famous for its fish restaurants – and, best of all, at **SÃO PEDRO DE MUEL**, where the tents are sheltered in the woods from the Atlantic winds. The São Pedro **youth hostel** (☎044/592 36) has a marvellous location on the sea, but is seasonal (May 1–Sept 30); **buses** to Leiria are rather erratic (less so in summer and at weekends; last one back at 6pm) and involve a change at MARINHA GRANDE.

Sadly, the northern part of this coastline – indeed the whole coast north from PRAIA VELHA almost as far as FIGUEIRA DA FOZ (see Chapter Three) – is now **severely polluted**. This is due to the noxious emissions of two paper plants at LEIROSA: a correspondent who walked the coast all the way from Figueira to São Martinho do Porto described seeing the beaches polluted red, the sea foaming red and stinking along the whole stretch, and PEDROGÃO a ghost town inhabited only by protest posters.

Even in PRAIA VELHA, a delightful local resort with some great restaurants, the sea is rather dubious, which may explain the handy showers on the beach. So stick to the area between Praia Velha and São Pedro de Muel, where there are several charming beach-hut settlements populated largely by Portuguese holidaymakers. **South of São Pedro**, too, you can find sheltered stretches of beach – especially around VALE DE PAREDES, an area popular with Portuguese, camping outside the established campsites – though here you're no longer in the forest.

Batalha

The **Mosteiro de Santa Maria da Vitória**, better known as **BATALHA** (Battle Abbey), is the supreme achievement of Portuguese architecture – the dazzling richness and originality of its Manueline decoration rivalled only by the Jerónimos Monastery at Belém, with which it shares UNESCO world monument status. An exuberant symbol of national pride, it was built to commemorate the battle that sealed Portugal's independence after decades of Spanish intrigue.

Some history

With the death of Dom Fernando in 1383, the royal house of Burgundy died out; in its wake there followed a period of feverish factional plotting over the Portuguese throne. Fernando's widow, Leonor Teles, had a Spanish lover even during her husband's lifetime, and when Fernando died she betrothed her daughter, Beatriz, to **Juan I of Castile**, encouraging his claim to the Portuguese throne. **João, Mestre de Aviz**, Fernando's illegitimate stepbrother, also claimed the throne. He assassinated Leonor's lover and braced himself for the inevitable invasion from Spain. The two armies clashed on August 14, 1385, at the **Battle of Aljubarrota**, fifteen kilometres south of Batalha. Faced with seemingly impossible odds, João struck a deal with the Virgin Mary, promising to build a magnificent abbey in return for her military assistance. It worked: **Nuno Álvares Pereira** led the Portuguese forces to a memorable victory and the new king duly summoned the finest architects of the day.

The Abbey

The honey-coloured **Abbey** (Tues–Sun: summer 9am–7pm; Oct–April 9am–5pm) was transformed by the uniquely Portuguese Manueline additions of the late fifteenth and early sixteenth centuries, but the bulk of the building was completed between 1388 and 1434, in a profusely ornate version of French Gothic. Pinnacles, parapets, windows, and flying buttresses are all lavishly and intricately sculpted. Within this flamboyant framework there are also strong elements of the English perpendicular style. Huge pilasters and prominent vertical decorations divide the main facade; the nave, with its narrow soaring dimensions, and the chapter house, are reminiscent of church architecture in the English cathedral cities of Winchester and York.

The Capela do Fundador

Medieval architects were frequently attracted by lucrative foreign commissions, but there is a special explanation for the English influence at Batalha. This is revealed in the **Capela do Fundador** (Founder's Chapel), directly to the right upon entering the church. Beneath the octagonal lantern rests the joint tomb of Dom João I and Philippa of Lancaster, their hands clasped in the ultimate expression of harmonious relations between Portugal and England.

In 1373, Dom Fernando had entered into an alliance with John of Gaunt, Duke of Lancaster, who claimed the Spanish throne by virtue of his marriage to a daughter of Pedro the Cruel, King of Castile. A crack contingent of English longbowmen had played a significant role in the victory at Aljubarrota, and in 1386 both countries willingly signed the **Treaty of Windsor**, "an inviolable, eternal, solid, perpetual, and true league of friendship". As part of the same political package Dom João married Philippa, John of Gaunt's daughter, and with her came English architects to assist at Batalha. The alliance between the two countries, reconfirmed by the marriage of Charles II to Catherine of Bragança in 1661 and the Methuen Commercial Treaty of 1703, has become the longest-standing international friendship of modern times – it was invoked by the Allies in World War II to establish bases on the Azores, and the facilities of those islands were offered to the British Navy during the 1982 Falklands war.

The four younger sons of João and Philippa are buried along the south wall of the Capela do Fundador in a row of recessed arches. Second from the right is the **Tomb of Prince Henry the Navigator**, who guided the discovery of Madeira, the Azores, and the African coast as far as Sierra Leone. Henry himself never ventured further than Tangiers but it was a measure of his personal importance, drive, and expertise that the growth of the empire was temporarily shelved after his death in 1460.

Concerted maritime exploration resumed under João II (1481–95) and accelerated with the accession of Manuel I (1495–1521). Vasco da Gama opened up the trade route to India in 1498, Cabral reached Brazil two years later, and Newfoundland was discovered in 1501. The momentous era of burgeoning self-confidence, wealth, and widening horizons is reflected in the peculiarly Portuguese style of architecture known (after the king) as Manueline. As befitted the great national shrine, Batalha was adapted to incorporate two masterpieces of the new order: the Royal Cloisters and the so-called Unfinished Chapels.

The Claustro Real

In the **Claustro Real** (Royal Cloister) stone grilles of ineffable beauty and intricacy were added to the original Gothic windows by Diogo de Boitaca, architect of the cloisters at Belém and the prime genius of Manueline art. Crosses of the Order of Christ and armillary spheres – symbols of overseas exploration – are entwined in a network of lotus blossom, briar branches and exotic vegetation.

Off the east side opens the early fifteenth-century **Sala do Capítulo** (Chapter House), remarkable for the audacious unsupported span of its ceiling – so daring, in fact, that the Church authorities were convinced that the whole chamber would come crashing down and employed criminals already condemned to death to build it. The architect, Afonso Domingues, could only finally silence his critics by sleeping in the chamber night after night. Soldiers now stand guard here over Portugal's **Tomb of the Unknown Warriors**, one killed in France during World War I, the other in the country's colonial wars in Africa.

The **Refectory**, on the opposite side of the cloisters, houses a Military Museum in their honour. From here, a short passage leads into the **Claustro de Dom Afonso V**, built in a conventional Gothic style which provides a yardstick against which to measure the Manueline flamboyance of the Royal Cloisters.

The Capelas Imperfeitas

The **Capelas Imperfeitas** (Unfinished Chapels) form a separate structure tacked on to the east end of the church and accessible only from outside the main complex. Dom Duarte, eldest son of João and Philippa, commissioned them in 1437 as a royal mausoleum but, as with the cloisters, the original design was transformed beyond all recognition by Dom Manuel's architects. The portal rises to a towering fifty feet and every inch is carved with a honeycomb of mouldings. Florid projections, clover-shaped arches, strange vegetables; there are even stone snails. The place is unique among Christian architecture and evocative of the great shrines of Islam and Hinduism: perhaps it was inspired by the tales of Indian monuments that filtered back along the eastern trade routes. Although conveniently referred to as Manueline, it is really in a class by itself and illustrates the variety and uninhibited excitement of Portuguese art during the Age of Discovery.

The architect of this masterpiece was Mateus Fernandes, whose tomb lies directly outside the entrance to the Capela do Fundador. Within the portal, a large octagonal space is surrounded by seven hexagonal chapels, two of which contain the sepulchres of Dom Duarte and his queen, Leonor of Aragon. An ambitious upper story – equal in magnificence to the portal – was designed by Diogo de Boitaca but the huge buttresses were abandoned after a few years.

The Village: practicalities

The Battle Abbey stands alone, the huddle of cottages that once surrounded it swept away and replaced by a bare concrete expanse. There's not much else here but a sprinkling of tourist shops, bars, and restaurants, which all do brisk business during the Fátima weekend in early October, when the place is packed.

Accommodation is a choice between the *Pensão Vitória* (☎044/966 78; ①), just off the main road to Fátima, next to the petrol station, which is okay if basic; *dormidas*, advertised within a few paces of the bus stop; and the new *Pousada Mestre Afonso Domingues* (☎044/962 60; ⑤), beside the abbey. Most people, however, visit Batalha on a day trip from Leiria: on the whole, the best idea.

Porto de Mós and some caves

High above the small, white village of **PORTO DE MÓS**, just eight kilometres south of Batalha but well off the tourist trail, a grandiose thirteenth-century **Castle** of the Knights Templar stands guard (daily 10am–1pm & 2–4pm). Bright green cones crown its turrets and from a noble balcony you can gaze down over the village. Bars, restaurants, and a solitary, ramshackle **pension**, the *Rio Alcaide* (☎044/421 24; ①), are grouped around the bus stop on the main road.

More significantly, Porto de Mós is the nearest base from which to visit three of Estremadura's fabulous **underground caves**. If you're doing this, there's a convenient bus to Mira d'Aire which leaves around 8am (last one back around 5pm); Porto de Mós also has a small, helpful **Turismo**.

Mira d'Aire

The largest, most spectacular, and most accessible caves in Portugal are **Grutas de MIRA D'AIRE** (9.15am–9pm), ten minutes' walk from the bus stop in the drab textile town from which they take their name. Discovered in 1947, they comprise a fantasy land of spaghetti-like stalactites and stalagmites and bizarre rock formations with names like "Hell's Door", "Jelly Fish", and "Church Organ". Rough steps take you down and the excellent 45-minute guided tour (in French or Portuguese, or even English on occasion) culminates in an extravagant fountain display in a natural lake 110 metres underground. You might have to wait some time for a group of acceptable size to gather.

Alvados and Santo António

There are similar *grutas* or caves in open country near the hamlets of **ALVADOS** and **SANTO ANTÓNIO** (both open 9am–9pm). Three buses a day run between Porto de Mós and Mira d'Aire, passing within 3km of Alvados and 7km of Santo António. Hitching along the main road is not too difficult but there's a good chance you'll have to walk part of the way.

Grutas da Moeda

The labyrinthine **Grutas da Moeda** (9am–9pm) at **SÃO MAMEDE** are also well worth seeing, not least because one of the chambers has been converted into a unique bar with rock (!) music, subtle lighting, and stalactites nose-diving into your glass of beer. They're best visited from Fátima, 6km away, where, with concerted haggling, you should be able to arrange a reasonably priced taxi. The whole area, full of old salt mines and pits, forms part of the **Parque Natural das Serras d'Aire e dos Candeeiros**, which has a head office in the nearby town of RIO MAIOR.

Fátima

FÁTIMA is the fountainhead of religious devotion in Portugal and one of the most important centres of pilgrimage in the Catholic world. Its cult is founded on a series of six **Apparitions of the Virgin Mary**, in the first of which, on May 13, 1917, three peasant children from the village were confronted, while tending their parents' flock, with a flash of lightning and "a lady brighter than the sun" sitting in the branches of a tree. According to the memoirs of Lúcia, who was the only one who could hear what was said – and the only one of the children to survive into her teens – the Lady announced, "I am from Heaven. I have come to ask you to return here six times, at this same hour, on the thirteenth of every month. Then, in October, I will tell you who I am and what I want".

News of the miracle was greeted with scepticism, and only a few casual onlookers attended the second appearance, but for the third, July 13, apparition, the crowd had swollen to a few thousand. Although only the three children could see the heavenly visitor, Fátima became a *cause célèbre*, with the anticlerical government accusing the Church of fabricating a miracle to revive its flagging influence, and Church authorities afraid to acknowledge what they feared was a hoax. The children were arrested and interrogated but refused to change their story.

By the date of the final appearance, October 13, as many as 70,000 people had converged on Fátima where they witnessed the so-called **Miracle of the Sun**. Eye-witnesses described the skies clearing and the sun, intensified to a blinding, swirling ball of fire, shooting beams of multicoloured light to earth. Lifelong illnesses, supposedly, were cured; the blind could see again and the dumb speak. It was enough to convince most of the terrified witnesses. Nevertheless the three children remained the only ones actually to see the Virgin, and only Lúcia could communicate with her.

To her only were revealed the three **Secrets of Fátima**. The first was a message of peace (this was during World War I) and a vision of Hell, with anguished, charred souls plunged into an ocean of fire. The second was more prophetic and controversial: "If you pay heed to my request", the vision declared, "Russia will be converted and there will be peace. If not, Russia will spread her errors through the world, causing wars and persecution against the Church" – all this just a few weeks before the Bolshevik takeover in St Petersburg, though not, perhaps, before it could have been predicted. The **third secret*** has never been divulged – it lies in a drawer of the Pope's desk in the Vatican, read by successive popes on their accession but supposedly too horrible to be revealed, though the present incumbent has hinted that the day may not be far off when he will announce its contents.

The Basílica and the town

To commemorate the extraordinary events and to accommodate the hordes of pilgrims who flock here, a shrine has been built; it has little to recommend it but its size. The vast white **Basílica** and its gigantic esplanade are capable of holding more than a million devotees. In the church the **tombs of Jacinta and Francisco** – Lúcia's fellow witnesses, both of whom died in the European flu epidemic of 1919–20 – are the subject of constant attention in their chapels on either side of the main exit. Long, neoclassical colonnades flank the basílica and enclose part of the sloping esplanade in front. This huge area, reminiscent of an airport runway, is twice the size of the piazza of Saint Peter's in Rome. On its left-hand side the original holm oak tree in which the Virgin appeared was long ago consumed by souvenir-hunting pilgrims; the small **Chapel of the Apparitions** now stands in its place, with a new tree a few yards away.

Whatever your feelings about the place, there is an undeniable (and to some people suffocating) atmosphere of mystery around it, perhaps created by nothing

---

* In 1984 an Irish priest tried to hijack an *Aer Lingus* plane to persuade the Pope to reveal the secret. Unfortunately the crisis was defused with no one any the wiser.

more than the obvious faith of the vast majority of its visitors. It's all at its most intense during the great **annual pilgrimages** on May 12–13 and October 12–13. Crowds of up to 100,000 congregate, most arriving on foot, some even walking on their knees in penance. Open-air mass is celebrated at 5am and an image of the Virgin is paraded by candlelight as priests move among the pilgrims hearing confessions. The fiftieth anniversary of the apparitions attracted one-and-a-half million worshippers, including Pope Paul VI and Lúcia – who is still alive, a Carmelite nun in the Convent of Santa Teresa near Coimbra. Lúcia was again part of the vast crowds that greeted John Paul II here in 1982 and 1991.

A multitude of hospices and convents have sprung up in the shadow of the basílica, and inevitably the fame of Fátima has resulted in its commercialisation. As each year goes by, the grotesquely kitsch souvenirs on sale move into hitherto unexplored territories of taste – look out for the Fátima ballpoint pens, which tilt to reveal the Virgin in Glory. Business is particularly brisk on Sunday, when thousands of local families converge by bus, car, lorry, and cart – yet the shrine itself is in no way swamped.

There is a pleasant walk up to the place of the **"Apparitions of the Angel"**, outside the village, along which pilgrims follow the Stations of the Cross.

Accommodation and food

Pensions and **restaurants** abound in Fatima, most of them decked out in tasteful shades of Marian blue. Outside the major pilgrimages – or weekends – there's enough accommodation to go round. A particularly good restaurant is *O Zé Grande*, on the road up to the Basilica. But frankly there's little reason to stay except during the **pilgrimages** (when the pensions are booked months ahead) to witness the midnight processions. At these times people camp all around the back and sides of the basílica. Beware of thieves during the pilgrimages.

The regular **bus services** to Fatima from Leiria and Tomar make a relaxed daytrip easy. Coming from Batalha you'll pass REGUENGO DO FÉTAL, another pilgrimage site that's host to a torchlit procession (lit by burning oil carried in shells) up to a hilltop sanctuary around October 3. Coming by **train**, you'll need to get a taxi or local bus (not always a ready connection) from the Estação de Fatima, 10km from town; the station is on the main Lisbon–Porto line.

Tomar

The **Convento de Cristo** at **TOMAR**, 34km east of Fátima, is an artistic *tour de force* which entwines the most outstanding military, religious, and imperial strands in the history of Portugal. The *Ordem dos Templários* (Knights Templar) and their successors, the *Ordem de Cristo* (Order of Christ), established their headquarters here and successive Grand Masters employed experts in Romanesque, Manueline, and Renaissance architecture to embellish and expand the convent in a manner worthy of their power, prestige, and wealth.

In addition, Tomar is an attractive town in its own right, well worth a couple of days. It is split in two by the Rio Nabão, with almost everything of interest on the west bank. The **train** and **bus** stations are in easy walking distance of the centre. Head directly north and you'll hit Avenida Dr. Candido Madureira, where there's a very helpful **Turismo** (☎049/31 32 37), facing the park in which the **Convento de Cristo** complex stands.

Practicalities

Tomar has a good range of accommodation and finding a room should be pretty straightforward. Among the **pensions** are:

Pensão Nun'Álvares, Avda. Nuno Álvares Pereira 3–1º (☎049/31 28 73). Very cheap and friendly – but book ahead for one of just eleven rooms. ①.

Pensão Bonjardim, Praçeta de Santo André (☎049/31 31 95). Basic but okay. ①.

Pensão Tomarense, Avda. Torres Pinheiro 13 (☎049/31 29 48). Not a first choice: bare, rather tatty rooms and a noisy position. ①.

Pensão Residencial Luz, Rua Serpa Pinto 144 (☎049/31 23 17). A notch up the scale and excellent value, especially for multiple-person rooms. On a pedestrianised street. ②.

Pensão Luanda, Avda. Marqúes de Tomar 13–15 (☎049/31 29 29). Nice enough modern pension building by the river; again, all rooms with bath. ②.

Pensão Residencial União, Rua Serpa Pinto 94–1º (☎049/31 28 31). Nice rooms around a courtyard, all with private bath. Excellent value. ③.

In addition, there are *quartos* near the Mercado and the Câmara Municipal, and a pleasant municipal campsite(☎049/31 39 50), out towards the football stadium. An alternative campsite, if you have transport, is at CASTELO DE BODE (13km from Tomar and 7km from the train station at Santa Cita, the stop before Tomar; ☎041/942 44). Bode reservoir is Lisbon's main water source, set amid pine woods and with boats for rent to reach the islands in the lake.

For **meals**, the *Nun'Álvares* has the edge on its pension rivals, with a fine house wine and local dishes. Alternatively, try the *Restaurante Nabão*, across the Ponte Velha on Rua Fonte Choupo; *Restaurante Piri-Piri* at Rua dos Moinhos 54 (closed Sun); or the very cheap and filling *Pica Pau*, just off Rua dos Arcos. The town's most elegant **café** is the 1930s-interior *Paraiso* on Rua Serpa Pinto. Nightlife is a straight choice between two **disco-bars**: *Ping Ping*, just over the Ponte Velha, and the less crowded *Pôr de Sol*, further out along the same road.

Finally, on the practical front, it's worth being aware of Tomar's major **festival,** the *Festas dos Tabuleiros*, held tri-annually at the beginning of July (1993 is the next date due), when the place goes wild. Lack of available accommodation should be compensated by all-night fun.

The Town

Built on a simple grid plan, Tomar's old quarters preserve all their traditional charm, with whitewashed, terraced cottages lining narrow cobbled streets. On the central Praça da República stands an elegant seventeenth-century town hall, a ring of houses of the same period, and the Manueline church of **São João Baptista**, remarkable for its octagonal belfry, elaborate doorway, and six panels attributed to Gregório Lopes (circa 1490–1550), one of Portugal's finest artists (see p.65).

Nearby at Rua Joaquim Jacinto 73 is an excellently preserved fourteenth-century **Synagogue** (closed Wed), interesting in a town dominated for so long by crusading Defenders of the Faith; you can get the key down the street at no. 104 or at the Turismo. Its stark interior, with plain vaults supported by four slender columns, houses a collection of thirteenth- to fourteenth-century Hebraic inscriptions. In 1496 Dom Manuel followed the example of the *Reis Católicos* (Catholic Kings) of Spain and ordered the expulsion or conversion of all Portuguese Jews. The synagogue at Tomar was one of the very few to survive so far south – there's another at Castelo de Vide in the Alentejo. Many Jews fled northwards, especially to Trás-os-Montes where Inquisitional supervision was less hawk-eyed.

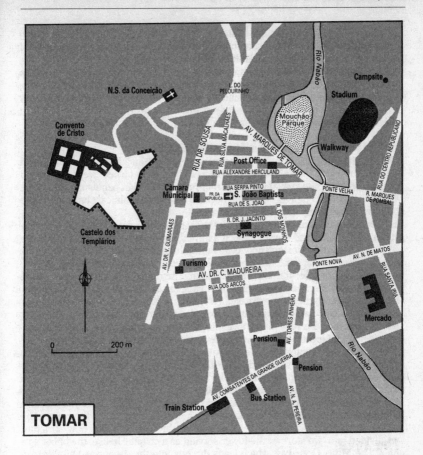

TOMAR

Midway between the town and the Convento de Cristo, it's worth taking the time for a look around the unassumingly beautiful Renaissance church of **Nossa Senhora da Conceição**. It is attributed to Diogo de Torralva, architect of the Convento's Great Cloisters. The Turismo again has keys for the church.

The Convento de Cristo

The **Convento de Cristo** (Tues–Sun 9.30am–12.30pm & 2–6pm; 300$00) is set among pleasant gardens with splendid views, about a quarter of an hour's walk uphill from the centre of town. Founded in 1162 by Gualdim Pais, first and grandest Master of the **Knights Templar**, it was, as headquarters of the Order, and, as such, both a religious and a military centre.

One of the main objectives of the Templars was to expel the Moors from Spain and Portugal, a reconquest seen always as a crusade against the Dark Forces – the defence of Christianity against the Infidel. Spiritual strength was an integral part of the military effort and, despite magnificent additions, the sacred heart of the whole complex remains the **Charola**, the twelfth-century temple from which the knights drew their moral conviction. It is a strange place, more suggestive of the occult than of Christianity. At the centre of the sixteen-sided, almost circular, chapel stands the high altar, surrounded by a two-storeyed octagon. Deep alcoves, decorated with sixteenth-century paintings, are cut into the outside walls; the Templars are said to have attended mass on horseback. Like almost every circular church, it is ultimately based on the Church of the Holy Sepulchre in Jerusalem, for whose protection the Knights Templar were originally founded.

The Order of Christ – and Dom Manuel's additions

By 1249 the reconquest in Portugal was completed and the Templars reaped enormous rewards for their services. Tracts of land were turned over to them and they controlled a network of castles throughout the Iberian peninsula. But as the Moorish threat receded, the Knights became a powerful political challenge to the stability and authority of European monarchs.

Philippe-le-Bel, King of France, took the lead by confiscating all Templar property in his country, and there followed a formal papal suppression of the Order in 1314. In Spain this prompted a vicious witch-hunt and many of the Knights sought refuge in Portugal, where Dom Dinis coolly reconstituted them in 1320 under a different title: the **Order of Christ** They inherited all the Portuguese property of the Templars, including the headquarters at Tomar, but their power was now subject to that of the throne.

In the fifteenth and sixteenth centuries, the Order of Christ played a leading role in extending Portugal's overseas empire and was granted spiritual jurisdiction over all conquests. Prince Henry the Navigator was Grand Master from 1417 to 1460, and the remains of his **Palace** in the Convento de Cristo can be seen immediately to the right upon entering the castle walls. Henry ordered two new cloisters: the **Claustro do Cemitério** and the **Claustro da Lavagem**, both reached via a short corridor from the Charola and attractively lined with *azulejos*.

Dom Manuel succeeded to the Grand Mastership in 1492, three years before he became king. Flush with imperial wealth, he decided to expand the convent by adding a rectangular **nave** to the west side of the Charola. This new structure was divided into two storeys: the lower serving as a chapter house, the upper as a choir. The **Main Doorway**, which leads directly into the nave, was built by João de Castilho in 1515, two years before Dom Manuel appointed him Master of Works at Belém. Characteristically unconcerned with structural matters, the architect profusely adorned the doorway with appliqué decoration. There are strong similarities in this respect with contemporary Isabelline and Plateresque architecture in Spain.

The crowning highlight of Tomar, though, is the sculptural ornamentation of the windows on the main facade of the **Chapter House**. The richness and self-confidence of Manueline art always suggests the Age of Discovery, but here the connection is crystal clear. A wide range of maritime motifs is jumbled up in two tumultuous window frames, as eternal memorials to the sailors who established the Portuguese Empire. Everything is here: anchors, buoys, sails, coral, seaweed, and especially the ropes, knotted over and over again into an escapologist's nightmare.

The windows can only be fully appreciated from the roof of the **Claustro de Santa Bárbara**, adjacent to the Great Cloisters, which unfortunately almost completely obscure a similar window on the south wall of the Chapter House.

A new style: João III

João III (1521–57) transformed the convent from the general political headquarters of the Order into a thoroughgoing monastic community, and he endowed it with the necessary conventual buildings: dormitories, kitchens, and no less than four new cloisters (making a grand total of seven). Yet another, much more classical, style was introduced into the architectural mélange of Tomar. So meteoric was the rise and fall of Manueline art within the reign of Dom Manuel that, to some extent, it must have reflected his personal tastes. João III on the other hand had an entirely different view of art. He is known to have sent schools of architects and sculptors to study in Italy, and his reign finally marked the much-delayed advent of the Renaissance in Portugal.

The two-tiered **Great Cloisters**, abutting the Chapter House, are one of the purest examples of this new style. Begun in 1557, they present a textbook illustration of the principals of Renaissance neoclassicism. Greek columns, gentle arches, and simple rectangular bays produce a wonderfully restrained rhythm. At the southwest corner a balcony looks out on to the skeletal remains of a second Chapter House, begun by João III but never completed.

Santarém

SANTARÉM, capital of the Ribatejo, rears high above the Rio Tejo, commanding a tremendous view over the rich pasturelands to the south and east. It ranks among the most historic cities in Portugal: under Julius Caesar it became an important administrative centre for the Roman province of Lusitania; Moorish Santarém was regarded as impregnable (until Afonso Henriques captured it by enlisting the aid of foreign Crusaders in 1147); and it was here that royal *Cortes* (parliaments) were convened throughout the fourteenth and fifteenth centuries.

All evidence of Roman and Moorish occupation, though, has vanished and – with the notable exceptions of two exquisite churches – modern Santarém has little to show for its history. Even so, a visit is rewarded by the famous view from the *miradouro* known as the **Portas do Sol**, and, if you can plan your stay to coincide, by a whole series of **festivals** held in the town and region (see overpage).

Arriving and accommodation

The **railway station** lies several hundred feet below the town but local buses are usually ready to ferry passengers to the **bus station** in the centre. Rua Pedro Canavarro, across the gardens opposite the bus station, leads into **Rua Capelo e Ivens**, the main pedestrian street of the old town. Excellent maps (with all the pensions, hotels and restaurants keyed) are available here from the **Turismo** at no. 63 (☎043/231 40).

Finding a place to stay can be hard during festival times – when your best bet is to turn up early and see if Turismo can find you a **private room** – but should be little problem at other times of year.

Pension and hotel options are:

Pensão do José, Travessa do Froes 14 (☎043/230 88). A clean, basic pension, on a quiet alleyway just off the Rua Capelo e Ivens. ①.

Hotel Central, Rua Guilherme de Azevedo 24 (☎043/220 28). Large, pleasant rooms – and a pool room downstairs. Close by the Turismo. ②.

Pensão O Beirante, Rua Alexandre Herculano 3–7 (☎043/225 47). Inexpensive rooms, all with private bath. ②.

Hotel Abidis, Rua Guilherme de Azevedo 4 (☎043/220 17). A slice of nineteenth-century style. Highly recommended and excellent value. ③.

Residencial Vitoria, Rua 2 Visconde de Santarém 21 (☎043/225 73). Fifteen minutes' walk from the centre: decent, if small, rooms – all with bath. ③.

Residencial Muralha, Rua Pedro Canavarro 12 (☎043/223 99). Central and confortable. ③.

Residencial Jardim, Rua 2 Visconde de Santarém 21 (☎043/271 04), Santarém's plushest – not very characterful. ⑤.

Quinta de Sobreira, Vale de Figueira (☎043/422 21). Part of the manorhouse accommodation scheme, this is located 12km north of the town. ⑤.

Around the town

At the heart of the the old town is the **Praça Sá da Bandeira**, overlooked by the many-windowed Baroque facade of the Jesuit **Seminário** (1676). Rua Serpa Pinto or Rua Capelo e Ivens lead from here toward the signposted **Portas do Sol**, about fifteen minutes' walk, with the best of the churches conveniently en route.

First of these is the Manueline **Igreja de Marvila**, at the end of Rua Serpa Pinto, with its brilliant seventeenth-century *azulejos* and lovely stone pulpit, comprising eleven miniature Corinthian columns. From here, Rua J. Araújo, at right angles to the side of the church, descends a few yards to the architectural highlight of Santarém: the early fifteenth-century **Igreja da Graça** (9.30am–1pm & 2.30–5.30pm). A spectacular rose window dominates the church and overlapping "blind arcades" above the portal are heavily influenced by the vertical decorations on the main facade at Batalha. Pedro Álvares Cabral, discoverer of Brazil in 1500, is buried within, but his austere tomb-slab is overshadowed by the elaborate sarcophagus of Pedro de Menezes (died 1437), first Governor of Ceuta.

Continuing toward the *miradouro*, a third sidetrack is the twelfth-century church of **São João de Alporão**, now an archaeological museum. Take a look at the Flamboyant Gothic tomb of Duarte de Menezes (died 1464). So comprehensively was he butchered by the Moors in North Africa that only a single tooth was recovered for burial! Avenida 5 de Outubro eventually finishes at the **Portas do Sol** (Gates of the Sun), a large garden occupying the site of the Moorish citadel. Modern battlements look down on a long stretch of the Tejo with its fertile sandbanks. And beyond, a vast chunk of the Ribatejo disappears into the distance – green, flat, and monotonous.

Bulls and festivals

This thinly populated agricultural plain is the home of Portuguese **bullfighting**. The very best horses and bulls graze in the lush fields under the watchful eyes of *campinos*, mounted guardians dressed in bright eighteenth-century costume. Agricultural traditions, folk dancing (especially the *fandango*), and bullfighting all come together in the great annual **Feira Nacional da Agricultura**, held at Santarém for two weeks starting on the fourth Sunday in May, while dishes from every region in Portugal are sampled at the **Festival de Gastronomia** (last week in Oct, first one in Nov). For a fixed price (low) you can eat as much as you like.

More bullfights are staged here during the **Milagre Fair** (2nd Sun in April for two weeks; fights on Sat), the **Piedade Fair** (2nd Sun in Oct for two weeks), and throughout the summer, and there are cattle markets on the second and fourth Sunday of every month.

Vila Franca de Xira and the Tejo Nature Reserve

The mecca for aficionados of the Portuguese bullfight is **VILA FRANCA DE XIRA**. A Pamplona-style running of the bulls, with the usual casualties, takes place here on the first and second Sunday in July at the **Festa do Colete Encarnado** ("Red Waistcoat" – a reference to the costume of the *campinos*), and on the first Sunday in October at the **Annual Fair**.

Accommodation on these occasions is difficult to find and it's easier to visit the festivals on a day trip from Santarem or Lisbon. It's best to take the train to Vila Franca – the station is in the town centre – as traffic is chaotic at festival times. When not hosting these events Vila Franca is a drab industrial city; the only reason to visit would be for the major **bullfights**, staged throughout the season.

Tejo Nature Reserve

South and southeast from Vila Franca de Xira, the banks of the Tejo are classified as a **Reserva Natural**, as protection for the thousands of wild birds that gather in the estuary. The best access point for viewing is the **Reserva de Pancas**, near BENAVENTE, approached on the EN10 from Porto Alto; the reserve has its head office, the *Herdade de Pancos*, here.

OTHER RIBATEJO FESTIVALS

During August, dozens of other small festivals and bullfights take place in the strip of bull-rearing towns down along the other side of the Tejo – the nearest to Santarém are ALMEIRIM (6km) and ALPIARÇA (9km). Posters should advertise such events well in advance.

Other towns to keep an eye out for include CHAMUSCA (on the left bank of the Tejo, northeast from Santarém); GOLEGÃ (right bank of the Tejo, near Chamusca – with a **Feira Nacional do Cavalo** in the first week of Nov); SALVATERRA DE MAGOS (south from Santarém on the left bank of the Tejo); BENAVENTE (see above); and MONTIJO (easily reached by ferry from Lisbon, with plenty of action and few tourists).

Up the Tejo: Almourol and Beyond

As if conjured up by some medieval-minded magician, the **Castle of ALMOUROL** stands deserted on a tiny island in the middle of the Tejo, 35km northeast of Santarém. Built by the Knights Templar in 1171, it never saw military action – except in sixteenth-century romantic literature – and its double perimeter walls and ten small towers are perfectly preserved. There is a beautiful rural panorama from the tall central keep.

Railway lines hug the banks of the Tejo at this point and there are two convenient stations, Almourol and Tancos, fifteen and thirty minutes' walk respectively from the island. The former is stuck in the middle of nowhere but **TANCOS** is actually a small village with a couple of bars catering for a nearby army barracks. There's no accommodation anywhere but unofficial camping shouldn't be too difficult in such deserted territory, so long as you avoid the rifle range.

To **reach the castle** from Tancos, strike out along the railway tracks: the river banks are an impassable forest of eucalyptus trees, cacti, and assorted bushes. For around 250$00 per person, one of two old **ferrymen** will row you around the island and deposit you on a miniature beach to explore the castle at leisure. Your day is very much determined by the temper of your ferryman – usually there's no problem about taking picnics over to the island.

Constância

CONSTÂNCIA, 3km upstream of Almourol, is a useful place to stay the night after a visit to the castle. A sleepy whitewashed village, arranged like an amphitheatre around the Tejo and the mouth of the Rio Zêzere, it is best known in Portugal for its association with **Luís de Camões**, Portugal's national poet. In fact Camões was here for only three years (1547–50), taking refuge from the court of Dom João III, whom he had managed to offend by the injudicious dedication of a love sonnet to a woman on whom the king himself had designs. Constância, however, is said to have remained dear to the poet's heart until the end of his life. In more troubled times, the town served the Duke of Wellington in 1809: he amassed his forces here and prepared for the Battle of Talavera in Spain.

If you want to stay in Constância, ask for *dormidas* in the central cafés or, if you have the money, book ahead for a manorhouse stay at *O Palácio* (☎049/932 24; ⑥), run by the English-speaking Azevedo family. The nearest **campsite** is in an attractive lakeside setting at Castelo de Bode, 9km up the Rio Zêzere (see Tomar).

Abrantes

ABRANTES occupies a position similar to Santarém, perched strategically above the Tejo, 15km upstream of Almourol. But the streets and *praças* here are prettier and the views more varied and just as extensive, making the town more of a worthwhile base in its own right. Additionally, the town has useful train connections linking up with the lower Beiras and the Alto Alentejo.

The highpoint – in all respects – is the town's well-battered **Castelo** (Tues–Sun 10am–12.30pm & 2–5pm), constructed in the early fourteenth century. As at Santarém, Romans and Moors established strongholds here – and the citadel was again sharply contested during the Peninsular War. The chapel of **Santa Maria do Castelo**, within the fort, houses a motley **archaeological museum**, its prize exhibits being three tombs of the Almeidas, Counts of Abrantes.

From the battlements there's a terrific view of the countryside and the rooftops of Abrantes and the gardens around its walls. Two large, whitewashed churches tower above all else; both were rebuilt in the sixteenth century.

Practicalities

Abrantes has a **Turismo** at the entrance to the town from the Tejo, where Rua do Montepio turns off the main road and climbs to the central Praça Barão da Batalha; the **bus station** is a few yards from here along Rua N. S. da Conceição.

There are two local **train stations**, both out of town. The main one is 2km south, across the Tejo, and offers the possibilities of the **Leste line** either to Valencia de Alcântara in Spain (via Castelo de Vide and Marvão stations) or to Crato, Portalegre, and Badajoz (in Spain). Trains also run to Portalegre, with *CP* buses (rail passes valid) on from there to Estremoz.

The other station is northeast of the town at ALFERRAREDE. This is the first stop on the **Beira Baixa line** to Belver (see "Alentejo") and Castelo Branco and Guarda (see "Mountain Beiras").

Accommodation is generally easy enough to find, with three decent-priced pensions, a hotel and an *agroturismo* lodging. These are:

Pensão Central, Praça Raimundo Soares 15 (☎041/224 22). Pleasant and inexpensive. ①.

Pensão Abrantes, Rua Miguel de Almeida 17, off the Praça Soares (☎041/221 19). Very rundown but rockbottom prices. ①.

Pensão Aliança, Rua Cidade das Caldas (☎041/223 48). ②.

Hotel de Turismo de Abrantes, Largo de Santo Antonio (☎041/212 61). The upmarket option, with all the facilities. ⑥.

Quinta dos Vales, Tramagal (☎041/973 63). Manorhouse accommodation in a village just south of the town, across the Tejo. ⑥.

One of the most stylish and inexpensive restaurants in all Portugal is the **Restaurante Huambo**, on the corner of the main *praça* and Largo Avelar Machado. This also may have a few rooms available.

travel details

Trains from Lisbon and Entroncamento
OESTE LINE

From Lisbon, 13 trains daily to Torres Vedras (70–90min), 12 to Óbidos (1hr 50min) and Caldas da Rainha (2hr–2hr30min), 6 to Leiria (3hr–3hr30min), and 4 to Figueira da Foz (3hr45min). For most of the trains, you have to change at Cacém on the Sintra line.

From Lisbon to Entroncamento 25 daily (1hr 30min–2hr), via Vila Franca de Xira (25min) and Santarém (1hr 10min).

From Entroncamento there are trains to Porto, Coimbra, Guarda, Portalegre etc – and to Tomar (16 daily; 20–30min) and to Almourol/Abrantes (9 daily – not all stop at Almourol; 15min/50min).

Trains from Abrantes
BEIRA BAIXA LINE

From Abrantes 7 daily to Belver/Castelo Branco (45min/1hr15min–2 hr), 6 to Covilhã (3hr30min), and 4 to Guarda (5hr15min).

LESTE LINE

From Abrantes 5 daily to Crato and Portalegre (1hr 40min/2hr), 4 to Elvas (2hr 50min), 3 to Badajoz, Spain (3hr 20min). Change at Torre das Vargens for Castelo de Vide (2hr), Marvão (2 daily;

2hr 30min), and Valencia de Alcântara, Spain (2 daily; 3hr).

PORTALEGRE LINE

From Abrantes 2 trains daily to Portalegre (3hr 15min), with *CP* bus service to Estremoz .

Buses
From Lisbon to Mafra/Ericeira (hourly; 1hr 30min–1hr 45min); Torres Vedras/Areia Branca/Peniche (hourly; 1hr 40min/2hr 25min/3hr); Vila Franca de Xira/Santarém (every 30min; 50 min/2hr); Leiria (8 daily; 2hr 30min).

From Peniche to Consolação/Areia Branca (hourly; 15/35min); Óbidos/Caldas da Rainha/São Martinho do Porto (hourly; 40min/50min/1hr 20min).

From Nazaré to Alcobaça (hourly; 20min); Leiria (10 daily; 1hr 10min).

From Leiria to Batalha/Alcobaça (8; 20min/50min); Batalha/Fátima/Tomar (4; 20min/50min/2hr); Porto de Mós/Mira d'Aire/Santarém (4; 30min/50min/1hr 50min); Coimbra (hourly; 1hr 40min).

From Ericeira to Sintra (8; 45min).

From Tomar to Abrantes (4; 45min).

From Abrantes to Santarém (6; 1hr 25min).

CHAPTER THREE

COIMBRA AND BEIRA LITORAL

T he province of **Beira Litoral** is dominated by the city of **Coimbra**, which, with Lisbon and Porto, forms the trio of Portugal's historic capitals. Sited on a hill above the river Mondego, it's a wonderfully moody place, full of ancient alleys and lanes, and diverting both in terms of monuments and museums, and in a strong cultural life, based around the country's oldest university. As a base for exploring the region, the city can't be beaten, with Portugal's most extensive Roman site, **Conímbriga**, on the outskirts, and the delightful spa town of **Luso** and ancient **forest of Buçaco** under a half-hour's journey to the north.

Beira's **coastline**, from Figueira da Foz up as far as Porto, has been dubbed the **Costa de Prata** ("Silver"). Although slowly succumbing to development, most noticeably around **Praia de Mira**, it remains one of the least spoiled in Portugal – an endlessly sandy reach, with predominantly small-scale towns and resorts. Indeed the only resorts of any real size are **Figueira da Foz** and **Aveiro**, and even these have kept an enjoyably old-fashioned feel. In many of the smaller villages, coastal life remains highly traditional, with the whole community still involved in hauling in the fishing boats and their catches.

Inland, the villages and towns of the fertile plain have long been conditioned by the twin threats of floodwaters coming down from Portugal's highest mountains, and silting caused by the restless Atlantic. Drainage channels have had to be cut to make cultivation possible and houses everywhere built on high ground. At Aveiro, positioned on a complex estuary site, a whole network of canals was developed to cope with the currents, and to facilitate salt production and harvesting of seaweed – still the staples of the local economy.

The Beira region also hints at the river valley delights to come, in the Douro and Minho, further north. Following the **Rio Mondego** upstream from Coimbra, you'll come to see why it has been celebrated so often in Portuguese poetry as the *Rio das Musas* – River of the Muses. An equally beautiful road journey trails the **Rio Vouga**, from Aveiro, up into the **Cambarinho Nature Reserve**; unfortunately, as of 1990, the Vouga's even lovelier train line has been closed.

Coimbra

COIMBRA was Portugal's capital for over a century (1143–1255) and its famous **university**, founded in 1290 and permanently established here in 1537 after a series of moves back and forth to Lisbon, was the only one in Portugal until the beginning of this century. It remains highly prestigious – though Lisbon has far more students nowadays – and provides the greatest of Coimbra's monuments.

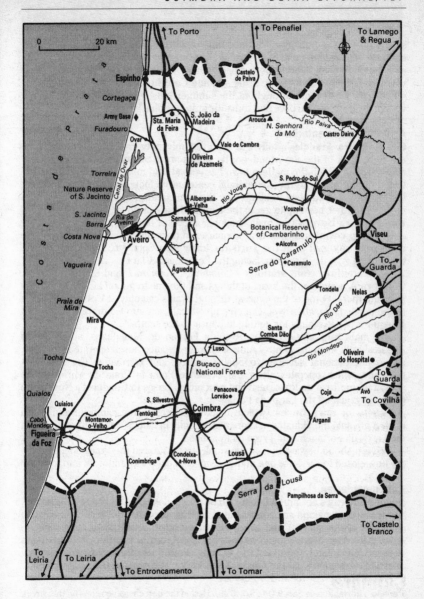

For a small, provincial university town, however, there are a remarkable number of other riches: two cathedrals, dozens of lesser churches, and scores of ancient mansions, one housing the superb **Machado de Castro** sculpture museum. Besides which, the town is a lot of fun in itself, packed with student bars and taverns, and very pleasantly small scale, with a population of just 56,000.

The city is at its most lively when the students are in town, and can be decidedly sleepy during the holidays. The best time of all to be here is in May, when the students celebrate the end of the academic year in the **Queima das Fitas**, graduates ceremoniously tearing or burning their gowns and faculty ribbons. This is when you're most likely to hear the genuine **Coimbra fado** (though the tourist office organises events throughout the summer), distinguished from the Lisbon version by its mournful pace and romantic or intellectual lyrics.

Arriving and orientation

Old Coimbra straddles a hilly site, with the university crowding its summit, on the right bank of the Rio Mondego. Its slopes are a convoluted mass of ancient alleys around which the modern town has spread, and most of interest is concentrated on the hill or in the commercial centre at its foot. Chances are you'll get lost as soon as you start to climb past the remains of the city walls, but it's no problem – either head up to get to the **Universidade** or down, and you can't miss **Rua Ferreira Borges** (the main shopping street) or the river.

Our **map** covers only this central quarter of town; for a free plan showing the rest of the city, call in at the **Turismo** (daily 9am–8pm; ☎039/238 86), on the triangular Largo da Portagem, facing the Ponte Santa Clara.

There are three **train stations** – *Coimbra A, Coimbra B* and *Coimbra Parque*. **Coimbra A** is right at the heart of things and the one to get off at, if your train is stopping there. Some of the express through trains call only at **Coimbra B**, 3km to the north, from where you can pick up a local train into Coimbra A. **Coimbra Parque** is of use mainly for getting to Lousa, to the south.

The main **bus station** is on Avenida Fernão de Magalhães, about fifteen minutes' walk from the centre. Almost all long-distance buses operate from here, as do international services to Spain, France, and Germany. The *Avic* bus company, which operates along the Costa de Prata to Praia da Mira, has its station in Rua João de Ruão, near the post office. Buses to Condeixa-a-Nova leave from a stop just off the Largo da Portagem.

Tickets for **town buses** (which include services to the campsite and youth hostel) are sold individually, or more conveniently in blocks (*módulos*) at kiosks in the Largo da Portagem and Praça da República.

Drivers shoud beware that all the small streets around the Praça do Comércio are now closed to cars; use one of the signposted car parks and walk into town.

Accommodation

Much of the city's accommodation is to be found close by Combra A train station. The cheaper pensions are concentrated in **Rua da Sota** (left and immediately right out of the station) and the little streets off it: a central, if rather sleazy-looking location. More expensive ones line the **Avenida Fernão de Magalhães** (left and immediately left out of the station), **Avenida Emídio Navarro** (directly ahead of the station) and the **Largo das Ameias**, between the two.

Pick of the **pensions and hotels** are:

Pensão Vitória, Rua da Sota 9 (☎039/240 49). Best of the best cheap pensions on this street, with a good restaurant downstairs. ①.

Pensão Lorvanense, Rua da Sota 27; **Pensão Sota**, Rua da Sota 41. Two Rua da Sota fallbacks, neither especially recommended. ①.

Pensão Flôr de Coimbra, Rua do Poço 8, off Rua da Sota. Nothing special, though the very cheap meals for residents may appeal. ①.

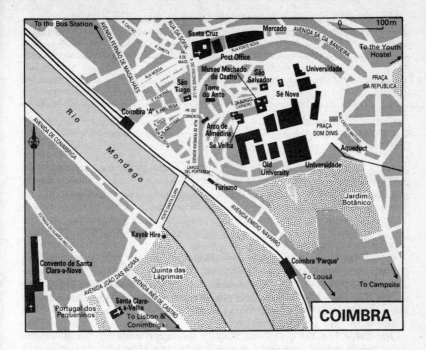

Hospedaria Simões, Rua Fernandes Tomás 69 (☎039/346 38). Clean, basic lodgings on a quiet back street. ①.

Pensão Gouveia, Rua João de Ruão 21 (☎039/297 93). Away from the centre, but quiet, and convenient for the bus stations. ①.

Pensão Diogo, Praça da República 18-2°. An old-fashioned sort of place in the student area of town, with views over the square. ①.

Pensão Rivoli, Praça do Comércio 27 (☎039/255 59). Excellent value rooms and (pedestrianised) location. ②.

Pensão Jardim, Avda. Emídio Navarro 65 (☎039/252 04). Has seen better days, but a nice riverbank location. ②.

Pensão Parque, Avda. Emídio Navarro 42 (☎039/292 02). Much better rooms both here and in its **Residencial Universal** annexe (☎039/224 44), at no. 47. Both ②.

Residencial Internacional, Avda. Emídio Navarro (☎039/255 03). Noisy location opposite the train station, but the rooms have a bit of old-style character. ②.

Residencial Larbelo, Largo da Portagem 33 (☎039/290 92). Right by the Turismo and a very good deal; all rooms with private bath. ③.

Pensão Antunes, Rua Castro Matoso 8, beneath the aqueduct (☎039/230 48). One of Coimbra's nicest budget pensions – though a bit of a haul from the centre. ③.

Residencial Lusa Atenas, Avda. Fernão de Magalhães 68 (☎039/264 12). Clean, spacious rooms, with private bath. ③.

Hotel Astoria, Avda. Emídio Navarro 21 (☎039/220 55). The only recommendable upmarket option – a 1930s building by the river; rooms are around 14,000$00. ⑥.

Additional budget alternatives include a youth hostel and campsite:

Pousada de Juventude, Rua António Henriques Seco 14 – above the Parque Santa Cruz, signposted off to the top right on our map (☎039/229 55). A decent, if not overwlecoming, modern hostel. Reception 9am–noon and 6pm–midnight; midnight curfew. It's about twenty minutes' walk, or bus #7/8/29/46, from Coimbra A.

Camping Municipal, at the municipal sports complex (☎039/729 97). A highly municipal site, but has the attraction of the adjacent town **swimming pool**. Bus #5 runs there from the Largo Portagem, or, if you're coming from Lousa, you can get off at São José station, 250m from the entrance. Open all year.

The City

It's best to start your exploration of Coimbra with the **Velha Universidade** (old university), not only because of its importance but because it's the easiest place to find, and from its balcony the city is laid out below you like a map. Before leaving there, set your sights on your next destination and with luck you should be able to find it when you get down.

The Velha Universidade

The main buildings of the **Velha Universidade** (summer 10am–2pm & 5–7pm; winter 10am–5pm; occasionally closed from 12.30–2pm throughout the year) date from the sixteenth century when João III declared its establishment at Coimbra permanent. They're set around the **Patio das Escolas**, a courtyard dominated by the Baroque clocktower nicknamed **A Cabra** – the goat – and a statue of the portly João III.

The elaborate stairway to the right of the main court leads into the administrative quarters and the **Sala dos Capelos**; tickets are sold here for visits to each of the main sections of the university. The hall itself is used for conferring degrees and is hung with portraits of Portugal's kings and has a fine wood-panelled ceiling with gilded decoration in the Manueline style. The highlight of this part of the building though is the narrow **catwalk** around the outside walls.

The central door off the courtyard leads past the **Capela**, not the finest of Coimbra's religious foundations but one of the most elaborate – covered with *azulejos* and intricate decoration including twisted, rope-like pillars, a weirdly frescoed ceiling, and a gaudy Baroque organ.

To the left is the famous **Library**, a Baroque fantasy presented to the faculty by João V in the early eighteenth century. Its rooms telescope into each other, focusing on the founder's portrait in a disconcertingly effective use of trompe l'oeil. The richness of it all is impressive, such as the yards of cleverly marbled wood, gold leaf, tables inlaid with ebony, rosewood and jacaranda, Chinese-style lacquer work, and carefully calculated frescoed ceilings. The most prized valuables, the rare and ancient books, are locked away out of sight and, impressive multilingual titles notwithstanding, the volumes on the shelves seem largely chosen for their aesthetic value; no one seems likely to disturb the careful arrangement by actually reading anything.

The Museu Machado de Castro

After the university a good first stop is at the **Museu Machado de Castro** (Tues–Sun 10am–1pm & 2.30–5pm; 350$00; free Sun am), just down from the unprepossessing **Sé Nova** (New Cathedral). The museum, named after an eighteenth-century sculptor, is housed in the former archbishop's palace – which would be worth visiting in its own right even if it were empty. As it is, it's positively stuffed with treasures: sculpture (especially a little medieval knight, riding home with his mace slung over his shoulder), paintings, furniture, and ceramics.

Underneath all this is the Roman **Cryptoportico**, a series of subterranean galleries probably used by the Romans as a granary and subsequently pressed into service for the foundations of the palace.

The Cathedral

The **Sé Velha** squats about halfway down the hill; an unmistakable, heavy, fortress-like bulk. Started in 1162, it's one of the most important Romanesque buildings in Portugal, little altered and seemingly unbowed by the weight of the years; the one significant later addition – the Renaissance *Porta Especiosa* in the north wall – has, in contrast to the main structure, almost entirely crumbled away. Solid and square on the outside, it's also stolid and simple within, the decoration confined to a few giant conch shells holding holy water and some unobtrusive *azulejos* from Seville around the walls. The Gothic tombs of early bishops and the low-arched cloister are equally restrained.

Santa Cruz

Restraint and simplicity certainly aren't the chief qualities of the **Mosteiro de Santa Cruz** (9am–12.30pm & 2–6pm), at the bottom of the hill past the old city gates. Although it was originally founded by São Teotónio even before the cathedral, nothing remains that has not been substantially remodelled. Its exuberant facade and strange double doorway set the tone. In the early sixteenth century Coimbra was the base of a major sculptural school that included the French artists Nicolas Chanterene and Jean de Rouen (João de Ruão), as well as the two Manueline masters João de Castilho and and Diogo de Boitaca, all of whom had a hand in rebuilding Santa Cruz.

These artists designed a variety of projects: **tombs** to house Portugal's first kings, **Afonso Henriques** and **Sancho I**; an elaborate **pulpit**; and. most famously, the **Cloister of Silence**. It is here that the Manueline theme is at its clearest, with a series of airy arches decorated with bas-relief scenes from the life of Christ. From the cloister a staircase leads to the raised *coro*, above whose wooden benches is a frieze celebrating the nation's flourishing empire.

There is a superb **café** built into the Gothic valuts to the east of the church.

The Santa Clara convents

It was in Santa Cruz that the romantic history of Dom Pedro and Inês de Castro (see "Alcobaça") came to its ghoulish climax. Pedro, finally proclaimed king, had his lover exhumed and set up on a throne in the church, where his courtiers were forced to pay homage to the decomposing body.

Inês had originally lain in the **Convento de Santa Clara-a-Velha**, across the river, alongside the convent's founder, the saint-queen Isabel, Coimbra's patron. Isabel was married to Dom Dinis, whom she infuriated by constantly giving away his wealth to the poor. She performed one of her many miracles when, confronted by her irate husband as she smuggled out yet another cargo of gold, she claimed to be carrying only roses: when her bag was opened that was exactly its contents. The Gothic hall church she built was almost entirely covered by silt from the Mondego but the ruin – an amazing sight – is slowly being restored.

The two tombs have long since been moved away, Inês's to Alcobaça and Isabel's to the **Convento de Santa Clara-a-Nova**, higher up the hill and safe from the shifting river. The new convent, built in 1650, doesn't have much of the charm of the old and the fact that the nuns' quarters now house a Portuguese army barracks doesn't help. Its two saving graces, which make the climb worthwhile, are **Isabel's tomb** – made of solid silver collected by the citizens of Coimbra – and the vast **cloister** financed by João V, a king whose devotion to nuns went beyond the normal bounds of spiritual comfort.

Portugal dos Pequeninos and the Jardim Botânico

Between the two convents extends the parkland site of **Portugal dos Pequeninos**, a 1950s themepark where scale models of many of the country's great buildings are interspersed with "typical" farm houses and sections on the overseas territories, heavy with the White Man's Burden.

Historically and architecturally accurate it's not, but the place is fun and great for kids who can clamber in and out of the miniature houses. It's open daily from 9am to 7pm in the summer; out of season times vary.

A short distance beyond is a somewhat more sombre little park, the **Quinta das Lágrimas** (Garden of Tears), in which, so legend has it, Inês de Castro was finally tracked down and murdered.

If you like gardens though, the most rewarding site in Coimbra is the **Jardim Botânico**, on the far side of the hill from Portugal dos Pequeninos. Founded in the eighteenth century, these botanical displays once enjoyed a worldwide reputation and, even if they've seen better days, it's still very pleasant to stroll among the formally laid out beds of plants from around the world. Nearby are impressive remains of the sixteenth-century **Aqueduct of São Sebastião**.

Food, drink and practicalities

Whatever the size of your budget, you're unlikely to starve in Coimbra. With its student presence, it has some of the best value **restaurants** in the country. There is also a fair bit of **café and nightlife**, as well as all the usual city **facilities**: banks, post offices, travel agents, and so on.

Restaurants

The city's cheapest meals are to be found in the pensions – most of which serve residents only; in the atmospheric little dives on Beco do Forno, Beco dos Esteireiros, or Rua dos Gatos, a trio of tiny alleys between the Largo da Portagem and Rua da Sota; or in the workers' canteens along the Rua Direita.

For slightly more sophisticated fare, try the following:

Adega Paço do Conde, tucked out of the way on the Largo do Paço do Conde. Always buzzing with Coimbrans: barrel wine and great barbecued fish at low prices.

O Funchal, Rua das Azeiteiras. A place to go for substantial stews and the like – try *chanfana*, the house special.

O Pingão, on the outskirts of the town at Rua Figueira da Foz 166. A very fine chef, and an outdoor grill in summer.

O Palácio, Praça Sé Velha (closed Sun). Surprisingly good food and reasonable prices for a restaurant with such a touristy location.

Trovador, Praça Sé Velha. A rather more chi-chi place, which features evening fado sessions – with a balcony for those just wanting to drink.

Cafés, bars and nightlife

At some stage of the day, try to visit one of the traditional **coffee houses** along Rua Ferreira Borges and Rua Visconde da Luz – the banks and big shops are all near here and the cafés are filled with business types and package-laden shoppers. *Arcadia*, on Rua Ferreira Borges, is a personal favourite.

The Praça da República, across town by the Parque de Santa Cruz, is also surrounded by cafés and **bars**, this time populated with students. The *Associação Académica* on Rua Castro Matoso stays open lunchtime and late in the evening, and offers excellent value drinks and snacks.

Nightlife is less predictable, but you can occasionally find fairly impromptu **fado sessions** taking place on the steps of the cathedral at about 11pm. The *Café Santa Cruz*, on Praca 8 de Maio, and *Bar Diligência*, on Travessa da Rua Nova, have regular nightly fado sessions. For up-to-the-minute news on concerts and events, it's best to talk to one of the students in the *Associaçao Académica*, above.

Listings

Market. Weekday mornings off Rua Olímpio Nicolau Rui Fernandes, above the post office.

Crafts. The *Torre de Anto*, at the bottom of the old town near the Arco de Almedina, now houses a handicraft co-op with fine, well-priced goods.

Travel agencies. *Abreu* (Rua da Sota 2) and *Visa* (Avda. Fernão de Magalhães 11) both sell international bus and flight tickets.

Swimming pool. The *Piscina Municipale* is at the municipal sports complex: take bus #5 from the Largo Portagem.

Post office. The main post office is on Avda. Fernão de Magalhães.

Currency exchange. Banks are grouped along the avenues west and east of Coimbra A station. The *Hotel Astoria* on Largo da Portagem will change currency outside bank hours.

Conimbriga

The ancient city of **CONIMBRIGA** (daily 9am–1pm & 2–6pm; 300$00), 16km southwest of Coimbra, is by far the most important Roman site in Portugal. It was almost certainly preceded by a substantial Celto-Iberian settlement, dating back to the Iron Age, but the excavated buildings almost all belong to the latter days of the Roman Empire, from the second to the fourth century AD. Throughout this period Conimbriga was a major stopping point on the road from Olisipo (Lisbon) to Bracara Augusta (Braga). Although by no means the largest town in Roman Portugal, it has survived better than any other – principally because its inhabitants abandoned it, apparently for the comparative safety of Coimbra, and never resettled there. That the city came to a violent end is clear from the powerful wall thrown up right through its heart – a wall thrown up so hurriedly and determinedly that it even cut houses in two.

It is the **wall**, with the **Roman road** leading up to and through it, that first strikes you – little else, indeed, remains above ground level. In the urgency of its construction anything that came to hand was used and a close inspection reveals pillars, inscribed plaques and bricks thrown in among the rough stonework. Most of what has been excavated is in the immediate environs of the wall; the bulk of the city, still only part-excavated, lies in the ground beyond it.

What you can see is impressive enough, though. **Houses** with excellent mosaic floors, **pools** whose original fountains and water-ducts have been restored to working order, and a complex series of baths with their elaborate – and beautiful – below-floor heating systems have been revealed. To make sense of it all, it's worth investing in the official guide at the entrance. In the summer you may find students on site to explain the finer points.

The **museum**, opposite the site entrance (closed Mon), displays fascinating finds from the dig, including bronze jewellery and coins, and fragments of statues. Around the back is an excellent **café** with views from its terrace down into the valley, whose steep sides were for many years Conimbriga's main defence.

Getting there – and Condeixa

There's at least one daily **bus** direct to the site from Coimbra (leaving from the Largo de Portagem). In summer, the first bus of the day is at 9am – the one to go for if you want to avoid the sometimes overwhelming school parties.

Alternatively, you can take one of the hourly buses from Coimbra (again leaving from the Largo da Portagem) to the small town of **CONDEIXA-A-NOVA**, half an hour's walk to the south of Conimbriga. Condeixa is the centre of the Berias' **hand-painted ceramics** industry and eight local factories are open to visits. It's a pleasant place in its own right, too, with several bars and cafés around the central square. Arriving in the early afternoon at Condeixa, you could walk to the site, spend a leisurely few hours there, and then catch the direct bus back to Coimbra or arrange a lift with other tourists.

Lousã and the Serra da Lousã

Another popular daytrip, southeast from Coimbra, is to the medieval-looking village of **LOUSÃ** and its surrounding **serra** (mountain) countryside. Going by train, sit on the right, facing the engine, for maximum scenic enjoyment. Some of the trains from Coimbra stop (or just halt) first at Lousã A; if they do, hold on for the next stop, which is higher up, in Lousã proper. From this main **station**, the road opposite, slightly to the right, leads directly into town.

The village

Wandering along Lousa's **main street**, you pass a succession of intricately decorated **chapels** and **casas brasonadas** (heraldic mansions), and a little **museum** that doubles up as the **Turismo**. Customarily helpful, this can supply you with maps of the Serra da Lousã, vital if you want to explore the range, and useful, too, for the walk up to Lousa's ruined **castle**, too – a route erratically signposted from the village as *Castelo & Ermidas*.

Following this path up from the village brings you out, after around 3km, at a spot where a tributary of the Mondego curls around a narrow gorge between two splendid wooded hills. On one there sits a miniature **castle**; on the other is a small hermitage dedicated to **Nossa Senhora da Piedade**. Pilgrims mingle with swimmers, who come to bathe in the chilly river pool between the two; picnickers abound; and there's a café. There are springs midway, bubbling up beautifully clear water that locals drive up to collect.

The village has two **pensions**, both pleasant and moderately priced: the *Residencial Martinho* (②) in Rua Movimento das Forças Armadas, and *Pensão Bem Estar* (☎039/99 14 45; ②) on Avenida Coelho da Gama. There is also a municipal **campsite**. During your stay, don't forget to try the delicious **Licor Beirão** – herb-flavoured firewater – which comes from Lousã.

The Serra da Lousã

A hike to the top of the Serra da Lousã will reward you with stunning views and a sequence of eery sights, in the range's **abandoned villages**. The most direct path runs through the woods above Lousã and is marked, rather intermittently, with yellow and white blazes on the trees.

There are six villages on the range, all of them deserted in the 1950s as a result of rural emigration. It's quite an unsettling experience to wander through the empty streets and into the open houses. In the first village you come to, **Casal Novo**, a few of the houses are being renovated as holiday homes – and it's possible that you may be able to stay the night; check first with the Turismo in Lousã.

Upriver to Penacova – and Lorvão

Northeast of Coimbra, the **Rio Mondego** is a delight, with its hilly, wooded valley. It is trailed by the minor D110 road (four buses daily) and in summer it's possible to rent a **kayak** from Coimbra for the trip upriver to **Penacova** – or downriver if you do the trip in reverse (which is rather easier going). For details of the kayaks, contact the Coimbra *Turismo*, or the campsite at Penacova; kayaks leave Coimbra from the Quinta das Lágrimas.

Penacova

PENACOVA is a small town high above the river, with a good **campsite** on the bank, a single **pension**, the *Avenida*, and a superb **restaurant**, the *Panorâmica* (go for the veal stew, its cheapest dish).

These facilities apart, there is little enough to the place – the appeal is in the river and woods around – though an oddity, as elsewhere in this region, are the highly elaborate **toothpicks** on sale. These are hand-carved by local women and are genuinely beautiful artefacts – the more delicate like feathered darts.

Lorvão

A strange and sad side trip from Penacova, or Coimbra, could also be made to the **Convento de Lorvão**, at the village of **LORVÃO** (bus to Rebordosa, then walk the remaining 4km). This very ancient complex was founded by Benedictines in the ninth century, predating the arrival of the Arabs, and later taken over by Cistercian nuns. The abbesses are buried horizontally in the graveyard; the lesser sisters are buried vertically, in twos and threes.

Most of what remains of the convent is the product of heavy restoration in the eighteenth century. If you ring for admission, you can visit the **church**, which displays the skull of an Arab king in its treasury, and with luck climb up to the *zimbório* or domed roof, with its splendid views over the village. The visit, however, is a disturbing one, as Lorvão serves as a distressingly old-fashioned mental institution; the inhabitants lower paper cups down on pieces of string to visitors in the courtyard, to receive money or cigarettes.

The Forest of Buçaco

The **Forest of Buçaco** is something of a Portuguese icon. The country's most famous and most revered woods were a monastic domain through the Middle Ages, and the site in the Peninsular War of a battle that saw Napoleon's first significant defeat. They are today a little undertended and overvisited, but remain an enjoyable spot for rambling.

From Coimbra it is easy enough to visit Buçaco as a daytrip, or en route to Viseu. All of the non-express **buses** from Coimbra to Viseu take a short detour from Luso through the forest, stopping at the *Palace Hotel* and again by the Portas da Rainha. Alternatively, you could stay in the nearby spa town of **Luso**, a short walk from the forest, or, if you have money to burn, stay in the old royal forest lodge, the *Hotel Palace do Buçaco* (see below).

Some history

Benedictine monks established a hermitage in the midst of Buçaco forest as early as the sixth century, and the area remained in religious hands right up to the dissolution of the monasteries in 1834. The forest's great fame and beauty, though, came with the **Carmelite monks** who settled here in the seventeenth century, building the walls which still mark its boundary.

In 1643 Pope Urban VIII issued a papal bull threatening anyone who damaged the trees with excommunication; an earlier decree had already protected the monks' virtue by banning women. The monks, meanwhile, were propagating the forest, introducing varieties new to Portugal from all over the world. Nowadays there are estimated to be over seven hundred different types of tree, but the most impressive remain some of the earliest – particularly the mighty Mexican Cedars.

Walks around the forest

Walks are laid out everywhere in Buçaco: along the **Vale dos Fetos** (Valley of Ferns) to the lake and cascading **Fonte Fria**, for example, or up the **Avenida dos Cedros** to the **Coimbra Gate**. But you can wander freely anywhere in the forest, and in many ways it is at its most attractive when it's wildest, away from the formal pathways.

The **Via Sacra**, lined with chapels in which terracotta figures depict the stages of Christ's journey carrying the cross to Calvary, leads from the *Palace Hotel* to the Cruz Alta, a giant cross at the summit of the hill. From here, as from the Portas de Coimbra, there are magnificent panoramas of the surrounding country. It's a lovely place, if not always the haven of peace the monks strove to create – at weekends and holidays the woods are packed with picnicking Portuguese.

The Palace Hotel and the Battle of Buçaco

The **Hotel Palace do Buçaco** (☎031/931 01; ⑤) stands at the heart of the forest, built on the site of the old Carmelite monastery as a summer retreat for the Portuguese monarchy. Since it was only completed in 1907, however, three years before the declaration of the Republic, it saw little royal use. An enormous imitation Manueline construction, it charges upwards of 22,000$00 for a double room, but anyone can stroll in, have a drink or a meal, and admire the Afonso Mucha prints, or the sequence of *azulejos* depicting the Battle of Buçaco and the Portuguese conquest of Ceuta.

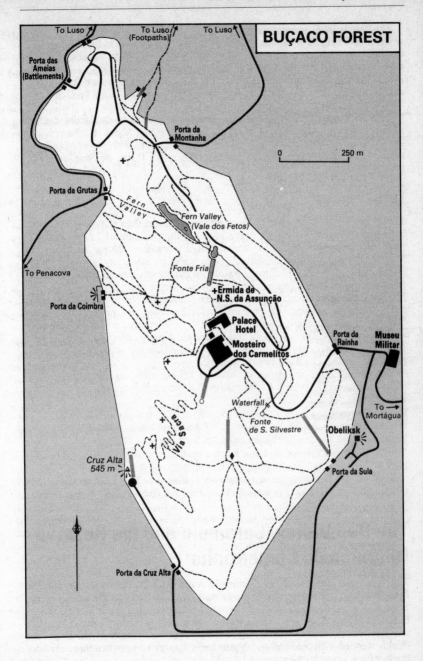

BUÇACO FOREST

To Luso

To Luso (Footpaths)

To Luso

Porta das Ameias (Battlements)

Porta da Montanha

0   250 m

Porta da Grutas

Fern Valley

Fern Valley (Vale dos Fetos)

To Penacova

Fonte Fria

Porta da Coimbra

+Ermida de N.S. da Assunção

Palace Hotel

Mosteiro dos Carmelítos

Porta da Rainha

Museu Militar

To Mortágua

Via Sacra

Waterfall

Fonte de S. Silvestre

Obeliksk

Cruz Alta 545 m

Porta da Sula

Porta da Cruz Alta

The **Battle of Buçaco** was fought largely on the ridge just above the forest, and it marked the first serious reverse suffered by Napoleon in his campaigns on the Peninsula. The French under Massena launched a frontal assault up the hill on virtually impregnable Anglo-Portuguese positions, sustaining massive losses in what for the Duke of Wellington amounted to little more than a delaying tactic, which he exploited in order to give himself time to retreat to his lines at Torres Vedras (see p.101).

A small **Museu Militar**, outside the forest near the Portas da Rainha, contains maps, uniforms, and weapons from the campaign. Just above it a narrow road climbs to the obelisk raised as a memorial to the battle, with vistas inland right across to the distant Serra da Estrêla, from where the **Porta de Sula** leads back into the forest.

Luso

LUSO lies on the main road to Viseu and on the Beira Alta rail route to Guarda, 3km downhill from the forest. A spa town for the past hundred or so years, its radioactive waters still draw crowds of Portuguese, taking the cure for rheumatism and other complaints. As such places go, it's pretty enjoyable, with a a series of elegant spa buildings, a wonderful nineteenth-century **Salão do Chá** – all white wicker, potted palms, and art nouveau – and a casino.

Taking **the waters** can be fun, too. It costs about 600$00 for the basics, with a full session of massage, electrolysis, and other therapies priced up to about 3000$00 maximum; the only serious expenditure is incurred if you see one of the spa's consultants. There's also a fine **swimming pool** (attached to the *Grande Hotel das Termas*), whose somewhat stiff admission fee is more than recompensed if you feel like a few hours basking.

You should have no problem finding a **room**, with excellent, inexpensive choices all over the centre; the **Turismo** in the central *praça* can help if there's any difficulty. Good choices include:

Pensão Portugal, Rua Dr. Marinho Pimenta (☎031/931 58). Best of the cheapies. ③.

Pensão Astória, Rua Emídio Navarro (☎031/931 82). Very pleasant, with a decent bar. ①.

Pensão Central, Rua Emídio Navarro (☎031/932 54. A little more character. ②.

Grande Hotel das Termas do Luso, Rua dos Banhos (☎031/934 50). A spot of luxury if you want to take the spa experience seriously. Doubles for around 11,000$00. ⑤.

Most of the pensions have **restaurants** attached. The *Central* has a nice terrace and a good cook. For a splash upmarket, the *Grande Hotel* is your place.

The Dão Valley, Caramulo and the Reserva Botânica do Cambarinho

The route east from **Luso to Caramulo** leads through the **valley of the Rio Dão**. The road follows the valley assiduously, with the river on the right, and the Serra do Caramulo on the left, all the way to Tondela (and on to Viseu). This is the heart of the region where **Dão wines** – some of the country's finest and richest reds – are produced. Where they're not covered with vineyards, the slopes are thickly wooded with pine and eucalyptus trees, though all too often there are bare tracts where forest fires have raged.

To the north stretches the **Reserva Botânica do Cambarinho**, a vast area of great natural beauty. The central **valley of Lafões**, again covered by vineyards, is reminiscent of the terraced hills of the Minho and Douro; other parts are densely wooded and dark, more like the Beiras countryside around Luso.

Getting to Caramulo – and Tondela

Public transport links to Caramulo, from **Luso**, involve something of a detour. You need first to take a bus to TONDELA, where you should be able to pick up one of the two daily buses to Caramulo/Águeda (7.35am and 6pm), a majestic if rather bumpy drive straight across the centre of the Serra do Caramulo. From **Coimbra**, there are also three daily buses to Caramulo, via Águeda. If you're detained by choice or necessity in Tondela, the *Residencial Tondela de Severino Gonçalves* (☎032/822 411; ①) is excellent value, and there's a good restaurant right opposite in the square.

A rather easier approach to Caramulo is from **Vouzela** (see the following section). On weekdays, two buses daily run between Vouzela and VARZIELAS, 4km north of Caramulo; from there you can either walk, hitch, or with luck pick up a local bus connection. If you are approaching from the south, Vouzela is an obvious next destination after Caramulo.

Cambarainha villages

There are three tiny villages at the heart of the reserve – **CAMBARINHO**, **ALCOFRA**, and **Caramulo**.

Cambarinho and Alcofra are of interest really for their environs, full of rhododendrons, brightly coloured azaleas, and thick green shrubs growing wild on the hillside. If you feel like staying off the beaten track, both have **rooms** to rent, since the villagers have wised up to the financial advantages of taking an interest in tourism.

The third village, Caramulo, has similar attractions, plus a couple of wonderful museums.

Caramulo

Tucked beneath the peaks of the high Beiras *serra*, **CARAMULO** is a great walking base – the loftiest Serra de Caramulo peak, *Caramulinho* (1062m), is less than an hour's walk away. It's also a very striking village – a diminutive, rather ghostlike place, apparently in the middle of nowhere, that seems an almost surreal setting for a couple of the country's major museums.

Principal of these is the **Fundação Abel Lacerda**, a wonderfully jumbled art collection, with everything from primitive religious sculpture to sketches by the greatest modern masters – minor works by Picasso and Dali among them. There's an exquisite series of sixteenth-century Tournai tapestries depicting the earliest Portuguese explorers in India, full of weird animals and natives based on obviously very garbled reports. A painting by British portraitist Graham Sutherland, donated to Portugal by the queen, and symbolising the long alliance with Britain, is accompanied by its letter of authenticity from Buckingham Palace. Elsewhere there's a large *John the Baptist*, painted by Grão Vasco, and quantities of beautiful furniture and jewellery.

Next door, and even more incongruous, is a collection of **vintage cars and motorcycles**, including a pack of chrome-plated American dream machines.

Caramulo has a fine **pension**, the *São Cristovão*(☎032/86 13 94; ②), though phone first to ascertain whether this is open. The only alternative is the six-bedroom **pousada**, São Jerónimo (☎032/85 12 91; ⑤), just outside the village; doubles here run at 10,000$00 – cheaper than most in the chain.

Along the Vouga

The **Rio Vouga** is one of the most beautiful, somnolent rivers in Portugal and until the railway closures of the late 1980s was trailed along its course by the Vouga rail line, a ride scenic enough to justify a trip for its own sake. The train services have been replaced by *CP* **buses** (on which rail passes are valid), and although these lack the romance of the train, the route remains worthwhile, if you feel like taking in a little of backwater Portugal. Coming from Coimbra or Aveirro, the place to leave the train for the bus is ALBERGARIA-A-VELHA, rather than SERNADA (which involves some backtracking on the bus).

Alternatively, as indicated in the previous section, you can approach from the south, from Luso or Caramulo.

Vouzela

VOUZELA is a small provincial town with an almost palpable sense of civic pride. The locals – and the tourist board – boast of the peculiar sweet cakes, or *pasteis de Vouzela* (only for the most sweet-toothed), richly flavoured traditional dishes like *Vitela de Lafões*, and the heady local *vinho Lafões* (similar to *vinho verde*). Vouzela also has its own local paper, which is quite a feat for a town with little over two thousand inhabitants.

The old centre is built around a sluggish stream, the backdrop to the main morning activity – washing clothes. Beneath a low **Romanesque bridge**, garments are spread to dry on the tall grass and soap suds run blue in the clear water. Houses around the bridge are all of the small town manor-type, with granite steps and balconies and whitewashed plaster-work. Topping this scene, a viaduct gracefully loops its way across the roof tops, whilst beyond it the *serras* of Arada and Caramulo rise up, dark and green, to north and south.

Back along the lane toward the main through-road, the **Turismo** is housed in a former prison. On the floor above, there's a **museum** (free) offering insights into local preoccupations such as weaving, photography, and painting. It's a small, rather odd collection, ranging through anthropological and historical exhibits, traditional craftwork, and Romanesque fragments, to an array of old dolls. Nearby is the town **Pelourinho**, popularly referred to as the *forca* or scaffold, from its days as a site of executions during the Inquisition.

Practicalities

Finding a **room** in Vouzela shouldn't be much of a problem at the *Pensão Ferreira* (☎032/776 50; ②) on the main street. There are also a couple of local **campsites**: the nearest is on an attractive site one kilometre up toward **Senhora do Castelo** (3km), a low hill which is the location for much merrymaking and picnicking on the first Sunday after August 5. An alternative is at SERRAZES, 8km north: follow the old railway station road and then turn right in order to reach either of these.

Another **feira** happens on May 14 when flowers are strewn in the streets in honour of **São Frágil**, and everyone drives up into the hills to witness the blossoming of the rare *loendreiros*, a kind of rhododendron peculiar to this wildflower reserve area (see the following entry on the *Reserva Botânica de Cambarinho*).

Other details are easily summarised. There is a **street market** every first Wednesday in the month; the *Snack-Bar Pub* (Rua Teles Loureiro) is a friendly place where you can eat or play cards until late; the *Casa de Camilinha*, not far from either of these stops, offers cheap food and has the bus timetables. **Buses** for Viseu leave from outside the old train station; for Caramulo from the crossroads just beyond the viaduct.

São Pedro do Sul

Eight kilometres north of Vouzela are the **TERMAS DE SÃO PEDRO DO SUL**, possibly the oldest spa in Portugal. It was a great favourite with the Romans, a popular haunt of Portuguese royalty – Dom Afonso Henriques is said to have bathed his wounded leg here after the battle at Badajoz – and remains today among the grandest and most attractive.

The spa's position beside the Vouga, and the pine trees all around, certainly lends it charm, and it makes for a pleasant brief stop between buses – you can pick up connections here to Viseu and Lamego – or an afternoon trip from Vouzela. If you plan to stay, though, you'd be wise to book ahead. The seven **hotels and pensions** are all on the expensive side and frequently full. Cheapest options are the *Pensão Ultramarino* (☎032/71 12 11; ③) and *Hotel Vouga* (☎032/71 12 63; ④).

Figueira da Foz

FIGUEIRA DA FOZ is one of the liveliest towns on the west coast, a major resort and deep-sea fishing port. Sited at the mouth of the Mondego, roughly equidistant from Lisbon and Porto and only an hour by train from Coimbra, it attracts people from all over the country. And with good reason, for Figueira has a superb beach and surf, and the town has a bubbling good humour about it, even when it's packed to the gills. Don't be put off by the somewhat industrial approach from the south: the centre of Figueira is atmospheric, reasonably affordable, and as close to a typical Portuguese resort as you'll find.

Arriving and accommodation

It can take time to find a room in Figueira in high season, but with persistence you should be able to get something – there's no lack of places to try. If you need help, the **Turismo** (☎033/226 10), on the seafront promenade Avenida 25 de Abril, is even more helpful than most. If you end up some way out of town, you might want to **rent a bike** from *AGFA* at Rua Miguel Bombarda 79.

A couple of the cheaper **pensions** are just in front of the **railway station** on Rua Fernandes Tomás and Rua da República, but these are some way from the beach. It's better to keep walking next to the river until you see the ocean, then cut down into the town centre. Along here both **Rua Bernardo Lopes** and **Rua da Liberdade** are lined with possibilities, though those nearer to the casino tend to be booked well in advance.

Recommended **pensions and hotels** include:

Pensão Figueirense, Rua Direita do Monte. Large, light rooms, a lovely owner, and the cheapest prices in town. Three minutes' walk from the train station. ①.

Pensão Bela Figueira, Rua Miguel Bombarda 13 (☎033/227 28). Close to beach and town centre. Not remarkable in any way, but a reasonable fall-back. ②.

Pensão Europa, Rua Cândido dos Reis 40 (☎033/222 65). Very central, above a cheap fish restaurant. Bare, adequate rooms with basin. ②.

Pensão Central, Rua Bernardo Lopes 36 (☎033/223 08). Healthy, spacious *pensão* just down from the casino. Rooms with shower. Breakfast extra. ③.

Hotel Universal, Rua Miguel Bombarda 50 (☎033/262 28), near the casino. Worth trying if you arrive early in the day, a beautiful hotel run by a Portuguese Indian *retornado* from Mozambique, with rooms equipped with phone, TV, and bath. ③.

Residencial Pena Branca, Rua 5 de Outubro 42 (☎033/236 65). At the northern end of the beach, about 1km from the town centre. Worth the location for a splendid, high quality set-up with private bathrooms, phone, TV, fridge, and balcony and breakfast included. Good regional restaurant below. ④.

Hotel Wellington, Rua Dr. Calado (☎033/267 67). Genteel sort of place, highly recommended if you can afford it. Everything included. ④.

There are also two **campsites**, both well run:

Camping Municipal de Figueria da Foz (☎033/231 16). Located 2km inland – follow the signs – this is a large, well-equipped site with a huge swimming pool and tennis courts.

Camping Orbitur (☎033/314 92). Located at Gala, 4km to the south, across the estuary.

The town and beaches

The town doesn't offer much in the way of sightseeing – the most impressive sight is the beach – but there are a couple of places to look out for. The brand new **museum** on Rua Calouste Gulbenkian has an impressive archaeological section, as well as a large number of photographs of nineteenth-century bathing belles. The inside walls of the **Casa do Paço** are covered with thousands of Delft tiles, part of a ship's cargo which somehow got stranded in Figueira. Just along the river from the latter on Rua 5 de Outubro is the **market**, good for food and just about anything else you might need.

Figueira's **town beach** is enormous, not so much in length as in width: it's a good five-minute walk across the sand to the sea and unless you wear shoes or stay on the wooden walkways provided, the soles of your feet will have been burned long before you get there. If it's **surfing** you're after, then just step over the barrier to the next stretch of sands to the south, where fans gather to admire the breakers. By contrast, **Cabadelo beach**, behind the mole on the Mondego rivermouth's south bank, is small and sheltered and good for families – though to reach it you have to go right out through the town and over the bridge.

You can have a quicker dip in the Santa Catarina park's fee-paying **swimming pool** on the north side of town: about a 15-minute walk along Avenida Dr. Manuel Gaspar de Lemos or, coming from the beach side, a 10-minute walk along Rua Alexandre Herculano.

Restaurants and entertainment

The centre of town is packed with **places to eat**, with any number of seafood restaurants offering *ementas turísticas* at reasonable prices. The following are some less obvious alternatives:

Cozinha Nova, Rua Direita do Monte. This amazingly inexpensive canteen is always packed with locals. Service is a bit brusque but the food rivals most in town.

O Escondidinho, hidden away (as the name suggests) on Rua Dr. F.A. Dinis. Superb Goan food.

Pizzaria Cristal, Rua Académico Zagalo 26–28A. Tasty, cheapish pizzas and pasta dishes with some vegetarian options. Good house red too – Bairrada.

Café/Snack/Restaurante/Salão de Jogos Nicola, Rua Bernardo Lopes, opposite the casino. A bustling downtown rendezvous, big on snacks.

Restaurante Tahiti, Rua da Fonte 86, five minutes from the casino. Good food and friendly staff.

Snack-Bar Marujo, Rua Dr. Calado 51A, just up the street from the Turismo. Again, decent food in a warm atmosphere.

Restaurante Cacasolo, Rua Cândido dos Reis. Highly recommended.

Dory Negro, Largo Cavas Direitas 16, on the way to Buarcos. Pricey but great for fish.

Nightlife and events

Nightlife, for the wealthy, centres on the **Casino**, for which semi-formal dress – and an initial outlay on chips – is compulsory. The casino also houses a couple of cinemas, which generally have quite up-to-date releases.

Alternatively, there are several central **discos,** among them:

Disco Bergantim, Rua Dr. Lopes Guimarães 28. Very lively, open 10.30pm–4am. 1500$00 minimum expenditure on drinks.

Silver Spring, Rua Maestro David de Sousa 42. Smaller and more select but similar prices and opening hours.

For locals, however, *the* place to go is *Flashen* disco in QUIAIOS, 8km north of Figueira; it is hidden in the pine trees outside the village.

As for **events**, there's almost always something going on – Figueira likes to promote itself. One of the best of the year's parties is **Saint John's Eve** (June 23/24) with bonfires on the beach and a "Holy Bathe" in the sea at dawn. **Bullfights** are often held during the season and in the first couple of weeks of September the casino hosts an **International Film Festival** – a little uneven in its organisation, but always with a good selection of new films shown in their original language.

North of Figueira – Praia de Mira

The coastline immediately **north of Figueira** is remarkable only for its air of total desertion. Beyond **BUARCOS** – a fishing village which has become more or less part of the resort of Figueira (and is served by regular local buses) – there's very little, and for long stretches hardly even a road. Off the main north–south road you can get to the coast at just three points before Aveiro: **Quiaios**, **Tocha**, and **Praia de Mira**.

Quiaios and Tocha

With a car you can find virtually empty beaches around either **QUIAIOS** or **TOCHA**, though the low-lying coastal plain offers no protection against the Atlantic winds. Occasional buses – rarely more than one a day – run to both places. Nor is there much accommodation once you get there, other than the excellent **campsite** at Quiaios, which has its own swimming pool.

Praia de Mira

Set on a small lagoon – the southernmost point of a system of waterways and canals centered around Aveiro – **PRAIA DE MIRA** is the focus of increasing development. On the plus side, though, it is also much more accessible than Quiaias or Tocha, with four buses a day from Figueira and five daily *Avic* buses from Coimbra. You couldn't describe Mira as a beautiful place, despite its traditional wooden stilt-houses, but the beach that stretches around it is seemingly endless and backed by dunes: ideal if your sights extend no further than beach lounging and walks.

There are two official **campsites** a short way from town – the municipal one is closer and considerably cheaper, though less well equipped. Alternatively pick from a couple of good **pensions**, the *Arco-Iris* (☎034/471 44; ②) and *Pensão do Mar* (031/471 44; ③), both overlooking the sea, or any number of places offering cheap, basic *dormidas* along the main street. For the latter, just ask in any bar.

TRADITIONAL FISHING METHODS

Praia de Mira is one of the very few places in Portugal where traditional fishing methods have just about survived. Even if it's too cold to swim, you can spend a day or two on the beach, watching the techniques in action.

There is no real harbour, so the few remaining fishing boats are hauled across the beach, rolled on small tree trunks. They have very high prows and slightly lower sterns, so that they can be launched through the crashing breakers. Once clear of the surf they head out a kilometre or two offshore, drop their nets, and come back in – the nets are then slowly trawled in, traditionally by teams of oxen marching up and down the beach, nowadays by more prosaic tractors. This can take more than an hour and once the haul has come in the fish are taken out, sorted, and auctioned there and then on the beach. It's a process that involves the whole village, either in the boats, driving the tractors, coiling ropes, or sorting the catch.

On a good day you can pick up a huge fish for virtually nothing and cook it yourself over a fire on the beach. Not surprisingly the local restaurants also have really good seafood, especially the thick, bouillabaisse-like soups and stews.

Aveiro

Like Figueira da Foz, **AVEIRO** is a sizeable resort, with a series of excellent beaches to north and south. However, it's also a place of some antiquity and of interest in its own right. It was a thriving port throughout the Middle Ages, up until the 1570s, when the mouth of the Vouga silted up, closing its harbour and creating vast fever-ridden marshes.

Recovery only began in 1808 when a canal was cut through to the sea, reopening the port and draining much of the water; only the shallow lagoons you see today were left. These form the backbone of a modern economy based on vast **salt-pans**, fishing, and the collection of seaweed (*molico*) for fertiliser. The occasional pungent odour wafting across town, seemingly from the lagoon, is actually from the large paper factory nearby – this is one of Portugal's chief industries.

The town's big annual event is the **Festa da Ria**, celebrated in the last two weeks of August with boat races, folk-dances, and competitions for the best decorated *barcos moliceiro*, the flat-bottomed lagoon boats used to collect seaweed.

Arrival and accommodation

Aveiro is on the main Lisbon to Porto **rail line**, by far the easiest way to arrive; the bus companies use the train station as their terminus anyway. From the station, walk straight down the broad main street in front of you – **Avenida Dr. Lourenço Peixinho** – and you'll eventually hit the river and town centre. Note that the Vouga line to Viseu has been closed, although narrow gauge trains still (at least at time of writing) run from Aveiro as far as Sernada do Vouga, where *CP* buses (passes valid) take over for the rest of the route.

Finding a room in Aveiro isn't easy. The **Turismo** (☎034/236 80), in the central Praça da República, can help, and supplies free maps, but options are distinctly limited. If at all possible, bok ahead at one of the following:

Adega San Gonçalinho, Rua das Salinheiras 28 with an annexe at Travessa do Arco 17. Cheapest lodgings in town. ①.

Pensão Palmeira, Rua da Palmeira 7–11 (☎034/225 21). Decent rooms and a convenient location, close by the train station. ②.

Pensão Residencial Estrela, Rua José Estevão 4 (☎034/238 18). Just across the bridge from the Turismo. Confortable rooms. ②.

Residencial Beira, Rua José Estevão 18 (☎034/242 97). A second choice to the above. ②.

Residencial Santa Joana, Avda. Lourenço Peixinho 227 (☎034/286 04). Larger and slightly pricier rooms. ③.

Hotel Arcada, Rua de Viana do Castelo 4 (☎034/230 01). A nice old-fashioned hotel. ④.

Residencial Pomba Blanca, Rua Luís Gomes de Carvalho 23 (☎034/225 29). Very pleasant rooms in a gracious townhouse. ⑤.

Alternatives are to stay out of town, in one of the lagoon beach resorts (described overpage): out towards Torreira (to the north) or Praia da Barra (south), or at **Bunheiro**, a little inland. Possibilities here include:

Pensão Moliceiro, Avda. Hintze Ribeiro, between São Jacinto and Torreira (☎034/482 35). Decent enough. ②.

Pousada da Ria, Bico do Muranzel, between São Jacinto and Torreira (☎034/483 32). Mid-priced *pousada*, with doubles around 15,000$00. ⑥.

Albergue A Mansão, Bunheiro (☎034/460 00). A good choice if you have transport. Bunheiro is an inland village towards Murtosa and the *Mansão* has pleasant rooms and a very fine, reasonably priced restaurant, run by a Parisian chef. ②.

Pensão A Marisqueira, Avda. João Corte Real, Gafanha da Nazaré (☎034/392 62). Just inland of Praia de Barra. ③.

The local campsite is also out at São Jacinto:

Orbitur São Jacinto (☎034/482 84). A substantial site with good facilities.

Around the town and Rias

Around town the only sight of real note is the fifteenth-century **Convento de Jesus**, in which has been installed the **Regional Museum** (Tues–Sun 10am–12.30pm & 2–5pm). Its finest exhibits all relate to Santa Joana, a daughter of Afonso V who lived in the convent from 1475 until her death in 1489. She was barred from becoming a nun because of her royal station and her father's opposition, and was later beatified for her determination to escape from the material world (or perhaps simply from an unwelcome arranged marriage). Her tomb and chapel are strikingly beautiful, as is the convent itself, and there's a fine collection of art and sculpture – notably a series of seventeenth-century naive paintings depicting the saint's life.

During July and August there are organised **boat trips around the Rias** (usual departure 10am, returning at 5pm); at any time of year a group of people can rent a boat to tour the river; information, again, from the Turismo.

Cafés and restaurants

The main activity in town is hanging around in the **cafés**, watching life on the Ria: try some of the celebrated local sweets, especially *ovos moles*, candied egg yolks which come in little wooden barrels.

More substantial food is surprisingly hard to come by for a town with pretensions to being a resort. **Restaurants** are few, far between, and often full. Good standbys are *El Mercantel*, just off the Rossio, the *Zico Snack Bar* on Rua José Estevão, and the **vegetarian** restaurant below the Tourist Office. For slightly pricier meals, try *Centenário* on the Largo do Mercado; *Alexandre*, a grillhouse, at Rua Caid do Alboi 14; or *Galo d'Ouro* at Travessa do Mercado 2. Local specialties include eels and shellfish from the lagoons and powerful *Bairrada* wine.

The lagoon and beaches

There's no beach in Aveiro itself but the coast to north and south is a more or less continuous line of sand, cut off from the mainland for much of the way by the meandering lagoon. Roaming about this area, note that the pine forests shelter several military bases, so stick to the roads, and don't camp outside proper sites.

See the Aveiro listings (on the previous page) for details of **accommodation** at the lagoon beaches.

South to Barra and Costa Nova

The most accessible points from Aveiro are **PRAIA DA BARRA**, at the mouth of the Vouga, and **COSTA NOVA**, just to its south, both of which are served by local buses. Neither, however, are anything more than functional daytrip beaches, enormously crowded on summer weekends. If you're headed south, Praia de Mira (see p.144) is a far preferable place to stay.

North to São Jacinto and Torreira

Going north is rather more fun, with a choice of **ferries** across the lagoon to São Jacinto and Torreira, plus the inland attractions of Ovar and Santa Maria da Feira.

SÃO JACINTO is a thriving little port with good swimming and dockside cafés. Beautiful it's not, but it is an atmospheric sort of place, and backs onto an extensive **bird reserve** (two-hour guided tours each morning and afternoon).

Buses run north from here through **TORREIRA**, a lively little resort with several small pensions, a campsite, and a highly recommended restaurant, *Casa Passoeira*, on the main road. The buses at this point loop back round to Aveiro; to go on to Furadouro (see below) means a detour through Ovar.

Ovar and Furadouro

OVAR, 25km north of Aveiro, is on the main rail line to Porto, and connected by buses every fifteen minutes in the height of summer; the train station is about fifteen minutes' walk from the centre and the bus depot is right in front of it. The place is an attractive market town, with the asset of a fine beach at Furadouro, 5km walk (or local bus) away. In the main square is a helpful **Turismo**, and nearby is a surprisingly good **Museu Ethnographica**, with an international collection of pottery, plus traditional clothing and the usual folklore displays. Perhaps more compellingly, while you're here try some of the local *pão-de-ló* sponge cake – every bit as good as it looks.

FURADOURO marks pretty much the northern extent of the system of waterways, and like its neighbours to the south is a long stretch of pine-backed dunes. There are a few rooms available above the *Café Amadeu* and a summer campsite.

Santa Maria da Feira

AT **SANTA MARIA DA FEIRA** (or simply FEIRA), easily reached by bus from Aveiro or Espinho (see Porto chapter), is one of the most spectacular castles in Portugal – a sight not to be missed travelling up this coast.

The **Castelo da Feira** towers above the town, its skyline a fanciful array of domes, added to a very solid Moorish keep. Its principal room is the **Great Hall**, a magnificent Moorish structure, beyond which you can climb to the domes. Beyond the keep, a tunnel links the two parts of the castle in such a way that no direct or easy access can ever have been offered to intruders. In some of the walls you may notice a few stones with Roman inscriptions incorporated, and you can make out the familiar straight Roman road through the wooded hills above.

On the way down from the castle, you pass the **Convento de Loios** (now a conference centre), at the back of which is an incredibly tacky cement **Grotto** and garden of faked bridges and pebble-lined paths. This apart, there's not much else to the place, except during the annual **Festa das Fogaceiras** (Jan 20), when files of little girls parade through the town carrying castle-shaped *fogaça* cakes. It's a custom – much revived in recent years – which dates back to the plague of 1750 when the Infante Pedro made a *vota* to Santa Maria that cakes in the shape of his castle would be baked in thanksgiving for those who survived.

If you want to stay in Feira, the tumbledown *Hospedaria* at Dr. Santos Carneiro 5 (①) offers exceptionally cheap **rooms**, and there's also the *Pensão Ferreira* on Rua Dr. Vittorino de Sá (☎056/328 59; ②). Decent and inexpensive **meals** are to be had at the *Café Moderno* or *Restaurante Parque*.

Arouca

AROUCA, a further 20km or so inland of Feira, is a small town overshadowed by a vast and magnificent **convent**. It makes a pleasant trip into the hills, with bus links from OLIVEIRA DE AZEMEIS on the main N1 highway – which, if you get stuck there overnight, has a couple of pensions and a campsite. However, if you can make it, Arouca would be the beter place to stay, with the very friendly *Pensão Alexandra* (①), on the main street, and pricier *Residencial São Pedro* (☎056/945 80; ④), further up the street. For meals, try *Cheiro Verde*, beneath the modern shopping complex.

Convento da Arouca

The **Convento da Arouca** (Tues–Sun 9am–noon & 2–5pm) was founded as early as 1091, though most parts surviving are rather later medieval. In the kitchen there are huge **fireplaces** along Alcobaça lines; in the vast **baroque church** there are richly carved choir stalls and a great **organ** with 1352 notes, played on rare occasions by one of the country's few experts; and off the central courtyard there's an airy **Sala Capítula** lined with *azulejos*, where the abbesses once held court.

The convent peaked in importance when Queen Mafalda, of whose dowry it had formed a part, found her marriage with Dom Henrique I of Castille annulled and retired here to a life of religious contemplation. In the extensive **museum** upstairs, you can see some of Mafalda's treasures, including an exquisite thirteenth-century silver diptych, along with a series of paintings by Josefa de Óbidos (see p.104) and Diogo Teixeira, a notable Portuguese Primitivist. Four centuries after Mafalda's death, in 1792, villagers claimed to have witnessed her saving the convent from a terrible fire. She was promptly exhumed and beatified.

During the **Festa de Nossa Senhora da Mó**, the whole town turns out for a picnic on the crown of the hill 8km east of the town. Everyone takes food and drink, plays their own music, and parades about – it's a lot of fun..

The Serra da Arada: rocks that pop

If you have your own transport, consult the Turismo for details about places to visit in the **Serra da Arada**, a beautiful countryside, terraced like the Minho and abundantly littered with dolmens, crumbling villages, and waterfalls with ancient bridges. While you're in the area, watch (or listen) for the local geological phenomenon of **"jumping stones"**. A "parent" rock literally gives birth to a small disk of "baby" rock, flinging it into the world with an impressive pop.

travel details

Trains

BEIRA BAIXA LINE

From Guarda 4 trains daily to Covilhã (1hr 10min), Castelo Branco (3hr 20min), Belver (4hr 45min), Abrantes (5hr 30min), Entroncamento (6hr 30min), Santarém (6 hr 45 min), and Lisbon (8hr).

NORTE LINE

From Lisbon 4 trains daily to Coimbra B (2hr), Aveiro (3hr), and Porto (4hr), plus 7 daily *rapidos* to Porto stopping at Coimbra B (2 hr) and Aveiro (2hr 30min): twice as fast and twice the price. Also *suburbanos* from Aveiro to Porto (roughly every hour from 6am to midnight).
From Lisbon 2 trains daily to Braga (5hr 15min).

OESTE LINE

From Figueira da Foz 8 trains daily to Leiria (45min–1hr 15min), 4 continuing to Óbidos (2hr 45min), and Lisbon (4hr 45min).

From Figueira da Foz to Coimbra A, 15 daily (1hr).

VOUGA LINE

From Aveiro trains run only to Sernada do Vouga (9 daily; 1hr).
CP **buses** follow the old Vouga line from Aveiro through Sernada to Viseu. *CP* buses also run from Sernada do Vouga to Espinho (3 daily; 2hr).

Buses

All the major towns have an express service at least once a day, and there are frequent, regular bus services throughout the region. In addition, there are express buses from Coimbra, Viseu, Guarda and Aveiro, usually three or four times daily, to **Lisbon and Porto**.
International buses from Lisbon to Paris also pass through Coimbra, Viseu, and Guarda, and you can pick them up there, though seats must be reserved in advance.

CHAPTER FOUR

MOUNTAIN BEIRAS

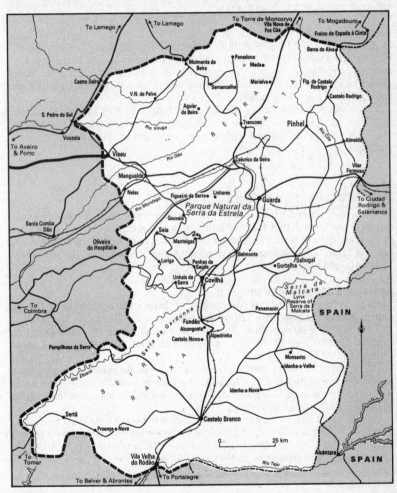

C omposed of two provinces, the **Beira Alta** (Upper) and **Beira Baixa** (Lower), the **Mountain Beiras** region offers some of the least explored country in the Iberian peninsula. It is also perhaps the most quintessentially Portuguese part of the country. Little touched by outside influence, and the historic heartland of **ancient Lusitânia** where the Iberian rebel Viriatus made his last stand against the Romans. You'll see many signs of this patriotism in the fine old town of **Viseu**, in **Beira Alta**, where every other café or hotel is called the *Viriato* or *Lusitânia*. Here too, in the heights of the stunningly beautiful **Parque Natural da Serra da Estrela**, lies the source of the **Rio Mondego**, the only large river with its origins in the country. The whole region in and around the park is excellent walking country, especially if you strike off from one of the two main routes which cross the range.

As far as towns go, **Guarda** is a must. Though diminutive in size for somewhere of such renown, it has one of the highest locations of any provincial capital in the country and it bristles with life, especially on *feira* days. To the north and east stretch a whole series of high-sited castle-towns and some of the country's most remote villages. Over to the south lies the more sombre plain of the **Beira Baixa** with its capital at **Castelo Branco** and, its most obvious highlight, the ancient hilltop town of **Monsanto**.

The whole Mountain Beiras region is very little visited by tourists and travellers: if you've spent some days in the fleshpots of Lisbon, Porto, or the Algarve, you'll find a very different **atmosphere** here – and almost exclusively Portuguese company.

Viseu

From its high plateau, **VISEU** surveys the country around with the air of a feudal overlord; and indeed, this dignified little city is capital of all it can see and a place of great antiquity to boot. There was a Roman town here and on the outskirts you can still make out the remains of an encampment claimed to be the site where Viriatus fought his final battle.

Arrival and accommodation

Viseu is no longer on the rail line, though *CP* **buses** still operate along the old routes, linking the town with Lisbon and Guarda on the Beira Alta line at Nelas and the Coimbra–Aveiro–Porto line at Sernada. All buses use the station on Avenida António José de Almeida, a short walk from the centre. Buses on to Lamego run via Castro Daire.

The centre of town is marked by the **Praça da República**, an elongated square that is also known as the **Rossio**. The **Turismo** (☎032/279 94), just south of here on the Avenida Calouste Gulbenkian, is helpful for maps and information on the Beira Alta region as a whole.

Most of the **places to stay** are in the old quarter, though the cheaper pensions in Viseu seem uniformly poor. You might be better off with a room in a private house (try Rua Chão de Mestre 107) or above one of the cafés in Rua Direita. Among **hotels and pensions**, pick from the following:

Casa de Hóspedes Central, Rua Dr. Luís Ferreira 65. Just about tolerable rooms, right by the market. ①.

Pensão Bocage, Travessa de São Domingos 5, off Rua Direita (☎032/223 75). Not much better – definitely see the room before you take it. ①.

Pensão Viseense, Avda. Alberto Sampaio 31, off the Rossio (☎032/279 00). Large clean rooms, despite the shabby appearance. ②.

Pensão Bela Vista, Rua Alexandre Herculano 510 (☎032/260 26). Functional pension in the street behind the Turismo; has some cheaper, bath-less rooms. ③.

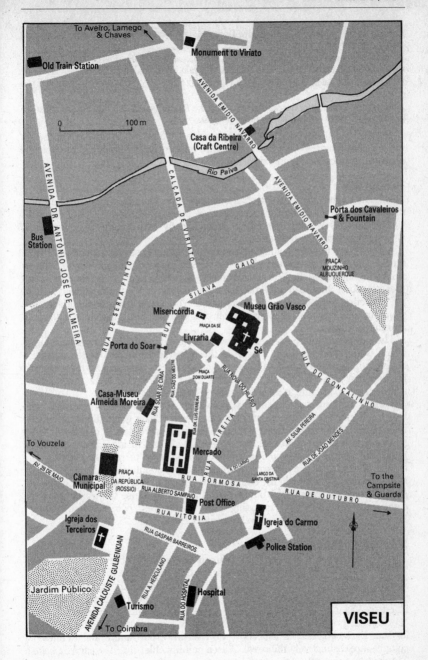

To Aveiro, Lamego
& Chaves

Monument to Viriato

Old Train Station

AVENIDA EMÍDIO NAVARRO

0   100 m

Casa da Ribeira
(Craft Centre)

CALÇADA DE VIRIATO

Rio Paiva

AVENIDA EMÍDIO NAVARRO

Porta dos Cavaleiros
& Fountain

Bus
Station

AVENIDA DR ANTÓNIO JOSÉ DE ALMEIRA

PRAÇA
MOUZINHO
ALBUQUERQUE

GAIO

RUA DE SERPA PINTO

SILAVA

Misericórdia

Museu Grão Vasco

RUA

PRAÇA DA SÉ

Livraria

Porta do Soar

Sé

RUA DO GONÇALINHO

RUA CAÇO DO MESTRE

RUA SOAR DE CIMA

PRAÇA
DOM DUARTE

RUA NOVA DO PILÁRIO

Casa-Museu
Almeida Moreira

RUA DR LUÍS FERREIRA

AV. SILVA PEREIRA

RUA DE JOÃO MENDES

To Vouzela

RUA DIREITA

AV. 28 DE MAIO

PRAÇA
DA REPÚBLICA
(ROSSIO)

Mercado

R. DO CAIXO

Câmara
Municipal

RUA FORMOSA

LARGO DA
SANTA CRISTINA

To the
Campsite
& Guarda

RUA ALBERTO SAMPAIO

Post Office

RUA DE OUTUBRO

Igreja dos
Terceiros

RUA VITÓRIA

Igreja do Carmo

AVENIDA CALOUSTE GULBENKIAN

RUA GASPAR BARREIROS

Police Station

Jardim Público

RUA A. HERCULANO

RUA DO HOSPITAL

Hospital

Turismo

To Coimbra

VISEU

Pensão Dom Duarte, Rua Alexandre Herculano 214 (☎032/257 81). Another reasonable *residencial*; all rooms with bath ④.

Pensão Rossio Parque, Rua Soar de Cima 55, again off the Rossio (☎032/257 85). Characterful old hotel that has seen better days; again, all rooms with bath. ④.

Hotel Avenida, Avda. Alberto Sampaio 1 (☎032/234 32). A fairly pleasant hotel with a few cheap rooms. ④.

Hotel Grão Vasco, Rua Gaspar Barreiros, off the Rossio (☎032/235 11). Viseu's finest – a grand central hotel with bar and swiming pool. ⑤.

There's a well-equpped *Orbitur* **campsite** (☎032/255 47) in the Parque do Fontelo, ten minutes' walk from the centre on the Guarda road, and a municipal **swimming pool** in the same direction, on the Avenida José Relvas.

The Old City

The heart of the medieval city has changed little, though it's approached now through the broad avenues of a prosperous provincial centre. Parts of the walls survive and it's within their circuit, breached by two doughty gateways, that almost everything of interest lies.

A good place to start looking around town are the old streets around the **Praça da Sé**. On the approach here, from the Rossio up through the Porta do Soar, or along the shop-lined Rua Dr. Luís Ferreira, a certain amount of restoration and "beautification" has been undertaken, but the jumble of alleys immediately behind the cathedral remains virtually untouched. You come upon sixteenth-century stone mansions proudly displaying their coat of arms in the middle of a street of crumbling shacks.

The cathedral square itself is lined with noble stone buildings, most striking of which is the white baroque facade of the **Misericórdia**. Silhouetted against a deep blue sky it looks like a film set – you expect to walk around the back and find wooden props holding it up. There's some truth to that feeling: behind the symmetry of the facade, it's a very ordinary, rather dull church.

There's nothing two-dimensional, however, about the **Sé**, a weighty twin-towered Romanesque base on which a succession of later generations have made their mark. The granite frontage, remodelled in the seventeenth century, is stern and makes the church look smaller than it actually is – inside it opens out into a great hall with intricate vaulting, twisted and knotted to represent ropes. The cathedral's Renaissance **cloister**, of which you get no intimation from outside, is one of the most graceful in the country. The rooms of its upper level, looking out over the tangled roofs of the oldest part of the town, house the treasures of the cathedral's art collection, including naive sculptures, two thirteenth-century Limoges enamel coffers, and a twelfth-century Bible.

Museu Grão Vasco

The greatest treasure of Viseu is the **Museu Grão Vasco** (Tues–Sun 10am–5pm; 200$00; free at weekends), right next door to the cathedral in the **Paço dos Três Escalões** – once the Bishop's palace. **Vasco Fernandes** (known always as *Grão Vasco*, The Great Vasco) was the key figure in a school of painting which flourished at Viseu in the first half of the sixteenth century. The style of these "Portuguese primitives" is influenced heavily by Flemish masters and in particular Van Eyck, but certain aspects – the realism of portraiture and richness of colour – are distinctively their own. Vasco and his chief rival Gaspar Vaz have a fair claim to being two of the greatest artists Portugal has produced.

The museum is spread over three floors with the works of the Viseu School on the uppermost. The centrepiece of the collection is the masterly *Saint Peter on his Throne*, one of Grão Vasco's last works and painted, it is said, to rival Gaspar Vaz's treatment of the same theme for the Convent of São João at Tarouca (see Chapter Five). It shows considerably more Renaissance influence than some of the earlier paintings but its Flemish roots are still evident, particularly in the intricately – and sometimes bizarrely – detailed background.

Other works attributed to Vasco include a *Calvary* and a *Pentecost*, but there's considerable argument over what is actually his. Several pictures are clearly the fruits of collaboration – most obviously the fourteen panels of the former cathedral altarpiece. These, now exhibited in a room of their own, depict the life of Christ and some sections are clearly better executed than others – notice *The Adoration of the Magi* in which Balthazar, traditionally an African king, is depicted as an Indian from newly discovered Brazil.

Food and festivals
Some of the best **meals** in the province are to be had (at not too inflated prices) at *Contico*, at Rua São Hilário 47, which is popular enough for tables to be hard to get. Alternatively, follow the EN2 out into the suburbs (in the Coimbra direction) and you'll reach another superb restaurant, *Rodízio*, to which diners come from far afield. For an upmarket fado evening, try the *Restaurante Solar do São Gonçalinho* on Rua do São Gonçal. Wherever you eat, or drink, bear in mind that locally produced **Dão wines**, especially the reds, are some of the best you'll find anywhere in the country.

Viseu's **Feira de São Mateus** – held throughout September – is largely an agricultural show, but enlivened by occasional bullfights and folk-dance festivals.

Into the Serra da Estrela: Celorico

All along the **Beira Alta rail line** – from Santa Comba Dão to Guarda – the high and austere territory of the **Serra da Estrela** spreads itself as far as the eye can see: a landscape of great jagged boulders and rough, dry grass – often singed in patches by summer fires. The wilderness of the area, as so often in mountain regions, belies its inhabitants, who, though a little abrupt, have none of the suspicion of outsiders often encountered in Portuguese cities and coastal regions.

Celorico da Beira, the first main stop on the line, lies at a nexus of routes, with bus connections to **Linhares**, perhaps the most attractive of the *serra* villages. **Guarda**, beyond, has a more extensive network of trains and buses to the outlying villages, as well as connections east into Spain.

Celorico da Beira

Most approaches to Guarda, whether by rail or road, will be via **CELORICO DA BEIRA**. An unprepossessing town – its one claim to fame is as the birthplace of the aviator Sacadura Cabral – it is not the most attractive *serra* base, split as it is by heavy traffic along the east-west road from Spain and the north-south route to Lisbon. It does, however, have a fine castle and, if you're passing through at the right time, it's the best place to pick up a pungent *queijo da serra*, the famed round cheese of the Serra da Estrela district.

The castle and town

A key can be obtained from the *Câmara Municipal* (town hall) to open the south gate of the **Castelo**. If you trust the rickety construction strung up outside the large keep you can climb to impressive views from the roof. On a clear day the Sé and single tower of the castle at Guarda are both visible, while all around stretches the extraordinary wasteland of the mountains, split only by a small river and a couple of Portuguese highways.

The castle has a long military history, forming, together with Trancoso and Guarda, a triangle of defensive fortifications against Spain. In its day, a garrison of three hundred, well equipped with arms and an ample supply of food, were able to hold out with relative ease against border skirmishes. Only on one occasion, in 1198, did they have to call for assistance – which was provided by the stout men of nearby Linhares.

Feiras – held on alternate Fridays for cheese, and on Tuesdays for the ordinary covered market – are the times to catch the town's cheery provinciality. You'll see some of the more rugged mountain types coming in to sell their *queijo da serra*. Market-going is their only form of income, enabling them to reinvest in their impoverished hilltop farms – the farmers of the Serra da Estrela must have the harshest agricultural lifestyle in Europe.

Practicalities

Celorico's **train station** is 4km north of town; bus connections are erratic, so you'll probably need to take a taxi, hitch or walk (there's a possible shortcut across country). The **bus stops** are more central, along the town's main road: one in front of the *Residencial Parque*, the other in front of the *Café Central*, where you can consult timetables. Three buses daily travel in the Guarda and Gouveia directions.

The town's best and most central **pension** is the *Residencial Parque* (☎071/ 721 97; ②). A couple of other cheaper places – the *Nova Estrela* (②) and *Boa Hora* (②) – are located out on the road toward Viseu. There is a possible freelance **campsite** by the river, near the station. The nearest official site is seven kilometres east, off the road to Guarda, at LAJEOSA DO MONDEGO.

Guarda

GUARDA, at an altitude of over 1000m, is claimed by its inhabitants to be the highest city in Europe – an assertion to be taken with a modest pinch of salt. It is high enough, though, to be chilly and windswept all year round – and to offer endless views, especially to the east into Spain.

The city was founded in 1197 by Dom Sancho I, to guard (as the name implies) his borders against both Moors and Spaniards. It was a heftily fortified place and, despite the fact that castle and walls have all but disappeared, still has something of the grim air of a city permanently on war footing. It is known in Portugal as the city of the four Fs – *Fria, Farta, Forte e Feia* – cold, rich, strong and ugly.

The Town

The last, at least, of these proverbial anecdotes is unfair. With its arcaded streets and little *praças*, the centre of Guarda can be distinctly picturesque. At the heart of it all is the dour grey **Cathedral**, one of those buildings that took so long to

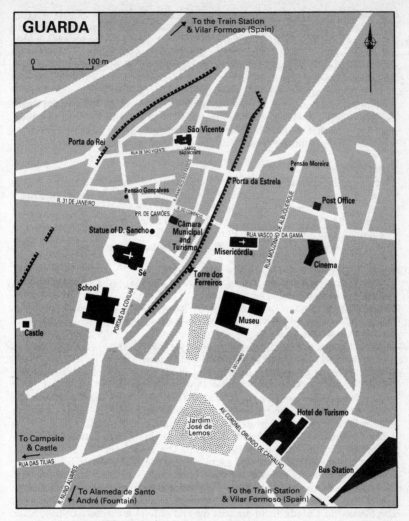

complete (1390–1540) that several architectural styles came and went during its construction, all of them incorporated somewhere into the work. The castellated main facade, with its two heavy octagonal towers, looks like the gateway of some particularly forbidding castle, but around the sides the design is lightened by flying buttresses, fantastic pinnacles, and grimacing gargoyles – the ones facing Spain are particularly mean-looking.

Inside it's surprisingly long and lofty, with twisted pillars and vaulting influenced by the Manueline style of the later stages of its development. The huge carved stone **retábulo** is the work of João de Ruão, a leading figure in the sixteenth-century resurgence of Portuguese sculpture at Coimbra.

It's amazing, for a place of its size and importance, that, the cathedral aside, there's little else to see in Guarda. The displays of local archaeology, art, and sculpture in the **Museu Regional** are, frankly, dull; of the **castle**, on a bleak little hill nearby, only the plain square keep survives, while the **walls** are recalled by just three surviving gates – the most impressive of them the **Torre dos Ferreiros** (Blacksmiths' Tower).

The cobbled streets of the old town, though, are fascinating in themselves, and the tangled area between the other two portals – the **Porta da Estrela** and **Porta do Rei** – can have changed little in the past 400 years. Like Celorico, the town also has a market, busiest on Saturdays, where you'll find delicious *queijo da serra*, the local mountain cheese. It's located by the bus station.

Practicalities

Guarda's main **railway** station is 3km out of town but there's a bus (the stop is opposite) to meet all the major trains. The **bus station** is fairly central (see map) and ultra-efficient; services are operated by a variety of companies. There is a **Turismo** (☎071/222 51) behind the cathedral on Praça Luís de Camões,

Rooms are fairly easy to come. **Pensions and hotels** include:

Residencial Gonçalves, Rua Augusto Gil 17. Centrally located, off the Praca de Camões; clean but a bit down-at-heel. ①.

Pensão Guardense, Rua Serpa Pinto 15 (☎071/215 11). ①.

Pensão Moreira, Rua Mouzinho de Albuquerque 47 (☎071/241 31). Again pretty central – and rather more comfort. ②.

Pensão Gare, Avda. João de Ruão 104 (☎071/294 88). By the train station. ②.

Pensão Residência Filipe, Rua Vasco da Gama 9 (☎071/226 58). A more upmarket pension, near the Misericórdia. ④.

Solar de Alarcão, Rua Dom Miguel de Alarcão 25–27 (☎071/212 75). Pleasant rooms in a town mansion that's part of the *Turismo de Habitação* scheme. ⑤.

Hotel Turismo da Guarda, Avda. Coronel Orlindo de Carvalho (☎071/222 05). Guarda's grandest: big and reasonably well run; doubles around 13,000$00. ⑥.

Guarda's *Orbitur* **campsite** (☎071/212 64) is in a park a short way from the castle; it is open-all-year remember, though beware that the nights can get extremely cold. The town's heated **swimming pool** is in the same park.

Most of the town's **restaurants** are to be found in the area between the Porta da Estrela and the church of São Vicente. The *Belo Horizonte*, at Largo São Vicente 1, is among the best – and inexpensive. Good food is also to be had at the first floor restaurant of the *Pensão Filipe*.

Numerous **festivals** take place in the Guarda area. The biggest events are the great **Feiras** (June 24 and October 4), extended markets full of life and character. The **Festas da Cidade** (held towards the end of July) are a more cultural affair with exhibitions and folk-dancing, a little too highly organised for their own good.

The Serra da Estrela

The peaks of the **Serra da Estrela** – the highest mountains in Portugal and the last of the four central Iberian *serras* – rise to the south of Guarda. There is a choice of approaches. From the west/north, you can follow RN-17 down from Celorico da Beira to enter the park at the quirky village of **Linhares**, or via the larger towns of **Gouveia** and **Seia**. Alternatively, from the east/south, the railway and RN-18 road skirt the eastern slopes, with access to the park from **Belmonte** and **Covilhã**. If you're intent on serious hiking the best base is **Penhas da Saúde,** just northwest of Covilhã, where there's a large year-round hostel and access to the valleys north to **Manteigas** or south to **Unhais da Serra**.

Public transport into the area is erratic at the best of times, though a little easier in winter when Penhas de Saúde has Portugal's only **skiing** facilities.

Linhares

LINHARES perches on a sunny slope overlooking the Rio Mondego valley, one of the most accessible of the *serra* villages, with a trio of attractions in its castle, a series of troglodyte-like dwellings, and a stretch of Roman road. To reach it, take a through **bus** either from Celorico da Beira to Gouveia, or vice versa, and stop at CARRAPICHANA, 2km distant.

If you want to **stay**, ask at Linares's only café, the *Linharense*, in the central square near the church. They will know who has a spare room or where best to pitch your tent – most probably above the village near a rustic football pitch.

The village and castle

If you arrive in Linhares in the early morning the village appears deserted, its only sounds of life the animals grunting and kicking their stable doors to be let out. Later in the day you'll see the donkeys being brought in from the fields and, depending on the time of year, seeds laid out to dry in the sun, wine casks being washed for the next year's vintage, and, whatever the season, village gossips on their doorsteps, keen as ever to meet a stranger.

A little-known secret of the village's **Church** is that it contains three paintings almost certainly executed by **Grão Vasco** and belonging to a larger series which is now lost. Propped up behind vulgar wooden statues and, in one case, stuck in one of the side aisles, the panels, depicting the *Adoration of the Magi*, *Descent from the Cross* and *Annunciation*, shine out in the obscurity. They reveal all the qualities of the great painter – his skill as a portraitist and his deft handling of tone and colour, particularly in the depiction of clothing and folds of material.

Barely distinguishable at first, the lofty keep of the **Castelo** (keys from the hairdresser who lives above the village church) soon rises into reality, in command of all that lies before it. It dates from 1169 when Linhares, then more of a town, was claimed for Portugal. Afonso Henriques realised its potential as a defensive post, and soon the men of Linhares were trained up and equipped to carry out such feats of bravery as the rescue of Celorico da Beira from the Spaniards in 1198. In the walls are traces of the *cisternas* which would have given the village a constant supply of water at times of siege. You can still see the course of the spring which now runs along the gully beneath the great slabs of rock on which the castle was constructed.

The Roman Road

Near the schoolhouse in Linhares a path branches off the road toward Figueiró da Serra. Following it, you'll soon realise that you are walking along an old **Roman road** – part of the one which ran to Braga – with heavy slabs of rock for paving stones looking like something out of an Asterix cartoon. The walk is a beauty, the hedgerows lined with flowers in the spring and blackberries in the autumn.

Gouveia

GOUVEIA has lost the rural *serra* feel that once constituted its charm, as it has developed into a fair-sized provincial town. However, it has a Thursday market that's worth coinciding with, and it houses the Serra da Estrela park headquarters and an interesting modern art museum.

The town

Arriving by bus, walk up from the bridge (where you're dropped), veer right and you'll soon come across the **Turismo**, established along with the municipal library in the basement of a *casa brasonada*. They hand out maps of the town and will point walkers towards the elegant **Casa da Torre** on Rua Direita, the Serra da Estrela park office, which has further maps and leaflets on the area.

Above the Turismo is the **Museu de Abel Manta**, a modern art museum with a broad selection of contemporary Portuguese pictures all donated by Gouveian-born artist **Abel Manta** (1888–1982). There's a small room dedicated to the man himself, a figure of some stature who frequented groups which included Amadeo de Sousa Cardoso (see "Amarante") and Almada Negreiros (see "the Museu da Cidade" in Lisbon) – some of whose works are also here – and who represented Portugal in the Venice Biennale. This selection of Manta's work features only one outstanding picture, but the collection as a whole is enjoyable.

Portugal's sense of heraldry comes out in manor houses of every shape and size, where sets of arms are tacked up over doorways, on cornices, beneath the corners of the roof, and any other empty space. Gouveia boasts several examples, the finest of which is the **Câmara Municipal**. This hosts open-air concerts in its courtyard during the summer months, but you are generally free to walk in.

Finally, you may have noticed a **statue** of a shepherd with his dog, at the entrance to the town, which is proudly illuminated at night. Though not perhaps the finest piece of sculpture, it is significant for what it represents. The people in the hills around here live a harsh and impoverished existence and have, as the Portuguese put it, "an unlimited capacity for suffering". There is never a break in the agricultural year, for when the summer is over and the harvest is stored away it is time to begin the cheesemaking, an activity which brings in their only serious income. The shepherd's friend in this harsh lifestyle is his dog, the *Cão da Serra da Estrela* – a fearsome looking breed said to be cross-bred from wolves.

Accommodation

Gouveia offers half a dozen **accommodation** possibilities:

Café Cruzeiro, Avenida 25 de Abril. On the way up to the Câmara Municipal; pleasant and inexpensive rooms above the café. ①.

Restaurante A Regional, Avenida da República 45. Modest rooms but an excellent restaurant. ①.

Casa da Rainha, Rua Direita 68 (☎038/421 32). A *Turismo de Habitação* lodging. ③.

Pensão Estrela, Avenida da República 36 (☎038/421 71). A dusty old hotel with modern prices, but again a restaurant with something of a reputation. ③.

Hotel de Gouveia, Avenida 1º de Maio (☎038/428 90). The town's most upmarket option; decent if not very characterful rooms. ④.

The local **municipal campsite** is at CURRAL DO NEGRO, around 3km from the centre of town; to get there, turn right immediately after the Câmara Municipal, then right again, before finally forking to the left for 2km.

Seia

Cut out **SEIA** from your itinerary and you would miss very little, but it can be, like Gouveia, a useful jumping-off point, with bus connections to the Serra da Lousã (see "Beira Litoral") and for the Estrela *parque natural*. If you decide to stay, you'll find rooms rented above the *Restaurante Miranda*, next to the town hall, and three rather upmarket **hotels**: the excellent *Hotel Camelo*, Rua 1º de Maio 16 (☎038/225 10; ④); the *Estalagem de Seia*, Avda. Dr. Afonso Costa (☎038/ 226 66; ④); and the *Albergaria Senhora do Espinheiro*, Lugar do Espinheiro (☎038/220 73; ④).

With enough time, or transport, however, it's better to press on **into the Parque Natural**, where there are various *turismo rural* and *agroturismo* lodgings, as well as a handful of pensions and campsites. SABUGUEIRO, 8km east of Seia, has three such places, all priced around 8000\$00 for a double room: the *Casa do Cruzeiro*, *Casa Nova* and *Casa da Sofia* (all on ☎038/228 25; ⑤).

Before setting out, call in at Seia's **regional park office** in the *Casa da Janela Bonita*, Praça da República 28. Roads from Seia branch off to MANTEIGAS at the centre of the range, and to COVILHÃ via PENHAS DA SAÚDE; there is no regular transport along these routes, but you can make do with a mix of walking and hitching. Alternatively, two **buses** daily cover the southern route to Covilha, looping around the fringes of the park, via the little spa-village of UNHAIS DA SERRA. See below for more on these destinations.

Belmonte

BELMONTE was the birthplace of Pedro Álvares Cabral, the discoverer of Brazil, and is a village of considerable charm, commanded by a heavily restored thirteenth-century **castle**. It is a pleasant stopping-off point on the route south, and for those with transport, provides access to the Estrela *parque natural* as well as to the barren and medieval region of the Beira Baixa (covered later in this chapter). There are limited bus services, running to the two main Beira Baixa towns of Fundão and Castelo Branco, but not to Sabugal and the Transylvanian-like fortress-village of Sortelha, for which you'd do better to return to Guarda. Despite Belmonte's proximity to both of these, the region between them is deserted and wild with roughly surfaced roads and few cars.

If you want to **stay** in Belmonte, the *Hotel Belsol* (☎075/913 45; ③) offers reasonably priced rooms.

Covilhã

COVILHÃ, immediately below the highest peaks of the *serra*, is the most obvious base for exploring the park. The train station is 5km from the town, but buses shuttle new arrivals from there into the centre. There's a **Turismo** in the main Praça do Município, which can provide maps, arrange guides, and fill you in on transport details, and the town has plenty of shops for stocking up on hiking provisions – beyond this point there is just one small store in Penhas da Saúde.

If you want to stay, there are half a dozen **pensions**, among them: *A Regional*, Rua das Flores 4 (☎075/225 96; ②); *Solneve*, Rua Visconde da Coriscada 126 (☎075/230 01; ④); and *Montalto*, Praça do Municipio 1 (☎075/250 91). The best of the bunch for **meals** is the *Sol Neve* – a restaurant in its own right.

Into the *parque natural*

The most obvious – and enjoyable – hike from Covilhã is the route up the glacial valley from here to **PENHAS DE SAÚDE**, an energetic walk well worth the effort. As a major hiking trailhead, Penhas has a campsite and a large 160-bed youth hostel, which should have space at most times of year.

From Penhas, you are within striking distance of the chief beauty spots of the *serra*, with the highest peak in Portugal – **Torre** (1993m) – just a couple of miles up the road; it can be climbed quite easily. Nearby is the vast statue of **Nossa Senhora da Boa Estrela**, carved into a niche in the rock, to which there's a massive procession from Covilhã on the second Sunday in August. A little west of Torre is the narrow rock cone known as the **Cântaro Magro** (Slender Pitcher), which conceals the source of the Rio Zêzere; there's an excellent summer **camp-site** below it at COVÃO DE AMETADE. Further still are the waters of the **Lagoa Comprida**, a huge artificial lake. Keep on heading west and you will eventually emerge – past the **pousada** at PENHAS DOURADA (*Lourenço*, ☎075/981 50; doubles around 16,000$00; ⑥) – at SABUGUEIRO and SEIA (see previous page).

Alternatively, you can strike **north** at NAVE DE SANTO ANTÓNIO, between Penhas and Torre, and follow the glacial **valley of the Rio Zêzere** down to the spa of CALDAS DE MANTEIGAS and, 5km beyond, the larger *serra* town of **MANTEIGAS** proper. Accommodation here includes the *Hotel de Manteigas* (at Caldas; ☎075/981 51; ⑤); and the *Pensão Estrela* (☎075/982 88; ②) and *Pensão Serradalto* (☎075/981 51; ②) at Manteigas. Heading out of the park from here, there is a campsite at **VALHELHAS** on the Belmonte road.

Circumnavigating the Serra da Estrela

There's a beautiful track that circumnavigates the whole Serra da Estrela range. It is not well marked but is easy to find and quite spectacular. It goes right across the high plains, through countryside of shepherds (and their dogs) and ringing bells. The walk takes a couple of days and there are plenty of camping opportunities along the route – which *has* to be adhered to. Hitching some, or all, of this route is generally easy, with the reverse law of hitching coming well into play: the fewer the vehicles, the more chance of getting a lift in any one of them.

Sabugal, Sortelha and Serra da Malcata

The area **east of Covilha**, over toward the Spanish borderland, is worth explor-ing for the chance to visit **Sabugal** and, more particularly, **Sortelha**, whose amaz-ing circuit of walls rise amid one of the bleakest locations in all Portugal. Depending on buses, you'll need to backtrack to Guarda for connections. However, if you have your own transport, the two towns are an easy sidetrip from Covilha and the Serra da Estrela, and you can continue into the **Serra da Malcata** – wild terrain which, believe it or not, harbours a **lynx reserve**.

Sabugal

SABUGAL, like most towns in Beira Alta, has a **castle**. It's a good one, too, with massively high walls, a vast hollow centre, and a pentagonal tower with three arched chambers piled one on top of the other. Trust the rickety staircase and you could be on top of the world; trust the wobbly stonework (personally, I didn't) and you could walk right around the walls.

The village has a couple of **pensions**, the *Sol-Rio* and *O Século,* and a fine *Turihab* lodging, the *Casa do Palheiro* on Rua das Escadinhas (no phone). There's no official campsite, though nobody should object if you put a tent up by the river, on its out-of-town stretch. In June there's a **festa** on the 24th and a grand **feira** on the 29th; at other times of year it's all pretty quiet.

Regular **buses** run by *Viúva Monteiro* leave from the main square for Guarda, and others go north to VILAR FORMOSO and south to Penamacor and Castelo Branco via Penamacor. To get to **Sortelha**, 15km west, public transport is limited to school buses (5.30pm Mon, Tues, Thurs, Fri; 1pm Wed); these, obviously, don't run during the holidays. If you decide to try and hitch, start walking and be prepared to possibly continue for the distance. More

Sortelha

SORTELHA is isolated and rather eerie, especially when mist drifts down from the *serra*. It is an ancient town, with Hispano-Arabic origins, and was also the first *castelo roqueiro* ("rock fortress") to be built this side of the Côa. Mystery and legend have grown up with the castle and its fortifications (*sortelha* means "ring"), with stories spun around the figure of an old lady, *a velha*, whose profile you can see on rocks from outside the top gates.

At first sight the town seems nothing special. Walk uphill from the new quarters, however, and you arrive at the fantastically walled **old town**. Within the grid, take a look at the **Igreja Matriz** (keys from the house next door) with its beautiful ceiling, executed by medieval Moorish workmen. Arabic script can be seen, too, on several house lintels near the top of town.

It's also worth taking time to browse around the **antique shop** on the road up to the **castle**, and the **carpet workshop** on the route back down toward Sabugal. Both offer insights into the way life used to be, but above all they show a healthy attitude to present-day tourism. Even if their continuing existence depends entirely on the foreign visitor, you never get the feeling that the show is laid on just for you. The chance to work with the fine materials and coloured wools seems to be enjoyed by all in the workshop, and the antique dealer is as happy to chat about the curious customs and folk tales as strike a bargain.

Festivals

Sortelha's major event is a **bullfight**, which takes place on August 15, once every two or three years, when the local council has money to stage it. It retains the ancient and peculiar custom of the *forca* – a rudimentary defence against the bull, using branches – which has been handed down from father to son. The order of events for the day has never changed, beginning with a *forca* involving all the young boys of the village – at least 25 of whom are needed to carry the device to prevent it from being tipped up by the bull. Later, solo performers strut the stage with their red capes to take the bull's charges. Onlookers are also frequently involved – many a young bull has hopped up onto the terrace of rocks, only to find himself sniffing at discarded hats and bags while nervous laughter rises up from behind the safety of the nearest wall.

In non-bullfight years there's still a **festa** on August 15, and a **romaria** in honour of Santo António takes place each June 13.

Rooms and practicalities

Sortelha has three superb and inexpensive *Turihab* **lodgings,** the *Casa do Vento que Soa*, *Casa do Patio* and, best of all, the *Casa da Escadinha* (all ②). For advance booking – which is recommended in summer – phone ahead (☎071/681 82 or 681 13). If you just turn up, ask for Maria da Conceição Marquês, one of three women in charge. Each of the *Turihab* houses is a traditional village home in the old town, replete with massive walls, wooden furniture, hot baths, cobwebs – all in all a splendid mix of modern comforts and medieval surroundings.

If you're out of luck, try asking for **rooms** at the *Restaurante Celta*. Alternatively, there are any number of promising areas to pitch camp above and beyond the old town, where the terrain is rocky and sheep take shelter beneath massive boulders. Best bet for **meals** is the wood-beamed *Restaurante Típico*, which often has *javali* (wild boar) on the menu.

Buses back to Sabugal leave at 7.30am on schooldays, and sometimes at 9am on Tuesdays and Thursdays – check times the day before in the café.

The Serra da Malcata

The **Serra da Malcata** has its reserve's headquarters at Penamacor (Rua dos Bombeiros Voluntários), 33km south of Sabugal. They are full of advice about how to approach the area and where best to go at different times of the year. The **lynx** – a graceful spotted feline with the build of a domestic cat but the dimensions of a labrador – is notoriously difficult to see, especially without the aid of the park keepers, but the countryside is compensation enough if you don't get a sighting. If you're fortunate you might also see the back of a wild boar disappearing into the forests of black oak.

The reserve contains a newly opened **barragem** (dam), currently a scar on the landscape, though it will hopefully heal in time; it has good swimming spots.

Penamacor

PENAMACOR is a rather dull place, split in two by constant noisy traffic, but it has several small **pensions** to choose from and numerous cafés where you can get a snack. There's also a **castle** – nothing out of the ordinary if you've come from Sabugal and Sortelha, though the climb up is rewarded by views over the Serra da Malcata toward Spain, and tremendous sunrises and sunsets.

Unless you are hanging around to explore the Serra da Malcata, you would really do better to move on for the night to the extraordinary villages of **Monsanto** and **Idanha-a-velha** which lie off the route to Castelo Branco (see following sections). For **bus** times consult the **Turismo** (next to the main through-road) and with any luck you'll be there on the right day.

South from Covilha: Serra da Gardunha

Fundão and the neighbouring villages of **Alpedrinha** and **Castelo Novo** lie sunk into a ridge, the **Serra da Gardunha**, south of Covilhã. All have magnificent views and are healthy, rural places, with delicious local fruit and, at Castelo Novo, healing waters. Without your own transport, a route through Fundão is an easier approach to Monsanto than cutting across country from Sabugal and Penamador.

Fundão

FUNDÃO is the largest town in the area and a pleasant place to stock up on supplies. As far as sights are concerned, though, even the local tourist pamphlet admits that the town has "no monuments of note". Fundão's rural tranquility, however, does much to make up for its touristic shortcomings, as does its glorious abundance of fresh fruit and vegetables. The villages around the *serra* are celebrated for their produce and this is the local market centre.

Moving **on to Alpedrinha** is a pleasure in itself: a three-hour walk along an old, cobbled Roman road via the hamlet of ALCONGOSTA. Given this option, it seems a shame to use the bus. However, Beira Baixa line trains will deposit you on the plain below Alpedrinha – with an approach along another section of Roman road.

Alpedrinha

ALPEDRINHA is set into the side of the *serra*, overlooking fields of olives and fruit trees. In spring the hillside flowers, fruit-tree blossoms, and springwater oozing from every crack in the road make it as idyllic a spot as you could hope to find – notwithstanding the rumbling lorries crashing through the village on the main road to the south. It is easy to escape the noise though, once you wander up to the older quarters or on into the *serra*.

Around the town

A good first stop is at the museum in the former **Paços do Concelho**. This displays an interesting collection of tradesmen's tools – from cobbler to baker to tinsmith – and traditional clothing, including a striking, black wedding dress, the customary colour in this part of the world. A short way beyond, the **Capela do Leão**, in the courtyard of the Casa de Misericórdia, provides Alpedrinha with its current talking-point. Something of a mystery surrounds a series of valuable **sixteenth-century panels** which disappeared from the chapel. The panels were last spotted at a Primitivist exhibition in Lisbon, which coincided with renovation work due to be carried out on the chapel.

At the top of the same street, above the plain **Igreja Matriz**, you'll come across Alpedrinha's highlight: an elaborate fountain known as the **Chafariz de Dom João V**. When the king passed through in 1714 he found the water so good that he commissioned the *chafariz* as a sign of royal approval. The little village flourished and grand houses such as the now-deserted **Palácio do Picadeiro**, which towers above the fountain, were constructed during the eighteenth century. In front of this spectre of a palace the old **Roman road** (from the times when Alpedrinha was called Petratinia) begins to wind its cobbled way up the side of the *serra* toward Fundão.

Other architectural delights abound, all detailed in the "Friends of Alpedrinha" booklet (available from the library below the museum). Above all, don't miss the **furniture workshop**, situated below the main road on the way out of town toward Castelo Branco. Ask inside and someone will show you around António Santos Pinto's **sala de arte**, with some of the most consummate singlehanded marquetry ever produced. Pinto moulded Louis XV chairlegs to Napoleonic dressers and threw the odd carved African page-boy into his structures for good measure. There's even a set of tableaux depicting the first six cantos of Camões's *Lusíadas* – all in the most incredible detail.

Rooms and practicalities

The best of Alpedrinha's **pensions** is the *Clara* (☎075/573 91; ①), run by a sprightly old lady of the same name; there's an old wing in the centre and a modern building on the road in from Belmonte. Pricier alternatives include the *Estalagem São Jorge* (☎075/571 54; ③), and a gorgeous *Turihab* mansion, the *Casa do Barreiro* (☎075/571 20; ④), set amid rambling gardens. **Campers** can pitch tents near the **swimming pool**, off the main road in from the north. The *Estalagem São Jorge* **restaurant** serves up great pizzas and huge salads which make a refreshing change from the usual solid country fare.

Lastly, a miscellany of details. The town hosts a tremendous **feira** (market), on the first Sunday in every month, and a full-blown festival, the **Festa do Anjo da Guarda**, each August 3. Information on **buses** is available from the newspaper kiosk on the side of the main through-road. The Alpedrinha **train station**, on the plain below, is unstaffed but you can buy tickets on the trains (Beira Baixa line).

Castelo Novo

In northern Portugal **CASTELO NOVO** is best known as the source of *Alardo*, a bottled mineral water reputed to possess healing properties. At the **spa**, marked by just a single café-restaurant, the water gushes from every crack in the earth's surface. There is no accommodation, but there's scope for camping – and no shortage of sparkling, clear, water.

The village proper, like Alpedrinha, has ancient origins, and a few crumbling remains to prove it: a **castle**, an attractive **Paços do Concelho** (above the main square), and a Manueline **pelourinho**. Off to the sides of the square, narrow alleyways and heavy stonework constitute the village's principal charm. Although there is no **bus** to the village, four daily run along the main N18 road; you can be dropped or picked up at the crossroads, 4km out.

Castelo Branco, Monsanto and Idanha

After the surpassing beauty of most of Beira Alta, the flat plain of the lower province comes as something of an anti-climax. For the most part it's monotonous, parched country, dotted here and there with cork and carob trees or the occasional orchard. However, from **Castelo Branco**, Beira Baixa's capital and only sizable town, you can make rewarding and fairly easy excursions to two strange and atmospheric villages – **Monsanto** and **Idanha-a-Velha**.

Castelo Branco

CASTELO BRANCO is a predominantly modern town – and attractive for it. Set out around wide boulevards, large squares, and small parks, it has an air of prosperityand activity in contrast to the somnolent villages round about.

What's left of its **old town** – beaten about by successive frontier wars – is confined within the narrow cobbled alleyways and stepped sidestreets leading up to the ruins of the **Castle**. Around its twelfth-century walls, a garden-viewing point, the **Miradouro de São Gens**, has been laid out.

Nearby is the **Palácio Episcopal**, the old Bishop's palace, with its formal, eighteenth-century garden – a sequence of elaborately shaped hedges, baroque statues, little pools, fountains, and flowerbeds. The balustrades of the grand stair-case are peopled with statues – the Apostles on the right, kings of Portugal on the left. Two of the latter are much smaller than the rest: the hated Spanish rulers, Felipe I and II.

The palace itself houses a **regional museum** (daily 9.30am–noon & 2–5.30pm), its collections roaming through the usual local miscellany, save for a large and splendid collection of finely embroidered bedspreads, or *colchas*, a craft for which the town is known throughout Portugal. Until quite modern times, these were made of locally produced silk, and formed the part of every bride's trousseau. The finest in the museum date from the seventeenth and eighteenth centuries, with designs clearly based on cloths brought back from the east. There are also some modern examples; the same building houses a school of embroidery which is striving to revive the craft.

Worth seeing, too, are the elegant sixteenth-century **Câmara Municipal** in the Praça Luís de Camões and the many seventeenth- and eighteenth-century mansions in the streets around it.

Practicalities

There is a **Turismo** (☎072/210 02) right in the centre of Castelo Branco, in a little park off the Alameda da Liberdade. The **bus station** is on the corner of Rua Rebelo and Rua do Saibreiro, the latter leading straight up to the Alameda. It's a little further to the **train station**, but equally simple – straight down the broad Avenida de Nuno Álvares.

The few **pensions** are nothing to write home about. The *Pensão Martinho* at Alameda da Liberdade 41 (☎072/217 06; ②) is the most central and conspicuous – and also the least recommended. Marginally better are the *Residencial Caravela* (☎072/239 39; ③), near the bus station at Rua do Sabreiro 24, and the *Residencial Arriana* at Av 1º de Maio 18 (☎072/216 34; ③).

Monsanto

MONSANTO, 45km northwest of Castelo Branco (buses twice daily), claims to be the most ancient settlement in Portugal. It is a claim easy enough to believe, for the old village – there's a newer settlement at the bottom of the hill – looks as if it has barely changed since the Iron Age. Its houses cower beneath a huge forti-fied granite outcrop, the stone from which they are themselves constructed. From a few hundred yards, they disappear entirely into the grey, boulder-strewn background, with only the odd splash of whitewash, added in these more peace-ful times. It is all incredibly basic and beautiful – flowers are everywhere and the streets, barely wide enough even for a mule, are simply carved out of the rock.

The **castle** too is impressive, though tumbledown. As you climb up through the village you're quite likely to meet someone who'll insist on guiding you up, showing you the views and expounding some of the legends. A big celebration takes place every May 3, when the village girls throw baskets of flowers off the ramparts. The rite commemorates an ancient siege when, in desperation and close to starvation, the defenders threw their last calf over the walls: their attack-ers, so disheartened at this evidence of plenty within, gave up and went home.

There is a small **bar** on the road below Monsanto which sometimes lets out rooms (they turned down my request as the rooms "would be too hot"). They'll give you a meal anyway, and if you're stranded no one will mind if you camp.

Idanha-a-Velha

IDANHA-A-VELHA is another tiny backwater, sited midway between Castelo Branco and Monsanto. It sees just one bus a day (mid-afternoon) from Castelo Branco, which promptly turns around and leaves; however, if you don't have transport, it shouldn't be too hard to hitch from Monsanto.

The village is certainly worth a little effort to reach. It's possibly of a similar age to Monsanto, but has a considerably more illustrious history. Known as Igaetania, it was once a major Roman city, and subsequently, under Visigothic rule, was the seat of a bishopric – which endured even Moorish occupation. Wamba, the legendary King of the Goths, is said to have been born here. During the reign of Dom Manuel, however, early in the fifteenth century, it is said that a plague of rats forced the occupants to move to Monsanto or nearby Idanha-a-Nova.

The village looks much as it must have done when the rats moved in, and not far different to when the Romans left, either. It retains still a section of massive Roman wall, the **Roman bridge** is still in use, and odd Roman relics lie about everywhere. In the very ancient **Basílica**, which is at least part Visigothic, there's a collection of all the more mobile statues and lumps of inscribed stone found about the place; another small chapel contains an exhibition of coins, pottery, and bones, all found more or less by accident. Another oddity, whose history nobody seems to know, is a Moorish-inspired balconied mansion.

North of Guarda: the *planalto* of Beira Alta

North and east of Guarda, and beyond the mountains of Estrela, stretches a rough and barren-looking territory known as the **Planalto** – tableland – of the Beira Alta. Villages here are spread far apart, with much of the land between untamed by agriculture, strewn with boulders and great slabs of granite. The odd valleys and settlements, though, are fertile, with a local speciality of roast or dried **chestnuts**. Once a replacement for potatoes, and now a dessert, they come from vast, shady trees growing beside the roads on almost any approach to a village.

In medieval times the region was home to prosperous Jewish settlements such as **Trancoso** and **Sernancelhe**, though their merchant trade went into decline from the Age of Discovery onwards as business moved to the coast. In successive centuries, the *planalto* towns became closely associated with Portuguese independence from Spain, and in particular with Afonso Henriques' march south down the length of the country. **Penedono, Trancoso**, and **Pinhel** are just three of the towns which he fortified. Their **castles** are today the highlight of the region. Penedono's castelo roqueiro is especially magnificent, with seventeenth-century reconstructions on top of the original article. Spectacular, too, is the star-shaped fortress at **Almeida**, the site of the penultimate battle in the Peninsular Wars against Napoleon.

If you're travelling in the **winter**, take to heart the proverb that *O frio almoça em Penedono, merenda em Trancoso e ceia na Guarda* – "The cold lunches in Penedono, takes tea in Trancoso and dines in Guarda" – and come suitably prepared. You will at least be rewarded by some extraordinary landscapes: the frost (*sincelo*) can have an extraordinary effect on the *planalto*, with massive trees linked by boughs of crystal and metre-long icicles hanging from every house.

BANDARRA: A COBBLER'S PROPHECY

Trancoso takes its place in Portuguese history through the legend of one **Bandarra**, a shoemaker-prophet who lived in the town in the fifteenth century.

The cobbler began his prophetic career with local horoscopes and poems, but after a while moved to more national matters – foretelling, among other things, the end of the Portuguese kingdom. In an age of religious dilemma and disillusionment with monarchical rule, they struck a chord – and attracted the attention of the authorities. Their circulation was banned and Bandarra condemned to death, a sentence commuted, after popular outcry, to a punishment of walking barefoot around town carrying a massive candle until it burned to the wick.

There the matter might have rested, but twenty years after Bandarrra's death, Dom Sebastião did indeed die – along with most of the Portuguese nobility, on the battlefield at Alcáçer-Quibir – leaving no heir to the throne. Portugal subsequently lost independence to Spain, and Bandarra was pronounced the **Nostradamus** of his time.

Trancoso

TRANCOSO, still largely contained within a circuit of medieval walls, is an atmospheric little town, full of dark alleyways and interesting architectural details.

The presence of a large **Jewish community** during the Middle Ages is apparent from the facades of the more ancient homes. Each has two doorways – one broad for trade, the other narrow for the family – and above the carefully crafted and bevelled stonework, some have clumsy crosses, inscribed by the Inquisition to indicate the family's conversion to Christianity. The most striking is the former **rabbi's house** (known as the *Casa do Gato Negro*), near the restaurant *São Marcos*, which is decorated with the Lion of Judea, the Gates of Jerusalem, and a figure of *Preguiça,* or Sloth.

At the centre of the fortifications is the **castle**, with its squat, almost triangular, tower – a distinctive silhouette visible from many miles away. It's a Moorish design and a reminder of the Saracen domination of the town in the tenth century, following the town's conquest by al-Mansur. The following two centuries saw frequent siege and battle, with the fortress taken by Fernando Magno in 1033, and finally by Afonso Henriques and Egas Moniz in 1139 – an event celebrated by the construction of the monastery at São João de Tarouca (see Chapter Five). Trancoso's later military history includes the usual invasions and billeting during fourteenth-century Castillian troublemaking and nineteenth-century Peninsular Warring – look out for a charming corner house with an open stone stairway on the central square, with the tellingly British name, *Quartel do General Beresforde*.

An equally historic site is the small **Chapel of São Bartolomeu**, on the side of the dusty *avenida* leading into town, where Dom Dinis married the twelve-year-old Isabel of Aragon. Outside the walls from here, in front of the law courts, **Celtic tombs** attest to very early origins indeed. Here and there a coffin-cover lies askew; the rest of the mound is a carved mass of human-shaped pits of varying sizes – one obviously for a child.

Practicalities

The town offers a choice of two **pensions**. *Residencial Rico* on Rua Dr. Fernandes Vaz (☎071/914 11; ①) is central, old-fashioned, and down-at-heel, while *Residencial Dom Dinis*, outside the walls, next to the *Correio*; ②) is modern and clean. A third alternative are rooms at the *Café Bandarra*, near the main gateway. There is a summer **Turismo**, opposite the Bartolomeu chapel.

Feiras are held on Fridays, with the big annual bash, the **Feira de São Bartolomeu**, on August 20–22, following the **Festa de Nossa Senhora da Fresta** on August 15.

Buses leave at 10am and 1pm for Pinhel; at 1.45pm for Penedono; and at 3.15pm for Pinhel, Almeida and Figueira de Castelo Rodrigo. Lamego-bound buses, via Sernancelhe, pass by several times a day – though you may have to go out to the main road to catch them. For Guarda and major towns en route to Lisbon there's a 5.15pm weekday service.

Sernancelhe

Sited a couple of kilometres off the Guarda–Lamego road, **SERNANCELHE** is not exactly the hub of Beira Alta. But it's a quietly impressive place, in the manner of Trancoso, with further reminders of the area's Jewish past, and a fine riverside location. The village is also said to have the *planalto*'s finest chestnuts. The trees, broad-boughed and spreading across the road, dominate the landscape as you approach the village. Carnivals, love songs, recipes, and folk tales all centre on the fruit, and if you coincide with the **Festa of Nossa Senhora de Ao Pé da Cruz** on May 1 you'll witness a curious mixture of religious devotion, springtime merrymaking, and, above all, folkloric superstition. There's a dance of the chestnuts, a blessing of the trees, and the exchange of handfuls of blossom by local lovers, aside from the religious procession.

Should you want to know more, the local cultural expert, Padre Cândido Azevedo, in his majestic, castle-like home overlooking the town, is more than pleased to greet a stranger. The walk up there takes you through the **old quarter** of town, now only semi-populated, and coming alive only for the weekly Thursday market. Following the main road, you pass the **Igreja Matriz**, an attractive Romanesque church with a curious facade. Fixed into twin niches on either side of the main doorway, are six weathered apostles – said to be the only free-standing sculptures of the period in the whole of Portugal. Inside the church are several sixteenth-century panels, including a magnificent *John the Baptist*.

Wandering about this part of town you'll see the same features of medieval **Jewish settlement** as in Trancoso – canted lintels, pairs of granite doorways of unequal size, the occasional cross for the converted. Equally noticeable are a number of large **townhouses**, dating from the sixteenth and seventeenth centuries. One of these is the supposed birthplace of the Marquês de Pombal. Another was the birthplace of Padre João Rodrigues, an eminent and influential missionary who founded a series of mission houses in Japan in the sixteenth century. Japanese tourists often make the pilgrimage here to see the building.

Practicalities

The village has two **pensions** – the *Flora* and *Trasmontana*, both fairly basic and inexpensive (②). Alternatively, you could put a tent up by the river, just outside Sernancelhe, or at the **Barragem do Tavora**, a man-made barrage 3km to the north, which is said to be okay for swimming.

Buses on to Lamego (see "Trás-os-Montes") leave from the *Estrada Nacional 226*, 4 kilometres away – there are four a day in the week, fewer at the weekend. There are also weekday buses to Penedono (1pm and 7pm) and Trancoso (9am).

Penedono

PENEDONO is another one-horse town, but again a likable place, and with a fantastic **Castelo Roquiero** – visible from miles around. The *roqueiro* ("rock") part of the name is due to the castle's emergence from its granite base, as if the rock and the walls were one and the same. From the top, as you might imagine, there are grand views, with the village's old quarter laid out below. Keys are available from the village shop, who will warn you to rattle the doors in order to get the pigeons in the air – rather than flying straight at your face.

The castle, in times of war, and the **Solar dos Freixos** (now the Town Hall), in times of peace, were supposed to have been home to Álvaro Gonçalves Coutinho, the legendary **King Magriço**, ("Lean One"), sung of in Camões' *Os Lusíadas*. It's a claim fought over fiercely with the inhabitants of Trancoso, who likewise are prepared to swear he is their man. Penedono, though, has the edge, as its name, from *pena* and *dono*, means literally "King of the Rock". According to Camões the *Magriço* led eleven other men to England to champion the cause of twelve noble English ladies, who found themselves without knights, and fought a joust on their behalf. Such tales of chivalry made them the subjects of numerous allegorical murals and panels of *azulejos* around the country.

Practicalities

The village has just one **pension**, the *Solneve* (☎054/542 39; ②), with friendly management, though you could also find rooms above the *Café Gomes* or the *Café Avenida* on the main road; the latter has excellent food. **Feiras** are held every other Wednesday, and there's a **Romaria** on September 15–16.

Buses leave at 2pm and 7.30pm on weekdays for Vila Nova de Foz Côa, and at 8.30am for Trancoso (connection to Coimbra).

Pinhel

PINHEL is big enough to run both a wine cooperative (producing an excellent red) and a cake factory (churning out *cavaca* sweetmeats). But, digestibles apart, it's also small enough to have left the old centre of town virtually untouched. You can walk right around the crumbling castle walls, across the top of five intact archways, through vegetable plots and back gardens, and remain almost unaware of the twentieth century. From one corner of the **walls** you look down on the shell of a ruined **Romanesque Church** – whose facade alone merits closer inspection. On another stretch you will discover what is left of the original **fortress**, a soaring tower with an intricately carved Manueline window.

Down in town further architectural pleasures are in store, with numerous **manor houses** clustered about magnificent gardens. One of the largest is now the **Câmara Municipal**, its hallway bedecked with a series of excellent photographs of local buildings of interest. An adjacent building houses the town **museum** (Mon–Fri 10am–noon & 2–6pm; free), with a pile of **Celtic tombstones** on the ground floor and, upstairs, remnants of a local convent.

Practicalities

Pinhel has two modest-priced pensions: the *Residencial Pinhelense* (☎071/423 73; ②), with superb meals, and the *Residencial Falcão* (☎071/421 04; ②). If you want to camp, no one seems to mind tents being pitched around the castle walls.

Buses leave from the centre of the municipal gardens – ask in the museum or shop nearby for schedules. One useful connection is the *Berrelhas* bus which you can flag down at about 4.15pm (every day) to go to Almeida or on to Figueira de Castelo Rodrigo.

The local **Festa de Santo Antonio** is held on the Sunday closest to June 13.

Almeida

ALMEIDA is perhaps the most attractive of all the fortified borderland towns. A beautifully preserved stronghold, its **walls** are in the form of a twelve-pointed star: a Dutch design, influenced by the French military architect Vauban. A four-kilometre walk around the walls takes in all the peaks and troughs, and if you stay overnight, there's an irresistible charm in watching the sun go down and the lights come on in a hundred tiny villages across the plateau of the Ribacôa. This was one of the last stretches of land to be recognised as officially Portuguese, in the Treaty of Alcañices with the Spanish in 1297, and it's easy to see why boundaries were not clearly staked out in the broad, flat terrain.

Inevitably, perhaps, tourism has been catching up with the place. A new government *pousada* was built here a couple of years ago and the number of cafés in town has risen from three to twenty-three. Locals seem grateful, if intrigued, by the phenomenon of rich tourists and foreign ministers turning up in their long-forgotten town, to fork out more than a villager's weekly earnings to ride in a souped-up pony cart, or to pay through the nose (relatively speaking) for a coffee on the balcony overlooking the humble dwellings below.

The Casamatas and fortifications

The arrival of the **Pousada**, sadly, resulted in the hacking out of a fourth gateway in Almeida's **fortifications**. The original three are the town's most splendid features – long shell-proof tunnels with emblazoned entrances and sizeable guard rooms – and for years they have stood as an effective barrier against modernisation within the walls. However the new *pousada* gateway, smashed through eighteenth-century walls, is bus-size, lorry-size, delivery-van-size – in fact the size and price of door-to-door service to a *pousada* in a "quaint village setting".

The **Casamatas** (9am–noon & 2–5pm; tip expected), or barracks, is second in size only to Elvas, with a capacity for five thousand men and their supplies. Its layout explains how it withstood lengthy sieges. With its own water supply, rubbish chute, breathing holes, hidden escape routes, munitions chamber (there's a range of cannonballs and gunshot still on view), and dormitory space, the possibilities were limitless. One hazard which no one foresaw, however, was the potential for an explosion within the fortress itself. In 1810, after the Luso-Brittanic forces had held out for seventeen days against Massena, a leaky barrel of gunpowder, carried from the cathedral–castle in the centre of town to the *Praça Alta* (an artillery platform on the northern walls), left a fatal trail of powder. Once ignited this began a fire that killed hundreds, and the survivors gave themselves up to the French. Wellington, on his victorious return from Buçaco, subsequently took the fortress with no bloodshed. The French army scuttled away during the night, probably making use of one of three *portas falsas* – narrow slits in the ramparts allowing for a discreet exit.

You can find out more about the campaign from the **museum** (same hours as Casamatas) in the old guard's room within the main town gates.

One other curiosity, not far from the *pousada*, is an inscription on the side of a small house declaring it to be the dumping ground for illegitimate children. At the **Rodo dos Eispostos** (literally the "Circle of the Deserted") anyone could come and claim an unwanted child for themselves – a convenient arrangement for both mother and foster parent.

Rooms and other practicalities

For those with the means, the *Pousada Senhora das Neves* (☎071/542 83; ⑥) provides the town's finest **accommodation** – priced at around 14,000$00 for a double. This apart, staying in the old town is a question of getting talking with the villagers. A good first stop is the *Casa da Amelinha*, which serves as the **bus office** and unofficial gathering place. Ask for Amélia, who has a number of rooms and, if full, will probably be able to direct you elsewhere; if you stay, be sure to try her *ginginha* (morello cherry liqueur).

Otherwise, there are two new *residencials* by the crossroads outside the fort – *A Muralha* and *Morgado* – and further rooms for rent at the *Café Tertúlia*. The *Tertúlia*, and the *Restaurante Portas de Almeida* nearer town, are the best **places to eat**. A personal favourite of the **cafés** within the fort is the *Terreiro Velho*, near the market stalls; it stays open till 2am most nights and, despite fairly modern tastes in music, seems popular with old as well as young.

For **camping or swimming**, make your way to the Rio Côa, two kilometres' stroll downhill on the Pinhel road. Just above the old Romanesque bridge (and its present-day equivalent), you'll find some idyllic spots. It's important to swim below the barrier, as the water above is for town consumption.

If you can possibly do so, try to coincide with one of the twice-monthly **feiras** (on the 8th day and last Saturday) or – best of all – visit at Pentecost (fifty days after Easter) for the grand **picnic** at the **Convento da Barca**, a former Franciscan monastery, with a distinctively Tuscan feel about its domed chapel and setting. It's the only time you can visit the convent, but at other times of the year you can try the excellent red wine, apples, peaches, nuts, and various other produce for which it is famous, at shops in town.

Buses on to the north come from Vilar Formoso twice on weekdays and go as far as Figueira de Castelo Rodrigo. One sure service to catch is the *Berrelhas* bus which passes through on the main road 200 metres from the gates to Almeida at about 5pm every afternoon. Going south there are local services as far as Vilar Formoso (14km), which has trains to Guarda or Spain, and three daily buses to Sabugal and Castelo Branco.

travel details

Trains

BEIRA BAIXA LINE

From Guarda 3 trains daily to Covilhã (1hr 10min), Fundão (1hr 40min), Alpedrinha (2hr 20min), Castelo Branco (3hr 20min), Belver (4hr–4hr 30min), Abrantes (4hr 30min–5hr), Entroncamento (5–6hr), Santarém (5hr 30min–6hr 30min), and Lisbon (6hr 30min–7hr 30min).

BEIRA ALTA LINE

From Guarda 5 trains daily to Celorico da Beira (1hr), Nelas (1hr 45min; change for buses to Viseu), Sta Comba Dão (2hr), Luso-Buçaco (2hr 40min) Pampilhosa (3hr; change for Figueira da Foz, Aveiro and Porto), Coimbra B (3hr 30min), Entroncamento (5hr), and Lisbon (6hr 30min).

Most **Beira Baixa and Beira Alta trains** also run from Guarda to the **Spanish border** at Vilar Formoso-Fuentes de Oñoro (1hr), from where there are two onward connections to **Salamanca** (2hr 30min).

Buses

From Coimbra to Castelo Branco (3 daily; 5hr); Guarda (2; 4hr); Viseu (3; 3hr); Covilhã (1; 4hr).

From Covilhã to Castelo Branco (4; 2hr 30min); Guarda (4; 1hr 30min).

From Guarda to Lamego (4; 4hr); Viseu (4; 2hr).

From Viseu to Lamego (5; 2hr); Porto (2; 5hr).

All the major towns have at least one express service a day to **Lisbon** and **Porto**, usually three or four. **International** buses from Lisbon to Paris also pass through Coimbra, Viseu, and Guarda and you can pick them up there, though seats must be booked in advance.

Flights

From Viseu to Lisbon, 2 flights a week.

From Covilhã to Lisbon 2 or 3 flights a week; to Porto, once a week.

CHAPTER FIVE

PORTO AND THE DOURO

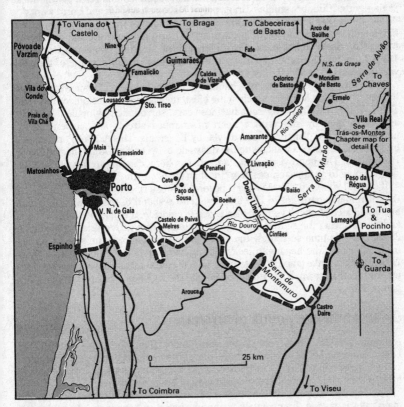

The **River Douro** (*Rio d'Ouro* – river of gold) dominates every aspect of this region. Its valley, a spectacular rocky gorge as it approaches the sea, nourishes in its upper reaches the **port** vineyards. Even though the wine no longer shoots down the river's rapids in barges, a trip up the valley remains one of the best scenic routes in the country. You can cover most of its course by train, or by car, while to the north a series of **narrow gauge rail lines** – sadly truncated in recent years – follow a trio of tributary river valleys. Covered in this chapter, too, though technically in Mountain Beiras, is the elegant town of **Lamego** – most easily reached by bus from Régua on the Douro rail line.

Above all, of course, there's **Porto** itself, a massively atmospheric city, almost Dickensian in parts, and its port-producing suburb of **Vila Nova de Gaia**; to the north of the city, excellent beaches front **Vila do Conde** and **Póvoa de Varzim**.

PORTO (OPORTO)

Portugal's second largest city, **PORTO** is magnificently situated on the great gorge of the Douro, its old quarters scrambling up the rocky north bank in tangled tiers. Although the capital of the north, it's a very different city from Lisbon – unpretentious, inward-looking, unashamedly commercial. As the local saying goes: "Coimbra studies; Braga prays; Lisbon shows off; and Porto works".

The city's monumental sights are its **bridges**: four of them, two modern, two nineteenth century, and each spectacular. The two old ones are the metalwork Maria Pia railway link, designed by Eiffel, and the dizzying, two-tiered **Ponte de Dom Luís**, which connects the city with **Vila Nova de Gaia**, home of the port wine lodges – all of which offer tours and tastings to visitors.

In the city "proper", there are a handful of buildings to direct your wanderings, but the fascination lies very much in the life of the place: a bizarre mix of First and Third World, with its prosperous business core, surrounded by opulent suburbs and villas, side by side with a heart of cramped streets and ancient alleys, untouched by the planners – and, as yet, by EC grants. This side of Porto comes into focus if you take a walk along the quayside between the Dom Luís and Maria Pia bridges. The improvised sheds and shacks here, clinging to the sides of the gorge, could to all appearances be a Brazilian shanty town.

It's a real shock to discover such poverty in western Europe. However, for all that, it remains hard not to like the city, or to respond to the crowds, tiny bars and antiquated shops. If you can plan a visit to coincide, the place is at its earthiest and finest during the riotous celebration of **Saint John's Eve** (the night of June 23–24). At this time seemingly the entire population takes to the streets, hitting each other over the head with leeks, plastic hammers, or anything else to hand. Lesser festivals take place in September, and, of course, at any time when the city's brilliant football team, **F.C. Porto**, overcome their Lisbon rivals or big European competition.

Orientation and points of arrival

Although modern Porto sprawls for some miles along the north bank of the Douro, most sights of any interest are within the compact and very hilly centre, and all are within walking – or perhaps more accurately *climbing* – distance. For trips further afield, there's a reliable network of buses and trams.

The "centre" is perhaps best regarded as the **Estação de São Bento**, the main railway station. Immediately to the northwest of here is the **Avenida dos Aliados**, the commercial hub of the city, fronted by banks and offices, and, at its north end, by Praça General Humberto Delgado, where you can pick up a large-scale city plan from the **Turismo** (Mon–Fri 9am–5.30pm, Sat 9am–4pm, Sun 10am–2pm; ☎02/31 27 40). Another, smaller tourist office (☎02/31 27 40) is located on the Praça de Dom João I, a block to the southwest.

The streets leading off the Avenida dos Aliados are the city's major shopping areas: to the west, the busy **Rua da Fábrica** with its stationers and bookshops; to the east, **Rua de Passos Manuel**, which runs into the elegant **Praça Dom João I**, and beyond into **Rua de Santa Catarina**, full of fashion and shoe shops.

South of São Bento, a labyrinth of medieval streets and seedy-looking alleyways group below the **Sé**, or cathedral, and slope down to the waterfront **Cais da Ribeira**, lined with fish tavernas and cafés, and the **Ponte Dom Luís I**.

City transport

A brief word on Porto buses and **bus and tram stops** will help you get around more easily. There are three main terminals/destinations:

■ **Cordoaria**. By the Universidade building. Stops are in Campo dos Mártires da Pátria and (for trams) Praça Gomes Teixeira, across the gardens.

■ **Praça**. The central Praça da Liberdade, at the bottom of the Avenida dos Aliados.

■ **Bolhão**: Rua Sá da Bandeira – stops in front of the theatre and halfway up at Bolhão itself.

Single **tickets** are available on buses or trams but it works out cheaper to buy them in blocks, *módulos* (20 tickets for 1120$00), or, if you're staying for a few days, a four- or seven-day *Passe Turístico* (Tourist Pass). These are available at kiosks and in the *papelaria* on Avenida dos Aliados, next to the *Café Imperial*.

There are three **trams**: #1 runs from Alfândega to Matosinhos (the most scenic ride – along the estuary to the mouth of the Douro and then upcoast); #18 from Cordoaria to Boa Vista; and #19 from Boa Vista to Matosinhos.

Points of arrival

Coming into Porto by train or bus, you'll find yourself deposited fairly centrally. If you are driving, try to avoid getting caught up in the downtown grid, whose streets are best negotiated on foot or in a tram or taxi.

TRAIN STATIONS

■ **Coming from the south**, trains drop you at the **Estação de Campanhã**, some way out from the centre. You should change here for a local train into **São Bento** – it takes about five minutes and there should never be more than a twenty-minute wait.

■ **Trains from the north** run directly to **São Bento**.

■ **Narrow gauge trains** from **Minho** (Guimarães) and the **north coast** (Póvoa de Varzim) use the smaller **Estação da Trindade**, north of the Avda dos Aliados.

If you're leaving Porto on an international connection – Paris especially – in the summer, be sure to reserve a seat several days in advance.

BUS STATIONS

Bus companies have no single terminal and a first glance at the schedules suggests that each company operates from a different street in a different part of town. Most, though, are fairly central, and a large number operate from a common terminal below the landmark Torre dos Clérigos at **Rua das Carmelitas**. Other services heading south tend to leave from around **Rua Alexandre Herculano** (just east of São Bento), and those heading north (Viana do Castelo, Barcelos, Braga) from around the **Praça Filipa de Lencastre**. Before setting out, it's well worth checking times and details with the Turismo.

Major companies and their terminals include:

■ **Rodoviária do Porto**, Praça Filipa de Lencastre. The rump of the region's old national bus company serves most destinations in northern Portugal, both by express and local bus.

■ **Cabanelas**, Rua Ateneu Comercial do Porto, off the Rua de Passos Manuel, north of São Bento. Useful express services to towns in Trás-os-Montes (Vila Real, Chaves, Bragança).

■ **Rede Nacional de Expressos (Renex)**. The best express service to Lisbon.

■ **InterNorte** operate international buses to most parts of Europe from their head office on Praça da Galiza and, more conveniently, from Rua das Carmelitas.

THE AIRPORT

From the airport, 13km north of the city, bus #56 shuttles to and from **Praça de Lisboa**, by the Universidade building; the journey usually takes forty minutes, but allow an hour at peak times of day. On the way into Porto, the bus passes the youth hostel and Boavista.

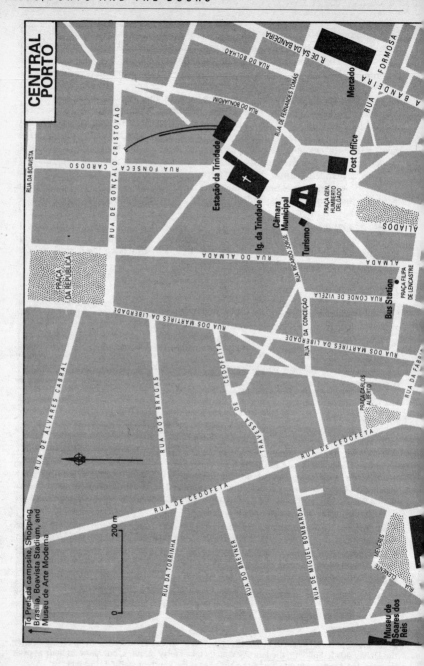

CENTRAL PORTO

RUA BOAVISTA

RUA DE GONÇALO CRISTOVÃO

RUA FONSECA CARDOSO

RUA DO BONJARDIM

RUA DO BOLHÃO

R DE SÁ DA BANDEIRA

RUA DE FERNANDES TOMAS

FORMOSA

Mercado

RUA A BANDEIRA

Estação da Trindade

Ig. da Trindade

Câmara Municipal

Turismo

PRAÇA GEN. HUMBERTO DELGADO

Post Office

PRAÇA DA REPÚBLICA

RUA DO ALMADA

RUA RICARDO JORGE

ALMADA

ALIADOS

RUA DA CONCEIÇÃO

RUA CONDE DE VIZELA

PRAÇA FILIPA DE LENCASTRE

Bus Station

RUA DE ÁLVARES CABRAL

RUA DOS MÁRTIRES DA LIBERDADE

RUA DOS MÁRTIRES DA LIBERDADE

RUA DA FÁBR

RUA DOS BRAGAS

TRAVESSA DE CEDOFEITA

RUA DE CEDOFEITA

PRAÇA CARLOS ALBERTO

RUA DE CEDOFEITA

200 m

RUA DA TORRINHA

RUA DO BREYNER

RUA DE MIGUEL BOMBARDA

RUA CLEMENTE MENERES

0

◄ To Prelada campsite, Shopping Brasília, Boavista Stadium, and Museu de Arte Moderna

Museu de Soares dos Reis

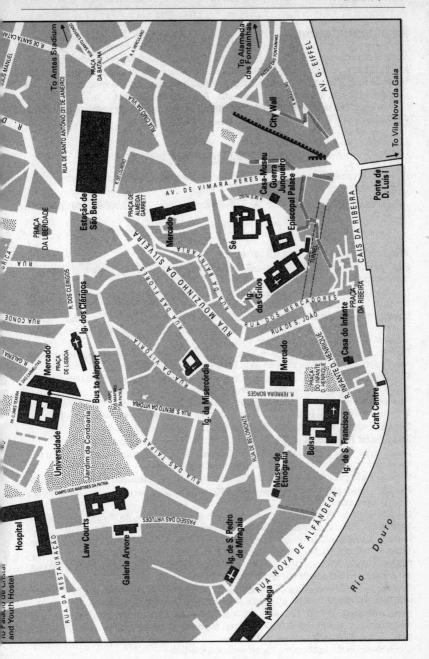

Accommodation

Porto's **accommodation** is generally good value. The cheapest rooms in the city
are in the area south of São Bento station; for rather more salubrious places, your
best bet is to ignore bargainers at the stations and head for the recommendations
detailed below in areas west or east of the Avenida dos Aliados.

In winter, it's worth the investment in one of our more expensive – ③ or above
– rooms, or you'll freeze. Very few hotels have any heating.

ROOM PRICE SCALES

The symbols used in our hotel listings denote the following price ranges.

① 2000–2500esc	③ 3500–5000esc	⑤ 8000–12,000esc
② 2500–3500esc	④ 5000–8000esc	⑥ 12,000esc and upwards

For a fuller explanation, see p.21.

West of the Avenida dos Aliados

Residencial Continental, Rua Mouzinho da Silveira 14 (☎32 03 55). Pleasant, inexpensive
pension on the main street running southwest of São Bento station. ②.

Pensão Universal, Avda. dos Aliados 38 (☎200 67 58). Basic pension, somewhat overpriced
due to its highly convenient position. ③.

Pensão Monumental, Avda. dos Aliados 151–4º (☎200 39 64). Huge but rather decrepit
rooms in the top floors of a huge turn-of-the-century building; dank in winter, okay in
summer, though a noisy location late at night. ②.

Pensão dos Aliados, Rua Elísio de Melo 27, off Avda. dos Aliados (☎248 53). Very comfortable budget pension; all rooms with bath. Book ahead in summer. ③.

Residencial Vera Cruz, Rua Ramalho Ortigão, off Avda. dos Aliados (☎32 33 96). A hike in
quality, this is more of a hotel than a pension – elegant if a bit pricey. ④.

Pensão Pão-de-Açucar, Rua do Almada 262 – parallel to Avda. dos Aliados, behind the
Turismo (☎200 24 25). Stylish 1930s hotel with quiet rooms and private bathrooms. ③.

Pensão Europa, Rua do Almada 398 (☎200 69 71). A second choice on this street . . . ②.

Residencial Porto Rico, Rua do Almada 237 (☎31 87 85). . . . and a third. ②.

Residencial Porto Chique, Rua Conde de Vizela 26 – the next street west (☎38 00 69).
Large, quiet rooms: all with private bath, some with balconies. ③.

Pensão Novo Mundo, Rua Conde de Vizela 92 (☎200 54 03). Clean and popular pension. ②.

Pensão União, Rua Conde de Vizela 62 (☎200 30 78). Again, very popular – bookings are
wise in midsummer. ②.

Pensão d'Ouro, Praça Parada Leitão 41, off Praça Gomes Teixeira, by the Universidade
(☎38 12 01). Rooms with differing facilities at a range of prices. Noisy location. ②–③.

Pensão Duas Nações, Praça Guilherme Gomes Fernandes 59, again off Praça Gomes
Teixeira (☎200 68 07). Dingy and cheap – but likely to have rooms at any time. ②.

Pensão Grande Oceano, Rua da Fábrica 45 – north of the Universidade (☎38 24 47). Again,
not pretty, but a fallback that generally has rooms available. ②.

Pensão São Marinho, Praça Carlos Alberto 59 (☎32 54 99). Efficient and friendly; all rooms
with bath; set in a pleasant, small square 300m from the Torre dos Clérigos. ③.

Pensão Estoril, Rua de Cedofeita 193 – further north again (☎200 27 51). Large, well-
maintained rooms, with private baths, phones, radio, etc. Unbeatable value. ②.

Pensão Residencial Rex, Praça da República 117 (☎200 45 48). A once-grand hotel that still
seems rooted in the last century. Highly recommended. ④.

All numbers in the Greater Porto area are prefixed with the code ☎02.

East of Aliados

Pensão Madariz, Rua Cimo da Vila. Right by São Bento station and as cheap as you could wish with excellent café-bar next door and restaurant opposite. ①.

Hotel do Imperio, Praça da Batalha 130 (☎200 68 61). Modern, comfortable hotel on the square immediately east of São Bento. ⑤.

Pensão do Norte, Rua de Fernandes Tomás 579, on the junction with Rua de Santa Catarina (☎200 35 03). Pleasant, rambling old place with masses of rooms. ②.

Pensão Castelo de Santa Catrina, Rua de Santa Catarina 1347 (☎49 55 99). Right at the end of the street – about a mile from São Bento – this is a most peculiar pension: a walled mansion, built in the 1920s, with loads of azulejos and even a private chapel. ④.

Grande Hotel do Porto, Rua de Rua Santa Catarina 197 (☎200 81 76). Large, neat hotel with a touch of grandeur, just down the street from São Bento. ⑤.

Residencial São Torcato, Rua Guedes de Azevedo, just off Rua Santa Catarina (☎200 6449). Slightly expensive but extremely comfortable and well-kept. Private baths and TVs and breakfast included. ③.

Pensão Astória, Rua Arnaldo Gama 56 (☎200 81 75). Lovely, old-fashioned place behind the city wall in an un-touristy, terraced part of town; be sure to reserve in advance. ③.

Hotel Peninsular, Rua Sá da Bandeira 21 (☎200 30 12). Central (under a minute's walk from São Bento station) and comfortable two-star hotel. ④.

Albergaria Girassol, Rua Sá da Bandeira 133 (☎200 18 91). A tiny little inn, further up the street; rates are a fraction cheaper then at the *Peninsular*. ④.

Campsites

Parque de Campismo de Prelada, Rua Monte dos Burgos (☎81 26 16; bus #9 from Bolhão until 9pm, bus #50 from Cordoaria until midnight). The closest site, 3km northwest of the centre; open year round.

Parque de Campismo de Salgueiros, Praia de Salgueiros, Vila Nova de Gaia (☎781 05 00). Across the river, near the Salgueiros beach – not a place to swim! Open May–Sept.

Youth Hostel

Pousada de Juventude, Rua Rodrigues Lobo 98 (☎655 35); buses #3, #20, or #52 from Praça da Liberdade (ask for Praça da Galiza). Large, clean and functional. ②.

The Town

Taking the **Estação de São Bento** as the centre of downtown Porto, don't be too eager to start your explorations. The station itself is one of the city's grandest buildings in its own right, and it's worth taking a while to view its magnificent *azulejos* by João Colaço; these, somewhat arbitrarily, take on two great themes – the history of transport and the battle of Aljubarrota (see Batalha, p.112).

West to the Torre dos Clérigos and Cordoaria

The stifled streets of the old town rarely permit any sort of overall view of the city, so it's a good idea to climb the Baroque **Torre dos Clérigos** (9am–noon & 2–5.30pm; closed Wed) to get your bearings. This landmark, 200m west of São Bento, characterises the Porto skyline above all else. It was designed, like the curious oval church beneath it, by the Italian architect Nicolau Nasoni, and was once the tallest structure in Portugal. The dizzying vistas from the top take in the entire city, Vila Nova de Gaia south across the river, and sometimes even the distant mouth of the Douro and the coast.

The area immediately below the tower comprises the older sections of the university, and the gardens of the **Cordoaria** – a useful reference point. This area is a fairly prestigious quarter of town, housing, for example, most of the city's commercial art galleries – which are grouped together on the **Rua Galeria de Paris**, which leads off to the north, behind the Cordoaria. At the main dealers here, *Galeria Nasoni* at no. 68–80 (closed Aug–Sept), you're free to wander in and take a look at four floors of the best (and priciest) paintings on sale in the country.

There is more modern art across the Cordoaria from here at the **Galeria Árvore** on Passeio das Virtudes. This is a cooperative of painters, sculptors and designers who run their own art school in close competition with the official Escola das Belas Artes (itself housed in a nearby mansion). They pride themselves on the vitality of the teaching and the freedom they allow their pupils – the results of which are on view in a punchy summer show in June/July.

The Sé and down to the riverside

There are fine views, too, from the broad flagged courtyard in front of Porto's cathedral, the **Sé** (9am–12.30pm & 3–6pm). The building, externally reminiscent of the Sé Velha at Coimbra, is a bluff, austere fortress, set on a rocky outcrop.

Despite attempts to beautify it in the eighteenth century it retains the hard, simple lines of its Romanesque origins – more impressive from a distance than close up. Inside it's depressing, even the vaunted silver altarpiece failing to make any impression in the prevailing gloom. For a small fee, however, you can escape into the neighbouring cloisters, and climb a Nasoni-designed Renaissance staircase leading up to a dazzling chapterhouse, with more views from the casement windows over the old quarter.

Beside the Sé stretches the fine facade of the **Archbishop's Palace** (not open to the public) while around to the back, along Rua de Dom Hugo, is the **Casa Museu de Guerra Junqueiro** (Tues–Sat 11am–12.30pm & 2.30–6pm; 96$00). This is the former home of the poet Guerra Junqueiro, housing his collections of artwork and furniture. The tours around these are not very enthralling, though the mansion and its gardens happily outshine their contents.

Rua de Dom Hugo curls back around to the Sé to merge with the crumbling, animated old alleys which lead down to the riverside. From the prancing statue of Vimara Peres, **Calçada de Vandoma** plunges downwards, lined with the stalls of an authentic **flea market** (at its best on Saturday mornings). A few of the stalls sell fruit or homemade foods but most have a spread of unremitting junk – torn clothes, broken transistor radios, used batteries. This area is the most fascinating and atmospheric part of the city: a medieval ghetto of back streets that would have been demolished or prettified in most other cities of Europe. Tall, narrow, and rickety, the houses have grown upwards into every available space, adapting as best they can to the steep terrain.

Not much goes on down at the waterfront since the big ships stopped calling here, but along the **Cais da Ribeira** old men still sit around as if they expect to be thrown a line or set to work unloading some urgent cargo. Cafés and restaurants line the quayside, too, providing some of Porto's best and most enjoyable fare (see p.173), alonside a weekday **market**. A post-modern cube of a fountain adds a slightly surreal air to the quarter.

Following the Cais westward, past the Praça da Ribeira, you reach Rua da Alfândega, which turns in from the sea, past the **Casa do Infante** (currently closed for restoration), the house where Prince Henry the Navigator is said to have been born. It's an impressive mansion which, when in use, tends to house prestigious touring exhibitions. Further along the Cais, you pass an imaginative regional **Crafts' Centre** before meeting the first major road in from the sea – **Rua Infante de Dom Henrique**. This runs into a square of the same name, where a statue of Henry faces the **Bolsa** – Porto's stock exchange.

The Bolsa and around

The **Bolsa** is a pompous nineteenth-century edifice with a vast neoclassical facade – and its keepers are inordinately proud of the place. On the guided tours (June–Sept: Mon–Fri 10am–5.30pm, Sat & Sun 9am–12.30pm & 2–5pm; Oct–May: Mon–Fri only 9am–11.30am & 2–5.30pm; 300esc) they dwell, with evident glee, on the enormous cost of every item, the exact weight of every piece of precious metal, and the intimate details of anyone with any claim to fame ever to have passed through the doors; President Kennedy, apparently, was one. The tour's nadir is the "Arab" Hall, an oval chamber that misguidedly attempts to copy the Moorish style of the Alhambra; here the guide's superlatives achieve apotheosis. Should you not want to bother with the tour you can see the main courtyard, easily the most elegant part, without having to buy a ticket.

Adjoining the Bolsa is the church of **São Francisco** (Tues–Sat 10am–12.30pm & 2.30–5pm; 100$00), perhaps the most extraordinary in Porto. From its entrance on Rua de São Francisco it looks an ordinary enough Gothic construction, but the interior has been transformed by an unbelievably ornate eighteenth-century refurbishment. Altar, pillars, even the ceiling, drip with gilded rococo carving which reaches its ultimate expression in an interpretation of the Tree of Jesse on the north wall. If it has reopened, don't miss the church's small **museum**, housed in a separate building next door and consisting of artefacts salvaged from the former monastery. Beneath the flags of the cellar is an **osseria** – thousands of human bones, cleaned up and stored to await Judgement Day.

Two other churches in this neighbourhood have small museums. Pride of the **Igreja da Misericórdia**, a couple of blocks to the north, is a remarkable *Fons Vitae*, depicting King Manuel I with his wife Leonor and eight children, richly clothed, kneeling before the crucified Christ. It's an exceptional example of fifteenth-century Portuguese Realism – a style which was heavily influenced by Flemish painters like Van Eyck and Van der Weyden. To gain admission, knock at the government offices next door and ask for permission to enter the *Sala das Sessões*. Over to the west, in the **Igreja de São Pedro de Miragaia**, there's another fine fifteenth-century triptych; the church is kept locked but someone with a key is usually near at hand.

Between these two churches, a **Museu de Etnografia e História** (Tues–Sat 10am–noon & 2–5pm; free) occupies a beautiful noble house in the quiet Largo de São João Novo; it is unmarked: you just have to spot the building and push open the door. Within is a fascinating collection of jewellery, folk costumes, ancient toys, and almost anything of interest that has defied easy definition. One room houses a collection of nineteenth-century childbirth chairs, another is a reconstruction of a rural kitchen, and in yet another is a display of boats used on the Douro. It's the most attractive of Porto's museums and now more or less back to its former glory after severe fire damage in 1985.

The Soares dos Reis and De Castro museums

Northwest of the Cordoaria, on Rua de Dom Manuel II, is the **Museu Nacional Soares dos Reis** (Tues–Sun 10am–5pm; 200$00). The first designated national museum – dating from 1933 – it occupies the former royal *Palácio das Carrancas*; a building that was the French headquarters in the Peninsular War and from where they fled so hurriedly that the Duke of Wellington, leading his troops across the Douro, was able to sit down and eat the celebratory banquet that had been laid out for Marshal Soult and his officers. The museum's excellent collections include glass, ceramics and a formidable display of Portuguese art of the eighteenth and nineteenth centuries. Highlights include the paintings by Henrique Pousão and sculptures by Soares dos Reis (*O Desterrado* – The Exiled – is probably his best-known work), and his pupil, Teixeira Lopes.

While at the Soares dos Reis, it's worth enquiring about the currrent opening hours (currently Tues only) of the **Casa-Museu de Fernando de Castro**, which the museum maintains at Rua de Costa Cabral 176 (an extension of Rua de Santa Catarina), way over to the east of São Bento. This extraordinary house is crammed with treasures and in particular with pieces of gilded wood salvaged from the city's convents following the 1910 dissolution of the monasteries. The culmination of de Castro's own gothic vision is a minute ballroom. It's wonderful and dreadful and shouldn't be missed.

The Palácio de Cristal park and the Solar do Vinho do Porto

Closer to hand, you can follow the road past the Museu Soares dos Reis, or take any bus from *Cordoaria* except #6 and #18, to reach the **Jardim do Palácio de Cristal**, a beautiful stretch of park dominated by a huge domed pavilion; this was built to replace the original "Crystal Palace", and now serves as an exhibition hall. In summer the park is home to a vast funfair.

On the far side of the park, across Rua Entre Quintas, stands the **Quinta da Macieirinha**, which houses both the **Romantic Museum** (a collection of mid-nineteenth-century furniture and artwork; Tues–Sat 10am–noon & 2–5pm), and the **Solar do Vinho do Porto** (Mon–Sat 11am–midnight).

At the latter, in air-conditioned splendour, you can sample one of hundreds of varieties of **port wine**. The list is the same as at the Port Wine Institute in Lisbon but the service is considerably friendlier and the wine, after all, is at home. It's a good prelude to a visit to the port lodges across the river in Vila Nova de Gaia (see facing page).

The Museu de Arte Moderna

About half an hour's bus journey west of the centre, at Rua de Serralves 977, is a more recent addition to the art scene of Porto: the highly contemporary **Museu de Arte Moderna** (Tues–Sun 2–8pm). It can be reached by bus #78 from *Cordoaria* or from near the Palácio de Cristal.

Established and administered by the Gulbenkian Foundation, and housed in a 1930s palace known as the *Casa de Serralves*, the museum displays the work of a number of Portuguese architects and designers. No public collection in the country gives you a more accurate picture of Portugal's modern art scene, and the setting manages to be at once majestic and personal. Exhibitions run for a month at a time, and the **gardens** (meriting a visit in themselves) remain open from 2pm to 5pm daily (7.30pm in summer), even during the two-week rehanging closures.

The Rotunda

The road directly west at the top end of the the the Praça da Republica, Rua do Boavista, leads to the landmark Praça Mouzinho de Albuquerque, popularly known as the **Rotunda da Boavista**. This is overlooked by a huge column, with a lion astride a much flatttened eagle, erected to celebrate the victory of the Portuguese and British over the French in the Peninsular War, and by a flash modern shopping centre, the **Centro Comercial de Brasília** – Porto's answer to Lisbon's Amoreiras complex.

A couple of blocks before you reach the Rotunda, you pass the very simple **Igreja de Cedofeita** (from *cito facta*: "built quickly"), a church that is reputed to be the oldest Christian building in the entire Iberian peninsula. It was supposedly built by the Suevian king Theodomir in 556, though the current building is a twelfth-century Romanesque refashioning.

Out to the beach: Matosinhos

Going on from the Rotunda, you could catch a #18 tram to the beachfront suburb of **Matosinhos** and then loop back into town to the Cordoaria. Matosinhos itself is unremittingly ugly, built around the industrial port of Leixões, and you'd be well advised to keep clear of the sea hereabouts. However, there's a swimming pool, at the mouth of the river Leça, and the trip out is thoroughly enjoyable, the trams shuttling alongside the river and up the coast.

Alternative **trams** to Matosinhos are #1 (from Rua Nova da Alfândega – the continuation of Cais da Ribeira) and #19 (from Praça da Liberdade).

Vila Nova de Gaia

The suburb of **Vila Nova de Gaia** is taken over almost entirely by the port trade. Walking across the **Ponte Dom Luís I** from central Porto, the names of the old **port lodges**, spelled out in huge white letters across their roofs, dominate the views. The most direct route to the wine lodges is across the bridge's lower level from the Cais da Ribeira, but if you've a head for heights it's an amazing sensation to walk over the upper deck some two hundred feet above the river.

There's a beautiful view of the tiered ranks of Porto's old town from here and an even better one from the terrace of **Nossa Serra do Pilar** high above the bridge. From this former convent, Wellington planned his surprise crossing of the Douro in 1809, and it's a barracks again today. The round church is open to the public, but sadly the unusual circular cloister rests in a sort of no-man's-land between church and army territory. It's being restored, so perhaps there's a chance of its being opened soon.

Touring the lodges

Most of the **port wine lodges** were established in the eighteenth century, in the wake of the treaty of 1703 between England and Portugal, and although on the whole they have long since been bought by multinational brewing companies, they still try hard to push a "family" image. Almost without exception, they offer free **tasting** and a tour of the manufacturing process, though not all are open to visits year-round. Most have visiting hours of approximately 10am to 8pm (5pm in winter), Monday to Friday. Only a few – they include *Calém* and *Sandeman* – open on Saturdays; all except *Sandeman* are closed on Sunday. It's in any case better to go on a weekday when the houses are at work.

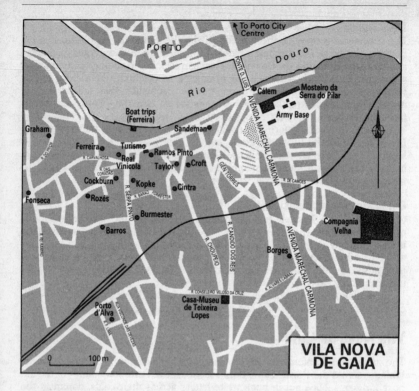

It's interesting to contrast one of the large manufacturers, like **Sandeman** or **Real Vinícola** – which operate virtually a production-line process – with the smaller, more traditional lodges such as *Calem, Croft, Taylor* or *Kopke*. **Calém** has a particularly pleasant riverside bar and takes small groups. **Taylor** – a bit of a hike uphill – gives a very informative talk on the processes and is happy to take just a couple of visitors at a time, as is **Fonseca** (whom they own). There are distinct contrasts, too, between the "British" names and the Portuguese-founded establishments, like **Ramos Pinto** or **Borges**. The attentions of the latter tend to be concentrated on French and Nordic, rather than British, tourists.

At the **Companhia Velha** lodge the Swedish Consulate is actually tucked into the grounds; the company led the first Portuguese challenge to the British port monopoly in the nineteenth century. Also in the grounds are numerous warehouses storing casks for the rich and famous (Generalissimo Franco – or his descendants – among them), and a six-kilometre-long tunnel – intended to form part of a rail link but found to be built at the wrong angle – which now serves as a perfect cold storage for Velha's famed sparkling wines and vintage ports.

Casa-Museu de Teixeira Lopes

A more sober visit in Vila Nova de Gaia could be made to the **Casa-Museu de Teixeira Lopes** (9am–12.30pm & 2–5.30pm, free admission; bus #36 across the bridge as far as "Hospital"). Lopes was Soares dos Reis's principal pupil and formed the centre of an important artistic and intellectual set that lived in Gaia at the turn of the century. The circle is well represented in the second part of the museum's display, the first being devoted to Lopes's work – much of it preoccupied with the depiction of children. His masterpiece is considered to be the enigmatic portrait of an Englishwoman, *A Inglesa*.

River trips and walks

The *Cruzeiro das Três Pontes* company operate regular **river trips** (May–Oct: Mon–Fri on the hour from 10am to 6pm, except at 2pm; Sat at 10am, 11am and noon) leaving from the dock outside the *Ferreira Port Company*. The standard half-hour ride ride takes you through most of the city, and under all four bridges. Longer – three-hour – **journeys along the Douro** leave twice daily from the Cais da Ribeira, across the river.

Another rewarding excursion is the **walk downriver** past the port houses to the coast at the small fishing port of **Afurada**. Small ferries, bedecked with *Sandeman* hoardings and pursuing erratic courses against the currents, cut across the rivermouth between here and the grubby Porto suburb of **Foz do Douro**. From there, you can take a #1 or #18 bus back to the centre of town.

Food, drink and nightlife

Porto is a city where you can eat well and cheaply. In most **restaurants** 1500$00 will get you a good meal, and in many places you'll spend a lot less. **Cafés and bars** in the city rival Lisbon's, with some lovely old art nouveau survivals, and Porto's **nightclubs** are highly regarded too – although most, frustratingly, are way outside the centre.

Meals

You may be shocked to discover that the city's speciality is *tripas* (tripe) and that the people are affectionately referred to by the rest of the country as *tripeiros* – little tripe. Don't let this put you off – there's always plenty of choice on the menu, and the cooking is as good as any in Portugal.

At the basic level, Porto has **workers' cafés** galore, all with wine on tap, and often with a set menu for the day. They are mainly lunchtime places, though most serve an evening meal through to 7 or 7.30pm, and a few stay open later; prime areas are the grid of streets **north and south of the Cordoaria**: especially the Rua do Almada (north) where three-course meals are offered for little more than 300$00, and the Dickensian Rua de São Bento da Vitória (south). Through the day, popular **snacks** include *lanches* – pieces of sweetish bread stuffed with ham – and *pasteis de carne* – puff-pastry sausage rolls.

Moving slightly upmarket, into the restaurant league, the **Cais da Ribeira** is hard to beat for atmosphere – or for its fish, with any number of café-restaurants installed under the arches of the first tier of dwellings. Other of our recommendations cover restaurants in most of the central areas of the city; unless stated otherwise, all are modestly priced.

CAIS DA RIBEIRA

Casa Filha da Mãe Preta, Cais da Ribeira 39 (open daily to 10.30pm). Built into the arches – the azulejo-decorated upper floor gives you a view over the river. An excellent *ementa turistica* features mackerel, sardines and all the business.

Taverna do Bebobos, Cais da Ribeira 24 (open Mon–Sat to 9.30pm; ☎31 35 65). Established in the nineteenth century, this has a real old *tasca* feel, with its barrels of wine on the walls. Fish specialities. Very popular, so book ahead if possible. Full meals around 3000$00.

AROUND TRINDADE STATION

Vigo no Porto, Rua Fernandes Tomás 959. Excellent cheapie, up behind the post office.

Pedro dos Frangos, Rua da Bon Jardim 219–223 (closed Tues). Down to earth grillhouse, where you can sit at the bar or in the upstairs restaurant. A *meia frango* (half chicken), chips, salad and wine will leave plenty of change for a night's entertainment.

A Brasileira, Rua do Bonjardim 116 (daily to 10.30pm). Elegant restaurant attached to a beautiful art deco café. Around 3000$00.

AROUND THE SÉ AND DOWN TOWARDS THE BRIDGE

O Castiço da Sé, Rua da Bainharia 18. Bar with a tiny restaurant upstairs which serves superb and inexpensive lunches for local office workers; open evenings, too.

Restaurante Chinês, Avda. Vimara Peres 38 (daily to 10.30pm). The city's best Chinese food – served in a modern building just at the entrance to the Ponte Dom Luís I.

AROUND PRAÇA DA BATALHA/AVENIDA DOS ALIADOS

Café Java, Praça da Batalha 97. Good cheap standby on the square.

Aquário Marisqueiro, Rua Rodrigues Sampaiso 179 – just off the Avda. dos Aliados to the east, one block south of Rua Formosa (☎222 31; open until 10.30pm, closed Sun). One of the city's best seafood restaurants – and not expensive for the quality of cooking. Around 3000$00.

Restaurante O Escondidinho, Rua de Passos Manuel 144 – east off the Avda. dos Aliados (open Mon–Sat to 10pm; ☎210 79). A place for an extravagance: French-influenced Portuguese cuisine and superb fish. Around 5000$00 for a feast. Book ahead.

Don Guilon, Rua de Passos Manuel 241. Good budget-priced restaurant.

Restaurante Adega, Rua Cimo da Vila 60–62 – south of Praça da Batalha. Simple, excellent fare at very low prices.

Restaurante/Snack Bar Kinary, Rua Dom João IV 8, east of Praça da Batalha. Friendly place that offers a good variety of well turned-out meat and fish dishes; the *bacalhau* is superb.

Restaurante Ribeiro, Rua Santo Ildefonso 128, east of Praça da Batalha. Moderately priced Portuguese cuisine, specialising in northern dishes. 2500–3000$00.

Mesa Antiga, Rua Santo Ildefonso 208 (open to midnight; ☎264 32). More excellent regional specialities. Around 4000$00.

Casa Casais, Avenida Rodrigues de Freitas 359 – the main avenue east of Praça da Batalha. A very male bar upfront, where you can wash down wine from the barrels on marble-topped tables. A more mixed clientele crowds the restaurant behind the partition.

UP RUA DE SANTA CATERINA

Montecarlo, Rua de Santa Catarina 17-2° (daily until 10pm or later). This looks like a 1930s tearoom, has views over the Praça da Batalha, buzzing television, good food and, particularly at Sunday lunchtime, very noisy locals.

Café Majestic, Rua de Santa Catarina 112. One of the city's most beautiful cafés – all mirrors and bent wood. Specialises in steaks.

Restaurante Retiro Desportivo, Praça Marquês de Pombal 226-r (top of Rua de Santa Catarina). Angolan-run chicken grillhouse, specialising in fast service and outrageously cheap prices – 500$00 tops. A long walk from the centre – take a taxi.

NEAR THE SOARES DOS REIS MUSEUM

O Assador Típico, Rua Dom Manuel II 15 (closed Mon). Bustling cavern of a restaurant.

AROUND THE CORDOARIA

A Tasquinha, Rua do Carmo 23 (open until 9.30pm, closed Sun). "Olde worlde" sort of place, a block north of the gardens.

Casa Costa, Campo dos Mártires da Pátria 166. Very cheap workers' diner on the square immediately south of the gardens. Open until 10pm.

Cafés and port

Porto's **cafés** include some elegant art deco rivals to the turn-of-the-century places in Lisbon. For their atmosphere and appearance, try: the *Majestic*, Rua de Santa Caterina 112; the *Imperial*, on the Avenida dos Aliados; and *A Brasileira*, Rua do Bonjardim 116 (closed Sun), a sister branch to the one in Lisbon.

Less venerable interiors – but more of a cross section of life – can be found down on the **waterfronts** on either side of the river, though beware that riverside cafés in Vila Nova de Gaia can be fiendishly expensive. The area around the Cais da Ribeira is always fruitful, and you'll also find numerous clubs and sometimes live music at the places on nearby Rua São João or Rua da Reboleira.

Not to be missed, at some point in a Porto stay, is a visit to the *Solar do Vinho do Porto*, where you can sample hundreds of varieities of **port** (see p.170).

Food shops

Whether you're buying anything or not, a number of the city's food shops are worth looking inside. A personal favourite is the **bakery** at Travessa de Cedofeita 20b. This is one of the oldest in the country, using traditional methods such as burning *carqueja* – a variety of broom which reaches high temperatures while producing very little ash. Specialities are *pão-de-ló*, a round sponge cake, and the *marmelada*, or quince jelly, sold after the September harvest.

The *Casa Africana*, Rua dos Clérigos 112, is another delight, a combined **bacalhau and port wine shop** which advertises itself by hanging its wares outside. The *bacalhau* (codfish split open to dry and be salted) is bundled up in stacks all around the counter, alongside just about every type of port available.

Nightlife: music bars, clubs and discos

As with Lisbon, most of Porto's **clubs** stay open until 3 or 4am. Prices, however, are generally cheaper, with a standard 1000–1500$00 admission levied; at most places you can present the entrance ticket as a voucher for your first couple of drinks. Note that all these destinations are distinctly far-flung and require taxis.

BOAVISTA

Griffon's, Centro Comercial Brasília, Avda. da Boavista. Always busy dance bar, overflowing with pretentious types, redeemed by non-stop good music. Free entrance, but dress up for it.

Swing, Centro Comercial Brasília, Avda. da Boavista (☎69 00 19). Not to be missed for the music and drinks alone. Fairly lively clientele.

VILA NOVA DE GAIA

Rocks, 228 Rua Rei Ramiro, Vila Nova de Gaia (☎30 12 08). Built in old port cellars, this does indeed rock. Fantastic terrace with a view over the Douro, and barbecues in the summer.

FOZ DO DOURO/MATOSINHOS

Indústria, Avda. do Brasil 853, Centro Comercial da Foz, Foz do Douro (☎67 68 12). Porto's fashion-conscious at their most vapid (11.30pm–4am).

Cais 447, Avda. Menéres 447, Matosinhos. Won't appeal to all; the *Cais* seems proud of its go-go-dancers-on-marble-columns image and comparisons with the *Alcântara* in Lisbon.

ELSEWHERE IN THE CITY

Batô, Largo do Castelo 13 (11pm–4am). High camp pirates' galleon interior, just needs Errol Flynn sliding down one of the masts. Trendy clientele, and high prices.

Loko Moskito, Rua Eugénio de Castro, Galeria Foco (10pm–2am). Small, down-to-earth bar laid out to cater for only a few people. Nice atmosphere and usually good music.

Labirinto, Rua Nossa Senhora de Fátima 334 (9.30pm–3am). A "bar-arcade" catering for a wide range of tastes with shows, concerts, exhibitions, live music.

Directory

Airlines/airport information *TAP*, Praça Mousinho de Albuquerque 105 (☎69 98 41); *British* Airways, Rua Júlio Dinis 778–2º (☎69 45 75). **Airport information** ☎948 2141.

American Express c/o *Star Travel*, Avda. dos Aliados 202.

Bookshops There is an English-language bookshop in Rua da Picaria; try also *Livraria Internacional*, Rua 31 de Janeiro 43, or the lovely old shop at 144 Rua dos Clérigos.

Banks Main branches are concentrated around Praça da Liberdade.

Car hire Companies include: *Jumbo Travel*, Rua de Ceuta 47 (☎38 15 61); *AutoCerro*, Rua do Monte 130 (☎941 35 13); and *Inter Rent*, Rua do Bolhão 182, ☎38 19 64). Several companies maintain offices at the airport, where cars can usually be booked on the spot.

Car repairs Addresses from the *Automóvel Clube de Portugal*, Rua Gonçalo Cristovão 2 (☎200 92 73). They also run a breakdown service.

Chemists Late-night services are detailed in the *Jornal de Notícias*, next to the TV section.

Consulates include: **UK**, Avda. da Boavista 3072 (☎684789); **USA**, Rua Júlio Dinis 826–3º (☎69 00 08); **Holland**, Rua da Reboleira (☎362 00); **Sweden**, Largo do Terreiro 4 (☎200 7243).

Emergencies General ☎115 (free); Red Cross ☎60 720; Police ☎200 6821.

Festivals The biggest event is Saint John's Eve and Day (23 & 24 June).

Football The city's principal team, **F.C. Porto**, were winners of the European Cup in 1987 and have alternated with Benfica over recent years in winning the league championship; they play at the 90,000-capacity *Estádio das Antas*; bus #6/78 from "Praça". First Divison football is on view, too, from two other Porto sides: **S.C. Salgueiros**, who play over in Vila Nova de Gaia at the *Sport Comércio e Salgueiros*, on Rua Álvares Cabral, and **Boavista F.C.**, whose *Estádio do Bessa* is on Rua Primeiro de Janeiro.

Hospital Santo António, Rua José de Carvalho (☎200 7254).

Maps Ordnance survey-type maps are available from *Porto Editora*, Rua da Fábrica.

Markets General market daily in the Praça de Lisboa by the Torre dos Clérigos and in the market building on Rua Sá da Bandeira, behind the main Post Office; the latter is a must. Flea markets (best on Saturday mornings) are held along the Calçada de Vandoma, below the Sé, and the Alameda das Fontaínhas, overlooking the river.

Newspapers English-language papers are available from *Tabacaria Senador* on Praça da Batalha, the subway kiosk below São Bento station and *Livraria Bertrand* in the Centro Comercial de Brasília, Praça Mousinho de Albuquerque (bus #3 from "Praça"). Porto's leading paper, the *Jornal de Notícias*, and the local edition of *Público*, are useful sources of information on cinemas, clubs, football matches, late-night chemists, etc.

Post office Main post office (open until 10pm weekdays, 8pm weekends) is opposite the town hall in Praça General Humberto Delgado; *posta restante* mail is held here, and you can also make international phone calls.

Travel agencies *Jumbo Travel*, Rua de Ceuta 47 (☎38 15 61) is useful for budget/student travel.

Upcoast from Porto

If you read the Tourist Board handouts in Porto they'll tell you there are splendid beaches and sea bathing in the city's northern suburbs of Foz do Douro and Matosinhos. Don't believe it. The stretch of coast around the mouth of the Douro is severely polluted, and you need to head at least as far as **Vila Chã**, 18km north of Porto, for a dip in the ocean; despite encroaching development, this retains a fishing village identity, and has a fine sandy beach with pools at low tide. Press on a few kilometres further north from here to **Vila do Conde** or **Póvoa de Varzim** and you may be tempted to stay; indeed, in summer, you might prefer to visit Porto while based at one of these resorts.

Access to Vila Chã, Vila do Conde and Póvoa de Varzim is straightforward from Porto, with a choice of **trains** (hourly from the Estação da Trindade) and **buses** (Praça Filipa de Lencastre terminal).

Vila do Conde

VILA DO CONDE has become quite a significant resort over the last few years, but it has lost refreshingly little of its character in the process. It remains an active fishing port with a bustling Friday market and, as well as a long sandy beach, boasts an atmospheric medieval quarter – complete with traditional boat-building industry. If you're interested in Portugal's regional crafts, there's a bonus, in the annual **crafts fair**, held the last week of July into the first week of August.

The **medieval quarter** juts out into the sea beside the Rio Ave. The narrow streets are at their best on Saints' Days, when the little street corner votive chapels are illuminated by worshippers. Dominating everything, on a rise behind, is the enormous bulk of the **Convento de Santa Clara**. This is now a reformatory for boys but it is open to visits at weekends. One of the inmates will be designated to show you around its early Gothic church, which contains fine relief carvings, especially on the tombs of the founders. There's an elegant cloister, too, with a fountain fed by the long aqueduct – now partly ruined – which stretches from here into the hills. Back in town, the sixteenth-century **Igreja Matriz** is also a beauty, with a soaring, airy interior and – thanks to the Basque workmen who helped with its construction – an unusual but very effective mix of Spanish and Portuguese styles.

DOWNCOAST FROM PORTO: A WARNING

The coastline immediately **south of Porto** is one of the worst polluted in Europe, with industrial effluent and inadequate sewage plants constituting a major health hazard. In recent years, there have been several outbreaks of hepatitis in Porto and Vila Nova de Gaia, linked with bathing in these waters.

Most people consider the first safe place to swim is **ESPINHO**. This is a major resort – though not a very attractive one. Windswept and overcrowded, it has a feeling of a suburb rather than a town, with a casino, a few high-rise hotels (many more are on the way), hordes of tourist shops, a dull grid of numbered streets, and a railway right through the centre. But most of all Espinho is characterised by the piped Eurodisco blaring out along the main road behind the beach.

If you're heading south along the coast from Porto, it's better to keep going as far as **ESMORIZ, CORTEGAÇA** or **FURADOURO** (see previous chapter).

Much of your time at Vila do Conde, however, is likely to be spent on the clean, long **beach**, or in the **bars and restaurants**. Recommended among the latter are *La Fruits*, a stylish fondue place on the Cais das Lavadeiras, and *Villageois* (closed Mon), which serves up serious steaks on a site overlooking the Praça da Republica. Neither of these are cheap. For budget meals, the best bets are *Restaurante Saõ Roque* in Rua do Lidador, *Restaurante Ramon* (closed Tues) in Rua 5 de Outubro, and the enormous *Pioneiro* on the seafront.

The extremely helpful **Turismo** (☎052/634 27), on Rua 25 de Abril, has a lengthy list of private rooms, which is likely to be all you'll find in the summer. If you're booking ahead, or travelling out of season, try the *Pensão A Princesa do Ave* (☎052/63 20 65; ④) on Rua Dr. Antonio José Sousa Pereira, or the *Estalagem do Brasão* (☎052/63 20 16; ④) on Avda. Dr. João Canavarro; both are good value, the latter especially, with its *pousada*-quality furnishings.

Buses from Porto arrive at (and leave from) in front of the Igreja Matriz. The **train station** is a five-minute walk from the centre.

Póvoa do Varzim

PÓVOA DO VARZIM is within walking distance to the north of Vila do Conde – but the two couldn't be more different. Although Póvoa, too, retains a small harbour, along with the ruins of a fortress, it is very much the out-and-out resort. A casino and a line of concrete hotels open onto the beach, which is crowded throughout the year with Portuguese holidaymakers.

None of which should discourage you. The crowds here help to create a lively, enjoyable seaside feel, restaurants are plentiful and excellent value (despite the multilingual menus), and there usually seems enough **accommodation** to go round. The cheaper pensions are to be found mostly along Rua Paulo Barreto and Rua Caetano de Oliveira. A pleasant mid-range option is the *Hotel Luso-Brasileira*, Rua dos Cafés 16 (☎052/62 41 61; ④). If you have problems, the **Turismo** (☎052/64 609), Avda. Mouzinho de Albuquerque 166, can help with lists of rooms.

The beach apart, Póvoa's only real point of interest is its **Museu Etnográfico** (daily 10am–12.30pm & 2.30–6pm), an unusually interesting and well-presented display on the lives and times of local fishing and farming communities.

Buses operate from the central Praça do Almada; the **train station** is a few minutes walk from here, along the Rua Almirante Reis.

THE DOURO RIVER AND ITS TRIBUTARY VALLEYS

The valleys of the **Rio Douro** and its tributaries are among the loveliest and most spectacular landscapes in the whole of Portugal. The Douro itself is the best of all: a narrow, winding gorge for the major part of its long route to the Spanish border, with port wine lodges dotted about the hillsides, and a series of tiny villages, visited by few except their inhabitants and seasonal wine trade workers.

If you're **driving**, you can follow minor roads along the river practically all the way from Porto to the border-crossing at Miranda do Douro. Taking the **train**, though, is probably more fun. The **Douro line** joins the course of the river about 60km inland from Porto and sticks to it from then on, cutting into the rockface and criss-crossing the water on a series of rocking bridges: one of those journeys that needs no justification other than the trip itself. Sadly, trains no longer run the whole way to the border, but there are services as far as **Pocinho** – and you could always walk, along the rails, on the stretch beyond.

To the north, three **narrow gauge rail lines** follow the river's tributaries into Minho and Trás-os-Montes. These, too, have been severely curtailed in recent years. However, the **Tâmega** line still runs as far as **Amarante** – and has further hiking possibilities along the redundant track; the **Corgo** line connects with Vila Real, a useful bus terminal for exploring Trás-os-Montes; and the **Tua** line runs as far as Mirandela, where you can catch buses on to Bragança in the northeast. The Tua is covered in the Trás-os-Montes chapter, through which it steers its course; details on Amarante and the Tâmega, and the Corgo as far as Vila Real, follow in this one. Also covered, at the end of this chapter, is the delightful Baroque town of Lamego, the home of Portugal's champagne-like wine, *Raposeira*, and just 13km south of **Régua**, the capital of the Alto Douro province.

The Douro Line from Porto to Livracão

This section follows the first stretch of the **Douro railway line** – which in fact runs for an initial 40km or so alongside the Rio Sousa. At **Livraçao**, with the line still to meet the Douro proper, the **Tâmega line** heads off to **Amarante**.

Paço de Sousa

If you're on one of the slow trains, it will stop at CETE, a dozen stations out of Porto. This is just a mile away from the vilage of **PAÇO DE SOUSA**, the former headquarters of the Benedictines in Portugal and, set beside the Rio Sousa, a popular picnic spot for Porto locals.

The principal sight, inevitably, is the old **abbey church**, a dank and dark medieval building in the process of restoration. In one corner is the **tomb of Egas Moniz**, tutor and adviser to the first king of Portugal, Afonso Henriques, and a great figure of loyalty in Portuguese histories. In 1127, shortly after Afonso Henriques had broken away from his grandfather, the king of León, Egas was sent to negotiate a settlement, thus enabling Afonso to concentrate his efforts on the Moors in the south. Within three years, the king of León considered the treaty to be broken on the Portuguese side and threatened all-out war. Egas made his way to León, presented himself and his family, and, as can be seen on the panels around the tomb, offered to receive the punishment due to his master. Mercy was granted and the king sent the loyal minister home unscathed.

There are a couple of cafés in the village and plenty of possible camping spots. If you're looking for a bed, it's not much further down the line to Penafiel.

Penafiel

At **PENAFIEL** you enter **vinho verde** country. The wine's origins lie with the Benedictine monks, who were famed in this region for their laborious terracing along the valley slopes. A further legacy of the Benedictine presence are a dozen of the finest Romanesque churches in the country, each gorgeously sited in hamlets hidden away in folds of the countryside.

Penafiel itself, split by main road traffic, is not that enticing, and getting to it involves a connecting bus from the station – some way down the hill. But it has a saving grace in its fabulous local **wine**, served from massive barrels in the down-at-heel *adega* in the central Largo do Padre Américo; this also offers basic fare, washed down with pints of wine at a time; a stream of old men in black hats moves regularly through its doors. Right next door is a good-value **pension**, the *Casa João da Liza* (☎055/251 58; ②). Nearby, too, is a fine covered **market**.

If you are interested in exploring the area's **churches**, call in at the **Turismo** (in a modern complex at Avda. Sacadura Cabral 50), which dispenses advice and stacks of leaflets. Most of the churches are hard to reach without your own transport. The most accessible by bus (departure at 11am; return mid-afternoon) is at BOELHE. This is reputedly the smallest Romanesque church in the country: a simple building, without much architectural detail, which gains its power from a stunning position on the brow of a hill.

The Tâmega: Amarante and beyond

At LIVRAÇÃO, about an hour from Porto, the **Tâmega line** cuts off for Amarante, hugging the ravine of the Rio Tâmega, a Douro tributary. There is scarcely more than the station here. If you're changing trains, keep your eyes open.

The rail line, until its curtailment in 1990, had services from Livração through Amarante and up into the into the Serra do Marão – following the course of the Rio Tâmega through the villages of **Celorico** and **Mondim de Basto** and up to Arco de Baúlhe. Today, the nine daily trains terminate at Amarante. From here, four buses daily run to Celorico and on to the next crossroads at **Fermil**, where a local bus picks up passengers for Mondim. To explore the valley, the best idea is to take a bus to Celorico and walk, following the increasingly overgrown tracks, to Mondim: a pleasant two hours' hike, through woods and over viaducts.

If your time is limited, the **half-hour trip to Amarante** is worthwhile in itself. From the start it's an impressive scenic ride, with pine woods and vines clinging to incredible slopes, and goats scrambling across the steep terrace walls to nibble at the haystacks constructed to hang from the branches of living trees.

Amarante

AMARANTE is set immaculately along the Tâmega river, the wooden balconies of its old houses leaning over the water. It's a fine place to stop, with any number of bars and cafés along the riverside, mostly on the opposite side from the station. Sadly, the polluted river beaches can no longer be recommended – at least for swimming – though, in summer, pedalboats (*barcos a pedal*) or rowing boats can be hired for an hour or two's dawdling.

The Town
The **Convento de São Gonçalo**, beside the very elegant town bridge, is Amarante's most prominent monument. It forms the heart of an ancient fertility cult – probably with pagan origins – which still persists here at the grand *Festa de São Gonçalo*, celebrated on the first Saturday in June. At this time, traditionally, the local unmarried youth exchange phallus-shaped cakes as tokens of their love. In the church, the saint's tomb is said to guarantee a quick marriage to anyone

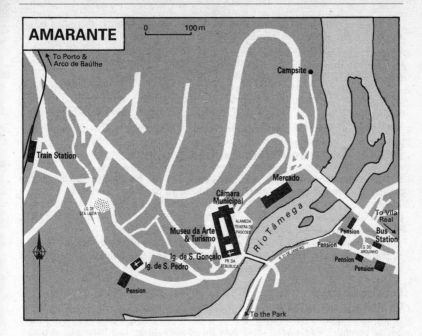

who touches it – his face, hands, and feet have been almost worn away by hopeful suitors. Another chapel, devoted to Gonçalo's healing miracles, is festooned with wax models of every conceivable part of the body as well as entire artificial limbs, bottles full of gallstones, and other votive offerings.

Around the side of the church, in the cloister of the former monastery, is the **Museu Municipal Amadeo de Sousa Cardoso** (Tues–Sun 10am–12.30 & 2–5.30pm; free). This is a surprising exhibition to find out in the sticks – dominated by the Cubist works of local boy Amadeo de Sousa Cardoso, one of the few Portuguese painters of this century to achieve international renown.

Rooms and restaurants

Amarante is quite a popular town and **rooms** can be hard to come by in summer; if at all possible, phone ahead and book. Your first call should be to the *Hotel Silva*, Rua Cândido dos Reis 53 (☎055/42 31 10; ②), comfortable and pleasantly sited, with a balcony (and several rooms) overlooking the river. Second choices would be the *Residencial Estoril*, Rua 31º de Janeiro 49 (☎055/42 22 91; ③), a pleasant new pension, and the *Residencial Rio* (☎055/42 45 72; ②), best of a trio of pensions on the Largo Conselheiro António Cândido.

The cheapest rooms in town are above the *Casa Avião* on Rua 31º de Janeiro, where there is also *vinho verde* on tap from massive barrels. Additionally there are a couple of **campsites**, one on the riverbank below the town, another, newer and more spacious, a little further upstream. The **Turismo** (☎055/429 80), housed in the Câmara Municipal, may be able to suggest further accommodation possibilities.

Most pensions have **restaurants**, of highly varying quality: extremes represented by the *Estoril* (wonderful) and the *Príncipe* (dire). Among non-pension restaurants, try the outwardly un-tempting *Adega Regional* on Rua de Olivença, off the main praça, where, to fine music – and no TV – the proprietor serves well-spiced dishes washed down with jugs of heavy local red wine.

Should you happen to be in Amarante on a summer Saturday evening (July–Sept) you could join in one of the **festivals** in the gardens of the Casa da Calçada, with as much food and wine as you can handle for around 2500$00. There's also a year-round Wednesday **market**, held beside the *mercado* building (see map).

Into the Serra do Alvão: the Basto villages

Beyond Amarante you really feel the climb into the **Serra do Marão** on the approach to the villages of **Celorico** and **Mondim de Basto**, both set astride the Tâmega. To their north – and technically in the Minho region – is the larger, provincial town of **Cabeceiras de Basto**, which provides a useful transport link to Braga and the Gerês national park (see Minho chapter).

This region, the **Terras do Basto**, is a fertile countryside that produces a strong *vinho verde*. The name ("basto" meant "I claim") comes from a group of Celtic statues, symbolic of power, which have been found in several local spots.

Celorico de Basto

CELORICO DE BASTO is an attractive little village, full of civic pride in its neatly laid-out lawns and formal flower beds. It has a single **pension**, and lots of hiking potential. For a brief foray into the **woods**, there is a labyrinth of paths, heading off from behind the village church, while in the distance is the prospect of **Monte Farinha**, the highest peak in the region. The mountain is actually easier approached from Mondim de Basto, accessible from Celorico on a roundabout 11km road (sporadic buses), or by hiking six kilometres along the old rail line. Mondim's train station is two kilometres away from the village proper.

Mondim de Basto

Unless you're intent on hiking, there's little enough to **MONDIM DE BASTO**, though the views are majestic enough to wake up to after a night's stay, and there's good river swimming. There are three **pensions**: the *Mondinense*, which has huge rooms, the best views, and erratic plumbing; the *Parque Dormidas*, near the bus terminal; and a new and rather good-value *residencial* by the petrol station on Avda. Dr. Augusto Brito. There's also an excellent **campsite** – about 1km from the centre along the Vila Real road. For **meals**, try the *Churrasqueira Chasselik*.

The **Parque Natural do Alvão** maintains a branch office in Mondim on the Rua do Retiro. The park lies beyond the Monte Farinha and stretches to Vila Real. It is covered in more detail following the section on Vila Real (which offers easier approaches and has the park HQ; see Chapter Seven, "Trás-os-Montes").

Monte Farinha and the Cabril Valley

Monte Farinha is surprisingly easy to climb – less than three hours' easygoing walking. If the times coincide, you can get a headstart by taking the bus to the foot of the ascent, three-and-a-half kilometres from Mondim. Walking, follow the Cerva road out of town, then take a path up to the right shortly after Pedra Vedra; you may lose this among the pines, but on the whole, the way is clear enough.

Once you reach the mountain, there's a stone path (leading up from the road below) that runs straight to the summit. The panoramic views well repay your efforts, and at the summit is the attractive parish church of **Nossa Senhora da Graça**, centre of a major **festa** on the first Sunday in September.

Another good hike from Mondim is into the **valley of the Cabril**. Only about twenty minutes beyond the village campsite, this stream is crossed by a **Roman bridge** – impressive in itself and set near a little waterfall, where there's a good swimming hole. From here, follow the river upstream to a working watermill or take the stone track (about 200m upriver) along what must have been a Roman road. Follow this, cross a road, and you're at the start of a maze of small paths cutting between the fields and vineyards of the Cabril valley, and leading higher into the pine-forested slopes.

On from Mondim: buses and Arco de Baulhe

There are regular bus connections from **Mondim to Vila Real** (a spectacular ride, skirting the Parque Natural de Alvão), Guimarães, and Porto (changing buses at FERMIL, just across the Tâmega valley). Alternatively, you could catch a **bus** – or hitch or walk – the 7km on to the lively provincial town of **Cabeceiras de Basto** (see below), from where there are regular buses to Braga and the Gerês national park (see Chapter Six, "The Minho").

En route to Cabeceiras, you pass through **ARCO DE BAÚLHE**, the old terminal of the Tâmega rail line. A bleak and unwelcoming village, its former points of interest – a steam train and royal railway carriage display at the old station – have been shunted off to Bragança. However, it's worth a trip if you can coincide with the *Festas de São Miguel*, a huge **agricultural show** held in late September.

Cabeceiras de Basto

CABECEIRAS DE BASTO is at the heart of the *Terras de Basto*, and proudly displays the finest of the *basto* figures – which has sported a French head since a prank during the Napoleonic Wars – in the gardens across from the bus station.

The main local monument, just outside the town, is the Baroque **Mosteiro de Refojos** – one of the few religious institutions not to have succumbed to the temptation to bludgeon faith into the populace through a quartet of loudspeakers. If you pay your respects to the sacristan, not only can you visit the treasury (a collection of statues and religious garments) but also gain privileged access to the clocktower, from which you can view the church's highlight – the *zimbório* (dome). From here, too, you can look down over the peeling houses of the region's old landowners, reminders of the glory and elitism of Portugal's Age of Absolutism; they were hard hit by the revolution and its aftermath.

There is reasonable **accommodation** to be had at the café-restaurants *A Cafil* and *São Miguel*, in the modern quarter of the town. A short way up the road at the back of the Refojos monastery, the *Restaurante O Avenida* has no rooms but very good meals. Another area of town to explore is beyond a patch of ground set aside for the Monday **feira** – a left turn after the school takes you into the Campo do Guinchoso, where there's a **nightclub** (Thurs–Sat 10pm–2am, Sun 4–7pm), a *pastelaria*, and **swimming** in the river – past the new housing development.

Buses connect Cabeceiras with Celorico and Mondim de Basto; Póvoa de Lanhoso in central Minho (which has links with Braga and Gerês destinations); Chaves in Trás-os-Montes; and Porto (Mon–Sat only).

The Douro Line proper: Régua, the Corgo, the Tua, and on to the Spanish border

Shortly after Livraçao, the Linha do Douro finally reaches the **Douro river** and heads upstream. At MESÃO FRIO, the river temporarily leaves its confined channel and broadens into the little plain commanded by **Régua**, the terminus for trains up what remains of the **Corgo line** – a brief excursion through marvellous vine and granite landscape to Vila Real (see *Trás-os-Montes*).

Régua is also the jumping-off point for buses to **Lamego**, 13km to the south, at the tip of Beira Alta; as this is by far the easiest link with the town, it is covered, along with its immediate region, in the section following.

Régua

RÉGUA (or, more fully, PESO DA RÉGUA) is a small and very provincial town that has been known for over two centuries as the "Capital of the Upper Douro", after its role in the port industry. In fact, the centre for quality port wines has shifted to Pinhão, half an hour further down the line; Régua is simply the junction and the depot through which all the wine must pass on its way to Porto.

The **Turismo** on the riverbank can, nonetheless, inform you about visits to local **port lodges** – open, as is the tourist office, from Monday to Saturday. The easiest to visit are in Régua itself, the *Casa do Douro* and *Ramos Pinto*, each of which runs more personalised and interesting tours than their Vila Nova de Gaia equivalents. Apart from these alcoholic diversions, there's not much to do in Régua except wander through the upper village and along the riverbank. It's as well to be sure of your train connection or next bus out; **buses to Lamego** run every hour up until 9pm, from in front of the station.

Accommodation

If you need to **stay**, the *Pensão Império* at Rua José Vasques Osório 8 (☎054/223 99; ②) has nice rooms and views. A cheaper alternative is the *Pensão Borrajo* on Rua Custódio José Vieira 32; ①), and **camping** is possible, free of charge, below the swimming pool down by the river; ask in the Turismo for Senhor Pereira, who owns the land. There are plenty of **restaurants** along the main street.

On to the border – and Torre de Moncorvo

Just beyond Régua, and past the massive dam of a hydroelectric power station, you begin increasingly to see the terraced slopes where the **port vines** are grown. They're at their best in August, with the grapes ripening, and September, when the harvest has begun.

Quotas for wine production have been in force around here since the mid-eighteenth century, and some terrace walls from that period have withstood the assault of the diggers and dynamite that are used nowadays to clear the way for the vineyard tractors. Grape-treaders and *barcos rabelos* (the river's traditional barges) have also been replaced by machines and cistern lorries, though there's still a demand for large groups of hand-pickers (*rogas*) when there's a bumper crop, and some treading still goes on in small villages.

The country continues craggy and beautiful, with the softer hills of the interior fading dark green into the distance, past **PINHÃO**, the main centre for quality ports (*Pensão Douro*, ☎054/724 04; ②), **TUA**, where the narrow-gauge **Tua railway** begins its journey to Mirandela (see *Trás-os-Montes*), and on to the isolated station of **POCINHO**, where the trains come to a halt.

It is a shame that it's no longer possible to travel the line into Spain, though walkers might enjoy following the rails for the twenty kilometres to **BARCA D'ALVA**, and thence across the frontier to the villages along the Spanish Río Duero. Note that the rail line from Barca, on the Spanish side of the border, to LA FUENTE DE SAN ESTEBAN has also been closed.

Torre de Moncorvo

Train arrivals at Pocinho are met by buses to **TORRE DE MONCORVO**, 10km to the northeast; several of these buses continue on to Mogadouro and Miranda do Douro, deep into Trás-os-Montes. A couple of other daily connections run to remote Freixo de Espada à Cinta, virtually on the Spanish border, and south to Vila Nova de Foz Côa, and thence into Beira Alta.

Torre de Moncorvo was until very recently the last place in Portugal where you could still see steam engines at work, shuttling freight to nearby Duas Igrejas – another line to bite the dust in recent years. The town's other claim to fame is more enduring – in the form of its almond trees, which draw crowds of Portuguese in February and March to witness the blossoming. At other times, aside from the **Cathedral**, there is little to see.

Best value of the **pensions** is the *Campos Monteiro*, at Rua Visconde de Vila Maior 55 (☎079/223 55; ①), with a good restaurant downstairs. If it's full, head uphill and turn right and you come to *Pensão Passarinho* at Rua Infante Dom Henrique (☎079/223 55; ②). The *Roboredo* on Rua Constantino has the cheapest rooms in town and occupies the top two floors of the *Adega O Caneco* (The Mug). Sadly, the place doesn't reflect Moncorvo's high reputation for wine – which is owed to the *Barca Velha* from the nearby and internationally renowned Quinta do Vale de Meão – but the stuff comes in jugs and the prices are fair enough.

Heading **to Porto,** there are bus connections to meet trains at Pocinho. All the buses operate from the central square, just across from the *Santos* office.

Lamego and its region

Although technically in Beira Alta, **LAMEGO** is isolated at the tip of its mountain province, and greatly more accessible from Régua and the Douro. The town itself has more in common with the Douro region, too, spreading over gentle slopes of the rich agricultural land fed by the river, a terrain which the locals put to good use in the production of such gastronomic delights as hams and melons, as well as **Raposeira** – the closest thing to champagne you will find in Portugal.

Lamego is a wealthy place, and long has been, as evidenced by the graceful white *quintas* and villas on the hillsides, and the luxuriant architecture of the centre, where Baroque mansions seem to stand on every corner and lavish decorations are found within the smallest chapel. Lamego also has one of the very greatest Baroque structures in Europe – the pilgrimage church of **Nossa Senhoria dos Remédios**, which, with its monumental stairway, dominates the whole west–east axis of the town.

Arriving and accommodation

Buses arrive in Lamego at an efficient new station, behind the museum, right in the centre of town. In addition to the Régua connections (hourly, 7am–7.30pm), there are services linking Viseu, Guarda and other points in Beira Alta. The **Turismo** (☎054/620 05) is just across the main square, the Largo de Camões.

Accommodation can be tricky to find and is on the expensive side. Booking ahead is strongly advised, though if you turn up on spec, the Turismo may be able to sort you out a private room. Possibilities include:

Private rooms: Rua de Santa Cruz 15 (☎054/625 56); the cheapest rooms in town. **Rua da Olaria 61**: more cheap lodgings, above a smoked-ham shop and café. **Restaurante Espírito-Santo**, Avda. Visconde Guedes Teixeira: rooms above the restaurant. All ①.

Pensão Silva, Rua Trás-da-Sé 26 (☎054/629 29). Decent rooms, though be warned that the cathedral bells strike every quarter of an hour all night long. ②.

Residencial Solar, Avda. Visconde Guedes Teixeira (☎0541/620 60). A fraction further from the clock – though still with fine views over the cathedral. ③.

Residencial São Paulo, Avda. 5º de Outubro (☎0541/231 14). Again reasonably central, and reasonable quality. ③.

Pensão Império, Travessa dos Loureiros 6, off Avda. Visconde Guedes Teixeira (☎054/627 42). Pleasant if rather overpriced rooms. ④.

Hotel Parque, by the church of Nossa Senhora dos Remédios, at the top of the hill (☎054/621 05). An unbeatable location and lovely hotel, set in its own gardens. ⑤.

Albergaria do Cerrado, on the outskirts of town – on the Régua road (☎054/631 64). Lamego's top hotel – well-equipped but a bit characterless. ④.

The local **campsite** is four kilometres out – and up – along Rua Marquês de Pombal: a lofty position on the Serra das Meadas, where there is a weekend of pilgrimages, picnics and general revelry on the second Sunday in June. There are no buses, but hitching in summer is no problem. There's also a very good restaurant just before the campsite, with fine views over the Douro.

The Town

The **Sé** clearly delineates the centre of Lamego. It is basically a Renaissance structure, though with a twelfth-century tower surviving from a predecessor. The mixture works well and the **cloister** is a beauty.

Facing the cathedral, occupying an eighteenth-century palace, is the town's excellent **Museu Regional** (10am–12.30pm & 2–5pm; Tues–Sun). Its exhibits include five of the remaining panels of a polyptych commissioned from Grão Vasco by the Bishop of Lamego in 1506. Judging by the lack of correlation between the various panels – for instance the *Creation of the Animals* and the prodigiously executed *Annunciation* – some of the work must be attributed to the great man's school. Also on show are a series of sixteenth-century Flemish tapestries (including a marvellous *Life of Oedipus* sequence), three curious statues of a conspicuously pregnant Virgin Mary (a genre peculiar to this region), a fine assembly of *azulejos*, piles of ecclesiastical treasure from the Episcopal Palace, and a group of chapels rescued from the decaying *Convento das Chagas*. It's all beautifully laid out and more than justifies the small fee.

Across the square, the Rua da Olaria, a narrow street of tiny shops, leads into Rua do Almacave, which follows the walls of the old inner town. The route takes you past the **Igreja do Almacave**, a very ancient foundation said once to have been a mosque, to the Praça do Comércio. From here you can pass through the walls of the **Old Citadel** and climb up to the castle.

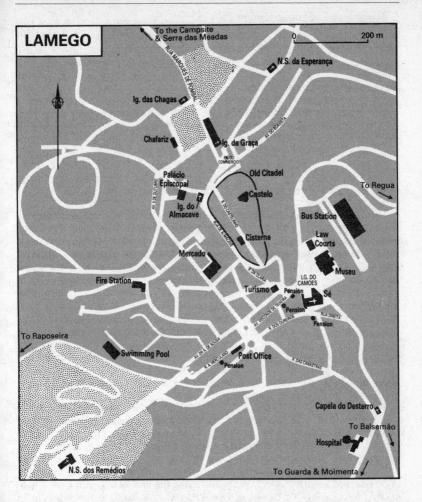

LAMEGO

To the Campsite & Serra das Meadas

N.S. da Esperança

RUA MARQUES DE POMBAL

Ig. das Chagas

Chafariz

Ig. da Graça

R. DO BRASISTA

R. DO COMMERCIO

Palácio Episcopal

Old Citadel

Castelo

To Regua

AV. 5 DE OUTUBRO

Ig. do Almacave

R. DO CASTELINHO

RUA D. AVEIRO

Cisterna

Bus Station

Law Courts

Museu

Mercado

R. DA LAPA

LG. DO CAMOES

Fire Station

Turismo

Pension

Sé

AV. VISCONDE DE TEIXEIRA

Pension

RUA DIREITA

Pension

To Raposeira

AV. DR. A. DE SOUSA

R. DOS QUEIROS

Pension

R. A. HERCULANO

Swimming Pool

Post Office

Pension

R. DAS CANASTRAS

Capela do Desterro

To Balsemão

Hospital

N.S. dos Remédios

To Guarda & Moimenta

0   200 m

The **Castelo**, surrounded by a cluster of ancient stone houses, has been pressed into service as the local scout hut (open to visits 10am–noon & 2–5pm). The boys do have a fairly legitimate claim on the place, having – so they say – cleared eighteen lorryloads of garbage away in the 1970s and saved the building from ruin. For a small entrance fee you can watch their displays of knot-tying and campcraft on your way up to admire the view. Sadly, what you'll probably see are a lot of burned hillsides: once known as the *Vila Verde*, the Lamego region suffers up to three forest fires a day in the height of summer.

Below the castle, and still within the upper town, there's a thirteenth-century **Cisterna**, one of the strangest buildings in the country. If your powers of persuasion are up to it (French may help), the Chief Fireman's wife, down below at Rua do Almacave 30, will lead you up four storeys to the top of her house and out into the back garden – and there stands what appears from the outside to be a half-sunken toolshed. Inside, it looks like a perfectly preserved Romanesque chapel, its walls still bearing the original stonemasons' marks; it is in fact the town's ancient water source. Even today, in emergencies, it proves useful as an extra supply.

Nossa Senhora dos Remédios

The celebrated shrine of **Nossa Senhora dos Remédios** is a major point of pilgrimage – a reputation for healing miracles drawing devotees from all over the country. Standing on a hill overlooking the city, it's approached by a magnificently elaborate eighteenth-century stairway, modelled on the one at Bom Jesus near Braga. Its seven hundred steps – ascended on their knees by the most committed – are punctuated by a *via santa* of devotional chapels, *azulejos* and allegorical fountains and statues. After the approach, and its own facade, the church itself is simply a detail in the architectural ensemble: an assembly hall for the ever-present faithful.

The great **pilgrimage** here takes place on September 8, an occasion for several weeks' celebration in Lamego, starting in the last week of August and continuing into mid-September. Apart from the pilgrimage and its associated processions – some with cavalcades of young children in white – there's a traditional "Battle of Flowers", torchlit parades, rock concerts with some of the country's top bands, dances, car races, and a fair on the Recinto da Feira, below the sanctuary.

Balsemão

At the hamlet of **BALSEMÃO**, a three-kilometre hike from the back of the Lamego cathedral, is a seventh-century chapel founded by the Suevi. The route requires three left turns in all: the first is at the Capela do Desterro down into the old quarters of town and across a bridge; the second, a fork on to the hillside road; and the third comes a little while later, taking you down into the valley and above a rushing river. After three large curves, a village school, a collection of outhouses, and the chapel appear.

The undistinguished facade and dark interior of the **Capela de Balsemão** give it the air of a family vault, an impression strengthened by the imposing **sarcophagus** of Dom Afonso of Porto. Florid fourteenth-century capitals encircling the tomb make the few remaining Suevi curls on the archway into the choir seem subdued by comparison. A profoundly pregnant statue of *Nossa Senhora do Ó* (that's Ó as in *O! Nossa Senhora, Mãe de Deus . . .*) is being restored, but is due to be returned shortly. Slightly problematically, the chapel may still have a note on the door saying it's closed and referring visitors back to the museum in Lamego – not an instruction you're likely to comply with if you've just slogged out from town. Make gentle enquiries in the hamlet, and a woman should appear with a key and show you around.

Meals – and champagne

Restaurants in Lamego, like pensions, are on the expensive side. The one at the *Pensão Império* is probably the best, if funds will stretch. If not, try the *Novo* (opposite the cathedral), or the *Combinado* on Rua da Claria (behind the Turismo), which does wonderful trout stuffed with smoked ham. The bus station has a good restaurant open weekdays and a café that's useful for early morning breakfasts. A fine **picnic** can be put together from the ham shop and nearby grocers on Rua da Olaria. For drinking, a couple of saloon-door **bars** are to be found on the way to the castle – at the top of Rua do Almacave, and at Rua do Castelinho 25 – though both close at 9pm.

Finally, wine buffs or champagne enthusiasts may want to visit the **Caves Raposeira**, a kilometre out of town on the Castro Daire road. These are open for free tours and tasting, though the guides are grudging and the hours of opening unpredictable; check with the Turismo before setting out.

South from Lamego

Continuing south from Lamego, in the direction of Guarda and Viseu, the country of the **Leomil** and **Montemuro** ranges is high, wild and sparsely inhabited. This territory was among the earliest to fall to Afonso Henriques, the first king of Portugal, in his march south against the Moors. It is said that he laid the first stone of the monastery of **São João de Tarouca** after his victories at Trancoso and Sernancelhe in Beira Alta. The region's three other rewarding sights – the monastery of **Salzedas**, the fortified bridge at **Ucanha**, and the church at **Tarouca** – were also founded at this time.

São João de Tarouca

The small village of **SÃO JOÃO DE TAROUCA**, off the southeast route from Lamego to Guarda, was the site of the first Cistercian monastery to be founded in Portugal (1124).

Only the simple **Romanesque Church** is really intact, and even here the greatest treasure – Gaspar Vaz's renowned altarpiece of Saint Peter – is no longer on display. Villagers complain that the authorities in Lisbon removed the painting for cleaning in 1978 and have refused to return it ever since. Being less portable, the medieval tomb of Dom Dinis' illegitimate son, the Count of Barcelos, with elaborate hunting scenes carved into the sides, still lies in a side aisle.

THE INSTITUTE OF CULTURAL AFFAIRS

The **Montemuro** district, between Lamego and Castro Daire, suffers enormously from unemployment and depopulation, but has long traditions of **handicraft industries**, including weaving, knitting, basketry, honey and cheese production, pottery, and cape-making. And there's still a thriving **cultural life**, which with theatre, folk dance, and religious festivals – not to mention live music in the bars – occupies a central place in Montemuro life.

The **Instituto dos Assuntos Culturais** is an international development organisation with a staff of six foreign and eight Portuguese workers supporting the initiatives of local people. Some twenty villages, with a total population of about 11,000, are currently involved with the IAC's work. It's based at the village of **Mezio**, about 20km southwest of Lamego on the N2 Castro Daire road.

If you're interested in having a look at what the Institute does – and it seems there's not much it doesn't take an interest in – you might like to stop off en route between Lamego and the Mountain Beiras and stay for a day or two: visitors are actively encouraged. Facilities are basic, but there are showers and toilets and plenty of organic food. Contributions are around 1500esc per person per day, but that's pretty much all-inclusive. If you want to make enquiries in advance, write to the *IAC* at Rua Central 45, Mezio, 3600 Castro Daire, or Apartado 35, Lamego Codex, or telephone ☎054/68246.

In summer there are usually students working on the site, who will probably be happy to show you around. There's a pleasant spot for rest and recuperation – and a nice café – down by the river not two minutes' walk from the church.

Buses leave Lamego every Thursday at 8am and 1.30pm to pick up shoppers from São João. On other days, you have to take one of the daily Guarda- or Moimenta-bound buses to MONDIM DA BEIRA, a half-hour hike from São João, high above the brook that waters the remote valley.

Ucanha

In UCANHA – north of Tarouca, on the opposite side of N226 – life revolves around the water. Down below the main road, two ingenious ducts have been made to tap the river upstream in order to provide adequate washing facilities in the centre of the village. The wash houses are practically in ruins, but the system of one tank for suds and another for rinses, common to the Mediterranean, has been preserved. Running below the pools, the river looks so tempting that on a sunny day, regardless of what trash might be floating by, the village children are constantly nipping in and out.

The real beauty of the scene stems from the majestic **tollgate** (free admission) and single-arched **bridge**. They date from shortly after 1163, when the diocese of Salzedas was awarded to Teresa Afonso, erstwhile nursemaid to Afonso Henriques' five sons and heirs, and widow of Egas Moniz, the first king's tutor and closest adviser. Besides marking and protecting the border of her domain, these structures were also, of course, an ostentatious mark of manorial power. Today, clothes are hung out to dry under the arches.

Salzedas

SALZEDAS lies four kilometres further along the Ucanha road, past another "champagne" cooperative, a rival to *Raposeira*. The **Monastery** here was once the greatest of its kind, grander even than São João. The complex was rebuilt with money donated by Teresa Afonso in 1168, when the order was Augustinian; it became Cistercian during a later period of administration from Alcobaça.

Unfortunately, eighteenth-century renovation has largely altered its original appearance into a clumsy mixture of Baroque and pseudo-Classical styles. The monastery's main facade presides over the small square of the diminutive village. As at São João de Tarouca, students work here in the summer, and though they may seem surprised to see casual visitors, they will follow you around and open the relevant doors.

The smell of decay is strong inside and the two dark and dusty **paintings** of *Saint Peregrine* and *Saint Sebastian* by Grão Vasco, either side of the choir, are easily overlooked. More conspicuous are the fifteenth-century tombs of the Coutinho family – dominant nobles in these parts in the early years of the Portuguese nation – near the entrance. Out through a side door, a succession of courtyards, once fronting formal gardens, bear the scars of a period of extensive pillage and decay, which began in 1834 at the dissolution of the monasteries.

travel details

Trains

NORTE LINE

From Porto, 5 trains daily to Espinho (25min), Ovar (40min), Aveiro (1hr–1hr 15min), Coimbra "B" (1hr 45min–2hr; change for Coimbra "A", just a 4min ride), Entroncamento (3hr 15min), and Lisbon (4hr 20min). Also "*Rápido*" (express trains) from Porto to Lisbon – twice as fast (3hr) but twice as expensive – and *suburbano* trains to Aveiro (hourly from 6am to midnight).

NB: Change at **Aveiro** for *CP* bus connections to Viseu (3 daily; 4hr); at **Pampilhosa** for the Beira Alta; at Alfarelos (2hr) for Figueira da Foz (15 daily; 20min); and at **Entroncamento** for the Alto Alentejo, Beira Baixa, and Madrid (2 daily; 11–13hr). For Baixo Alentejo, it is better to travel via Lisbon.

DOURO LINE

From Porto, 19 trains daily run to Livração (1hr 10min; change for **Tâmega line**) with 13 continuing to Régua (2hr 30min; change for **Corgo line**), 7 to Tua (3hr 30min; change for **Tua line**), and 4 to Pocinho (4hr 30min).

PÓVOA LINE

From Porto, hourly to Vila do Conde (50min) and Póvoa do Varzim (55min). From Póvoa 4 trains daily go to Famalicão (45min) for connections along the Minho line.

CORGO LINE

From Régua to Vila Real (5 daily; 1hr).

TUA LINE

From Tua 5 trains daily (3 at weekends) to Mirandela (2hr; buses for Bragança).

GUIMARÃES LINE

From Porto (Trindade station), hourly to Santo Tirso (1hr) and Guimarães (1hr 45min).

MINHO LINE

From Porto, 12 daily to Nine (1hr; change for Braga), Barcelos (1hr 30min), and Viana do Castelo (2hr).

TÂMEGA LINE

From Livração to Amarante (4 daily; 30min).

Buses

From Porto there are a combination of express and ordinary buses to most northern towns, as well as to major cities in Galicia, across the border in Spain, and to Lisbon. Times vary greatly between the two: a motorway bus from Porto to Viseu, for example, can take just 1hr 45min, as opposed to 4hr 30min on an ordinary bus. *Renex* leaves for Lisbon every hour, on the hour, between 1pm and 9pm.

More **local services from Porto** include:

Vila do Conde/Póvoa do Varzim (every 30–60min, taking 40–45min); Viana do Castelo (3 daily; 1hr 10min); Braga (10; 1hr 20min); Guimarães (5; 1hr); Amarante (hourly; 1hr 30min); Vila Real (6; 3hr 40min).

From Lamego Régua (hourly; 30min); Viseu (daily; 1hr 20min); Guarda (2 daily, Mon–Fri only; 2hr).

Flights

From Porto Faro (weekly), Funchal (3 times a week), Lisbon (12–20 flights daily), plus numerous international flights .

CHAPTER SIX

THE MINHO

The Portuguese consider the **Minho** to be the most beautiful part of their country, and with its river valleys, wooded hills, trailing vines and barely developed coastline, the attractions are obvious. It's a small, thoroughly rural province, conservative (and at times reactionary) in politics, and deeply suspicious of change. Wooden-wheeled ox-carts still creak down its lanes and age-old traditions are maintained in dozens of local **festas** and **romarias**. In

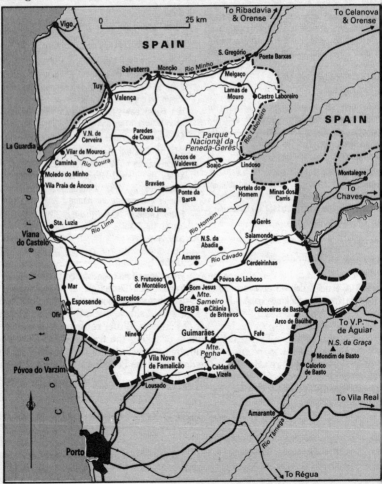

summer you'll probably just happen on these carnivals or saints' days, though most of the larger events are detailed in the text: they're worth coinciding with. The region is also known for its huge country **markets**, selling local produce and traditional handicrafts: the Thursday market at **Barcelos** is a prize example.

The main monuments and museums are concentrated in the southern Minho, in the neighbouring historic towns of **Guimarães** and **Braga** – the region's major centres. Between them lie the extensive Celtic ruins of the **Citânia de Briteiros**, one of the most impressive archaeological sites in Portugal, while a short drive to the west brings you to the Minho coast, the **Costa Verde**. This offers wonderful beaches, though the sea here is cold – and the weather overall can be cool, too, even in midsummer. However, the principal resort of **Viana do Castelo** is enjoyably low-key, and, if it's isolation you're after, there are strands to the north and south that scarcely see visitors.

Inland from Viana, the beautiful **Rio Lima** runs east through a succession of gorgeous small towns where there's little to do but soak up the somnolent scenery. On the whole, much of the Minho is like this – outrageously picturesque and full of quiet charm and interest. In the Lima valley, and particularly around the town of **Ponte de Lima**, these characteristics have been exploited by a scheme known as *Turismo de Habitação*, whereby local manor houses, farms and country estates offer rooms to tourists on a bed-and-breakfast basis – a highly enjoyable (and comfortable) way of seeing the countryside.

In the far north of the province, the **Rio Minho** forms the border with Spanish Galicia, and a string of small fortified towns stares across the river at Spain. South of the river, the highlights are all scenic, with waterfalls, river gorges, reservoirs, and forests of oak and cork contained within the protected **Parque Nacional da Peneda-Gerês**. This is superb camping and hiking territory, including a spa at **Caldas do Gerês** where you can recuperate from your endeavours.

Approaches to the Minho

There are several possible approaches to the Minho, though since the province is fairly small you needn't worry unduly about your point of arrival: regular, efficient buses link up most inland towns and villages, while the train from Porto runs north, through Viana do Castelo, to the end of the line at Valença.

Coming **from Porto or Lisbon**, the best initial destinations are Guimarães, Braga and Barcelos, after which you can move on easily enough to Viana do Castelo and the coast, or inland to the Peneda-Gerês.

Arriving **from Spain**, the most straightforward border crossing – with train and road links – is at **Tuy–Valença**; a little used alternative is the car ferry from **Goyan to Vila Nova de Cerveira**, east of Caminha. Either route puts you on the course of the Minho river, with the option of taking the train down the coast towards Viana do Castelo, or cutting south by bus towards the Lima valley. Arriving from the north, you're also within the domain of the Peneda-Gerês park. Arriving in the region **from Trás-os-Montes** (by bus from Chaves via Montalegre), you'll run through the southern section of the park before reaching Braga.

MINHO MARKET DAYS

Mon: Ponte de Lima (fortnightly) p.236. **Thurs**: Barcelos p.221; Monção p.233.
Tues: Ponte da Barca p.238; Braga p.211. **Fri**: Viana do Castelo p.225;
Wed: Arcos de Valdevez p.239; Valença p.232. Melgaço p.235.

EMIGRATION AND THE MINHO

Travelling around the Minho, you'll see much new building – even in the smallest and most isolated villages. This is accounted for mainly by **Minho emigrants**, who return to their homes after working abroad in France or Germany, sometimes the United States. Minho, more than any other area of Portugal, suffered severe depopulation from the late 1950s, as thousands migrated in search of more lucrative work.

The new-found prosperity of the emigrants has transformed their homeland in two ways: money sent back from abroad to support the family members left behind (a mainstay of the local economy), and the return of some of the emigrants themselves to enjoy a well-heeled retirement in *minha terra* (my land). August is the time when most people race back from abroad to see their families – making it a particularly hairy period on the region's roads. If you drop in on a *festa*, don't be surprised to see groups of well-dressed emigrant kids speaking English, German, or French. If you don't speak Portuguese, it can be worth brushing up on your **French** to use in travelling through the region – it is understood a great deal more often than English.

SOUTHERN MINHO

The **southern Minho** contains the region's two chief towns, **Guimarães** and **Braga**. They are both small enough to walk around in a busy day's sightseeing, though a night's stay has greater rewards, especially if you want to explore the **Citânia de Briteiros** and other local sights. Barcelos, too, is a great place to stay, if you can find a room on a Wednesday night before the weekly market.

Guimarães and Braga are on separate branch lines of the main **rail route**, which starts in Porto and passes through Barcelos on its way to Viana do Castelo. You may need to change at Lousado for Guimarães (though there are also direct trains from Porto) and Nine for Braga; to move between the two places it's far quicker to use the direct bus rather than fiddle about with connections between the train lines.

Guimarães

Birthplace of Afonso Henriques in 1110, and first capital of the fledgling kingdom of Portucale, **GUIMARÃES** has a special place in the story of Portuguese nationhood: from here began the reconquest from the Moors and the subsequent creation of a united kingdom which, within a century of Afonso's death, was to stretch to its present borders. Although Guimarães subsequently lost its pre-eminent status to Coimbra – which became the Portuguese capital in 1143 – it never relinquished its sense of self-importance, something that's evident from the careful preservation of an array of impressive medieval monuments. There's a grandeur to the town, and a tangible sense of history in the narrow medieval streets, all of which conspires to make Guimarães one of the most attractive and enjoyable places in the country.

If you can afford to stay at one of the two local pousadas – both occupying superb, converted historical premises – then the experience is complete. Otherwise, decent accommodation is hard to come by, though this matters little since Braga, or even Porto, is close enough to make your visit an easy day trip.

Arriving and accommodation

Arriving by **train**, you'll find yourself ten minutes' walk south of the centre; head into town past the university (occupying the grounds of a former *palácio*) and you'll pass the **Turismo** (Mon–Sat 9.30am–1pm & 2–5pm), at the edge of a stretch of gardens, opposite the main town square, the **Largo do Toural**.

The **bus station** is a fifteen-minute walk from the centre, at the bottom of Avenida Conde de Margaride (the Famalição road); walk up the avenue, past the market and turn right for the centre. There are express services from Porto and Lisbon, and regular weekday connections with Braga, Amarante, Cabeceiras and Mondim de Basto, and Póvoa do Lanhoso.

Accommodation

Good budget accommodation is scarce in town, and even more so during Guimarães' main festivals (see p.211). It's best to book ahead – especially if you're planning a splurge in one of the pousadas.

PENSIONS

Casa dos Retiros, Rua Francisco Agra 163 (☎053/41 22 53). A clean and functional hostel, attached to the church of São Francisco, and run by padres, who impose an 11pm curfew. It is sometimes booked up by groups. ③

Pensão-Residencial São José, Rua de Campos 84. Dingy but cheap. ②

Pensão Imperial, Alameda Dr. Sá Carneiro 111 (☎053/41 51 63). A variety of small rooms are available over the restaurant; the food is better than the accommodation. ③

Residencial São Mamede, Rua de São Gonçalo 1 (☎053/51 30 92). Very neat and professional approach, with bath and TV in all rooms. ④.

POUSADAS

Pousada de Santa Maria da Oliveira, Rua de Santa Maria (☎053/51 41 57). Converted from a row of sixteenth-century houses, right in the medieval centre, this sixteen-room *pousada* is beautifully furnished – and worth every *escudo*. Doubles around 15,000$00. ⑥

Pousada de Santa Marinha da Costa, Penha, 4800 Guimarães (☎053/51 44 53). This is reckoned one of the top *pousadas* in the country, set in a medieval monastery, 6km southeast of town (see p.210); it is also one of the priciest at upwards of 20,000$00 for a double room. ⑥

CAMPING

Camping Penha, Penha. Sited close by the pousada above, this is a pleasant (if distant) site, with a small swimming pool. Buses leave for Penha every half-hour between 6am and 10pm (8pm on Sun) from the gardens near the Turismo.

The Town

The old centre of Guimarães is an elongated kernel of small, enclosed squares and cobbled, medieval streets. It is buttressed at its southern end by the town gardens and overlooked from the north by the imposing castle, an enduring symbol of the emergent Portuguese nation.

The castle

The **Castelo** (Tues–Sun 9am–12.30pm & 2–5pm; free) was built by Henry of Burgundy, though its fame stems from the establishment of the first Portuguese court here, by his son, **Afonso Henriques**. Afonso is reputed to have been born

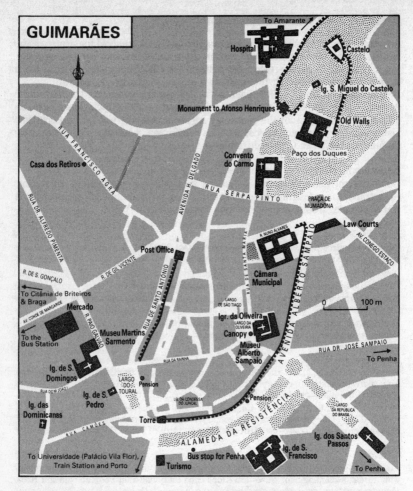

GUIMARÃES

To Amarante

Hospital

Castelo

Ig. S. Miguel do Castelo

Monument to Afonso Henriques

Old Walls

Paço dos Duques

RUA FRANCISCO AGRA

Casa dos Retiros

Convento do Carmo

AVENIDA H. DELGADO

RUA SERPA PINTO

PRAÇA DE MUMADONA

RUA DR. ALFREDO PIMENTA

Law Courts

AV. CONEGO ESTAÇO

R. DE S. GONÇALO

Post Office

R. DE GIL VICENTE

R. DE SANTO ANTONIO

RUA SANTA MARIA

AV. NUNO ALVARES

AVENIDA ALBERTO SAMPAIO

To Citânia de Briteiros & Braga

AV. CONDE DE MARGARIDE

Mercado

R. PAÇO GALVÃO

Câmara Municipal

LARGO DE SÃO TIAGO

0   100 m

To the Bus Station

Museu Martins Sarmento

Igr. da Oliveira

LARGO DA OLIVEIRA

RUA DR. JOSÉ SAMPAIO

Canopy

To Penha

Ig. de S. Domingos

RUA DA RAINHA

Museu Alberto Sampaio

RUA DOM JOÃO

LARGO DO TOURAL

Pension

Ig. de S. Pedro

LG. DA CONDESA DO JUNCAL

Pension

Ig. das Dominicanas

RUA CAMÕES

Torre

ALAMEDA DA RESISTÊNCIA

LARGO DA REPUBLICA DO BRASIL

Ig. dos Santos Passos

To Universidade (Palácio Vila Flor), Train Station and Porto

Bus stop for Penha

Turismo

Ig. de S. Francisco

To Penha

in the great square keep which is surrounded now, as then, by seven castellated towers. It's a splendid structure, made all the more impressive by its juxtaposition with the diminutive Romanesque chapel of **São Miguel** (erratic opening times), on the grassy slope below, in whose font Afonso was probably baptized.

Just across from the chapel is the **Paço dos Duques** (daily 9am–5.30pm; 300$00, Oct–May 200$00), once the medieval palace of the Dukes of Bragança. Under the Salazar dictatorship, its ruins were "restored" as an official residence for the president, and today, with such memories fading, it looks rather ludicrous – like a mock-Gothic Victorian folly. It houses an extensive collection of portraits, furniture and porcelain, around which perambulate lengthy guided tours.

Perhaps more attractive are the **children's toys** – hammered out from old tin and no doubt lethal, but beautiful objects nonetheless – on sale in a number of shops opposite the castle; there's a **café** here, too.

Along Rua de Santa Maria

From the castle, **Rua de Santa Maria** leads down into the heart of the old town, a beautiful thoroughfare, with its iron grilles and granite arches. Many of the town's historic buildings have been superbly restored, and as you descend to the centre you'll pass one of the loveliest: the seventeenth-century **convent of Santa Clara**, which today does service as the town hall.

On a much more intimate scale are the buildings ranged around the delightful central squares at the end of the street, **Largo de São Tiago** and **Largo da Oliveira**. The latter is dominated by the **Colegiada**, a convent church built (like the great monastery at Batalha) in honour of a vow made by João I before his decisive victory over Castile. Its unusual dedication is to "Our Lady of the Olive Tree" and before it stands a curious Gothic **canopy-shrine**. This marks the legendary spot where Wamba, unwillingly elected king of the Visigoths, drove a pole into the ground swearing that he would not reign until it blossomed. Naturally it sprouted immediately. João I, feeling this a useful precedent of divine favour, set out to meet the Castilian forces from this very point.

At the heart of the Colegíada is a simple Romanesque cloister with varied, naively carved capitals. This, and the rooms off it, comprise the splendid **Museu Alberto Sampaio** (Tues–Sun 10am–12.30pm & 2–5.30pm; 200$00), essentially the treasury of the collegiate church and convent, but outstandingly exhibited and, for once in such displays, with pieces of real beauty as well as weight-value. The highlight is a brilliantly composed and humanized silver-gilt *Triptych of the Nativity*, said to have been found in the King of Castile's tent after the Portuguese victory at Aljubarrota (1385). Close by this is displayed the tunic worn by João I in the battle. Unfortunately, you have to take a guided tour of the museum, which – if you don't speak Portuguese – becomes reduced to a dull litany of substances and dates ("wood, sixteenth-century") intoned by someone following two steps behind you, switching on and off the lights.

The Museu Martins Sarmento and São Francisco

The **Museu Martins Sarmento** (10am–noon & 2–5pm; closed Mon) is another superb collection, again housed in a former convent, just off the Largo do Toural. Here, finds from the neighbouring *citânias* of Briteiros and Sabroso are displayed in the fourteenth-century Gothic cloister of São Domingos.

They include a remarkable series of bronze votive offerings, (amongst them, a "coach", pulled at each end by men and oxen), ornately patterned stone lintels and door jambs from the huts; most spectacular of all are the two *Pedras Formosas* ("beautiful stones") and the *Colossus of Pedralva*. The Pedras, once taken to be sacrificial altars, are in fact the portals to funerary monuments – one of which survives in situ at the Citânia de Briteiros. The Colossus is more enigmatic and considerably more ancient, a vast granite hulk of a figure with arm raised aloft and an oversized phallus. It shares the bold, powerfully hewn appearance of the stone boars found in Trás-os-Montes (in Bragança, for instance) and like them may date from pre-Celtic fertility cults of around 1500 to 1000 BC.

Among the numerous other churches scattered about the centre of Guimarães, the finest is the **Igreja de São Francisco** (closed noon–3pm), on the south side of the town gardens. It features a series of huge eighteenth-century *azulejos* of Saint Francis preaching to the fishes, and an elegant Renaissance cloister and fountain. Once again, the church was attached to a monastery of considerable size until the 1834 dissolution.

Santa Marinha da Costa: the pousada

You have to travel a short way outside Guimarães for the best preserved medieval building in the region, the former monastery – and nowadays *pousada* – of **Santa Marinha da Costa**. It is set on the slopes of **Penha**, six kilometres to the southeast of town, and can be reached by taking the São Roque bus from the Turismo (every half-hour until 11.15pm); get off at COSTA, and then follow the signs.

The monastery was founded in 1154 by order of Dona Mafalda, the wife of Afonso Henriques, in honour of a vow to Santa Marinha, patron saint of pregnant women. Originally Augustinian, the foundation passed into the hands of the Order of Saint Jerome in the sixteenth century. In the **church** (July–Sept 9am–1pm & 2–7pm; small fee), Jerome's twin emblems of the skull and the lion are recurring motifs. They are surrounded by an oddly harmonious mixture of styles – tenth-century doorways on the south wall, sixteenth-century panels in the sacristy (Jerome beating his breast with a stone against the temptation of women), and an eighteenth-century organ and stone roof in the choir.

Strictly, the monastic buildings are off limits except to guests of the *pousada*, but you can peek into the magnificent **cloister**, with its Mozarabic doorway. For more of a look around it would be diplomatic to buy a meal, or at least a drink at the bar.

Food and entertainment

Guimarães has no shortage of places to **eat and drink**, although – as with accommodation – it's difficult to get excited about the choice. However, there's an easygoing feel about the place, a bit of **nightlife**, a great **festival** in August, and a lot of partying at weekends when the local **football** team, **FC Guimarães**, is at home. They have been causing a few raised eyebrows over the last couple of years, contending with the big boys of Lisbon and Porto at the top of the First Division; their stadium is northwest of the centre, along Rua Dr. A. Pimenta.

Restaurants

Bom Retiro, Rua de Avelino Germano. Don't be put off by the rather touristic look of this place: the food is good and you find yourself effectively sitting in a kitchen, while your meal is prepared around you.

Nicolino, Largo do Toural 106. Modest-priced local dishes in a central location.

Oriental, Largo do Toural. Central bar-restaurant serving up standard Portuguese dishes.

Pinguim, up the steps off Rua Francisco Agra. Just out of the centre, this serves local dishes, but there's not much atmosphere.

Solar da Rainha, Rua da Rainha D. Maria II. The daily set menu here is good value.

Pousada de Santa Maria da Oliveira, Rua de Santa Maria. Unquestionably the best restaurant in town, with fine traditional fare served in a wonderful antique dining room. Book a table in advance – and bring enough money!

Entertainment and nightlife

A trio of nightclubs that might reward a visit:

Crocodile Club, Rua de São Gonçalo. The big young hangout, open July–Sept only (Fri–Sun 10.30pm–3am); fairly steep admission charges.

Disco Traca's, Rua Gil Vicente. Similar to the *Crocodile*. Open from mid-afternoon.

Casa do Arco, opposite the town hall. Possibly more enjoyable, for foreign tastes, this has an art gallery, live music and lower admission charge. Open 3–7pm & 9.30pm–2am.

Festivals

Guimarães' major festival is the **Festas Gualterianas** (for São Gualter – aka Saint Walter, Aug 5–8), when all public buildings will be closed. It takes place from August 5th to 8th and has done since 1452. If you miss the festival you can catch most of the same stall-holders, and something of the atmosphere, the week-end after in CALDAS DE VIZELA, a spa-town 10km south of Guimarães.

Next in importance, after the *Gualterianas*, is the long-established *romaria* to **São Torcato** (6km northeast, first weekend of July), which, in the curious lingo of the Turismo leaflet, "includes procession with archaic choirs of virgins".

East of Guimarães: towards Trás-os-Montes

Heading east towards Trás-os-Montes, the minor N206 runs across country towards the Rio Tâmega (see previous chapter).

FAFE is the first place you happen upon, 14km away. Little more than an over-grown bus station (you'll almost certainly need to change here for Trás-os-Montes destinations), it has a couple of *pensões* and a large revolutionary statue of a worker violently clubbing his bowler-hatted boss.

Beyond Fafe lies some magnificent countryside, dotted with huge boulders. You might want to stop at GANDARELA, which is famed for its topiary. At ARCO DE BAULHE, a road leads 7km north to Cabeceiras de Basto (see p.195), while a dozen kilometres or so further east you reach the Tâmega river itself. The route south from here used to be accessible by train, though the Tâmega line now stops at Amarante. By car, you're just 30km from the main Vila Real–Chaves road, one of Trás-os-Montes' finest routes.

Braga

BRAGA, the Turismo pamphlet claims, is the Portuguese Rome. This is clearly going a bit overboard – the Portuguese Canterbury might be more appropriate – though it neatly illustrates the city's ecclesiastical pretensions. One of the most ancient towns in Portugal, founded by the Romans in 279 BC, Braga was an important Visigothic bishopric before its occupation by the Moors. Reconquered early in the Christian campaigns, by the end of the eleventh century its archbish-ops were pressing for recognition as "Primate of the Spains", a title they disputed bitterly with Toledo over the next six centuries.

The city is still Portugal's religious capital – the scene of spectacular **Easter celebrations**, with torchlit processions and weirdly hooded penitents – while Braga's outlying districts boast a selection of important religious buildings and sanctuaries, including that of **Bom Jesus**, one of the country's most extravagant Baroque creations. Braga also has a reputation as a bastion of reactionary politics. It was here, in 1926, that the military coup leading to Salazar's dictatorship was launched, while in the more recent past, after the 1974 revolution, the Archbishop of Braga personally incited a mob to attack local Communist offices.

Such memories don't seem so distant when you look around at the weight of church power in Braga – including an archbishop's palace on a truly presidential scale. However, overall the city is an enjoyable place, and it seems recently to have acquired a new energy that reflects less of the church than its position as a fast-growing commercial centre.

Arriving and accommodation

Braga is a fair-sized city, though the old town – an oval of streets radiating from the Sé – is a compact area. The main **bus station** is just over five minutes' walk from the centre; follow Rua dos Chaos downhill into Praça da República, north of the Sé. The **train station** is west of the centre, reached down Rua Andrade Corvo, a fifteen-minute walk from the old town.

The **Turismo** – housed in a wonderful Art Deco building – is at Avenida da Liberdade 1 (Mon–Sat 9am–12.30pm and 2–7pm, Sun 9am–12.30pm and 2–5pm; Oct–May closed Sun; ☎053/22550); it offers an impressive large-scale map of the city. If you are heading for **Gerês**, the park headquarters in Braga is at Rua de São Geraldo 19 (Mon–Fri 9am–5.30pm).

Accommodation

There are plenty of *pensões* and hotels in Braga (though beware of turning up without a reservation during local festivals – see p.216) and it makes a decent base for touring the southern Minho. An alternative to staying in the city is to stay at the hotel or Turismo de Habitacão lodging up at Bom Jesus (see p.217).

PENSIONS AND HOTELS

Pensão Comercial, Rua dos Chãos 33 (☎053/226 28). Small *pensão*, on the way in from the bus station, whose box-rooms (some windowless) tend to fill early in the day. ②

Residencial Inácio Filho, Rua Francisco Sanches 42 (☎053/238 49). Central, spotless *residencial*, cluttered with wonderful artefacts. Most rooms come with a bath. You'll find the pension to the left off Rua do Souto, heading down from the Turismo. ③

Pensão Grande Residencial Avenida, Avda. da Liberdade 738 (☎053/229 55). Fine old pension in a great location, just by the Turismo. Once grand, it's beginning to fade a little these days, but remains a good bet. Reservations esssential in summer. ③

Hotel Francfort, Avda. Central (☎053/226 48). Just across from Praça da República, this charming and friendly place dates from 1879, and features a lot of built-in furniture and an amazing stairwell. The Art Deco dining room is worth a visit, too. ③

Residencial São Lázaro, Rua 25 de Abril 457-6° (☎053/298 74). Neat and modern, although slightly spartan rooms, all with balcony and private bathroom. Reasonable value. ③

Residencial Centro Comercial Avenida, Avda. Central 27 (☎053/757 22). Good value if you want all the extras – TV, lots of space, attached bathroom and kitchenette. Definitely upmarket, but friendly with it. ④

Residencial dos Terceiros, Rua dos Capelistas 85 (☎053/704 66). Another recommended upmarket option with a bar and a nice atmosphere. ④

YOUTH HOSTEL

Casa de Juventude, Rua de Santa Margarida 6 – off the Avda. Central (☎053/781 63). An excellent youth hostel, very popular in the summer with hikers heading for the national park. There's a kitchen for preparing meals, and state-of-the-art pressure showers. Reception is open from 9–11am and 6pm–midnight.

Casa Santa Zita, Rua São João 20 (☎053/234 94). A pilgrim-hostel, hidden behind the Sé; look out for the brass plaque. Large and peaceful, with nice rooms and an altogether religious aura, curfew and dress code. Not for hell-raisers, but good value. ②

CAMPING

Camping Parque da Ponte. This is the nearest site – a two-kilometre walk out from the town centre, down Avenida da Liberdade; it is right next to the municipal swimming pool.

The City

The obvious point to start exploring Braga is the **Praça da República**, a busy arcaded square at the head of the old town. It's backed by the former town keep, the **Torre de Menagem**, while in the arcade itself you'll find two fine coffee-houses which look out down the length of the long central gardens. From here,

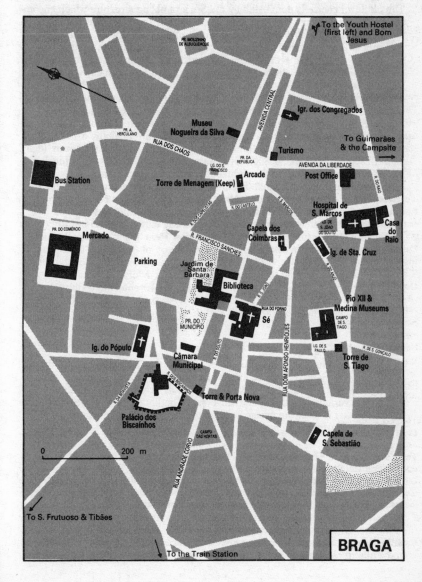

almost everything of interest is reached down narrow **Rua do Souto**, the main pedestrianised street which runs down to the Sé. The street is Braga's main shopping district, though few commercial centres are like this one, with shoe shops rubbing shoulders with places selling candles, icons and other religiana.

The Sé

The old town centre is dominated by the **Sé**, a rambling structure which encompasses Gothic, Renaissance and Baroque additions to an original Romanesque building, founded in 1070 with the restoration of the bishopric after the Christian reconquest. The cathedral's south doorway is a survival from this earliest building, carved with rustic scenes from the legend of Reynard the Fox. The most striking element of the structure, however, is the intricate ornamentation of the roofline, commissioned by Braga's great Renaissance patron Archbishop Diogo de Sousa and executed by João de Castilho, later to become the architect of Lisbon's Jerónimos Monastery, the greatest of all Manueline buildings.

Inside, the cathedral complex is disorientating: you enter through a courtyard fronting three Gothic chapels, a cloister and, most prominently, a ticket desk, where you can gain access to the treasury, now the cathedral **museum** (daily 9am–12.30pm & 2–6pm; 200$00). One of the richest collections in Portugal, this has pieces from the tenth to the eighteenth centuries, though the display does its best to make it all look dull. Eventually you emerge alongside magnificent Baroque twin organs in the **Coro Alto** to gaze down into the cathedral proper – unexpectedly small and, when you descend, remarkably uninteresting.

The tour of the treasury aside, each of the three outer chapels is worth a visit, particularly the fourteenth-century **Capela dos Reis** (King's Chapel), built to house the tombs of the cathedral's founders, Henry of Burgundy, first Count of Portucale, and his wife Teresa – the parents of Afonso Henriques, founder of the kingdom. Exposed beside them is the mummified body of Archbishop Lourenço, found "uncorrupt" when his tomb was opened in the seventeenth century; he had fought in the great victory over the Castilians at Aljubarrota (1385), riding around bestowing indulgences on the ranks, and there sustained a scar on his cheek – which he himself is said to have carved proudly on his effigy.

The Archbishop's Palace

Opposite the cathedral, across Rua do Souto, you won't be able to miss the old **Archbishop's Palace**, a great fortress-like building, which in medieval times actually covered a tenth of the city. Today it easily accommodates the municipal library and various faculties of the university. The library is open weekdays and inside you can inspect the ornate ceilings of the medieval reading-room and the *Sala do Doctor Manuel Monteiro*.

Braga's churches, mansions and museums

Unless you have an academic interest, you're unlikely to find Braga's other **churches** very inspiring: most, like the cathedral, were stripped and modernized in the late-seventeenth and eighteenth centuries. The most interesting, architecturally, is the small Renaissance **Capela dos Coimbras**, another of Archbishop de Sousa's commissions, sited on the Largo Carlos Amarante.

On the whole more inspiring are the numerous **mansions** from earlier ages, with their extravagant Baroque and Rococo facades. The **Câmara Municipal** and **Palácio do Raio**, both by André Soares, are good examples; look out, too, for the apostle-clad roofline of the **Hospital de São Marcos**. Best of all perhaps, and visitable, is the mid-seventeenth-century **Casa dos Biscaínhos** (Tues–Sun 10am–noon & 1–5.30pm; 200$00), whose flagstoned ground floor is characteristically designed to allow carriages through to the stables. Nowadays, it houses a small museum of period furniture.

Across town, in the Campo de São Tiago, a former seminary has been turned into the **Museu Pio XII e Medina** (Tues–Sun 10am–12.30pm & 3–6pm; 150$00). It in fact consists of two distinct collections: the **Pio XII**, housing dusty religious regalia, and the **Medina**, named after the Portuguese painter and donated on the understanding that it would be housed separately from any other exhibits. Save your energy for the collection of fonts and capitals gathered in a courtyard like standing stones, or for the small excavation of a first-century Roman water tank – and try persuading the guide to hold back on a few of the endless locked doors.

If you feel in a mood for museums, the city also boasts the **Museu Nogueira da Silva** on Avenida Central (Tues–Fri 10am–noon & 3–5pm, Sat 3–5pm), with a variety of paintings, Chinese porcelain and carpets.

Cafés, restaurants, nightlife and festivals

You can eat pretty well in Braga, though the city's most characterful locales are its nineteenth-century cafés – busy through the day and into the evening. For details of local events, get hold of a copy of the *Correio do Minho* newspaper; the Turismo generally has one on the counter and is happy to advise on listings. Don't miss out on tickets to anything that's on at the *Teatro Circo*, on the Avenida da Liberdade, if only for a chance to view the sumptuous Art Deco interior.

Cafés

Café Astória, Avda. da Liberdade. By far the best of the old coffee houses, mahogany-panelled and with cut-glass windows, going very beautifully to seed; occasional live music and invariably tasty snacks add to the attractions.

O Brasileiro, Rua Dom Marcos. Another superb old-style café, at the top of Rua do Souto, full of crusty old waiters dealing out brandies to a similarly aged clientele. In summer, you can sit in the open window-terrace – virtually on the street.

Café Avenida, in the gardens of the Avenida Central. All Art Deco curved glass, chrome and black leather.

Prégão, Largo da Praça Velha 18. Lovely place for a snack and a drink. Chatty barman, good wines and sangria.

Restaurants

A Ceia, Rua do Raio (closed Sun). This is always crowded with locals, so arrive early, especially at weekends, or you'll have to eat at the bar. Spit-roast chickens and steaks served up in enormous portions, plus a fine wine list. Moderate prices.

Restaurante A Marisqueira, Rua do Castelo 15. The rather shabby-looking interior belies a menu of well-presented (and inexpensive) seafood dishes.

Restaurante Bem de Quer, Campo das Hortas. Again, fine-value seafood dishes.

Café Talismã, Rua do Souto, opposite Largo do Paço. Good Portuguese standards served in generous quantities and at very low prices.

Restaurante Moçambicana, Rua Andrade Corvo 8, just outside the town gate. As the name suggests, a spattering of African dishes feature on the menu. Cheap.

Rio Este, Rua das Barbarosas – first left having crossed the river down Avda. da Liberdade (convenient for the **campsite**). The house speciality – possibly the nastiest dish in Portugal – is *Papas de Sarrabulho* (giblets in pig's blood), but they serve seafood dishes as well.

Pizzeria Papalloni, Rua da Taxa 8 (close to the **youth hostel**). A dependable place for cheap and tasty pizzas.

Restaurante Inácio, Campo das Hortas 4 – through the town gate at the end of Rua do Souto and off to the left. A very pleasant, upmarket restaurant that specialises in local dishes and wines: probably the best place in town for a treat.

Bars and discos

Pub John Lennon, Centro Comercial Freeway, Rua do Raio. Disco-bar with 60s music and a busy clientele. No dancing, but genuinely worth a visit for novelty value.

O Corêto Disco-Pub, Centro Comercial Avenida. Open all hours. A small, low-key dance floor and very nice bar staff.

Indústria, beneath the *Hotel Turismo* on Avda. da Liberdade. Braga's most fashionable club, with a reputation that stretches as far as Lisbon; the rather punctilious door policy favours well-dressed couples.

Salsa, Rua de Diu (just around the corner from the *Indústria*). The obvious retreat if the trendies were too much for you. Comfortable, relaxed, and spacious, with a mixed bag of music and an unpretentious crowd. Minimum consumption, 500esc.

Trigonometria, at *O Nosso*, Avda. da Liberdade. A rather staid bar in the afternoon, this undergoes a remarkable metamorphosis after dark, providing the main competition for *Indústria* and still audibly humming at 4am. Strong dance tracks; pricey but very much worth it if you can get past the identical twin bouncers.

Festivals

In addition to the **Semana Santa** (Holy Week) celebrations – which are at their best in Braga – the whole city is illuminated for the **Festas de São João** (June 23–24), which provides the excuse for ancient folk dances, a fairground and general partying. The main **pilgrimage to Bom Jesus** (see below), takes place over Whitsun (six weeks after Easter). Don't expect to find a room at any of these times, unless you book well ahead.

Throughout the year, there's popular entertainment in the recently installed **Feira Popular Bracalandia**, a kilometre out of town on the Bom Jesus road. This is a permanent fairground, with a ferris wheel, rides and the like, popular with locals and tourists in the early evening. A regular **Tuesday market** is held at the new exhibition centre, at the end of Avenida da Liberdade, just off our map.

Around Braga: Bom Jesus and other sites

There are a trio of fascinating religious sites around Braga. The Baroque stairway and pilgrim church of **Bom Jesus do Monte** is a good enough reason to come to the city in the first place, while just to the northwest of Braga is a Visigothic church, **São Frutuoso**, and a ruined Benedictine monastery, **Tibães**.

You can reach all these sites on **public transport**. Buses to Bom Jesus leave every half-hour (at 10 and 40 minutes past each hour) from near the Hospital de São Marcos. Buses to São Frutuoso/Tibães leave from the corner of Rua do Carvalho/Rua de São Vicente (they are marked *Ruães*). If you want to make things easy by hiring a **taxi** for a few hours, Antonio Fanil da Silva (☎053/61 40 19 or 235 35) offers reasonable rates.

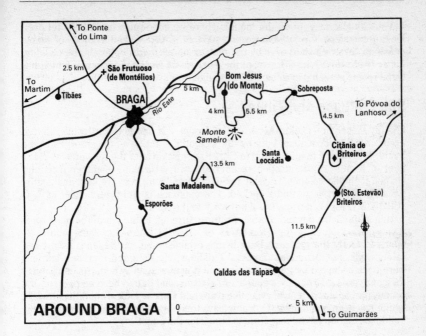

AROUND BRAGA

Bom Jesus do Monte

BOM JESUS DO MONTE is one of Portugal's best-known images, and as much concept as building. Set in the woods high above the city, it comprises a glorious ornamental stairway of granite and white plaster, a monumental homage created by Braga's archbishop in the first decades of the eighteenth century. There is no particular reason for its presence – no miracle or vision – yet it remains the object of devoted pilgrimage, with many penitents climbing on their knees.

Buses run the three kilometres from Braga to the foot of the stairway. At weekends they are packed, as seemingly half the city piles up to picnic in the woods. Most of the local families, armed with immense baskets of food, ride straight to the top in an ingenious hydraulic funicular (50$00). If you resist temptation and make the climb up the stairway, Bom Jesus's simple allegory unfolds.

Each of the **stairway** landings has a fountain: the first symbolises the wounds of Christ, the next five the Senses, and the final three represent the Virtues. At each corner, too, are chapels with mouldering, larger-than-life wooden tableaux of the Life of Christ; these are arranged chronologically, leading to the Crucifixion at the altar of the church. As a design it's a triumph – one of the greatest of all Baroque architecture – and was later copied at Lamego.

Food and rooms

Bom Jesus is a very pleasant place to spend an afternoon or, best of all, early evening. There are wooded gardens, grottoes and miniature boating pools behind the church, and (at the far end) several cheap, lively **restaurants** – filled on Saturdays with parties from a constant stream of weddings.

You can also stay up on the mount. There's a good-value one-star **hotel** overlooking the steps, the *Sul-Americano* (☎053/67 67 01; ③), and a couple of simple pensions, less well sited over by the restaurants. A fourth option is the *Casa dos Lagos* (☎053/67 67 38; ④), part of the *Turismo de Habitação* scheme, which has three rooms available in a splendid old building.

São Frutuoso and Tibães

Slightly closer in – 3.5km northwest of Braga – is another worthwhile church excursion: **São Frutuoso**, built by the Visigoths in the seventh century, adapted by the Moors, and then restored to Christian worship after the Reconquest. It is a gem of a church, set in open countryside with a flanking eighteenth-century chapel. It should be open Tuesday to Sunday until 5pm; keys are kept in a nearby house if you arrive to find it locked. The approach is from the hamlet of SÃO JERÓNIMO REAL, down a (marked) track to the right.

Half a kilometre beyond the São Frutuoso turning, to the left of the main road, a paved track leads to the **Monastery of TIBÃES** (Turs–Sun 9am–noon & 2–5pm), formerly the grandest Benedictine establishment in the land. A vast and ruined hulk, its abandoned medieval buildings, cloisters and rambling gardens were once occupied by gypsy families, but it is now state-owned, the entrance to the courtyards guarded by a couple of Alsatians, and due to become part cultural centre, part *pousada*. It is an evocative place and you can look around the **church**, which has been maintained. On some days there is a guided tour of the monastic buildings, on others you may have to knock for the priest.

Póvoa do Lanhoso and the road to Gerês

Heading **east from Braga** along the N103 to the Peneda-Gerês park (see the last section in this chapter), you will pass, after 16km, the turning for **Póvoa do Lanhoso**, 3km south of the main road. If you have transport, and time to spare, this small provincial town is worth a detour for a castle and Romanesque church. Another sight, revered in Portugal though perhaps of more peripheral interest to visitors, is the shrine of **Nossa Senhora da Abadia**, to the north of the Braga–Gerês road, turning off at Santa Maria do Bouro.

Povoa do Lanhoso

The modern quarters of **PÓVOA DO LANHOSO** aren't up to much, but they lie sandwiched between two ancient sites. At the northern end of town (the approach from Braga), a steep mound rises up to one of the smallest **castles** in Portugal (open most afternoons) and a scattering of chapels and picnic tables. In the fourteenth century, the lord of the shire was reported to have locked up his adulterous wife, her lover, and their servants in the castle and ordered it to be burned; it was substantially rebuilt in the eighteenth century. The **restaurant** nearby keeps a set of keys and offers reasonable food and good views, if you can squeeze in between their regular parties of christening and wedding guests.

In the opposite direction, 3km out of town, the small church of **Fonte Arcada** is a short walk from the main road (past the white statue). The simple interior, characteristic of the Romanesque style, is in marked contrast to the complications of the doorway with its centrepiece relief of a large sheep.

Lanhoso has a central **pension**, though you would be wiser to move on. The town provides useful transport links to the east into Trás-os-Montes; south to the Douro, via the village of Cabeceiras de Basto (see p.195); and also to Porto, via Famalicão. Regular **buses** also connect with Braga, Caldas do Gerês, Guimarães and Cabeceiras de Basto. To pick up one of the four daily Chaves buses, you have to walk the 3km out to PINHEIRO, on the main road, the N103.

Nossa Senhora da Abadia

Turning off at SANTA MARIA DO BOURO – which has a shell of a monastery and a large Baroque church – you arrive at the shrine of **Nossa Senhora da Abadia**. This is said to be the oldest sanctuary in Portugal and, like Bom Jesus, is a centre of pilgrimage (the main festival is on August 15). The focus of devotions is a twelfth-century wooden statue of the Virgin and Child. The church itself is largely an eighteenth-century rebuilding, though outside are two elegant wings of monks' cells, and, usually, some market stalls.

The Citânia de Briteiros

Midway between Guimarães and Braga is one of the most impressive and exciting archeological sites in the country, the **Citânia de Briteiros**.

Citânias – Celtic hill settlements – lie scattered throughout the Minho: remains of twenty-seven have been identified along the coast, plus some sixteen in the region between Braga and Guimarães alone. Most date from the arrival of northern European Celts in the Iron Age (circa 600–500 BC), though some are far older – having merged with an existing local culture established since Neolithic times (circa 2000 BC). The one at Briteiros was occupied from about 300 BC, and seems to have been a last stronghold against the invading Roman forces, resisting colonisation until around 26–19 BC.

Getting there

There are two **buses** direct to Briteiros **from Braga** (at 8.15am and 6pm). Otherwise you have to **hitch or walk**, either from Bom Jesus (set out along the road beyond the gardens and pensions; 9km from the site), or from CALDAS DAS TAIPAS (on the Braga–Guimarães bus route; 6km from the site). Alternatively, you might be able to catch one of the buses which run **from Guimarães** through Caldas das Taipas to Póvoa do Lanhoso.

Leaving the Citânia, hitching a lift from other visitors, either to Braga or Guimarães, should be fairly easy.

The excavations

The site excavations (open daily from 9am to dusk) have revealed foundations of over a hundred and fifty **huts**, a couple of which have been rebuilt to give a sense of their scale and design. Most of them are circular, with porches for their fires, though some are rectangular, among them a larger building which may have been a prison or meeting house – it is labelled the *casa do tribunal*.

There's also a clear network of paved **streets** and paths, two circuits of **town walls**, plus **cisterns**, stone **guttering**, and a **public fountain** (the *fonte*). Most of these features are identifiable as you wander around the place, though the site is more evocative in its layout and extent than for any particular sights.

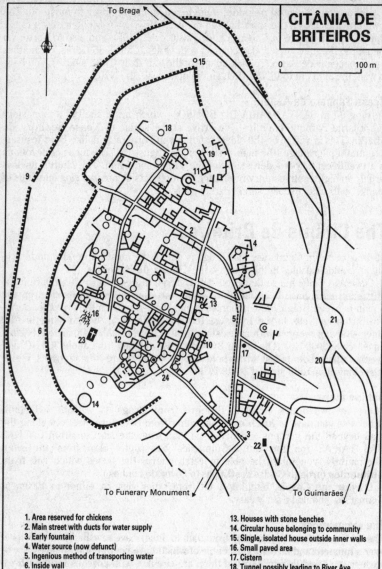

CITÂNIA DE BRITEIROS

To Braga

15

To Funerary Monument

To Guimarães

1. Area reserved for chickens
2. Main street with ducts for water supply
3. Early fountain
4. Water source (now defunct)
5. Ingenious method of transporting water
6. Inside wall
7. Second (of four) walls
8. Gateway
9. Gateway
10. House with various rooms
11. House with helix
12. Houses reconstructed by Martins Sarmento
13. Houses with stone benches
14. Circular house belonging to community
15. Single, isolated house outside inner walls
16. Small paved area
17. Cistern
18. Tunnel possibly leading to River Ave
19. Law courts(?), prisons(?)
20. Entrance
21. Parking
22. Guard's room
23. Chapel of S. Romão
24. Cross and Christian cemetery

One feature not to be missed, however, is the **funerary chamber** (no. 17 on the plan: a fair walk down the hill to the left of the settlement) with its geometrically patterned stone doorway. Similar examples, along with carved lintels from the huts and other finds from the *citânia*, are displayed at the Museu Martins Sarmento in Guimarães. These indicate that the settlement was abandoned as late as 300 AD and – unlike Conimbriga, another Celtic site near Coimbra – show little Roman influence other than the presence of coins.

The Roman historian Strabo gave a vivid description of the northern Portuguese tribes, who must have occupied these *citânias*, in his *Geographia* (circa 20 BC). They organised mass sacrifices, he recorded, and consulted prisoners' entrails without removing them. Otherwise, they liked to:

> *live simply, drink water and sleep on the bare earth . . . two-thirds of the year they live on acorns, which they roast and grind to make bread. They also have beer. They lack wine but when they have it they drink it up, gathering for a family feast. At banquets they sit on a bench against the wall according to age and rank . . . When they assemble to drink they perform round dances to the flute or the horn, leaping in the air and crouching as they fall.*

Entrails aside – and they may have been literary licence – none of this seems far removed from the Minho and Trás-os-Montes of recent memory.

Barcelos

It's worth a little planning to arrive in **BARCELOS**, 20km west of Braga, for the great Thursday market, the **Feira de Barcelos**. The great weekly event of southern Minho, it takes place from around dawn until mid-afternoon on the Campo da República. This, also known as the **Campo da Feira**, is a vast open square that's about the first place you come upon walking into town from the railway station.

Arrival and accommodation

The **railway station** is at the eastern edge of town; follow the street straight ahead for fifteen minutes and you'll eventually emerge on the Campo da República. **Buses** use a terminal at the southeast corner of the square; among other services, there's an hourly run to Braga. For more obscure routes and local villages, the services of the green buses of the *Linhares* bus company may come in handy: they're located at the top of our map, on the Viana do Castelo road.

The **Turismo** is housed in the town's old castle keep, the **Torre de Menagem**, on the Largo da Porta Nova (Mon–Sat 9am–6pm; ☎053/81 18 82). In addition to its information counter, it features a permanent display and sales of Barcelos handicrafts (see overpage).

The town has three **pensions** and a hotel:

Pensão Bagoeira, Avda. Sidónio Pais 57 (☎053/81 12 36). Located on the southeast corner of the Campo da República, this is a real old market inn, with a handful of spotless rooms; phone ahead if you want to secure one on a Wednesday night, before the market. ③.

Pensão Arantes, Avda. de Liberdade 32 (☎053/81 13 26). Cheaper option on the west side of the Campo. ②.

Residencial Dom Nuno, Avda. Dom Nuno Alvares Pereira 76 (☎053/81 50 84). A fancier place, off to the right as you approach the Campo da República from the station. ④.

Albergaria Condes de Barcelos, Avda. Alcaides de Feria (☎053/820 61). Upmarket hotel on the road in from the station to the Campo. ⑤.

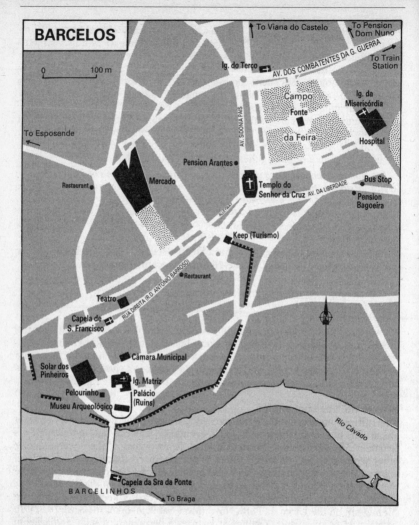

BARCELOS

The Feira

The Minho's markets are always interesting and the **Feira de Barcelos**, which must be one of the largest in Europe, is both a spectacle (which makes it something of a tourist attraction in summer) and a crash course in the region's economics. There are stalls for virtually everything – yokes for oxen, sausage skins, whole avenues of ducks and rabbits (treated as live meat and enough to turn you vegetarian) – as well as row upon row of village women squatting behind baskets of their own produce. Minho is made up of hundreds of tiny, walled smallholdings, rarely more than allotments, many people here are just selling a few vegetables, some fruit, eggs, and maybe even cheese from the family cow. It all looks unbelievably wholesome.

THE BARCELOS COCK

A crucifix in Barcelos' archaeological museum depicts the legend of the **Galo de Barcelos**, a miraculous roast fowl which rose from the dinner table of a judge to crow the innocence of a pilgrim he had wrongly condemned to the gallows. The pilgrim, having wisely proclaimed "I'll be hanged if that cock don't crow", got his reprieve. It's a story that occurs in different forms in northern Spain – at Santo Domingo de Calzada a cock is even kept in the church – but the Barcelos rooster has taken a special hold on popular folk art, becoming a national symbol of Portugal and now, usually in pottery form, the ubiquitous emblem of Portuguese tourism.

Apart from produce, clothes and kitchen equipment, the *feira*'s big feature is local **pottery** and handicrafts, for Barcelos is the centre of Portugal's most active *artesanato* region. The pottery ware – *louça de Barcelos* – is characteristically brown with distinctive yellow dots, and has been highly acclaimed since the 1950s, when the imaginative earthenware figurines of Rosa Ramalho began to be collected throughout Europe. In comparison most of today's pieces look rather production line (some, indeed, are Far East imports), but there are good items to be found, if you look around, and at half the price of outlets elsewhere.

Other crafts, too, are impressive – especially the basketwork, traditionally carved yokes (*cangas*), and wooden toys.

The rest of town

At the southwest corner of the Campo is Barcelos's most striking church, the **Templo do Nosso Senhor da Cruz**, fronted by a Baroque garden of obelisks and box-hedges. Built in 1708, its distinctive exterior, created by a simple contrast of dark granite and white plasterwork, was to be influential in the design of churches throughout the region. It sets an odd tone to the old part of town, though, which is essentially Gothic and medieval – a small, hillside web of streets spun above the River Cávado.

Heading south from the Campo, you'll soon end up at the **river**, as beautiful as any in the Minho, overhung by willows, fronted by gardens, and spanned by a fifteenth-century bridge. Just above it loom the ruins of the **Paço dos Condes**, the former Palace of the Counts of Barcelos, wrecked by the Great Earthquake of 1755, and now providing a shell for the **Museu Arqueologico** (daily 10am–noon & 2–6pm). This is a miscellaneous outdoor assembly of stone crosses, including a fourteenth-century crucifix locally famed for its connection with the *Senhor do Galo* – the Gentleman of the Cock (see box); it also has a small display of **Rosa Ramalho's ceramics**. Just outside the museum, in the riverside gardens, stands the town's Gothic **pelourinho**.

Eating and drinking

On market day, be sure to have lunch at the *Bagoeira*'s **restaurant**, which sees a constant stream of stallholders bringing in pots and pans for takeaways. It's open in the evening, too, and meals are excellent value. Both *Dom António*, on the main Rua Dom António Barroso, and *Casa dos Arcos*, in the Rua Duques de Bragança, just north of the Solar dos Pinheiros, also have local reputations.

Other, cheaper places to eat include a bargain-basement café-restaurant around the corner from the Campo da República, in the alleyway opposite the *Templo*; and the grill-restaurant *Furna* on Largo da Madalena (closed Mon).

THE COSTA VERDE

Spurred by the flow of foreign currency into the Algarve, the Portuguese Tourist Board is energetically trying to promote the Minho's almost continuous line of sandy beaches as the **Costa Verde** – a zone which seems to stretch inland along the left bank of the river itself and covers much of the Minho hinterland. So far, the seaside element of the campaign hasn't quite worked, for despite the enticing promises of "unpolluted beaches with a high iodine content . . . health for the whole year", Costa Verde is green for a reason. It can be drizzly and overcast right through midsummer and the Atlantic here is never too warm. Still, if that doesn't bother you and the weather's looking good there's amazing potential; you can pick almost any road, any village, and find a great **beach** virtually to yourself.

The coast between Póvoa de Varzim and Caminha is actually an almost continuous beach, with the road running for the most part a kilometre or so inland. There are at least four **buses** a day in each direction, most using the resort of **Viana do Castelo** – very much the main event on this coast – as an axis. In addition, there are regular **trains** along the coast from Viana to Caminha.

North from Porto to Viana

The section of coast immediately **north of Póvoa de Varzim** (see p.190) is really only accessible by those with their own transport, since the train doesn't touch the coast between Póvoa and Viana do Castelo. There are buses, but it's slow going. The route, however, has its rewards, not least because much of this part of the Costa Verde is protected from development by law: the coastline between the Rio Neiva estuary and south to Apúlia comes under the *Área de Paisagem Protegida do Litoral de Esposende*.

Esposende and Ofir

The easiest place to reach by public transport is **ESPOSENDE**, 20km north of Póvoa. A rather drab sprawl of buildings, it is actually sited inland on the estuary of the Rio Cávado, with the nearest beaches 4km by road across the estuary at **OFIR**, where a couple of large luxury hotels have been built on a beautiful spit of pine-backed sand. If you are driving, this could be a good place to stop and swim, but it's not enticing enough for a stay.

Mar

North of Ofir, you probably won't see another tourist all the way to the little fishing village of **MAR** (or, more fully, SÃO BARTOLOMEU DO MAR), which fronts one of the best stretches of the Costa Verde. It's just 15km south of the resort of Viana, but there is still refreshingly little to the place: just a church, shop and café (with a few **rooms** to let), and good unofficial camping amid the pines.

As well as fishing, the local economy revolves around gathering **seaweed**. Traditionally, whole families harvest it on the beach using huge shrimping nets, which are then hauled across the sands by beautiful wooden carts pulled by oxen. Although the methods are changing, and tractors are supplanting beasts, the seaweed is still stacked at the edge of the village to dry before being spread as fertiliser on the coastal fields.

Viana do Castelo

VIANA DO CASTELO is the one town in the Minho you could describe as a resort – and it's in fact all the more attractive for it. A lively, elegant place, it has an historic old centre, above-average restaurants and, some distance from the town itself, one of the best beaches in the north. It's also beautifully positioned, spread along the north bank of the Lima estuary and shaped by the thick wooded hill of Monte de Santa Luzia, which is strewn with Celtic remains.

If you can be in the area toward the end of August, Viana's **romaria** (see box overpage) is the biggest and most exciting festival of the Minho.

Orientation and accommodation

The **train station** is at the north end of the main Avenida dos Combatentes da Grande Guerra, a street which cuts right through the town and down to the river. There's a seasonal **Turismo** stand at the station, though the main office is in the centre: walk down the avenue and look for the sign pointing to the left; it's at Rua do Hospital Velho, off Praça da Erva (Mon–Sat 9am–12.30pm & 2.30–6pm; Sun 9.30am–12.30pm; ☎058/226 20).

Apart from at *festa*-time, there is a **bus stop** in the centre by the river, on Largo 5 de Outubro, from where you can catch services to Braga and Ponte de Lima. Otherwise, all buses depart from the *Central de Camionagem*, at the top end of Rua da Bandeira, some twenty minutes' walk from the centre.

Accommodation

Pensions are easy enough to find, though in summer, and particularly during the *romaria*, **rooms** in private houses offer the best deals; for possibilities, ask at the Turismo, or look in the windows of houses. You might also ask there about accommodation at **farms** and **manorhouses** in the surrounding villages: they're an ideal way to get to know the countryside, if you have transport.

Camping is a poor alternative, given the range of accommodation available, though the town's two sites (both open all year except Christmas) do at least have the advantage of being by the Cabedelo beach; take the ferry across the river and walk from there.

PENSIONS

Residencial Dolce Vita, Rua do Poço 44 (☎058/248 60). Excellent-value rooms above a fine pizza restaurant. ②

Pensão Guerreiro, Rua Grande 14-1° (☎058/82 20 99). Down-at-heel place with shared bathrooms, but friendly (and with good meals in the restaurant). ②

Residencial Laranjeira, Rua General Luís do Rego 45 (☎058/82 22 61). A good choice, just off the main avenue, with small, pleasant rooms. Friendly, fresh and comfortable, and with breakfast included in the price. ③

Pensão Laranjeira, Rua Manuel Espregueira 24 (☎058/82 22 58). A cheaper annexe of the *Residencial Laranjera*. Unexceptional rooms, but plenty of them if you're desperate. ②

Residencial Magalhães, Rua Manuel Espregueira 62 (☎058/82 32 93). Twin and triple rooms, with or without bath, furnished in best Minho tradition, with dark, carved headboards on the beds. ③

Residencial Terra Linda, Rua Luís Jácome 11–15 (☎058/82 89 81). Average and adequate, but tries hard to please. Only its rooms without bath are in this price category. ③

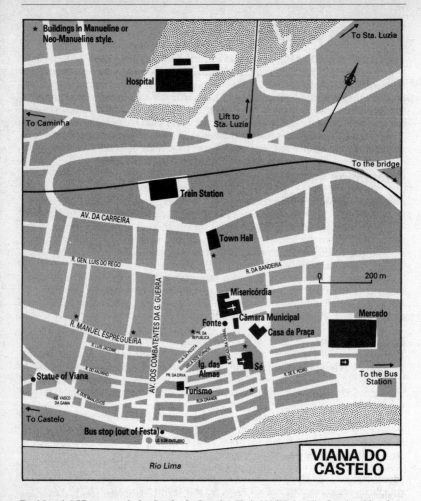

★ Buildings in Manueline or Neo-Manueline style.

To Sta. Luzia

Hospital

To Caminha

Lift to Sta. Luzia

To the bridge

Train Station

AV. DA CARREIRA

Town Hall

R. GEN. LUIS DO REGO

R. DA BANDEIRA

0   200 m

Misericórdia

Fonte

Câmara Municipal

Mercado

R. MANUEL ESPREGUEIRA

Casa da Praça

AV. DOS COMBATENTES DA G. GUERRA

R. LUIS JACOME

PÇ. DA REPUBLICA

R. DO ANJINHO

Ig. das Almas

Sé

R. DE S. PEDRO

Statue of Viana

PÇ. DA ERVA

To the Bus Station

LG. VASCO DA GAMA

R. DOS MANJOVOS

Turismo

RUA GRANDE

To Castelo

Bus stop (out of Festa)

LG. S DE OUTUBRO

Rio Lima

VIANA DO CASTELO

Residencial Vianense, Avda. Conde da Carreira 79 (☎058/82 31 18). Comfortable, clean and near the train station. ③

Residencial Jardim, Largo 5º de Outubro 68 (☎058/82 89 15). Overlooking the river, at the bottom of town, this has spotless, well-furnished rooms with bath and TV. Good views if you get a balcony. ④

Pensão Viana Mar Avda. dos Combatentes da Grande Guerra 215 (☎058/82 89 62). Another reasonably good place, with warm rooms in winter, though not quite up to top Viana standards. ④

CAMPSITES

Inatel (☎058/32 20 42). For carnet-holders only, and used by Porto families for summer-long camping holidays.

Orbitur (☎058/32 21 67). Overpriced for what you get, but closer to the beach.

The Town

Viana has long been a prosperous and seafaring town. It produced some of the greatest colonists of the "discoveries" under Dom Manuel, and in the eighteenth century was the first centre for the shipment of port wine to England. Many of the buildings reflect these times and, unusually for the north, you'll notice Manueline mouldings around the doors and windows of Viana's mansions. The Turismo in **Praça da Erva** is next to an especially fine example and makes a good first stop.

At the heart of Viana's old town is the distinctive and beautiful **Praça da República**, a square enclosed by a wonderfully elegant ensemble of buildings. You'll see copies of its showpiece Renaissance fountain in towns throughout the Minho, but few structures as elegant and curious as the old **Misericórdia** (almshouse) that lines one side of the square. Built in 1598, this is one of the most original and successful buildings of the Portuguese Renaissance, its upper storeys supported by deliberately archaic, primitive-looking caryatids. The adjacent sixteenth-century Town Hall has been brightly restored, and stands foursquare above a medieval arcade, while just off the square is the **Igreja Matriz**, Viana's parish church, which retains a Gothic door of some interest.

The **Museu Municipal** (Tues–Sun 9.30am–noon & 2–5pm; 100$00) adds further to these impressions of Viana's sixteenth- to nineteenth-century opulence, contained within an eighteenth-century palace and housing a notable collection of ceramics and furniture. It stands near the end of Rua Manuel Espregueira, ten minutes' walk from the square on the far side of Avenida dos Combatentes da Grande Guerra.

If you continue past here, you'll eventually reach the old **fort** by the sea, in an area known as the **Campo do Castelo**. Outside the walls, on Fridays, Viana's **market** takes place; it's much smaller than the famous one at Barcelos but attracts many of the same stallholders.

Monte de Santa Luzia

Wherever you stand in Viana, **Monte de Santa Luzia** makes its presence felt, an ugly modern basilica glowering from its summit like an evil eye. But don't let this – the ostensible highlight of the town – put you off. It's a great walk up, through the pines and eucalyptus trees (take the shortcut over the railway tracks), or you can be hauled to the top by an old **funicular**. This starts its haul (hourly 10am–noon, and half hourly 12.30–7pm; 60$00) from just behind the railway station; to reach it, walk through the station and cross the tracks. En route, there are tremendous views down the coast and along the River Lima.

At the summit of the Monte, there's a café and plenty of wooded walks. While the **basilica** itself is of little interest, look for the side-entrance (marked *Zimbório*), where steps climb right through the building and out on top of the dome itself. It's very narrow, very steep, and – at the top – very scary if the wind has picked up, but the views are magnificent.

Behind the basilica, amid the woods and just below the luxury *Hotel Santa Luzia*, lie the ruins of a Celto-Iberian **citânia** (see "Citânia de Briteiros", p.219). These include the foundations of dozens of small, circular stone huts, a thick village wall, and partly paved streets. Occupied from around 500 BC, they were only abandoned with the Roman pacification of the north under Emperor Augustus (circa 26 BC). The ruins have recently been fenced off but there should be access from the approach road to the hotel.

Praia do Cabedelo

Praia do Cabedelo, Viana's town beach, lies across the river, connected by a seasonal and very rickety ferry, the *Saudade*, which leaves from wooden steps down from the Largo 5 de Outubro. The only road access from town to beach is over the old metal bridge, with its half-metre wide sidewalks nudged by lorries. Given sun, the beach is more or less perfect – a low curving bay with good (but not wild) breakers, and a real horizon-stretching expanse of sand. From here the beach extends northwards, virtually unbroken, to the Spanish border at Caminha, and south to Póvoa de Varzim. For the energetic, either of these routes makes a memorable and enjoyable hike. For details of the northern route, see below.

If you're interested, Viana's **docks** are accessible through gaps in the fence near the ferry terminal and there seems to be no objection to your wandering around by the large ships and the smaller vessels of the fishing fleet.

Food and practicalities

There's a wide choice of places to eat and drink in town, as you might expect from a busy resort. Some are lunchtime workers' cafés, and very cheap, and there's a full range of tourist **restaurants**, too, many of which are extremely good since they have to cater mostly for demanding Portuguese visitors rather than foreigners. There is a permanent **market** at the eastern end of town, on Rua Martim Velho, for general provisions.

Restaurants and bars

Casa de Pasto Trasmontano, Rua Gago Coutinho 12, behind the old town hall in the Praça da República. An incredibly low-cost establishment for basic meals.

Dolce Vita, Rua do Poço 44. The wood-fired pizzas are a bit disappointing, but there's pasta, too, and a fine winelist. Don't worry if it looks full – there is plenty of space downstairs.

Laranjeira, Rua Manuel Espregueira 24. The restaurant here, below the *pensão*, receives varying reports, without doubt partly because it's always busy and sometimes very slapdash. Worth chancing, though, for reasonably priced Portuguese meals.

Marisqueria Almoço, Rua General Luís do Rego. Carefully cooked, generous dishes – highly recommended.

Restaurante Pekim, Rua General Luís do Rego. Open daily for large portions of economical Chinese food.

Os Três Arcos, Largo João Tomás da Costa 25, by the Jardim Marginal (closed Mon). The best restaurant in town, with excellent food, a full list of *vinhos verdes*, and a bar where you can eat much more cheaply from the same menu – mostly seafood, but the turkey is good. If you want a table, call in earlier to book.

Os Três Potes, Beco dos Fornos 7 (☎058/234 32). Incredibly popular in high season, with national costumes and music at weekends. Good traditional food, but relatively pricey, with full meals running to at least 3000$00. Again, book ahead in summer.

SNACKS AND BARS

Pastelaria Paris, Avda. dos Combatentes da Grande Guerra. Great cakes, pool room, and decent toilets for a change!

Asturias, by the docks. A snack bar serving hearty soup and the biggest *tostas mistas* you'll ever have the good fortune to encounter. A great place for lunch.

O Triângulo, Rua dos Manjovos 14. Quiet and pleasant seafood and snack joint.

Girassol Café, Jardim Marginal. Lovely spot for a *bica*; closes at 7pm.

THE VIANA ROMARIA

Viana's main *romaria*, dedicated to **Nossa Senhora da Agonía** – Our Lady of Sorrows – takes place for three days around the weekend nearest to August 20. A combination of carnival and fair, fulfilling an important business function for the local communities, it's a great time to be in town.

Events kick off with an impressive **religious parade** on the Friday. But the best day is probably **Saturday**, when there's a massive parade of floats with every village in the region providing an example of a local craft or pursuit: a marvellous display of incongruities, with threshers pounding away in traditional dress while being pulled by a new Lamborghini tractor. If you want a seat in the stands, get a ticket well in advance.

Each of the three days there are lunchtime **processions** with *gigantones* (carnival giants), folk dancing, remarkably loud drum bands, pipe bands and, needless to say, concerted drinking. The blessing of the fishing boats on Monday morning is quite moving – women in the fishing quarter decorate their streets with pictures in coloured sawdust on religious and quotidian themes. And there are nightly **firework displays** too, of immense brilliance and noise.

Nightlife

Romaria time aside, there's not an awful lot going on after dark in Viana. But if you're bubbling with energy, the following are worth a try:

Ministério Music Bar, Rua do Tourinho 41, just off Praça da Erva. Groovy music in a dimly lit and vaguely "alternative" youth hangout. Pricey cover charge but fun.

Disco-Pub-Clube-Viana Sol, off Largo Vasco da Gama by *Hotel Viana Sol*. Open from the afternoon until 3am, or 4am on Saturday nights. Another very youthful crowd. 800$00 cover.

Listings

Banks Several main banks have branches on the Praça da República.

Boat trips *AVIC*, Avda. dos Combatentes (☎058/82 97 05) runs trips up the Rio Lima.

Car rental Avis, Rua do Gontim (☎058/82 39 94); Hertz, Avda. Conde da Carreira (☎058/82 22 50).

Chemists *Nelsina*, Praça da República; *Central*, Rua Manuel Espregueira.

Cinemas *Palácio*, Rua de Aveiro; *Verde Viana*, Praça 1° de Maio.

Hospital Avda. 25 de Abril (☎058/82 90 81).

Swimming pool There's a municipal pool on Avda. 28 de Setembro.

Taxis Available from ranks along Avda. dos Combatentes.

Viana to Caminha

North of Viana the **railway line** follows the coast all the way to Caminha, the trains stopping at all the villages en route, and offering easy access to a sequence of – for the most part deserted – beaches. An alternative, if you're feeling active, is to **walk**; one of our readers covered the stretch in a couple of days, camping overnight among the sheltered dunes at Afife, 10km north of Viana.

Afife

AFIFE, whichever way you get there, is certainly a good goal: a tiny village with a fort, a small **pensão-restaurante** (the *Compostela*; ③) and a useful café-shop at the railway station. The dunes – and a particularly wonderful expanse of beach –

are fifteen to twenty minutes' walk from the village, the least frequented parts being to the south. On the north side, there is an official **campsite** in the pine woods at GELFA.

Vila Praia de Âncora

Five kilometres up the coast from Afife, and the next stop on the railway line, is **VILA PRAIA DE ÂNCORA**. This is larger – almost a real resort – and popular with the locals at weekends. The beach, which is right alongside the railway line, is again superb, sheltered by hills and drifting back into a beautiful river estuary, where you can swim enjoyably even when the Atlantic breezes are blowing towels around the sands. A seafront fort adds a bit of character.

Finding **accommodation** for a few days here should not be hard. Choices include the *Pensão-Restaurante Sereia da Gelfa*, Pinhal da Gelfa (☎058/91 16 30; ②); the rather pricey *Hotel Meira*, Rua 5 de Outubro 56 (☎058/91 11 11; ⑤); and private rooms, arranged through a summer **Turismo** office. There's also unofficial camping by the fort on the beach. **Restaurants** are plentiful, as is fresh fish; the *Café Central*, opposite the train station, has the cheapest meals.

Moledo

North of Vila Praia de Âncora, **MOLEDO** offers the railway traveller's last chance of sea swimming (though there are river beaches all along the Minho; see section below). Very much in the same mould, it again has a fort – this time half-ruined, guarding the river from a long, sandy spit – and is predominantly a Portuguese family resort. If you're heading for Caminha, Valença, or Spain, you could easily stop off here, wander down to the beach, and catch the following train on.

ALONG THE RIO MINHO

At Moledo, the **train line** finally leaves the coast to follow the south bank of the **Rio Minho**, which meanders northeastwards forming the country's border with Spain. **Caminha** is the first river town you reach, a pleasant stopover, either for a night or for a meal between trains. Beyond here, several small fortified towns guard the Portuguese side of the river, with the Minho rail line coming to a halt in perhaps the best of the lot, **Valença**, which is also the major crossing-point into Spain. The best section of the river route, however, is from Valença east to **Melgaço**, a minor border crossing, with buses on the Spanish side to Orense.

The rail line no longer extends east of Valença, though local buses run on east to Monção and Melgaço.

Caminha

Resembling a smaller version of Viana do Castelo, **CAMINHA** is a quiet river port with a few reminders of better days. These are principally in the main square, with its battlemented town hall and Renaissance clocktower. In previous years the town had a ferry link across the river to La Guardia in Spain, though this is currently suspended; meanwhile, a service still operates to the east at Vila Nova de Cerveira (see facing page).

The town and the Island-Fort

Caminha's most distinguished building is the **Igreja Matriz**, a couple of minutes' walk away toward the river; take the street through the arch, past the Turismo. This church was built toward the end of the fifteenth century when the town was reputed to rival Porto in trade, and it still stands within part of the old city walls. Try and find someone with a key, for it has a magnificent inlaid *artesanato* ceiling – a rare burst of Moorish inspiration in the north. Note also the figures carved on the two Renaissance doorways, one on the north side giving the finger to Spain across the river!

A couple of kilometres south of town, the river-island of **Fortaleza da Ínsua** makes an enjoyable trip – local fishermen run trips across on Sundays. If you want to arrange something during the week (for the next morning), ask in the *Café Valadares* for directions to António Garrafão's house. He will only go if there is a reasonably large – or affluent – group gathered.

Practicalities

The town has a choice of two **pensions**: the new and excellent-value *Residencial Arca Nova* (③), by the station, and the more upmarket but rather dreary *Galo d'Ouro*, Rua da Corredoura 15 (☎058/92 11 60; ④). Alternatives include a few private **rooms** in houses near the station (turn right and head for the water, then turn left), and the local member of the *Turismo de Habitação* scheme: the *Casa de Esteiró* (☎058/92 13 56; ⑤), a small neighbourhood house with lovely gardens.

There are also two nearby **campsites**. The better of them is a little inland at VILAR DE MOUROS (weekday buses 11.30am and 6.30pm from the café/stop 200m left out of the station), which is nicely positioned, by a small river, and has a swimming pool. The other, which tends to be crowded in summer, is an *Orbitur* site (☎058/92 12 95), 2km to the south, next to the river and opposite the Fortaleza island (weekday buses from the town hall in the main square at 11.30am, 1pm and 6pm stop close by).

Among the town's restaurants, the *Caminhense* (in the main square) has superb regional specialities, and there's good food, too, at the more reasonably priced *A Lareira* and *Adega do Chico* on Rua Visconde de Sousa Rego (head up the right-hand side of the main square, away from the clocktower).

Near Caminha: Vila Nova de Cerveira

More or less hourly **trains** run along the banks of the Rio Minho to **VILA NOVA DE CERVEIRA**, 12km to the northeast. A small walled town, this has an important local function in its car- and passenger-ferry – actually little more than a floating platform – which drifts every half-hour across the river to GOYAN in Galicia. The ferry (60$00 passengers, 400$00 cars) has turned the village into something of a shopping centre for Spaniards, but it remains a pleasant and accessible place and in many respects is more enticing than the bigger and better known Valença further upstream. It has a fair bit of life through the presence of an art college.

If you wanted to stay, there's accommodation available at both ends of the scale. For budget travellers, there is a pleasant **youth hostel** at Largo 16 de Fevereiro 21 (☎051/79 61 13), which boasts its own kitchen and a terrace. And if you have money to blow, there is also an excellent **pousada**, the *Dom Dinis* (☎051/79 56 01; ⑥), built within the old fortress walls and overlooking the ramparts. Though not a historic building, this would provide a memorable first or last night in Portugal.

Valença and around

The beautiful old border "town" – in reality a village – of **VALENÇA** is quite absurdly quaint, clumped amid perfectly preserved multi-layered seventeenth-century ramparts on a hillock above the river. There are great walks down by the river and along the **ramparts** (watch out for hidden stairwells) and, an equally fine sight just inside the walls, a fire station with a couple of gleaming red engines straight out of a 1950s children's book.

In the daytime these charms are exploited by myriad souvenir shops, catering for the day-trippers who cross the border from Spain to pick up Portuguese linen and low-duty electrical goods. Small-scale smuggling of such items is probably Valença's major industry and, increasingly, the extent of this commercialism is reducing the appeal of the town – Tuy, across the river in Spain, is probably nicer. By late afternoon, though, the crowds are gone and at night it's almost a ghost town.

The newer part of town, to the south of the ramparts, has nothing of interest but it's here that you'll track down all the basic necessities. Come on Wednesday and you'll encounter the huge weekly **market** held beside the **Turismo** (daily 9am–7pm; ☎051/233 74), between the station and town.

Practicalities

Arriving by train, there are no obvious signs to the old town; turn right at the avenue that leads away from the station. The train line stops at Valença and to continue eastwards, following the river, you'll have to take the bus.

Valença isn't a bad place to stay, and there are **rooms** available throughout the town: try asking at the *Bar Cantinho* on Rua Conselheiro Lopes da Silva, or in any of the countless restaurants. More formally, Valença has several **pensions**, including the *Rio Minho* (Largo da Estação, ☎051/223 31; ③), down by the train station: a bit the worse for wear and often full, it has a good restaurant. And on a different scale altogether, there are the comforts of the swanky *Pousada de São Teotónio* (☎051/82 40 20; ⑤), which is located inside the fortress itself, overlooking the border with Spain. Even if this is out of your range, a drink in the bar – or even lunch in the excellent restaurant – is money well spent.

Alternatively, you could **camp** below the ramparts at the western end, as numerous summer travellers do, or find your own hidden corner between the fortifications themselves.

Recommended among the **restaurants** is the *Monumento*, by the gateway to the old town, which does a wonderful, spicy *arroz de marisco*.

Crossing to Spain: Tuy

Just a mile from Valença, Spanish **TUY** is an ancient, pyramid-shaped town with a grand battlemented parish church. It, too, is partly walled and it looks far sturdier than Valença, though the first English Guide to Portugal (*Murray's* in 1855) reported that "the guns of Valença could without difficulty lay Tuy in ruins". If you're not planning to go on by train, walk across the frontier bridge to explore Tuy's old quarter by the river.

By **rail** you can go direct from Valença to Vigo, which is in easy reach – by road or rail – of Santiago de Compostela, the ancient and beautiful pilgrimage town of Galicia.

Inland: Paredes de Coura

PAREDES DE COURA, 28km south of Valença, claims to be the oldest village in Portugal – and also declares itself a centre of trout fishing. The first claim is conceivable, the second a bit stretched, as these days it's all done from a feed-pen. If you are headed for Ponte da Barca or Ponte de Lima (see "The Lima Valley"), it's a pleasant enough detour, nonetheless. You can climb up to the top of the town for views over an almost Swiss landscape, with chalet-style houses and white church spires, or follow the track down beyond the football field to the river for the town's best swimming spot (at lunchtime no one is around).

The best **place to stay** is the *Pensão Miquelina* on Rua Conselheiro Miguel Dantas (☎058/921 03; ②), which is not far from the **Turismo**, itself housed in an old prison. A daily **bus** runs to the town from Valença, leaving at around 5pm from the old market, on the way to the train station.

Monção and around

MONÇÃO, 16km east of Valença, also preserves a **fortress**, though it doesn't quite make the grade – there being little more than a doorway, a section of walling above the bus station, and a high defensive walkway that runs along the northern, river-facing side of town. Perhaps for this reason, Monção has escaped much of the daytime tourist attention that bedevils the towns to the west – the liveliest day to visit is probably Thursday, market day. But there's an attractive old centre, which is always worth a stroll, and the town's history, in which two local women played a prominent part, provides a colourful backdrop to the surviving fortifications and buildings.

The principal figure in this is **Deu-la-deu Martins**, who is commemorated by a statue in the Largo da Loreto (opposite the Turismo, close to the central Praça da República). Her tale, similar to a number of other siege accounts across Portugal and Spain, recalls a crucial moment in the fourteenth century, when the Spanish troops had besieged the townspeople to the point of starvation. Deu-la-deu baked some cakes, using much skill and next to no flour, and had them presented to the Spanish camp with an offer to "make more if they needed them". The psychological effect of this bluff was so great that the enemy promptly gave up and went away. Local *pãozinhos* (little bread cakes) are still baked in her honour; her birthplace is off the praça, above the butcher's shop on the arched side road.

A second Spanish siege, in the seventeenth-century Wars of Restoration, was relieved in 1659 when the **Countess of Castelo Melhor**, perhaps inspired by earlier example, resorted to psychological warfare once again. The story goes that, having negotiated a ceasefire on condition that full military honours be given to her men, the Countess relinquished her 236 surviving fighters to the Spanish army; knowing nothing of the town's two thousand fatalities, the enemy assumed they had been kept at bay by this paltry platoon, and duly retreated in shame.

In the town, behind the mask of new paint and building work, there are a couple of interesting older places to visit. The seventeenth-century **Misericórdia** on the central square contains some magnificent *azulejos*, as does the Romanesque **Matriz** – at the centre of a maze of ancient streets – which houses various tombs, including that of Deu-la-deu herself. The local **festivals** of *Corpo de Deus* (Corpus

Christi; June 18) and particularly of *Nossa Senhora das Dores* (Sept 19–22) are interesting times to visit – though you are unlikely to find a room. The former perpetuates medieval superstition in an elaborate enactment of the Fight against Evil, a battle that looks something like the tale of Saint George and the Dragon.

Transport and rooms

The Monção **bus station** stands in front of the defunct train station, with the town centre straight ahead. There's a **Turismo** in the Largo do Loreto (☎051/527 57). For travellers to Spain, there's a simple **car ferry** across the Minho.

Pensions raise their rates with each passing day, but you can still find a reasonably priced bed at the *Pensão Central,* Largo Deu-la-deu (☎051/65 23 14; ②) or at *Residencial Esteves*, Rua General Pimenta de Castro, near the station, ☎051/65 23 86; ③). There are also **rooms** available above the *Pastelaria Raiano* next to the *Central*, or above the *Galeria Melis*, on Praça Deu-la-deu. Better still for price and atmosphere is the *Casa Constantino*, Rua da Independência 24, with a couple of rooms overlooking the river. Or finally, in the rock-bottom range, there's *Ponte de Lima* (near the *Esteves*), which promotes itself as "an ancient house with modern service" – don't believe it!

For an upmarket *Turismo de Habitação* accommodation, *Casa de Rodas* (☎051/521 05; ⑤) is a lovely, low, eighteenth-century building, just out of town, with four guest rooms. The Turismo will find out if there's space and give directions.

Big dinners

The town is an excellent place to push the gastronomic boat out. Minho trout and salmon are always tremendous and between January and March the rich, eel-like **lamprey** are in season – avoid them in other months, as they can be toxic if they're not absolutely fresh. The local **wine**, the finest *vinho verde* in the country, is available on draft in a couple of bars off the main square; the most delicious bottled variety is *Palácio da Brejoeira Alvarinho*, which, as another splendid Monção tourist leaflet one-liner puts it, "someone in France once classified as being the best in the world".

Among the cheapest **places to eat** are the Spanish-run *El Pollo Rico* (opposite the station), for good grilled chicken. Fancier, though not overly expensive, are *Restaurante Mané*, on Rua General Pimenta de Castro, which has the best fish dishes in town but no atmosphere, and the pleasant *Quinta da Oliveira*, 400m down the road to Braga on the Estrada dos Arcos.

Around Monção: the Spa, Cortes and Lapela

The presence of a **thermal spa** to the east of Monção (follow the walls) has turned the town into something of a resort for Spanish day-trippers and Portuguese weekenders. Aside from the dubious pleasures of the alkaline water, there's a park and a free **campsite** by the river; if you swim in the latter, take care with the currents.

Further afield to the west of the town, a pleasant walk trails off into the woods from the stop at *Senhora da Cabeça* to the hamlet of **CORTES**, which was Monção's medieval site. About 3km further west is **LAPELA**, whose river beach is safer for swimmers. The village is dominated by a lofty **tower**, all that remains of a fortress destroyed in 1706 to provide materials for the restoration of the battered walls of Monção.

East to Melgaço

An historic incident in Anglo-Portuguese relations took place on the fragile-looking bridge over the Rio Mouro just before **CEIVÃES**, 10km along the road from Monção to Melgaço. Cascades of garbage tumble down the banks below the spot where John of Gaunt, the Duke of Lancaster, arranged the marriage of his daughter Philippa to King Dom João I in 1386, an arrangement that resulted in the signing of the **Treaty of Windsor** between the two countries. It gave rise to an alliance lasting over six hundred years and to the naming of numerous public places in honour of "Filipa de Lencastre".

Thermal spa enthusiasts might want to stop at **PESO** (5km short of Monção). This is a tiny spa town, spread along the main road and looking down on a magnificent curve of the river. There's a lovely (and free) **campsite** set in lush riverside gardens, a **Turismo**, and several **pensions**, of which the *Rocha* (☎051/423 56; ②) and *Águas de Melgaço* (☎051/422 62; ②) are best value.

Melgaço

MELGAÇO – the country's northernmost outpost – is a small town sitting high above the Rio Minho. If its rural origins are somewhat obscured by the modern developments that sprawl along the main road, the accent and the mentality remain unchanged. With the exception of a few *festa* days in mid-August when a display of tractors, an array of the town's long-reputed smoked hams (*presunto*), a craft exhibition, and a performance from the school banjo band are organised, very little happens. Try to arrive for the **Friday market** when chickens, ducks, sticky buns, furniture, pottery, cabbages and corsets cover the stretch of road around the old walls.

At other times the reasons for coming to Melgaço are that it is so obviously off the tourist track, and that it gives easy access to the northern part of the Parque Nacional da Peneda-Gerês and to Spanish Galicia (see below for access details). Its one historic feature is the ruined **fortress**, much fought over during the Wars of Restoration, but now little more than a tower and a few walls handy for hanging out washing.

In the alleys below the fort, a couple of **café-restaurants** offer good food at reasonable prices, while there are two **pensions** toward the main road: the pleasant and astonishingly cheap *Flôr do Minho*, south of the central square in Rua Velha (①), and the *Pemba*, near the bus stop on Largo da Calçada (☎425 55; ③).

Buses leave for Monção every day (7.45am, 2.30pm, 4.40pm, and Mon–Fri 8.40am & 11.45am), and connect with services to Braga, Coimbra, Porto and Lisbon.

Romanesque churches and the Spanish border

Short **excursions** from Melgaço might include the two **Romanesque churches** of PADERNE (3km, off the road to Monção) and NOSSA SENHORA DA ORADA (1km east).

The Spanish **border post** at PONTE BARXAS (open April–Oct 7am–midnight, Nov–March 8am–9pm) is a kilometre away from **SÃO GREGÓRIO** (10km to the east; inexpensive taxis from Melgaço). Across the frontier, buses leave for RIBADAVIA and ORENSE at 7am and 1pm (weekdays only).

Both RIBADAVIA (along the Minho and with superb red wine) and CELANOVA (on a different route to Orense and dwarfed by a vast medieval monastery) are within striking distance, and must be two of the most lovely and characteristic towns of Spanish Galicia. The Minho itself – or Miño as it becomes known – is more placid in the further reaches, as it is dammed shortly after the point when both of its banks are within Spain.

THE LIMA VALLEY AND PARQUE NACIONAL DA PENEDA-GERÊS

The **Rio Lima**, whose valley is perhaps the most beautiful in Portugal, was thought by the Romans to be the Lethe, the mythical River of Oblivion. Beyond it, they imagined, lay the Elysian Fields – and to cross would mean certain destruction, for its waters possessed the power of the lotus, making the traveller forget country and home. The Roman Consul Decimus Junius Brutus, having led his legions across most of Spain, had to seize the standard and plunge into the water shouting the names of his legionaries from the far bank – to show his memory remained intact – before they could be persuaded to follow.

There are roads along both banks of the Lima from **Viana do Castelo** (see p.225), where the river meets the sea. Travelling this way, regular buses pass through a series of highly attractive towns – like **Ponte de Lima** and **Ponte da Barca** – from any of which you could have fine walks into the hilly and wooded surrounding countryside, perhaps exploring one or two of the many Romanesque churches in the region, such as that at **Bravães**.

Further east, the Lima runs into the heart of the **Parque Nacional da Peneda-Gerês**, the largest nature reserve in Portugal. The easiest point of access to the central section of the park is from Ponte da Barca or nearby **Arcos de Valdevez**, though there's a possible northern approach, too, from Melgaço .

Ponte de Lima

An hour's ride east of Viana do Castelo, **PONTE DE LIMA** lies at the end of a low stone bridge, Roman in origin and said to mark the path of their first hesitant crossing. It's a delightful small town, whose crumbling old centre – as is often the way – has no specific attraction other than its air of sleepy indifference to the wider world. You might disagree if you visit in July or August, when Ponte de Lima begins to show worrying signs of midsummer tourist strain – which the local authorities plan to capitalise on by building a huge, highly un-ecological golf complex nearby. In the meantime, though – and at almost any other time of year except high summer – the town remains one of Portugal's most pleasing.

The river here offers fine swimming and has wide sandbanks where the town's bi-monthly Monday **market**, the oldest in Portugal, has been held since a charter of 1125. So, too, have the curiously named **"New Fairs"** (second/third weekend of September), a tremendous festival and market, seemingly attended by half the Minho, with a traditional bull-taunting game by the bridge, fireworks, a fairground, wandering accordionists and *gigantones*, and a large brass band competition.

At other times the evening focus is a long riverside **Alameda** shaded by magnificent plane trees; it leads to the rambling old convent of Santo António, which has a small museum of treasures in its church. In the town itself there are sixteenth-century **mansions** with stone coats of arms, and interesting remains of the old **keep**, used into the 1960s as a prison (the occupants were allowed to hang cups down from the windows for money and cigarettes).

Transport and accommodation

The **bus station** is behind the market, just a minute or so from the river. A few minutes' walk away, in Praça da República in the centre of the town, the **Turismo** (daily 9am–8pm, winter Mon–Sat 9am–1pm and 2–6pm; ☎058/94 23 35) hands out brochures and a map of town, though you're hardly lilkely to need one. It shares its premises with the headquarters of the Minho's **Turismo de Habitaçao** scheme (see box below), which provides some of the finest accommodation you'll find for rent in northern Portugal.

TURISMO DE HABITAÇÃO

The Ponte de Lima **Turismo de Habitação** (*Turihab*) organisation arranges rented accommodation in local manor houses, farms and country estates throughout the Minho. There are nearly thirty properties available in the Ponte de Lima area alone, each with usually just two or three rooms and offered on a bed-and-breakfast basis: you can find yourself staying in some extraordinary historical buildings, and even rubbing shoulders with Portuguese aristocrats who have turned their ancient seats over to the scheme. Bookings have to be made through *Turihab* (☎058/94 27 29, fax 058/94 18 64); stays are usually for a minimum of three nights; and you can expect to pay from 8–10,000$00 per room, sometimes a few thousand more for the really exclusive country houses.

Properties particularly worth enquiring about include the *Moínho de Estorãos* (an old mill); the amazing *Paço de Calheiros* country seat; the stone *Casa do Tamanqueiro*; and the eighteenth-century *Casa do Outeiro*. You'll need to your own transport to reach most of these houses, which lie from one to ten kilometres away from Ponte de Lima.

Other *Turihab* houses are scattered throughout the Minho: some are mentioned elsewhere in this chapter; or ask at local Turismos for details.

The town has just a couple of regular **pensions**: the *São João*, in Largo de São João (☎058/94 12 88; ②), near the Roman bridge, which is excellent and serves good food downstairs; and the comfortable *Isaura*, on the waterfront, directly opposite the beach, with grandstand views of the comings and goings before – and after – the market. However, there are budget **rooms** above the *Restaurante Catrina* (①), on the riverfront.

Alternatively, you could **camp** across the bridge on the riverbank, where during the New Fairs a rainbow-coloured site emerges, with families washing clothes, auctioning cattle, and letting off fireworks through the night.

Bars and restaurants

Ponte de Lima's **bars** serve wine straight from the barrel into handleless porcelain cups. There are a few inexpensive café-**restaurants** along the riverfront – the *Catrina* is a good one – but the best place to eat traditional local food is the *Restaurante Encanada*, Praça Municipal (closed Thurs), which is close to the market and has a terrace overlooking the river. The food is good and very modestly priced.

Walks around Ponte de Lima

All around Ponte de Lima is beautiful **walking country**, especially along both banks of the river east of the town. The Turismo has gone to some pains to produce a set of nominally marked trails, accompanied by the leaflets you pick up from them. Keep your wits about you, however, as directions and left/right details are not all they might be.

One walk goes over the bridge and up a winding, dusty road to the TV-mast-topped summit of the hill opposite the town. Here stands the chapel of **Santo Ovidio**, patron saint of ears. If, as is likely, it is closed, you can still peep through the grille and see the walls strung with wax ears and a table covered in them. Each is a model of the afflicted ear of a parishioner, brought here for saintly treatment, or as thanks for relief received.

East to Bravães and Ponte da Barca

In almost any village in the Lima region you'll come upon a **Romanesque church**, simple and rustic in design but often with beautiful naive carvings on its doorways and columns. Most were built in the twelfth and thirteenth centuries under the supervision of the Cluniac monks, who brought their architecture to Spain and Portugal along the pilgrimage routes to Santiago de Compostela in Galicia; the main Portuguese route ran through Braga and so Minho has the highest concentration.

They are really best encountered by chance, hidden among the trees of some once-remote roadside village: and this, even if you plan the visit, is what it feels like to arrive at the twelfth-century church at **BRAVÃES**, 14km east of Ponte de Lima along the N203. The church, **São Salvador**, stands just to the right of the road in this small hamlet – a lovely walk through low hills traced everywhere with vines, often suspended in trellises above some other crop. The church's two sculpted **doorways** are perhaps the best in the country, filled with carvings of doves, griffins, monkeys and two of the local wide-horned oxen. The interior is kept locked but ask at the cottage behind and the doors will be flung open for you, lighting up medieval murals of Saint Sebastian and the Virgin.

There's a **bar** in Bravães where local transport-users can debate the chances of a bus going on to Ponte da Barca, 4km further east; it's probably quicker to walk.

Ponte da Barca

Ignoring the modern suburbs of **PONTE DA BARCA**, and heading for the river, the old town quarters form a quintessential pastoral vision. The Lima is spanned here by a lovely, fifteenth-century bridge; alongside is a splendid *mercado* and, on the corner, a seasonal **Turismo**. On Tuesdays there's a superb **market**, which again spreads out by the riverbanks, drawing hundreds of people from outlying hamlets, in an almost medieval atmosphere. Walk down to the other end of the main road and you'll come to the cattle market area. It's worth noting that the town's great **romaria** takes place around the weekend closest to August 19.

There are two top-value **pension–restaurants** overlooking the bridge: the *Pensão Maria Gomes*, Rua Conselheiro Rocha Peixoto 13 (☎058/422 88; ②) is especially recommended, and worth phoning ahead to book. If you don't eat here, the *Pensão Panorama*, Centro Comercial Emigrante 1, up the hill at the east end of town, is a fair deal better than you might expect from its address. For meals, you have also have the choice of the slightly upmarket *Varanda de Lima*, Largo do Curro 17 (close to the bridge), and the *Bar do Rio*, close to the Praia Fluvial – a beach on the left bank of the river, which is a nice place to dine watching the sunset. If you want to camp, it's possible to pitch a tent (fairly discreetly) along the river bank and enjoy perfect, pink-hazed, evening light.

From the **bus stop** by the bridge, near the arches of the town hall, there are connections to Lindoso (Mon–Fri 7.35am, 5.20pm, and 6.30pm, plus 12.10pm every day) and Braga (5 daily).

Walks from Ponte da Barca

The Ponte da Barca Turismo publishes a useful pamphlet on the town and region, which, like that of Ponte de Lima, features several fine walks. The **seven-hour circuit** described from SÃO MIGUEL is highly recommended: an uphill hike most of the way, but passing through some gorgeous villages – SOBREDO, especially, which seems unchanged from centuries past – and with food available at several points along the way (midway at GERMIL, for example).

Arcos de Valdevez

As an alternative to the main Minho river route – or a diversion from it – you might contemplate exploring the Rio Vez, which can be reached just 5km north of Ponte da Barca, at **ARCOS DE VALDEVEZ** ("Arches of the Valley of the Vez"). This town comes alive in mid-August with a three-day **festival**, featuring *gigantones* (giant figures), *zés pereiras* (red-caped drummers), horse races and fireworks. Traditionally these celebrations should take place on the last weekend of the holiday month, but they've been shifted to take account of local emigrants who return to work abroad at the end of August; one of the festival days is actually named the *Dia do Emigrante*. At other times, it is a sleepy little place, with a weekly spot of animation for the **Wednesday market**.

Practicalities

Like Ponte da Barca, Arcos de Valvedez is a useful point of departure for the Peneda-Gerês national park; the **Turismo** opposite the bridge (July–Sept 9am–1pm & 2–7pm, except Sun 9am–noon) has free maps and advice on this. For information on the **bus** service to Lindoso, ask at the depot above the Largo da Lapa, from where there are also regular services to Monção, Ponte de Lima and Viana do Castelo. Buses to Soajo and Braga leave from a stop by the Turismo.

The town has several good and reasonably priced **pensions**, including the *Pensão Ribeira*, Largo do Milagres (☎058/651 74; ②), and the more expensive *Pensão Tavares*, Rua Padre Manuel José da Cunha Brito (☎ 058/662 53; ④). A third, attractively sited in Rua de São João in Valeta, the upper part of town (second left up to Largo da Lapa and down the left-hand side of the church), is the small and unpretentious *Pensão Flor do Minho* (Largo da Valeta 11–15, ☎058/652 16; ②). You can **camp** unofficially on the riverbank, downstream from the town.

There is a nice cluster of restaurants in Rua São João. For a real treat, though, visit *Casa Delfim*, down the right-hand side of the church in Largo da Lapa, run by an aging "world-famous" accordionist and stacked with his instruments, any of which are liable, suddenly, to be snatched up for in impromptu jam.

Parque Nacional da Peneda-Gerês

The magnificent **PARQUE NACIONAL DA PENEDA-GERÊS** is hardly a secret. Caldas do Gerês, the main centre of the park, attracts more tourists than anywhere else in the Minho, with the possible exception of Viana, and at weekends, when Portuguese campers arrive in force, parts of it can seem a bit too close to civilisation. The park as a whole, though, is large enough to absorb the great numbers of visitors. It's split into two distinct parts, based around the southern **Serra do Gerês** and the wilder northern section containing the **Serra da Peneda**; this latter area, particularly (best approached from Melgaço, on the Minho), remains largely undiscovered.

Maps and information

A **survey map for the Gerês** is available from the *Instituto Geográfico e Cadastral* (see Lisbon "Directory"), or *Porto Editora* (see Porto "Directory"). It is not very reliable, dating as it does from 1959, since when dams have been built and whole areas submerged. Very much better is the **new map** available from the park information office, which details altitudes and all roads (even the footpaths); the park's head office in Braga (Rua de São Geraldo 19) should have copies available, or you can pick it up on the spot in Caldas do Gerês. Maps aside, if you plan a long hike, take boots, a compass, food (for the remoter areas) and a water bottle (plenty of streams). Beware of fog in spring and winter.

Picking flowers and – more important – **lighting fires** are forbidden in Gerês. The Portuguese have an alarming habit of lighting them whenever and wherever they picnic, no doubt a factor in disastrous fires such as those that destroyed over 800 square kilometres of forest in 1985 alone – a spate that caused particular damage to the landscape of the Minho.

Staying in the park

Hotels and pensions in **Gerês** are concentrated in the town of CALDAS DO GERÊS, though there are rooms available at Campo do Gerês, Ermida and a few other villages. The best **campsite** (open May–Oct and Easter week) is at Caldas, too, though there's a second official campsite at ENTRE AMBOS-OS-RIOS, and wild camping is permitted at Lamas de Mouro, Lindoso and Mezio. Note that at Albergaria there is now *no* campsite – despite its presence on the maps – and camping in the area is not permitted. On longer walks into the wilder areas of the park, so long as you're discreet, no one will mind you putting up a tent.

In the **Peneda** section of the park, there's a new **youth hostel** (☎053/353 39) – and a good **pension** – at SÃO JOÃO DO CAMPO, close to the dam of Vilarinho das Furnas, along the road between Ponte da Barca and Lindoso.

Caldas do Gerês and hikes in the central Gerês

The Parque Nacional is centred around the old spa town of Caldas do Gerês (commonly known just as Gerês), which is reached most easily by bus from Braga – a two-hour journey. From here, there are a couple of interesting and accessible hikes, though, frustratingly, this central section is not well equipped with footpaths and walking off the tracks can be difficult and painful, with small shrubs slashing the legs.

Caldas do Gerês

Weekends aside, when Portuguese picnickers arrive en masse, **CALDAS DO GERÊS** is a relaxed and very elegant base. "The Spa of Gerês", it became fashionable in the early years of the last century – an epoch convincingly evoked by a row of Victorian grand hotels along the sedate old main street. The **spa** still functions, attracting the infirm in the holiday season, though most visitors nowadays are younger and healthier, up from the northern cities to picnic in the woods – or, in the case of eccentric foreigners, to hike.

There is no shortage of **pensions** but predictably enough they're not cheap. Note, too, that many are open only from May to October. The *Flôr de Moçambique* (③) is clean and amiable; *Pensão da Ponte* (☎053/391 21; ③), behind the main street, is the long-established but increasingly expensive standby (with the extra lure of the town's best restaurant). Alternatively, try *Pensão Baltasar* (②), past the park office; *Pensão Príncipe*, Rua do Cemitério (☎053/391 21; ②); or *Pensão Central Jardim*, Aveinda Manuel Francisco da Costa (☎053/391 32; ③), which also has a few more expensive rooms with bath.

If you have the option, **camping** is greatly recommended. The site at VIDOEIRO, well maintained by the park authority, is just on the edge of town, set alongside a gushing river, with terraced areas for tents and good facilities. Open campfires are permitted here and most evening life takes place around them.

West of Caldas: around the mountain

This is an exhausting and long day's hike (10–12hr; or camp overnight) but a good one, taking you along the way of the **Roman road** that began at Braga and stretched ultimately to Rome and Byzantium. The route also runs alongside the **Rio Homem**, now a reservoir, with obvious swimming potential. In the height of summer you can see the submerged village of Vilarinho das Furnas (turn right after crossing the dam) and even swim through its doors and windows. From there you could reach the **Louriça** summit (5hr; see p.246) by following the path above the cemetery along the brook and heading for the TV masts.

Setting out from Caldas, follow the road north toward Portela do Homem. You'll have to keep on it for a while, despite apparent shortcuts, past the defunct campsite at ALBERGARIA and beyond, veering left, by which time the signs are for Campo do Gerês and the **reservoir** looks increasingly enticing. There is a road off to this, but the main road heads southwest – first along gladed paths and then suddenly into the open, following stretches of the old Roman road. Fires here have seared the foliage and given the granite crags an almost apocalyptic grandeur. Staying with the road (past an old stone building housing a weaving project run by the park), you veer left into **CAMPO DO GERÊS**, a small group of houses with a **pension**, a very good restaurant and, nearby, a bus stop (six daily connections with Braga).

Soon after Campo do Gerês you come to the crucifix of **São João do Campo**. Turn off the road here, to the left, on to a dirt track. This will take you around the southern tip of the mountain and, apart from the occasional obsessive car driver, you'll be pretty much alone – eerily so at times, amid the Neolithic boulders. Follow the sign to Calcedónia, a Celtic and Roman *citânia* with an impressive cave. This stretch can be hard going in the midday heat, as there is no shelter, so save it for the late afternoon. At the end of the circuit the way back to Caldas is signposted (right at the first junction, then right again at the water fountain).

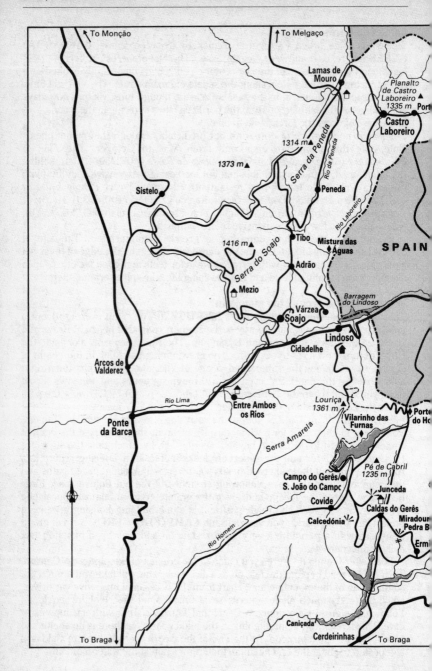

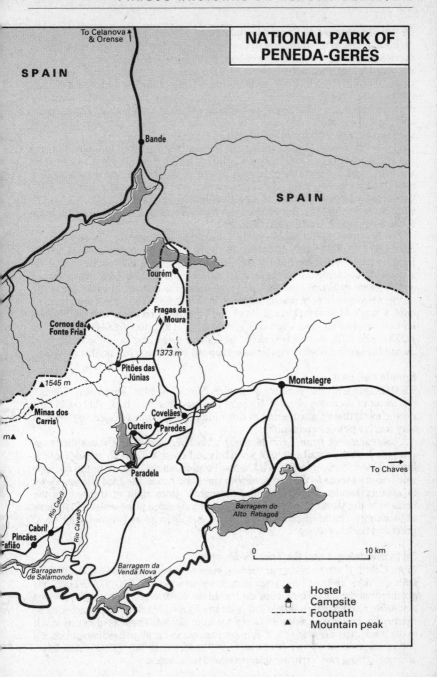

NATIONAL PARK OF PENEDA-GERÊS

SPAIN

To Celanova & Orense

Bande

SPAIN

Tourém

Fragas da Moura

Cornos da Fonte Fria

▲ 1373 m

Pitões das Júnias

▲ 1545 m

Minas dos Carris

m▲

Covelães

Outeiro
Paredes

Montalegre

To Chaves

Paradela

Rio Cabril

Rio Cávado

Cabril
Pincães
Fafião

Barragem do Alto Rabagoã

Barragem de Salamonde

Barragem da Venda Nova

0   10 km

🛏 Hostel
⌂ Campsite
----- Footpath
▲ Mountain peak

To the Miradouro and Caniçada reservoir

An hour's walk to the southeast of Caldas do Gerês, the **Miradouro do Gerês** is *the* destination for Portuguese weekend picnickers. And small wonder, with its site overlooking the vast reservoir of Caniçada and a good part of the Gerês range. The only catch, if you're intent on following suit, is the extent of local enthusiasm. This is not a road to walk unless you're immune to inhalation of exhaust fumes and dust; better to hitch up and then start hiking. The quickest approach to the Miradouro road is to follow the road behind the petrol station at Caldas, where it becomes an uphill path.

The most obvious, and probably the most attractive, route to follow **beyond the Miradouro** is to ERMIDA and CABRIL. Though this is marked as a road on the maps, and has sections of tarmac, it is to all intents and purposes a country path. Walking between the Miradouro turning and Cabril (nearly 30km; 5–6hr), you'll pass a lot more oxen than cars. Just before arriving at Ermida is a sign to CASCATA DO ARADO, left off the main track; follow this and a brief walk leads to the magnificent **Arado waterfalls**.

The best base for the **Albufeira da Caniçada** – the reservoir – is the village of **RIO CALDO**, 8km south of Caldas do Gerês, where a number of local houses have been converted for holiday lets. If you turn up and ask around, it may be possible to negotiate one of these. Alternatively, you could head for the *Pousada de São Bento* (☎053/571 90; ⑥), sited high above the dam at Sonegas; this is one of the more reasonably priced lodgings in the chain. At the reservoir, there is quite a range of **watersports** facilities and equipment on offer, with possibilities for both windsurfing and waterskiing; swimming is fine, too. At SÃO BENTO DA PORTA ABERTA, there's a weekend of **festival** picnicking in July (usually held during the second week); regular buses run out from Braga during this period.

Ermida and east

ERMIDA, despite its proximity to Caldas (90min) and the Miradouro (30min), has an air of seclusion about it. If you're looking for a quiet base, this could be a good choice: there's a scattering of **dormidas** and a couple of cafés, but it is still very much a farming community.

Continuing **east from Ermida**, along a blackberry-lined lane above the reservoir, you'll pass a small group of waterfalls and cross a distinctly unsafe-looking bridge before coming to **FAFIÃO,** a tiny farming hamlet. Past here the countryside becomes more fertile, terraced with vines and maize, the road winding down to another hamlet, **PINCÃES**, and through it (turn right at the end of the houses) to the slightly larger **CABRIL.** A lovely, isolated place with odd attempts at modernity (100m of tarmac), its centre is still sauntered through by oxen, goats and flocks of sheep.

On to Montalegre and the Trás-os-Montes

From Cabril, if you're hiking or driving, you could go on to OUTEIRO, PITÕES DAS JÚNIAS (with a decaying monastery nearby), or MONTALEGRE, via another vast dam, the **Barragem da Paradela**. Montalegre (see p.258) provides a suitably remote and dramatic link with the Trás-os-Montes region, and can be reached by bus from Caldas do Gerês (or from Braga). The appeal lies as much in the road up as the place itself. Bumpy, narrow, and at all points incomplete, it's one of those journeys that seem to trigger madness in bus drivers, simultaneously delighting and terrifying unaccustomed passengers.

The route takes you through **VENDA NOVA**, a tiny group of houses, with a friendly **pension** (not always open), a rather rundown motel, and a good-value luxury establishment on the shore of the reservoir. There are some lovely walks in the vicinity and exceptionally bracing **swimming**. Buses from Venda Nova continue regularly to Montalegre, passing the hydroelectric plant of **Pisões** – the largest dam in the country, and an unexpectedly modern development in this otherwise very remote region.

Soajo and Lindoso

The neighbouring villages of **Soajo** and **Lindoso**, midway between the Peneda and the Gerês areas of the park, are reached most easily from (respectively) Arcos de Valdevez and Ponte da Barca. There are buses from both towns (weekdays only from Arcos de Valdevez to Soajo). Approaching from the Minho river, to the north, you can reach Arcos de Valdevez and Ponte da Barca by travelling due south from Monção for 40km down the N101.

Both Soajo and Lindoso are fine centres for **hiking**, and the walk between the two is enjoyable, too, crossing the Rio Lima dam – a route not yet open to traffic.

Soajo
SOAJO is a small village tucked into the folds of a hilly landscape. Its highlight is a collection of eighteenth- and nineteenth-century **espigueiros** (grain houses), over twenty of which are clumped together on a stony platform, their roof-crosses (intended to bless the annual crop) giving them the look of a graveyard.

In addition to providing a ready-made, breezy threshing ground, the *espigueiros* site offers a degree of protection from rats, though the tall stone mushrooms that raise the houses from the ground do not appear to keep vermin entirely at bay. Their grouping together is a vestige of the days when the isolated village depended heavily on communal effort for its survival. Even now there are several flocks of sheep and goats that belong to the whole community and are tended by the village shepherds. If you set off on a hike at the crack of dawn you will walk up into the hills to the sound of small brass bells.

Changes are not accepted easily and the village takes its traditions very seriously. Folkloric groups are maintained by those who stay behind, while the emigrants all try to inculcate a sense of *minha terra* (my homeland) into their modern-minded (and in many cases American) offspring. The local **festival** has a special feel, with the period of "madness" essential for everyone's sanity and the fun and games spontaneous. Owing to a lack of horses, the *corrida* is a race on foot – balancing blue plastic amphoras full of water on their heads, the contestants compete for the honour of being ceremoniously drenched by all the others. Large, homemade fireworks are set off all over the place without warning.

Staying in Soajo is simple as long as there aren't many others in town. The only café-restaurant, the *Casa do Adro*, next to the bus stop (☎058/673 27; ③) has extremely nice **rooms** upstairs and should be able to suggest alternatives if it's full. There's a **campsite** 8km west along the Arcos road at MEZIO.

Lindoso
Set high above the Rio Lima, **LINDOSO** is one of the most attractive villages in Peneda-Gerês. It is easiest reached from Ponte da Barca, though buses also run directly from Braga.

All along **the route from Ponte da Barca** there are perfect spots for swimming and camping (the official campsite at ENTRE-AMBOS-OS-RIOS is open very erratically), until you reach the turning to Soajo, where the banks rise above a gorge that stretches to the hydroelectric dam below Lindoso. Here you can cross on foot and walk up the Rio Laboreiro (see "Lamas de Mouro", p.247).

Like Soajo, Lindoso is dominated by a cluster of *espigueiros* (grain houses), and its life is again very traditional. The rearing of **livestock** is central. Every morning starts with the lowing of cows or the clattering of the communally herded sheep and goats, and the smell of animals lies thick on the air. The traditional method of baking bread in these parts involved removing the hot coals and sealing the oven door with an ash and dung mixture, and it's a technique still in use in the old part of the village.

You can see a restored oven in the heavily-restored **Castle**, whose keys are kept at the village pension-restaurante, the predictably-named *Castelo* (☎058/47 405; ③); sited off the main road, at the edge of the village, this is a bit overpriced, and guests are likely to be disturbed by the noisy camaraderie of the damworkers who often drink downstairs until 2am. A better bet is the *Pensão-Restaurante Três Cabanas* (☎058/472 18), a two-kilometre walk across the dam, whose English-speaking owners provide wonderfully individual and friendly hospitality. The local **youth hostel**, a three-kilometre walk out of the village – follow the trail of pale red arrows – is at the time of writing closed indefinitely.

To the east of Lindoso, the **border post with Spain** is currently open in summer only, though an all-year opening is planned, following the recent upgrading of the road.

A hike across the Serra Amarela

Lindoso Youth Hostel is the starting-point for a **two-day walk across the Serra Amarela** via PORTELA DO HOMEM or VILARINHO DAS FURNAS to GERÊS, an adventure for which you should take provisions for three days, in case of fog. The journey is in two stages: a dirt track (13km) to the bottom of the **Louriça summit** (1361m), and two less obvious routes across the hills to Portela do Homem (14km), or Gerês (15km). You'll need walking boots, a water bottle (last water for the second day is below the road up to Louriça or up at the top for those going on to Vilarinho das Furnas), a stick (to drive off cattle or wild horses), and something warm (for the night cold).

Setting out from the hostel site, you could take a shortcut on the second sighting of the Louriça television aerials, roughly in line with the pylons, up to the next bend, or else put your trust in the road and follow its winding course all the way to the deserted cottage below the summit. This is where the two routes split.

If you're going on to Vilarinho, the **forest guard** and his family, who live on top of the hill, will point out the reservoir from the plateau in front of the station, and advise you on the best route down. Ignoring their suggestions could get you stuck behind the sheer cliff faces above the deserted, half-sunken village of Vilarinho. Once at the reservoir, you can cross the dam and join the route detailed in the Gerês section to Campo de Gerês.

The **alternative route to Portela do Homem** follows the road (so overgrown as to be barely distinguishable) that lies below the more obvious track from the cottage to the old lookout post. After a large zigzag down into the valley, a wooded patch, and a long stretch pushing through chest-high tree heather along the other side, you break out into a rocky landscape. From here, follow the dry stone wall a short way (200m), turn left (north) along the ridge or just behind it, and walk down into the first valley. Before descending, you'll catch sight of the glacial rounded valley of the Rio Homem (up to Minas dos Carris); a useful landmark away in the distance, Portela do Homem is tucked into a fold of land at its foot.

Cutting across country, you should hit the old road (you can see part of this from back up on the ridge), which ends at the border post (open June–Oct 7am–9/12pm). If you're having problems finding your way, use the Spanish border, a stone wall with marker posts (E and P) as a guideline, but cut down to the road as soon as you see it. A couple of hours later you should come upon the border café. At **PORTELA DO HOMEM** there is a collection of Roman milestones. Gerês is 13km further, but you can hitch; don't miss the **river pool** nearby at the bottom of the Minas dos Carris valley.

The northern section: Peneda

Peneda, the northern section of the Parque Nacional da Peneda-Gerês, sees far fewer tourists than Gerês to the south, partly because of the difficulty of access. Without your own transport, you have to rely on the infrequent buses which seem to take a perverse delight in seeing how early they can leave Melgaço. However, the route from here is one of the best approaches to this area of staggering scenery and awesome rock formations.

Weekday **buses** leave Melgaço for LAMAS DE MOURO and CASTRO LABOREIRO between 5 and 7am (with additional noon service on Fridays) and return at 6.45pm – check times with the parcel depot just around the corner from the *Pemba*. If you're driving, note that the route south of Lamas de Mouro into the park, along the **valley of the Peneda**, though unsurfaced, has been improved, and presents no problems for cars; previously, it was a track strictly for Landrovers. After SOAJO, the road is paved.

Lamas de Mouro and walks south

LAMAS DE MOURO, 19km southeast of Melgaço, has a beautifully situated but minimally-equipped **campsite**. Beyond here, you pass the sanctuary of **Nossa Senhora da Peneda** (9km), full of devotees at the beginning of September (especially on the 7th and 8th), but pretty much deserted the rest of the year. You can take a two-hour **walk** from the sanctuary up to the peak of **Penameda** (1258m), where there are freshwater lagoons and extraordinary views across the whole of the Parque Nacional.

Alternatively, you might consider setting out on the first stage of a **two-day hike** (approximately 25km, allow an extra day in case of fog) to either **Soajo** or **Lindoso** (see previous accounts), from either of which you can cross the Serra Amarela to Gerês. The Soajo route, which is marginally the easier, follows the Rio Peneda until it meets the Rio Veiga (7km), crosses over to the tiny village of TIBO, and takes the dusty road to Soajo (18km). The second trek (for which you'll definitely need a survey map) continues down the Rio Peneda to the *Mistura das Águas* (Mixing of the Waters, 11km); from there use the Rio Laboreiro as a guideline down to the Rio Lima (15km), where you can cross over the barrage to Lindoso.

Castro Laboreiro

The main road through Lamas takes you up to the ancient village of **CASTRO LABOREIRO** (9km further), a place that's best known for the breed of mountain dog to which it gives its name. The village is practically deserted in summer, being made up of *inverneiras* (winter houses), the pastoral community having gone off to find greener fields and build *brandas* ("soft" houses) for the warmer months. If you can speak Portuguese and want to learn more about the area, contact the village priest, who knows everything. In the summer when it's open there are **rooms** at *Pensão Abrigo* (☎051/451 26; ②).

To get to the ruins of the town's **castle**, you have a steep twenty-minute walk: left at the roundabout on the other side of the village, then left up a path where the road drops to the right, past a large rock known as the *Tartaruga* (Tortoise), and through heather and between boulders, with sheer drops to each side and steps hacked out of the rock face.

travel details

Trains

GUIMARÃES LINE
From Porto (Trindade station), hourly to Santo Tirso (1hr) and Guimarães (1hr 45min).

MINHO LINE
From Porto, 12 daily to Nine (1hr; change for Braga), Barcelos (1hr 30min), and Viana do Castelo (2hr); 8 continue to Caminha (2–3hr) and Valença (2hr 30min–4hr).

VIGO (SPAIN) LINE
From Valença 3 trains daily to Vigo (1hr 10min). Connections to Santiago de Compostela and La Coruña.

Buses

From Porto to Fão/Esposende/Viana (3 daily; 50min/1hr/2hr 10min), Vila Real (6 daily; 3hr 40min), Braga (10 daily; 1hr 15min).

From Braga to Guimarães (half-hourly until 8.30pm; 45min), Arcos de Valdevez (7 daily; 1hr 15min), Ponte de Lima (7 daily; 1hr), Ponte da Barca (7 daily; 1hr), Caldas do Gerês (6 daily; 90min), Barcelos (7 daily; 1hr), Monção (4 daily; 2hr 30min), Chaves via Montalegre (4 daily; 3hr).

From Viana do Castelo to Ponte de Lima (16 daily, 1hr); Ponte da Barca/Arcos de Valdevez (4 daily; 1hr 30min/1hr 45min),

From Monção to Braga (2 daily; 2hr); Melgaço (4–5 daily; 1hr) .

From Arcos de Valdevez to Ponte de Lima (6–8 daily; 1hr), Soajo (15 each weekday, fewer on weekends; 30min), Viana do Castelo (6–8 daily; 1hr 45min), Braga (7 daily; 1hr 15min).

International Buses

From Porto and Valença to Spain and France
Saturday buses leave Porto (3.30pm) and Valença (5.30pm) for Vigo/Santiago (2hr/4hr 15min). Tues, Thurs, and Fri buses pass through Monção (11am), Melgaço (11.30am) for Ponte Barjas in Spain and for France.

Flights

From Lisbon to Braga to Lisbon, weekly flight, currently Wednesday: dep Lisbon 9am, arr Braga 10.15am; dep Braga 10.30am, arr Lisbon 11.45am (11,000$00 one-way).

CHAPTER SEVEN

TRÁS-OS-MONTES

rás-os-Montes – literally "Beyond the Mountains" – is Portugal's Lost Domain. For centuries this remote and rural province has been a place to hide and practise one's beliefs in peace: its peculiar traditions and dialects have been formed by a diversity of populations, from the prehistoric tribes who carved the *porcas* (stone pigs) to Jews who sought refuge here from the Inquisition. The extremity of the climate – "Nine months of winter and three months of hell", as the local proverb puts it – and the aridity of much of its land have kept it well apart from the mainstream. Even today, with new highways being built and some industry coming to the major towns, the province has a population half the size of Minho's in almost twice the area.

A sharp **natural divide** cuts across the province. In the south is the fertile territory officially entitled the Upper Douro, but known unofficially as the **Terra Quente** (Hot Land). Encompassing the terraced stretches of the Douro, Corgo and Tua rivers, this area produces peaches, oranges, melons and wine. By contrast, the bitter winters of the north have earned it the name of **Terra Fria** (Cold Land). Out beyond Mogadouro, the most visible features of this wild and rugged terrain are the countless pony carts, pigeon houses (*pombais*) and almond trees, whose fleeting blossom time in late February and early March draws weekenders to the border town of Miranda do Douro.

Travelling into and around the province can be a slow business, with few remaining train services and very localised buses. However, almost any route in Trás-os-Montes has its rewards, and the fortified frontier towns of **Chaves** and **Bragança** – the former an attractive spa, the latter an amazing medieval ensemble – should feature on any northern Portuguese itineraries. Chaves can be reached, a little tortuously, from the Gerês park (see *Minho* chapter), but the most obvious approach to the region is **from the Douro** – whose eastern reaches, covered in the Douro chapter, are technically a part of the province. From the river railway line, two truncated but still functioning **narrow gauge rail lines** cut some way north: the **Corgo line** runs from Régua to Vila Real (where you can catch buses north to Chaves), and the **Tua line** runs from Tua to Mirandela (where since January 1992 trains have been replaced by buses for the journey on to Bragança).

Chaves and Bragança aside, Trás-os-Montes' sights are low-key: a succession of hardworking mountain or valley villages, and tiny, fortified towns guarding the border with Spain, whose appeal lies above all in their remoteness and situation. The only town of any real size is **Vila Real** – a good starting point for a tour of the province, especially for hikers, with its access to the dramatic granite scenery of the **Parque Natural de Alvão**. A second natural park has been designated in the far north of the province, beyond Bragança, in the **Serra de Montezinho**, where walkers can experience Trás-os-Montes at its most rural and remote.

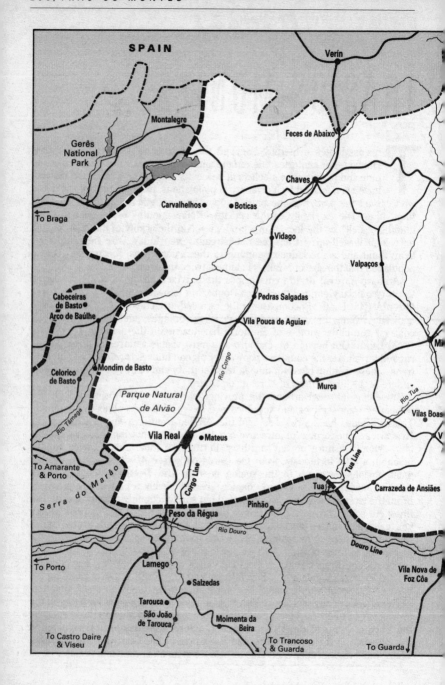

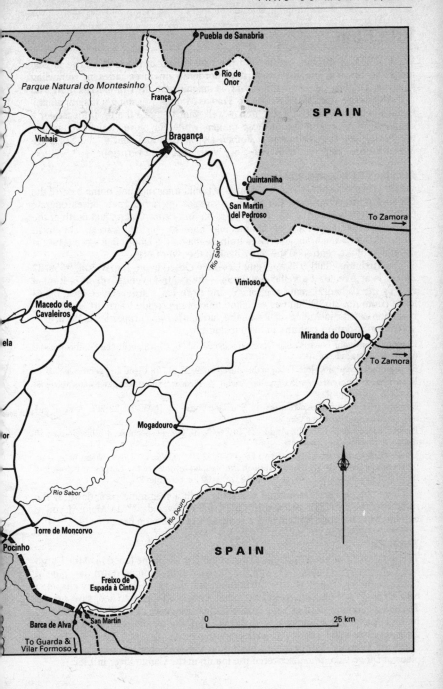

Vila Real

VILA REAL is the one break from the pastoralism of the Corgo. The largest industrial town in the northeast, it is bordered on three sides by sprawling suburbs. The broader setting, however, is magnificent, the twin **serras** of **Marão** and **Alvão** (the so-called "Gateway to Trás-os-Montes") forming a natural amphitheatre behind the town. Walkers may well want to make the town a base for a couple of days' exploration of these ranges, while, for more casual exploration, the town gives easy access to a Roman site at **Panóias**, and to the **Solar de Mateus** – the castle on the Mateus Rosé wine label (see overpage).

Arriving and accommodation

Vila Real is the nexus of Trás-os-Montes regional transport, and home base of the *Cabanelas* **bus company**, the province's major operator. Their buses operate from a station behind the *Hotel Cabanelas* on Rua Pedro Castro, just north of the centre; it's worth picking up a timetable here for further travels. The **train station** (Corgo line branch services from Régua on the Douro line – see p.196) is 500m east of the centre, on the other bank of the river Corgo.

The **Turismo** (daily 9.30am–7pm; Oct–June closed noon–1pm & Sun; ☎059/32 28 19) is at Avenida Carvalho Araújo 94 – the central avenue, which is fronted also by the cathedral, main post office, and town hall – from where local buses leave (from no. 26). Helpful as ever, the office can provide transport and accommodation details, including advice on the various *Turihab* properties in the area.

Accommodation options in town include:

Pensão Mondego, Travessa São Domingos (☎059/32 30 97). Opposite the Sé, this has the cheapest rooms in town. ①

Residencial Excelsior, Rua Teixeira da Sousa (☎059/22 24 22). Clean and good value. ②

Restaurante Encontro, Avda Carvalho Araújo 78. Pleasant, apartment-like rooms above an excellent restaurant. ②

Pensão São Domingos, Travessa de São Domingos 33 (☎059/32 20 39). A nice, old-fashioned market town pension. ②

Hotel Tocaio, Avda Carvalho Araújo 45 (☎059/32 31 06). Respectable if a bit gloomy; all rooms with private bathroom. ④

Hotel Mira Corgo, Avda. 1º de Mayo 76 (☎059/32 50 01). Vila Real's swankiest hotel is an ugly modern block but its rooms overlook the stepped terraces of the Corgo, far below, and there's an indoor swimming pool. Around $12,000.00 for a double. ⑤

There is a pleasant **municipal campsite**, with a swimming pool, down by the river (☎059/32 47 24). From the centre, follow Avenida 1º de Maio; if you're coming from the train station, take a right after crossing the bridge.

The town

The old quarter of Vila Real, built on a promontory above the junction of the Corgo and Cabril rivers, is attractive, with the main **avenida** running down the spine of the promontory. The view from the bottom, past the fourteenth-century chapel of **São Brás**, is not for vertigo sufferers, but there's little else to see, save for the **Turismo** building – formerly the palace of the Marqueses of Vila Real, and fronted by four Manueline windows – and the **Sé**, opposite, which has modern stained glass windows and a simple, fifteenth-century interior.

By the **Câmara Municipal**, a plaque on the café opposite recalls the birthplace of Diogo Cão, who discovered the mouth of the Congo River in 1482.

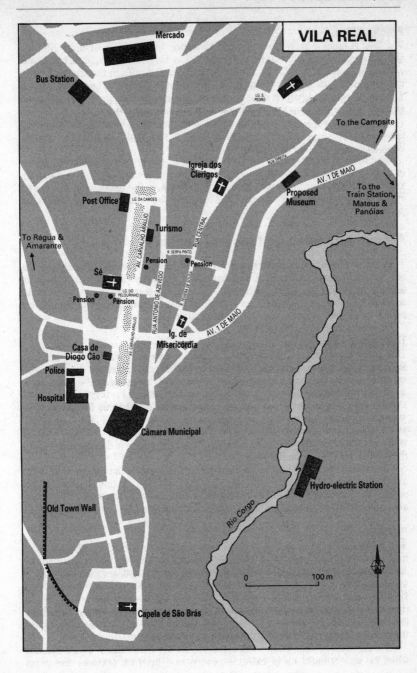

VILA REAL

Mercado

Bus Station

LG. S. PEDRO

To the Campsite

RUA SERETA

AV. 1 DE MAIO

Igreja dos Clerigos

Proposed Museum

To the Train Station, Mateus & Panóias

Post Office

LG. DA CAMÕES

AV. CARVALHO ARAÚJO

RUA CENTRAL

Turismo

To Régua & Amarante

Pension

R. SERPA PINTO

Pension

Sé

LG. DO PELOURINHO

RUA ANTÓNIO DE AZEVEDO

R. TEIXEIRA DE SOUSA

Pension

Pension

Ig. de Misericórdia

AV. 1 DE MAIO

Casa de Diogo Cão

AV. CARVALHO ARAÚJO

Police

Hospital

Câmara Municipal

Hydro-electric Station

Old Town Wall

Rio Corgo

0   100 m

N

Capela de São Brás

Practicalities

Vila Real is quite a lively place – above all during the **festivals** of Santo António (June 13) and São Pedro (June 29) – and it has an enticing range of **bars and restaurants**. Good bets for inexpensive meals are the cafés in the streets behind the Turismo; particularly recommended here is the *Churrasqueria Real*, at Rua Texeira da Sousa 14, which does wonderful and inexpensive grills and spit-roast chicken. For something a bit fancier, try the *Restaurante O Aldeão*, at Rua Dom Pedro de Castro 7 – just down from the bus station; this is popular and very reasonably priced, with a changing daily menu of standards, including a *bife* dish that comes with absolutely everything.

The liveliest **nightspot** is the unnamed bar at Largo do Pelourinho 11 (open until 1am; Fri & Sat 2am), which, for this part of the country at least, is distinctly avant garde. Another good bar, open until midnight, is the *Excelsior* at Rua Serpa Pinto 30–36 – a huge, elaborate pool hall featuring the strangest timing meters for your game you'll ever see.

Around Vila Real: Mateus and Panóias

Trips out to the palace of **Mateus** and Roman remains at **Panóias** make good use of a night's stopover in Vila Real. Both are easily visited by car and Mateus is quite feasible by public transport, with regular *Cabanelas* services along the Sabrosa road. For Panóias, *Cabanelas* runs a weekday bus at 3pm, though to return you need to walk back down to the stop on the main road.

The Solar de Mateus

The **Solar de Mateus** (signposted "Palácio de Mateus") is just 4km from Vila Real, along the road to Sabrosa. Described by Sacheverell Sitwell as "the most typical and the most fantastic country house in Portugal", it's certainly the most familiar, being reproduced on each bottle of *Mateus Rosé*, one of Portugal's major wine exports. The facade keys well enough with the wine's soft-focus image, its twin wings "advancing lobster-like", as Sitwell put it, across a formal lake. The architect is unknown, though most authorities attribute it to the Italian, Nicolau Nasoni, who built the landmark Clérigos church in Porto; the palace is dated around 1740, the heyday of Portuguese Baroque.

The villa charges a handsome admission fee for a somewhat limited tour of its interior (summer only: daily 9am–1pm & 2–6pm; 400$00). Although there are no special treasures, the building is an enjoyable evocation of its period, full of draperies, aristocratic portraits and rural scenes. The **gardens**, too, are a delight.

Panóias

You might combine a visit to Mateus with the Roman site of **PANÓIAS**, 5km further along the Sabrosa road. The sole remnant of the once powerful *Terras de Panóias*, ancient forerunner of Vila Real, it doesn't at first appear much of a site – a few slabs of rock with odd-shaped cavities that are often full of water and rubbish. However, if you know a little French or Portuguese, the tour offered by the old man in the nearby house is worth accepting (tips gratefully received). He brings the three **sacrificial slabs** to life with gory descriptions of the filter systems for the blood and viscera created by the offerings to Serapis, a pre-Roman deity.

As a digression, your guide may elaborate on the harsh times under Salazar, when he was brought up in extreme poverty and lived off potatoes and grass soup. The region, in fact, happens to be where the first potatoes from South America were introduced, and appropriately enough, **Magellan's birthplace** is at nearby SABROSA, a village better known nowadays for its wine.

Parque Natural de Alvão

The **Parque Natural de Alvão** can be glimpsed if you are travelling by road between Vila Real and Amarante. A granite basin formed around the **Rio Olo** – a tributary of the Tâmega – the park has some spectacular waterfalls at FISGAS DE ERMELO, and a handful of quiet, rural hamlets, whose houses are made from the layered rock of the hillsides.

The whole district has a dramatic, boulder-strewn scenery reminiscent of a Western movie. Good targets might include LAMAS DE OLO, with its mill and primitive aqueduct; the waterfall (and another mill) at GALEGOS DA SERRA; and the dammed lakes of Alvão itself.

The problem in exploring Alvão is **transport**. Without a car, you're dependent on very sketchy bus services: *Tâmegatur* goes only as far as LORDELO, and *RN* to nearby BORBELA. Serious walkers intending to cross the whole reserve should obtain maps in advance from Porto or Lisbon and consult the Park Headquarters in Vila Real (Rua Alves Torgo 22–3º).

North towards Chaves: the Corgo Valley and Vidago

One of the sins of Portuguese modernisation is that the old narrow gauge railways of the north have been curtailed or closed. The **Linha do Corgo**, which until 1990 ran from Régua through Vila Real and north to Chaves, was one of the best, trailing the Corgo river valley almost all the way, through a landscape where everything from cowsheds to vine posts is made from granite, and where the luscious green of the vines belies the apparent barrenness of the earth.

Now that the line stops at Vila Real, you've little choice but to take the N2 road, which is a less romantic route, but follows the valley pretty closely as far as the village of VILA POUCA DE AGUIAR – famous in the north for its bread. Beyond here, the road cuts through the edge of the Serra da Padrela, before reaching the upper valley of the **Tâmega** river, which it traces for the rest of the route to Chaves, at Vidago.

VIDAGO, a summer spa town, is the most interesting stop along the route. If you can afford it, the place to stay is the sublimely old-fashioned *Palace Hotel* (☎076/973 56; ⑤), an Edwardian pile with its own post office (now defunct), a magnificent pump room, a bandstand amid the trees, and one of the best wine cellars in the country. More modest lodgings include the *Pensão Alameda* (☎076/972 46; ②) and *Pensão Primavera* (☎076/972 30; ②). The spa and most hotels and pensions open from mid-June to mid-October, closing for the winter months.

Chaves

CHAVES stands just twelve kilometres from the Spanish border and its name, which means "Keys", reflects a strategic history of occupations and ownership. Between 1128 and 1160 the town was an Islamic enclave, and in the following seven centuries it was fought over in turn by French, Spaniards and Portuguese.

One of its greatest overlords, **Nuno Álvares Pereira**, was awarded the "keys" of the north by João I for his valiant service at the Battle of Aljubarrota, and from him the town passed into the steady hands of the House of Bragança. However, as recently as 1912 Chaves bore the brunt of a Royalist attack from Spain – two years after Portugal had become a republic.

The town is today considerably less significant, a market centre for the villages of the fertile Tâmega plain – the richest agricultural lands in the provence – and regional capital for the northern Trás-os-Montes. For visitors, its principal attractions are its setting, a modest array of monuments, a **spa**, and its gastronomy. Chaves is famed in Portugal for its smoked hams, delicious meat cakes (*bôlas de carne*), stuffed sausages and a strong red wine. The town also hosts an important **winter fair**, held on November 1.

Arriving and accommodation

The old quarter of Chaves is highly compact, grouped above the river, and with the spa just below the old walls to the west. From this central area, the **bus station** is a five-minute walk to the north; coming into town, follow the main road directly ahead, then straight past the roundabout, and you'll emerge near the **Turismo** on Rua de Santo António (☎076/210 29).

Accommodation is well worth booking in the summer months, when you're quite likely to arrive in town to find the pensions full (and overpriced) and space restricted even in the campsite. Out of season there should be no problem, save for the intense cold in winter if you're in a cheap, unheated room.

Hotel and pension options, in ascending order of price, include:

Pensão Imperial, Rua Direita 158 (☎076/231 42). Central location, near Praça de Camões. ①
Pensão Jorge, Rua do Loureiro, off Rua S António. Best bet for cheap rooms. ②
Pensão Jaime, Avda. da Muralha (☎076/212 73). Nicely sited below the city walls. ③
Hotel de Chaves, Rua 25º de Abril (☎076/211 18). Comfortable, 1920s-era hotel which retains a few trappings of grandeur from its better days; the lack of a dining room (and slight seediness) ensure a low official classification and prices. ③
Pensão Flavia, Travessa Candido dos Reis (☎076/225 13). Not worth the extra money. ④
Hotel Trajano, Travessa Candido dos Reis (☎076/224 15 or 25). The town's most expensive hotel – modern, comfortable, and a bit dull. ⑤

There are **private rooms** (look for the *dormidas* signs) just past the Turismo on the corner of Rua de Santo António, and over towards the bridge.

The Town and spa

Chaves' military past is still much in evidence. There are two seventeenth-century **fortresses**, built in the chracteristic Vaubanesque style of the north, and a four-teenth-century keep, near the bridge, that houses a small **Museu Militar** (Tues–Fri 9.30am–12.30pm & 2–5pm, Sat & Sun 2–4.30pm).

Tickets for the latter entitle you to admission to the **Museu da Região Flaviense** (same hours) on the Praça de Camões, a haphazard assortment of material tracing the history of the town and its customs, including quite an assembly of remains from the old Roman spa settlement. The town was known to the Romans as *Aquae Flaviae*, after its spa waters, and was an important point on the imperial road from Astorga, in Spanish León, to Braga. In the first century AD it was the army headquarters under Aulus Flaviensis, who was responsible for developing the thermal stations here and elsewhere in the region – at Vidago, Carvalhelos and Pedras Salgadas.

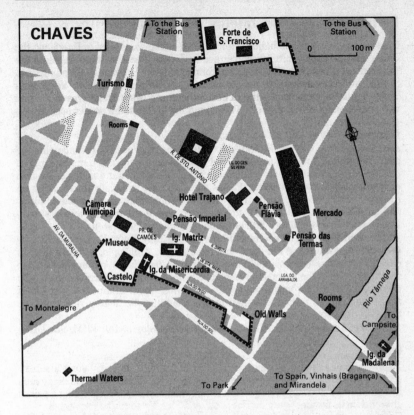

You can still take the waters in summer at the Chaves **spa**, built around the *nascente* (spring) below the city walls, toward the river. The water emerges at a piping 73°C and is not very tasty. It is reckoned to be good for gout and obesity. Unfortunately, the river itself is polluted – frustrating any chance of a swim – though the gardens around are well kept and attractive.

Back in town, further traces of the Roman past are to be seen in the form of the **Ponte Trajano** – the Roman bridge – and its ancient milestones. The two churches in the Praça de Camões are worth a look, too: the **Matriz**, which is partly Romanesque, and the **Misericórdia**, distinguished by vast *azulejo* panels.

Restaurants

Most of the pensions and hotels have **restaurants**. Recommended are those attached to the *Pensão Jorge* – which is very cheap – and the *Hotel Trajano* – a very slick operation in the basement and not too expensive. The pavement restaurant opposite the Torre de Menagem serves huge portions very cheaply. Try the local speciality, *folar*, an interesting and wholesome pork bread.

Out of town, a kilometre or so over the bridge on Bragança road, the *Restaurante Pote* (closed Mon) serves up local dishes to an enthusiastic clientele. Also recommended is the *Restaurante Campismo*, opposite the campsite.

On from Chaves: Montalegre and Vinhais

Chaves is quite a fulcrum of bus services, with connections west to Braga and the Gerês national park via **Montalegre** (see below), and east to **Mirandela** (on the Tua railway line) and **Vinhais** (for connections to Bragança). Heading **into Spain**, you could pick up an *Internorte* express coach to Orense, via Verin, on a Thursday or Sunday (originating in Porto, these pass through Chaves at 3.15pm; book ahead if possible). There is no currency exchange at the border post.

Montalegre

Approached from Chaves, **MONTALEGRE** looms up suddenly, commanding the plains all around. Looking at its isolated position on the map, you might expect a frontier town, rooted in past centuries. In fact, there is a fair amount of modern development, due to the nearby Pisões dam, which is gradually encroaching on the medieval centre and castle. However, it remains quite an atmospheric place, and an enjoyable night or two's stopover, set amid good walking territory, scattered with dolmens and the odd Templar and Romanesque church.

Accommodation choices include the surprisingly fancy *Residencial Fidalgo* (④), uphill to the left at the main square, Largo do Município, and a number of cheaper pensions out on the Chaves road. The *Brasilieira* **restaurant** on the southwest side of the Largo do Municípiois a good bet for an excellent meal. You might ask at the local bars about *Vinho dos Mortos* – Wine of the Dead – so called as it is fermented in bottles buried in the ground at the nearby villages of the Serra do Barroso.

North of Montalegre, there is a minor border crossing at TOURÉM/SENDIM.

Vinhais

To the east of Chaves, three buses a day roll through the hills along a superb scenic route to Bragança. Midway is the village of **VINHAIS**, which is dominated by the Baroque convent of **São Francisco**, a vast building incorporating a pair of churches in its facade.

There's a clutch of **pensions** if you get stuck in Vinhais; a good one to try is the *Residencial Ribeirinha* (☎073/724 90; ①), which has lovely old rooms with balconies overlooking the valley. Alternatively, you could **camp** at VILA VERDE, 8km east of the town. To the north of here – and accessible also from Vinhais – is the **Serra de Montesinho**, now protected as a natural park (see p.265), a fine area for walkers, right away from any tourist route.

The Tua valley and Mirandela

Although the narrow gauge **Tua rail line** now covers the route only from TUA, on the Douro line (see p.197), up as far as **Mirandela**, it remains one of the most enjoyable rides in the country. Improbably engineered, it cuts a rocky course following the Tua valley for virtually its entire distance. Four trains daily (three at weekends) cover the route in both directions.

At Mirandela, you have a choice of **buses**: northeast to Bragança; northwest to Chaves; and southwest to Vila Real. The rail line used to cover the former, trailing across the **Serra de Nogueira**, a route which has been largely circumvented by a fast new highway.

Mirandela

MIRANDELA is an odd little town with a medieval centre, a scattering of Baroque mansions, and a brand new modern art gallery. It makes a good place to break the rail journey – with the option of staying, or continuing on a later train to Bragança. There is also a range of **buses**, most of which leave from a terminal between the bridge and the train station – though *Cabanelas* buses operates from beyond the fire station on the Rua da República. There is a seasonal **Turismo** by the bridge.

The best time to visit Mirandela is during its **festa** – one of the longest in Portugal (July 25–Aug 15) – or, failing that, for one of the weekday **markets**, held as close as possible to the 3rd, 14th, or 25th of every month.

Around the town

The modern art gallery, the **Museu de Arte Moderna** (Mon–Fri 2.30–6pm), is in fact combined with the town's library. It has two collections of paintings: one dedicated to local artist Armindo Teixeira Lopes' images of Mirandela and Lisbon; the other, rather more exciting, to a fairly representative – if slightly too slick – display of twentieth-century Portuguese painting and printmaking.

In contrast to the clean lines of this modern building, the **old town** is in a state of considerable decay. The chapel next to the town hall, at the summit of the ancient citadel, simply fell down in 1985. Scavengers have pilfered the most useful or attractive pieces of stonework, leaving a pile of rubble and an altarpiece open to the skies. The **old gate** to the town can still be seen on Rua do Arco.

In a rather better state is the grandiose **Câmara Municipal** – the town hall, but formerly the *Palácio dos Távoras*. This was one of several flamboyant townhouses here associated with the **Távora** family, who controlled the town between the fourteenth and seventeenth centuries. Pêro Lourenço de Távora rose to power in 1385 at the Battle of Aljubarrota, where he fought against the Castilians at the side of the future João I. Unfortunately, his distant grandson, Luís Álvares Távora, was to accompany Dom Sebastião in 1578 on the disastrous trip to Morocco, and the subsequent decline in the family fortunes went so far that in 1759 Pombal ordered the Távora insignia to be removed from all the palaces.

Prior to all this baronial activity, the Romans, as usual, were building bridges. Mirandela's **bridge** – renovated in the fifteenth century – is by far its most striking feature, stretching a good 200m across the sluggish river.

Rooms and meals

Somewhat surprisingly, Mirandela has half a dozen pensions and hotels, so rooms are pretty easy to find, except during the festa. The local **campsite** is several kilometres out of town , on the Bragança road.

Pick of the **pensions and hotels** are:

Residencial Flórida, Rua da República 77 (☎078/222 54). This looks very run-down from the outside, but once inside it's friendly and comfortably, and wonderfully quiet. ①

Pensão Sá Moreno, Avda. das Amoreiras (☎078/224 34). A bit pricier, but probably the first choice pension; located on the right coming from the station to the bridge. ③

Residencial O Viajante, Rua da República 209 (☎078/228 66). ③

Hotel Mira Tua, Rua da República 20 (☎078/224 03). Reasonable. ④

For **meals**, try the *Sá Moreno* pension or the *Restaurante Universo* on the Travessa de São Cosme, above the *Residencial Florida*.

Toward Bragança: Macedo de Cavaleiros

At Mirandela the Tua broadens and the Bragança road veers east along the Rio Azibo, past **MACEDO DE CAVALEIROS**. Unless the shooting and fishing parties at the *Estalagem do Caçador* are your bag, this is not much of a place to linger. If you want a lunch stop from driving, or get stranded trying to make a bus connection east to Mogadouro, you might check out the delicious Italian **pizzas** at the *Marisqueira* at Rua Fonte do Paço 5. There are inexpensive **rooms** available above the *Churrasqueira* restaurant 8 (②) and at the *Pensão Monte-Mel* (☎078/423 78; ③) on the main street.

Carrezeda de Ansiães and Vila Flôr

Travelling by road between the Douro and Mirandela, the main route runs to the southeast of the Tua valley, through **Carrezeda de Ansiães** and **Vila Flôr**. Both are rewarding halts, if you have your own transport and can move on later in the day; relying on public transport, you may judge the times between bus connections (the most regular are between Tua railway station and Vila Flôr) excessive.

Carrezeda de Ansiães

CARREZEDA DE ANSIÃES is a modern town with a single pension (if you get stuck) and little intrinsic interest. However, three-and-a-half kilometres to its south are the intriguing ruins of a medieval **walled town**. Little remains within the perimeter of walls except rocks and boulders, but two **chapels** stand outside, the better preserved of which, twelfth-century **São Salvador**, has a Romanesque **portal**, extravagantly carved with leaves, animals and human figures.

Local myth has it that a tunnel connects this enceinte to another castle beyond the Douro, twelve kilometres distant; a gaping, fly-ridden hole beneath an impressive slab is the principal piece of supporting evidence. What is undoubtedly true, however, is that the town was a base for five different kings, including the King of Léon and Castile, before Portuguese independence; they're listed by the gateway on a plaque unveiled by Mário Soares in February 1987.

People lived in old Carrezeda only until the mid-eighteenth century. In 1734, a gentleman named Francisco de Araújo e Costa managed to transfer the official council seat to the new town below. He replied to protests by ordering the castle *pelourinho* (pillory) to be destroyed. With this symbol gone and deprived of a sufficient supply of water, the hill community had no hope of putting up effective resistance. The medieval town went into decline and was soon totally abandoned.

Vila Flôr

Over to the east of Carrezeda, towards the projected Torre de Moncorvo–Bragança highway, **VILA FLÔR** is a larger and vaguely historic town. Its name, Town of Flowers, was given by Dom Dinis, when on his way to meet Isabel of Aragon in the thirteenth century. His favouritism was short-lived though, in practical terms, for soon Vila Flôr was forced to contribute a third of its revenue to rebuilding the walls of rival Torre de Moncorvo. Nowadays the only striking features of the Vila Flôr townscape are a piece of old town wall known as the *Arco Dom Dinis*, and a so-called "Roman" fountain.

The place merits a visit principally for its eccentric **Museu Municipal** (9.30am–12.30pm & 2–5pm; closed Mon). Three eminent Vilaflôrians donated the contents of their houses to the museum when it was founded in 1946, and the result is an incredible hodge-podge: a much-glued stone *porca* (see "Bragança") and a few dusty pictures by Manuel Moura are the only items of value. The enveloping clutter contains typewriters, sewing machines, snake skins, a set of broken percussion instruments, religious sculptures, teacups, stuffed animals and an ensemble of zebra-hide furniture.

The town is not a bad place to break a journey. There are three **pensions** at the new end of town, among which *Pensão Campos* (☎079/523 11; ②) is most pleasant; a little to the south, 2km along the Moncorvo road, is an excellent **campsite** – one of very few in this area, and equipped with a swimming pool. For meals, the best bet is the *Campos*, though they like you to warn them in advance. Otherwise, you may find sustenance at one of the cafés down by the museum. The local red **wines**, from the *Co-Op Vila Flôr*, are regarded as among the best in the country.

The town **festa** runs from August 22 to 28, with amateur live bands and open-air stalls on the last weekend. Couples insist on traditional slow dancing whatever the rhythm of a song. There's also an extensive **street market** on the weekday closest to the 15th and 28th of every month. An important romaria takes place at a hilltop sanctuary at nearby VILAS BOAS, 8km northwest, on August 15 (Nossa Senhora da Assunção).

Vila Flôr boasts a useful **bus company**, *Soc de Transportes* (Avda. Marechal Carmona), with pale green buses and the resources to print their timetables.

Bragança

On a dark hillock above **BRAGANÇA**, the remote capital of Trás-os-Montes, stands a circle of perfectly preserved medieval walls, rising to a massive keep and castle, and enclosing a white medieval village. Known as the **Cidadela**, this is one of the most memorable sights in Portugal, seemingly untouched by the centuries, with crops still grown within the walls, and a hamlet size wonderfully at odds with the royal connotations of the town's dynastic name. The Braganças were the last line of **Portuguese monarchs**, ruling from 1640, when they replaced the Spaniards, until the end of the monarchy in 1910. To the British, the name is most readily associated with Catherine, queen to Charles II. For the Portuguese, the town also represents the defence of the liberty of the people, for the Braganças were the first to muster a popular revolt against Junot in 1808, and have always defended their power to make their own decisions.

The citadel, along with an excellent **historic museum**, provides the principal reason for a visit to the town. For anyone interested in a bit of wilderness hiking, or fishing though, the nearby **Parque Natural de Montesinho** provides an additional draw (see section following), while a **cultural festival**, held from August 14 to 22, is another very good reason to be in town.

Arriving and accommodation

Modern Bragança, set along the valley below the Cidadela, is a pleasant base, despite an eruption of blocks of flats on the outskirts. Most **buses** operate from the old **train stations** (where the *Cabanelas* company maintain a kiosk), from where it's a short walk along the Avenida João da Cruz to the **Praça da Sé**, essentially the centre of town. From here, it's a couple of hundred metres north to the **Turismo** (☎073/222 71), on the Avenida Cidade de Zamora.

Pensions and hotels are grouped mainly around the Praça da Sé. They include, in ascending order of price:

Pensão Transmontano, Avda. João da Cruz 168 (☎073/228 99). Located opposite the train station, this is the cheapest pension in town, and the rooms are not so bad. ①

Pensão Caracol, Rua Alexandre Herculano 132 (☎073/254 77). Reasonable. ②

Hospedaria Bragantina, Rua Alexandre Herculano (next door). Rundown external appearance belies quite acceptable rooms. ②

Residencial Poças, Rua Combatentes da Grande Guerra 200 (☎073/221 75). Excellent value for money – as long as you pick your room. Book in at the grocery across the street. ②

Residencial São Roque, Rua da Estacada (☎073/234 81). Annexe owned by the *Poças*, with more good-value rooms, often taken long-term by students. A little out of the centre. ②

Pensão Rucha, Rua Almirante dos Reis 42 (☎073/226 72). Characterful and welcoming – more of a family home than a pension. ③

Residencial Cruzeiro, Travessa do Hospital, off Rua Emidio Navarro (☎073/226 33). Again, highly recommended. ③

Residencial Tulipa, Rua Dr Francisco Felgueiras 8 (☎073/236 75). Highly recommended as a slightly pricier, but very well-run, *pensão*. Good restaurant below. North of the post office – follow signs. ④

Pousada de São Bartolomeu, south of the river and about 1km by road – follow the signs (☎073/224 93). This is one of the country's best value *pousadas* at around 11,000$00 for a double; it's a modern building but with brilliant views of the Cidadela. ⑤

The nearest **campsite** is 6km out of town on the França road (left from the station; no bus) and has pretty sparse facilities. However, there are also plenty of open spaces beyond the walls of the upper town.

The Cidadela

At the heart of the Cidadela stands the thirteenth-century council chamber, the **Domus Municipalis**. Very few Romanesque civic buildings have survived, and none other has this pentagonal form. Its meetings – for solving land disputes and the like – took place on the arcaded first floor; below was a cistern. Rising to its side is the church of **Santa Maria**, whose interior is distinguished by an eighteenth-century barrel-vaulted, painted ceiling – a feature of several churches in Bragança. Keys for both are kept locally if you find the doors shut.

Facing these buildings is the town keep, the **Torre da Menagem**, which the royal family rejected as a residence in favour of their vast estate in the Alentejo. It was one of the first works of restoration by the Society of National Monuments in 1928, and houses a fine little craft shop.

At the side of the keep, a curious **pelourinho** (pillory) rises from the back of a prehistoric granite pig. The town's museum has three more of these crudely sculpted **porcas**, the most famous of which is to be seen at Murça. They are thought to have been the fertility idols of a prehistoric cult, and it's easy to understand the beast's prominence in this province of wild boars and chestnut forests, where the staple winter diet is smoked sausage.

Look over the furthest walls of the castle and you'll see the **Parque Natural de Montesinho** stretching to Spain, a view which seems to stress the town's remoteness. One group who made the most of this isolation were the **Jews**, who escaped over the border in the sixteenth century from the terrors of the **Inquisition** in Spain. Despite the common rule by Spaniards over the two countries during this period, the Inquisition in Portugal was relatively inefficient – administered in municipalities, the organisation spread slowly northwards with ever-decreasing zeal. The Jewish community has left its mark in the names of local families and in

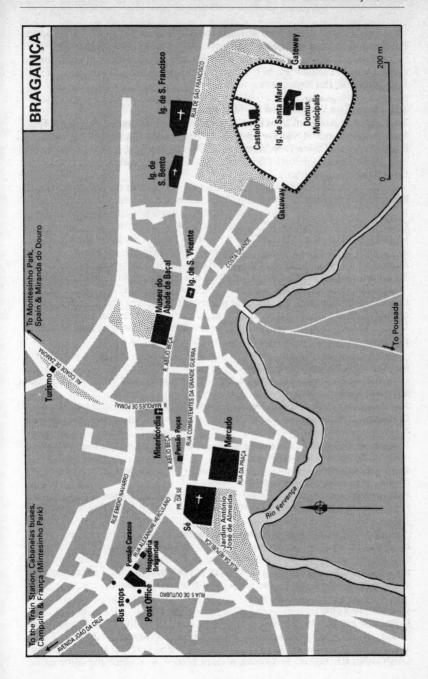

BRAGANÇA

To the Train Station, Cabanelas buses,
Campsite & França (Mintesinho Park)

To Montesinho Park,
Spain & Miranda do Douro

Ig. de S. Francisco

Ig. de
S. Bento

Gateway

Castelo

Ig. de Santa Maria

Domus
Municipalis

Gateway

200 m

0

RUA DE SÃO FRANCISCO

COSTA GRANDE

Ig. de S. Vicente

Museu do
Abade de Baçal

R. ABILIO BEÇA

AV CIDADE DE ZAMORA

Turismo

R. MARQUES DE POMBAL

Misericórdia

Pensão Poças

R. ABILIO BEÇA

RUA COMBATEMTES DA GRANDE GUERRA

Mercado

RUA DA PRAÇA

RUE EMIDIO NAVARRO

PR. DA SÉ

Sé

Jardim Antonio
José de Almeida

RUA DA REPÚBLICA

Rio Fervença

To Pousada

Pensão Caraíços

RUA ALEXANDRE HERCULANO

Hospedaria
Bragamina

Bus stops

Post Office

RUA 5 DE OUTUBRO

AVENIDA JOÃO DA CRUZ

the town's cuisine (the *alheira* sausage is made from chicken rather than pork); but the once thriving synagogue is no more.

You can get a superb **view** of the Cidadela from the bottom of the steps of the church of São Bartolomeu; to get there, follow the signs to the *pousada*, a half-hour walk from the town centre.

The Town: São Vicente and the Museum

Heading back into town from the Cidadela, the narrow, stepped Rua Serpa Pinto leads to the church of **São Vicente**, where Dom Pedro I claimed to have secretly married Inês de Castro (see "Alcobaça" for the legend, p.108). A little way to the east is **São Bento**, the town's finest church – a simple Renaissance structure with three contrasting ceilings.

A similar distance to the west of São Vicente is the **Museu do Abade de Baçal**, the town's distinguished museum (10am–12.30pm & 2–5pm; closed Mon). It is installed in the former Bishop's Palace, and in its gardens Celtic-inspired medieval tombstones rub shoulders with a menagerie of *porcas*. Inside, the collection of sacred art and the topographical watercolours of Alberto Souza are the highlights, along with the displays of local costumes – especially the female dress of the *Pauliteiros* ("stick dancers"), who still perform at festivals around Bragança and Miranda do Douro. Further down the street is a fine Renaissance **Misericórdia**.

One last, incidental sight, which rail buffs will want to check out, is the tiny **transport museum** at the old train station. This features the first steam train operative in northern Portugal, and the royal carriage of Portugal's second-to-last king, Dom Carlos; both were recently brought here from Arco de Baulhe, following the closure of the upper reaches of the Tâmega rail line.

Restaurants, bars and swimming

Bragança has a promising array of bars and restaurants, at most budgets. The following are all recommended:

Machado Cura, Rua Almirante Reis. Basic, disarmingly friendly and not to be missed.

O Bolha, Jardim Dr António José de Almeida. Cheap set menus and a homemade pink liqueur which go down very nicely.

Residencial Poças, Rua Combatentes da Grande Guerra 200. Excellent food – family run and popular enough to fill a couple of floors.

O Manel, Rua Orobio de Castro 27, near the market. Possibly the best cooking in town, though a sweltering hot environment in summer.

Solar Bragançeno, Praça da Sé (closed Mon). An upmarket but excellent *casa típica*, where you dine in oak-panelled rooms to the accompaniment of classical music. Nice bar, too, if you want to spend rather less.

For the town's rather limited **nightlife**, the place to try is *Bô*, a late bar with Brazilian bands and local guitarists in summer, on Rua Combatentes da Grande Guerra .

And lastly, there's an indoor **swimming pool**, on the road in from the north, just by the football stadium. It's open every afternoon, from 3pm; bathing caps are compulsory for both sexes – and hired out if you don't have one.

Crossing to Spain

If you can get tickets, the easiest access to Spain is on the *Internorte* **express bus** from Porto to Zamora, which passes through Bragança at 2.45pm (Tues–Sat). Failing that, you can get a *Cabanelas* bus to the Portuguese border post at QUINTANILHA (34km; departures at 5pm Mon–Fri), or take the Miranda do

Douro bus as far as the border road crossroads and hitch the 12km on to the frontier. At the Spanish frontier village of SAN MARTIN DEL PEDROSO, there's a single, combined, pension-restaurant, the *Evaristo*, and a 7am bus to Zamora.

An alternative crossing is to take the road **through the Parque Natural de Montesinho** (see below), through the border villages of PORTELO (Portugal) and CALABOR (Spain) to the Spanish town of PUEBLA DE SANABRIA (which is on both bus and train lines and has accommodation). Using public transport, you can catch *Cabanelas* buses to Portelo at 2.15pm (Mon, Wed, Fri) and irregular Spanish buses (Mon–Fri) between Calabor and Puebla de Sanabria; you would have to walk or hitch the 6km between Portelo and Calabor.

Hitchhikers will find the **Miranda do Douro** route to Zamora marginally busier than either of these crossings.

Parque Natural de Montesinho

Occupying the extreme northeastern tip of Portugal, the **Parque Natural de Montesinho** is the only sector of the *Terra Fria* where the way of life and the appearance of villages have not been changed by the new wealth of the emigrant workers. The *Terra Fria*'s predominantly barren landscape is here disrupted by microclimates which give rise to the **Serra de Montesinho**'s heather-clad hills, wet grass plains and thick forests of oak. Another curious feature of the region is the round *pombal*, or pigeon house – a structure which, no matter how well established its position, invariably seems to have dropped in from another world. The ethnographic museum in Miranda do Douro can fill you in on these and other aspects of traditional village life such as the black cape and the cloaks of straw – as much protection against heat as against cold.

For leaflets and advice for walkers of all grades, contact the **Montesinho Park Office** in Bragança (Rua Alexandre Herculano 1959; 10am–noon & 2–5pm). They can advise on transport in the area, too; the most useful bus links are to França/Portelo and Rio de Onor. It is not too hard to hitch on the França road in summer, and walking beyond here, alongside the **Rio Sabor**, is idyllic, with wonderful and deserted spots for camping and swimming.

Rio de Onor
RIO DE ONOR, right up on the Spanish border, provides perhaps the most fascinating insight into the village life of the Serra de Montesinho. There are in fact two Rio de Onors – one in Spain, one in Portugal – but a simple chain slung between two stone blocks labelled "E" and "P" is all that delineates the frontier. The villagers have come and gone between the two for generations, intermarrying and buying goods; both sides speak a hybrid Portuguese-Spanish dialect known as *Rionorês*. Their extreme isolation encouraged systems of justice and mutual co-operation which are independent of the state and which still exist. The aging villagers share land, flocks, wine-presses, mills and ovens.

The two villages are set on either side of a stream: the granite steps and wooden balconies of rough stone houses line narrow alleyways, and straw creeps out across the cobbles. If you want to **stay**, you can pitch a tent, or there's the possibility of basic shelter in the *Casa do Povo* (parish rooms) if you contact the village *presidente* on arrival. *STUB* **buses**, fluctuating with local school and market timetables, connect the village twice daily with Bragança.

Miranda do Douro

The route from Bragança to **MIRANDA DO DOURO** runs across the *Planalto Mirandês* – a breathtaking journey in late February and early March, when the sudden blossoming of the **almond trees** transforms the countryside. Some say that it was the beauty of this vista – and Miranda do Douro itself – that decided Afonso Henriques, the future first king of Portugal, to turn against his Spanish kinsmen, refortify the border, and begin his victorious sweep across Lusitânia at the start of the twelfth century. Facing Spain across the deep gorge of the Douro, Miranda do Douro played a key role in all of the country's subsequent wars. After valiant service in the Independence, Spanish Succession, and Seven Year wars, it ended its fighting days in 1762 when an explosion during a Spanish attack destroyed the castle, the town and 400 inhabitants.

The "city"

Today, with a population of less than two thousand, Miranda seems scarcely more than a village. Yet it has the status of a city, and a sturdy sixteenth-century **Sé** overlooks its cobbled streets and low white houses. This cathedral and the city status came about in the sixteenfth century with the Portuguese church authorities' decision to make Miranda the capital of the diocese to counteract the feudal power of the House of Bragança in Trás-os-Montes. At the end of the eighteenth century, however, the see was transferred to the larger of the two towns, leaving Miranda cathedral as a cumbersome memento of past glory. To the bitter comment "The sacristy is in Bragança, but the cathedral is in Miranda", the astute Bragançans reply, "If ever you go to Miranda, see the cathedral and come home".

The cathedral aside, Miranda has a certain neat charm, despite a rather offputting rash of frontier tourist shops. The tidied-up ruins of its **Episcopal Palace**, now a café, and the medieval facades of the **Rua da Costanilha** set the tone, and there is a small medieval bridge, too, over the diminutive Rio Fresno. Beyond here you reach an eighteenth-century fountain, the Fonte dos Canos.

The focus of interest in town, however, is the **Museu de Terra de Miranda** (Tues–Sun 9am–noon & 2–4.45pm), just off the Rua da Constanilha. This is literally bursting with curiosities, from lumps of stone to pistols, and features a couple of reconstructed rooms in traditional Mirandês style – an illustration of local life that's inaccurate only in that the agricultural labourers of the region generally live, sleep and die in a single room.

Apart from the **festa** periods (*Santa Bárbara* on the third Sunday in August; *Romaria Nossa Senhora do Nazo*, Sept 7–8; *Pauliteiros*, Dec 27–28) and the **feira** held on the first weekday of every month, not a lot happens in Miranda besides the occasional football match. In summer, a folk group from nearby Duas Igrejas, the *Pauliteiros de Miranda*, occasionally performs the **stick dance** in a whirl of dust and to the sound of the tambourine and the bagpipes, but their world tours (if you can believe that) have put an end to their regular Sunday afternoon displays.

Rooms and food

The town has several attractive **accommodation** options – though nothing is very cheap – and a well-maintained **campsite**.

Pensions and hotels include:

Pensão Santa Cruz, Rua Abade de Baçal 6l (☎073/424 74). The only pension in the old part of town; fine rooms and a chatty parrot in the restaurant. ③

Residencial Douro Azul, Rua do Mercado. An excellent new hotel. ③

Residencial Planalto, Rua 1º de Maio (073/423 62). Reasonably priced, modern rooms above the fire station. and a very good restaurant; the fire station itself has a bar, open to the public in the evening. ③

Pousada Santa Catarina (☎0073/422 55). Sited on the edge of the gorge, overlooking the huge Miranda do Douro dam, 3km from town. ⑤

In addition to the pension/hotel **restaurants**, you might like to check out the menus at *O Mirandês* or the cheaper *Balbina*; the latter has a collection of grandfather clocks, serves excellent wine and a local *posta assada á mirandesa* (beef) which is plenty to feed two or three. Alternatively, if you have transport, and are prepared to pay for some of the country's top cooking, try *Restaurante Gabriela*, in the nearby village of Sendim, on the Mogadouro road; it is run by Alicia, an award-winning chef who appears on many a Portuguese TV show.

Transport – and on to Spain

Moving on from Miranda do Douro, *Santos* operate **buses** from the museum square to Mogadouro, Moncorvo and Pocinho at 5.45am and 3.15pm (daily) and 11am (Mon–Fri only). At Mogadouro station (14km from Mogadouro town), you can pick up *FS* bus connections to Freixo de Espada à Cinta, Figueira de Castelo Rodrigo and Guarda. A weekday would be best for Guarda.

The **Spanish border** lies just across the Barragem de Miranda, on the other side of a vast **hydroelectric dam** – at 528m the highest in the country, and the last before the Portuguese Douro becomes the Spanish Duero. If you have transport or fancy hitching, you might take advantage of this crossing (3km to the border post) to approach Zamora; there are no buses along the route.

Mogadouro

For a more unkempt and authentic picture of town life in the *Terra Fria*, take a look at **MOGADOURO**, 47km southwest of Miranda do Douro, and, specifically, head for its **Castle**. This is unexceptional as a monument, but the ground in front is a common where children play and farmers sort out their produce. During the harvest period the area is stacked high with dried *tremoços* bushes, which are consumed as beer-time snacks and used in soups. The castle hill also commands terrific views over a long, low horizon and a patchwork of fields and *pombais*.

Mogadouro would never be listed for its ancient buildings. The **Câmara Municipal** occupies a former convent, but is treated by the townspeople as their own backyard, herding cows home in the evening, saddling up pony carts, and playing at tossing coins for hours at a time. The one building to visit is the **Casa de Cultura**, on the Avenida da Espanha, which has small exhibitions upstairs; to find it, follow the signs for the hospital and then walk right down.

Should you want to **stay**, the are cheapish rooms at the *Pensão Russo*, Rua 5 de Outubro 10, ☎079/32134; ②), and, more enticingly, in the stone house below the far walls of the castle. There's a good café-restaurant (*Café Estoril*) below the castle: try to sample the delicious *posta à mogadourense* – steak with potato pancake. Another fine and unnamed restaurant is to be found behind the Turismo.

Be warned that the town is busy (and rooms at a premium) in August, when the emigrants are back home with their families. There is a **festa** on the penultimate weekend, before they leave the country again.

Freixo de Espada à Cinta

The twentieth century recedes even further as you travel south to **FREIXO DE ESPADA À CINTA**, reached by changing buses off the Miranda do Douro–Pocinho route at Freixo station, 14km away. The town feels end-of-the-worldish as the bus climbs down to its valley, hidden on each side by wild, dark mountains, a backdrop against which you might glimpse the occasional hawk or black kite. Arrive at dusk and you'll see donkeys being led back to their stables in the lower storeys of the houses.

Curiously, for such a remote outpost, there is a very rich parish church, or **Igreja Matriz** – part Romanesque, part Manueline – with a *retábulo* of paintings by Grão Vasco (see Viseu, p.152). Across the way from the church is a magnificent hexagonal **keep**, a landmark for miles around. Another, unpublicised, attraction is a mansion in the Largo do Outeiro, which maintains a garden of mulberry worms for silk production; ask around and you may be taken for a look.

Unexpectedly, too, there are a couple of decent **places to stay** – a good modern *hospedaria* (②) in the square where you arrive, and the *Pensão Paris* (③), 100m south of the church in a small square next to the *Banco Espirito Santo & Comercial*. For meals, try the very good café-restaurant on the way out of town to the south, up the hill on the left.

travel details

Trains

DOURO LINE

From Porto, 19 trains daily run to Livração (1hr 30min; change for **Tâmega line**) with 13 continuing to Régua (2hr 30min; change for **Corgo line** to Vila Real), 7 to Tua (3hr 30min; change for **Tua line**), and 4 to Pocinho (4hr 30min).

CORGO LINE

From Peso da Régua 5 trains daily to Vila Real (1hr).

TUA LINE

From Tua 4 trains daily (3 at weekends) to Mirandela (2hr; buses on to Bragança).

SABOR LINE

Buses have replaced trains on the route **from Pocinho** to Freixo de Espada à Cinta station

(1hr), Mogadouro (2hr) and Miranda do Douro (3hr). All departures are from the old train stations.

Buses

From Chaves to Vinhais/Bragança (3 daily, 2hr/3hr); Montalegre/Braga (4 daily, 1hr/3hr).

From Bragança to Miranda do Douro (3 daily; 1hr 30min).

From Lamego to Peso de Régua (12 daily; 30min).

From Lamego to Viseu, for Coimbra (6 on weekdays, 3 at weekends; 1hr 15min/3hr 45min).

Flights

From Lisbon to Vila Real, Bragança, and back, flights every weekday, 3 a week in winter .

From Lisbon to Chaves and back, 2 flights a week.

CHAPTER EIGHT

ALENTEJO

The **Alentejo** is an overwhelmingly agricultural region, dominated by vast cork plantations – the one crop that is well suited to the low rainfall, sweltering heat, and poor soil. It is traditionally one of the poorest parts of the country, (indeed one of the poorest parts of Europe), with a sparse population who scratch a living on huge feudal estates, known as *latifúndios*. Many of these were collectivised in the wake of the 1974 Revolution, but the workers possessed neither the financial nor the technical know-how to cope with a succession of poor harvests, and increasingly the original *latifundio* owners have been clawing back their estates at depressed prices. Jobs today are said to be scarcer than ever, despite European Community grants for modernisation programmes and new methods.

For visitors, the region's standout attraction is **Évora**, an historic city whose medieval walls and cathedral, and Roman temple, have put it very much on the tourist map. Elsewhere in **Alto Alentejo** – the "Upper Alentejo" province – few towns see more than a handful of visitors in a day. Yet there is much to see and enjoy: the spectacular fortifications of **Elvas**; the eagle's nest hilltop sites of **Monsaraz**, **Évora-Monte** and **Marvão**; and the marble towns of **Estremoz**, **Borba** and **Vila Viçosa**, to the northeast of Évora, where even the humblest homes are made of fine stone from the local quarries. This region is also scattered with **prehistoric remains**, sheltering over a dozen megalithic sites with dolmens, standing stones and stone circles.

South of Évora, the plains of **Baixo Alentejo** – the "Lower" province – have rather less appeal, and the towns, with the notable exception of **Beja**, once an important Moorish stronghold, can seem rather dull. The only features to make much impression here are the fading revolutionary slogans, daubed on buildings in even the smallest communities. The Beja district is known in Portugal as the reddest region of the country – its government still controlled by the Communists, who have gradually lost sway in the rest of Alentejo.

The Alentejo coastline here, though, almost as long a stretch as that of the Algarve, more than compensates for the lack of urban pleasures and the tedium of the inland landscape. Whipped by the Atlantic winds, its **beaches** can seem pretty wild, but in summer at least the sea is warm enough for swimming, and few of the resorts attract more than weekend crowds. Particularly enticing are the lagoons of **Melides** and **Santo André** – between Setúbal and the eminently avoidable industrial port of Sines – and the long beaches further south at **Ilha do Pessegueiro**, **Vila Nova de Milfontes** and **Zambujeira do Mar**. If you want to head straight for these southern resorts, there are express buses in summer from Lisbon. Accommodation is somewhat limited as yet, but there are plenty of campsites strategically positioned along the coast.

Another pull for the area – both upper and lower Alentejo – is the strength of **ornithological interest**. The region is home to hundreds of types of birds, from black storks to great bustards, all finely adapted to the mix of varied agriculture and marginal wilderness.

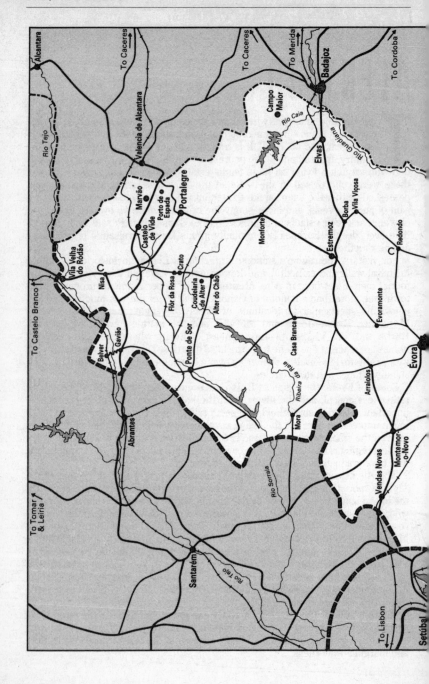

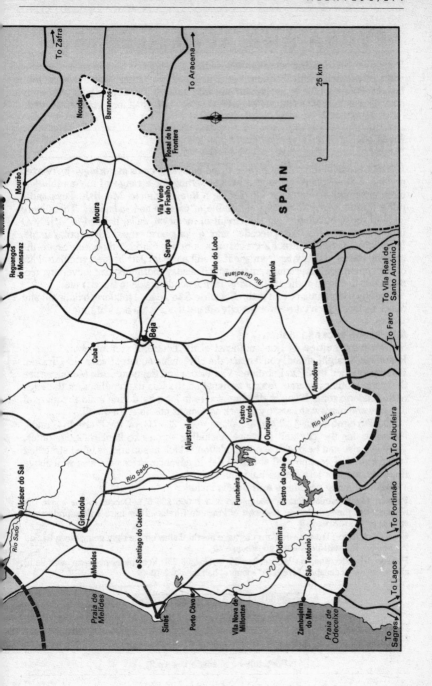

ÉVORA AND ALTO ALENTEJO

Unless you are heading south to the beaches, **Évora** provides the easiest starting point in Alentejo, with frequent and fast buses, or rather slower trains, from Lisbon. There is little to detain you en route, though if you have your own transport, the castle at MONTEMOR-O-NOVO is worth the halt for a clamber around.

Évora

ÉVORA is one of the most impressive and enjoyable cities in Portugal, its relaxed provincial atmosphere forming a perfect setting for a range of memorable and often intriguing monuments – including a Roman temple, Moorish alleys and a rather grand sixteenth-century ensemble of palaces and mansions. The superb state of these buildings, and the circuit of medieval walls, has led to UNESCO protection over the past decade, and a long-term restoration programme. Inevitably, they also attract a great many summer tourists; though, despite the crowds, the city is very far from spoilt. It still plays its part in the agricultural life of the region, with a produce market on Tuesday mornings; the university, too, re-established here in the 1970s, adds an independent side to the city life.

The city's big annual event is the **Feira de São João**, a folklore, handicraft and music festival which takes over the city during the last ten days of June.

Arrival and accommodation

Évora's **train station** is 1km southeast of the centre; if you follow the Rua da República, straight ahead, you'll reach the city's main square, **Praça do Giraldo**. **Buses** operated by *CP* to Estremoz, Vila Vicosa and Reguengos de Monsaraz use the station; others operate from a terminal on the Rua da República, at the edge of the historic zone. If you're **driving**, you're in for a hard time amid the maze of one-way and narrow streets; try to park as soon as possible, then walk.

The **Turismo** (9am–12.30pm & 2–7pm; ☎066/226 71), on the Praça do Giraldo, has maps for the city and province, including some excellent walking routes. They can also can help with accommodation, which in summer is often stretched to the limit and best booked at least a day in advance. Prices are also well above the odds, more or less comparable with Lisbon.

Recommended **pensions and hotels** include:

Pensão Os Manueis, Rua do Raimundo 35A (☎066/228 61). Decent rooms above the restaurant of the same name, just west of Praça do Giraldo. They have a (less preferable) annexe across the road. ②

Casa Portalegre, Travessa do Barão 18 (take the third alley on the right going down Rua do Raimundo). Reasonable, budget guesthouse. ②

Pensão Giraldo, Rua dos Mercadores 15 (☎066/258 33). Very pleasant rooms with bath; also some much cheaper, "overspill" rooms at half the price. ②–③

ROOM PRICE SCALES

The symbols used in our hotel listings denote the following price ranges.

① 2000–2500esc	③ 3500–5000esc	⑤ 8000–12,000esc
② 2500–3500esc	④ 5000–8000esc	⑥ 12,000esc and upwards

For a fuller explanation, see p.21.

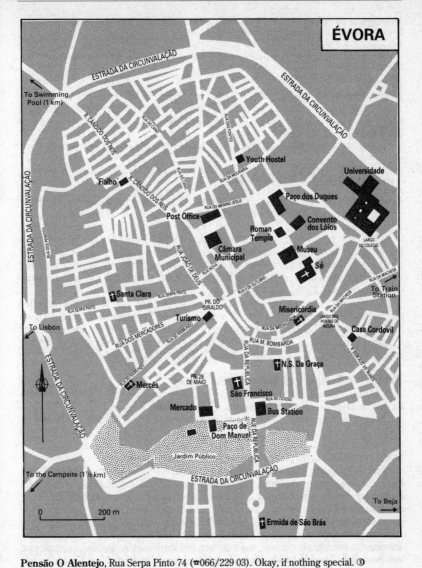

Pensão O Alentejo, Rua Serpa Pinto 74 (☎066/229 03). Okay, if nothing special. ③

Pensão Policarpo, Rua da Freira de Baixo 16 (☎066/224 24). Nice location, in a sidestreet near the cathedral. Comfortable, medium-range rooms, in a converted sixteenth-century townhouse; most rooms have bathrooms, though there are a few cheaper ones without. ③–④

Pensão-Residencial O Eborense, Largo da Misericórdia 1 (☎066/220 31). One step up from the *Policarpo*, this is a former ducal mansion – elegant , spacious and relaxed. Excellent breakfasts included in the room rates . ④

Pensão-Residencial Diana, Rua Diogo Cão 2 (☎066/220 08). Pleasant enough rooms in a house between the Sé and Praça do Giraldo. ④

Residencial Riviera, Rua 5º de Outubro 49 (☎066/233 04). Another reasonable if unexciting pension between the Sé and Praça do Giraldo. ④

Pousada dos Lóios, Largo do Conde de Vila Flor (☎066/240 51). One of the country's loveliest pousadas (see below), in the old monastery; double rooms are 20,000$00. ⑤

Camping

Évora's *Orbitur* **campsite** (☎066/251 90) is a couple of kilometres out of town on the Alcáçovas road. There's no reliable bus service and you're best off taking a taxi if you can't face the trudge. The campsite itself is clean, well equipped and open throughout the year.

Note that the **youth hostel** was closed, apparently indefinitely, in 1990.

The city and its monuments

Évora was shaped by **Roman** and **Moorish** occupations: the former is commemorated by a temple, the latter by a characteristic tangle of alleys, rising steeply among the whitewashed houses. Most of the city's monuments, however, date from the fourteenth to the sixteenth centuries, when Évora prospered under the patronage of the ruling **House of Avis**. To their royal display of wealth are owed the many noble palaces scattered about the town; the Jesuit **university**, founded in 1559 by Cardinal Henrique – the future "Cardinal King"; and a wonderful array of Manueline and Renaissance buildings.

That the city has survived so intact was due, in large part, to its decline after the Spanish usurpation of the throne in 1580. Future Portuguese monarchs chose to live nearer Lisbon, and the university was closed down; for the next four hundred years, Évora drifted back into a rural existence as a provincial market centre. Even today, the 40,000 population is only half its medieval level.

The Roman Temple and Convento dos Loios

The **Templo Romano** at the heart of the old city stands out as a kind of progenitor of the later monuments around it. Dating from the second century AD, it is the best-preserved temple in Portugal, despite (or perhaps because of) its use as a slaughterhouse until 1870. The stark remains consist of a small platform supporting more than a dozen granite columns with Corinthian capitals and marble entablature. Its popular attribution to Diana is apparently fanciful.

Directly opposite the temple, the magnificent fifteenth-century **Convento dos Lóios** has been converted into a top-grade, government-owned *pousada* hotel. Its cloisters now serve as a dining area in summer, and the hotel staff can be sniffy about allowing non-residents (or non-diners) in to look around. However, dress up as formally as you can – a tie is a help for men – and walk in regardless. The dual horseshoe arches, slender twisted columns and the intricate carvings on the doorway to the chapter house, midway around the cloister, are fine examples of the so-called Luso-Moorish style and have been attributed to Francisco de Arruda, architect of the aqueduct in Évora and the famous Belém tower in Lisbon.

To the left of the *pousada* lies the former conventual church, dedicated to **São João Evangelista**. This is today the private property of the ducal Cadaval family, who still occupy a wing or two of their adjacent ancestral palace. Ring the bell and you should be admitted (for a fee) to see the *azulejos* within, created early in the eighteenth century and the masterpiece of one António Oliveira Bernardes.

The Sé and Municipal Museum

Évora cathedral, the **Sé** (closed 12.30–2pm, 150$00), was begun in 1186, about twenty years after the reconquest of Évora from the Moors, and the Romanesque solidity of its original battlemented towers and roofline contrasts sharply with the pointed Gothic arches of subsequent and less militaristic additions, like the porch and central window.

The interior is more straightforwardly Gothic, although the choir and high altar were remodelled in the eighteenth century by the German Friedrich Ludwig, architect of the Convent at Mafra. For a nominal fee you can clamber onto a terrace above the west entrance and take an unusually close look at the towers and the *zimbório* (the lantern above the crossing of the transepts). Don't miss the cathedral museum, either: it's stuffed with treasures and relics, the prize exhibit being a carved statue of the Madonna whose midriff opens out to display layered scenes from the Bible.

Immediately adjacent to the Sé is the former archbishop's palace, now the **Museu Municipal** (10am–12.30pm & 2–5pm; closed Mon), housing important collections of fifteenth- and sixteenth-century Flemish and Portuguese paintings assembled from the city's churches and convents. These give a good illustration of the significance of Flemish artists in the development of the "Portuguese School", and reflect the strong medieval trade links between the two countries. Frei Carlos, probably the most important Flemish artist known to have worked in Évora, is well represented – but the centrepiece of the museum is a series of thirteen panels by an anonymous fifteenth-century Flemish artist, portraying scenes from the Life of the Virgin. This was once the cathedral altarpiece.

Up behind the museum, a quick stroll to the north will take you to the beautiful entrance courtyard of the **Antiga Universidade** – one of the liveliest corners of the city.

Elsewhere in the city

Great Portuguese and European architects likewise gravitated to Évora, and the **Ermida de São Brás,** just outside the city walls on the road to the train station, has been identified as an early work by Diogo de Boitaca, pioneer of the flamboyant Manueline style. Its tubular dunce-capped buttresses and crenellated roofline bear scant resemblance to his masterpieces at Lisbon and Setúbal, but they certainly foreshadow the style's uninhibited originality.

No less bizarre is the mid-sixteenth-century facade of the **Igreja da Graça**, out behind the bus station. At each of the corners of its Renaissance pediment, grotesque Atlas-giants support two globes – the emblem of Dom Manuel and his burgeoning overseas empire.

Close by here is the most memorable monument in Évora – the **Capela dos Ossos** ("Chapel of Bones") in the church of **São Francisco** (Mon–Sat 8.30am–1pm & 2.30–6pm; Sun 10am–1pm & 2.30–6pm, with winter closing at 5.30pm; small fee for taking photos). A timeless and gruesome memorial to the mortality of man, the walls and pillars of this chilling chamber are entirely covered in the bones of more than 5000 monks. There's a grim humour in the neat, artfully planned arrangement of skulls and tibias around the vaults, and in the rhyming inscription over the door which reads *"Nós ossos que aqui estamos, Pelos vossos esperamos"* ("We bones here are waiting for your bones"). Such macabre warnings to the faithless can be encountered in a couple of other locations in Portugal – at Campo Maior, to the north of Évora, and at Faro in the Algarve.

Another interesting feature of this fifteenth-century church is its large **porch**, which combines pointed, rounded, and horseshoe arches in a manner typical of Manueline architecture. Appropriately enough, the restored **Palácio de Dom Manuel** (1495–1521) – the king who gave his name to the style – lies no more than a minute's walk away, in the Jardim Público. It too incorporates inventive horseshoe arches with strange serrated edges.

Directly opposite São Francisco, on the Praça 1 de Maio, the rich craft traditions of the Évora district are well displayed in the **Museu do Artesanato Regional** (10am–noon & 2–5pm daily). The collections include pottery, weaving, tapestry, and carvings in wood cork and bone; modern pieces are on sale, too.

Lastly, it's worth following the **Rua do Cano**, north of the old centre, behind the Câmara Municipal. Here, you can travel the course of the medieval **Aqueduto**, into whose arches a row of houses has been incorporated.

Food, drink and the market

Évora goes to bed pretty early, as if exhausted by the tourgroups. For a late evening drink, you'll find just a couple of outdoor cafés in summer in the Praça do Giraldo, the very pleasant *Gelateria Zoka* at Rue Miguel Bombarda 10, and an occasional event at the university. Finding a place to eat, however, is no problem, with a range of decent restaurants, at most budgets, around the centre.

Restaurants

Restaurante A Choupana, Rua dos Mercadores 20. Best of a trio of modest-priced restaurants in this central old city street.

Restaurante O Túnel, Alcárcova de Baixo 59, just off Rua Miguel Bombarda.

Restaurante Guerreiro, Travessa Afonso Trigo 19, at the far end of Rua Cândido dos Reis. Spotless and packed with locals, this offers very tasty and inexpensive meals.

Restaurante Alcoucel, Rua Serpa Pinto 125. A little pricier but still very good value.

Restaurante Fialho, Travessa do Mascarenhas 14, off Rua Cândido dos Reis (see map). Reckoned by some to be one of the ten best restaurants in Portugal. Starters are superb.

Pousada dos Lóios, largo Conde de Vila Flor. Elegant and upmarket dining in the cloisters.

The market

On Tuesday and Saturday mornings the city hosts a thriving **market**, held on an open space past the bus station; from the centre, follow Rua da República south. The gathering is as much for locals as tourists, with a large livestock component (especially on Tuesdays), as well as domestic goods, junk and crafts – with plenty of the coarse Alentejan terracotta ware in evidence.

Arraiolos and some megaliths

The administrative district of Évora contains over a dozen **megalithic sites** dating from around 3000 BC. The dolmens, standing stones and stone circles found here have their origins in a culture which flourished in the peninsula before spreading north as far as Brittany and Denmark.

Two of the most accessible sites lie to the west and northwest of Évora, which makes them possible visits in conjunction with the carpet town of Arraiolos. For descriptions of – and directions to – other sites, ask at the Turismo in Évora for the leaflet entitled *Roteiro Turístico de Alguns Monumentos Megalíticos do Distrito do Évora*. A couple of other menhirs are covered with Monsaraz on p.281.

Os Almendres

One of the sites nearest to Évora is the **stone circle** and three-metre-high **menhir** (upright stone) at a cork plantation called **Os Almendres**, about 3km out of GUADALUPE, just south of the N114 Évora–Montemor road. Ask for directions in the village, and then it's a stiff uphill walk through wild country. Those interested in unusual birds will have the additional pleasure of seeing the **hoopoes** of the area.

Back on the N114, you can cut north across country to Arraiolos on the minor N370 road.

Arraiolos

ARRAIOLOS has been famed since the seventeenth century for its tapestries – and the craft has survived. Nowadays the designs tend to be simple and brightly coloured but the originals were based on elaborate Persian imports. Some of the workshops' most luxuriant eighteenth-century creations can be seen hanging on the walls of the Royal Palace at Queluz, near Lisbon.

Apart from the carpet shops – the carpets are expensive, but a lot less so than elsewhere – Arraiolos is a typical Alentejo village with its ruined castle, whitewashed houses, seventeenth-century pillory and fading anti-fascist graffiti. It is connected by **bus** with Évora four times a day.

Pavia

In the hamlet of **PAVIA**, 20km north of Arraiolos, is a massive **dolmen**, within which the tiny sixteenth-century chapel of São Dinis has been built. The effect is a bit grotesque and out of keeping with Pavia's traditional Alentejan architecture, but impressive nonetheless.

Estremoz and the marble towns

Northeast of Évora, quarry trucks and tracks announce your entry into marble country. Around Estremoz, the area is so rich in marble that it replaces brick or concrete as a building material, giving butchers' stalls and simple cottages the sort of luxurious finish you generally see only on churches and the grandest houses. **Estremoz**, **Borba** and **Vila Viçosa** are all distinctive marble towns, and the latter has an additional attraction in its **ducal palace** – the last residence of the Portuguese monarchy. An additional attraction, en route to Estremoz from Évora, is **Évora-Monte**, with its superb Renaissance castle.

Évora-Monte

The sixteenth-century **castle** of **ÉVORA-MONTE** stands on fortifications going back to Roman times and occupies a spectacular position, atop a steep mound. Its keep is constructed in Italian Renaissance style with four robust round towers, and adorned with a simple rope-like relief of Manueline stonework. Within are three vaulted chambers, each displaying intricately carved granite capitals. The town – predominantly medieval in appearance – rings the castle mound.

Estremoz

ESTREMOZ is the largest and liveliest of the three marble towns, and comes into its own every Saturday when the **market** takes over the **Rossio** – the main square of the lower town. This is a classic marketplace of huge dimensions, surrounded by bars, restaurants and churches; among the produce on sale are what are renowned as the best cheeses in Portugal, mainly made from ewes' and goats' milk. For centuries Estremoz has been famous, too, for the manufacture and sale of earthenware jars, and the shapes and styles of the pottery have remained basically unchanged since Roman times. The most distinctive products are the porous water coolers known as *moringues*, globe-shaped jars with narrow bases, two short spouts, and one handle.

Around the Rossio

Arriving by bus, you'll be dropped at the Rossio, next to the twin-towered marble facade of the **Câmara Municipal** . Originally this was one of the three convents on the square. It is worth a look inside for the grand staircase, decorated with late seventeenth-century *azulejos*.

At no. 62 on the Rossio is a **Museu Rural** (Tues–Sun 10am–noon & 2–6pm), with a display of earthenware figurines from the town potteries, and an illuminating ethnographic collection of locally produced artefacts in clay, wood, rush, straw, cork, textile and metal. Nearby at Rua de Serpa Pinto 87 is a **Museu Agricultura** (same hours) with a fascinating display of old kitchen equipment.

The Upper Town

In its heyday the population of Estremoz was ten times its current size and the town one of the most strongly fortified in the country. An army garrison is still stationed here, and the inner star-shaped ramparts of the **upper town** are well preserved.

On the hill within these fortifications stands a white, prison-like building, easily visible from the Rossio; despite its external austerity, it was once a **palace** of Dom Dinis, the king famous for his administrative, economic and military reforms. It is now a *pousada*, but you're free to wander in and look around; there's a splendid panoramic view from the tower.

Beyond loom the deep-cut battlements of the thirteenth-century keep, the **Torre de Menagem** – which bears a close resemblance to the great tower of Beja, its exact contemporary. From this part of town the castle of Évora-Monte is clearly visible on the horizon, thirty kilometres to the southwest. Opposite the tower, in an old almshouse, is a small **Museu Municipal** (Tues–Sun 10am–noon & 2–6pm),with more displays of Estremoz pottery and Alentejan life.

Practicalities

An enthusiastically-staffed **Turismo** (Mon–Fri 9.30am–12.30pm & 2–5.30pm, Sat 9.30am–12.30pm, Sun 2–5.30pm) is to be found on Largo da República, a small square just off the Rossio at the southwest end; if it's closed, try the tourist kiosk at the corner of Rossio.

Unless you're stopping over on Friday night, before the market, **accommodation** should be easy enough to find. Options are:

Café Alentejano, Rossio 15 (☎068/223 43). Modest rooms above the café . ①

Casa Miguel José, Travessa da Levada 8 (☎068/223 26). Characterful private house. ①

Pensão Mateus, Rua Dr. Gomes Resende 26 (☎068/222 262). ②
Residencial Carvalho, Largo da República 27 (☎068/227 12). A fairly pleasant pension. ③
Hotel Alentejano, Rossio 50 (☎068/227 17). ④
Pousada da Rainha Santa Isabel, in the Upper Town (☎068/226 18). One of the grandest Portuguese *pousadas*, with a regal feel to the rooms and stairway. Doubles at 20,000$00. ⑤

There's no shortage of **restaurants** either. On a budget, the best deal has to be a tiny, nameless place at Rua Dr. Gomes de Resende Junior 15, on the way to the upper town. Other good alternatives include the *Pensão Mateus*, which does a wonderful *ensopado de borrego* – the local lamb stew speciality – and the rather pricier *Restaurante Zé Varunca* on Avenida Tomás Alcaide. For a treat, the *Pousada* restaurant has all you could ask for in atmosphere and cooking.

Borba

Eleven kilometres east of Estremoz is **BORBA**, a dazzlingly white little place, where just about anything not whitewashed is white marble. The town seems not to have exploited the wider commercial possibilities of its quarries, though, and with the exception of a fine eighteenth-century fountain there are no particular signs of wealth, no extravagant mansions or remarkable churches. All this only serves to make more extraordinary the extensive use of marble in even the most commonplace cottages, shops and streets. Borba is simply an unassuming town which happens to be built of marble. The town's other main attribute is the wine of the local cooperative, which is marketed throughout Portugal. **Rooms** are available at the *Restaurante Lisboeta* at Rua de Mateus Pais 31.

Vila Viçosa

The road from Borba to **VILA VIÇOSA** is lined on either side with enormous marble quarries, and everything from the pavements to the toilets in the bus station are made of the local marble. The town is justly famous, too, for its **Paço Ducal**, the last palace-residence of the Bragança dynasty.

Orientation is straightforward, with the **Old Town** straight ahead of you, walking from the bus station, and the Paço Ducal beyond it.

The Paço Ducal

The dukes of Bragança were descended from the illegitimate offspring of João I of Avis, and established their seat at Vila Viçosa in the fifteenth century. For the next two centuries they were on the edge of the ruling circle but their claims to the throne were overridden in 1580 by Philip II of Spain. Sixty years later, while Spanish attention was diverted by a revolt in Catalonia, Portuguese resentment erupted and massive public pressure forced the reluctant João, eighth Duke of Bragança, to seize the throne; his descendants ruled Portugal until the foundation of the Republic in 1910.

Despite a choice of sumptuous palaces throughout Portugal – Mafra, Sintra and Queluz are the most renowned – the Bragança kings retained a special affection for their residence at Vila Viçosa, a relatively ordinary country home, built in the sixteenth and seventeenth centuries. Dom Carlos spent his last night here before his assassination on the riverfront in Lisbon in 1908, and it was a favourite haven of his successor, Manuel II, the last king of Portugal.

The **palace** (Tues–Sun 9am–1pm & 2–6pm; guided tour lasts 1hr; 300$00) has a simple rhythmic facade. Inside, the standard regal trappings of the more formal chambers are tedious, but the private apartments and mementos of Dom Carlos and his wife Marie-Amélia have a *Hello* magazine fasincation. Faded family photographs hang on the walls, changes of clothing are laid out, and the table is set for dinner: the whole scene seems to await the royals' return. In reality, Dom Duarte, present heir to the nonexistent throne, spends his days in experimental eco-farming at his estate near Viseu.

The old town and castle

The **old town**, still enclosed within walls on its hilltop site, was built by Dom Dinis at the end of the thirteenth century and reinforced four centuries later. Originally the population of Vila Viçosa was based within these walls and a few of the cottages are still lived in.

The **Castle**, in one corner of the ensemble, was the seat of the Braganças before the construction of their palace. Its interior (Tues–Sun 9am–1pm & 2–6pm; guided tour 45min; 150$00) has been renovated beyond recognition and houses an indifferent archaeological museum. However, from the roof there's a good view of the Braganças' old **Tapada Real** (Royal Hunting Ground), set within its eighteen-kilometre circuit of walls.

Practicalities

Vila Viçosa is a quiet town and despite its attractions there's very little available **accommodation**. Your best bet is to arrange private rooms through the **Turismo** (☎068/983 05) by the bus station on the elongated Praça da República. There are budget rooms (①) at Praça da República 27 and at Rua Públia Hortênsia de Castro 2 by the Santa Cruz church (both ①). Alternatively, there's an upmarket *Turihab* lodging, the *Casa dos Arcos* on Praça Martim Afonso de Sousa 16 (☎068/98518; ④). Although it's officially discouraged, you could also camp around the old town; alternatively, the bus services make daytrips feasible from Évora or Estremoz.

Best of the town's **restaurants** is the *Framar* at Praça da República 35, near the bus station.

South to Monsaraz

The road **south from Vila Viçosa** provides great insights into the Alentejo, taking you past ALANDROAL and TERENA, both quite prosperous villages, set below a castle, before entering a region of scattered farming communities, where the walls are still daubed with slogans from the 1974 Revolution. A couple of buses daily cover the route, with numerous diversions along crumbling back-roads, to the town of REGUENGOS DE MONSARAZ (which is also connected by a dull road with Évora, to its west). From here, there are sporadic local connections 17km further east to the dramatic fortified village of **Monsaraz** – known to the locals as "Ninho das Águias" (Eagles' Nest).

If you're stranded in **REGUENGOS DE MONSARAZ**, there are some dirt-cheap rooms (unadvertised) just off the Praça da Liberdade and directly opposite the *Café Central*, itself the liveliest place to sample the splendid wine of the local cooperative.

Monsaraz

MONSARAZ stands perched high above the border plains, a tiny village, fortified to the hilt and entirely contained within its walls. From its heights, the landscape of the Alentejo takes on a magical quality, with absolutely nothing stirring
amid a sensational panorama of sunbaked fields, neatly cultivated and dotted with
cork and olive trees. To the east, you can make out the Rio Guadiana, delineating
the frontier with Spain.

There's something peculiarly satisfying, too, about such a small village. From
the clocktower of the main gateway, the only real street leads past the only bar
(unmarked, on the left, next to the post office) to the village square. Here you'll
find an unusual eighteenth-century pillory topped by a sphere of the universe.

The keep, or **Torre de Menagem**, stands at the far end of the village, part of a
chain of frontier fortresses continued to the south at Mourão, Moura and Serpa,
and to the north at Alandroal, Elvas and Campo Maior. When the Moors were
ejected in 1167 the village was handed over to the Knights Templar, and later to
their successors, the Order of Christ; their fort has been converted to a bullring.

A few **rooms** are available at the bar in Monsaraz, where you can also get basic
meals. There's also a *Turismo Rural* lodging on the main street, the *Casa Dom
Nuno*, at Rua Direita 6 (☎066/551 46; ③), and a rather fancy hotel, the Estalagem
de Monsaraz (☎066/551 12; ④), with a pool and restaurant, in the settlement
below the castle walls. Freelance camping outside the walls isn't encouraged.

Menhirs around Monsaraz

There are two giant *menhirs* close by Monsaraz, just off the Reguengos road: at
Outeiro, and at **Bulhoa**, where the stone is covered with symbolic engravings.
Details of these sites are included in the Évora Turismo leaflet.

A further menhir is to be found between Monsaraz and the Guadiana river, at
MONTE DO XAREZ. This one is four metres high, surrounded by a square of
standing stones, and was probably the site of neolithic fertility rites.

East to Elvas and Campo Maior

The hilltop town of **ELVAS** was long one of Portugal's mightiest frontier posts, a
response to the Spanish stronghold of Badajoz, 15km east across the Rio ·
Guadiana. Its star-shaped walls and trio of forts are among the most complex military fortifications surviving in Europe – and superbly preserved. If you make a
special detour to see just one Alentejo castle, Elvas is the natural choice; in addition, the town itself is a delight – all steep cobbled streets and mansions.

Some history

Elvas was recaptured from the Moors in 1230, and withstood periodic attacks from
Spain through much of the following three centuries. It succumbed just once,
however, to Spanish conquest, when the garrison was betrayed by Spanish bribery
in 1580, allowing Philip II to enter and, for a period the following year, establish his
court. The town subsequently made amends, during the war over the succession
of Philip IV to the Portuguese territories. In 1644, the garrison resisted a nine-day
siege by Spanish troops, and in 1658, with its numbers reduced by epidemic to a
mere thousand, saw off a 15,000-strong Spanish army.

During this period, the fortifications underwent intensive rebuilding and expansion, and they were pressed into service twice more: in 1801, when the town withstood a Spanish siege during the War of the Oranges, and ten years later, during the Peninsular War, when the fort provided the base from which Wellington advanced to launch his bloody but successful assault on Badajoz. Perhaps out of tradition as much as anything, a military garrison is still stationed in the town.

Arriving and accommodation

The walls make Elvas a pretty easy place to get your bearings. Arriving by bus, you'll find yourself right in the centre of town, in the Praça da República; the Turismo (Mon–Fri 9am–7pm, Sat & Sun 9am–1pm; ☎068/62 22 36) is next door. Shuttle buses also run into this square from the train station, 4km down the Campo Maior road at Fontaínhas; the station is on the Lisbon–Badajoz line.

The Turismo can help with **private rooms**, which you may need, given the dearth of **pensions and hotels**. Choices include:

Quartos: *Joaquim Dias*, Rua João d'Olivença 5 (☎068/634 22); *Lucinda Travancas*, Rua Aires Vareza 2 (☎069/62 47 22); *Maria Garcia*, Rua Aires Vareza 5 (☎069/62 21 26). A trio of private room lodgings, just off the Praça da República. ①

Casa de Hóspedes Arco do Bispo, Rua Sineiro 4 (☎068/634 22). Cheapest guesthouse in town: from the Praça da República, turn right down the hill and past the police station. ①

Pensão Luso-Espanhola, Rua Rui de Melo (☎068/62 30 92). Comfortable but rather overpriced pension. ④

Estalagem Dom Sancho II, Praça da República 20 (☎068/62 26 84). Characterful hotel in the main square, with a fine restaurant downstairs. ④

Hotel Dom Luís, Avda. de Badajoz (☎068/62 27 56). Pricey hotel, with doubles at a most unwelcoming 13,000$00. ⑥

Pousada de Santa Luzia, Avda. de Badajoz (☎068/62 21 94).One of the country's more missable pousadas – a modern building, outside the town walls . ④

The town

Any exploration of Elvas has to start with its **fortifications**. The earliest stretches of the walls date from the thirteenth century, but most of what you see today is the result of the Wars of Succession with Spain in the seventeenth century. Under the direction of the great French military engineer, Vauban, the old circuit of walls was supplemented by extensive moats and star-shaped ramparts, their bastions jutting out at irregular but carefully judged intervals to maximise the effects of artillery crossfire. Echoes of these designs are to be seen at Estremoz and throughout Portugal.

The aqueduct and central Elvas

WIth its jagged and ungainly course, the **Aqueduto Amoreira**, at the entrance to the town, looks at first like a bizarre extension of the fortifications. Despite its stark and awkward appearance, it is an imaginative and original feat of engineering: monstrous piles of masonry, distinctive cylindrical buttresses, and up to five tiers of arches support a tiny water channel along its seven-kilometre course, until it is finally discharged at the fountain in Largo da Misericórdia. It was built between 1498 and 1622 to the Manueline designs of Francisco de Arruda.

Arruda was also responsible for the **Igreja de Nossa Senhora da Assunção**, dominating the Praça da República, which was the cathedral until Elvas lost episcopal status in 1882. Alterations in the seventeenth and eighteenth centuries left a ragged hodge-podge of styles, but its original Manueline inspiration remains evident on the south portal and in the unusual conical dome above the belfry.

Behind the cathedral lies the **Largo de Santa Clara**, a tiny cobbled square built on a slope around a splendid sixteenth-century **pelourinho** (pillory). Criminals were chained from the four metal hooks toward the top but, aside from the grisly technicalities, it's also a work of art, with typically Manueline twisted column, and rope-like decorations.

Directly opposite stands the strange and beautiful church of **Nossa Senhora da Consolação** (Tues–Sun 9am–12.30pm & 2.30–6pm). From the outside it's nothing more than a whitewashed wall with a mediocre Renaissance porch, but the interior reveals a sumptuous octagonal chapel: richly painted columns support a central cupola and virtually all surfaces are decorated with magnificent seventeenth-century *azulejos*. The chapel was built between 1543 and 1557, on the site of a Knights Templar chapel – the insipiration for its octagonal design.

The Largo de Santa Clara tapers upwards to a restored tenth-century archway flanked by fortified towers and surmounted by a **loggia** or gallery. Originally part of the old town walls, this was built by the Moors, who occupied Elvas from the early eighth century until 1226. The street beneath the gateway leads to the **Castle** (9.30am–12.30pm & 2.30–7pm; closed Thurs), also constructed by the Moors, on an old Roman fortified site, but strengthened by Dom Dinis and João II in the late fifteenth century.

Peripheral forts

Further chains in the fortifications remodelled by Vauban are the **Forte Nossa Senhora da Graça**, a couple of kilometres north of Elvas, and the superb star-shaped **Forte de Santa Luzia**, a few minutes' walk to the south of the town.

Festivals and food

Elvas' weekly event is its **Monday market** – a vibrantly chaotic affair attracting people from miles around, held just outside town behind the aqueduct. The town's big annual bash is its **Festa de São Mateus**, which lasts a week in late September, encompassing a programme of agricultural, cultural and religious events. It's worth seeing, although accommodation is at a premium at this time.

The rest of the time, the town is a fairly quiet place, with sparse diversions beyond the sights and a cluster of **restaurants**. Best of the budget places is the invariably packed *Canal Sete* at Rua dos Sapateiros 16 – off the main square, opposite the Turismo. More expensive, but with good reputations for cooking, are *O Alentejo* on Rua da Cadeia, *O Aqueduto* on the Avenida da Piedade, and the *Estalagem Dom Sancho* on the Praça da República. If you want to put your own picnic together, the place to buy supplies is a small, early-morning food **market** held Monday to Saturday at the bottom of Rua dos Chilões.

Campo Maior

The road to the fortress town of **CAMPO MAIOR**, 18km north of Elvas, passes through olive groves and sunflower fields. It's a pleasant trip, though the town would be unremarkable were it not for the presence of its **Capela dos Ossos** (daily 9am–noon & 2–5pm), a diminutive version of the Chapel of Bones in Évora .

This stands immediately to the right of the large parish church just off Rua 1 de Maio: ask for the key in the church itself or try the door next to the chapel. Adding to the surreal effect, the entrance is through a neat local government office.

The walls and vaults in the claustrophobic chapel interior are completely covered in human bones, while two skeletons hang from the walls, and three rows of skulls are positioned on the window ledge to inspect passers-by. The chapel is dated 1766 and its purpose is indicated by two verses from the Book of Job traced out in collarbones near the window: "My bone cleaveth to my skin and to my flesh, and I am escaped with the skin of my teeth". Job is complaining of his horrific physical and mental suffering, but takes solace in the knowledge that "though after my skin worms destroy this body, yet in my flesh shall I see God".

The chapel may have been "furnished" by the disaster which devastated Campo Maior in 1732, when a powder magazine in the town's **Castle** was struck by lightning, killing 1500 people and destroying 823 houses. Today it is little more than a ruin, though with fine views over the borderlands.

Practicalities

The journey from Elvas takes just 35 minutes (5 buses daily, 2 on Sun), making it an easy sidetrip. There's a simple **pension**, *A Tentadora*, at Rua 1 de Maio; and a pleasant **restaurant**, *O Faisão*, opposite the parish church.

Portalegre

PORTALEGRE is the capital, market centre and transport hub of the northern district of Alto Alentejo. It is an attractive town, crouched at the foot of the Serra de São Mamede, and endowed with the province's usual contingent of white-washed and walled old quarters, along with some interesting reminders of industrial history. These include a couple of cork factories, whose great twin chimneys greet you on the way into town, and a tapestry workshop, the last remnant of a thriving period of textile production in the seventeenth and eighteenth centuries. The wealth produced in these years, in particular from silk workshops, has a further legacy in an ensemble of grand mercantile mansions and townhouses, which give the town an air of faded affluence.

Arriving and accommodation

All the main roads converge on the **Rossio**, a large square at the centre of the new town. Uphill from here, the Rua 5º de Outubro runs into the walled **old town**. The **bus station** is just a few blocks from the Rossio on Rua Nuno Alvarez Pereira. Shuttle buses to and from here meet **trains** at the Estação de Portalegre, 12km out of town to the south, on the Lisbon–Badajoz line.

There is limited **accommodation** available, and it's advisable to book a day ahead to be sure of a bed. Options are:

Pousada de Juventude: Antigo Convento de São Francisco, Praça da República (☎045/ 235 68; open 8–10am & 6–11pm). Excellent youth hostel, housed in a converted Franciscan monastery near the cork factories.

Pensão Nova, Rua 31º de Janeiro 28 (☎045/216 05). Cheap but decidedly rundown pension; the reception also runs the nearby **Pensão São Pedro** boarding house. ①

Pensão Alto Alentejo, Rua 19º de Junho (☎045/222 90). Comfortable pension near the Sé, with reasonably priced rooms with private bath, and heating in winter. ②

Hotel Dom João III, Avda. da Liberdade (☎045/211 92). A dull, functional hotel, opposite the Jardin Municipal in the new town. ②

Camping is quite an attractive alternative. The *Orbitur* site (☎045/228 48; open mid-Jan to mid-Nov) at Quinta da Sáude, 4km into the hills, is well equipped, with electricity, showers, a few bungalows for rent, and a surprisingly good restaurant.

The town

The town's boom years in the seventeenth century are immediately apparent as you walk up Rua 19 de Junho – the main thoroughfare of the Old Town – which is lined by a spectacular concentration of late Renaissance and Baroque mansions.

At the south end of the street, and dominating the quarter, is the **Sé**, an austere building save for a flash of fancy in the pyramidal pinnacles of its towers. To one side of this an eighteenth-century palace houses a **Museu Municipal** (Mon & Wed–Sun 10am–12.30pm & 2–5.30pm; one-hour tour; 50$00). It's not exactly a compelling visit, with much routine furniture and fittings, though there are some lovely ceramics and ivories.

The most interesting visit in town is to the **Fábrica Real de Tapisseria** (Mon–Fri: tours on the half-hour from 9.30–11am & 2.30–4pm), the single surviving tapestry factory. It's housed in the new town, in a seventeenth-century former Jesuit convent on Rua Gomes Fernandes, just off the Rossio. The guided tour conducts you through the studios and weaving hall – where 5000 shades of wool are used in the reproduction of centuries-old patterns – and on to a gallery displaying works about to be dispatched to their very well-heeled patrons.

Bars and restaurants

The Rossio is the liveliest place for a drink, by day or evening; there's not much life in the Old Town. Among the restaurants, try:

Restaurante O Cortiço, Rua Dom Nuno Alvares Pereira 17, near the Rossio. Very reasonable fare draws nightly crowds of locals; a speciality is the typically Alentejan dish of *migas*.

Restaurante Alpendre, Rua 31º de Janeiro 19. Another, somewhat pricier recommendation just off the Rossio.

Restaurante O Abrigo, Rua de Elvas 74 (closed Tues). An inexpensive and reliable choice up in the old town.

Crato, Flôr da Rosa and Alter do Chão

Directly to the east of Portalegre, **Crato** has small-town charms and, nearby, an impressive **dolmen**, as well as the beautiful honey-stone convent of **Flôr da Rosa**. Horse enthusiasts may also want to make the 13km detour south of Crato to **Alter do Chão**, home of a prestigious *coudelaria* (stud farm).

Buses run intermittently from Portalegre to both Crato and Alter do Chão, while the **Estação de Crato** gives access to **Lisbon–Badajoz line**, with its connections west to Abrantes and east to Elvas.

Crato

CRATO is an ancient agricultural town which has clearly seen better days and larger populations. A trio of imposing and ornate churches, and the elegant **Varanda do Grão Prior** in the main square, attest, like Portalegre's monuments, to the textile boom years of the sixteenth century. The *varanda* is the most interesting of the structures – built for the outdoor celebration of mass. Also worth a look is a town mansion a couple of streets away, by the public gardens, which houses a small **museum** (erratic hours) of Alto Alentejo handicrafts and domestic traditions. Well into this century alms were handed out to the local poor from a balcony-chapel upstairs.

The town castle was once among the mightiest of the Alentejo, but today it's a gorgeous pastoral ruin, overrun by farm animals, fig trees and oregano plants. It is normally locked, but keys are generally kept beneath an abandoned blue cart in the field in front; if they're not there, ask at one of the nearby farm dwellings. From the ramparts, there is a splendid view over the town and across the countless rows of olive trees to the hills of Portalegre.

For a good rural walk from Crato, follow the by-road towards Aldeia da Mata. On the left hand side of the road, about 5km from town, is what is reckoned to be the best-preserved **dolmen** in Portugal. On the corner of the road leading out of town, you'll find an excellent **adega**, with delicious home cooking and a crowded bar where everyone plays *belho* – a kind of miniature version of *boules*.

Rooms and transport

The town has just one small **pension**, above the *Café Parque* on Avenida Dom Nuno Álvares Pereira (☎045/97223; ②), though the seasonal **Turismo**, in a hut near the public gardens, may be able to fix you up with rooms in private houses. **Campers** can pick their own spots by the old Roman bridge near the train station, or up by the castle.

If you arrive at the **train station**, 3km from town, the station master will telephone for a taxi, which is not expensive.

Flôr da Rosa

Two kilometres north of Crato lies the village of **FLÔR DA ROSA**, traditionally a centre for **pottery**, with seventy families in the trade in the early part of this century. Today the distinctive *olaria* of the region is made in only two workshops, whose shared kiln is near the convent, high above the broad streets and low houses. Their methods of manufacture haven't changed in centuries, though the clay – yellow for waterproofing, grey for ovenware – has to be sought further and further afield. Purchases break easily, but it's nice to know that these functional (and inexpensive) pieces aren't designed for the tourist trade.

The **Convento de Flôr da Rosa**, founded in the fourteenth century and much endowed over the next two hundred years, was abandoned in 1897, due to leaking roofs and a decaying structure. Over recent years, however, a sizeable injection of state aid has been used to restore the main conventual building, whose church and reception rooms can be visited. Around the main building, you can also make out vestiges of stables and a kitchen, and trace the plan of the gardens, laid out in the insignia of the Order of Malta, in honour of the famous warlord **Nuno Álvares Pereira**, whose family founded the convent.

Father Pereira's tomb (dated 1382) is prominent in the narrow, soaring convent **church**. Adjoining it, on the ground floor, is the sixteenth-century **Sala do Capítulo**, distinguished by fine brickwork, fan-vaulting and a **Gothic cloister**. On the first floor are the monks' **dormitories**, whose open casements offer sweeping views across acres of olive trees.

Alter do Chão

ALTER DO CHÃO, 13km to the south of Crato, is another town that did well in the sixteenth-century textile years: a past attested to by an attractive Renaissance marble fountain and an array of handsome townhouses. There is a **castle**, too, whose central tower can be climbed for an overview of the region, but the chief reason for a visit is the **Coudelaria de Alter-Real** stud farm, 3km out of town.

If you can time a visit, April 25 is the best day to be at the Coudelaria, when the annual sale takes place. The town's main festival – the **Festa de Nossa Senhora da Alegria** – occurs on the following day.

The Coudelaria

The **Coudelaria de Alter-Real** was founded in 1748 by Dom João V of the House of Bragança, and remained in the family until 1910 when the War Office took it over. Today, maintained by the state, it is open for public visits daily, from around 9am to 5pm. To see the horses in action it's best to arrive in the morning; between 10am and noon you can watch them filing in from the fields to feed, accompanied by the ringing of forty bells.

The tours of the stud are also interesting with a museum display of carriages and horse regalia, through wihich you are conducted at a stately pace by a retired cavalry officer (tips welcomed). Alter-Real horses have been sought after since the stud's foundation – one is depicted in the equestrian statue of Dom José in Lisbon's Praça do Comércio, for example – and they remain the favoured breed of the Portuguese mounted police and the Lisbon Riding School at Queluz.

Practicalities

Several **pensions** are clustered in the road opposite the castle in Alter do Chão. Ask for rooms above the *Café Simas* or at the *Pensão Ferreira* (Avda. Dr. João Pestana, ☎045/62254). Get up before 9.30am if you're interested in seeing the Coudelaria coach and horses come in to town to collect the mail.

For **meals**, the *Café Simas* is pretty good, and there are wonderful cakes at the nearby *Pastelaria Ateneia*. **Buses** connect the town with Estremoz and Crato.

Castelo de Vide and Marvão

The upland district **north of Portalegre** is a bucolic landscape, with tree-clad mountain ranges and a series of gorgeous hilltop villages. Among these, the best targets are **Castelo de Vide** and **Marvão**, both with castles, and the former with a spa. Castelo de Vide is the most easily accessible, connected by bus five times daily with Portalegre; Marvão has two daily services, Monday to Friday only. Getting between the two, the 9.20am and 6.15pm buses from Castelo de Vide to Portalegre connect with buses to Marvão at the junction of PORTAGEM.

Castelo de Vide

CASTELO DE VIDE covers the slopes around a fourteenth-century castle, its blindingly white cottages delineated in brilliant contrast to the greenery around. Arriving by bus, you'll be dropped at a **pelourinho** outside the **Turismo** in the centre of town. From here, half a dozen parallel streets make a sharp climb up to the aptly named **Praça Alta** on the edge of town. The main road, meanwhile, peters out into a narrow path, descending past a tranquil Renaissance fountain to the twisting alleyways of the **Judiaria** – the old Jewish quarter. Amid the cottages, most of which preserve Gothic doorways and windows, is a thirteenth-century **synagogue** – the oldest surviving in Portugal. From the outside it doesn't look very different from the cottages, so you will probably need to ask directions; its key is to be found in a special compartment on the outside wall.

On a hill above the Judiaria, the **Castle** (summer 8am–6pm; winter 10am–5pm) squats within the wider fortifications of the original medieval village. While there, chat to the castle guide and he'll probably show you the elaborate moving wooden toys that he produces, and his workshop; his neighbour is a lacemaker who trains young women in the art. Samples of both crafts are for sale at a nearby crafts centre, known as **O Ouriço**.

Accommodation

Given its size, the town has a surprising amount of accommodation, with three **pensions**, two **hotels** and a couple of *Turismo Rural* lodgings. Options are:

Pensão O Cantinho Particular, Rua Miguel Bombarda 7–9 (☎045/917 51). Friendly if a bit on the basic side. ①

Pensão Xinxel, Largo do Paço Novo 5 (☎045/914 06). Very much a family boarding house. ①

Pensão Casa do Parque, Avda. da Aramenha 37 (☎045/912 50). Nicest of the pensions. ③

Albergaria Jardim, Rua Sequeira Sameiro (☎045/912 17). Pleasant hotel flanking the municipal gardens; fine restaurant attached. ④

Hotel Sol e Serra, Estrada de São Vicente (☎045/912 50). Comfortable but soulless. ⑤

For details of *Turismo Rural* rooms, contact the **Turismo** (☎045/916 63).

Marvão

Beautiful as Castelo de Vide is, **MARVÃO** surpasses it. The panoramas from its remote, eyrie site are unrivalled and the atmosphere even quieter than a population of less than a thousand would suggest. No more than a handful of houses – each as scrupulously whitewashed as the rest – lie outside the seventeenth-century walls.

Originally the village seems to have been an outlying suburb of *Medobriga*, a mysterious Roman city which has vanished almost without trace. Its inhabitants fled before the Moorish advance in around 715 but later returned to live under Muslim rule, when the place was renamed after Marvan, the Moorish Lord of Coimbra. It fell to the Christians in 1166 and the present **Castle** was built by Dom Dinis in 1229 – another important link in the chain of outposts along the Spanish border. The castle stands at the far end of the village, its massive walls blending into the sharp slopes of the serra. It appears dauntingly impenetrable and was indeed captured only once, in 1833, when the attackers entered by means of a secret gate.

The village makes a superb night's stop, as several houses within the walls are rented out under the **Turihab** scheme. In some of these you can get just a room, while others are rented out as a unit; prices range from ② to ⑤; for details and bookings, contact the **Turismo** (☎045/932 26). Additional, more upmarket accommodation is provided by the *Estalagem Dom Dinis* (☎045/932 36; ④) and the attractively converted *Pousada de Santa Maria* (☎045/932 01; ⑥).

Marvão-Beirã: on into Spain

Lisbon–Madrid trains stop at the station of MARVÃO-BEIRÃ, 9km north of Marvão village. Heading for Spain by public transport, this is the easiest way to go; the station cantina has a few rooms upstairs if you need to stay overnight between connections. The road border at GALEGOS, 14km east of Marvão, is open to traffic but very few cars use it.

In addition, there's one daily bus from Portalegre direct to the Spanish border town of Valencia de Alcantara.

Northwest of Portalegre: Belver Castle

Travelling northwest from Portalegre, the N18/N118 roads – the latter in atrocious condition – take you up to the Tejo valley, and, of course, the Alentejo border. The most interesting targets on this route are the **castles** of **Abrantes** and **Almourol** in Ribatejo (see p.123–124) and **Belver**, which, although sited with its town on the north bank of the Tejo, is technically a part of Alentejo. If you are dependent on public transport, it is easiest to take a train or bus to Abrantes, and approach Belver from there.

Belver

The **Castle** of **BELVER** is one of the most famous in the country, its fanciful position, name and tiny size having ensured it a place in dozens of Portuguese legends. The name comes from "belo ver" (beautiful to see), the supposed exclamation of some medieval princess, waking up to look out from its keep at the river valley below.

The castle dates from the twelfth century, when the Portuguese frontier stood at the Tejo, the Moors having reclaimed all the territories to the south, save Évora, that Afonso Henriques had conquered for his kingdom. Its founder was Dom Sancho I, who entrusted its construction and care to the knight-monks of the Order of Saint John. Its walls form an irregular pentagon, tracing the crown of a hill, with a narrow access path to limit attackers to virtual single file.

If you find the castle locked, search out the jovial guard who lives at no. 1 on the main square in Belver village. For a small fee, he will unlock the **chapel** to show you its formidable fifteenth-century reliquary. All the pieces of bone were stolen during the French invasions in the nineteenth century, but fortunately for the villagers there was still a casket of "spares" hidden away by the priest, and these substitutes are nowadays paraded around town at the **Festa de Santa Reliquária**, held during the last five days in August. At the beginning of August there is also a **folk-dancing** competition.

Rooms and transport

You're very likely to track down the castle guard sharing a few jokes over a glass of *bagaceira* (Portugal's cheapest hangover) in Belver's single **café-restaurant-pension**. Rooms (②) are usually available, outside the August festival times.

Buses leave from the Praça or from above the **train station**, which is directly below the village beside the river. If you take the **train** north along the valley towards Castelo Branco, look out for the striking rock faces before Vila Velha de Ródão known as the **Portas do Ródão** (Gates of Ródão).

BAIXO (LOWER) ALENTEJO

The hot, dry inland routes of southern Alentejo have little to offer beyond a stop at **Beja** – the most interesting southern Alentejo town – en route to the Algarve, or at the frontier villages of **Serpa** or **Mértola**, if you're heading for Spain. The **coast-line**, however, is another matter, with resorts like **Vila Nova de Milfontes**, **Almograve** and **Zambujeira do Mar** providing an attractively low-key alternative to the summer crowds on the Algarve. Their only disadvantage – and the reason for a very patchy tourist development – is their exposure to the Atlantic winds, which at times creates huge breakers and dangerous swimming conditions. However, as long as you're prepared to spend occasional days out of the water, they are relaxed and enjoyable places to take it easy for a few days by the sea.

All the beaches are situated along minor roads, but there are functional local **bus services** from Santiago do Cacém and Odemira. Alternatively, coming from Lisbon, you can take the *Zambujeira Express* bus direct to Vila Nova de Milfontes, Almograve and Zambujeira do Mar; it leaves Lisbon twice a day from the Casal Ribeiro terminal and, as with all *expressos*, it's wise to buy tickets in advance.

South from Lisbon: Alcácer do Sal

Heading south into the Alentejo from Lisbon or Setúbal, the main road loops around the **Rio Sado estuary**, through **Alcácer do Sal**, at the mouth of the river, and on through the agricultural town of **Grândola**. The latter was made legendary through the song *Grândola vila morena*, the broadcasting of which was the pre-arranged signal for the start of the 1974 Revolution. At Grândola the roads diverge: southwest to the coast; east to Beja, Serpa and, ultimately, Spanish Andalucía.

An enjoyable alternative approach for drivers to Grândola and the coast is to take the ferry from Setúbal to Tróia and make your way down the long sand-fringed **Pensinsula de Tróia** along the N253 (see p.93).

Alcácer do Sal

ALCÁCER DO SAL is one of Portugal's oldest ports, founded by the Phoenicians and a regional capital under the Moors – from whence its name (*al-Ksar*, the town) derives. The other part of its name, *do Sal*, "of salt", reflects the dominace of the salt industry in these parts; the Sado estuary is still fringed with salt marshes.

The town today is slightly seedy-looking, but attractively so, particularly along its waterfront promenade. At the end of the promenade is the part-ruined Moorish **castle** (10am–noon & 2–5pm), from which there are striking views of the lush green paddy-fields which almost surround the town, and of the storks' nests on the church rooftops.

There are a couple of good restaurants and bakeries – try the *pinhadas,* a honey and pine-seed sweet – facing the river. If you decide to stay the night, the *Pensão Alcacerense* is just a few doors from the bus station, though rather noisy; good private **rooms** can be arranged through the *Restaurante Flor,* on the other side of the main road.

On the first Saturday in October the town hosts a major **regional fair** which lasts for three days. It's one of the most enjoyable in the south.

East towards Beja: Viana do Alentejo

Heading towards Beja, the main road runs via Grândola, 23km south of Alcácer do Sal. If you have transport, you could instead drive directly east, cutting across a succession of country roads. The first of these – the N5 to TORRÃO – curves around the Rio Sado, past the **Barragem de Vale do Gaio**. Sited on the edge of the reservoir is the *Pousada de Vale do Gaio* (☎065/661 00; ⑥), a fairly simple conversion of the lodge used by the dam engineers.

Continuing east, along the N383, you pass through **VIANA DO ALENTEJO**, a sleepy and typically southern Alentejan village which preserves a highly decorative **castle-ensemble**, full of Mudejar and Manueline features. The castle walls were built, on a pentagonal plan, by Dom Dinis in 1313, and the ensemble expanded under Dom João II and Dom Manuel I in the late fifteenth century. To this latter period belong a sequence of elaborate battlements and the parish church, part of a striking group of buildings within the walls, encompassing a Misericórdia, town hall, cistern and pelourinho.

From Viana do Alentejo, the N384 runs east, past another huge reservoir, to meet the main Évora–Beja road.

Beja

On the inland route through southern Alentejo, **BEJA** appears as a welcome oasis amid the sweltering and featureless wheatfields. It's the most interesting stop, south of Évora, on the way to the Algarve, and once past the modern suburbs reveals an unhurried old quarter with a cluster of peculiar churches, a beautiful convent and a wonderfully fancy thirteenth-century castle.

Arrival and accommodation

The old quarter is a circular tangle of streets, enclosed within a ring road that has replaced the town walls. At its heart are a pair of interlocking squares – the Largo de Santa Maria and Largo dos Duques de Beja. The **bus station** lies five minutes' walk southeast of this quarter; the **train station** five minutes' northeast. A very helpful **Turismo** (☎084/236 93) is located just south of the central squares at Rua Capitão J. F. de Sousa 25.

Most of the town's **accommodation** is to be found within a few blocks of the Turismo. There is not a lot of choice, however, and in summer it is well worth booking ahead. Options are:

Pensão Rocha, Rua Dom Nuno Álvares Pereira 12 (☎084/242 71). Basic but clean. ①

Pensão Pax Julia, Rua Pedro Victor 8. Marginally superior. ②

Residencial Bejense, Rua do Capitão J.F. de Sousa 57 (☎084/250 01). Another pretty basic pension, close by the Turismo. ①

Pensão Tomás, Rua Alexandre Herculano 7 (☎084/246 13). Recently renovated pension, with pleasant rooms and a friendly owner. ③

Residencial Coelho, Praça da República 15 (☎084/240 31). Decent-value pension, with a few rooms overlooking the square; all rooms have private showers. ③

Residencial Santa Barbara, Rua de Mértola 56 (☎084/220 28). Functional pension out from the centre, just off the road to Faro. ③

Residencial Cristina, Rua de Mértola 71 (☎084/230 35). A rather soulless, modern hotel – but Beja's most comfortable, if it's comforts you're after. ④

The town's **Camping Municipal** (☎084/243 28) is located on the south side of town, past the stadium on the Avenida Vasco da Gama. It's a fairly pleasant, shaded site, and adjoins the local **swimming pool**.

The town

Beja has a pretty compact historic centre and you can take in a good tour of the sights in half a day. In summer, the heat in this plains town will probably turn you towards a bar within an hour or so.

Convento de Nossa Senhora da Conceição

Beja is best known in Portugal for the love affair of a seventeenth-century nun who lived in the **Convento de Nossa Senhora da Conceição**, just off the Largo dos Duques de Beja. Sister Mariana Alcoforado is believed to have fallen in love with Count Chamilly, a French cavalry officer, and is credited with the notorious (in Portugal anyway) *Five Love Letters of a Portuguese Nun*, first published in Paris in 1669. The originals have never been discovered, and a scholarly debate has raged over the authenticity of the French "translation". Nonetheless, English and Portuguese editions soon appeared and the letters became internationally famous as a classic of romantic literature.

Sentimental associations aside, the **convent** is quite a building. Founded in the fifteenth century, it has a panoply of Manueline fripperies, with elaborate portals and a rhythmic roofline decorated with balustrades and pinnacles. The walls of the cloisters and chapter house are completely covered with multicoloured sixteenth- and seventeenth-century *azulejos*, and present one of the finest examples of this art form. The other highlight is a magnificent Rococo chapel, sumptuously gilded and embellished with flying cherubs.

The convent was dissolved in 1834 and today houses the **Museu Regional** (Mon–Sat 9.30am–1pm & 2.30–5pm). Compared to the architecture of the building, the museum pieces are comparatively lacklustre, though they include a wide-ranging display on the town's past eras – Roman and Visigothic stone, fifteenth- to eighteenth-century Portuguese painting, and the grille through which the errant nun first glimpsed her lover.

The Castle and around town

Beja's **Castle** (10am–1pm & 2–6pm) rises decoratively on the edge of the old quarter. It was built – yet again – by Dom Dinis and is remarkable for the playful battlements of its keep, or *Torre de Menagem*. Similarly, an exaggerated horseshoe window halfway up hints at the architect's artistic intent. In the shadow of the keep stands the Visigothic basilica of **Santo Amaro**, today a small archaeological museum. The building is a rare survival from pre-Moorish Portugal; the interior columns are carved with seventh-century geometric motifs.

Among other churches in Beja, the most distinctive is the mid-sixteenth-century **Misericórdia** in the Praça da República; its huge projecting porch served originally as a meat market and the stonework is deliberately chiselled to give a coarse, "rustic" appearance. Earlier, fortress-inclined Gothic elements are to be seen on the church of **Santa Maria**, in the heart of the old quarter, and on the fifteenth-century **Ermida de Santo André**, on the road out to Lisbon, which is endowed with gigantic tubular buttresses, similar and contemporary with those on the Ermida de São Brás at Évora.

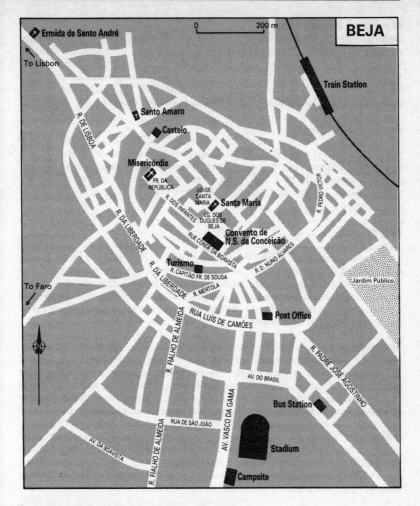

Practicalities: food and transport

There's a fair selection of **restaurants and bars** around the old town. Pick from the following:

Casa Primavera, Largo do Correio – opposite the post office. A real gem: cheap and filling.

Restaurante Alentejano, Largo dos Duques de Beja. Another good local.

Restaurante Pena, Praça de Diogo Fernandes de Beja 21 – between the pedestrian shopping district and the castle. Modest prices and dependable cooking.

Restaurante Tomás, Rua Alexandre Herculano. Excellent restaurant below the *pensão* – the quality is much higher than a "pension restaurant" would suggest.

Restaurante O Portão, off Rua dos Infantes. Nothing much to look at but arguably the best meals in town.

Moving on: buses and trains

Beja has good transport connections to the rest of central and southern Portugal, as well as a bus link to Sevilla in Spain. In most cases you have a choice of bus or train: for Lisbon and the western Algarve take the **train**, while for Évora, Vila Real de Santo António (for the eastern Algarve) and Santiago do Cacém (for the western Algarve) it's quicker to go by **bus**. **Car hire** is available through the *Agência de Viagens Pax-Júlia*, across the road from the Turismo.

Around Beja: Pisões

The only point of interest in the immediate vicinity of Beja is at **PISÕES**, 8km to the southwest, just past PENEDO GORDO. Here the remains of a first- to fourth-century AD **Roman villa** include well-preserved mosaics, a heating system under the floor, a pool and baths. The site is sporadically closed for further excavation, so check opening times first with the Turismo in Beja.

Serpa

The small market town of **SERPA** lies 30km east of Beja, midway to the border with Spanish Extremadura. It's an enjoyable stop if you are heading towards Spain, or feel like a roundabout but scenic approach to the Algarve, via Mértola. In addition to its classic Alentejan attractions – a walled centre, a castle and narrow whitewashed streets – it offers access (for drivers, anyway) to the Pulo do Lobo waterfall, 18km to the south.

The town

Serpa was at various times occupied by Celts, Romans, Moors and Spaniards, and inevitably is dominated by a **Castle**, predominatnly Moorish, which offers spectacular vistas of the Alentejan plain to the north and the hills to the south. There is a tiny archeological museum in the keep and, close by, the thirteenth-century church of **Santa Maria**, with an altarpiece of intricate wood carving, surrounded by seventeenth-century *azulejos*.

From the castle, you can track the course of the well-preserved eleventh-century **aqueduct**. It is worth a look from close up, too, with the remnants of a *nora* or chain-pump are at one end. If you have time to fill, you might also wander down to the **Museu Etnographica** near the hospital, which offers an interesting account of the changing economic activity of the area.

Practicalities

The **bus station**, with three connections a day to Beja and one through bus to Sevilla, is on the central Largo do Rossio, where – unmarked at no. 75 – you'll also find the town's one **pension**, the *Virgínia* (☎084/901 45; ②). At the southwest corner of town there's a new and well-equipped **campsite** (open year-round) and **swimming pool** complex.

Out of town, there is also a modern **pousada**, the *São Gens* (☎084/903 27; ⑤), 2km south, on a hill known as Alto de São Gens; and a British-run **Turihab** lodging, the *Quinta de São Bras* (☎084/902 72; ③), 5km south, on the road to the Pulo de Lobo waterfall (see following).

Among Serpa's **restaurants**, the *O Zé* at Praça da República 10 is highly recommended for its atmosphere, *gaspacho* and delicious local cheese.

The Pulo do Lobo waterfall

If you have transport, the **Pulo do Lobo** (Wolf's Leap) waterfalls are an easy half-day's excursion from Serpa, or a diverting route heading south to Mértola and the Algarve. They are sited amid stark, rocky scenery, 18km south of Serpa.

From Serpa, the road to the falls is signposted behind the Jardim Botanico. It is well surfaced as far as the village of SÃO BRÁS (6km); as it climbs into the mountainous countryside, it deteriorates suddenly to a rough track, which becomes narrow and vertiginous as it leads down, around the 16km mark, to a stream – a tributary of the Guadiana. Cars can cross this stream quite easily and, following the track, after a couple of kilometres you can turn left to arrive very close to the Pulo do Lobo. Around the falls – which you'll probably have to yourself – the river has carved a deep gorge through the hills, and the valley is made up of strikingly eerie rock formations.

If you want to make a circuit of it, you can reach the EN122, 3km northwest of Mértola, via a pair of hamlets, Amendoeira da Serra and Corte de Gafo de Cima.

South to the Algarve – and Mértola

There are three main routes south from Beja to the Algarve. The most interesting and enjoyable is the **N122** to Vila Real de Santo António, right on the eastern border of the province with Spain; this passes through the old Moorish fortress town of **Mértola** and a scenic stretch of the Guadiana river valley. Two buses daily cover the route.

Alternatives, more convenient if you are heading for the western or central Algarve, are to take the N391 across the plains to **Castro Verde**, then the fast E1 to **Albufeira** or the more mountainous N2 to **Faro**. Again, these routes are served by two buses daily.

Via Castro Verde

If you're a birder, you may consider the route from **Beja to Castro Verde** a must, for the chance to see **great bustards** winging across the plains. This apart, the road has few attractions, with a handful of small agricultural towns set amid interminable parched tracts of wheatfields.

Following the N2, directly south of Castro Verde, the route continues in similar vein until you hit the lush greenery of the **Serra do Malhão** and the **Serra do Caldeirão** around Ameixial – just across the border in the Algarve.

To the west, the N264 provides faster access to the Algarve, as well as an interesting detour in the **Castro da Cola**, the remains of a small, Romano-Celtic village, similar to the *citânias* of the north. This is located to the west of the road, a few kilometres beyond the village of ALDEIA DOS PALHEIROS. There is a pilgrimage at the site on September 7–8.

Via Mértola

The N122 gets a green edge on the Michelin map as it approaches **MÉRTOLA** – a sure sign of rising gradients and an escape from the plains. The town is in fact as beautifully sited as any in the south, set high above the Rio Guadiana, around the extensive ruins of a Moorish frontier castle. It's a quiet, isolated place, certainly worth a night's stopover – more if you feel like a walking or birding base. The region is home to the rare black stork.

The obvious focus for a visit is the **Castle**, views from whose keep sweep across the Guadiana valley. To the north, you may be able to make out the copper mines a few kilometres down the Serpa road at Mina de São Domingos. These were until recent decades the source of the town's meagre employment. Up until the war, they were owned by a British company, which employed a private police force and treated the workers with appalling brutality. Older residents in the bars still recall these times.

Back in town, take time to look around the **Igreja Matriz**, which started life as a Moorish mosque and retains its *mihrab* (prayer niche) behind the altar on the eastern wall. Also worth searching out is the little **Museu Arqueológico** (Mon–Sat 9am–12.30pm & 2–5.30pm), a well-presented collection of recoveries from local digs, notably Roman pottery, jewellery and needles, plus a set of strange-looking religious figures retrieved from the castle.

Orientation is straightforward, with **buses** stopping by the bridge, close to the centre of town and the **Turismo** (Mon–Fri 9am–noon & 2–5.30pm), who organise **boat trips on the Rio Guadiana** in summer. Staying overnight, you have a choice of two fairly simple **pensions**: the *Residencial Beira Rio*, Rua Dr. Afonso Costa (☎086/623 40; ②), has the edge on the *San Remo*, Av. Aureliano Mira Fernandes (☎086/621 84; ②) in character and situation. The *Restaurante Boa Viagem*, opposite the bus stop, offers a good and inexpensive selection of **meals**.

Santiago do Cacém

Heading south from Lisbon or Setúbal, **SANTIAGO DO CACÉM** is the first place that might tempt you to stop. A pleasant little provincial town, it is overlooked by a castle, and has on its outskirts – half an hour's walk – the fascinating Roman ruins of Mirobriga. In addition, it's only a short bus journey to the **Santo André and Melides lagoons**, two of the Alentejo's finest beaches.

The town

In the town, there are a couple of minor sights to be found. The Moorish **Castle**, presently under restoration, was rebuilt by the Knights Templar and now serves as a cemetery. There are splendid views over to the sea from the battlements, whose crumbling masonry provides the habitat for a curious species of large golden beetle.

It's also worth making your way to the **Museu Municipal** (Tues–Fri 9am–12.30pm & 2–5pm), one of the most interesting of its kind, housed in one of Salazar's more notorious prisons in a small park just northeast of the centre. A suitably political strain pervades its display: one of the spartan prison cells has been preserved while two others have been converted into a "typical country bedroom" and "a rich bourgeois bedroom". Even a drawing in the section devoted to the local primary school shows a child's impression of the "Great Revolution" of 1974.

Mirobriga

The archaeological section in Santiago's museum should whet your appetite for a visit to **Roman Mirobriga** (Tues–Sat 9am–12.30pm & 2–5pm; 150$00). From the centre, follow the Rua de Lisboa for about a kilometre up the hill, then take the marked turning to the right, and, after another ten-minute walk, turn left at a sign marking the entrance to the site, which lies isolated amid arcadian green hills.

At the highest point of the site a **Temple of Jupiter** has been partly reconstructed, overlooking a small forum with a row of shops built into its supporting wall. A paved street descends to a **villa and bath complex** whose underground central heating system is still intact.

Practicalities

If you want to base yourself in the town, rather than at the beaches, there's a rather thin spread of **accommodation**, including a few private rooms advertised in windows. There is no Turismo in the town.

Pensions and hotels include:

Pensão–Restaurante Covas, Rua Cidade de Setúbal 10 – by the bus station (☎069/226 75). Cheap and unpretentious rooms and meals. ②

Pensão Esperança, Largo 25 de Abril 17–21 (☎069/221 93). Basic but adequate. ②

Residencial Gabriel, Rua Professor Egas Moniz 24 (☎069/222 45). Not a bad choice, but try to avoid being placed in its inappropriately named annexe – the clean but utterly soul-destroying **Pensão Ideal** on Rua Calouste Gulbenkian. ②

Albergaria Dom Nuno, Avda. Dom Nuno Álvares Pereira (☎069/233 25). A rather dull modern hotel. ④

Pousada de São Tiago, Estrada Nacional – just out of town on the Lisbon road (☎069/224 59). Pleasant if not over-memorable *pousada*, with a pool and a decent restaurant. ④

Two good **restaurants** are *O Grelhador*, Rua de Camilo Castelo Branco 26, and *O Braseiro*, Rua Prof. Egas Moniz 15. There's also a fine covered **market** in the centre of town – useful for stocking up for a stay at one of the beaches.

Santo André and Melides lagoons

There are seven buses a day from Santiago do Cacém to **LAGOA DE SANTO ANDRÉ**, and it's a short walk from there along the shore to **LAGOA DE MELIDES**. These two **lagoon beaches**, separated from the sea by a narrow strip of sand, are named after the nearest towns inland, but each has its own small, laid-back community entirely devoted to having a good time on the beach. The **campsites** at both places are of a high standard and there are masses of signs offering rooms, chalets and houses to let. There's a premium on space in July and August, but at other times accommodation should be no problem at all. People still camp on the beach, too, though the authorities áre taking an ever-harder line on this.

At either beach, the social scene centres around the beach-cafés and ice-cream stalls. Beyond these is the sand – miles and miles of it, stretching all the way to Comporta in the north and down to Sines in the south. The sea is very enticing with high waves and good surf, but be warned and take local advice on water conditions: the undertow can be fierce and people are drowned every year.

Sines, Porto Covo and Pessegueiro

SINES – the cape just south of Santiago do Cacém – is the one place *not* to go to on this stretch of coast. Vasco da Gama was born here, but he'd probably turn in his grave if he could see the massive **oil refinery** and the sacrifice of the environment to new roads, railways, pipelines and wells.

The ugliness around Sines is short-lived and just south of here there's a whole new set of untouched little beach settlements. The best of all of them is the furthest south, the area around Ilha do Pessegueiro, reached from the road heading down to **PORTO CÔVO** – which is served by three buses daily from Sines. Porto Covo itself is a simple, unassuming little place with a small cove harbour, a pension (*Abelha*, ☎069/951 08; ②), a few rooms to let . . . and a sewage plant right on the oceanfront. The compensation is that Ilha do Pessegueiro is within easy walking distance.

Ilha do Pessegueiro

ILHA DO PESSEGUEIRO (Peach Tree Island) can be reached by road from the Porto Covo–Vila Nova de Milfontes road – but the nicest approach is to walk, following the coastal path south from Porto Covo. It's only a couple of kilometres.

The resort's name actually applies to the beach facing the island, which is less than a kilometre offshore (and reachable on local fishing boats). On the mainland, there's a wonderful bar-restaurant, a small seaside **fort** and an increasing number of **campsites**. Quite a few people – a good mix of Portuguese and foreign travellers – camp out at Pessegueiro, but if you want to get away from them, it's no problem at all. There are facilities in the form of toilets and showers, and basic provisions are easy to come by. All in all, it makes an excellent place to hole up for a while if the very simple (and inexpensive) life appeals.

Odemira and the south Alentejo resorts

On the southern half of the Alentejo coast, **Odemira** is the main inland base, offering local bus connections to the beach resorts of **Vila Nova de Milfontes**, **Almograve** and **Zambujeira do Mar**.

Odemira

In summer, unless you're camping, you'd be lucky to find accommodation in any of these southern Alentejo resorts, so it's not a bad idea to stay in **ODEMIRA** and take daytrips to the seaside. The town has several **pensions**, best of which are the *Residencial Rita* (Largo do Poço Novo; ☎083/224 23; ②) and *Residencial Idálio*, both off to the left when you come out of the bus station. The ancient *Pensão Dionísio* is a poor fallback, a couple of minutes away in the centre, at Rua Serpa Pinto 4.

Among **restaurants**, try *O Escondidinho* – cheap and reasonable, at the lower end of town.

Vila Nova de Milfontes

VILA NOVA DE MILFONTES lies on the estuary of the Rio Mira, whose sandy banks gradually merge into the coastline. It is an advantage of geography for sailors (the port is reputed to have harboured Hannibal and his Carthaginians during a storm) and swimmers: if the waves of the Atlantic are too fierce you can always swim in the estuary – though beware of very strong currents.

The resort is not exactly undiscovered – the Germans, especially, built villas here through the 1980s – and it is perhaps the most crowded and popular resort in the Alentejo. It's a pretty place, though, with a striking little castle; Portuguese families on holiday from the big cities of the north give it a homely atmosphere quite distinct from the cosmopolitan trendiness of the Algarve. If you want to escape some of the crowds, take the ferry from the little jetty to the far side of the estuary to beaches nearby.

All the **pensions** are likely to be fully booked in summer, but off season you can take your pick of excellent and inexpensive rooms. If you fancy a spot of luxury, the best lodgings in town – indeed the best on the whole Alentejo coast – are at the Castelo de Milfontes – the fort, which is privately owned and offers highly atmospheric full board (its owner, Dona Margarida, is said to be very picky about her guests; ☎083/961 08; ⑥). More affordable alternatives include the *Casa dos Arcos* (☎083/962 64; ③) and the English-run *Boavista Hotel* (③), 2km from the centre behind the petrol station on the main road. There's a large **campsite** just the north of the village.

Almograve

The coastline south of Vila Nova de Milfontes becomes ever more rugged and spectacular. At the tiny resort of **ALMOGRAVE**, five kilometres west of the Odemira–Vila Nova de Milfontes road, huge waves come crashing down on the rocks and for most of the day swimming is impossible. It can get very crowded at high tide, too, when the beaches are reduced to thin strips with occasional waves drenching everybody's belongings; but, for all that, it's an exhilarating place.

You could camp virtually anywhere back from the beach at Almograve, and there are a few cafés and bars, but the bus service from Odemira is just right for a day-trip. If you are interested in a **month-long stay** in the village, a Danish woman, Henja Listner (Almograve, 7630 Odemira), offers bed-and-breakfast, catering mainly to writers and painters; write in advance.

Zambujeira do Mar

At the village of **ZAMBUJEIRA DO MAR**, south of Odemira and 7km west of the main road, a large cliff provides a dramatic backdrop to the beach, which, like that of Vila Nova de Milfontes, can get very crowded in July and August.

The scenery more than compensates for the winds and the sea – which can get positively chilly, even in summer – but can't disguise the rundown state of the village and the encircling villas. There are a couple of small **pensions**, the *Naresol* and *Residencial Mar-e-Sol*, a few *quartos*, and a couple of bars, and the schedule of the buses from Odemira makes a daytrip impossible. A reasonable **campsite** is being redeveloped about 1km from the cliffs; if you want to rough it meanwhile, make sure you've got enough rocks to hold the tent down. Good seafood is alleged to be available at the harbour 3km along the road to the north of the village.

On to the Algarve

Zambujeira is the southernmost Alentejo beach, and an attractive road twists its way into the hills of the Algarve from the river crossing at ODECEIXE. For the most dramatic approach, however, take the road from Odemira through the **Serra de Monchique**, descending to the Algarve coast at Portimão.

travel details

Trains

BEIRA BAIXA LINE

From Lisbon 4 trains daily through Abrantes to Belver (3hr), 3 continuing to Castelo Branco and Guarda.

LESTE LINE

From Lisbon 7 trains daily to Abrantes: 2 go on to Marvão (3hr), Valencia de Alcantara (3hr 15min), and Madrid (11hr); 4 go on to Crato (3hr 40min), Portalegre (4hr), and Elvas (4hr 30min), with 3 continuing to Badajoz, Spain (5hr 30min).

SUL LINE (ALENTEJO)

From Lisbon 4 trains daily to Casa Branca (2hr), Évora (2hr 30min) and Beja (3hr 30min). 2 continue from Beja to Faro, Lagos and Vila Real de Santo Antonio in the Algarve.

SADO LINE (LISBON–ALGARVE)

From Lisbon 4 trains daily to Tunes (5hr; connections on Algarve line) via Alcácer do Sal (2hr), Grandola (2hr 20min) and Ermidas-Sado. From Ermidas-Sado 2 connections daily by bus to Santiago do Cacém (40min) and Sines (1hr).

Buses

INLAND ALENTEJO

From Évora bus station to Lisbon (6 daily; 3hr) of which 2 go on to Porto (7hr 35min) and Braga (9hr); Vila Viçosa/Borba/Elvas (5; 1hr 25min/1hr 35min/2hr); Monsaraz (2; 2hr 30min); Estremoz (3; 1hr – via Évora-Monte); Portalegre (2; 3hr); Beja (2; 2hr); Arraiolos (4; 35min).

From Évora train station *CP* buses: 4 daily to Estremoz (1hr 20min), Borba (1hr 35min) and Vila Viçosa (1hr 40min); 4 daily to Reguengos de Monsaraz (1hr).

From Portalegre to Elvas (3 daily; 1hr 30min); Castelo de Vide (5; 30min).

From Elvas to Estremoz (4 daily; 1hr); Badajoz (4; 30min).

From Beja to Santiago do Cacém (3 daily; 2hr 30min); Faro (4; 3hr 30min); Serpa (3; 45min); Seville, Spain (1; 5hr).

From Estremoz 2 daily to Portalegre (1hr 30min).

COASTAL ALENTEJO

From Lisbon to Vila Nova de Milfontes/Almograve/Zambujeira (2 daily expresses; 4hr/4hr 30min/4hr 50min).

From Odemira to Zambujeira (2; 30min), Lagos (2; 1hr 45min), Almograve/Vila Nova de Milfontes (8; 40–50min).

CHAPTER NINE

THE ALGARVE

With its long, sandy beaches and picturesque rocky coves, the **Algarve** has attracted more tourist development than the rest of the country put together. In parts, this has all but destroyed the charms that it was intended to exploit. The strip of coast from Faro west to Lagos has suffered most, with its endless villa complexes creating a rather depressing Mediterranean surburbia. On the fringes, though, especially around Sagres and Tavira, things are far better, with small-scale and relaxed resorts and the odd undeveloped beach or island sandbank.

The **coastline** in fact has two quite distinct characters. To the **west of Faro** you'll find the classic postcard images of the province – a series of tiny bays and coves, broken up by weird rocky outcrops and fantastic grottoes. They're at their most exotic around the resort towns of **Lagos** and **Albufeira**, the major resorts. For fewer crowds, better bases here would be the beach village of **Salema** or the historic cape of **Sagres** – site of Henry the Navigator's naval school.

East of Faro, there's a complete change as you encounter the first of a series of sandy offshore islets, the *Ilhas*, which front the coastline virtually all the way to the Spanish border. Overall, this is the quieter section of the coast – developers haven't yet come to grips with the islands – and it has the bonus of much warmer waters than those further west. First- choice bases along this stretch would be Faro, Olhão and Tavira, all of which offer access to sandbank-islands.

Inland, there are scattered attractions in the Roman ruins of **Estói**, north of Faro, and the old Moorish town of **Silves**, easily reached from Portimão. The outstanding area, however, is the **Serra de Monchique**, the highest mountain range in the south, with cork and chestnut woods, remote little villages, and a beautiful old spa in **Caldas de Monchique**.

Seasons and accommodation

The Algarve is an all-year-round destination, with sunny and relatively mild winters. In many respects the region is at its best in **spring** or **winter**. Most pensions and restaurants stay open, so rooms are easy to find – if often unheated at the cheaper end of the scale – and people are genuinely welcoming of visitors. May has an added attraction in the Algarve's **International Music Festival**, sponsored by the Gulbenkian Foundation, and hosting major classical artists.

If you come in the summer, without a booking, finding **accommodation** can be a real struggle. Over the last couple of years, there has been scarcely a hotel vacancy on the coast in July or August, and little on offer from the touts for private rooms (*quartos*). Your own transport is a great help at these times, with more vacancies inland, though car hire, again, is best booked in advance.

Be prepared, too, for very high summer prices relative to the rest of the country. Conversely, **off-season travel** in the Algarve will get you some of the best deals in the country, with luxury hotels offering all-in packages at discounts of up to 70 percent; check out the latest deals at the local tourist office.

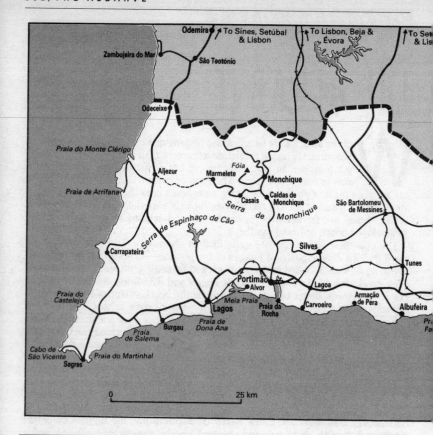

FARO AND THE EAST ALGARVE

The administrative capital of the Algarve, **Faro** hosts the international airport and acts as a transport hub for the region. The city is connected with Lisbon by fast express coaches and offers efficient access to most Algarve towns by **bus** and – a little slower – on the Algarve **rail line**. Although no great holiday destination in itself, the centre of the town is more attractive than the ugly concrete suburbs might suggest and has some good beaches of its own within easy reach.

The Algarve coastline to the **east of Faro**, protected by an elongated sandbank for much of its length, has suffered less from intensive tourist development than the west. The towns of **Tavira** and **Vila Real de Santo António** preserve a fair bit of character, while most of the resorts are fairly small-scale, with boats (or sometimes a wade) out to the wonderful beaches on the seawards side of the *ilhas*.

Inland, the eastern Algarve offers few diversions, with the nearest towns of interest – Mértola, Serpa and Beja – across the border in **Alentejo**. With longer detours in mind, you might find equal rewards in travelling across the frontier **into Spain**, with Sevilla only a couple of hours from Vila Real de Santo António.

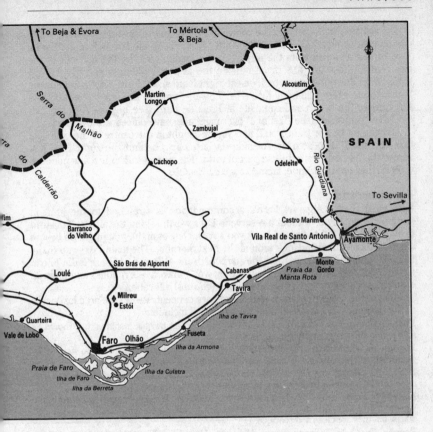

Faro

FARO has been transformed from a sleepy provincial town into a centre of tourism, trade and commerce within twenty years. Ranged around its attractive harbour, it has all the facilities of a modern European resort, with a bustling, pedestrianised shopping area, and chic restaurants and bars. Excellent **beaches**, too, are within easy reach, and in summer there's quite a **nightlife** scene, as thousands of travellers pass through on their way to and from the airport. There are certainly better places to spend a holiday on the Algarve, but for a night or two's stay at either end, it can be an enjoyable enough base.

Arriving and orientation

In the summer months, flights land at Faro **airport** (☎089/242 01), six kilometres west of the town centre, 24 hours a day. Here, you'll find a police and first aid post, bank, post office and tourist office, but no shops to speak of and nothing much in the provisions line apart from the routine airport restaurant. When flying out again, take food supplies as insurance against flight delays.

The easiest way to get into the centre of Faro from the airport is by **taxi**, which should cost about 800$00, or 1000$00 after 8pm; check the fare before getting in. Two **buses** also run from the airport to the Jardim spot, by the harbour in the city centre; these are #18 (from outside the airport buildings) and #16 (which stops 200m down the main road, on the right hand side); from May to September both operate every half-hour (Mon–Fri 7.30am–8pm). In the other direction, the #16 runs to the beach and campsite at Praia de Faro (see below). A number of **car hire** companies (see "Listings" overpage) also have offices at the airport.

Arriving by bus or train, you'll find yourself right in the centre of the city. The **bus terminal** is located on Avenida da Republica, behind the *Hotel Eva*, just across the harbour from the old part of town. The **train station** is a few minutes' walk further up the avenue, facing Largo da Estacão.

Accommodation

Like most of the Algarve, Faro's accommodation is stretched to the limit in summer. If you fly in without a reservation, it's worth asking the airport **Turismo** desk (☎089/225 82) to try and book you a room; late at night, you might do best to sleep at the terminal and look around the next morning. The main **Turismo** (daily 9am–8/7pm; ☎089/254 04), on the harbour front at Rua da Misericórdia 8, can provide full lists of pensions (though they won't make reservations) and have an efficient, pot-luck system of private rooms (*quartos*) allocation.

Most of the city's **pensions and hotels** are concentrated in the area just north of the harbour. Recommendations for a first call include:

Pensão Dandy, Rua Filipe Alistão 62 (☎089/247 91). Not terribly inspiring, but should be able to find you a room even if you arrive late. ③

Pensão Madalena, Rua C. Bivar 109 (☎089/208 06). One of the better places to stay – ever-expanding and increasingly upmarket, but still the same friendly reception. ④

Pensão Condado, Rua Gonçalo Barreto 14 (☎089/220 81). Recommended *pensão* which often cuts its prices for backpackers – sometimes by up to 50 percent. ④

Pensão O Farão, Largo da Madalena 4 (☎089/82 33 56). Well-kept *pensão* in a lovely little square. The rooms are not as impressive as the grand marble entrance hall and potted plants, but they are clean and spacious. ④

Pensão Casa da Lumena, Praça Alexandre Herculano 27 (☎089/80 19 90). Highly attractive townhouse with a courtyard bar and pleasing, individually furnished rooms. Advance bookings recommended. ⑤

Hotel Faro, Praça Dom Francisco Gomes 2 (☎089/80 32 76). The cheapest place on the waterfront, this comfortable three-star hotel has harbour views from the front rooms and from the first-floor bar. ⑤

Hotel Eva, Avenida da República 1 (☎089/80 33 54). The town's best hotel, with a superb harbourfront position and rooms whose balconies look across to the old town. There's a pool, too, and a courtesy bus to the local beach. ⑥

In summer, Faro's **campsite** at Praia de Faro is always full and very cramped; if you want to stay, phone ahead (☎089/248 76); it is open all year and requires an *Auto Club camping card*.

ROOM PRICE SCALES

The symbols used in our hotel listings denote the following price ranges.

① 2000–2500esc	③ 3500–5000esc	⑤ 8000–12,000esc
② 2500–3500esc	④ 5000–8000esc	⑥ 12,000esc and upwards

For a fuller explanation, see p.21

FARO

To Estádio de São Luis

Mercado

AV. CINCO DE OUTUBRO

RUA ALMEIDA GARRET

RUA DA GRACA

RUA DO BOCAGE

RUA HORTA MACHADO

RUA DE PORTUGAL

PR. DA LIBERADE

Museu Etnográfico

PR. ALEXANDRE HERCULANO

RUA DA TRINDADE

RUA DO LETHES

RUA VASCO DA GAMA

RUA REBELO DA SILVA

RUA SANTO ANTONIO

RUA DA ALMEIDA

RUA DO ALPORTEL

PR. ALMEIDA

RUA

Igreja do Carmo (Capela dos Ossos)

RUA BAPTISTA LOPES

LARGO DO CARMO

LARGO DE S.PEDRO

RUA FILIPE ALISTAO

RUA 1° DE MAIO

PR. AFONSO III

Museu Arqueológico

Turismo

Sé

Bishop's Palace

Post Office

RUA SERPA PINTO

RUA DA BOAVISTA

RUA DO TRICA

RUA DUT RICA

Arco da Vila

Jardim Manuel Bivar

LARGO DA SE

PR. D. FRANCISCO GOMES

RUA CONSELHEIRO BIVAR

Harbour

Boats to Praia de Faro & Campsite

RUA ASCENCAO

RUA INFANTE D. HENRIQUE

RUA FRANCISCO BARRETO

RUA DOM JOAO

Hotel Eva

Bus Station

AVENIDA DA REPUBLICA

PR. D.

To Lisbon, Lagos, Praia de Faro, Airport (EN125)

LARGO DA ESTACAO

Train Station

0   200 m

The town

Faro's Roman predecessor was eight kilometres to the south – at Ossonoba (see p.308). The present city here was founded by the Moors, under whom it was a thriving commercial port, supplying the regional capital at Silves. Following its conquest by the Christians, under Afonso III in 1249, the city had a checkered few centuries, amid a series of conquests and disasters. Sacked and burned by the Earl of Essex in 1596, and devastated by the Great Earthquake of 1755, it is no surprise that the modern city has so few historic buildings. What interest it does retain is contained within the **Cidade Velha** (Old Town), which lies behind a series of defensive walls, across the harbour from the main part of town.

The Cidade Velha

The old town is entered through the eighteenth-century town gate, the **Arco da Vila**, next to the Turismo. From here, cobbled Rua do Município leads up to the majestic Largo da Sé, flanked by the cathedral (Sé) and a group of palaces – including the former bishop's palace – and lined with orange trees.

The **Sé** itself (Mon–Fri 10am–noon, Sat evening service only, Sun 8am–1pm) is a squat, white mis-match of Gothic, Renaissance and Baroque styles, all heavily remodelled after the 1755 earthquake. It's worth looking inside mainly for the fine eighteenth-century *azulejo* tiling.

More impressive is the **Museu Municipal** (Mon–Sat 9am–noon & 2–5pm; 150$00) in nearby Praça Afonso III, an archeological collection installed in a sixteenth-century convent. The most striking of its exhibits is a superb third-century AD Roman mosaic of Neptune surrounded by the four winds, unearthed a few metres back near the Faro railway station. Other items include a collection of Roman statues from the excavations at Estói (see p.308), a four-foot Roman phallus, and a selection of local paintings, militaria and sixteenth-century naive multicoloured tiles upstairs in the art gallery.

For the rest, the old town streets have mostly been scrubbed clean of interest, though some of the cobbled side streets provide entertaining strolling, with their decorative balconies and tiling.

The rest of town

Having done your historical duty in the old town, the **harbour** is the most interesting area. The town gardens and a cluster of outdoor cafés overlook the moored yachts, while in the back streets around Rua de Santo Antonio, shops, bars and restaurants do their best to keep you off the local beach. The most intriguing of Faro's museums is here too: the **Museu Etnográfico** (Mon–Fri 9.30am–12.30pm & 2.30–5.30pm; 100$00) on Rua Pé da Cruz, which has a display of local crafts and industries, including reconstructions of typical cottage interiors, and models of the net systems still used in fishing for tuna.

By far the most curious sight in town is the Baroque **Igreja do Carmo** (Mon–Fri 10am–noon & 3–5pm, Sat 10am–1pm) near the central post office on the Largo do Carmo. A door to the right of its altar leads around to a macabre **Capela dos Ossos** (Chapel of the Bones). Like the one at Évora, its walls are decorated with human bones – in this case disinterred from the adjacent monks' cemetery. Nearby, in Largo de São Pedro, the sixteenth-century **Igreja de São Pedro** mixes Renaissance and Baroque with startling modern images of Christ.

Eating, drinking and nightlife

The heart of the city is a modern, pedestrianised shopping area around **Rua de Santo António**, where you can find a multi-screen cinema and innumerable restaurants, cafés and bakeries – the latter stocked with almond delicacies, the regional speciality. Both here, and in the other streets around the harbour, there are **restaurants** to meet most budgets, and though they tend to be touristy, it's possible to find some very acceptable places.

Restaurants

Adega Nova, Rua Francisco Barreto 24. Near the train station, this is an old-fashioned *adega* with solid Portuguese food and jugs of wine. An inexpensive choice.

Café Aliança, Rua F. Gomes 7–11. Along the lines of a down-at-heel coffee house, the *Aliança* has seats outside in summer, and a full menu of snacks and light meals.

Café Boéma, Travessa da Mota 10. This place adds an African touch to its Portuguese cooking. Try the African *bacalhau*.

Caldinho Rua Cruz de Mestras 51. On a road leading east from the Largo de São Pedro, the *Caldinho* is a small, plain restaurant which serves highly rated Portuguese food, popular with locals. 1000$00 and upwards. Closed Sun.

Caracoles, Largo Terreiro do Bispo 26–28. A reasonably priced, though touristy, fish and seafood restaurant, serving all the standard dishes.

Cidade Velha, Rua Domingos Guieiro 19 – by the Sé (☎089/271 45). The only restaurant in the old town, this serves elegant French and Portuguese cooking in a fine eighteenth-century building. Expensive.

Esplanada-Bar As Parreiras, Rua Rebelo da Silva 22. An outdoor patio shaded by grape-bearing vines; eat the barbecued fish, done in the open air.

Restaurant Dois Irmãos, Largo Terreiro do Bispo 13–15 – next to Praça Ferreira de Almeida. One of the oldest of the city's fish and seafood restaurants, this moderately priced place specialises in tasty *cataplanas*. Try the sardines, too. Around 2000$00 a head and up.

Bars and discos

The best of Faro's nightlife is found along Rua do Prior, three blocks back from the harbour and parallel to Rua Conselheiro Bivar. Things here get going around midnight; soon afterwards, as the bars fill up, drinkers tumble out onto the cobbled alleys to party. Apart from the many **bars** which feature loud, late-night music as a matter of course, Faro also frequently hosts big name gigs by British bands at the football stadium – details from the Turismo.

Adega dos Argos, Rua do Prior. Large bar which gets packed out as drinkers sing along to live Portuguese music.

Chaplins, Rua do Prior – ring the bell by the imposing doorway. A large bar with a club-like feel; drink prices are slightly above the average, as, usually, is the DJ.

Kingburger Bar, Rua do Prior. A small, relaxed but cool bar, known for its hamburgers.

Megahertz, Rua do Prior. Glitzy disco open until 4am. Take a ticket as you enter and you'll be charged 400$00 plus whatever you spend on drink when you leave – beware!

Rocha Bar, Rua do Prior. Attracts a young, trendy and friendly crowd who sit on floor cushions around wells in the floor. Cheap beer, too.

Sheherazade, at the *Hotel Eva*, Avenida da República. Established disco nights in the club to the side of the hotel every Wednesday, Friday and Saturday.

Listings

American Express c/o *Star Travel*, Rua C. Bivar 36 (Mon–Fri 9am–12.30pm and 2–6pm).

Car rental *Avis* (airport, ☎089/81 85 38); *Budget* (airport, ☎089/24 888; *Hotel Eva*, ☎089/26 195); *Europcar* (airport, ☎089/81 87 77); *Hertz* (Rua 1 de Maio, ☎089/248 77).

Fairs Occasional fairs are held on the Largo de São Francisco, in the old town.

Football The Algarve's only First Division team, Sporting Club Farense, play at the Estádio de São Luís, in the north of the city, a twenty-minute walk from the centre. Matches are on Sundays.

Police Rua Serpa Pinto.

Post office Largo do Carmo (Mon–Fri 9am–6.30pm, Sat 9am–1pm).

Around Faro

Faro marks a geographical boundary on the Algarve. The **coastline** east from here to Manta Rota, near the Spanish border, is protected by thin stretches of mud flats, fringed in turn by a chain of long and magnificent sandbanks. Often accessible only by boat, they're usually far less crowded than the small rocky resorts of the western Algarve. Ornithologists should take binoculars, as the shores are thick with various types of wading birds in winter and spring.

Inland, at Estói, you can divide your time between a delightful eighteenth-century country estate and the remains of a Roman settlement at Milreu. Further north, the hilltop town of São Brás de Alportel makes a pleasant excursion.

Praia de Faro

Faro's "town beach" – Praia de Faro – is typical of the sandspit *ilha* beaches, at least in its make-up. It's less characteristic in being both overcrowded and overdeveloped. Hotels, bars, restaurants (*Camané* is excellent), and a campsite have all been jammed onto a sandy island far too narrow to cope, and you have to walk miles to escape the human press.

Still, if you just want a few hours' swimming, it's functional. Inexpensive ferries (8 daily June–Sept; 4 daily off-season) shuttle across to the island from the jetty below the old town, through narrow marshy channels to the beach. You can also go by road (bus #16 runs from the harbour gardens; hourly), though it's a somewhat circuitous nine-kilometre trip.

Estói

Regular buses make the twenty-minute journey eleven kilometres north of Faro to ESTÓI . Just off the village square here is the Palácio do Visconde de Estói, a diminutive version of the Rococo palace of Queluz near Lisbon. At present only the grounds are open to the public but the palace has recently been bought by the state and there are plans to turn it into a museum.

The main reason for a visit to Estói, however, is the Roman site at Milreu, one kilometre west of the village (May–Sept 11am–12.30pm and 3–7pm, Oct–April 10am–12.30pm and 2–5pm; closed Mon). Known to the Romans as *Ossonoba*, the town was precursor to Faro, and inhabited from the second to the sixth century AD. The ruins are dominated by the apse of a temple, which was converted into a Christian basilica in the third century AD, making it one of the earliest of all known churches. The other recognisable remains are of a bathing complex with fragments of mosaic. The site was finally abandoned in the eighth century AD, after which date the Moors founded Faro to the south.

São Brás de Alportel

Seven kilometres north of Estói, SÃO BRÁS DE ALPORTEL, in a valley of the Serra do Caldeirão, makes an appealing detour for drivers with a couple of hours to spare. The Turismo on the main square will point you towards all the sights: the chapel of Senhor dos Passos, with its views of the surrounding valleys, the Costume Museum (Tue–Sat 10am–1pm and 3–6pm), and the local swimming pool, near which, on Rua Nova da Fonté, the former Bishop of Faro's palace and gardens now does duty as a school and playground.

The quiet surroundings entice a few visitors to make this their Algarve base. Accommodation isn't the good value it might be, but try for rooms at the *Residencial São Brás*, Rua Luis Bivar (③), or at the similarly priced *Ahorta*, on the Faro road. Big-spenders might want to check out the very comfortable *Pousada de São Brás* (☎089/84 23 05; ⑥), two kilometres north of town. The views from here are splendid, and there's an (expensive) restaurant, too; as there are only 29 rooms, advance booking is essential in summer.

Bars and **restaurants** are sparse but a couple of places are worth a mention. *Café Linião* on the main square is an easy option for drinks or snacks, while *Bar Roflin* on Rua Capitão Caiado attracts a vibrant crowd, occasionally puts on live music, and stays open late (closed Mon). For meals, the *Savoy Steakhouse*, next to the *Bar Roflin*, is reasonable value.

Olhão and its *ilhas*

OLHÃO, eight kilometres east of Faro, is the largest fishing port on the Algarve and an excellent base for visiting the surrounding sandbank *ilhas*. It's an otherwise uneventful place, notwithstanding the somewhat surreal prose of the local brochure, which proclaims Olhão home of the "amazing poodles of the Algarve . . . strong, muscular, and of invaluable assistance to the fishermen for whom they dive into the water to guide the fish into the nets". Unfortunately, the aquatic poodles were abandoned for more modern methods in the 1950s.

The town

Once past the run-down outskirts, Olhão with its shoreline and docks is quite an attractive town. There are no sights as such but the flat roofs, outdoor stairways and white terraces of the old town are striking and give a North African look to the place. No surprise, then, that Olhão has centuries-old trading links with Morocco, as well as a small place in history for its uprising against the French garrison in 1808. Following the French departure, the local fishermen sent a small *caíque* across the Atlantic to Brazil to transmit the news to the exiled king João VI. The journey, completed without navigational aids, was rewarded after the king's restoration to the throne with the granting of a town charter.

The best view of the whitewashed cube-houses is from the **belltower** of the seventeenth-century parish church of **Nossa Senhora do Rosário**, right in the middle of town. Look next door to find the chapel of **Nossa Senhora dos Aflitos** (daily 9.30am–noon & 4–5.30pm), where townswomen gather to pray for dead sailors amid candles and curious wax models of children and limbs. The other obvious focus of the town is the sprawling **market**, held along the riverfront, which is open from the crack of dawn every day except Sunday.

Practicalities

The **train station** and adjacent **bus terminal** are near the end of the Avenida da República, a wide boulevard leading into the city centre, a five-minute walk away. The **Turismo** is on Rua do Comércio, the main shopping street and an extension of the Avenida da República. It can provide a town map, advice on accommodation, and (not entirely reliable) sailing times for boats to the *ilhas*.

There are no *quartos* in town and consequently accommodation can be hard to find in the height of summer, despite a fair scattering of **pensions**. Among these, pick from:

Pensão Torres, Rua Dr. Paulo Nogueira 13 (☎089/71 26 81). Inexpensive but pretty average. Closed Nov–May. ①

Pensão Rosa, Rua Carlos da Maia 56 (☎089/71 38 31). Marginally preferable. ①

Pensão Bicuar, Rua Vasco da Gama 5 (☎089/748 16). A bit more character, including several rooms with small terraces. ②

Pensão Vasca de Gama, Rua Vasco da Gama 6. A fallback opposite the *Bicuar*. ②

Pensão Helena, Rua Dr. M. Bombarda 42 (☎089/71 26 34). Over on the west side of town, this has large, pleasantly furnished rooms. ②

Pensão Boémia, Rua da Cerca 20. Well-priced considering its comfortable interior. ②

Pensão Bela Vista, Rua Teófilo Braga 65–67 (☎089/71 25 38). Highly rated, first choice pension, if you're lucky enough to find space. It's on the east side of town – from the Turismo, turn left, then first left, and its sign is directly opposite. ③

Hotel Ria Sol, Rua General Humberto Delgado 37 (☎089/705 267). Upmarket and rather functional fifty-room hotel, out by the bus station. ④

The local **campsite** is at MARIM, three kilometres east along the railway tracks – if you walk – or five kilometres via the main road. It is equipped with a pool, and good views of Armona, though frustratingly devoid of any beach.

In town, there are a number of **restaurants** and **bars** around the Rua do Comércio, but the atmosphere here is fairly low-key; for a bit more life, try the *Taiti* at Rua Vasco da Gama 24. Clusters of cheap bars and restaurants also exist along the waterfront, on Avenida 5 Outubro, and over on Rua Almirante Reis, a poorer, less touristy area, where the houses are nonetheless beautifully tiled.

The *ilhas*: Armona and Culatra

Ferries leave for the *ilhas* of **Armona** and **Culatra** from the jetty at the far end of Olhão's municipal gardens, five minutes from the Turismo. The kiosk near the boats sells tickets and provides details of sailing times; fares are cheap.

The **boats** to Armona (15 min) leave between 9 and 12 times daily from June to September, five times daily in May and October, twice daily in winter. For Culatra and Farol (35–45min), on the Ilha da Culatra, boats leave seven times daily from June to September, once daily in winter.

Ilha da Armona

Ferries drop their passengers at the northern end of the single settlement on **ILHA DA ARMONA** – a long, crowded strip of holiday chalets and huts that stretches right across the island on either side of the main path. It's a ramshackle, cosy affair, a world away from the sterility of most of the Algarve's "holiday villages". There are a few **bar-restaurants** by the beaches at either end of the village, packed with a lively mix of holidaymakers – many Portuguese.

On the **ocean side** the beach disappears into the distance and a short walk will take you to attractive stretches of sand and dune: the further you walk, the greater the privacy. The beach **facing the mainland** is smaller and tends to get very crowded in summer, but the water here, sheltered from the Atlantic, is always warm and perfectly calm.

There are no campsites, pensions, or hotels on Armona. Camping on the beach is frowned upon, and if you want to stay, you're better off approaching the Turismo in Olhão, which rents out **chalets**: the more of you there are, the cheaper it becomes, though you'll be lucky to find anywhere in high season.

Ilha da Culatra

ILHA DA CULATRA is another huge sand spit, though very different in character from Armona. The **northern shore** is dotted with a series of very primitive fishing settlements, mixed with an incongruous sprinkling of holiday chalets.

The ferry's first port of call, CULATRA, is the largest settlement – a grim and distinctly unpleasant place. FAROL`, the second stop, is more agreeable. A rather commonplace, untidy village of holiday homes, it is edged by beautiful tracts of beach on the ocean side, though the mainland-facing beach is grubby.

Once again, **camping** on the island is not encouraged, and in any case tends to be conspicuous among the fishing villages. Basic **rooms** and **food** at not-so-basic prices are available at the all-year *Hotel Bar Tropical* – a lively, Norwegian-owned place that seems stuck somewhere in the 1960s.

Fuzeta

Armona is also accessible from the unkempt fishing village of **FUZETA**, ten kilometres east of Olhão. There is an official campsite here in summer, but it's very uninviting – you're better off heading straight for the islands.

There are no organised ferries over, but it's easy enough to pay for a ride across the channel. Take your own food and water.

Tavira

TAVIRA is one of the most beautiful towns on the Algarve, and a clear winner if you are looking for an urban base on the eastern stretch. It's sited on both sides of the broad Rio Gilão, which flows through the town and is overlooked by ancient balconied houses and straddled by two low bridges, one of Roman origin.

This is an eminently attractive ensemble, which many visitors use as a base to stay while making daytrips to the superb island beaches of the Ilha de Tavira, which lie within easy reach of the town; if this is your plan, keep in mind that the ferries to the island only operate from May to September. However, Tavira itself is certainly worth visiting, at any time of the year. Despite ever-increasing visitors and encroaching development, it continues to make its principal living as a tuna-fishing port, and fish dinners at restaurants along the palm-lined river are in themselves a powerful incentive to stop.

Orientation and accommodation

Arriving by **bus** you'll be dropped in the central **Praça da República**; from the terminal there are good connections to Vila Real, Faro and other eastern Algarve destinations. The **train station** is 1km from the centre of town, straight up the Rua da Liberdade.

The **Turismo** (☎081/225 11), in the Praça da República, has all the usual services, plus details of **bike and moped hire** if you want to explore the coast. It can sometimes help with **private rooms**, if you have no luck at the pensions listed below. As throughout the Algarve, be warned that places are at a premium during the summer season; if a tout offers you a room, take it, at least for the first night, and look around on your own later on.

Pension choices include:

Pensão do Castelo, Rua da Liberdade 4 (☎081/239 42). Very centrally located, across from the Turismo and with views of the castle; clean, good value rooms. ②

Residencial Mendonça, Rua dos Bombeiros Municipais (☎081/817 43). An excellent choice, run by the Mendonça family; it's south of the river, on the western edge of town. ②

Residencial Mirante, Rua da Liberdade 83 (☎081/222 55). Okay but some rooms are a bit noisy – ask to take a look before settling on a stay. ②

Residencial Lagôas, Rua Almirante Cândido dos Reis 24 (☎081/222 52). Situated on the north side of the river, across the bridge from Praça da República, this has attractive rooms and rooftop views, a wonderful manager, and the bonus of the top-notch budget restaurant, *Bica*, below. It's by far the best place to stay in town,. ③

Residencial Princesa do Gilão, Rua Borda de Agua de Aguiar 10–12 (☎081/32 51 71). A modern, white building, decorated inside with cool Portuguese tiles, this friendly *residencia* stands just across the river from the main square, right on the quayside. Go for a room at the front, with a balcony overlooking the river. ④

The town

Founded as long ago as 400 BC, Tavira's greatest period of prosperity came in the sixteenth to eighteenth centuries, the age which produced most of its graceful array of churches and mansions. In the old town streets on both sides of the river, numerous houses retain fine old doorways and coats-of-arms.

Buses drop you in the arcaded Praça da República, by the river, from where it's a short climb up to the **Castelo** (Mon–Fri 8am–5.30pm, Sat and Sun 9am–5.30pm; free), half hidden on a low hill in the centre of town. From the walls you

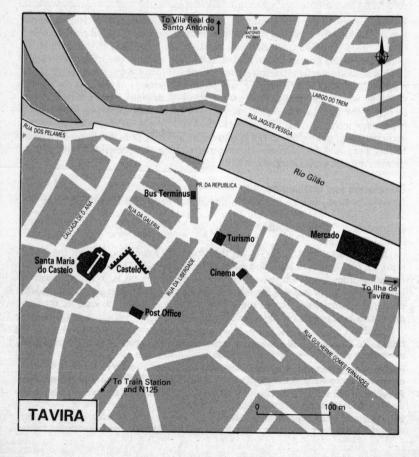

can look down over the peculiarly Oriental rooftops and the town's thirty-seven churches (most of which, sadly, are kept locked). Adjacent to the castle, the whitewashed **Santa Maria do Castelo** contains the tomb of Dom Paio Peres Correia, who reconquered much of the Algarve from the Moors, including Tavira in 1224. Fittingly, the church stands on the site of the former mosque.

The best part of Tavira is the **river**. Gardens lined with cafés run as far as the lively harbourside **market** (open mornings only), beyond which are moored the fishing boats that still operate out of the river port. This is a great place to wander, among the nets and marine clutter, stopping at one of the restaurants or more basic fishermen's bars, most of which serve up memorable meals, generally involving big tuna steaks.

Walks out of town

Most people's minds are set firmly seawards, but there are some beautiful **inland walks** you can do from Tavira. One, which follows the Rua dos Pelames out of town along the southwest (right) bank of the Rio Gilão, crosses the N270 Faro road, then becomes a minor road (N397) that leads through lovely countryside and eventually leaves the river bank and joins up with the N270 again (10km) before bringing you back south in a loop to Santo Estêvão (12km), whence you can return to Tavira (6km).

Food, drink and nightlife

A succession of **cafés and restaurants** line the gardens along the riverbank, while further down, on Rua José Pires Padhina, tables edge out on to the riverside. For a drink, there are a couple of cafés in the main square, plenty of nameless backstreet bars with matchstick-chewing old-timers for company, and a couple of trendier spots north of the river.

Restaurants

Restaurante Imperial, Rua do Cais 22. Just back from the riverside gardens, the *Imperial* is well-known for its fine seafood, but retains some notoriously unpredictable waiters. A decent meal here will cost around 2500$00.

O Barquinho, Rua José Pires Padhina. This unpretentious bar-restaurant, along the riverfront from the market, has seats outside and serves a mean tuna steak, with stewed onions and fries. A plateful, wine and coffee comes to well under 1000$00.

Restaurante Bica, Rua Almirante Cândido dos Reis 22–24. Inexpensive, excellent Portuguese meals on the north side of the river, under the *Residencial Lagoas*. From around 1000$00 a head.

La Pizza Corgo, Rua Álvares Botelho 3. A good but pricey French restaurant and pizzeria, on the north side of the river.

Churrasqueira Grill, Rua Almirante Cândido dos Reis. Reliable Portuguese grill restaurant near the *Bica*.

Anazu, Rua Jacques Pessoa 11–13. This large and friendly restaurant on the riverfront serves all manner of dishes – from fast food to feasts.

Bars and nightlife

Arco Bar, Rua Almirante Candido dos Reis 67. Friendly Portuguese bar on the north side of the river, attracting a laid-back crowd.

Coco-Coco, Rua Dr. August do Silva Carvalho 22. Also north of the river, this bar is aimed at those who don't mind shelling out 500$00 a time for cocktails.

Bar Cod'Oro, Rua José Pires Padinha. Upmarket bar-restaurant with live singing on certain summer evenings.

UBI. Tavira's only disco. You reach it by following Rua Almirante Candido dos Reis to the outskirts of town; look for the huge warehouse on the right, which conceals *UBI* within a shiny, metallic hangar. It's open 11pm–4am and costs 1000$00 to get in.

Ilha de Tavira

The **ILHA DE TAVIRA** stretches west from Tavira almost as far as Fuzeta (see p.311), some fourteen kilometres away. For most of its length the landward side of the island is a dank morass of mud flat, but at the eastern tip the mud disappears and the *ilha* ends in an expanse of sand and sea.

Boats cross from Tavira Beach (see below) to the island and dock at its eastern end, next to a rundown chalet settlement that incorporates an unappealing **campsite**. The beach is enormous but massively popular, and unless you're wise enough to be here out of the peak season, you may have to walk miles to escape the crowds.

Access

Buses marked *Quatro Águas* leave from outside the cinema in Tavira town for the ten-minute trip to the ferry terminal at Praia de Tavira (Tavira Beach). If you plan to do a lot of these bus trips, buy a block of ten tickets at the bus station – it pays for itself in three trips. Out of season, you've the choice of a two-kilometre walk from the town to the ferry terminus, or a taxi (around 600$00).

As for the **boats**, from early June to the end of August they're more or less a shuttle service (last departure from the beach of Ilha de Tavira at 6.45pm weekdays, 7.45pm Sundays), but there's only an hourly, or less frequent, service in May and September and none for the rest of the year.

Pedras d'El Rei and Barril

If you're after an isolated beach, in summer, it's better to head four kilometres west from Tavira to **PEDRAS D'EL REI**. This is a holiday village, designed expressly for the purpose, but while it's a bit sterile, it's not too big and is very pleasant for its type.

The sands spread for miles if you feel like laying down a sleeping bag for the night. Alternatively, chalets can be hired on a short-term basis at reasonable prices for small groups, though the complex is usually full in July and August. Regular summer **buses** connect the resort with Tavira, or you can walk up from the main coastal highway to Pedras in about fifteen minutes. The **reception and information desk** is well informed on topics such as bus times, organised tours, and much else.

From Pedras d'el Rei a **miniature railway** shuttles backwards and forwards across the mud flats to the beach of **BARRIL** on the Ilha de Tavira. It's a few minutes' walk right or left to escape the tourist facilities at the terminus, and there you are: miles of beautiful, peaceful, dune-fringed beach. This area constitutes the **Parque Natural da Ria Formosa**, a fairly new nature reserve. You can watch tens of thousands of fiddler crabs, scuttling about, silently waving their claws at the sky.

Tavira to Vila Real: Cacela Velha

Just to the east of Tavira, the sand spit that protects much of the eastern Algarve from the developers starts to thin out, merging with the shoreline beach at Manta Rota. The result is predictable: **CABANAS, MANTA ROTA, ALAGOA** and **MONTE GORDO** have all been intensively developed, robbing the coast of its allure. Monte Gordo's only saving grace is its **campsite** – the nearest to Vila Real de Santo António, with which it's connected by an hourly bus service. **PRAIA VERDE** is another place to avoid: the beach is pretty and the hills are attractively wooded, but sheltering under the branches are enough caravans to accommodate the Russian army.

However, there's one surprise. For some reason, the small hamlet of **CACELA VELHA** (not to be confused with VILA NOVA DE CACELA, 2km inland) is completely untouched by tourism. Perched on a rocky bluff overlooking the sea, surrounded by olive groves, and home to an old church and the remains of a fort, it is spectacularly pretty – a reminder of how the Algarve must have looked forty years ago. Naturally enough, the hamlet is short on facilities, but it's got a little restaurant and a handful of **rooms** that are snapped up in the summer. The beach is a delight and it's easy enough to arrange a lift over to the sand bar just offshore.

The only direct **bus** to Cacela Velha is from Vila Nova de Cacela and it isn't at all frequent. The best bet is to walk up from the main road, one kilometre away.

Vila Real de Santo António

The border town and harbour of **VILA REAL DE SANTO ANTÓNIO** is a lively place to end (or begin) your travels in Portugal. With its recently completed bridge across the Rio Guadiana, it's a major crossing point to Spain – offering access to Sevilla via Huelva. And with so many travellers passing through, and so many Portuguese coming here for their holidays, the town has something going on with popular bars and restaurants; there are regular bullfights and rock concerts in the Estádio do Lusitano; and there's always the odd chaotic festival with bands blaring through the streets.

The original town was demolished by a tidal wave at the beginning of the seventeenth century, and the site stood empty until it was revived in 1774 by the Marquês de Pombal. Eager to apply the latest concepts of town planning, Pombal used the same techniques he had already pioneered in the Baixa quarter of Lisbon and rebuilt Vila Real on a grid plan. The whole project only took five months – a remarkable achievement, but a startling waste of resources, as it transpired that the hewn stone that Pombal had dragged all the way from Lisbon could have been quarried a couple of miles up the road.

Practicalities

Vila Real is the eastern terminal of the Algarve railway, and **trains** pull up at the station on the riverfront, next to the Customs Post. Across from here, the **Turismo** (daily 8am–8pm; ☎081/444 95) can be persuaded to phone around for a vacant *quarto*, if you intend to stay. You may well need their help, for in general, there's a severe shortage of accommodation.

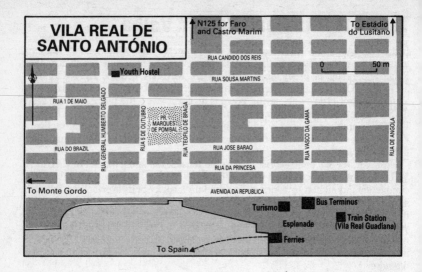

Looking around on your own for a **room**, try to arrive as early in the day as possible, leaving you the option of moving on if needs be. Two of the more pleasant places, worth trying to book ahead, are the *Residencial Felix*, across from the tourist office at Rua Dr. Manuel Arriaga 2 (☎081/347 91; ②), and *Residencial Baixa Mar*, Rua Teófilo de Braga 3 (☎081/435 11; ②). Alternatively, there's a modern **youth hostel** at Rua Dr. Sousa Martins 40, five blocks up from the tourist office; it's open all year round but again fills easily in summer.

Among **restaurants**, the *Caves do Guadiana* fronting the fishing port at Avenida da República 90 is outstanding and modestly priced.

Crossing into Spain

After years of planning and promises, a road bridge across the Guadiana to Ayamonte in Spain was finally opened to traffic in the summer of 1991. At the time of writing, however, there is no local bus service across it, so pedestrians have to continue to use the **ferries** – which run every half-hour, seven days a week from 7.30am to 11pm (and sporadically at night). The ferry trip takes about fifteen minutes and costs 100$00 per person. The ferry terminal is next to the bus station and the Vila Real–Guadiana train station.

From **Ayamonte** there's regular bus transport to HUELVA and SEVILLA – Vila Real's Turismo will provide up-to-date details.

Castro Marim

The little village of **CASTRO MARIM**, tucked away five kilometres north of Vila Real (two buses daily), makes a pleasant inland diversion. A key fortification protecting Portugal's southern coast, Marim was the first headquarters of the Order of Christ (1319) and the site of a huge castle built by Afonso III in the thirteenth century. The massive ruins are all that survived the earthquake of 1755, but it's a pretty place with fine views.

The marshy area around Castro Marim has been designated as a **nature reserve**, so there's no danger of its being despoiled. One of the area's most unusual and elusive inhabitants is the extraordinary, ten-centimetre-long, swivel-eyed, opposing-toed, **Mediterranean chameleon** – a harmless, slow-moving lizard that's severely threatened elsewhere by habitat destruction. Following the footpaths through the nature reserve is an enjoyable way to work up an appetite.

There's no regular accommodation in Castro Marim but ask around at the bars and you may find a **room** for rent. For **meals**, try the *Manuel d'Agua*, by the castle walls, which specialises in grilled fish.

THE WESTERN ALGARVE

The **western Algarve** stretches for a hundred kilometres from **Faro** to **Sagres** and encompasses Portugal's most intense tourist developments. The worst section is between Faro and Lagos, where the beaches and coves are fronted by an almost continuous stretch of villas, apartments and hotels. The purpose-built resorts feature marinas, golf links and tennis centres – all fine if you've booked a holiday but not especially inviting for casual visitors. Travelling along the coast, the most enjoyable stops are the towns of **Portimão** and particularly **Lagos**, both of which have a bit of local character. If you have transport, you might do better still to seek a base inland, either in a hillside villa, or at the historic towns of **Loulé** and **Silves**, and drive down to the nearest strip of beach.

West of Lagos the pace of development slackens and the resorts are smaller and generally more attractive. The best, perhaps, is **Salema**, beyond which the road and land cut high above the sea, across a cliff-edged plateau, and finally down to **Sagres**, with its dramatic scenery and busy nightlife.

On the coast **north of Sagres**, heading towards Alentejo, the sea is distinctly colder and often pretty wild, but the beaches accordingly less developed. If you can brave the climate, you might like to try low-key beach-villages such as **Vila do Bispo**, **Carrapateira**, **Aljezur** and **Odeceixe**. These attract a somewhat more youthful and "alternative" crowd than resorts on the Algarve proper – including, it seems, just about every German campervan in Portugal; their combination of nude sunbathing, surf and parties is not everyone's idea of an idyll.

Faro to Albufeira

The coast west of Faro is unremitting holiday village territory, with little promise for anyone simply in search of a quiet beach and an unsophisticated meal. This is territory for those into "Sportugal" – as the tourist board promotes the lesiure complexes – and none too fussy about a local environment.

Quinta do Lago to Vilamoura

The first of the resorts, **QUINTA DO LAGO** is a vast luxury holiday village with its own sports complex and opulent hotel. There's more of the same at **VALE DO LOBO**, next door, with serious-money hotels, golf courses, a riding school, and a swish **tennis centre** run by former Wimbledon-pro Roger Taylor.

Next along the coast is **QUARTEIRA**, which by contrast is quite a pleasant town with a good weekly market and attractive beach – though development from adjoining Vilamoura, the most extensive on the Algarve, increasingly threatens to overwhelm it.

Based around a king-sized marina, **VILAMOURA** is a constantly expanding resort, with a bewildering network of roads signposted to upmarket new hotels and leisure facilities, including some highly exclusive **golf courses**. The beach is impressive – as it should be considering all the development – and if you're not bothered by the crowds, and happy to pay for rather chi-chi beach-restaurants, is enjoyable. Oddly enough, there's quite often space to be found in the local pensions or private rooms – even in season; the local Turismo is helpful in directing you to vacancies. A pleasant **guest house**, five minutes' walk north of the centre, is *Os Pinheiros*, Volta do Pardal (☎089/30 13 32; ④).

Trafal

A kilometre to the east of Vilamoura begins a sequence of beaches known as **TRAFAL**. These are far less crowded and frequented mainly by the inhabitants of the beachfront **campsite**, the entrance to which is about two kilometres along the Quarteira–Faro road. Buses run here from Faro at least once an hour in high season, and there are services from Quarteira, too. For **eating** out, there are a few restaurants dotted along the road leading from the campsite to Almansil. The best is *Restaurante Marifo* – very popular, so come early.

Inland to Loulé

LOULÉ, eleven kilometres inland from Quarteira, has a history similar to most of the towns in southern Portugal – Roman and Moorish occupation – and **castle ruins** to match. If you are staying on the Quarteira strip of coast, it makes for a pleasant lunchtime or evening break from the coast.

The town
Loulé's castle walls are the best point to begin a look around town. They have been restored as a walkway and enclose a **Museu Municipal** of vaguely diverting historical bits and pieces.

Between the museum and the thirteenth-century Gothic Igreza Matriz – parish church – nearby, a grid of whitewashed cobbled streets reveals numerous handicraft shops at which you're free to watch the craftsmen at work – lacemaking, in particular, is a flourishing local industry. On Saturdays, the town is transformed as the whole region seems to arrive en masse for a busy **country market** that still owes surprisingly little of its animation to the tourist trade.

Loulé's most curious sight is a beehive-shaped monument on a nearby hilltop, out in the direction of Boliqueime, which you can't help but notice as you arrive in town. It turns out to be the abandoned skeleton of a modern church; adjacent is the faded sixteenth-century chapel of Nossa Senhora da Piedade.

Practicalities
Buses arrive in Loulé at a large new terminal, just off the main Avenida 25 de Abril, a five-minute walk from the old town area. The **Turismo** is inside the castle

The following account comes from an impeccably reliable correspondent:

"Driving with a Portuguese friend along N270 from POÇO DE BOLIQUEIME to LOULÉ, heading downhill after the *Eurocampina* factory, we noticed that the car began to slow down erratically, as if due to some mechanical failure. As this continued we felt the sensation of driving into some 'other force'. Putting the car into neutral, we slowed down and actually stopped before reaching the bottom of the hill! No brakes! After a few seconds of our stunned exclamations, the car began to move backwards, unaided, up the hill. We actually reached about 20mph until a lorry appeared on the horizon, at which point we slipped into gear and accelerated through 'the force'.

"I personally experienced this phenomenon on three separate occasions. Locals have no explanation – they prefer to create a mystery to amuse themselves and others. Non-believers are usually of the opinion that it is an optical illusion, and that the rock formations and horizon play tricks with the mind. Of this, I am somewhat dubious. I prefer the other, more inspired idea that some sort of magnetic force is in the area, created by friction at the quarry located further along the road. In fact many heavy-duty lorries use the road, so do pay attention while experimenting. If you can't get hold of a car try hitching a lift with holidayers in 'the force'."

walls at Largo Dom Pedro I; they can help you to find **accommodation** – which in summer is a bit more promising here than on the coast. Two decent places are the *Pensão Santa Teresa*, Rua do Comércio (☎089/955 25; ②), off the main Praça da República, and the Pensão Iberica at Avenida José da Costa Mealha 40 (③). If you have the money, a clear first choice is the extemely comfortable *Loulé Jardim Hotel* on Largo Manuel de Arriaga (☎089/41 30 94; ④).

There's a good choice of **places to eat**. Among a cluster of restaurants around the parish church, the *Casa de Pasta* serves salads and vegetarian meals, while *Aux Bons Enfants*, is known for its carefully prepared and pricey French cuisine (dinner only; closed Sun). More French-influenced food is on offer at *O Tacho*, Rua Maria Campinha 145, while for a real treat, try the intimate *Bica Velhas*, at Rua Bica Velhas 17 (closed Sun). Finally, there's the cheap and cheerful *Ja Está*, Rua Miguel Bombarda 60, and the *Avenida*, Avenida José da Costa Mealha 9, which is more upmarket but offers perhaps the best value in town.

Where Loulé falls down for the beach-going crowd is with its **nightlife**: there isn't any. Apart from a few habitués of the **bars** and cinemas around the Praça da República, the town is in bed by 11pm. One notable exception is at the *Copotonia Bar*, Rua Nossa Senhora da Piedade 37–39, in the northwestern part of town, where a cool clientele drink until the early hours.

Around Loulé: Alte

If you have transport, you can explore further inland: the village of **ALTE**, up the winding N124, 25km northwest of Loulé, is exceptionally pretty. Tacked across the hillside, a series of narrow, cobbled, mostly pedestrian streets focus on the church and nearby cafés near the top. Follow the signs to Fonte Grande and you'll come across a stream and a mill, which makes a pleasant picnic area. Adjacent is a **restaurant** with live music most lunchtimes.

Albufeira and its beaches

Every inch a resort, **ALBUFEIRA** tops the list of package-tour – especially British package-tour – destinations in the Algarve. It was once an unusually pretty resort with narrow, twisting lanes of whitewashed ancient houses criss-crossing the high grey-red cliffs above a beautiful spread of beaches. These still exist, but they are all but engulfed by hundreds of new apartment buildings. If you're looking for unspoiled Portugal, this isn't it – whatever the brochures might say. Nevertheless, Albufeira is still one of the nicer resorts, attracting a varied mix of holidaymakers: an ageing, well-heeled clientele who frequent the more expensive restaurants, and a younger contingent who seem to devote themselves to downing as much beer as is humanly possible.

Arriving and accommodation

In the last few years, resort sprawl has led to the creation of two town "centres" – Albufeira itself and Montechoro, two kilometres (500$00 taxi ride) to the east.

In "old" Albufeira, the main street, Rua 5 de Outubro, bisects the town and leads from the **bus station** to a tunnel, five minutes away, that's been blasted out of the rock to give access to the town beach. The **Turismo** (☎089/51 21 44) is on Rua 5 de Outubro, close to the tunnel. Albufeira's "local" train station is six kilometres north of town at Ferreiras; a bus connection meets every train.

If you need a taxi in town try *Rádio-táxis de Albufeira* (☎089/54395 or 55441).

Accommodation

Finding a room can be difficult in high season since most of the **hotels and pensions** are block-booked by package holiday companies. Those listed below are a few exceptions, which may have "independent" vacancies.

Pensão Limas, Rua da Liberdade 25–27 (☎089/540 25). A cheap, central choice, though the ten rooms fill quickly. Open from April to October only. ③

Pensão Silva, Travessa 5 de Outubro 18 (☎089/526 69). Almost opposite the Turismo, in an alleyway to the right as you face the beach, this is among the cheapest of the places to stay. It only has six rooms so call early. ③

Pensão Albufeirense, Rua da Liberdade 18 (☎089/520 79). A modern, comfortable *pensão*, with reasonably priced rooms. ④

Residencial Vila Branca, Rua do Ténis (☎089/58 68 04). A bit cramped but worth trying if the town is full. ③

Residencial Polona, Rua Cândido dos Reis 32 (☎089/558 59). A large, upmarket place; the *Residencial Baltum*, next door, is similarly priced. ④

Residencial Vila Bela, Rua Coronel Águas 15 (☎089/51 21 01). Situated on the west side of the centre, this is an attractive pension with balconied rooms overlooking a small swimming pool. Open April to October only. ④

If these are full, you'll have to do the rounds of the *Room to Let* signs, though these too are often at capacity in high season; if you are lucky, the Turismo will phone around on your behalf.

An attractive alternative is the finely appointed **Camping Albufeira** – complete with swimming pools, restaurants, bars, shops and tennis courts – 2km north of town, off the N395, and with regular connections from the bus station. It's open all year, and there are big off-season reductions when some of the facilities close.

The town

There's still a Moorish feel to parts of Albufeira, as well as the more tangible remnants of a Moorish castle – the original Arabic name of the town, *Al-Buhera*, means Castle-on-the-Sea. But the 1755 earthquake did for much of the town, and most of the modern centre is nondescript, though enlivened somewhat by a small **fishing harbour**.

None of this is of any consequence whatsoever to the summer crowds, who sleep and eat in town but spend their days at one of a dozen excellent cove-beaches in the vicinity. The **beach** fronting Albufeira itself – reached through the tunnel – is as good as any of these, flanked by strange tooth-like rock formations. But it gets crowded; a relatively short bus (or taxi) ride can open up a number of other possibilities. The best of these are detailed overpage.

Restaurants, bars and nightlife

Albufeira has **restaurants** to match every budget – and most tastes. You tend to get what you pay for, but for the better bargains head for the area around the old fishing harbour, east of the main beach. Stand around outside, perusing the menu, and you'll often be presented with enticements in the form of drinks vouchers and the like.

Restaurants

Ana, Rua Nova 7. Close to the fishing harbour, this little place serves up smashing, cheap dishes, which change daily.

A Ruina, Praia dos Pescadores. Rustic old restaurant on the beach, serving fish fresh from the market. Eat on the beach or inside on one of two floors. From around 2000$00 a head.

Cabaz da Praia, Praça Miguel Bombarda 7. Just west of the Turismo and overlooking the beach, this serves excellent but expensive meals. The menu mixes Portuguese and international dishes, and the roof terrace offers fine views – for which you're paying higher than usual prices.

Jardim d'Allah, Beco José Bernardino de Sousa. Reasonably priced family-owned Portuguese restaurant, decorated in Arabic style. Good fish dishes are available; meals run to about 2500$00 a head.

Sotavento, Rua São Gonçalo de Lagos 16. Back from the fishing harbour, this snack bar has counter seating and an affordable selection of Portuguese standards.

OUT OF TOWN

A Curva, Rua da Moinheta 25, in Algoz (☎089/55512; closed Sun). Ten kilometres inland of Albufeira, on the other side of the main N125 highway, this village restaurant has a deservedly high reputation for remarkably good-value country cooking.

La Cigale, Olhos de Água. Nine kilometres east of Albufeira, and right on the beach, this renowned restaurant has a lovely terrace and high-quality food, including great seafood. Open for dinner only, expect to pay around 3000$00.

Bars and nightlife

Like the restaurants, Albufeira **bars** are into promotion. There's not much to choose between them, and you may as well frequent those offering the cheapest drinks at the time. In this important connection, keep your eyes open for local free sheets, which carry a great number of Happy Hour (or more) coupons.

Among the more established bars are:

Bird's Nest, Largo Engenheiro Duarte Pacheco. Small-time British and American bands appear here at regular intervals.

Kiss, in Montechoro. At the southern end, this is regarded as the most attractive club in town. Entry, with a drink, is 1000$00, and though the music is good, the club tends to be overcrowded and very glitzy. Open till 4am.

Silver Screen, Avenida 25 de Abril. An established disco, open till 4am.

Sylvia's, Rua São Gonçalo de Lagos. Central Albufeira club, open till 4am. There's more late-night drinking and dancing at similar establishments nearby.

The morning after the night before is well catered for in most bars, with massive **English-style breakfasts** available until the sensible hour of 2pm.

Beaches west of Albufeira

The rocky red headlands just **to the west** of Albufeira are beautiful – and were inaccessible until the 1980s development of a strip of villa resorts, which have very much changed the landscape. There are no direct buses to these resorts, though the Albufeira–Portimão service drops passengers on the main road, a steep two kilometres' walk distant.

São Rafael, Castelo and Galé

This trio of resorts – **SÃO RAFAEL, CASTELO** and **GALÉ** – spread back from small cove beaches with craggy, eroded rock faces. Each is dominated by villa developments, competing at the more exclusive end of the European second-home market. Not all of the villas have been finished and the whole area can resemble a building site, with great gashes of red earth exposed by the bulldozers. If the developers were to show restraint it might not be so bad, but the indications are that now that the roads to the beaches have been finished, there'll soon be a chain of villas and chalets trailing right across the hills.

Vale de Parra

One corner of sanity open to those with a car, or who don't mind the walk, is the area of **VALE DE PARRA**, 1500m inland from Praia da Galé. It's reached from the main N125 highway by turning south at the village of PERA and driving three kilometres. Alternatively, if you're in Albufeira, follow the minor coast road out of town to the west six kilometres, through SESMARIA.

If you want to stay at Vale de Parra, try the *Residencial Mimosa* (⑤), a real haven, fifteen minutes' walk from the beach, with its own pool and roof terraces.

Beaches east of Albufeira

Overall, for the local beaches, it's better to head **east of Albufeira**, where you have several more choices. Immediately east of town, ochre-red cliffs divide the coastline into a series of bays and beaches, all within easy walking distance of the Albufeira–Faro bus route (a dozen buses daily) or directly along the town beach.

Praia da Oura and Olhos de Água

PRAIA DA OURA, which begins just two kilometres from Albufeira, is the longest and nearest beach, but has been terribly overdeveloped. Seven kilometres further along, **OLHOS DE ÁGUA**, an old fishing village, is smaller and nicer, with a lively bar-restaurant at the west end of the beach that often has live music at night. If this beach, too, is crowded, you can walk beyond it to other more isolated coves.

Praia da Falésia and Aldeia das Açoteias

At **PRAIA DA FALÉSIA**, ten kilometres east of Albufeira, the character of the coastline changes to produce one long tremendous stretch of sand. Unbroken red cliffs run its whole course – making it tricky to get down to, but worth the effort.

The simplest approach is to take the Faro bus to the *Touring Club* stop on the fringes of **ALDEIA DAS AÇOTEIAS**, a bewildering chalet and villa complex. Here you can just hop aboard the shuttle service to the beach and walk as far away from the crowds as you like.

West towards Portimão

Heading west from Albufeira along the main N125, you'll pass through **PORCHES**, about halfway between ALCANTARILHA and LAGOA. This is where the most famous of the Algarve's handmade **pottery** comes from. Thick, chunky, and handpainted, it has a good heavy feel, and if you're looking for thoroughly impractical and ridiculously cheap presents to take home, this is the place to stop. Further on, **LAGOA** is best known for its wine; tours of the local vineyards are arranged through local tourist offices.

Down to the coast: Armação de Pêra and Praia da Marinha

Off the main road, down on the coast, is the gargantuan resort of **ARMAÇÃO DE PÊRA**, about which little complimentary can be said, except for the fact that it claims the largest beach in the Algarve (not a unique claim in these parts, by any means). It is connected by frequent buses with Albufeira

There are better things to report about **Praia da Marinha**, however, reached from a turning south between Porches and Lagoa (no bus services). A path leads from a vaguely flat parking area on the clifftop down to an immaculate sandy beach with a string of secluded coves, beautifully warm sea even in winter, and relatively few people to share it with. There's a café of uncertain hours on the sand by the path.

Carvoeiro and Estômbar

Further west, the small resort of **CARVOEIRO** can be reached by bus from Lagoa and Portimão. Cut into the red sea cliffs, it remains quite an attractive place, despite a line of villa-apartments draped across the surrounding hills. The beach, however, is much too small to cope with the summer influx, and rooms are virtually out of the question in high season. If you phone well in advance, you might just get a bed at one of two small **pensions**, *Le Mistral* (☎082/573 82; ③) and *Pensão Baselli* (☎082/571 59; ③). The resort also has quite a number of bars and restaurants, a **tourist office** and boats offering fishing or beach trips. Accessible by the coast road, a kilometre east, are the impressive rock formations of **Algar Seco**, where the cliffs form dramatic overhangs above narrow beaches – though there's a monstrous hotel a little further along.

By way of contrast, a few kilometres inland is **ESTÔMBAR** (a stop for slow trains on the Algarve line), an unremarkable little town that was birthplace of the eleventh-century Moorish poet Ibn Ammãr. The town straggles down a steep hill in a confusion of narrow lanes – nothing very special, though at least you feel you're in Portugal.

Portimão

PORTIMÃO is one of the largest towns on the Algarve, with a population of 30,000-plus. It has made its living from fishing since pre-Roman times and with its site on the estuary of the Rio Arade, remains today a sprawling port, a major sardine-canning centre, and a base for the construction industries spawned by the tourist boom.

Its appearance is undistinguished – most of the older buildings were destroyed in the 1755 earthquake – and it is pedestrianised shopping streets and graceless high-rises that dominate. However, the riverfront and fishing harbour is a hive of activity with its bars and open-air restaurants, grilling sardine lunches.

Arriving

The **train station** is inconveniently located at the northern tip of town and there's no bus into town; a taxi costs about 300$00 or it's a twenty-minute walk.

Buses pull up much more centrally, on the Largo do Duque, close to the river, from where it's a five-minute walk to the **quayside**, which stretches as far as the bridge over to Ferragudo (see below).

Accommodation

The **Turismo** (☎082/236 95), on Rua Dr. João Vitorino Mealha, at the top of the central Largo 1 de Dezembro, helps with booking a **private room** and provides a list of **pensions**. Among the better value options are:

Residencias Roma, Rua Júdice Fialho 34 (☎082/238 21). ②
Pensão O Pátio, Rua Dr. João Vitorino Mealha 5 (☎082/242 88). Near the Turismo ③
Pensão São Roque, Rua das Oliveira 41 (☎082/243 05). Near the Turismo ③
Pensão Arabi, Praça Manuel Teixeira Gomes 13 (☎082/260 06) Spick-and-span. ④
Pensão Santa Isabel, Rua Dr. José Joaquim Nunes 4 (☎082/248 85). ③
Residencial Pimenta, Rua Dr. Ernesto Cabrita 7 (☎082/232 03). ④
Hotel Globo, Rua 5º de Outubro 26 (☎082/41 63 50). ④

Restaurants and bars

Any of the stalls that line the quayside, underneath the bridge, will charcoal-grill half a dozen huge sardines, and serve them up with a plate of chips and half a bottle of the local wine for around 700$00.

For more upmarket surroundings, try one of the places listed below.

Kómaaqui, Rua Infante Dom Henrique 136 (closed Tues). Portimão's most original restaurant, the *Kómaaqui* is a friendly African place with a varied menu. Try the *Gamba* special (tiger prawns) and follow with African-style coffee. Moderate prices.
Marcelo, Rua Júdice Fialho 25–27. African and Portuguese dishes, though pricier than the *Kómaaqui*.
Restaurante Rosamar, Rua da Barca 11. Down-to-earth Portuguese and Spanish dishes at low prices.
Tapas Bar, Rua França 10. Serves *tapas*-style cuttlefish and other spicy dishes. Open 11am–midnight daily except Tuesday.

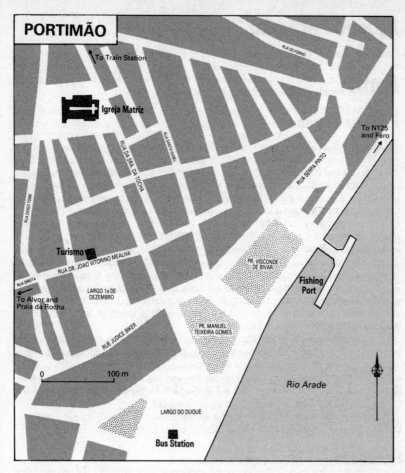

Most of the fancier **bars** are sited in Praia da Rocha (see overpage). The ones in Portimão are for the locals and at their best on Friday and Saturday nights. There is one place, though, worth the walk for locals and visitors alike:

Palco Bar, Avenida 25 de Abril, close by the *Centro Comercial Cedipraia*. This small, friendly bar on the outskirts of town is – oddly enough – busiest out of season. In summer, a local African band, Banda Icalulu, play Friday and Saturday nights; in winter, they have a residency, playing a couple of sets each night.

Other practicalities

There's a huge **market** on the first Monday of each month, held on the open land beyond the train station.

Note also that Portimão has a **British Consulate**, on Rua de Santa Isabel, one of the town's main shopping streets, which leads from the riverside Praça Visconde de Bivar.

Around Portimão

Praia da Rocha, three kilometres south of Portimão, more or less merges with the town these days, though keeps a highly distinct identity of its own as a fairly upmarket resort. Just across the estuary to the east of Portimão is the workaday town of Ferragudo, with a much smaller and less fancy beach.

Praia da Rocha

PRAIA DA ROCHA was one of the first Algarve tourist developments and it's easy to see why. The **beach** is one of the most beautiful on the entire coast: a wide expanse of sand framed by jagged sea cliffs and the walls of an old **fort** (housing a café-restaurant) that once protected the mouth of the river Arade. It was more beautiful still before a great chunk of cliff was blown away to improve access, and the high-rise hotels, discos and sports complex were built alongside the casino.

Surprisingly, **accommodation** is rarely hard to find, with an array of private rooms arranged through the **Turismo** (☎082/222 90), near the fort. The only inexpensive alternative is the *Pensão Oceano* (☎082/243 09; ③), on the main street, Avenida Tomás Cabreira. If you have thousands of *escudos* burning a hole in your pocket, however, *the* place to stay is the seafront *Hotel Bela Vista* (☎082/240 55; ⑥), a pseudo-Moorish mansion built in 1903 as a wedding gift by the wealthy Magalhães family; the interior is an exquisite mixture of carved woods, stained glass and yellow, white and blue *azulejos*. It is worth at least a drink on the hotel esplanade to take a look inside.

Restaurants are plentiful. The *Safari*, Rua António Feu, overlooks the beach and serves Portuguese dishes with an Angolan influence. *O Cloque* (follow the signs for Rocha dos Castelos) is a large candlelit venue, complete with several bars, a restaurant and a patio overlooking the sea. Bars include *Coconuts*, on Rua Bartolomeu Dias, and *Farmers*, behind the *Jupiter Hotel*, which are both as good (or bad) as they sound, depending on your viewpoint.

Bus connections from Praia da Rocha are excellent, with a half-hourly shuttle to Portimão and direct services to Lisbon; the stop is outside the *Hotel Jupiter*.

Ferragudo

FERRAGUDO, facing Portimão across the estuary, and connected by a regular bus service, is very different in character. Stuck on the side of a hill, it's a rundown, friendly little place that is only recently beginning to be fancied up for tourists. It sprawls around a fort – the partner to that in Praia da Rocha, built in the sixteenth century to defend Portimão against attack. It has good views of the port's skyline.

The town has a couple of small pensions and a few private rooms for rent through the local bars or at the tourist office (if it's open). There are a couple of lively bars – check out the *Caldeirão* which has jazz some nights – and an excellent **restaurant**, *A Lanterna* (☎082/239 48; closed Sun), which is to be found just across the bridge from Portimão; the smoked swordfish is particularly tempting.

The Ferragudo **beach** is about a kilometre to the south of town. It is popular in a small-scale way, with a windsurfing school and a scattering of restaurant-bars. A large and rather dreary **campsite** slouches next to the road ten minutes further to the south of the beach.

Alvor and Quinta da Rocha

The coast road west of Praia da Rocha, **towards Lagos**, has been engulfed by a series of massive and graceless tourist developments of very little interest. The ancient port of **ALVOR** may itself have been saved from this fate, but much of its appeal has been washed away under a tide of tourists from the surrounding hotels and holiday villages: the town's narrow streets and its multitude of bars and restaurants can hardly cope. Whitewashed houses and lovely views of the estuary are the last vestiges of Alvor's charm.

Nonetheless, the **beach** is enormous and if it's a bit on the dull side, at least you can escape the crowds. The west end is also an excellent place for catching *conquilhas* (shellfish). At low tide wriggle your feet under the sand in the shallows until you feel one move, then reach down and grab it – or simply copy the Portuguese who will be out there with you. They're good fried with oil and garlic for a few minutes (until they open).

In season, **rooms** at Alvor are hard to come by, but there are two **campsites**: a grim affair near the beach and the more pleasant *Campismo Dourado* about 1km north, toward Montes de Alvor. Restaurants are better, at least outside the peak season. The beach café *Rosemar* does good fish and basic meals.

Quinta da Rocha

The **Quinta da Rocha** nature reserve lies in the peninsula between the mouths of the rivers Alvor and Odiáxere, northwest of Alvor's huge beach. It is an extensive area which, in the parts not given over to citrus and almond groves, consists of copses, salt marsh, sandy spits and estuarine mudflats, forming a wide range of habitats for different plants and animal life – including twenty-two species of **wading birds**.

A Christian environmental group, *A Rocha*, runs a bird-ringing programme from a field centre known as *Cruzinha*, in the middle of the reserve. The warden, Peter Harris, is a valuable source of local natural history information and holds open house every Thursday lunchtime. The centre also has limited full board accommodation, in shared rooms, though as its aims are to increase the awareness in Portugal of the environment and Christianity, precedence is given to Portuguese visitors. Access to *Cruzinha* is from a turning south at MEXILHOEIRA GRANDE on the coastal N125 highway.

Silves

The medieval residence and capital of the Moorish kings of the al-Gharb, **SILVES** is one of the few inland towns in this province that merits a detour. It has a superb castle and a highly dramatic approach, with its red ring of walls gradually revealing their course as you emerge from the wooded hills.

Arriving and accommodation

The **train station** – an easy approach from either Lagos or Faro – lies two kilometres out of town; there is a connecting bus, but it's a pleasant walk if you're not weighed down with luggage. Arriving by **bus**, you'll be dropped on the main road, near the riverfront at the foot of town.

The **Turismo** (☎082/422 55), on Rua 25 de Abril, in the heart of the town, will help arrange **private rooms**. Recommended are those with Isabel Maria da Silva at Rua Cândido dos Reis 36 (☎082/44 26 67), which are spotless and share a little outdoor terrace; a second choice are the rooms in the same street at no. 9. Alternatively, there are three pensions and a hotel:

Residencial Sousa, Rua Samora Barros 17 (☎082/44 25 02). Comfortable old building. ②

Residencial e Pastelaria, Rua do Castelo – behind the fortress. Good value. ②

Estabelecimentos Dom Sancho, opposite the cathedral. Quite wonderful. Even if you have no intention of staying take a look at the hotel's souvenir shop – full of lime green plastic Virgins, terracotta copulating couples, various bits of stuffed animals . . . you name it. ③

Albergaria Marisqueira Rui, just across the river on the south bank (☎082/44 31 06). An excellent modern hotel, which incorporates one of the best restaurants to be found anywhere on the Algarve – see facing page. Modest prices out of season. ③–④

The town

Silves had its heyday under the **Moors**, a period when it was a place of grandeur and industry, described in contemporary accounts as "of shining brightness" within its three dark circuits of guarding walls. Such glories and civilised spendours came to an end, however, in 1189, with the arrival of **Sancho I**, at the head of a mixed army of Portuguese and Crusaders.

Sancho himself was a devout king, at least by the standards of his day, but, desperately in need of extra fighting force, had recruited a rabble of "large and odious" northerners, who had already been expelled from the holy shrine of Saint James of Compostela for their irreligious behaviour. The army arrived at Silves toward the end of June and the 30,000 Moors retreated to the citadel. There they remained through the long, hot summer, sustained by huge water cisterns and granaries, until September, when, the water exhausted, they opened negotiations.

Sancho was ready to compromise, but the Crusaders had been recruited by the promise of plunder, and were not prepared to accept the king's financial inducements to forgo the pleasure of wrecking the town. The gates were opened after Sancho had negotiated guarantees for the inhabitants' personal safety and goods; all were brutally ignored by the Crusaders, who duly ransacked the town, killing some six thousand Moors in the process.

Silves passed back into Moorish hands two years later, but by then the town had been irreperably weakened, and it finally fell to Christian forces in 1249.

The Fortress and Sé

The **Moorish Fortress** (always open) remains the focal point of Silves, dominating the town centre with its impressively complete set of sandstone walls, detached towers and elaborate communication system. The interior is a bit disappointing: aside from the great vaulted water cisterns that still serve the town, there's nothing left of the old citadel, which is planted with modern gardens. However, you can circuit the walls for impressive views over the town and surrounding hills. There's a "traditional festival" held here every Saturday night in summer, and a lively annual beer festival in June.

Just below the fortress is Silves' cathedral, or **Sé** (daily 8.30am–1pm and 2.30–6pm), built on the site of the Grand Mosque. Flanked by broad Gothic towers, it has a suitably defiant, military appearance, though the Great Earthquake and centuries of impoverished restoration have left their mark within.

The museum and market

Close by the Sé, in Rua das Portas de Loulé, is a new **Museu Arqueologia** (Mon–Sat 10am–1pm and 2–5pm; 250$00). It's engaging enough, despite a lack of English-language labelling, and romps through the history of Silves from the year dot to the sixteenth century, through displays of local archeological finds. At the centre of the museum is an Arab water cistern, discovered ten years ago; it's been left *in situ* and boasts a 30-foot-deep well.

Strolling around the rest of Silves is a pleasure. There's a **market** on the riverfront, near the narrow thirteenth-century bridge. This is a fine place to sit out at at one of the grill-cafés (see below) and watch life go by.

Practicalities

Silves is a pleasant alternative base to staying on the coast. If you have transport, it's easy enough to get down to the beach for the day – Carvoeiro is the nearest – or you can head inland to the **Barragem do Arade**, an artificial lake 12km northeast. Here you can hire a motor boat to cruise the waters behind the huge dam and hardly see a soul; the hilltop *Sunshine Café* provides drinks and snacks.

In town, there's a fair selection of restaurants and bars:

Restaurants and cafés

Restaurante Marisqueira Rui, on the south side of the river above the *Albergaria* (☎082/ 44 31 06; closed Tues). This had a reputation for its excellent, reasonably priced seafood long before it moved to these new premises. It continues to attract residents and tourists from all over the Algarve; if you manage to squeeze in – and you should try – order shellfish, the restaurant's speciality.

Churrasqueria Valdemar and **Café-Restaurante Cristal**. Best of a handful of grill-cafés on the riverfront road in front of the market. Outdoor seating and barbecues in summer, with piri-piri chicken, chips, salad and wine for around 1000$00.

Casa Velha, oppiste the Turismo. Decent restaurant serving typical Algarvian food.

Café Inglês, by the fortress. Delicious homemade snacks, ice cream and fruit juices, and seats outside.

Café Rosa, Praça do Municipio. Pleasant café with an elegant, stylish interior; serves drinks and cakes all day (closed Sun).

Inland to the Serra de Monchique

Seven buses a day leave Portimão for the ninety-minute journey to **Monchique** via **Caldas de Monchique**. Once clear of Portimão's ugly suburbs, the main road crosses the coastal plain, flanked by endless orchards of apples, pears, figs, almonds, pomegranates and citrus fruits.

At PORTO DE LAGOS the road divides, east to Silves and north into the foothills of the **Serra de Monchique**, a green and wooded mountain range of cork, chestnut and eucalyptus that gives the western Algarve a natural northern boundary. It is ideal **hiking country**, or a superb route to take if you can hire a moped for a couple of days at one of the Algarve resorts. Sadly, though, much of the area was damaged by a three-day fire which ravaged Monchique in 1990. Acres of land were destroyed and while the vegetation has started to peek back through the black patches, it will be some time before recovery is complete.

Caldas de Monchique

CALDAS DE MONCHIQUE, set in a ravine and surrounded by thick woods, has been a celebrated spa since Roman times. In 1495 Dom João II came here to take the waters (though he nevertheless died soon afterwards in the nearby village of Alvor), and in the nineteenth century the town became a favourite resort of the Spanish bourgeoisie. A casino from these times still stands in the main square, serving now as a handicraft centre, surrounded by lovely, fading nineteenth-century buildings.

The setting is as beautiful as any in the country, and the village's peace and quiet is only temporarily disturbed by the busloads of day-trippers who stop for a wander around and a cup of coffee. Architecturally, perhaps, it's a shame about the modern Thermal Hospital on the edge of the nearby cliff – an eyesore, despite its well-kept gardens – and the equally ugly *Oficina de Engarrafamento* where the famous water is bottled for sale around the country. But at least this maintains the town's tradition, and Caldas remains an active spa rather than being simply quaint.

There are two cheap **pensions** in the town. The better of the two is the *Hospedaria Central* (☎082/922 03; ②) in the main square. The other, *Pensão Internacional* (②) is out by the main road. Both are basic, but both also have a wonderful air of melancholic decay which seems to hang over these old spas, especially out of season. A third, more comfortable option is the *Albergaria do Lageado* (☎082/926 16; ④; May–Oct only), which has a pool and garden.

Out of season you may well find the pension-restaurants closed and service erratic, to put it kindly. However, climbing up from the spa you can follow the stream to sit under giant eucalyptus trees and picnic – and no doubt one could also camp around here without anyone being too bothered. Try taking along some of the local arbutus-berry-derived *aguardente* (fire water), which nicely complements the spring water.

Monchique and nearby villages

MONCHIQUE, six kilometres to the north of Caldas de Monchique, and 300m higher up the range, is a small market town with a huge monthly **agricultural fair**, famous for its smoked hams and its furniture.

There's not a great deal to see, but it's a busy town and makes a nice enough excursion. Of the buildings, the most impressive is the **Igreja Matriz**, the parish church, up a steep cobbled street from the main square, which has a Manueline porch and inside a little chapel with a facade of *azulejos*. The most evocative sight, though, is the ruined seventeenth-century monastery of **Nossa Senhora do Desterro**. Only a roofless shell of this Franciscan foundation survives, apparently quite uncared for, but it's in a great position overlooking the town and shows a beautiful blend of classical Renaissance facade with Moorish-influenced vaulting.

The town has three pensions. First choice, if you can afford it, is the very welcoming *Residencial Estrela de Monchique*, Rua do Porto Fundo 46 (☎082/931 11; ④), a stone's throw to the right of where the bus stops. The fallbacks are cheaper but a bit unappealing: the *Bela Vista*, in the main square, and the *Zé de Ferro*, about 150m down the Portimão road.

Monchique also has a handful of **restaurants**. *Restaurante Chorette* on Rua Samora Gil is highly recommended. If you have the chance, try the speciality of the *Ensopado de Enguias* – eels and bread baked in tomato sauce, which is a lot better than it sounds. *Café Montanha*, Rua do Revez Quente, is cheap and friendly, serving typical Algarvian meat and fish dishes, and local wine at giveaway prices.

There are also a couple of rather lively **bars** in town. One of them, *Barlefante*, just off Rua do Revez Quente, takes the elephant as its theme and serves coffee, drinks and snacks from 1pm onwards. For a quieter drink, try *Bar Travena* at Rua do Revez Quente 37.

Fóia

Fóia, eight kilometres west of Monchique, is – at nearly 900m – the highest of the Serra's peaks. There are no buses but you might be lucky in hitching a lift from a day-tripper. At the top there's a concrete obelisk, a radio tower, a few stalls selling knick-knacks and knitwear (it can be cool up here), a **pension-café**, *O Planalto*, a hotel, the *Estalagem de Santo António*, and a lot of bus tours . . .

What draws the latter is a **panoramic view of the Algarve**, taking in Portimão bay, Lagos, the foothills stretching to the Barragem da Bravura, and Cabo de São Vicente. The poet Robert Southey claimed to have caught a glimpse of the hills of Sintra, beyond Lisbon, but that must have been one of those legendary "clear days" – or maybe the air is never so clear now as it was in 1801.

Picota

Reaching 770 metres, **Picota** comes second in altitude to Fóia, though it's much more interesting in terms of its botany, and easier to reach without transport. You can reach the peak from Monchique in around one and a half hours, a walk that takes in cork trees (and cork collection points), eucalyptus and pines, peach, lemon and orange orchards, and even wild goats scurrying about the heights.

At the top there's nothing save a rickety watchtower occupied by a solitary guardian with a pair of binoculars. From here you can see the coastline stretching all the way to Sagres, and take in another magnificent view of the Monchique mountain range.

Marmelete

MARMELETE (2 buses a day from Monchique) is another fine excursion. It feels very remote: no pensions, nobody trying to sell you anything, old houses, old people. In short, nothing happens here, but the country around, and en route, is utterly tranquil; you can camp in the forest and hike among the woods or hills, and the village itself has two bars.

It might all change. There's a wonderful new road from Marmelete that swings down through the hills and forests to ALJEZUR (see p.342) providing a fast route to the west coast.

Santa Clara

Heading north from Monchique on the main N266 road, you pass the huge **Barragem de Santa Clara** and cut across the flatlands of the Alentejo to a fork with turnings for ODEMIRA and the west coast, or BEJA and the eastern Alentejo. **SANTA CLARA-A-VELHA** (30km from Monchique) makes a pleasant break in the journey, a compact little town with rooms and a few café-restaurants where you can get a meal of fresh fish from the Barragem.

Lagos

The attraction of **LAGOS** is that it's a real town – a fishing port and market centre, whose circuit of medieval walls and recall a past that long predates tourism. It has, of course, over the last two decades, developed into a major resort, attracting the whole gamut of visitors, from moneyed second-homers to *InterRail* backpackers. But for all the summer trade, the place retains a sense of independence and life of its own. In addition, it has some of the best beaches of the whole Algarve coast. To the east of the town is a long sweep of sand – Meia Praia – where there's space even in summer, while to the west is an extraordinary network of coves – sheltered by cliffs, pierced by tunnels and grottoes, and studded by weird and extravagantly weathered outcrops of purple-tinted rock.

Arriving and accommodation

Lagos is the western terminal of the Algarve railway line. Its **train station** is across the river, twenty minutes' walk from the centre; taxis are usually available if you can't face the walk. The **bus station** is a bit closer in, a block back from the main estuary road, Avenida dos Descobrimentos, and almost opposite the bridge to the train station. If you're just passing through Lagos on your way to Sagres, check at the train station before marching into town, since the bus on to Sagres from Lagos tends to call there first.

For those that are staying, it's probably wise to make straight for the **Turismo** in the Largo Marquês de Pombal (June–Aug 9am–8pm daily; otherwise Mon–Fri 9.30am–7pm, weekends 9.30am–12.30pm & 2–5pm; ☎082/630 31), which is the square adjacent to the central Praça Gil Eanes. They will help with booking private rooms, as well as dishing out maps, leaflets and timetables.

Private rooms, pensions and hotels

Most of the town's hotels and pensions are fully booked through the summer and unless you turn up very early in the day, your only chance of a bed will be a **room** in a private house. The Turismo (see above) will phone around and try to find you a space, if there's anything left on their books; arriving early in the day you'll probably be met by touts at the bus or railway stations. It's a good idea to take whatever's going (as long as it's central), and look round later at your leisure; expect to pay from 1500–3000$00 per person depending on season.

Out of season, or booking in advance, you could try for space at one of the established **pensions** and **hotels**, a selection of which are listed below. Prices are comparatively high in season; in winter, however, there are bargains to be had at many of the beach hotels west of town – ask at the Turismo for details.

Pensão Caravela, Rua 25 de Abril 16 (☎082/76 33 61). Reasonable rooms on the town's main pedestrianised street. ③

Residencial Mar Azul, Rua 25 de Abril 13 (☎082/76 97 49). The better establishment on this street. A few of the rooms have their own terrace. ④

Pensão Rubi Mar, Rua da Barroca 70 (☎082/631 65). There are only nine rooms here, but if you can find space it's a treat; some have sea views. ④–⑤

Residencial Baia, Rua da Barroca 70 (☎082/76 22 92). A slightly cheaper alternative on the ground floor of the same building. ④

Pensão Lagosmar, Rua Dr. Faria e Silva 13 (☎082/76 37 22). Upmarket *pensão*, close to Praça Gil Eanes, and reliable enough for the money. ⑤

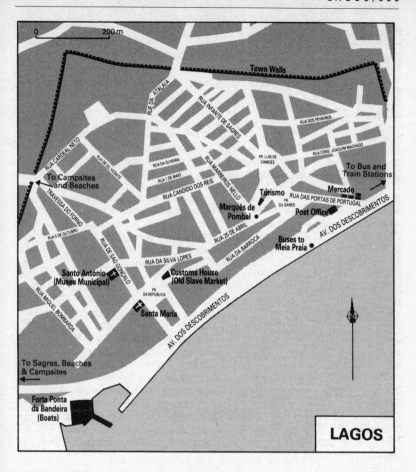

Pensão Dona Ana, Praia de Dona Ana (☎082/76 23 22). Situated at Lagos' finest beach, a 20–minute walk from town across the clifftops (see "Lagos Beaches", p.336). In summer, you'll need to book well in advance for one of the 11 rooms. ③

Camping

Lagos has two **campsites**, both located to the west of town, close by the Praia de Dona Ana. In season a bus marked "D. Ana/Porto de Mós" runs to the beach and sites from the bus station, and the *Imulagos* site provides its own free transport from the train station. On foot, follow the main Sagres road around the old town and it's about ten to fifteen minutes from the Forte Ponta da Bandeira to the sites.

Parque de Campismo Imulagos (☎082/76 00 31). The larger of the sites – huge, in fact, with good facilities and half-price entry to the nearby swimming pool.

Campismo da Trindade (☎082/76 38 92). Marginally closer to town and beach.

If these are full, or the crowds don't appeal, consider heading on west to Burgau, Salema or Sagres.

The town

Lagos is one of the most ancient settlements in the Algarve, founded by the Phoenicians, who were attracted to its superb natural harbour. Under the Moors it became an important trading post until its reconquest by Christian armies in 1241. Later it was a favoured residence of Henry the Navigator, who used the town as a base for the new African trade.

To this latter era is owed the town's least proud relic – Europe's first **slave market**, whose arcades survive alongside the old **Customs House** in the **Praça da República** near the waterfront. On the other side of this square is the church of **Santa Maria**, through whose whimsical Manueline windows the youthful Dom Sebastião is said to have roused his troops before the ill-fated Moroccan expedition of 1578. Fired up by militant Catholicism, the dream-crazed king was to perish on the battlefield of Alcácer-Quibir (modern Ksar el Kbir, between Tangier and Fes) along with almost the entire Portuguese nobility. It was a disaster that enabled the Spanish to absorb Portugal for sixty years, but it did Dom Sebastião's reputation a world of good among the aggressively devout. He's commemorated in the centre of Lagos, in **Praça Gil Eanes**, by a fantastically dreadful modern statue – pink, ridiculous and looking like a flowerpot man.

Much of the old town was devastated by the 1755 earthquake, though one rare and beautiful church that survived for restoration was the **Igreja de Santo António**. This really demands a look, even if you don't normally venture into churches. Decorated around 1715, its gilt and carved interior is wildly obsessive, every last inch filled with a private fantasy of cherubic youths struggling with animals and fish. Next door is the **Museu Municipal** (Tues–Sun 9.30am–12.30pm & 2.30–5.30pm; 100$00), whose bizarre displays range from Roman mosaics and folk costumes to misshapen animal fetuses.

The Praça da República, and the waterfront Avenida dos Descobrimentos, are the best vantage points for the remains of Lagos' once impregnable **walls** and fortifications, which include the seventeenth-century **Forte Ponta da Bandeira** (Tues–Sat 10am–1pm and 2–6pm, Sun 10am–1pm; 200$00), guarding the entrance to the harbour. Where the Avenida dos Descobrimentos meets Rua das Portas de Portugal, there's a diverting **fish and vegetable market** on Monday to Saturday mornings.

Food, drink and nightlife

The centre of Lagos is packed with **restaurants**, from basic to very posh. For a session of menu-browsing, don't miss the fish market area (see above) and ruas Afonso d'Almeida and 25 de Abril.

Restaurants

Ao Natural, Rua Silva Lopes 29. This lively Dutch-owned restaurant-bar specialises in vegetarian dishes with a difference. It also serves healthy breakfasts, from 10am.

Casa do Zé, Avenida dos Descobrimentos. Just around the corner from the market, this does excellent fish dishes at very fair prices. Very much a locals' choice, with the outdoor seating soaking up a brisk lunchtime trade.

Cervejaria O Sol do Algarve, Rua Infante de Sagres 56. Tucked away, out of the central eating area, this is an unpretentious place with great *prato do dia* bargains and a very hefty serving of *arroz de mariscos*.

O Cantinho Algarvio, Rua Afonso d'Almeida 17. Centrally located, this is again popular with locals for its wide range of modestly-priced Algarvian food.

Restaurante Piri Piri, Rua Afonso d'Almeida 10. Fresh fish served daily, as well as the spicy chicken dish that gives the restaurant its name. Inexpensive, given its central location, and with a pretty interior.

Pouso do Infante, Rua Afonso d'Almeida 11. Mid-range restaurant offering classic Portuguese and Algarvian cookery in an interior overwhelmed by rustic decoration.

Dom Sebastião, Rua 25 de Abril 20–22 (☎082/627 95). Arguably the town's finest restaurants, with outdoor seating, a stylish interior, superlative seafood, and a fabulous selection of starters. Phone or call in to reserve a table; a full meal runs to about 3500$00.

Bars and clubs

There are lots of **bars** around town, many of them owned by expatriates – in particular Irish and British; cocktails are almost universally generous.

Adega Portuguesa, Travessa dos Tanoeiros, just off Rua 25 de Abril. More of a bar than its "wine cellar" name would suggest, but retains a cosy atmosphere. Prices affordable by its predominantly young crowd. Open till 2am.

Aplauso, top end of Rua Infante de Sagres. Opens every night at 10pm for, often rather tacky, live music acts. Occasionally something better, including jazz. No cover.

Mullens, Rua Cândido dos Reis 86. The late night choice, this serves meals until 10pm (very good duck dishes), plays jazz on the sound system, and stays open until 2am. The bar staff are a show in themselves.

Roskos, Rua Cândido dos Reis – opposite *Mullens*.. Serious cocktails.

Zanzibar, Rua 25 de Abril 93. Modern, upbeat bar with good music.

Phoenix, Rua 5 de Outubro, 11. The best club in Lagos. Buy your ticket before midnight and it's 500$00, your first drink included; after midnight it's double. Two dancefloors play contemporary British sounds. Stays open till 4am.

Listings

Bike and motorbike hire *Motolagos*, Rua São José d'Armas (☎082/603 65).

Boat trips around the coast are easy to arrange with the fishing boats that gather around the Forte Ponta da Bandeira, or you can book a "cruise" at the Turismo.

Bullfights are held most Saturday afternoons in the summer, though they run strictly for the tourists and their "famous horsemen" are in reality quite unknown; don't encourage them, is our advice.

Car rental *Avis*, Largo das Portas de Portugal 11 (☎082/636 91); *Luz Car*, Largo das Portas de Portugal 10 (☎082/610 16); *Auto Ourique*, Avda. dos Descobrimentos (☎082/612 52).

Hospital Rua do Castelo dos Governadores, adjacent to the church of Santa Maria.

Markets In addition to the fish and vegetable market (see "The town"), there's a Saturday morning general goods market, held by the bus station.

Police Rua General Alberto Silveira.

Post office Behind the town hall, just off Avda. dos Descobrimentos; open Mon–Fri 8am–6pm, Sat 8am–1pm.

Telephones It's easiest to make long-distance calls at the post office; phone booths here are in operation from 9am to 11pm.

Travel agencies For tickets and tours, try *Joaquim Resende* on Rua António Barbosa Viana, or *Viagens Oásis* on Rua Victor Costa e Silva.

Watersports There's a windsurfing school at Meia Praia. For slides, pools and aquatic fun, take the bus from the bus station (around 9.30am) to *Slide & Splash*, a theme park 45 minutes away; adults 2000$00, children 1200$00.

Lagos beaches – and inland

The promontory **south** of Lagos is fringed by extravagantly eroded cliff faces that shelter a series of postage stamp-sized **cove-beaches**. All are within easy walking distance of the old town, though the beach tracks are increasingly confused by a multitude of paths leading to the hotels and campsites. In addition, the concentration of resort hotels near the beaches means that you may find the least crowded strand is the **town beach** itself, just beyond the Forte Ponta da Bandeira.

Cove beaches to the south

The easiest access on foot to the cove-beaches is to follow the Avenida dos Descobrimentos up the hill (toward Sagres) and turn left just opposite the fire station, where you see the signs to the tiny **Praia do Pinhão**. This is the first of the coves – around a twenty-minute walk from town. Five minutes further, across the cliffs, is the **Praia de Dona Ana** – one of the most photogenic of all the Algarve's beaches, with a superb restaurant, the *Mirante*, built into the cliffs.

Beyond here, despite the jostling hotels, you can follow a path around the cliffs and coast to **Praia do Camilo** – sometimes a bit less crowded – and right to the **Ponta da Piedade**, the point, where a palm-bedecked lighthouse makes a great vantage point for the sunset.

Meia Praia

To the **east** of Lagos, flanked by the railway line, is **Meia Praia**, a vast tract of sand that extends for four kilometres to the delta of the rivers Odiáxere and Arão. A regular **bus service** leaves from the Avenida dos Descobrimentos and travels the length of the beach; alternatively there's a seasonal **ferry** from the side of the Forte Ponta da Bandeira.

The Barragem da Bravura

If you'd rather get away from the crowds altogether, you could head instead for the **Barragem da Bravura** (or *Barragem de Odiáxere*), fifteen kilometres inland from Lagos and reached by three daily buses.

A huge reservoir built in Salazar's time to water the country behind Lagos, the lake is surrounded by forests, deserted except for a few picnickers and the occasional windsurfer. There's just one seasonal café.

Lagos to Sagres

A new highway is in the throes of construction from Lagos west to Vila do Bispo, and the erstwhile small settlements along the coast here are seeing an increasing amount of development. Among them, **Salema** – a superb beach and still recognisable as a former fishing village – promises most.

Luz, Burgau and Salema

Five kilometres west of Lagos you reach the resort of **LUZ**, an unappealing mass of chalets and villas that spreads in all directions from the beach, swamping the old village. There's a large luxury campsite, the *Valverde*, some way from the seafront and the full range of tourist facilities, but it's a charmless place.

It's best to keep heading west, past **BURGAU,** another intensively developed, very British holiday spot (though bound to lose its appeal with the recent loss of most of its sandy beach to the sea), and on to Salema, halfway between Lagos and Sagres. Buses cover this route several times daily from Lagos.

SALEMA was, until the mid-1980s, primarily a fishing community, with its old village trailing up the hill quite separate from the hotels. Now, sadly, a vast amount of apartment and villa construction has engulfed the whole area between the N125 main road and the sea. Still, the **beach** – a wide, rock-sheltered bay – is magnificent, and the development could have been worse.

Most of the accommodation in Sagres is in apartments, though there is a fair-sized and quite attractive hotel, the *Estalagem Infante do Mar* (☎082/651 37; ⑤) Cheaper alternatives include **private rooms** in the old village – ask at the bars and the post-office shop, or just stroll along the street – and a pleasantly landscaped **campsite** up toward the main road. Best of the restaurants is the *Mira-Mar* (open 9am–midnight), signposted off the main old street in the village; this serves up barbecued fish and meat on a terrace above the beach.

On towards Sagres

The beaches **between Salema and Sagres** are still unmarked on most tourist maps – a reflection of development that is yet to happen.

At the road village of **FIGUEIRA** on the N125 (the point at which the highway most closely approaches the coast between Lagos and Sagres) there's the very welcoming *Bar Celeiro* by the bus stop. From here, paths lead off to the lovely **Praia da Figueira** – a twenty- to thirty-minute walk– which is often more or less deserted except for a few campers.

Two other worthwhile beaches are accessible by road from the village of **RAPOSEIRA** (which also has a great-value restaurant, the *Artisanale*) though they are more of a walk. The turning to look out for is signposted "Ingrina": about 1km down the road, take the left fork that passes through Hortas do Tabual and after another 3km or so you'll reach two isolated, craggy beaches – **Praia do Zavial** and **Praia da Ingrina**. These have the bare minimum of tourist facilities, though there's a **campsite** at Ingrina, and there are no public transport connections from the main road. Zavial is large and sandy, with tumbles of rock at either end and a café-restaurant open daily (except Wed) in season. Ingrina is completely stony but good for beach-combing and rock pools.

West of Raposeira the road passes VILA DO BISPO and the turnoff for the west coast (see p.341), before heading across the flattened landscape for Sagres.

Sagres

Wild and windswept, **SAGRES** and its cape were considered by the Portuguese as the far limit of the ancient and medieval worlds. It was on these headlands in the fifteenth century that Prince Henry the Navigator made his residence and it was here too that he set up a school of navigation, gathering together the greatest astronomers, cartographers and adventurers of his age.

Fernão de Magalhães (Magellan), Pedro Álvares Cabral and Vasco da Gama all studied at Sagres, and from the beach at Belixe – midway between the capes of Sagres and São Vicente – the first long caravels were launched, revolutionising shipping with their wide hulls, small adaptable sails, and ability to sail close to the wind. Each year new expeditions were dispatched to penetrate a little further than their predecessors, and to resolve the great navigational enigma presented by the west coast of Africa, thereby laying the foundations of the country's overseas empire.

After Henry's death here in 1460, the centre of maritime studies was moved to Lisbon, and Sagres slipped back into the obscurity from which he'd raised it. Today, it remains little more than a one-street village, plus the inevitable trail of villas and apartments. It can be a great place to stay, especially out of season, when there's a bleak, desolate appeal to the scenery and hardly a tourist to be seen. Through the summer, by contrast, the village draws quite a lively and oddball social scene – including a concentration of backpackers and windsurfers from all across Europe and North America. They are well catered for by an ever-growing array of rooms for rent, restaurants and bars.

Arrival and accommodation

The nearest train station to Sagres is at Lagos. **Buses** from there generally call in at the bus and train station in summer. In Sagres, they drop and pick up passengers in the village square; timetables for onward connections are posted in various bars and shops. The petrol station on the roundabout hires out **bicycles** and **scooters** for getting around the cape and local beaches.

Orientation is straightforward, with the walls of the **Fortaleza** (fortress) standing at the end of the road, directly ahead of the village. There is a **Turistico** office (daily 10am–7pm; ☎082/641 25) in the village square – though signs still direct you to its old site in the Fortaleza.

Rooms and camping
"Rooms", "Quartos", "Chambres", "Zimmer": there are places to stay everywhere in and around Sagres village, and in high season, at least, it's basically a question of turning up and seeing what you're offered; prices range from around 2000–3500$00 for a double, according to season.

Generally, you'll be approached by people offering rooms and, if you want it, access to a kitchen too. There's little point in giving specific recommendations, since there's not much diference as far as price and location goes. However, if you have the time and inclination, ask around for directions to *Casa da Lidia*; her pleasant rooms and equipped kitchen are often touted by an old man called Francisco – quite a character – who drives new arrivals in the back of his motortrike and insists you wear a Biggles-like flying helmet to foil the attentions of the zealous local gendarmerie. You could, alternatively, visit one or two of the "old men bars" right near the square and ask them about rooms: they usually know.

Alternatives include a **youth hostel** and a scattering of regular **pensions** and **hotels** in Sagres, as well as a youth hostel. Check the list below for the options and note that – as with the private rooms – prices come down considerably out of season.

Youth hostel (☎082/642 19). This has recently moved out of the Fortaleza to a site 100m from the village square. It's packed in summer and a curfew puts a dampener on nightlife. ①
Residencia Pinheiro, Rua São Vicente (☎ 082/641 14). Good clean rooms. ②
Aparthotel Orquídea. Overlooks the fishing port and has fine views up the coast; flashy as the place looks, it's surprisingly cheap, especially out of season. ④

Residencial Dom Henrique (☎082/641 33). Located right on the village square and perfectly adequate. ⑤

Pousada do Infante (☎082/642 22). The best views of the fortress are from the bar-terrace of Sagres' *pousada*, an attractive clifftop mansion with Moorish elements. It's a wonderful location and offers special rates out of season. ⑥

The nearest **campsite** is two kilometres east of the village along the main road; it is convenient for Praia do Martinhal. Camping rough on the beaches is definitely not an option; the local police don't like it and, given the number of rooms available, you can see their point.

Sagres village, the Fortaleza and local beaches

Sagres village, rebuilt in the nineteenth century over the earthquake ruins of Henry's town, has nothing of architectural or historical interest and is little more than a line of houses connecting the fishing harbour with the square. Back from the main road, built to transport tourists straight to the headlands, trails virtually a new town of white villas and apartments, much of it still under construction. It says much for the surroundings of the village and cape that this seems to present no danger of turning Sagres into just another resort.

The Fortaleza

Henry the Navigator's **Fortaleza** dominates the whole scene near the village. An immense circuit of walls – only the north side survives intact – once surrounded its vast shelf-like promontory high above the Atlantic. With such explicit demands of secrecy and security, together with its wild remoteness, it must have seemed a kind of Aldermaston or Los Alamos of its day.

You enter through a formidable tunnel, before which is spread a huge pebble **Rosa dos Ventos** (wind compass) unearthed beneath a church in 1921 and said to have been used by Henry himself. Historians disagree – and are equally unimpressed by the claims of the adjacent tourist office and youth hostel to have been the **prince's house**. Still, it is all in all a wonderful, wild setting and the simple, much-restored chapel of **Nossa Senhora da Graça** is at least contemporary with Henry's explorations.

Local beaches

However impressive the fortress, most people's days in Sagres are spent on one of the excellent nearby beaches, five of which are within easy walking distance of the village. Three of them are on the more sheltered coastline east of the fortress: **Praia da Mareta** is just below the square, and the grubby **Praia da Baleeira** is by the harbour, from where it's a five-minute walk to the longest and best beach, the **Praia do Martinhal**, an ideal spot for windsurfing. West of the fortress, the beaches are longer and more impressive, and the one nearest the village is a good spot. It's a longer walk to the beautiful **Praia de Belixe** (see "Cabo de São Vicente" overpage), a couple of kilometres out of the village, where you are usually guaranteed plenty of sand to yourself.

Whichever beach you choose, the water is very cold and swimming must be approached with caution – there are some very strong currents. Before setting off for the more distant strands, stock up with drinks and picnic fixings since there are virtually no facilities. The village supermarket can oblige with most provisions, plus five-litre flagons of the local wine for evening parties.

Food and nightlife

Sagres' main street is lined with **restaurants and bars**, catering for a range of tastes and budgets. For breakfast, try either *Café Cochina* or *A Rosa dos Ventos* (see below), both on the main square.

Restaurants

A Grelha. Standard restaurant with the cheapest tourist menu in town.

A Tasca. Down by the fishing harbour, this serves marvellous seafood, tuna and *caldeirada* (fish stew) at fairly reasonable prices.

Atlântico. Excellent choice on the main street, with good grilled fish.

Bar O Pescador. Meals at prices much more reasonable than you'd expect from the sight of the lobsters patrolling their tanks at the entrance.

Bossa Nova. Off the main street, this place is noted for pizzas, salads and imaginative vegetarian meals.

Dromedário. An energetic bistro that serves drinks and snacks all day.

Restaurante O Descobridor. Calorific fish dishes at rock-bottom prices.

Mar A Vista. A bit pricey, though with excellent sea views, as the name suggests

Bars and discos

A Rosa dos Ventos, on the village square. In season, this is the place to be – a lively, loud, and drunken bar where Swedish teenagers, German bikers and Portuguese fishermen with berets stuck to their ears conduct fractured conversations, under the hazy gaze of novice boozers who've fallen at the first hurdle.

The Last Chance Saloon, around the corner, overlooking the sea. A Rosa's main rival, packed with the rest of the travelling youth contingent.

Disco Topas, near the campsite.

Disco Caravelo – in a strange mosque-like building, a short walk north of the village.

Cabo de São Vicente

The exposed **CABO DE SÃO VICENTE** – Cape Saint Vincent – across the bay from Sagres, was sacred to the Romans, who believed the sun sank hissing into the water beyond here every night. It became a Christian shrine when the relics of the martyred Saint Vincent arrived in the eighth century; watched over (some say piloted) by ravens, the remains were transferred by boat to Lisbon in 1173.

It was almost certainly at the cape that Henry established his School of Navigation, founded a small town, and built his Vila do Infante. Today only a **lighthouse**, flanked by the ruins of a sixteenth-century Capuchin convent, are to be seen. The other buildings, already vandalised by the piratical Sir Francis Drake in 1597, came crashing to the ground in the Great Earthquake of 1755, the monks staying on alone until the Liberal suppression of the monasteries in 1834.

The cape is nonetheless a dramatic and exhilarating six-kilometre walk from Sagres, a path skirting the tremendous cliffs for much of the way. This is a wonderful spot for **bird life** and at the right time of year you should be able to spot blue rock thrushes and peregrines nesting on the cliffs. Walking on the road is easier, and there's always the chance of a lift – if one doesn't materialise it'll take less than an hour and a half, with glorious views all the way. Try to be at the Cape for sunset – invariably gorgeous, though frequently also very windy.

Belixe

At **BELIXE**, just two kilometres down the road from Sagres to Cabo São Vicente, there's an excellent **beach** and a couple of bar-restaurants. Fifteen minutes' walk from here, at FORTE DO BELIXE, are the remnants of a prim little fortress, a fancy restaurant, and a small, four-room **hotel**, the *Fortaleza do Belixe* (☎082/ 64124; ⑤), an annexe of the Sagres *pousada*, perched high on the cliff edge.

Vila do Bispo and the coast to Odeceixe

Unlike the southern stretches of the "Algarve proper", the **west coast**, from Sagres to Odeceixe, is relatively undeveloped. There are several reasons: the coast is exposed to strong Atlantic winds, the sea can be several degrees cooler and swimming dangerous. However, if you can brave the climate, you might like to base yourself at low-key resorts such as **Vila do Bispo**, **Carrapateira**, **Aljezur** and **Odeceixe**, all of which have plenty of beach, plus an inexpensive network of private rooms and scope for freelance camping.

Like Sagres, these resorts attract a predominantly young and/or alternative crowd. At a few resorts – **Odeceixe**, in particular – this can be overwhelming, with summer crowds of German campervan-hippies strutting about nude on the beach. If this sounds more like purgatory than a holiday, you've been warned.

Vila do Bispo

VILA DO BISPO, at the junction of the west and south coast roads, is a pretty little town with a lovely parish church, every surface of which has been painted, tiled or gilded. Nothing much happens here, but the town could make a pleasant base if you have transport for daytrips to the beaches. There are some **rooms** above the restaurant in the square and a couple of **pensions** – *Pensão Mira-Sagres* on Rua do Hospital and *Pensão Casal da Vila* on Rua General Carmona. In the evening, *Café Correia*, opposite the church, is packed with travellers, while around the corner, down a small alley, is the much cheaper *Oasis*, a locals' haunt, where the house speciality is chicken.

The nearest beach, the cliff-edged **Praia do Castelejo**, is reached by a rough road – no buses and a backbreaking hike – leading five kilometres west, across a stretch of bleak moors and hills. In summer, there's a little bar-restaurant here.

Carrapateira

Fifteen kilometres to the north of Vila do Bispo (and connected with it by two daily buses) is the village of **CARRAPATEIRA**. This is better positioned for the beach but is itself rather dilapidated and not terribly inviting. It's possible to get a **private room** if you ask around the main square or at the *Bar Barroca*. However, the best accommodation is a couple of kilometres northeast of town at the *Residencial Casa Fajara* (⑤), a spruce modern villa with neat gardens, overlooking an empty river valley. It's a great location, open in the summer months only.

Carrapateira's local beach, a kilometre's walk from the *Casa Fajara*, is the **Praia da Bordeira**, a spectacular strand with dunes, a tiny river and crashing surf. The sandbanks provide shelter from the wind for a sizeable community of freelance **campers**, who seem to be tolerated by the local police. There is a seasonal **café-steakhouse** on the beach.

A second beach – quieter and with no facilities – is the **Praia do Amado**, 4km south of the Praia da Bordeira around the Carrapateira headland.

Aljezur and Vale da Telha

The village of **ALJEZUR** (2 buses daily from Lagos and Vila do Bispo) is divided into two distinct halves: to the west of the river is a rather drab old quarter, Moorish in origin and straggling along the side of a hill below ruins of a tenth-century **castle**, while to the east lies a more modern settlement. The **Turismo**, by the river, can sometimes help with private **rooms** – the only alternative if you find the town **pension**, the *Residencial Francisca Sirominho* (③) full.

A kilometre south of Aljezur, a road heads to the local **beaches** of MONTE CLÉRIGO (8km) and ARRIFANA (10km; served by a morning bus). The latter is magnificent, though its village, perched on the cliffs above, is a rather grubby affair. Midway between the beaches is the **VALE DA TELHA** tourist complex, which has planning permission for expansion to a site of 2500 chalets and villas. At present it's nowhere near that size, nor a great commercial success, with just a modest **hotel**, the *Residencial Vale da Telha* (☎082/981 80; ③), and a **campsite**, the *Municipal de Aljezur* (☎082/984 44), up and running. The **restaurant** near the develoment office is surprisingly good.

Odeceixe

ODECEIXE, hunched on a hill and cramped by the river, is the last village before the Alentejo (see p.299 for details of Zambujeira, just to the north). Situated near the head of a delightful curving estuary, it is a fairly quiet little place, at least outside July and August. At this time of year, it seems to attract – as mentioned earlier – just about every German hippy on the Algarve, a clientèle that creates its own rather exclusive presence. If you hit town outside the hippy season, though, it could be very pleasant, with a couple of simple restaurants, a number of houses offering **rooms**, and some small villas for rent by the beach.

The beach – **Praia de Odeceixe** – is a high-cliffed cove, stretching north of the estuary. It is one of the most sheltered beaches on this stretch of coast, with a minimum of tourist development and wonderful surf.

travel details

Trains

ALGARVE LINE

From Lagos 13 trains a day to Meia Praia (5min), Alvor (30min), Portimão (30min), Silves (50min), and Tunes (1hr 20min). 9 trains continue from Tunes to Ferreira–Albufeira (10min), Faro (50min), Olhão (1hr 10min), Tavira (1hr 50min), and Vila Real de Santo António (2hr 35min).

An additional 4 trains daily run from Faro to Vila Real.

TRAINS FROM TUNES STATION ("TUNES GARE") AND LISBON

From Tunes 4 trains daily to Lisbon **via Sado** (4hr–4hr 20min).

From Tunes 2 trains daily to Beja **via Sul** (3hr 20min) with connections for Casa Branca (4hr 40min); change for Évora (30min) and Lisbon (6hr 30min).

Trains from Lisbon continue beyond Tunes to either Lagos or Faro/Vila Real.

Night trains between Lisbon and Lagos and Faro/Vila Real.

Local buses

From Lagos to Sagres 9 daily (1hr); Luz/Burgau/ Salema 5 daily (15/20/50min); Aljezur/ Odemira 2 daily (1hr/1hr 45min); Portimão 12 daily (40min).

From Portimão to Silves 6 daily (20min); Ferragudo 12 daily (10min); Monchique 8 daily (1hr 30min); Albufeira 4 daily (1hr 10min); Lagos (hourly; 30min); Alvor (hourly; 20min); Faro (5 daily; 2hr), and Monchique (8 daily; 1hr).

From Albufeira to Faro via all stops 11 daily (1hr 20min); Armação de Pera (4 daily; 30min).

From Faro to Tavira/Vila Real 10 daily (50min/ 1hr 20min); Olhão 30 daily (20min); Estói 12 daily, fewer on weekends (20min); Quarteira/Vilamoura (hourly; 30min/40min); Albufeira (hourly; 1hr 20min); Loulé (half-hourly; 30min); Beja 4 daily (3hr).

From Sagres to Lagos (10 daily; 1hr) via Vila do Bispo, for Carrapateira and Aljezur (2 daily; 20 and 35min; unreliable on Sun).

Long-distance buses

Numerous companies operate **express buses** between Lisbon and the Algarve: ask at travel agents. Most are quicker than the *RN* buses between Faro and Lisbon which run 3 daily (7hr) and Lagos and Lisbon, once a day (7hr 30min).

Ferries

From Vila Real de Santo António to Ayamonte, Spain, every 30min (15 min).

Note that the ferry from **Faro to Tangier** *has been discontinued.*

Flights

From Faro to Lisbon 5 or 6 flights daily; **to Porto** once a week non-stop.

From Faro to London at least one daily scheduled flight; **to Manchester** one flight a week.

PART THREE

THE

CONTEXTS

HISTORICAL FRAMEWORK

The early history of Portugal – as part of the Iberian Peninsula – has obvious parallels with that of Spain. Division at this stage is somewhat arbitrary, an independent development only really becoming valid with Afonso Henriques' creation of a Portuguese kingdom in the twelfth century.

EARLY CIVILISATION

Remnants of pottery and cave burials point to tribal societies occupying the Tagus valley and parts of the Alentejo and Estremadura as early as 8000 to 7000 BC – but as yet there have been no finds in Portugal comparable to the Paleolithic caves of Altamira and northern Spain. More, however, is known of **Neolithic** Portugal and its *Castro* culture based on hilltop forts, a culture that was to be developed and refined after the arrival of Celtic peoples around 700 to 600 BC. These, the first permanent settlements, were concentrated in northern Portugal – and particularly in the Minho, where excavations have revealed dozens of **citânias**, or fortified villages. The most impressive is at Briteiros, near Braga, with its paved streets, drainage systems and circuits of defensive walls; like many of the *citânias* it survived, remarkably unchanged, well into the Roman era. Settlements in neighbouring Trás-os-Montes, in contrast, reflect less of a defensive spirit – but all that remains of this more pastoral **verracos** culture are the crude granite *porcas*, stone figures venerating wild sows as objects of a primitive fertility cult.

The potential for new trading outlets – and the quest for metals, in particular tin for making bronze – attracted a succession of peoples from across the Mediterranean but the emphasis of their settlement lay on the eastern seaboard and so fell within "Spanish" history. The **Phoenicians**, however, established an outpost at Lisbon around 900 BC and there were probably contacts, too, with Mycenaean Greeks. In the mid-third century BC, they were followed by **Carthaginians**, who recruited Celtic tribesmen for military aid against the Roman empire. Once again, though, their influence was predominantly on the eastern seaboard and in the south; with defeat in the Second Punic War (218–202 BC) they were to be replaced by a more determined colonising force.

ROMANS, SUEVI AND VISIGOTHS

Entering the peninsula in 210 BC, the **Romans** swiftly subdued and colonised the Mediterranean coast and the south of Spain and Portugal – the areas most affected by earlier trading links. In the interior, however, they met with great resistance from the Celtiberian tribes and in 193 BC the Lusitani rose up in arms. Based in central Portugal, between the rivers Tagus and Lima, they were, in the words of the Roman historian Strabo, "the most powerful of the Iberian peoples, who resisted the armies of Rome for the longest period." For some fifty years, in fact, they held up the Roman advance, under the leadership of **Viriatus**, a legendary Portuguese hero and masterful exponent of the feigned retreat who on several occasions brought the Romans to accept his autonomous rule. He was betrayed after a successful campaign in 139 BC and within two years the Lusitani had capitulated as the legions of Decimus Junius Brutus swept through the north. Still, over a century later their name was given to this most westerly of the Roman provinces and in the northern Celtic villages Roman colonisation can scarcely have been felt.

Integration into the Roman Empire came largely under Julius Caesar, who in 60 BC established a capital at Olisipo (Lisbon) and significant colonies at Ebora (Évora), Scallabis (Santarém) and Pax Julia (Beja). In 27 BC the Iberian provinces were further reorganised under Augustus, all but the north of Portugal being governed – as Lusitania – from the great Roman city of Merida in Spanish Extremadura. The Minho formed part of a separate province, later added to northwest Spain to create Gallaecia, with an important regional centre at Bracara Augusta (Braga). In general though it was the south where Roman influence was deepest; here they established huge agricultural estates (the infamous *Latifundia* which still survive in Alentejo) and changed the nature of the region's crops, as they introduced wheat, barley, olives and the vine to the area.

There are no great **Roman sites** in Portugal – at least nothing to compare with Spanish Merida, Tarragona, or Italica – though both Évora and Conimbriga have individual monuments of interest. The mark of six centuries of Roman rule consists more in their network of roads (used well into the middle ages) and their bridges, many of them still in use today. There is a more basic legacy, too, the Portuguese language being very heavily derived from Latin.

The **decline of the Roman Empire** in Portugal echoes its pattern elsewhere, though perhaps with greater indifference, the territory always being something of a provincial backwater. Christianity reached Portugal's southern coast toward the end of the first century and by the third century bishoprics were established at Braga, Évora, Faro and Lisbon. But the state was already disintegrating and in 409 the first waves of barbarian invaders crossed the Pyrenees into Spain. Vandals, Alans, Suevi and Visigoths all passed through Portugal, though only the last two were of any real importance.

The **Suevi**, a semi-nomadic people from eastern Germany, eventually settled in the area between the Douro and Minho rivers, establishing courts at Braga and Portucale (Porto). They seem to have coexisted fairly peacefully with the Hispano-Roman nobility and were converted to Christianity by Saint Martin of Dume – a saint frequently found in the dedications of northern churches.

Around 585, however, the Suevian state disappeared, having been suppressed and incorporated into the **Visigothic** empire, a heavily Romanised yet independent force which for two centuries maintained a spurious unity and rule over most of the peninsula. The Visigothic kings, however, ruled from Toledo, supported by a small and elite aristocratic warrior-caste, so in Portugal their influence was neither great nor lasting. And by the end of the seventh century their divisions, exacerbated by an elective monarchy and their intolerance (including the first Iberian persecution of the Jews), resulted in one faction appealing for aid from Muslim North Africa. In 711 a first force of **Moors** crossed the straits into Spain and within a decade they had advanced and conquered all but the mountainous reaches of the Asturias in northern Spain.

THE MOORS . . . AND CHRISTIAN RECONQUEST

In Portugal, Aveiro probably marked the northernmost point of the **Moorish advance**. The Moors met with little resistance but the dank, green hills of the Minho held little attraction for the colonizers-to-be and over the following century seem to have been severely depopulated. Most of the Moors were content to settle in the south: in the Tagus valley, the rich wheat belts around Évora and Beja and above all the coastal region of the **al-Gharb**. Here they established a capital at Shelb, modern Silves, and, by the middle of the ninth century, an independent kingdom, detached from the great Muslim emirate of al-Andalus which covered most of Spain.

They were a mix of ethnic races – for the most part Berbers from Morocco, but also considerable numbers of Syrians and, around Faro, a contingent of Egyptians, some of them probably Coptic Christians. In contrast to the Visigoths, the Moors were tolerant and productive, their rule a civilising influence. Both Jews and Christians were allowed freedom of worship and their own civil laws, while under Muslim law small landholders continued to occupy lands that they themselves cultivated. For most of these **"Moçárabes"**–Christians subject to Moorish rule– ife must have improved. Roman irrigation techniques were perfected and the Moors introduced the rotation of crops and cultivation of cotton, rice, oranges and lemons. Their culture and scholarship led the world – though less from al-Gharb than from Cordoba and Sevilla – and they forged important trade links, many of which were to continue centuries after their fall. Perhaps still more important, **urban life** developed, with prosperous local craft industries: Lisbon, Évora, Beja and Santarém all emerged as sizable towns.

The Christian **"Reconquista"** – at least by tradition – began at Covadonga in 718, when Pelayo, at the head of a small band of Visigoths, halted the advance of a Moorish expeditionary force. The battle's significance has doubtless been inflated but from the victory a tiny kingdom of the Asturias does seem to have been established. Initially only 40 by 30 miles in extent, it expanded over the next two centuries to take in León, Galicia and the "lands of Portucale," the latter an area roughly equivalent to the old Swabian state between the Douro and the Minho.

By the eleventh century **Portucale** had the status of a country, its governors appointed by the kings of León. In 1073 Alfonso VI came to the throne. It was to be a reign hard-pressed by a new wave of Muslim invaders – the fanatical Almoravides who crossed over to Spain in 1086 after appeals from al-Andalus and established a new Muslim state at Sevilla. Like many kings of Portugal after him, Alfonso was forced to turn to European crusaders, many of whom would stop in at the shrine of Saint James in Compostela. One of them, Raymond of Burgundy, married his eldest daughter and became heir-apparent to the throne of León; his cousin Henry, married to another daughter, Teresa, was given jurisdiction over Portucale. With Henry's death Teresa became regent for her son, **Afonso Henriques** and began to try to forge a union with Galicia. Afonso, however, had other ideas and having defeated his mother at the battle of São Mamede (1128), he established a capital at **Guimarães** and set about extending his domains to the south.

The reconquest of central Portugal was quickly achieved – Afonso's victory at Ourique in 1139 was a decisive blow and by 1147 he had taken Santarém. In the same year Lisbon fell, after a siege in which passing crusaders again played a vital role – though not sailing on to the Holy Land before murderously sacking the city. Many of them were English and some stayed on – Gilbert of Hastings became Archbishop. By now Afonso was dubbing himself the **first King of Portugal**, a title tacitly acknowledged by Alfonso VII (the new king of León) in 1137 and officially confirmed by the Treaty of Zamora in 1143. His kingdom spread more or less to the borders of modern Portugal, though in the south, Alentejo and the Algarve were still in Muslim hands.

For the next century and a half Afonso's successors struggled to dominate this last stronghold of the Moors. Sancho I (1185–1211) took their capital, Silves, in 1189, but his gains were not consolidated and almost everything south of the Tagus was recaptured the following year by al-Mansur, the last great campaigning vizier of al-Andalus. The overall pattern, though, was of steady expansion with occasional setbacks. Sancho II (1223–48) invaded the Alentejo and Eastern Algarve, while his successor **Afonso III** (1248–79) moved westwards, taking Faro and establishing the kingdom in pretty much its final shape.

THE BURGUNDIAN KINGS

The reconquest of land from the Muslims was also a process of **recolonisation**. As it fell into the king's hands, new territory was granted to such of his subjects as he felt would be able to defend it. In this way much of the country came to be divided between the church, the Holy Orders – chief among them the Knights Templar – and 100 or so powerful nobles or *ricos homens*. The entire kingdom had a population of under half a million, the majority of them concentrated in the north. Here there was little displacement of the traditional feudal ties, but in the south the influx of Christian peasants blurred the distinction between serf and settler, dependent relationships coming to be based on the payment of rent.

Meanwhile a **political infrastructure** was growing up. The land was divided into municipalities (*concelhos*), each with its own charter (*foral*). A formalised structure of consultation began to be seen, with the first **Cortes** being held in Coimbra in 1211. At first consisting mainly of the clergy and nobility, it later came to include wealthy merchants and townsmen, a development speeded both by the need to raise taxes and by later kings' constant struggles against the growing power of the church. The capital, which Afonso Henriques had moved to Coimbra in 1139, was transferred to **Lisbon** in about 1260 by Afonso III.

The Burgundian dynasty lasted, through nine kings, for 257 years. In the steady process of consolidating the new kingdom, one name stands out above all others, that of **Dom Dinis** (1279–1325). With the reconquest barely complete when he came to the throne, Dinis set about a far-sighted policy of stabilisation and of strengthening the nation to ensure its future independence. During his reign, fifty fortresses were constructed along the frontier with Castile, while at the same time negotiations were going on, leading eventually to the Treaty of Alcañices (1297) by which Spain acknowledged Portugal's frontiers. At home he established a major programme of forest planting and of agricultural reform; grain, olive oil, wine, salt, salt fish and dried fruit became staple exports to Flanders, Brittany, Catalonia and Britain. Importance, too, was attached to education and the arts: a **university**, later transferred to Coimbra, was founded at Lisbon in 1290. Dinis also helped entrench the power of the monarchy, forcing the church to accept a much larger degree of state control and in 1319 reorganising the Knights Templar – at the time being suppressed all over Europe – as the **Order of Christ**, still enormously powerful but now responsible directly to the king rather than to the pope.

Despite Dinis' precautions, fear of **Castilian domination** continued to play an important part in the reigns of his successors, largely due to consistent intermarrying between the two royal families. On the death of the last of the Burgundian kings, Fernando I, power passed to his widow Leonor, who ruled as regent. Leonor, whose only daughter had married Juan I of Castile, promised the throne to the children of that marriage. In this she had the support of most of the nobility, but the merchant and peasant classes strongly opposed a Spanish ruler, supporting instead the claim of João, Grand Master of the House of Avis and a bastard heir of the Burgundian line. A popular revolt against Leonor led to two years of war with Castile, finally settled at the **Battle of Aljubarrota** (1385) in which João, backed up by a force of English archers, wiped out the much larger Castilian army.

The great abbey of **Batalha** was built to commemorate the victory. **João I**, first king of the **House of Avis**, was crowned at Coimbra the same year, sealing relations with England through the 1386 Treaty of Windsor – an alliance which lasted into the twentieth century – and his marriage to Philippa of Lancaster, daughter of John of Gaunt, the following year.

DOM MANUEL AND THE MARITIME EMPIRE

Occupying such a strategic position between the Atlantic and the Mediterranean, it was inevitable that Portuguese attention would at some stage turn to **maritime expansion**. When peace was finally made with Castile in 1411, João I was able to turn his resources toward Morocco. The outpost at Ceuta fell in 1415, but successive attempts to capture Tangier were not realised until the reign of Afonso V, in 1471.

At first such overseas adventuring was undertaken partly in a crusading spirit, partly to keep potentially troublesome nobles busy. The proximity of North Africa made it a constant feature of foreign policy, giving a welcome boost to the economy of the Algarve. The first real advances in exploration, however, came about through the activities of **Prince Henry "the Navigator,"** third son of João and Philippa. As Grand Master of the Order of Christ, he turned that organisation's vast resources towards marine development, founding a School of Navigation on the desolate promontory of Sagres (then regarded as the end of the world) and staffing it with Europe's leading cartographers, navigators and seamen. As well as improving the art of offshore navigation, they redesigned the caravel, making it a vessel well suited to long ocean-going journeys. **Madeira** and the **Azores** were discovered in 1419 and 1427 respectively and by Henry's death in 1460 the **Cape Verde Islands** and the **west coast of Africa** down to Sierra Leone had both been explored.

After a brief hiatus, overseas expansion received a fresh boost in the reigns of João II, Manuel I and João III. In 1487 **Bartolomeu Dias** finally made it around the southern tip of Africa, christening it "Cabo da Boa Esperança" in the hope of things to come. Within ten years **Vasco da Gama** had sailed on past it to open up the **trade route to India**. This was the great breakthrough and the Portuguese monarchy, already doing well out of African gold, promptly became the richest in Europe, taking a fifth of the profits of all trade and controlling important monopolies on some spices. The small cargo of pepper brought back by Vasco on his first expedition was enough to pay for the trip three times over. Meanwhile Spain was opening up the New World and by the **Treaty of Tordesillas** in 1494 the two Iberian nations divided the world between them along an imaginary line 370 leagues west of the Cape Verde Islands. This not only gave Portugal the run of the Orient but also, when it was discovered in 1500, Brazil (though its development would have to wait nearly 200 more years). By the mid-sixteenth century Portugal dominated **world trade**; strategic posts had been established at Goa (1510), Malacca (1511), Ormuz (1515) and Macau (1557) and the revenue from dealings with the East was backed up by a large-scale **slave trade** between West Africa and Europe and Brazil.

The reign of **Manuel I** (1495–1521) marked the apogee of Portuguese wealth and strength. It found its expression at home in the extraordinary exuberance of the "Manueline" style of architecture – an elaborately decorative genre which found its inspiration in marine motifs. Notable examples can be seen in the Convent of Christ at Tomar and the Tower of Belém in Lisbon, while the best examples of civil architecture are probably the extensions made by Manuel to the royal palace at Sintra.

Enormous wealth there may have been, but very little of it filtered down through the system and in the country at large conditions barely improved. The practice of siphoning off a hefty slice of the income into the royal coffers effectively prevented the development of an entrepreneurial class and, as everywhere else in Europe, financial matters were left very much in the hands of the Jews, who were not allowed to take up most other professions.

Portugal had traditionally been considerably more tolerant than other European nations in its treatment of its **Jewish citizens** (and towards the Moorish minority who had been absorbed after the Reconquest). However, popular resentment of their riches, and pressure from Spain, forced Manuel – who had initially welcomed refugees from the Spanish persecution – to order their **expulsion** in 1496. Although many chose the pragmatic course of remaining as "New Christian" converts, others fled to the Netherlands.

This exodus, continued as a result of the activities of the **Inquisition** (from 1531 on), created a vacuum which left Portugal with an extensive empire based upon commerce, but deprived of much of its commercial expertise. By the 1570s the economy was beginning to collapse: incoming wealth was insufficient to cover the growing costs of maintaining an empire against increasing competition, a situation exacerbated by foreign debts, falling prices and a decline in domestic agriculture.

SPANISH DOMINATION

In the end it was a combination of reckless imperialism and impecunity which brought to an end the dynasty of the House of Avis and with it, at least temporarily, Portuguese independence. **Dom Sebastião** (1557–78), obsessed with dreams of a new crusade against Morocco, set out at the head of a huge army to satisfy his fanatical fantasies. They were crushed at the battle of **Alcácer-Quibir** (1578), where the Portuguese dead numbered over 8000, including Sebastião and most of Portugal's nobility. The aged **Cardinal Henrique** took the throne as the closest legitimate relative and devoted his brief reign to attempting to raise the crippling ransoms for those captured on the battlefield.

The Cardinal's death without heirs in 1580 provided Spain with the pretext to renew its claim to Portugal. **Philip II** of Spain, Sebastião's uncle, defeated his rivals at the battle of Alcântara and in 1581 was crowned Felipe I of Portugal, inaugurating a period of Hapsburg rule which lasted for another sixty years. In the short term, although unpopular, the union had advantages for Portugal. Spanish wheat helped alleviate the domestic shortage and Spanish seapower helped protect the far-flung empire. Philip, moreover, studiously protected Portuguese autonomy, maintaining an entirely separate bureaucracy and spending long periods in Portugal in an attempt to win popular support. Not that he ever did – throughout his reign pretenders appeared claiming to be Sebastião miraculously saved from the Moroccan desert, tapping a strong vein of resentment among the people. And in the long run, Spanish control proved disastrous. Association with Spain's foreign policy (part of the Armada was prepared in Lisbon) meant the enmity of the Dutch and the British, Portugal's traditional allies, losing the country an important part of its trade which was never to be regained.

Philip's successors made no attempt at all to protect Portuguese sensibilities – cynical and uninterested, they attempted to rule from Madrid while raising heavy taxes to pay for Spain's wars. The final straw was the attempt by Philip IV (Felipe III of Portugal) to conscript Portuguese troops to quell a rising in Catalonia. On December 1, 1640, a small group of conspirators stormed the palace in Lisbon and deposed the Duchess of Mantua, Governor of Portugal. By popular acclaim and despite personal reluctance, the Duke of Bragança, senior member of a family which had long been the most powerful in the country, took the throne as **João IV**.

THE HOUSE OF BRAGANÇA

At first the newly independent nation looked pretty shaky, deprived of most of its trade routes and with the apparently imminent threat of invasion from Spain hanging over it. As it turned out, however, the Spanish were so preoccupied with wars elsewhere that they had little choice but to accept the situation, though not formally until 1668 under the Treaty of Lisbon. João IV used the opportunity to rebuild old alliances and although the Portuguese were often forced into unfavourable terms, they were at least trading again. Relations with Britain had been strained during that country's Commonwealth, with Oliver Cromwell's particular brand of Protestant commercialism, but were revived by the marriage of Charles II to Catherine of Bragança in 1661.

At home Portugal was developing an increasingly centralised administration – the **discovery of gold and diamonds in Brazil** during the reign of Pedro II (1683–1706) made the crown financially independent and did away with the need for the Cortes (or any form of popular representation) for most of the next century. It was **João V**, coming to the throne in 1706, who most benefited from the new riches, which he squandered in an orgy of lavish baroque building. His massive convent at **Mafra**, built totally without regard to expense, employed at times as many as 50,000 workmen, virtually bankrupting the state. Meanwhile nothing was being done to revive the economy,

what little remained from João's grandiose schemes going mainly to pay for imports. The infamous Methuen Treaty, signed in 1703 to stimulate trade with Britain, only made matters worse – although it opened up new markets for Portuguese wine, it helped destroy the native textile industry by letting in British cloth at preferential rates.

The accession of João's apathetic son, José I (1750–77), allowed the total concentration of power in the hands of one man, the king's chief minister. The **Marquês de Pombal** became the classic "enlightened despot" of eighteenth-century history. It was the **Great Earthquake of 1755** that sealed his dominance over the age; while everyone else was panicking, Pombal's policy was simple – "bury the dead and feed the living."

Pombal saw his subsequent mission as to modernise all Portuguese life into an efficient and secular bureaucracy, renew the system of taxation, set up export companies, protect trade and abolish slavery within Portugal. It was a strategy that made him many enemies among the old aristocracy and above all within the Church, whose overbearing influence he fought at every turn. Opposition, though, was dealt with ruthlessly and an assassination attempt on the king in 1758 (which some say was staged by Pombal) gave him the chance he needed to destroy his enemies. Denouncing their supposed involvement, Pombal executed the country's leading aristocrats and abolished the Jesuits, who had long dominated education and religious life in Portugal and Brazil.

Although Pombal himself was taken to trial (and found guilty but pardoned on the grounds of old age) with the accession of Maria I (1777–1816), the majority of his labours survived him, most notably the reform of education along scientific lines and the completely rebuilt capital. Further development, however, was soon thwarted by a new invasion.

FRENCH OCCUPATION AND THE MIGUELITE YEARS

With **Napoleon's** appearance on the international scene, Portugal once more became embroiled in the affairs of Europe. The French threatened to invade unless the Portuguese supported their naval blockade of Britain, a demand that no one expected them to obey since the British ports were the destination for most of Portugal's trade. Only the protection of the British fleet, especially after the victory at Trafalgar in 1805, kept the country's trade routes open. General Junot duly marched into Lisbon in November 1807.

On British advice the royal family had already gone into exile in Brazil, where they were to stay until 1821, and the war was left largely in the hands of British generals **Beresford** and **Wellington**. Having twice been driven out and twice reinvaded, the French were finally forced back into Spain in 1811 following the Battle of Buçaco (1810) and a long period of near starvation before the lines of Torres Vedras. Britain's prize for this was the right to trade freely with **Brazil**, which together with the declaration of that country as a kingdom in its own right, fatally weakened the dependent relationship that had profited the Portuguese treasury for so long. Past roles were reversed, with Portugal becoming effectively a colony of Brazil (where the royal family remained) and a protectorate of Britain, with General Beresford as administrator. The only active national institution was the army, many of whose officers had absorbed the constitutional ideals of revolutionary France.

In August 1820, with Beresford temporarily out of the country and King João VI still in Brazil, a group of officers called an unofficial Cortes and proceeded to draw up a new **constitution**. Inspired by the recent liberal advances in Spain, it called for an assembly – to be elected every two years by universal male suffrage – and the abolition of clerical privilege and the traditional rights of the nobility. The king, forced to choose between Portugal and Brazil, where his position looked even more precarious, came back in 1821 and accepted its terms. His queen, Carlota, and younger son **Miguel**, however, refused to take the oath of allegiance and became the dynamic behind a reactionary revival which drew considerable support in rural areas.

With João VI's death in 1826, a delegation was sent to Brazil to pronounce crown prince Pedro the new king. Unfortunately Pedro was already Emperor of Brazil – having declared its independence some years earlier. He resolved to pass the crown to his infant daughter, with **Miguel** as regent provided that he swore to accept a new **charter**, drawn up by Pedro and somewhat less liberal than the earlier constitu-

tion. Miguel agreed, but once in power promptly tore up any agreement, abolished the charter and returned to the old, absolutist ways. This was a surprisingly popular move in Portugal, certainly in the countryside, but not with the governments of Britain, Spain, or France who backed the liberal rebels and finally put Pedro IV (who had meanwhile been deposed in Brazil) on the throne after Miguel's defeat at Évora-Monte in 1834.

THE DEATH OF THE MONARCHY

Pedro didn't survive long. The rest of the century – under the rule of his daughter Maria II (1834–53) and his grandsons Pedro V (1853–61) and Luís (1861–89) – saw almost constant struggle between those who supported the charter and others favouring a return to the more liberal constitution of 1822. In 1846 the position deteriorated virtually to a state of **civil war** between Maria, who was fanatical in her support of her father's charter, and the radical constitutionalists. Only a further intervention by foreign powers maintained peace, imposed at the Convention of Gramido (1847).

In the second half of the century, with relative stability and the two warring factions to some extent institutionalised into a revolving two-party system, the economy began at last to recover, with the first signs of widespread industrialisation and a major public works programme under the minister Fontes Pereira de Melo. The monarchy, however, was almost bankrupt and its public humiliation over possessions in Africa – imperial Britain and Germany simply ignored the Portuguese claim to the land between Angola and Mozambique – helped strengthen growing republican feelings.

Republicanism took root particularly easily in the army and among the urban poor, fuelled by falling standards of living and growing anger at government ineptitude. Dom Carlos (1898–1908) attempted to rule dictatorially after 1906, alienating most sectors of the country in the process and was assassinated, along with his eldest son, following a failed republican coup in 1908. Finally, on October 5, 1910, the monarchy was overthrown once and for all by a joint revolt of the army and navy. Dom Manuel went into exile and died, in Britain, in 1932.

THE "DEMOCRATIC" REPUBLIC

In the elections of 1911 republican parties won a clear majority, yet throughout the life of **the republic** political life was in chaos and the hopes, perhaps unrealistically high, of its supporters never began to be realised. Dominant from the start was the Democratic Party under **Afonso Costa**, who proved determined to retain power by any means – manipulating elections through patronage and deriding opposition, even from fellow republicans, as "anti-Democratic." The overblown, inefficient bureaucracy, too, clung to power; its employees, largely survivors from the monarchist era, proved unwilling or unable to carry out many of the government's policies. In office, meanwhile, governments became increasingly dependent on the armed forces for survival; since neither president nor prime minister had the power to dissolve parliament, **military intervention** came to be the normal means of governmental change – there were 45 such "changes" between 1910 and 1926.

The forces that had brought the republic into being had their base largely in the urban and rural poor, yet new electoral laws based on a literacy test led to a smaller electorate than under the monarchy, disenfranchising most of the republic's stongest supporters. Successive governments failed to fulfil the least aspirations. Anticlericalism had been a major plank of Costa's platform, but attempts to place **the Church** under state control misfired badly, arousing massive hostility in the countryside. Legalising the right to strike merely gave workers a chance to voice their discontent in a massive wave of work stoppages. Further fuel was given to the reaction by Portugal's economically disastrous decision to enter **World War I** on the side of the Allies in 1916 and by the vicissitudes of the postwar recession. By 1926 not even the trade unions were prepared to stand by the republic, preferring to maintain "proleterian neutrality" in the face of what at first seemed no more significant a military intervention than any other.

SALAZAR AND THE "NEW STATE"

While the military may have known what they wanted to overthrow in 1926, they were at first divided as to whether to replace it with a new republican government or a restored monarchy. From the infighting a Catholic monarchist, **General Carmona**, eventually emerged as president (which he remained until his death in 1951) with the republican constitution suspended. A pragmatic fear of popular reaction prevented Carmona from restoring the monarchy; his eventual solution was to formalise his position through elections, in 1928, in which he was the only candidate.

In the same year one **Dr. Salazar** joined the Cabinet as Finance Minister. A professor of economics at Coimbra University, he took the post only on condition that he would control the spending and revenue of all government departments. His strict monetarist line (helped by a change in the accounting system) immediately balanced the budget for the first time since 1913 and in the short term the economic situation was visibly improved. From then on he effectively controlled the country, becoming prime minister in 1932 and not relinquishing that role until 1968.

His regime was very much in keeping with the political tenor of the 1930s and while it had few of the ideological pretensions of a **fascist** state, it had many of the trappings. Members of the National Assembly were chosen from the one permitted political association, the National Union (UN); "workers' organisations" were set up, but run by their employers; education was strictly controlled by the state to promote Catholic values; and censorship was strictly enforced. Opposition was kept in check by the *PIDE* – a **secret police** force set up with Gestapo assistance – which used systematic torture and long-term detention in camps on the Azores and Cabo verde islands to defuse most resistance. The army, too, was heavily infiltrated by *PIDE* and none of the many coups mounted against Salazar came close to success. Despite remaining formally neutral throughout the **Spanish Civil War**, Salazar had openly assisted the plotters in their preparations and later sent unofficial units of the Portuguese army to fight with Franco. Republican refugees were deported to face certain execution at Nationalist hands.

At home Salazar succeeded in producing the infrastructure of a modern economy but the results of growth were felt by only a few and agriculture, in particular, was allowed to stagnate. Internal unrest, though, while widespread, was surprisingly muted and apparently easily controlled; the New State's downfall, when it came, was precipitated far more by external factors. Salazar was an ardent imperialist who found himself faced with growing **colonial wars** – costly and bringing international disapprobation. India seized Goa and the other Portuguese possessions in 1961 and at about the same time the first serious disturbances were occurring in Angola and Mozambique. The regime was prepared to make only the slightest concessions, attempting to defuse the freedom movements by speeding economic development.

The government's reign came to an end in 1968 when Salazar's deck-chair collapsed, and he suffered brain damage. Incapacitated, he lived for another two years, deposed as premier – though such was the fear of the man, no one ever dared tell him. His successor, **Marcelo Caetano**, attempted to prolong the regime by offering limited democratisation at home. However, tensions beneath the surface were fast becoming more overt and attempts to liberalise foreign policy failed to check the growth of guerilla activity in the remaining colonies, or of **discontent in the army**.

It was in the African-stationed army especially that opposition crystallised. There the young conscript officers came more and more to sympathise with the freedom movements they were intended to suppress and to resent the cost – in economic terms and in lives – of the hopeless struggle. From their number above all grew the revolutionary **Movimento das Forças Armadas** (MFA).

REVOLUTION

By 1974 the situation in Africa was deteriorating rapidly and at home Caetano's liberalisation had come to a dead end; morale, among the army and the people, was lower than ever. The **MFA**, formed originally as an officer's organisation to press for better conditions, then increasingly politicised, was already laying its plans for a takeover. Dismissal of two popular generals – Spínola and the defence minister, Costa Gomes – for refusing publicly to support Caetano, led to a first chaotic and abortive attempt on March 16.

Finally on April 25, 1974, the plans laid by **Major Otelo Saraiva de Carvalho** for the MFA were complete and their virtually bloodless **coup** went without a hitch, no serious attempt being made to defend the government.

The next two years were perhaps the most extraordinary in Portugal's history, a period of continual **revolution**, massive politicisation and virtual anarchy, during which decisions of enormous importance were nevertheless made – above all the granting of independence to all of the overseas territories. At first there was little clear idea of any programme beyond the fact that the army wanted out of Africa. Though the MFA leadership was clearly to the left and at first associated with the PCP (Portuguese Communist Party), the bulk of the officers were less political and **General Spínola**, whom they had been forced to accept as a figurehead, was only marginally to the left of Caetano and strongly opposed total independence for the colonies. Spínola's dream was clearly to "do a De Gaulle" in Portugal, while the army was above all determined not to replace one dictator with another.

In the event their hands were forced by the massive popular response and especially by huge demonstrations on May Day. It was clear that whatever the leadership might decide, the people, especially in the cities, demanded a rapid **move to the left**. From the start every party was striving to project itself as the true defender of the "ideals of April 25." Provisional governments came and went but real power rested, where it had begun, with the **MFA**, now dominated by Saraiva de Carvalho and Vasco Gonçalves. While politicians argued around them, the army claimed to speak directly to the people, leading the country steadily left. It was a period of extraordinary contradictions, with the PCP, hoping to consolidate their position as the "true" revolutionary party, opposing liberalisation and condemning strikes as counterrevolutionary, while ultra-conservative peasants were happily seizing their land from its owners.

Sudden **independence** and the withdrawal of Portuguese forces from the **former colonies** – while generally greeted in Portugal with relief – did not always work so well for the countries involved. Guinea-Bissau and

Mozambique, the first to go, experienced relatively peaceful transitions, but **Angola** came to be a serious point of division between Spínola and the MFA. When independence finally came, after Spínola's resignation, the country was already in the midst of a full-scale civil war. The situation was even worse in **East Timor**, where more than 10 percent of the population was massacred by invading Indonesian forces following Portuguese withdrawal. In Portugal itself the arrival of more than half-a-million colonial refugees — many of them destitute, most bitter — came to be a major problem for the regime, though their eventual integration proved one of its triumphs.

At home, the first **crisis** came in September 1974, when Spínola, with Gonçalves and Saraiva de Carvalho virtual prisoners in Lisbon's Belém Palace, moved army units to take over key positions. The MFA, however, proved too strong and Spínola was forced to resign, General Costa Gomes replacing him as president. By the summer of 1975 more general reaction was setting in and even the MFA began to show signs of disunity; the country was increasingly split, supporting the revolution in the south, deeply conservative in the north. The Archbishop of Braga summed up the north's traditional views, declaring that the struggle against communism should be seen "not in terms of man against man, but Christ against Satan." Nevertheless the revolution continued to advance; a coup attempt in March failed when the troops involved turned against their officers. The Council of the Revolution was formed, promptly nationalising banking and private insurance; widespread land seizures went ahead in the Alentejo; and **elections** in the summer resulted in an impressive victory for Mário Soares' Socialist Party (PS).

On November 25, 1975, elements of the army opposed to the rightward shift in the government moved for yet another **coup**, taking over major air bases across the country. Otelo Saraiva de Carvalho, however, declined to bring his Lisbon command to their aid; nor did the hoped-for mass mobilisation of the people take place. Government troops under Colonel Ramalho Eanes moved in to force their surrender and — again virtually without bloodshed — the revolution had ended.

DEMOCRACY AND EUROPE: THE 1980s

The period since November 1975 has been one of slow and sometimes shaky-looking, **retrenchment**. The Socialist Party was still in power at the end of the year and won further ground in the elections that followed, helping to shape the post-revolutionary constitution — a mildly socialist document, though providing for a fairly powerful president. Early fears of a right-wing coup led by Spínola failed to materialise, helped by the election of **Colonel Eanes**, a man whom the army trusted, as president. Saraiva de Carvalho came in second, despite the fact that no major party supported him — a token of the degree of popular following enjoyed by the MFA during the revolution.

Although parties of the right and centre have consistently polled higher votes, the Socialists had effective control until 1980 when Dr. Sá Carneiro managed to create the **Democratic Alliance**, uniting the larger groupings on the right. But within a few months he died in a plane crash. His successor as prime minister, Francisco Pinto Balsemão, barely managed to maintain the coalition for the two years of the term remaining and then only because the rightist parties were united in their determination to amend the constitution "to eliminate clauses which were appropriate in the post-revolutionary atmosphere of 1976 but not to today's needs."

The most enigmatic figure throughout this period remained **President Eanes**, a career soldier who supported the MFA in its early days, later led the forces who ended the revolution and is now accused by the right of being a "Marxist sympathiser." He above all seemed to be the figure of stability, with enormous popular support though (at least until recently) apparently little ambition, being happy to concentrate on developing Portugal's links with Africa, Asia and Latin America and overseeing a gradual normalisation process.

In elections held on the ninth anniversary of the revolution, April 25, 1983, **Mário Soares' Socialist Party** again became the largest single party in the national assembly, though requiring the support of the Social Democrats to maintain a coalition government. Soares' premiership was dogged by the unpopularity of his **economic austerity measures** (in part insisted on by the IMF) and by constant delays and breakdowns in the talks over Portuguese and Spanish **entry into the European Community**. These problems (now resolved) did at least have one positive result, namely closer relations with the traditionally hostile government in Madrid. But the government's economic problems led eventually to the withdrawal of Social Democratic support and to the collapse of the coalition.

New elections in October 1985 were barely conclusive: the left-wing vote split three ways and the Socialists lost their position as largest party to the **Social Democrats** (PSD), whose flamboyant leader, **Dr. Aníbal Cavaco Silva**, became prime minister. But the main feature of the election was disillusionment with the government and the choices on offer to the electorate. There was massive and countrywide abstention and, in rural districts (where people worried most about the effects of EC membership), attacks on polling booths.

In the months that followed, the revolutionary leader, **Lt-Colonel Otelo Saraiva de Carvalho**, was arrested and put on trial in Lisbon accused of being the leader of 73 suspected terrorists in the **FP-25** urban guerilla group. Proceedings were postponed following the shooting of one of the key witnesses and it was not until 1987 that Saraiva de Carvalho was sentenced to 15 years' imprisonment (50 others also received prison sentences). He was later conditionally released after a Supreme Court ruling that there had been irregularities at his trial. In February 1990 he renounced the armed struggle and requested an amnesty.

President Eanes, meanwhile – the other great figure at the end of the revolution – had been forced to resign the presidency on completion of his second term in January 1986. He was replaced by former socialist Prime Minister **Mário Soares** who, with the reluctant support of the Communists, narrowly defeated the candidate of the centre-right, becoming the first civilian president for 60 years.

Portugal's entry into the **European Community** in 1986 has brought with it the most important changes since the revolution. With the help of a massive injection of funds to help modernize infrastructure and increased foreign investment, Portugal has enjoyed unprecedented **economic growth**, running at above 4 percent per year and greater than most of its European partners. For many Portuguese, this has resulted in greater material wealth, but behind the trappings of the new prosperity are numerous pockets of Third-World poverty.

Prime Minister Aníbal Cavaco Silva's early attempts to introduce an economic reform programme were hampered by his lack of a majority, but in April 1987 a censure motion defeat caused the prime minister to resign, bringing about general elections. The PSD (Social Democrats) were returned to power in surprising numbers, enjoying the first absolute majority since the 1974 revolution and the strength to implement real changes.

The centre-right government's free enterprise drive for the removal of socialist structures and privatisation has not run unchallenged: the late 1980s were marked by **industrial unrest**. In March 1988 1.5 million workers took part in a 24-hour general strike in protest against labour reform laws freeing up employers to lay off workers. The law was eventually approved by both the assembly and the president, but strikes continued throughout 1989 in various sectors of the workforce, attempting to bring wages in line with inflation. The government was also able to reach an eventual agreement with the opposition to remove Marxist–Leninist elements from the constitution in August 1989.

The Portuguese **Green Party** won its first seat in the **European Parliament** elections in Strasbourg in June 1989 and the ruling PSD was successful in retaining most of its own seats, but suffered an enormous set-back six months later in municipal elections. The **socialist opposition** gained control of the capital, Lisbon; the northern industrial centre, Porto; and other significant cities. Four years of economic growth had benefited a new yuppie class, but voters were aware of accentuated social inequality and the continued inadequacy of health and education structures. Public opinion had also been influenced by **financial scandals** involving government ministers. Aníbal Cavaco Silva, however, avoided any dirt rubbing off on him personally and survived a motion of censure questioning the government's ethics. The ministers involved were summarily replaced in a surprise end-of-year reshuffle, along with three other ministers, in a move which was taken to indicate Cavaco Silva's firm grip on the reins.

INTO THE 1990S: THE PROSPECTS

Scandal was also in the air surrounding **President Mário Soares** in early 1990, when the socialist governor of Portuguese-administered **Macau** (Hong Kong's enclave neighbour), a man personally appointed by Soares, was accused of receiving back-handers from a German company trying to secure the contract for the building of an airport. The incident called Soares' integrity into question and strained relations with the prime minister, **Cavaco Silva**, but the president, popular for his down-to-earth image and his dislike of ceremony, retained his public support and won a landslide victory in presidential elections in January 1991.

At Cavaco Silva's insistence, the PSD had not put forward a candidate for the presidency, partly in acknowledgement of a successful relationship between the government and the incumbent president and partly to avoid any further humiliation of a figure who was guaranteed to win. In turn, Cavaco Silva won a convincing mandate in the elections of October 1991, when the **PSD returned to government** with over 50 percent of the vote.

The new decade took Portugal into the second stage of its ten-year transition phase for EC entry and into its **presidency of the European Community** in 1992, the year when (on December 31) all remaining trade and employment barriers are to be removed. The country adopted their EC task with considerable imagination, and expense, staging a superb exhibiton of its culture – *Europalia* – in Brussels, and building a grand presidency HQ in the Lisbon suburb of Belém.

On the domestic front, the PSD continued with privatisation and forged plans for the conversion of state-run banks in preparation for joining the European Monetary System in the mid-1990s.

Dealing with **inflation**, currently running at 13 percent, remained – and remains – at the top of their agenda. The government has to do this while coping with increased discontent over social issues, as the opposition calls it to account for statistics that show Portugal still has the highest **infant mortality** and **illiteracy** rates in Europe. Unemployment figures, too, although less than 5 percent, hide a high proportion of underpaid and part-time workers and disguise the fact that wages have failed to increase in real terms in spite of impressive economic growth. There are fears, too, that when the European Community opens up completely, fiercer competition is likely to force more Portuguese out of work.

The **opening up of Eastern Europe** is also going to expose Portugal to fiercer competition for trade and investment, although a modernized infrastructure and improved transport networks mean that it continues to be attractive to foreign investors. **Tourism**, which accounts for nearly a tenth of the country's GNP and over a quarter of all foreign investment, has flourished and one challenge will be finding alternatives to the Algarve, where restrictions have been imposed to control the industry's all too disturbingly obvious side-effects.

The main headache for the government, though, continues to be the inefficiency of **Portuguese agriculture**, which employs nearly one-fifth of the workforce but produces only a fraction of the country's wealth. So far, help from Brussels has buffered the less advantageous effects of EC membership, but the honeymoon period is over and although some modernisation has taken place, there is still a huge gap between Portuguese **prices** and European Community prices – a gap that is not likely to be eliminated until the end of the decade and one which will tend to keep Portugal among Europe's poorest nations.

MONUMENTAL CHRONOLOGY

2000 BC–1500 BC	**Neolithic** settlements in the north of the country – **Verracos Culture** in Trás-os-Montes.	*Porcas* (stone boars) of Bragança, Murça, etc.
700 BC–600 BC	**Castro Culture** of fortified hill-towns, or *citânias*, concentrated in the Minho; refined by the **Celtic** Iron Age invasions.	**Citânia de Briteiros** (near Braga) and other sites; best collection of artifacts in Sarmento Museum, Guimarães.
210 BC	**Romans** enter peninsula and begin colonisation; northern Portugal not finally pacified until 19 BC.	**Conimbriga**, 4th c Celtic town near Coimbra, adapted to Roman occupation (survives until 5th c AD).
60 BC	Julius Caesar establishes a capital at Lisbon and towns at Beja, Évora, Santarém, etc.	Walls and other remains at Idanha, in Beira Baixa; temple and aqueducts of Évora; bridges at Chaves, Ponte de Lima, Leiria and elsewhere.
4th c AD	Bishoprics founded at Braga, Évora, Faro and Lisbon.	
409–411	**Barbarian** invasions: Suevi settle in the north.	
585	**Visigoths** incorporate Suevian state into their Iberian empire.	Isolated churches, mainly in the north, include 7th-c São Pedro de Balsemão (near Lamego) and São Frutuoso at Braga.
711	**Moors** from North Africa invade and conquer peninsula within seven years.	Fortresses/walls survive at Silves, Lisbon, Sintra, Elvas, Mértola, Alcácer do Sal, etc.
9th c	**Al-Gharb** (Algarve) becomes an independent Moorish kingdom, governed from Silves.	Moorish legacy also includes *azulejos* (ceramic tiles), later designed by Muslim (Mudejar) craftsmen for royal palace at Sintra, etc.
868	Porto reconquered by Christian kings of Asturias-León.	
11th c	Country of **Portucale** emerges and (1097) is given to Henry of Burgundy.	Cluniac monks, administering pilgrimage route to Santiago, bring Romanesque architecture from France. 12th-c churches at Bravães, Tomar, etc. Council chamber at Bragança.
1143	**Afonso Henriques** recognised as first king of Portucale at the Treaty of Zamora.	Guimarães Castle.
1147	Afonso takes Lisbon and Santarém from the Moors; followed in 1162 by Beja and Évora and in 1189 (temporarily) Silves.	Fortress-like **Romanesque cathedrals** of Lisbon, Coimbra, Évora, Braga and Porto.
1212	First assembly of the Cortes (parliament) at Coimbra.	1153: Cistercians found abbey of **Alcobaça**: in this and other Cistercian churches, notably at Coimbra, Gothic architecture enters Portugal.
1249	Afonso III completes reconquest of the Algarve.	

1279–1325	Reign of **Dom Dinis** 1297: Castile recognises Portuguese borders.	Over fifty castles built along Spanish border, including Beja and Estremoz. Pinhal Real forest planted. Coimbra University founded.
1385	Battle of Aljubarrota: João I defeats Castilians to become first king of **House of Avis.**	Abbey of **Batalha**, the great triumph of mature Portuguese Gothic, built in celebration of victory. Paço Real built at Sintra.
1415	**Infante Henriques** (Henry the Navigator; d 1460) active at Sagres. 1419: Madeira discovered. 1427: Azores discovered. 1457: Cape Verde Islands discovered.	Navigation School at Sagres; Lagos fort. Painters: Flemish-influenced "Portuguese Primitives" include Nuno Gonçalves (fl 1450–71: see Arte Antiga museum, Lisbon).
1495–1521	Reign of **Dom Manuel I** ("The Fortunate"). 1497: Vasco da Gama opens up sea route to India. 1500: Cabral discovers Brazil. 1513: Portuguese reach China.	Late Gothic **Manueline style** develops, with strong marine motifs and flamboyance anticipating art nouveau. Greatest examples at Tomar, Batalha, Lisbon (Belém) and Sintra. By 1530s Renaissance forms are introduced and merged.
1521–57	Reign of João III.	Painters include Grão Vasco (fl 1506–42: see Viseu).
1557–78	Reign of **Dom Sebastião**. 1578: Disastrous expedition to Morocco, loss of king and mass slaughter of nobility at Alcácer-Quibir.	Important sculptural school at **Coimbra** (1520–70) centred on French Renaissance sculptors Nicolas Chanterenne, Filipe Hodart and Jean de Rouen.
1581–1640	Philip II brings **Spanish** (Hapsburg) rule.	
1640	**João IV**, Duke of **Bragança**, restores independence.	Severe late Renaissance style: São Vicente, Lisbon (designed by Felipe Terzi), etc.
1706–50	Reign of **Dom João V**. Gold and diamonds discovered in Brazil, reaching a peak of wealth and exploitation in the 1740s.	Baroque palace-monastery of **Mafra** (1717–35). Decoration of Coimbra University Library. High Baroque carved, gilt church interiors. Also simpler, more rustic Baroque style of plaster/granite – **Lamego** and **Bom Jesus**. Rococo Palace of **Queluz** (1752).
1755	**Great Earthquake** destroys Lisbon and parts of the Alentejo and Algarve.	"Pombaline" neoclassical rebuilding of Lisbon (Baixa).
1843–53	Maria II holds throne with German consort, Fernando II.	**Pena Palace** folly built at Sintra.
1908 1910	Assassination of Carlos I in Lisbon. Exile of Manuel II ("The Unfortunate") and **end of Portuguese monarchy**.	Cubist painter Amadeu de Sousa Cardoso (d 1918); museum devoted to him at Amarante.
1910–26	"Democratic" Republic.	
1932–68	**Salazar** dictatorship. Goa is seized by India; colonial wars in Africa.	
1974	April 25 **revolution**.	
1986	**Entry to European Community** (EC)	Permanent gallery of modern Portuguese artists at Lisbon's Gulbenkian Foundation.

BOOKS

Portugal has been covered very sparsely by British and American writers and publishers, and many of the works that do exist in English are out of print (o/p) and available only in libraries.

Publishing details below are in the form: British/American publisher, where both exist. Where books are published in one country only, UK or US (or Portugal) follows the publisher's name.

GENERAL/TRAVEL

Marion Kaplan *The Portuguese: the Land and its People* (Viking, UK/US). Published in 1991, this is a readable, all-embracing volume, covering everything from wine to the family, poetry and the land. The style is a bit old-fashioned – but it's the best general introduction to the country available.

Rose Macaulay *They Went to Portugal* (Penguin, UK/US). The book covers British travellers to Portugal from the Crusaders to Byron, weaving an anecdotal history of the country in the process. A serious study if you take it as such; a good read if you just feel like dipping into the stories.

William Beckford *Recollections of an Excursion to the Monasteries of Alcobaça and Batalha* (o/p); *Travels in Spain and Portugal (1778–88)* (o/p). Mad and enormously rich, Beckford lived for some time at Sintra and traveled widely in Estremadura. His accounts, told with a fine eye for the absurd, are a lot of fun.

Byron *Selected Letters and Journals* (Penguin/Harvard University Press). Only a few days of Portuguese travel but memorable ones – beginning with romantic enthusiasm, ending in outright abuse.

Almeida Garrett *Travels in My Homeland* (Peter Own/Dufour). A classic Portuguese writer, Garrett was exiled to Europe in the 1820s, came into contact with the Romantics and later returned to play a part in the liberal government of the 1830s. This is a witty, discursive narrative ramble around the country.

Sacheverell Sitwell *Portugal and Madeira* (o/p). Mix of art history/observation and rather pompous upper-class travelogue from the 1950s. Sitwell's great enthusiasm is Portuguese Baroque. He also "discovers" Mateus Rosé wine for the British . . .

HISTORY AND POLITICS

Harold Livermore *A New History of Portugal* (Cambridge University Press, o/p). The best single-volume coverage, taking events through to 1976. It's thorough if not exactly inspiring but was revised a little too soon after the 1974 revolution.

John Dos Passos *The Portugal Story* (Hale, UK); **Daniel J. Boorstin** *The Discoverers* (Penguin, UK/US); **C.R. Boxer** *The Portuguese Seaborne Empire 1415–1825* (o/p); **John Ure** *Prince Henry the Navigator* (o/p). Good texts on the Discoveries and colonisation.

António de Figueiredo *Portugal: Fifty Years of Dictatorship* (Penguin, o/p). An illuminating study which takes as its starting-point the 1926 military coup that brought the fascist Salazar to power and goes through to the 1974 revolution.

Tom Gallagher *Portugal: A Twentieth Century Interpretation* (Manchester U.P., UK). **Lawrence S. Graham and Douglas L. Wheeler, eds.** *In Search of Modern Portugal: The Revolution and Its Consequences* (University of Wisconsin Press, US). Two academic studies published in the early 1980s.

ART AND ARCHITECTURE

Júlio Gil and Augusto Cabrita *The Finest Castles in Portugal* (Verbo, Portugal). A superb illustrated survey, let down a little by a highly pededestrian translation/text.

Júlio Gil and Nuno Calvet *The Finest Churches in Portugal* (Verbo, Portugal). Another excellent volume in this series.

Marcus Binney *Country Manors of Portugal* (Scala Books/Harper & Row). Again, photos are the big thing in this solid volume.

Helder Carita and Homem Cardoso *Portuguese Gardens* (I.B. Tauris, UK). A huge and beautiful tome, lavishly illustrated with photos and plans, with a scholarly text.

Robert C. Smith *The Arts of Portugal 1500–1800* (o/p). Weighty academic tome.

FICTION

Fernando Pessoa *Selected Poems* (editions published by both Quartet and Serpent's Tail, UK). The country's best known poet (see below) wrote just this one work in prose: a kind of autobiography, posthumously compiled, in these selections, from a trunkload of material. Regarded as a modernist classic, the book's admirers include Jorge Luís Borges.

Eça de Queiroz *The Mandarin* (Dedalus/Hippocrene); *The Reliquary* (Dedalus/Hippocrene); *The Sin of Father Amaro* (Black Swan, UK); *The Maias* (Dent/Biblio). Queiroz is the classic Portuguese novelist, responsible for a string of nineteenth-century narratives. These are the only ones in print and form an entertaining introduction. Check out others in libraries; most have been translated.

António Lobo Antunes *An Explanation of the Birds* (Secker & Warburg, UK); *South of Nowhere* (Chatto/Random House, o/p). Many consider Antunes Portugal's leading contemporary writer. Both of these novels – there are five others, as yet untranslated – are first-person narratives of memory: the former of a political historian, the latter an ex-solider from the colonial wars. Recommended.

José Saramago *Baltasar and Blimunda* (Cape/Ballantine). Saramago is one of Portugal's major contemporary novelists. This, his first work to be translated into English, is a black comedy set in the reign of Dom João V. It brings alive the era of the inquisition, the building of Mafra and the climate of times before the Great Earthquake.

José Cardoso Pires, *Ballad of Dog's Beach* (Dent/Beaufort Books). Ostensibly a detective thriller but the murder described actually took place during the last years of Salazar's dictatorship and Pires' research draws upon the original secret-police files. Compelling, highly original and with acute psychological insights, it was awarded Portugal's highest literary prize and also filmed.

Maria Isabel Barreno, Maria Teresa Horta and Maria Velho da Costa *New Portuguese Letters: The Three Marias* (o/p). Published (and prosecuted) in 1972, pre-Revolution Portugal, this collage of stories, letters and poems is a modern feminist parable based on the seventeenth century "Letters of a Portuguese Nun."

POETRY

Luís de Camões *The Lusiads* (Penguin, UK/US). Portugal's national epic, celebrating the ten-month voyage of Vasco da Gama which opened the sea route to India. This is a good prose translation.

Fernando Pessoa *Selected Poems* (Penguin/Ecco Press). Pessoa, who died in 1933, wrote startling, lyrical verse in four quite different personas. Virtuoso stuff – and remarkable in the way he produces very simple poems from highly complex themes.

FOOD AND WINE

Edite Vieira *The Taste of Portugal* ((Robinson, UK). A delight to read, let alone cook from. Vieira combines snippets of history and passages from Portuguese writers (very well translated) to illustrate her dishes. Highly recommended.

Jan Read *The Wines of Portugal* (Faber, UK/US). Very full descriptions of every region and particularly of soon to be internationally recognised wines. Clear explanations, too, of why each region has its own flavour and much interesting social and historical background.

Alex Liddell and Janet Price *Port Wine Quintas of the Douro* (Sotheby's, UK). Highly erudite account of the wines and history; the superb photos put it beyond specialist interest.

FLORA

Oleg Polunin and B.E. Smythies *Flowers of South-West Europe: A Field Guide* (Oxford U.P., UK/US). Best guide to the Portuguese flora.

RESIDENCE

Rachael Robinson and Victoria Pybus *Live and Work in Spain and Portugal* (Vacation Work, UK). Invaluable handbook packed with details on permits, business, teaching, health, schools, renting and buying property, etc.

MUSIC

Portugal has a rich musical culture, with roots harking back to Provençal troubadours, continuing through ballads and the unique "blues" of the *fado* and encompassing, more recently, the rhythms of the country's five former African colonies.

Each of these elements has a currency in the sounds that you hear today – from the French Provençal strain in the folk music played at northern festivals, to the cosmopolitan rock and jazz of the larger cities. An additional element is added by the wealth of singer-songwriters, most of them from the highly political "New Song" movement fostered by the dramatic events of the 1970s, as the country threw off the 36-year dictatorship of Salazar and was forced to withdraw from its colonies.

INSTRUMENTS, VOICES AND RHYTHMS

There is a startling variety of Portuguese **folk instruments**: bagpipes, harmonicas, accordions, flutes, assorted drums (*caixas, bombos, adufes, pandeiros, sarroncas*) and countless percussion instruments (*reco-reco, ferrinhos, genebres, trancanholas*).

But the country's pride and glory is strings, which include violins, the classic twelve-stringed "Portuguese guitar," and six varieties of "**viola-guitars**," unknown elsewhere in Europe. Each of these has a character, tuning and design of its own. Best known are the little four-stringed *cavaquinho* and the bigger *guitarra portuguesa*, the standard accompaniments to Lisbon *fado*. Others range through elaborate combinations of single, double and triple strings.

One of the most common combinations of instruments is the **zés-pereiras**, made up of a large *bombo*, a *caixa* and a bagpipe or fife (depending on whether you're in the Minho or Beiras region) and often used to announce grand occasions. Another traditional combination popular throughout the country is the **rancho**, made up of violins, guitars, clarinets, harmonicas and *ferrinhos*, with the later addition of the accordion.

If the folk traditions are rich in instruments, its **singers** are unrivalled. In every town and district there is an amateur choir. After a good meal someone will start an **à desgarrada** (a cappella) song, followed intuitively by the other guests. It is not at all unusual, if you go to a **fado** performance, to find the entire staff of the establishment taking part, from the owner to the cloakroom attendant. To listen to a vocal ensemble of three women from Manhouce, or a rural male choir from **Alentejo**, is to hear genuinely popular roots music. Alentejo is home also to the *saia*, sung by women accompanying themselves on the *pandeireta*.

Since Portugal remains in large part a rural society, a great many **songs** survive reflecting the cycles of nature, such as *natal, reis* and *janeiras* – lullabies and tilling, sowing and harvest songs. They remain very much within a living tradition.

Equally authentic, if less harmonious, are the **singing contests** in which rival performers exchange improvisations on a theme, or the *fandango*, a dance where two men match their footwork. Among other popular **traditional dances** are *modas, despiques, chulas, rusgas, corridinhos, viras,* waltzes and the ritual steps of the *pauliteiros* (stick-dancers) of Miranda in the Douro region.

FADO

The *fado* is Portugal's most famous – though perhaps also its least accessible – music. Lyrical and sentimental, it is thought to have origins in African slave songs, though the influence of Portugal's own maritime and colonial past is equally apparent. After the 1974 revolution, when the empire disintegrated, it went through something of a crisis. Today, it has come to be identified with a general sense of frustration and, some would have it, with an endemic and peculiarly Portuguese fatalism.

There are two versions of the *fado*. That of the humble **Alfama and Mouraria districts of Lisbon** (performed mainly in the Bairro Alto clubs, these days) is highly personal and full of feeling. The more academic strand from **Coimbra** reflects that city's ancient university traditions and is performed mainly by students and Coimbra graduates. In both versions, the theme is usually love, though *fados* have been composed on all kinds of subjects.

By far the most famous of the *fado* singers and arguably its greatest performer, is **Amália Rodriguez**. She can be seen at prestige clubs and concerts in Lisbon, though keep in mind that in recent years she has strayed into other genres, even variety.

Other big traditional names include Florencio Carvalho, Alberto Prado, José de Câmara and Castro Rodrigo. Recent performers have adapted the form to a more modern rhythm, including, most recently, Manuel Osório and (a name to look out for in the clubs) **Carlos do Carmo**. The singer-songwriters, too, have looked toward *fado*. Following the lead of José Afonso (see below), nearly all the stars have produced one or two of their own interpretations of the form.

THE BALLAD

It was an attempt to update the Coimbra *fado* that resulted in the modern Portuguese ballad and which in turn, in the last years of the dictatorship, gave way to "New Song." This, from the revolution of April 25 1975 onwards, became a genuine political song movement, broadening in recent years to a movement known as *Música Popular* – essentially contemporary folk music, composed and performed by an impressive roster of singer–songwriters.

The **lyrics** generated by this movement were – and are – as significant as the music. Many artists turned to modern poetry that dealt with contemporary social and cultural issues. They also drew on music rooted in popular tradition, both rural and urban, that reflected influences of various kinds – colonial, French, English, or Spanish – but avoided the easy rhythms of commercial pop.

One of the forerunners of the genre was the 1956 LP *Canções Heróicas – Canções Regionais Portuguesas* ("Heroic Songs – Portuguese Regional Songs"), arranged by Fernando Lopes Graça and performed by the Choir of the Amateur Musicians' Academy. Although the harmonisations are a long way from New Song, two basic elements are already present: committed lyrics and respect for genuine **regional music**.

Another LP, *Fados of Coimbra* by José Afonso and Luís Gois, appeared in May of the same year. The *fado* was out of favour in radical circles at the time. It had become just another branch of "national song," with overtones of vulgar soap-opera.

José Afonso gradually abandoned the Portuguese guitar for the Spanish, which allows for more freedom in the accompaniment. His first solo records came out in 1960, including *Balada do Outono* (Autumn Ballad), which gave its name to the new genre and made it respectable. He was soon joined by Adriano Correia de Oliveira and the **poets** Manuel Alegre, Ary dos Santos and Manuel Correia, whose work provided the text for numerous songs.

After the onset of the **colonial wars** censorship began to wreak havoc. *Menino do Bairro Negro* (Black Slum Kid) and *Os Vampiros* (The Vampires), both by José Afonso, were withdrawn from the market and only instrumental versions allowed to be sold. Some singers chose to go into exile. Luís Cília released several records in Paris under the general title of *A Poesia Portuguesa de Hoje e de Sempre* (Portuguese Poetry of Today and All Times), on which he sung his own arrangements of poems by Camões, Pessoa, Saramago and others.

The release in 1968 of José Afonso's *Cantares do Andarilho* (Songs of the Road) marked the coming of age of the ballad. By now Adriano was making his first LPs, as were Manuel Freire, José Jorge Letria, José Mário Branco, Father Fanhais and soon afterwards Fausto, Pedro Barroso and the Angolan Rui Mingas. At the same time, the **social climate** was becoming increasingly suffocating. These singers were banned from television and hardly ever heard on the radio. There were very few venues and permits were granted sparingly. They had to take other jobs to make a living.

NEW SONG

José Afonso's *Cantigas de Maio* (Songs of May), José Mário Branco's *Mudam-se os Tempos, Mudam-se as Vontades* (Changing Times, Changing Wishes) and Adriano Correia de Oliveira's *Gente d'Aqui e de Agora* (People Here and Now) show an improvement in the quality of the material. The lyrics went further in their reflections on living conditions and were more open in their **protest**. The music explored new forms, rhythms and means of expression. José Mário Branco made a key contribution as an arranger and producer. Preproduction **censorship**, however, continued to be strictly imposed and some singers stopped recording to avoid it. Others, like José Afonso, resorted to ever more cryptic lyrics.

This was how things stood on the night of **April 24, 1974**. At 10.55pm João Paulo Dinis of the "Associates of Lisbon" radio programme played *E Depois do Adeus* (After the Goodbyes), Paulo de Caravalho's Eurovision Song Contest entry for the year. At midnight came the final signal – Leite Vasconcelos played *Grândola Vila Morena* on Radio Renascença's "Limit"

PORTUGUESE FOLK: THE KEY FIGURES

JOSÉ AFONSO The "father of modern Portuguese popular music" made a key contribution to song from the 1950s onwards and won fame far beyond his country's borders. He was born in Aveiro and as the son of a civil servant visited several colonies as a child, but it was not until later, when he made a trip to Angola as a student, that he became aware of the colonial realities.

His first records were collections of *fado* made with Luís Góis in 1956. In the 1960s he began to write songs on social issues. His records were censored and he was persecuted by the secret police. His whole life was dedicated to song and his personal crusade against fascism.

After the revolution, he continued to work prolifically and to consistently high standards, composing music for films and the theatre as well as producing nearly twenty LPs. His work was constantly evolving, yet his first compositions are still fresh today. With their careful attention to music, lyrics, arrangement and voice, any of his records is a miniature work of art. He lived modestly and died after a long illness in 1987.

FAUSTO The work of this singer combines the most diverse influences – modern and traditional, Portuguese and African – with a marked urban slant and a lyrical delivery. His skill lies in the subtlety with which he links African rhythms to Portuguese melodies and instruments and the delicacy of his singing.

His early songs provide a poetic analysis of the uncertain postrevolutionary period. Later ones use tales of the deeds of *conquistadores*, sailors and other Portuguese heroes to reflect on the country's history.

SÉRGIO GODINHO Born in Porto, Godinho went into exile as an economics student to avoid military service in the colonial war. He travelled in France, Switzerland and Canada, working at one time as an interpreter for the musical *Hair* and at another as a member of *Living Theatre*.

Due to these influences he is one of the more modern, cosmopolitan singers of his generation. His songs are usually narrative and he has a particular knack for affectionate character sketches. When dealing more directly with political issues he employs a fine sense of humour. His music is both loud and cheerful, intimate and sophisticated.

LUÍS CÍLIA Of the new songwriters, Luís Cília is the one who has devoted most attention to setting his poems to music. His work is rigorous and serious, showing a pronounced French influence. He is good at capturing the essence and general atmosphere of a given political moment in his lyrics. Músically, he has worked in two apparently contrasting fields: traditional song and experimental work with synthesizers from which he has produced a solo album.

JOSÉ MÁRIO BRANCO Another native of Porto, Mário Branco's chief contribution has been as an arranger and producer of records, though he has made important records himself, both individually and as a member of the *Grupo de Acção Cultural*. His skill in the studios has given an added dimension to the records of Portuguese singers.

VITORINO The songs of Vitorino are inextricably linked with the Alentejo region and its farming cooperatives and rural communities, though recently he has made more contact with the city. His early records were uneven in their development, a mixture of Alentejo folk songs, revolutionary anthems and love songs. It is with the latter genre that he has had most success in his recent work.

JANITA SALOMÉ Brother of Vitorino, he also has links with Alentejo, though he has concentrated increasingly on the Arab heritage there and in the Algarve. His music, full of percussion and gentle touches, also betrays the influence of José Afonso, with whom he worked closely in his last years.

programme. The army captains went into action and on the following day the coup was a reality: Portugal was returning to democracy.

There began an uncertain period during which it was unclear who held power. Singers like Sérgio Godinho, Luís Cília, José Mário Branco and Father Fanhais returned from exile. Now that censorship had been lifted, New Song gave way to **political song**. Everyone had slogans, analyses and solutions to offer in the process of clarification which followed.

Singers were suddenly in constant demand for the political and cultural events being improvised with a minimum of technical resources all over the country, giving performances in factories, cooperatives, squatters' settlements, etc. They set up various groups according to their political leanings: Free Song (*Canto Livre*), the October Group (*Grupo Outubro*) and the Group for Cultural Action – Voices for the Cause (*Grupo de Acção Cultural Vozes na Luta*, or *GAC*). The latter, in mixing traditional songs with its sloganeering political ones, set an unconscious pattern for future developments. Other artists slowly branched out into work with the numerous theatre groups of the time and on soundtracks for films. Some singers and musicians also formed cooperatives, such as *Eranova* (New Age) and *Cantarabril* (Sing of April).

FOLK GROUPS

As time passed and things returned to normal, **traditional music** enjoyed a revival, bringing with it the first commercial folk groups.

In the 1960s, much work had been done in studying and recording traditional Portuguese music, most notably by Fernando Lopes Graça and Michel Giacometti, who produced a five-volume *Antologia de Música Regional Portuguesa*. Over the last decade, the group **Almanaque** of Lisbon has followed in their footsteps, producing a series of records from the oral tradition, as well as reworking the traditional themes in a more modern form.

The **Brigada Victor Jara** of Coimbra also began by collecting folk tunes but soon turned to new directions, adapting the work of other folk writers. Although none of its original members are still in the lineup, this group is one of Portugal's best, producing well-crafted work based on sound ideas. Other active folk groups, adopting similar approaches, include *Raizes*

(Roots) from Vila Verde (Braga); the *Grupo Etnográfico de Cantares e Trajes* (Ethnographic Song and Costume Group) from Manhouce; *Terra Terra* (Land, Land); *Vai de Roda*, an ethnic arts cooperative from Oporto; *Trigo Limpo* (Clean Wheat) from Alentejo; and *Ronda dos Quatro Caminhos* (Crossroads) from Lisbon.

A more **contemporary** and ambitious folk music has also emerged over the last decade. **Trovante**, which was formed in 1975, is highly acclaimed in Portugal and has worked extensively with José Afonso and Fausto. Its work is full of uneven swayings and sudden changes of direction. Interesting, too, though less successful, are *Charanga*, *Pedra d'Hera*, *Construção*, *Disto e Daquilo* and *Rosa dos Ventos*.

Música Popular – as more recent folk has become known – owes much of its renewed popularity, however, to the work of some singer-songwriters who have dedicated themselves exclusively to it and to musicians who have made records devoted to individual folk instruments.

Among **instrumentalists**, perhaps the most outstanding figure is the guitarist **Carlos Paredes**. He explores both the folk and the classical sides of the Portuguese guitar, with surprising results; his records are a rare treat. Another excellent instrumentalist is **Júlio Pereira**, who began as a songwriter but became interested in traditional string instruments and has recently experimented to great effect in combining them with synthesizers, rhythm boxes and samplers in compositions inspired by folk tradition.

ROCK, JAZZ AND AFRICAN

Though Portuguese rock and jazz cannot even begin to match the maturity of its songwriting tradition, there have been some interesting developments recently. Two names to watch out for are the blues singer **Rui Veloso** and the pop singer **Mafalda Veiga**. Among groups, the most established include **GNR**, **Heróis do Mar**, **Madredeus**, **Chutos e Pontapés**, **Rádio Macau**, **Sétima Legião** and **Trovante**.

An intriguing figure, midway between jazz and "New Age," is the saxophonist **Rão Kyao**. As for jazz proper, there is the great vocalist **Maria João**, the **Lisbon Jazz Sextet**, the experimental trio **Shish**, and the ensembles led by **António Pinho Vargas** and **Mário Laginha**.

On the contemporary Portuguese rock scene, by far the most exciting development is the appearance of groups from the former African colonies of **Angola**, **Mozambique**, **Cabo Verde**, **Guinea-Bissau** and **São Tomé e Príncipe**. Many musicians, particularly from Cabo Verde (Cape Verde Islands), settled in Lisbon during the very hard years following the colonial wars and independence. Others spend part of the year based in Portugal, recording and touring Europe, drawn by the comparatively high fees to be made.

Staying in Lisbon, you're most likely to get a chance to see Cabo Verde groups, which include among their styles *morna*, similar to the Portuguese *fado* and the more danceable *moradeira*.

From **Guinea-Bissau** the sounds are an unusual mix of African and Latin, akin to zouk. Big names to look out for that may be in the country include **Justino Delgado**, **Super Mama Diombo**, **Manecas**, **Africa Libre** and **Jetu Katem**.

Finally, if you get a chance to see them, two outstanding southern African groups are **Guem** from **Angola** and **Fernando Luís** from **Mozambique**.

Manuel Dominguez

RECORDS

Records in Portugal are excellent value; the following is a personal selection of the most interesting.

Folk
Almanaque *Desafiando Cantigas; Sementes.*
Brigada Victor Jara *Marcha dos Foliões.*
Ronda dos Quatro Caminhos *Fados Velhos.*
Vai de Roda *Vai de Roda.*

Fado
Amália Rodrigues *O Melhor.*
Carlos do Carmo *Um Homem na Cidade; Un Homem no País.*

Portuguese Guitar
Carlos Paredes *Guitarra Portuguesa; Movimento Perpétuo; Concerto em Frankfurt; Espelho de Sons.*
Pedro Caldeira Cabral *Encontros; A Guitarra Portuguesa nos Salões dos sec. XVIII.*

Singer-Songwriters
Adriano Correia de Oliveira *Memória de Adriano.*
Fausto *Madrugada dos Trapeiros; Por Este Rio Acima; Despertar dos Alquimistas.*
Janita Salomé *Lavrar em teu Peito; Olho de Fogo.*
José Afonso *Cantigas de Maio; Venham Mais Cinco; Coro do Tribunais; Com as Minhas Tamanquinhas; Fura Fura; Fados de Coimbra e Outras Canções; Como se Fora Seu Filho; Galinhas do Mato.*

José Maria Branco *Ser Solidário.*
Julio Pereira *Cavaquinho; Braguesa; Cadoi; Os Sete Instrumentos; Miradouro.*
Luís Cília *Cancioneiro; Penumbra.*
Sérgio Godinho *De Pequenino se Torce o Destino; Coincidências; Na Vida Real.*
Vitorino *Romances; Negro Fado; Frol de la Mar.*

Rock/Pop
G.N.R. *Os Homems não se querem Bonitos.*
Heróis do Mar *Mãe.*
Madredeus *Os Dias da Madredeus.*
Radio Macau *Rádio Macau.*
Sétima Legião *Mar d'Outubro.*
Trovante *Terra Firme.*

Jazz
António Pinho Vargas *Variações.*
Maria João *Conversa.*
Rão Kyao *Fado Bailado; Danças de Rua.*
Sexteto de Jazz de Lisboa *Sexteto.*

African
Kaba Mane *Kunga Kungake* (Guinea-Bissau).
Guem *Dans Voyage* (Angola).
Fernando Luís *Bassopa* (Mozambique).

LANGUAGE

If you have some knowledge of Spanish and/or French you won't have much problem reading Portuguese. Understanding it when it's spoken, though, is a different matter: pronunciation is entirely different and at first even the easiest words are hard to distinguish – the sound is more like that of an East European language than of the Romance tongues it has its roots in. If you're stuck, most people will understand Spanish (albeit reluctantly) and in the cities and tourist areas French and English are also widely spoken. Even so, it's well worth the effort to master at least the rudiments; once you've started to figure out the words it gets a lot easier very quickly.

PRONUNCIATION

The chief difficulty with **pronunciation** is its lack of clarity – consonants tend to be slurred, vowels nasal and often ignored altogether.

CONSONANTS

The consonants are, at least, consistent:

C is soft before E and I, hard otherwise unless it has a cedilla – *açucar* (sugar) is pronounced "assookar."

CH is somewhat softer than in English; *Chá* (tea) sounds like Shah.

J is pronounced like the "s" in pleasure, as is *G* except when it comes before a "hard" vowel (A, O and U).

LH sounds like "lyur" (Batalha).

Q is always pronounced as a "k."

S before a consonant or at the end of a word becomes "sh," otherwise it's as in English – Cascais is pronounced "Kashkaish," Sagres is "Sahgresh."

X has the same sound – *caixa* (cash desk) is pronounced "kaisha."

VOWELS

Vowels are worse – flat and truncated, they're often difficult for English-speaking tongues to get around. The only way to learn is to listen – accents, ã, ô, or é, turn them into longer, more familiar sounds.

When two vowels come together they continue to be enunciated separately except in the case of *EI* and *OU* – which sound like a and long o respectively.

E at the end of a word is silent unless it has an accent, so that *carne* (meat) is pronounced "karn," while *café* is much as you'd expect.

The **tilde over Ã or Õ** renders the pronunciation much like the French -an and -on endings only more nasal.

More common is **ÃO** (as in *pão*, bread – *são*, saint – *limão*, lemon), which sounds something like a strangled yelp of "Ow!" cut off in midstream.

A FEW KEY WORDS . . .

Even if you speak no Portuguese at all there are **a few key words** which can help you out in an enormous number of situations.

● *Há* (the H is silent) means "there is" or "is there?" and can be used for just about anything. Thus: "*Há um pensão aqui?*" (Is there a pension here?), "*Há uma camioneta para . . ?*" (Is there a bus to . . .?), or even "*Há um quarto?*" (Do you have a room?).

● More polite and better in shops or restaurants are **"*tem . . .?*"** (do you have . . .?) or "*queria . . .*" (I'd like . . .).

● And of course there are the old standards "Do you speak English?" (*Fala Inglês?*) and "I don't understand" (*Não compreendo*).

PORTUGUESE WORDS AND PHRASES

BASICS

sim; não	yes; no	*agora; mais tarde*	now; later
olá; bom dia	hello; good morning	*mais; menos*	more; less
boa tarde/noite	good afternoon/night	*grande; pequeno*	big; little
adeus, até logo	goodbye, see you later	*aberto; fechado*	open; closed
hoje; amanhã	today; tomorrow	*senhoras; homens*	women; men
por favor/se faz favor	please	*lavabo/quarto de banho*	toilet
está bem	it's all right/OK	*banco; câmbio*	bank; change
*obrigado/a**	thank you	*correios*	post office
onde; que	where; what	*(dois) selos*	(two) stamps
quando; porquê	when; why	*sou Ingles/a*	I am English
como; quanto	how; how much	*Americano/a*	American
não sei	I don't know	*como se chama*	What's your name?
sabe . . .?	do you know . . .?	*(chamo–me . . .)*	(my name is . . .)
pode . . .?	could you . . .?	*como se diz isto em*	What's this called in
desculpe; com licença	sorry/excuse me	*Português?*	Portuguese?
aqui; ali	here; there	*o que é isso? quanto é?*	What's that? How
perto; longe	near; far		much is it?
este/a; esse/a	this; that		

* *Obrigado* agrees with the sex of the person speaking – a woman says *obrigada*, a man *obrigado*.

GETTING AROUND

para ir a . . .?	How do I get to . . .?	*a que horas parte?*	What time does it leave?
esquerda, direita,	left, right, straight ahead		
sempre em frente		*(chega a)*	(arrive at)
onde é a estação de	Where is the bus	*qual é a estrada para. ?*	Which is the road to . ?
camionetas?	station?		
a paragem de autocarro	the bus stop for . . .	*vou a (para onde vai?)*	I'm going to (Where are you going?)
para. . .			
a estação de comboios	the railway station	*está bem, muito obri-*	That's great, thanks a
donde parte o autocarro	where does the bus to . .	*gado/a*	lot
para. . .?	. leave from?	*pare aqui por favor*	Stop here please
é este o comboio para	Is this the train for	*bilhete (para)*	ticket (to)
Coimbra?	Coimbra?	*ida e volta*	round trip

ACCOMMODATION

há uma pensão aqui	Is there a pension near	*posso/podemos deixar*	Can I/we leave the
perto?	here?	*os sacos aqui até . . ?*	bags here until . . ?
queria um quarto	I'd like a room	*há um quarto mais*	Is there a cheaper
é para uma noite (semana)	It's for one night (week)	*barato?*	room?
é para uma pessoa (duas	It's for one person (two	*com duche (quente/frio)*	With a shower (hot/ cold)
pessoas)	people)		
posso ver?	May I see/look around?	*pode-se acampar aqui?*	Can we camp here?
está bem, fico com ele	OK, I'll take it	*chave*	key
quanto custa?	How much is it?		
é caro, não o quero	It's expensive, I don't want it		

DAYS AND MONTHS

domingo	Sunday	*janeiro*	January	*agosto*	August
segunda-feira	Monday	*fevereiro*	February	*setembro*	September
terça-feira	Tuesday	*março*	March	*outubro*	October
quarta-feira	Wednesday	*abril*	April	*novembro*	November
quinta-feira	Thursday	*maio*	May	*dezembro*	December
sexta-feira	Friday	*junho*	June		
sábado	Saturday	*julho*	July		

THE TIME

que horas são ?	what time is it?	*dez para as duas*	one-fifty
é/são . . .	it's . . .	*meio-dia*	midday, noon
a que horas	(at) what time?	*uma da tarde*	one in the afternoon
a/as . . .	at . . .		(1pm)
meia-noite	midnight	*sete da tarde*	seven in the evening
uma da manhã	one in the morning (1am)	*(dezanove)*	(7pm)
uma e dez	ten past one	*nove e meia da noite*	nine-thirty (pm)
uma e quinze	one-fifteen	*(vinte e uma e trinta)*	
uma e vinte	one-twenty	*meio-dia e quinze*	quarter past noon
uma e meia	one-thirty	*meia-noite e dez*	ten past midnight
quinze para as duas	one-forty-five		

NUMBERS

1	*um*	8	*oito*	15	*quinze*	30	*trinta*
2	*dois*	9	*nove*	16	*dezasseis*	40	*quarenta*
3	*três*	10	*dez*	17	*dezassete*	50	*cinquenta*
4	*quatro*	11	*onze*	18	*dezoito*	60	*sessenta*
5	*cinco*	12	*doze*	19	*dezanove*	70	*setenta*
6	*seis*	13	*treze*	20	*vinte*	80	*oitenta*
7	*sete*	14	*catorze*	21	*vinte e um*	90	*noventa*

100	*cem*
101	*cento e um*
200	*duzentos*
500	*quinhentos*
1000	*mil*
2000	*dois mil*
1,000,000	*um milhão*

PORTUGUESE TERMS: A GLOSSARY

AFONSINO of the reign of Dom Afonso Henriques, first king of Portugal.

ALAMEDA promenade (also called ESPLANADA along a seafront).

ALBUFEIRA reservoir.

ALDEIA village.

AZULEJO glazed and painted tile; originally used as geometric decoration around the base of doorways of a church or mansion; by the late sixteenth century whole pictorial blocks were created. From the late seventeenth until the mid-eighteenth century – the main period – tiles were exclusively blue and white.

BAIRRO quarter (of a town); ALTO is upper, BAIXO lower.

BAIXA commercial, shopping centre of town.

CÂMARA MUNICIPAL town hall (also PAÇOS DO CONCELHO).

CAPELA chapel; CAPELA-MOR is a chancel or sanctuary.

CENTRO COMERCIAL large shopping centre, where you can find almost anything.

CHAFARIZ public fountain (also FONTE).

CIDADE city.

CITÂNIA prehistoric/Celtic hill settlement (see *Minho* chapter).

CLAUSTRO cloister.

CORO central, often enclosed, part of church built for choir.

CORREIO post and telephone office, abbreviated CTT.

DOM, DONA courtesy titles (sir, madam) usually applied to kings and queens; INFANTE is prince, INFANTA princess.

ELÉCTRICO tramcar, found in Lisbon and Porto.

ELEVADOR elevator or funicular.

ERMIDA remote chapel – not necessarily a hermitage.

ESTAÇÃO station; . . . DE COMBOIOS railroad station; . . . DE AUTOCARROS bus station.

ESTRADA road; ESTRADA NACIONAL is a main road, designated EN on maps.

FEIRA weekly or monthly fair or market.

FESTA festival or carnival, as in Spanish *fiesta*.

GRUTAS caves

HORÁRIO timetable for trains or buses.

IGREJA church; IGREJA MATRIZ parish church.

LAGO lake.

LARGO square.

MANUELINO flamboyant, marine-influenced style of late Gothic architecture developed in the reign of Manuel I (1495–1521).

MERCADO market, often in covered buildings or an enclosure.

MIRADOURO belvedere or viewpoint of any sort.

MOÇÁRABE Moorish-Arabic (usually of architecture or a design).

MOSTEIRO not always a monastery, often an old church (can be CONVENTO instead); most orders were suppressed in 1834–38.

MUDÉJAR Moorish-style architecture and decoration.

NOSSA SENHORA (N.S.) Our Lady – the Virgin Mary.

PAÇO/PALÁCIO palace or country house, not necessarily royal (REAL).

PARQUE NACIONAL/PARQUE NATURAL National/Nature Park or Reserve.

PASTELARIA bakery .

PELOURINHO stone pillory, seen in almost every northern village.

POUSADA luxury state-run hotel, sometimes converted from a castle or monastery.

PRAÇA square (also LARGO and CAMPO); PRAÇA DE TOUROS bullring.

PRAIA beach.

QUINTA country estate, or its main house.

RETÁBULO altarpiece – usually large, carved and heavily gilt.

ROMARIA pilgrimage-festival.

SALA DO CAPÍTULO chapter house.

SÉ cathedral.

SENHOR Sir, man, or Mr; SENHORA woman, Ms or Mrs (MENINA means Miss).

SOLAR manor house or important town mansion.

TORRE DE MENAGEM keep of a castle.

INDEX

As indicated above, letters advising us of changes and errors are hugely appreciated. We're especially grateful for contributions from the following readers of the last edition:

Dixon Adams, Sharon Bainbridge, Stephen Ball, Malcolm Barton, Hugh Bayley, Pete Binfield, Paul Blarney, Paul Booton, Mick Bramich, Charlie Breindahl, Jeanette Brimblecombe, Mary Broere, Ian Buchanan, Tim Burford, Mary Lynn Buss, Vanessa Buxton, David Byers, Brenda Cathcart, Adam Caunt, John Cheshire, Judith Clifton, Nicki Coleman, Heather Collins, Margaret E. Cornwell, Miles Craven, Pamela Croston, Ben Crystall, Cathie Driver, Kay Dewsbury, Ann and Vivian Dunn, Paul Emmerson, Chris Esmond, Eileen Fisher, Shani Flint, Christopher Fox, Sandra and Peter Friedrich, Gill Gray, Romaine Gregory, Sheila Hakin, Matthew Hancock, Mike and Barbara Harding, Jo Hardy, Stephen Heneghan, Laurence Hicks, Barry Hill, Sandy Hills, Jane Honey, Hilary Hooper, Mike Ivy, Iain Jackson, Paul Jay, Christian Kerslake, Antoni Korris, Jess Lewis, Kirstin Lister, Kevin Low, Jane Lyons, Maya Manning, Peter Mair, G.A. Martin, Bernadette McAleer, Ian and Elizabeth McDougall, Guy Middleton, Frank Miller, Michael Miller, Elspeth Mitchell, D.W. Money, Pat Morgan, Sue Mowbray, Diana Musgrave, Marisa Nardella, Nigel Newman, Tim Nisbet, Jan Nordby, Michael O'Hare, Pádraig O'Neill, Chris Overington, Heather Paterson, Joanne Peak, John Peel, Anthony Phillips, Nicholas Philpot, Richard Priest, A.S.L. Rae, Graeme Pulleyn, Maria Jardim Hintze Ribeiro, Anna Richards, Catherine and Peter Robinson, Donald Robinson, Richard Robinson, W.P. Rook, Kevin Rose, James Salmon, Fritjof Sahlstöm, Chris and Joan Sayers, Haldi and Mairead Sheahan, Bee Shepherd, John W. Smith, Anita Stadelman, Carol Sterenberg, Paul Sutcliffe, Alan Thomas, Esther Thomson, Denver Thorpe, Jan Tielemans, Bill Todd, Amanda Tomlin, Chris de Voecht, Geoff Wallis, Geoff Ward, Tracey Ward, Sandy and Anne Webster, Sue Westwood, Dick Whiddett, Pip Whiteside, Paul Whitfield, Gail Whitney, R.B. Williams, Edna Wilson, Nan Wilson, John K. Wood, Geoff Wollen, Philip Wray, Nilce and David Wren, and N.F. Young.

MEDITERRANEAN LANDS

ITALY ✳ SICILY
TUSCANY & UMBRIA
GREECE ✳ CRETE ✳ SPAIN
BARCELONA & CATALUNYA
PROVENCE & THE CÔTE D'AZUR
ISRAEL & OCCUPIED TERRITORIES
TURKEY ✳ MOROCCO
TUNISIA ✳ EGYPT

ITALY: THE ROUGH GUIDE (1st edition) *992 pages; price £9.99*

SICILY: THE ROUGH GUIDE (1st edition) *336 pages; price £5.95*

TUSCANY & UMBRIA (1st edition) *576 pages; price £8.99*

GREECE: THE ROUGH GUIDE (5th edition) *752 pages; price £9.99*

CRETE: THE ROUGH GUIDE (2nd edition) *304 pages; price £5.99*

SPAIN: THE ROUGH GUIDE (5th edition) *672 pages; price £8.99*

BARCELONA AND CATALUNYA (1st edition) *384 pages; price £7.99*

PROVENCE & THE CÔTE D'AZUR (2nd edition) *448 pages; £8.99*

ISRAEL & OCCUPIED TERRITORIES (1st edition) *464 pages; price £5.95*

TURKEY: THE ROUGH GUIDE (1st edition) *752 pages; price £8.99*

MOROCCO: THE ROUGH GUIDE (3rd edition) *512 pages; price £7.99*

TUNISIA: THE ROUGH GUIDE (3rd edition) *400 pages; price £8.99*

EGYPT: THE ROUGH GUIDE (1st edition) *640 pages; price £9.99*

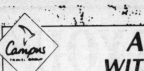

BEFORE YOU TRAVEL THE WORLD, TALK TO AN EXPERIENCED STAMP COLLECTOR.

At STA Travel we're all seasoned travellers so we should know a thing or two about where you're headed. We can offer you the best deals on fares with the flexibility to change your mind as you go – without having to pay over the top for the privilege. We operate from 120 offices worldwide. So call in soon.

74 and 86 Old Brompton Road, SW7, 117 Euston Road, NW1. London.
Manchester. Leeds. Oxford. Cambridge. Bristol.
*North America **071-937 9971**. Europe **071-937 9921**. Rest of World **071-937 9962***
*(incl. Sundays 10am-2pm). **OR 061-834 0668 (Manchester)***

WHEREVER YOU'RE BOUND, WE'RE BOUND TO HAVE BEEN.

STA TRAVEL